Group Work With Populations at Risk

Group Work With Populations at Risk

Third Edition

Edited by
Geoffrey L. Greif
Paul H. Ephross

UNIVERSITY PRESS
2011

OXFORD
UNIVERSITY PRESS

Oxford University Press, Inc., publishes works that further
Oxford University's objective of excellence
in research, scholarship, and education.

Oxford   New York
Auckland   Cape Town   Dar es Salaam   Hong Kong   Karachi
Kuala Lumpur   Madrid   Melbourne   Mexico City   Nairobi
New Delhi   Shanghai   Taipei   Toronto

With offices in
Argentina   Austria   Brazil   Chile   Czech Republic   France   Greece
Guatemala   Hungary   Italy   Japan   Poland   Portugal   Singapore
South Korea   Switzerland   Thailand   Turkey   Ukraine   Vietnam

Copyright © 1997, 2005, 2011 by Oxford University Press, Inc.

Published by Oxford University Press, Inc.
198 Madison Avenue, New York, New York 10016
www.oup.com

Oxford is a registered trademark of Oxford University Press

Library of Congress Cataloging-in-Publication Data
Group work with populations at risk / edited by Geoffrey L. Greif,
Paul H. Ephross. — 3rd ed.
    p. cm.
Includes bibliographical references and index.
ISBN 978-0-19-539856-4
1. Social group work.   2. Marginality, Social.   I. Greif, Geoffrey L.   II. Ephross, Paul H.
HV45.G73165 2011
361.4—dc22
2010010579

Printed in the United States of America
on acid-free paper

Preface

For this new edition, we considered what has changed in the American land-scape in the more than 6 years since we outlined the second edition. Many issues that are addressed in that edition—child abuse, hate crimes, cancer, community violence, and severe mental illness, to name a few—remain as areas of concern for social work with groups. We asked all the continuing authors to update their chapters with relevant interventions, citations, and website resources. We wondered about the need for chapters specifically about gays and lesbians. Are they still "at-risk" populations? Steven Ball, Ben Lipton, and Bonnie Engelhardt assured us that such chapters were still relevant given the shifting tides in relation to same-sex marriage and civil unions.

In two cases, we asked new authors currently working in the field to replace past chapters. Melissa Back Tamburo describes the changing landscape of the workforce and how Employee Assistance Programs can meet workers' needs through group work. With the recent economic downturn, the provision of mental health services in the workplace becomes even more crucial both for those that are remaining at a particular job as well as for those who need help with the transition out of their job site. Janice DeLucia-Waack shares her expertise in relation to children of divorce. While their numbers have not grown in the past decade, these children remain a large portion of the school-age population. Her chapter contains many good and specific interventions for social workers to consider whether they are working in the schools or in agencies.

Emerging areas of practice were also identified. First, we added a chapter on Latinos. Now the second largest population in the United States and a highly diverse one, Latinos present unique cultural challenges to many social workers. Luz López and Erika Vargas describe the experiences of Latino immigrants and what themes may arise for them in service provision in group settings.

Second, with the continuing wars in Afghanistan and Iraq, we wanted to prepare social workers for group work with returning veterans. Unlike veterans of past wars, these soldiers return home to a society where mental health services are rarely stigmatized. Julie Ellis and Matt Camardese, both with clinical experience in the Veterans Administration system, provide one of the first chapters to be written on this topic.

Third, Carolyn Knight has added a chapter on people who were abused as children. As more people come forth with childhood histories of abuse at the hands of family members and others, social workers need to be prepared to help this population through group work deal with the long-term consequences of maltreatment.

Finally, we have added a chapter on group work with men. While men's experiences are well covered in other chapters of this book, we believe that they can present challenges to social workers due to men's socialization against seeking help and appearing vulnerable. The first editor, who has written elsewhere about fathers and men's roles, contributed this chapter.

Other authors, Kay Connors, George Getzel, Geoffrey Greif, Susan Rice, and Joan Weiss, added co-authors to assist in bringing a fresh perspective to chapters they previously wrote. John Kayser substantially broadened his chapter to encompass more of a community focus in relation to violence. We also changed the titles of some of the chapters to reflect people first language.

As with the past editions, we hope this volume will help beginning practitioners and students to find their way through the initial sessions with these populations at risk. By knowing in advance what some of the key issues may be for the people and communities being served, the group worker should be well-positioned to assist with the difficult transitions that these people face.

G.L.G.
P.H.E.
Baltimore

Contents

Contributors

Melissa Back Tamburo, PhD, LCSW-C, CEAP, is the clinical supervisor for Business Health Services, a national workplace wellness vendor.

Steven Ball, ACSW, is a private practitioner and adjunct faculty member at Hunter College School of Social Work.

Margot Breton, MSW, is a professor emerita in the Faculty of Social Work, University of Toronto.

Matthew Camardese, LCSW-C, is a social worker in the Department of Veteran Affairs, Baltimore, Maryland.

Edna Comer is an associate professor at the University of Connecticut School of Social Work.

Kay Martel Connors, LCSW-C, is a social worker at the University of Maryland School of Medicine, Department of Psychiatry.

Barry M. Daste was a professor emeritus, School of Social Work, Louisiana State University, at the time of his death, January 30, 2010.

Janice L. DeLucia-Waack, PhD, is an associate professor and program director in school counseling in the Department of Counseling, School, and Educational Psychology, Graduate School of Education, University at Buffalo, SUNY.

Julie A. Ellis, LCSW-C, is a social worker in San Diego, California.

Bonnie J. Engelhardt, ACSW, LICSW, is a social group worker in private practice in Needham, Massachusetts.

Paul H. Ephross, PhD, is a professor emeritus at the School of Social Work, University of Maryland.

Charles Garvin, PhD, is a professor emeritus at the School of Social Work, University of Michigan.

George Getzel, DSW, is a professor emeritus at Hunter College School of Social Work.

Geoffrey L. Greif, DSW, LCSW-C, is a professor at the School of Social Work, University of Maryland.

Aminfu R. Harvey, DSW, is a professor at the School of Social Work, Fayetteville State University.

John A. Kayser, PhD, is a professor at the Graduate School of Social Work, University of Denver.

Carolyn Knight, PhD, is a professor in the Department of Social Work, University of Maryland Baltimore County.

Jessica Lertora, LCSW-C, is a social worker at the University of Maryland School of Medicine, Department of Psychiatry.

Kyla Liggett-Creel, LCSW-C, is a social worker at the University of Maryland School of Medicine, Department of Psychiatry.

Benjamin Lipton, CSW, is a private practitioner and adjunct professor at New York University Ehrenkranz School of Social Work.

Luz M. Lopez, PhD, MPH, LCSW, is an assistant professor at the School of Social Work, Boston University.

Andrew Malekoff, MSW, CAC, is associate director of North Shore Child and Family Guidance Center, Roslyn Heights, New York,

Jack McDevitt, MPA, is associate dean for research and graduate studies at the College of Criminal Justice at Northeastern University, where he also directs the Institute on Race and Justice.

Andrea Meier, PhD, is an emeritus research associate professor at University of North Carolina at Chapel Hill, School of Social Work.

Darnell Morris-Compton, MSW, is a doctoral candidate at the School of Social Work, University of Maryland.

Elizabeth Mulroy, PhD, is a professor emerita at the School of Social Work, University of Maryland.

Anna Nosko, MSW, is a social worker at Family Services Association of Toronto.

Phillip Osteen, PhD, is an assistant professor at the School of Social Work, University of Maryland.

Susan Rice, DSW, is a professor emerita at the Department of Social Work at California State University at Long Beach.

Steven R. Rose, PhD, is a professor at the School of Social Work, George Mason University.

Erika M. Vargas, MSW, is a social worker at La Alianza Hispana, Inc. in Roxbury, MA, Boston University.

Joan C. Weiss, MSW, is executive director of the Justice Research and Statistics Association, Washington, DC, and has a part-time private practice in psychotherapy.

Steve Wilson, PhD, LCSW, is an assistant professor at the Department of Social Work California State University, Long Beach.

Margaret M. Wright is an assistant professor at the School of Social Work and Family Studies, University of British Columbia.

Group Work With Populations at Risk

Social Work With Groups: Practice Principles

Paul H. Ephross

The past few years in social work may be characterized both as years of stability and as a time of dynamic and rapid change. In an ideal world, these changes would result in reducing risk for those in need through the provision of services and structural changes. For most, while services have improved, they remain in need of service. This book is about the practice of group work with a wide variety of people who remain at risk. The populations are defined by a particular physical or psychological condition, a social identity, an unmet need for a service or form of help, a condition that caused them to be stigmatized or discriminated against by society or social institutions, or by a challenge that arises from their stage of life or personal history. Many are affected by more than one of these factors. What unites the people described in the following chapters is that they share two characteristics. They are at risk for continued, intensified harm, pain, dysfunction, or unmet need. They can also benefit from participating in a group experience through which they can gain skills, understanding, and emotional learnings that can reduce their level of vulnerability, leaving them ideally better able to deal with stresses and demands of life roles and their own social relationships.

Each chapter author was asked to note ways in which the particular needs of his or her population may necessitate modifications or adaptations of traditional or mainstream social work practice in groups. This instruction and the chapter authors' responses suggest that there is a body of knowledge and skills, supported by a cluster of perceptions and attitudes, undergirded by a set of values and commitments about the nature of human beings and society that constitute mainstream group work. Each chapter assumes that the reader understands the bases of group work and uses those bases as a starting point. The purpose of this chapter is to provide an introduction to concepts that are generic to social group work, including the nature of group experience, values, perceptions, purposes and goals, and methods.

Defining *group* is not a simple matter. The word *group* has met with difficulties of definition, both in the social sciences and in social work literature. In one sense, it is defined by size; that is, the "small group" for treatment modification of individuals, is different than such large units as legislative committees or assemblies. In a second sense, *group* is linked to collectivity. In still another sense, *group* is tied to the term *social,* thereby contrasting the group with individuals. Yet all writers emphasize that groups, organizations, and collectivities consist of individuals, whom they influence through the concept of membership (Falck, 1988, p. 3).

THE NATURE OF GROUP EXPERIENCE

Human beings are born into groups, and their lives may be viewed as experiences in group memberships. As Falck has noted:

> *Every person is a member. A member is a human being characterized by body, personality, sociality, and the ability to comprehend human experience. Every member is an element in the community of men and women ... (p. 30).*

He proceeds to characterize a member as a "social being in continuous interaction with others who are both seen and unseen ... and ... a psychological being capable of private experience." Falck drew several inferences from the "fact that in speaking of a member one implicitly speaks of others, who are also members" (p. 30).

The term *member* refers to a person who is:

1. A physical being bounded by semipermeable membranes and cavities,
2. A social being in continuous interaction with others who are both seen and unseen, and
3. A psychological being capable of private experience.

In speaking of *member,* one implicitly speaks of others, who are also members, which leads to the following inferences (Falck, 1988, p. 30):

1. A member's actions are socially derived and contributory.
2. The identity of each member is bound up with that of others through social involvement.
3. A member is a person whose difference from others creates tensions that lead to individual and group growth, group cohesion, and group conflict.
4. Human freedom is defined by simultaneous concern for oneself and others.

Membership, in this view, is such an essential aspect of humanness that the one is virtually indistinguishable from the other. It is little wonder, then, that groups have been described as microcosms (Ephross & Vassil, 2004), participation in which can lead toward group healing, expanded and enhanced social functioning, learning, the expression of democratic citizenship, the practice of self-determination, mutual aid, mutual support, and progress toward achieving social justice. Of course, implicit in such statements is also the power of groups to mobilize less noble and more destructive purposes.

What can be mobilized in a group that can give group experiences for change the power to affect the group's members? Northen and Kurland (2001, pp. 25–27) list 10 factors that they label *dynamic forces* for change: mutual support, cohesiveness, quality of relationships, universality, a sense of hope, altruism, acquisition of knowledge and skills, catharsis, reality testing, and group control. They proceed to make important observations about these forces:

> *Findings from research generally support the importance of these forces in positively influencing the members' group experience. Findings also suggest that some factors are more important than others for different types of groups and even for different members of the same group.... Furthermore, these dynamic forces need to be viewed as potential benefits; they are not present automatically in groups but need to be fostered by the practitioner (2001, pp. 26–27).*

In this view, although groups are naturally occurring phenomena, the benefits of participation ought not be taken for granted but rather need to be nurtured by the social worker/practitioner.

Other writers may name the influential aspects of group life differently, but they agree both on the power of group experience and generally on the aspects that generate groups' power to affect members. For example, one list highlights nine mutual-aid processes as follows: "sharing data, the dialectical process, entering taboo areas, the 'all-in-the same-boat' phenomenon, mutual support, mutual demand, individual problem-solving, rehearsal, and the strength-in-numbers phenomenon" (Gitterman & Shulman, 1994, p. 14).

Focusing on "the group as an entity," Garvin developed a classification of the dimensions of group process.... [T]hese dimensions are the (1) goal oriented activities of the group, and the (2) quality of the interactions among the members. This list includes goal determination, goal pursuit, the development of values and norms, role differentiation, communication-interaction, conflict resolution and behavior control, changes in emotions, group culture, group resources, extra group transactions, group boundaries, and group climate (Garvin, 1987, pp. 113–121).

Henry first notes conflict between those who prefer analytic and organic approaches, respectively, to the question of what goes on in a group. She bases her answers on those identified by many early group work writers. She identifies as important criteria several aspects of group life, including group composition and criteria for membership; some level of consensus on group goals; the external structure, which consists of time, space, and size; time, or the time framework within which the group meets; internal structure; cohesion, communication, and decision-making; norms, values, and group culture; and group control and influence (1992, pp. 2–16).

GROUP WORK: VALUES AND PERCEPTIONS

This book addresses group work as part of social work. As such, it shares many values and perceptions with the entire social work profession. Getting our arms around group work is not easy. It is not surprising that three internationally renowned scholars who attempted to produce an exhaustive text on group work had to do so in a total of five substantive chapters authored by nine group work scholars. Then, they followed with five chapters, each of which is followed by a list of suggested readings (Garvin, Gutierrez, & Galinsky, 2004).

Northen and Kurland view social work as based on two fundamental values. They are "a conviction that each person has inherent worth and dignity" and "a conviction that people should have responsibility for each other"—the latter, they characterize as "the democratic spirit in action" (2001, p. 16).

On the other hand, it was pointed out, with both truth and wit, that contemporary group work stems from a symbolic total of no fewer than three parents (Weiner, 1964). One understands well the permutations and distortions of identity that can arise from interacting with only one or two parents. Imagine those that can arise from interacting with three! The "three parents" referred to are recreation, informal education, and social work. Each has left an inheritance of great value to group work.

From its recreational sources, group work has acquired an understanding of and a respect for the power of participation in activity, only one form of which is talking. Unlike other methods, which assume that talking is the highest form of interaction, group work understands that doing in interaction with others can have wonderful outcomes for individual group members, for groups, and for the society of which the group is part.

Related to this is both a positive valuation and a perception that it is important for people to do, to act, to interact with their environments. Group work has never even seriously considered a view of humans as only passive recipients of external influences. In group work, empowering group members to speak, to express opinions, to interact, to decide, and to act on their external environments are seen as essential purposes, always depending, of course, on the capacities of the group members. While assessment—especially self-assessment—is an important part of groups' lives, social work with groups emphasizes the assessment of strengths in addition to, indeed sometimes instead of, the assessment of weaknesses.

Partly for this reason, clinical diagnoses tend not to be seen as helpful by many group work practitioners. A great deal of practice experience teaches that categorical diagnoses are often inaccurate predictors of how people can and will act in groups. Also, although individual "intake" interviews are recommended by many of the authors in this book, some skepticism about the yield of such interviews may be warranted, because individual interviews do not always predict behavior in a group.

From its early years, group work has valued differences among group members, whether these differences be of race, class, sex, ethnicity, citizenship status, religious identity, age, or disability. Much group work took place in agencies and organizational settings identified with minority communities and/or with economically deprived and/or societally oppressed communities. Contemporary statements of perspective can be found, for example, in Toseland and Rivas (2005, pp. 131–135) and in Northen and Kurland (2001, pp. 221–237). Among the traditional sources of group work theory and practice, one of the most influential theorists of group dynamics was himself a refugee from totalitarian oppression and therefore was keenly aware of the potential for bigotry and intergroup violence (Lewin, 1948). A similar perspective can be found in the influential writings of another educator, herself a refugee from the same Holocaust, Gisela Konopka (e.g., 1983). An awareness both of women's needs and of various aspects of ethnicity can be found in early writings from the settlement-house field (e.g., Addams, 1909) through, one hopes, the present day.

As is true of other methods and fields of social work, group workers sometimes work with people with whom they quickly come to feel empathy. Sometimes one feels admiration for group members who struggle with handicaps, who are the victims of injustice, or who face difficult processes of rehabilitation. By contrast, with other populations, it may be difficult or even painful for a worker to attempt to relate helpfully to group members whose past or present behavior is personally abhorrent or is a reminder of painful experiences in the worker's own life or violates deeply held personal convictions of the worker. Supervisors, peers, and consultants may all be helpful in dealing with one's feelings about working with such groups.

In the extreme case, it may be impossible for a particular worker at a particular stage of life to work effectively with a particular population. The pain involved may be too great and the blocks to working with a group within the framework of "empathy, genuineness and warmth" (Garvin, 1987, p. 87) or "humanistic values and democratic norms" (Glassman, 2009) too intense. For example, a worker who has recently lost a family member to cancer may not be able, at this time, to work with a group of cancer patients or their relatives. Recognizing such a limitation is a sign of maturity and ethical decision making on the part of the worker and agency, not of incompetence or weakness.

Experience teaches that such situations are rare. Social workers often establish helping, empathic, genuine, and warm relationships with groups whose members have committed deeply antisocial acts. This certainly does not mean that workers approve of these acts. It means that, in groups, members' humanity tends to have more impact on group workers than their past or even present misdeeds and pathologies. The principle of unconditional positive regard for the worth of each person, at the same time that one disapproves of specific behaviors—sometimes stated in a religious context as "loving the sinner even when one hates the sin"—is an important component of group work. So, in a strengths perspective, one builds upon what group members can do and learn to do, rather than upon their limitation and disabilities.

GROUP WORK: PURPOSES AND GOALS

At one level, the purposes of group work are those of the social work profession, given the particular perspectives just sketched, providing the best possible services to clients in order to achieve the three purposes of social work: prevention of dysfunction, provision of resources for enhanced social functioning, and rehabilitation. At a suitably high level of abstraction, it is difficult to argue with these purposes. However, at a higher level of specificity, we have found it useful to take into account the typology of agency purposes and the emphasis on the importance of organizational factors introduced by Garvin (1997).

While emphasizing that no agency can be considered to have only one purpose, this typology views the major categories of purpose as being *socialization* and *resocialization*. Each category contains two subpurposes: *identity development* and *skill attainment* in the case of socialization and *social control* and *rehabilitation* in the case of resocialization. By emphasizing the importance of agency processes and structure to what happens with groups within that agency, Garvin's discussion, which is based on those of several organizational theorists, provides a useful perspective for the group work practitioner.

Many health care and social agencies seek to sponsor group work programs but are less receptive to the idea that their organizational structure, their emotional climate, how they are perceived by the community, their policies, or even their physical facilities operate in ways that can undercut or oppose the thrusts and objectives of the program. For this reason, conducting a group work program within an organizational context requires a group worker to have a broad vision: one that encompasses the organizational sponsor as well as the members of the groups within the broader context of client systems. In keeping with the general principle that group work always involves work with the group *and* work with the environment, the worker has an ongoing responsibility to address, and sometimes to help the group address, organizational factors such as those mentioned that can interfere with the accomplishment of the group's purposes.

GROUP WORK METHOD: AN OVERVIEW

Alissi (1982) defined what he referred to as a "reaffirmation of essentials" regarding group work method. It remains a useful platform from which to look at group work methods. He identified relationships, contracts, and programming as essential elements and as elements that distinguish social work with groups from other group methods

By *relationships,* Alissi meant those that are authentic, that involve an atmosphere in which "genuine feelings can be expressed and shared and by which
members can be encouraged to relate in similar ways within as well as beyond the
group…. The fundamental question to be asked throughout the process is what
kinds of relationship are best suited for what kind of ends?" (1982, p. 13).

The worker's relationship with group members and with the group as a whole
needs to be simultaneously conscious and spontaneous, a considerable challenge.
The principle of conscious use of self—knowing what one is doing and why one
is doing it—is basic. The countervailing principle of being oneself, of being spontaneous, of expressing feelings in a warm and accepting way, may seem like a
contradiction. In this writer's view, the bridging concept is one of focusing on
whose needs are being met primarily. The relationship between worker and group
needs to be a disciplined and focused one, and, of course, a nonexploitive one that
helps provide an atmosphere of safety, both physical and emotional, within the
group.

That exploitation and boundary violations are less often problems in group
work than in the one-to-one situation is due to the greater availability of support
for group members from each other. This in no way relieves the worker from
observing the boundaries set by ethics, by prevailing social standards, and by the
sensitivities of the members of a particular group or community.

Alissi's second aspect of method is that of *contracts,* or "working agreements"
between worker and group. "Unless members are involved in clarifying and setting their own personal and common group goals, they cannot be expected to be
active participants in their own behalf" (1982, p. 13). There is an egalitarian
flavor—a sense of worker and members working together to accomplish a common
goal that is overt and understood—that distinguishes social work with groups
from other therapeutic methods. Naturally, the capacity of group members to
understand the common goals often sets significant limitations on this part of
group work method, especially in the early stages of group development.

The third aspect, *programming,* refers to the point made earlier, about the ability of activities of various kinds, levels of intensity and skills, and activity media to
influence both interpersonal and intrapsychic processes within a group. With
many of the populations discussed in this book, verbal discussion is not the only
medium of communication, and it is often far from the best. Truly, one has the
opportunity to experience the truth of the old proverb that actions speak louder
than words.

GROUP WORK: SPECIFIC TECHNIQUES

Many of the specific techniques and skills of group work practice are discussed in
the chapters of this book as they relate to the population under discussion. As is
often the case, terminology can pose a problem. What one author calls *techniques,*

another calls *skills, technologies, worker behaviors,* or *interventions.* Despite the popularity of the last term, we think it is limited as a description of what social workers do in groups. Somehow *intervention* connotes entering group process from the outside and therefore portrays the worker as external to the group, at least most of the time. We think that the social worker is best understood as a person who is a member of the group, although a member with a difference: one with a specialized, disciplined, professionally and ethically bounded role. This role is defined in part by the structure and purpose of the sponsoring organization, in part by the personality and style of the worker, and in large part by the needs and developmental stage of group and members.

Many writers have attempted to list techniques. It is often useful to review these lists, both to free one's creativity and to remind oneself of the great range of possibilities open to a worker in a group. Among the useful lists of techniques are those developed by Garvin (1997), Northen and Kurland (2001), Brown (1991), Middleman and Goldberg Wood (1991), Bertcher (1994), and Toseland and Rivas (2004). Although Ephross and Vassil's list (2005) was originally intended for use with working groups, its contents are suitable for work with many other kinds of groups as well. Shulman's book on skills of helping (2008) contains a great deal of discussion of techniques.

Brown's list of 11 specific techniques may be particularly useful to beginning workers. Clearly referring primarily to verbal group processes, his typology is organized under three major headings:

Information Sharing

1. Giving information, advice, or suggestion(s); directing
2. Seeking information or reactions about (a) individual, group, or significant others, or (b) agency policies and procedures

Support and Involvement

1. Accepting and reassuring, showing interest
2. Encouraging the expression of ideas and feelings
3. Involving the individuals or group in activity or discussion

Self-Awareness and Task Accomplishment

1. Exploring with the individual or group the meaning of individual or group behavior, as well as life experiences
2. Reflecting on individual or group behavior
3. Reframing an issue or problem
4. Partializing and prioritizing an issue or problem
5. Clarifying or interpreting individual or group behavior, as well as life experiences
6. Confronting an individual or the group (Brown, 1991, p. 113)

Each of these techniques, of course, can be further subdivided and needs to be adapted to work with particular groups at particular stages of development in particular settings

What may be useful to add to the various lists are some techniques and principles of practice that are so basic that they are often overlooked. The first is the *ability to keep still*, sometimes referred to as the *ability not to interfere with group process and group development*. The problem here is not just that social workers in general and group workers in particular tend to be verbal people, but rather a more serious, more or less conscious misunderstanding of the purposes of helping to form a group. The issue is the locus of the helping dynamic. Contrary to the (more or less conscious) fantasies of beginning group workers, help in groups comes *from the group, not just from the worker*. For the group to develop and to provide members with the support, learning, growth, and healing referred to earlier in the chapter and throughout this book, the group needs "air time," room for members to talk and act, and silences that can represent reflective pause for groups or can stimulate participation by members.

Of course, workers need to be more active at the beginning of groups, with groups whose members have limited capacities, and in particular situations. After a while, though, we offer the following rough estimate: if the social worker is occupying more than 20% of the group's talking time—and with some groups even this proportion is high—the situation needs analysis and reflection. This figure, not to be taken too literally, is meant to apply over a period of time. But the technique of *not responding verbally*, which is really an expression of a participative and group nurturing skill, is an important one.

A second technique is that of *summarizing and bridging*. Often akin to the technique of *framing and reframing*, noted by other writers, *summarizing* consists of sharing an assessment of what the group has done and the point it has reached, while *bridging* consists of suggesting the work that lies ahead and assigning it a time frame. Nothing sounds simpler or demands greater concentration from the social worker. Because of the possibility that one may summarize inaccurately, social workers often will "ask" a summary rather than "tell" it, inviting correction and the expression of different views. Some experienced group workers refer to the summarizing-and-bridging process as serving as a road map for the group, helping its members see where it has arrived and where it has to go.

A third important technique is the use of limits. In group life, as for individuals, the absence of limits equals madness. Skill in the use of limits is, in part, the willingness of social workers to accept and feel comfortable with the authority they often have in groups. But skill in the use of limits means much more than comfort with the realities of administrative (and sometimes legal) authority as an internal process within the workers. Its other components include an ability to form clear and easily understood contracts with groups and an ability to help the group focus on why they exist and what they are about. Effective limits are those that have been internalized by group members and those that are defined by the reality of the group's situation, rather than merely those imposed by the social worker or agency, seemingly for arbitrary or irrelevant reasons.

Skilled group workers employ a range of approaches to developing consensual limits. Some people, situations, and matches between workers and groups seem to minimize conflicts about limits; others seem to intensify them. Also, one needs to recognize that there may be situations— as in a group in which attendance is legally mandated, for example—in which simply stating and enforcing a rule is the path to effective limits. One principle to keep in mind is that, for most members, most groups, and most sponsoring organizations, groups are transitory realities. The goal is for members to gain from their group participation knowledge and growth that they can take with them into the other areas of their lives and into future memberships, not merely to become the "best" possible members of the groups in which they participate with professional social work leadership.

Considerations of space limit us to a brief reference to the development of practice theory linked especially to the concept of the stages of group development (Garland et al., 1965, among others). One of the most useful developments is the connection that can be drawn between stage theory and specific worker roles and behaviors in the group. Particularly, one should note that often the worker needs to be considerably more active in the beginning stages of a group than later, when the group has developed some momentum (and some norms and structure) of its own. Schiller (1995) has raised the probability that many groups composed of women go through these steps of group development in a different order than had been described in men or mixed groups.

Let us turn now to some specific considerations about the behavior of the worker. First, the reader should note the use of the singular. In our view, the basis for professional helping in groups is one worker, one group. This is not to imply that there is no place for co-leadership. In an era of concern about resources, for one thing, and given the nature of group work, for another, there needs to be a positive reason for having more than one worker in a group. Several good reasons come quickly to mind. They include:

1. Physical safety. In a group that contains people with a tendency to act out, there may need to be two workers, one of whom can go for help or leave the group with a disruptive member, and the other worker.
2. Situations in which the co-leader is really a trainee. It is often very helpful for a student or an inexperienced worker to co-lead with a senior colleague. At other times, however, students and beginning workers can do very well in a solo worker situation.
3. Groups in which it is important to model differences, whether sexual, racial, ethnic, or any other kind. A male-female team may be effective in working with a group of heterosexual couples, for example.

Other situations that justify co-leadership can be described. In the absence of a positive reason, however, solo leadership is much less expensive and causes fewer logistical problems. Of equal importance is the fact that co-leadership can provide a fertile ground for various interpersonal processes that can impede group progress. These can be minimized in a solo worker format. Co-leadership requires planned communication between the workers (Weiss, 1988).

The basic reason for doing group work is the power of the group, *not the worker*. As long as one can keep this point clearly in mind and recognize that the worker in a group is the orchestra's conductor, not its concert master or principal bassist, the use of a solo worker will make greater sense in the absence of a positive reason for having more than one worker.

Various texts are available that supplement the brief overview given in this chapter. Many are listed in the references at the end of this chapter. All agree that no specific technique equals in importance the commitment of a group worker to enabling a group to form, allowing it to operate, and joining with the members in celebrating the individual and group growth, which is the raison d'être of group work.

REFERENCES

Addams, J. (1909). *The spirit of youth and the city streets*. New York: Macmillan.

Alissi, A. (1982). The social group work method: Towards a reaffirmation of essentials. *Social Work with Groups*, 5(3), 3–17.

Bertcher, H. J. (1994). *Group participation: Techniques for leaders and members* (2nd ed.). Thousand Oaks, CA: Sage.

Brown, L. N. (1991) *Groups for growth and change*. New York: Longman.

Ephross, P. H., & Vassil, T. V. (2004). *Groups that work: Structure and process* (2nd ed.). New York: Columbia University Press.

Falck, H. S. (1988). *Social work: The membership perspective*. New York: Springer.

Fatout, M., & Rose, S. R. (1995). *Task groups in the social services*. Thousand Oaks, CA: Sage.

Galinsky, M., & Schopler, J. (1989). Developmental patterns in open-ended groups. *Social Work with Groups*. 12(2), 99–104.

Garland, J., Jones, H., & Kolodny, R. L. (1965). A model of stages of group development in social work groups. In S. Bernstein (ed.), *Explorations in group work* (pp. 21–30). Boston: Boston University School of Social Work.

Garvin, C.D. (1997). *Contemporary group work* (3rd ed.). Boston: Allyn & Bacon.

Garvin, C. D., Gutierrez, L.M., & Galinsky, M.J. (eds.). (2004). *Handbook of social work with groups*. New York: Guilford Press.

Garvin, C. D., & Reed, B. G. (1994). Small group theory and social work practice: Promoting diversity and social justice or recreating inequities? In R. R. Greene (ed.), *Human behavior theory: A diversity framework* (pp. 173–201). New York: Aldine de Gruyter.

Gitterman, A., & Shulman, L. (1994). *Mutual aid groups, vulnerable populations, and the life cycle* (2nd ed.). New York: Columbia University Press. For a briefer but cogent and useful summary, see Gitterman, A. (2004). The mutual aid model. In C. D. Garvin, et al. (eds.), *Handbook of social work with groups* (pp. 99-118). New York: Guilford Press, 2004.

Glassman, U. (2009). *Group work: A humanistic and skills approach* (2nd ed.). Newbury Park, CA: Sage.

Henry, S. (1992). *Group skills in social work: A four-dimensional approach*. Pacific Grove, CA: Brooks/Cole.

Konopka, G. (1983). *Social group work: A helping process* (3rd ed.). Englewood Cliffs, NJ: Prentice-Hall.

Lewin, K. (1948). *Resolving social conflicts*. New York: Harper & Row.

Middleman, R. R. (1982). *The non-verbal method in working with groups: The use of activity in teaching, counseling and therapy* (enlarged ed.). Hebron, CT: Practitioners Press.

Middleman, R. R., & Goldberg Wood, G. (1991). *Skills for direct practice social work*. New York: Columbia University Press.

Northen, H., & Kurland, R. (2001). *Social work with groups* (3rd ed.). New York: Columbia University Press.

Schiller, L. Y. (1995). Stages of development in women's groups: A relational model. In R. Kurland & R. Solomon (eds.), *Group work practice in a troubled society: Problems and opportunities* (pp. 117–138). Binghamton, NY: Haworth.

Shulman, L. (2008). *The skills of helping individuals, families groups and communities* (6th ed.). Itasca, IL: Peacock.

Toseland, R., & Rivas, R. F. (2005). *An introduction to group work practice* (5th ed.). Boston: Allyn & Bacon.

Weiner, H. J. (1964). Social change and social group work practice. *Social Work, 9*, 106–112.

Weiss, J. C. (1988). The D-R model of co-leadership of groups. *Small Group Behavior, 19*, 117–125.

Part One

Health Issues

Chapter One

Group Work With People Who Have Cancer

Steven R. Rose and Barry M. Daste

Cancer is a disease that often has major psychological, physiological, and social consequences for patients, as well as for their families and friends. Lifestyle trends that could prevent cancer are not all positive. Since the early 1990s, there has been little improvement in the consumption of fruit and vegetables and in leisure-time physical activity among adults; also, fewer children are enrolled in physical education classes. The prevalence of overweight and obesity among children, adolescents, and adults has risen considerably since the early 1970s.

Cancer strikes differentially by demographic factors, including gender, socioeconomic background, race, and age. In the United States, men have a 1:2 lifetime probability of developing cancer, and women have a 1:3 lifetime probability (Groopman, 2007). African Americans are more likely to die of cancer than are whites, and men are more likely to die of cancer than are women. The American Cancer Society (ACS) estimated that about 1.5 million new cases of cancer will be diagnosed in the United States in 2009. Furthermore, the ACS estimated that about 292,540 cancer deaths of men and 269,800 cancer deaths of women would occur in 2009 in the United States, of which lung cancer remains the most common type of fatal cancer for both men and women.

Cancer is a pervasive illness that affects three of four families in the United States (Taylor et al., 1986). Although the treatment of cancer has become more successful in recent years, the emotional impact on individuals and their families remains great (Evans et al., 1992, p. 229). While half of all patients with cancer survived for at least 5 years in 1975–1977, two of three survived for that interval in 1996–2004 (see www.cancer.org for the most current statistics). Before diagnosis, the individual normally experiences general illness that progresses to the point where malignancy is suspected. Following this period of illness, the individual is subjected to numerous physiological tests that determine whether cancer is present. Testing leads to diagnosis. A cancer diagnosis is considered to be one of the most feared and serious events of an individual's life. It produces significant stress on all individuals involved (Daste, 1990). The stages that follow diagnosis include surgery and/or treatment, such as chemotherapy or radiotherapy; evaluation of the patient's prognosis; and medical follow-up (Gilbar, 1991, p. 293). During each of the stages of cancer detection, diagnosis, and treatment, patients with cancer face a number of questions about their vulnerability to the disease.

The specific issues that patients face include a sense of threat to their lives, their wholeness of body, sense of self-perception, mental balance, and social functioning (Gilbar, 1991, p. 293). Patients are often concerned about the implications of the disease for their future quality of life and for their relationships with family members and friends. In addition, they normally experience a wide spectrum of emotions, including anger, fear, sadness, guilt, embarrassment, and shame. Young adults are likely to struggle with anxiety about their physical well-being, fertility, and childrearing (Roberts et al., 1997).

Patients with cancer often express anger at their fate. Anger is frequently directed at the medical staff, who first inform the patient of the disease or treat the patient over the course of the illness, and at family members, who attempt to protect, coddle, or in general treat the patient differently than they did before the cancer diagnosis.

Sadness and depression, which are commonly experienced by patients with cancer, emanate from many sources. The latter include resignation about uncompleted tasks or goals, as well as fear and isolation often resulting from the disease. Physical losses associated with breast, colon, or laryngeal cancer may lead to depression. Often the patient with cancer is unable to discuss fears and emotions with family members, thereby increasing a sense of isolation. Studies have reported that both self-help and therapy groups for patients with cancer allow the expression of fears, as of death, and that such expression has numerous positive effects on the patients' sense of well-being and self-esteem (Ferlic et al., 1979; Spiegel & Yalom, 1978).

Patients who undergo radical surgical or treatment procedures that leave visible scars or signs of the disease are susceptible to embarrassment and shame. For example, appliances used by patients with a colostomy often have side effects such as odor, which can cause the patient great embarrassment (Gilbar & Groisman, 1991). Mastectomy or prostatectomy can cause patients to feel less sexually attractive and desirable to their spouses or lovers (Arrington, 2000; Gilbar, 1991).

Changes in bodily function resulting from such procedures also require some adjustment by the patient, as well as for family members and friends. These changes can serve as a major inconvenience in planning simple daily activities, as well as limiting access to activities in which the person previously participated.

Studies have documented the need for social support both as a means of preventing disease and as a factor in recovery from illness (Taylor et al., 1986). In dealing with the issues and emotions related to the diagnosis of cancer, family members and friends of the patient can serve as important sources of support (Palmer et al., 2000). However, family members or friends sometimes become overwhelmed with the patient's crisis and withdraw to protect themselves and to deal with their own emotional issues (Daste, 1989). If the supporting person and the patient have had previous relationship difficulties, the former may make attempts to rectify the situation for his or her own benefit without necessarily considering the needs or wishes of the patient. For example, a spouse who is about to leave a failed marriage decides to remain in it ostensibly to protect the patient but in reality to avoid the prospect of facing immense personal guilt. In other situations, family members attempt to support the patient but actually contribute to the patient's emotional distress (Daste, 1990). For example, this occurs when they attempt to treat the patient in the ways they would want to be treated in similar circumstances while ignoring the requests or desires of the patient to be treated as he or she wishes.

Both juvenile and adult patients with cancer often are reluctant to express their fear and sadness with family members because of their desire to protect the family system (Daste, 1990; Price, 1992). Siblings of juvenile patients with cancer often experience negative emotions and are unlikely to express these emotions to family members (Evans et al., 1992). Kaufman and his colleagues (1992) report that cancer diagnoses in children may exacerbate existing problems in dysfunctional families, and the resulting stress can increase the child's illness.

Complementary methods are increasingly being used in the United States by people with cancer. Support groups are one of the complementary methods frequently used by cancer survivors (Gansler et al., 2008). Support groups were reported to be used by 9.7% of a sample of 4139 survivors of 1 of 10 cancers that occur in adults.

Support or self-help groups designed to address the specific needs of patients with cancer and/or their families allow the patient to receive support and express emotions in a nonjudgmental and safe environment. These groups can provide education about the disease and about methods or techniques the patient can use to alleviate anxiety, stress, and depression (Forester et al., 1993; Montazeri et al., 2001; Vugia, 1991). Techniques such as visual imagery, self-hypnotic therapy, deep muscle relaxation, and systematic desensitization can also help to counteract the side effects of treatment methods like chemotherapy (Forester et al., 1993; Harmon, 1991).

To increase the likelihood that patients will attend and participate in cancer support groups, social workers should consider a wide range of individual and group factors, including the cancer patient identity, the presence of existing support, practical issues, coping styles, the match between the patient and the group, knowledge of and referral to groups, and solving problems experienced by particular groups (Ussher et al., 2008). Indeed, participation in support groups may be increased by involving the support network of the patient with cancer (Sherman et al., 2008).

Researchers have concluded that groups that provide intensive coping skills, such as those just discussed, are far more effective than traditional supportive group therapy (Telch & Telch, 1986). Self-help groups are prevalent (Gray & Fitch, 2001). Lieberman (1988) reported that client-led self-help groups appear to have "meaningful roles in helping individuals with psychosocial problems" (p. 168). Empirical studies of professionally led face-to-face cancer support groups for adults indicated that participants tended to be very satisfied with them (Gottlieb & Wachala, 2007). The groups were associated with improvements in morale and quality of life.

While much information is available about different types of cancer-focused treatment groups, studies continue to be performed in an attempt to substantiate the effectiveness of one group treatment method over another. Telch and Telch (1986) wrote that supportive group therapy is the most widely used and most intensively studied form of treatment. While a group may be primarily designed to provide education, psychological intervention is typically needed by group members.

PRACTICE PRINCIPLES

The practice principles that apply to group work with patients with cancer are similar to those that apply to group work in general. However, the issues that patients with cancer typically face tend to differ from those of other populations and should be kept in mind when composing and facilitating groups. One issue is the treatment status of each group member. Patients who receive chemotherapy or radiation therapy routinely experience side effects such as nausea, pain, or extreme fatigue. During this phase of their cancer treatment, these patients' attendance can be irregular, and they tend to be disoriented and distracted.

Contracting requires much flexibility; contracts should be tailored to each individual member. Given the nature and effects of cancer and its treatment, social workers must strive to understand when members can and cannot attend and participate, and continue to accept them in the group. The social worker should continually encourage members to attend and participate. Termination of these groups often entails flexibility, too. Often, members cannot predict with accuracy when and for how long they can continue to attend. Some groups formed expressly for terminally ill patients with cancer are open groups and continue to function after the deaths of individual members.

Other factors that are important to group work with patients with cancer include stage of the disease, type of cancer, amount of physical distress, age, religion, level and quality of support from family and friends, the development of mental disorders related to cancer, terminal versus nonterminal status, size of the group, and training of the leaders (Daste, 1990). For example, skilled group leadership has been shown to be an important factor in the success of prostate cancer support groups (Oliffe et al., 2009).

STAGE OF THE DISEASE

The stage of a patient's disease is important for a number of reasons. First, the issues faced by patients whose cancer is in remission are dramatically different from those of patients who are terminally ill. Patients whose cancer is in remission are primarily concerned with the potential recurrence of the disease, while patients who are terminally ill are often more concerned about their impending death, the process of dying, and the implications of these events for their family and friends. Understandably, patients who are dying may feel envious or resent those whose prognosis is more hopeful. Simonton and Sherman (2000) developed a treatment model that addresses patients with various stages of the disease.

DIFFERENCES AMONG AFFECTED GROUPS

Cancer, while having similar implications for all patients, strikes a heterogeneous group of individuals. Particular types of cancer often have specific implications for group composition. Patients with breast or colon cancer often have similar issues and can relate readily to other patients with the same concerns. Patients with breast cancer who have issues related to their sexuality and their perceived loss of femininity tend to feel more comfortable discussing such issues with other patients with breast cancer. Persons who have had sarcoma of a limb may have lost an arm or a leg due to amputation or have experienced more limited use of the limb. Issues such as limited mobility will often arise among these individuals.

Furthermore, age and stage of life are important considerations that differentiate responses to cancer. Adolescents with cancer are particularly vulnerable. They commonly experience many important losses and changes, including their former selves (prediagnosis person and prediagnosis family); relationships with parents, siblings, and girlfriends/boyfriends; body image; health; school life; independence; certainty about and indications of the future; and hope (Stevens & Dunsmore, 1996).

These issues and many other related concerns need to be kept in mind by the social worker. All such issues are often discussed with patients before they enter a group in order to offset the possible occurrence of problems at a later date.

DEMOGRAPHIC ISSUES

Members' age has significance for group work. Clearly, pediatric patients with cancer require a group setting that is age appropriate and allows them to discuss their unique concerns. Also, adult patients who are at different stages in life may feel more accepted by those in a similar stage. They may be better able to deal with issues that suit their particular needs.

Similarly, religion can significantly affect the sense of purpose and hope of patients with cancer. Their religious or spiritual orientation may affect their acceptance of various aspects of the disease. In addition, the religion or spirituality of significant others can affect how patients with cancer relate to them.

LEVELS OF SUPPORT

Support from family and friends affects the morale of the patient with cancer and can be an important factor in group work. Those patients who have less support available to them than do other patients are liable to feel even more depressed and alone in groups where family members and friends are allowed to attend. The social worker should be aware of situations where some patients may not have any supportive family members or friends while other patients seem to have an abundance of such support. One way of preventing the occurrence of this problem is to have separate groups for patients and for family members. As well meaning as family and friends may be, there are issues for which their attendance will inhibit discussion. For example, some patients may feel more comfortable discussing sexual issues among fellow patients without family and friends being in attendance.

There appears to be a relationship between level of support and benefits from group work. One study showed that peer discussion groups were helpful for women with breast cancer who lacked support elsewhere but were not helpful for women who had high levels of outside support (Gelgeson et al., 2000).

MENTAL DISORDERS

While in some cases mental disorders are present before the cancer diagnosis, patients often develop such disorders as a result of the disease (Fawzy et al., 1997). These disorders may be either new mental disorders and/or an exacerbation of previously existing disorders. These factors should be considered by the social worker who composes and facilitates the group. The appropriateness of including patients with major mental disorders should be considered in terms of their ability to interact with other members, engage in the group process, and benefit from it. Furthermore, the locus and type of treatment of mental disorders must be considered.

SIZE OF THE GROUP

Group size can have an impact on the effectiveness and level of intimacy within a group. Spiegel and Yalom (1978), in reporting on their group of patients with metastatic carcinoma, noted that the maximum effective size was seven. When the size of the group reached more than eight, the group was subdivided into two smaller groups (Spiegel & Yalom, 1978). Similarly, in a program designed by Cunningham and colleagues (1991), educational groups ranged in size from 12 to 15 members, but these groups were later subdivided to facilitate discussion (p. 44). Smaller groups are usually more cohesive and develop closer bonds than do larger groups (Daste, 1990).

Group size is often related to other issues, such as the presence of supportive family members and friends. As previously mentioned, the advisability of having family members present during discussions of subjects that the patients want to discuss privately should also be appraised.

WORKER SELF-AWARENESS

Practitioner self-awareness is an important aspect of providing high-quality, professional health care (Epstein, 1999). Among the most important issues in group practice with patients with cancer is the social worker's personal orientation to the disease. Often, the person diagnosed with cancer is afraid of death and dying. Because of the importance of this issue, it is often necessary for the practitioner to address this issue within the group. Consequently, the practitioner needs to face his or her own feelings regarding death (Firestone & Catlett, 2009). Often the full impact of this issue occurs when one is faced with it personally. This can be a very lonely time, and the issue becomes an existential one as opposed to an interpersonal one. Even in a group setting, members can feel alone and will require a lot of empathic understanding.

The social worker's interaction with the group should be clearly conceptualized and described in the planning phase of the group. The literature is divided on the role of the group facilitator. In a number of groups studied, the role is to educate the group members, while in other groups, researchers contend that it is to assist the members in expressing their emotions about their disease. Cunningham et al. (1991) noted that psychological interventions in cancer groups are becoming increasingly common. However, Vugia (1991) considered the role of leaders in self-help support groups as aiding members while allowing the members to maintain some authority (p. 94).

OPEN VERSUS CLOSED GROUPS

Opinions vary among professionals about whether cancer groups should be open or closed. The issue of open versus closed groups depends on the population being served. Both types of groups have advantages and disadvantages. Open groups, for example, allow more utilization, while closed groups provide a more intimate atmosphere and allow for more in-depth discussion of sensitive topics.

The literature indicates that cancer groups frequently are open, allowing new members to enter at any time (Daste, 1989). However, other research concludes that groups should be closed to new members after the first few sessions to enhance cohesion of the group and to "allow progressive work and promote good attendance" (Cunningham et al., 1991, p. 44).

Davidson (1985) notes that *burnout* is especially applicable to those working in the field of oncology because death and the threat of death create a large emotional burden. Group work with patients with cancer is challenging and often very trying (Daste, 1990).Persons who conduct group work with patients with cancer should be prepared to discuss such topics as death, dying, disfigurement, pain, and loss of function. Harmon (1991) presents the experience of one group in which a member died and the leaders consequently attempted to prevent the group from acknowledging or discussing it. Yalom and Greaves (1977) found that in their group, the therapists contributed to superficial group interaction because they felt that such topics might be too threatening for patients when, in reality, they were protecting themselves. According to Fobair (1997), open groups, such as drop-in groups, and closed groups, such as supportive-expressive existentialist groups, span a continuum.

COMMON THEMES

Some of the themes that social workers should keep in mind when conducting group work with patients with cancer include the following:

1. Fear of death
2. Fear of disease recurrence
3. Unique problems related to the long- and short-term effects of treatment
4. Changes in personal relationships
5. Economic issues

Other themes in conducting groups with patients with cancer include problems such as changes in sexual function during treatment, partners' reactions to loss of breasts or scarring, and loss of fertility due to some types of chemotherapy. Each of these problems has interpersonal manifestations that become significant in a group setting.

Fear of Death

Although cancer is a more treatable and survivable illness today than in the past, a cancer diagnosis frequently implies the possibility of death. Given cancer mortality rates, the patient's fear of death is often realistic. However, some cancers are more treatable than others.

As noted, often the patient's family or friends are also frightened by the diagnosis. Sometimes they inhibit the patient from discussing the possibility of death. However, group work can provide the patient with the forum for discussing it. Some authors have reported that patients' anxiety about death was often lessened when they were able to connect on a transcendent or spiritual level (Cunningham et al., 1991). Similarly, Spiegel (1992) found that allowing patients to discuss the possibility of death and its attendant anxieties lessened their fear of death and dying.

Fear of Disease Recurrence

Most patients with cancer experience a fear of recurrence of the disease. This is especially manifested for varying periods of time following initial diagnosis and treatment. Whenever a new pain occurs, an unexplained lump appears, a cough begins, or one of many other conditions arises, the patient with cancer will typically fear the worst. This is perhaps the single most difficult part of coping for those who have had cancer. It is as if a sword hangs over the patient's head from the time of initial diagnosis until the day he or she dies, even though the disease may never reappear. The fear of recurrence becomes a focal point, particularly for patients with cancer who have survived the initial cancer and are in remission.

Long- and Short-Term Effects of Treatment

Other common themes with patients with cancer are the short- and long-term effects of chemotherapy and radiation therapy, such as hair loss. Nausea and vomiting and the inability to maintain earlier eating patterns become recurrent themes.

Interpersonal Relationships

Interpersonal relationships often change when cancer enters the picture. Multiple interpersonal manifestations often provide surprises for group members. Some people with cancer become distanced from friends and family members. Some face constant questioning from others about the cancer, even when they would rather not talk about it. Some people find that their choice of partners becomes more limited, frequently due to fears about the patient's future. This problem may continue long after the person has survived cancer. Some experience either over-protectiveness or distancing from spouses or lovers.

Economic Issues

Often, financial issues arise for people with cancer in the present U.S. health care system. First, working persons who have cancer and take time off from work associated with their treatment can face a loss of income if they are unable to make up the missed work in an acceptable manner. Lost wages often create further difficulty for many persons with cancer who are faced with covering costs of living. Second, the cost of care frequently exceeds insurance benefits such that even those with insurance are likely to be faced with considerable financial hardship. Moreover, insurance companies sometimes attempt to drop clients who are proving very costly to continue to cover. Third, those persons who are fortunate to survive cancer often have great difficulty obtaining or transferring insurance plans due to preexisting condition limitations. Insurance generally becomes difficult or impossible to obtain following a cancer diagnosis, thereby limiting their job mobility (Nessim & Ellis, 2000). Fourth, patients with cancer and survivors also report job discrimination in hiring, promotion, and job assignments. Any person who has undergone treatment for cancer is considered legally handicapped and thus has some protection from job discrimination. However, this does not necessarily prevent the occurrence of discrimination.

RECOMMENDED WAYS OF WORKING

The cardinal practice principle is that social workers will be more effective if they compose and structure their groups to best meet the needs of the particular patients with cancer and/or survivors they wish to serve. Rather than placing everyone with a cancer diagnosis into a large group, it is far more beneficial to tailor each group to the specific needs of the prospective members. For example, 8- to 12-year-old children who undergone chemotherapy or radiotherapy have very different concerns than do women dying of breast cancer. People who have been cancer-free for 5 years have a different set of concerns than do those who have had a recurrence of the disease in that time span.

To a large extent, the population being served in the human service organization (HSO) will determine group composition. For example, a large hospital in a major metropolitan area usually has far more latitude in the numbers and types of groups that it can offer than does a small rural clinic, which may have to offer such groups in concert with other HSOs. The organizational context also determines other group parameters, including size, space considerations, availability of co-leaders, advocacy of services, and the accessibility of ancillary services such as delivery of meals or hospice care.

Group length is also population dependent. Indeed, group length often has to be tried and tailored to each HSO and the population it serves. Many social workers experience difficulty when they initially specify a certain number of sessions only to subsequently discover that the members, due to difficulties related to their cancer care or other factors related to their illness, find it difficult to work with the preset format. Many HSOs simply offer one large long-term group for all patients and significant others. This approach avoids many selection, time, and member availability issues because the group meets on a regular basis for all who care to attend. However, it also limits the potential that smaller, more carefully planned groups offer.

A case illustrating one of the problems of a large group that is open to all is as follows:

> During the weekly meeting of a large support group offered for patients with cancer, friends, and families by a metropolitan radiation treatment center, several newly diagnosed persons attended for the first time. John, a regular member, was suffering from a brain tumor and tended to dominate conversations without allowing others to speak. For this reason, the new members, who were uncomfortable in the group and who were very much in need of support, were denied an opportunity to participate.

A co-leader pattern is usually considered to be preferable to having one leader of the group for patients with cancer. For instance, if one worker is absent, the group can still meet. Co-leadership has many advantages over an individual worker pattern, assuming that the co-leaders work well together. Co-workers can complement and help each other in providing both technical expertise and emotional support.

Co-leadership allows more individual attention to be given to distraught members—one worker can attend to the individual while the other attends to the group process.

One key advantage of a co-worker pattern with these groups is that it allows the workers to deal with personal crises, which are often severe and require additional attention. If only one worker is present, the group as a whole must wait or must deal with the crises as a whole. In another type of therapy group this might be appropriate, but due to the nature of cancer and the potential for sudden life-or-death issues arising, the fear and panic may be so great that individual intervention is warranted. A case illustrating how co-leadership might be beneficial is as follows:

> During one of the sessions of a support group for women survivors of breast cancer, Jackie, who had been doing fine following breast cancer diagnosed and treated 2 years earlier, had just learned that her cancer had recurred. She bravely and patiently waited her turn to talk but finally felt overwhelmed by her fear, jumped up, and ran from the room. One of the co-leaders took off after her and spent a lot of time calming her down, as Jackie felt unable to return to the group. The other co-leader was able to continue without her.

EVALUATION MEASURES

Researchers have used many different methods to measure the effectiveness of groups in producing tangible benefits to patients. Instruments are available that measure quality of life, body image, self-esteem, support, and perceived personal control over illness (Helgeson et al., 2000). Scales such as those that measure quality of adjustment, stress levels, affect, optimism regarding disease treatment, and overall sensations of pain, discomfort, and anxiety are useful in determining the effectiveness of a cancer group intervention (Goodwin et al., 2001).

In a group organized by Spiegel and colleagues (1981), women with metastatic breast cancer were found to have less tension, depression, fatigue, confusion, maladjusted responses, and phobias than their control group counterparts.

In a postsurgery study of self-perception of women who had a mastectomy, Clarke and colleagues (1982) divided 40 patients into treatment and control groups. Ten weekly group psychotherapy sessions were offered. The authors used Q-sort tests and the Structured and Scaled Interview to Assess Maladjustment. While both groups showed positive change, the treatment group showed significantly greater improvement.

Other studies, such as one conducted by Kriss and Kraemer (1986), have examined patients periodically over several time periods—for example, three times over 12 months—to determine possible changes following group treatment. Longitudinal studies covering longer periods are also appropriate in determining changes following group treatment.

One of the difficulties in assessing evaluative research in this area is the great variety of methodology. Many ways exist to conduct research in this area. Accurately assessing outcome is difficult due to the number of variables involved. Both quantitative and qualitative methods are useful in assessing changes. Qualitative research on how cancer is experienced by patients and their families is useful in developing social workers' understanding and empathy, which is necessary for practice (Oktay, 2002). Questionnaires and scales measuring factors such as depression, fear, and coping can be administered on a pre- and post-treatment basis. Recording group attendance, degree of participation, and demographic representation by various ethnic/racial and socioeconomic groups will yield data that are useful to the social worker. Research questions should be addressed as early as possible to allow for gathering and analysis of more potential data. Much depends on what the social worker wants to know about the group members and how they cope with cancer.

CONCLUSION

Even though progress is occurring in the diagnosis and treatment of cancer, it remains a dreaded disease that places a great deal of emotional and physical stress on patients, their families, and friends. Many issues involving human relationships emerge when cancer appears. People with cancer are very heterogeneous. Usually, they have specific pressing concerns. This further mandates the need for groups designed to meet the specific needs of this population. In some groups, the social worker provides education and/or psychological intervention. Common themes among group members who are patients with cancer provide a basis for group discussion. Because there are so many variables in working with patients with cancer, the social worker must be flexible from the initial conceptualization of the group all the way to termination. Situations that are difficult to handle in a large, open group are often easier for the social worker to manage in a smaller, more carefully selected group.

RESOURCES

American Brain Tumor Association
2720 River Road
Des Plaines, IL 60018
(847) 827-9910

(800) 886-2282
Fax: (847) 827-9918
info@abta.org
www.abta.org

American Cancer Society
1599 Clifton Road NE
Atlanta, GA 30329
Cancer Answer Line: (800) 227-2345
www.cancer.org

American Institute for Cancer Research
1759 R Street NW
Washington, DC 20009
(202) 328-7744
(800) 843-8114
Fax: (202) 328-7226
aicrweb@aicr.org
www.aicr.org

Candlelighters Childhood Cancer Foundation
10400 Connecticut Avenue, Suite 205
Kensington, MD 20895
(301) 962-3520
(800) 366-2223
Fax: (301) 962-3521
staff@candlelighters.org
www.candlelighters.org

Colorectal Cancer Network
P.O. Box 182
Kensington, MD 20895
(301) 879-1500
Fax: (267) 821-7080
CCNetwork@colorectal-cancer.net
www.colorectal-cancer.net

CureSearch
Children's Oncology Group
440 E. Huntington Drive, Suite 400
Arcadia, CA 91006
(800) 458-6223
info@curesearch.org
www.curesearch.org

Kidney Cancer Association
1234 Sherman Avenue, Suite 203
Evanston, IL 60202
(847) 332-1051
(800) 850-9132
Fax: (847) 332-2978
office@kidneycancer.org
www.kidneycancer.org

National Alliance of Breast Cancer Organizations
9 East 37th Street, 10th Floor
New York, NY 10016
(888) 80-NABCO
Fax: (212) 689-1213
nabcoinfo@aol.org
www.nabco.org

National Breast Cancer Coalition
1101 17th Street, NW, Suite 1300
Washington, DC 20036
(202) 296-7477
(800) 622-2838
Fax: (202) 265-6854
www.stopbreastcancer.org

National Children's Cancer Society
1 South Memorial Drive, Suite 800
St. Louis, MO 63102
(314) 241-1600
(800) 532-6459
Fax: (314) 241-1996
www.children-cancer.com

National Foundation for Cancer Research
4600 East West Highway, Suite 525
Bethesda, MD 20814
(301) 654-1250
(800) 321-CURE
Fax: (301) 654-5824
info@nfcr.org
www.nfcr.org

National Ovarian Cancer Coalition, Inc.
2501 Oak Lawn Avenue, Suite 435

Dallas, TX 75219
(214) 273-4200
(888) OVARIAN
Fax: (214) 273-4201
NOCC@ovarian.org
www.ovarian.org

Support for People with Oral and Head and Neck Cancer
P.O. Box 53
Locust Valley, NY 11560
(800) 377-0928
Fax: (516) 671-8794
info@spohnc.org
www.spohnc.org

REFERENCES

Arrington, M. I. (2000). Sexuality, society, and senior citizens: An analysis of sex talk among prostate cancer support group members. *Sexuality & Culture, 4*(4), 45–74.

Clarke, D. L., Kramer, E., Lipiec, K., & Klein, S. (1982). Group psychotherapy with mastectomy patients. *Psychotherapy: Theory, Research, and Practice, 19*(3), 331–334.

Cunningham, A. J., Edmonds, C., Hampson, A., Hanson, H., Hovanec, M., Jenkins, G., & Tocco, E. (1991). A group psychoeducational program to help cancer patients cope with and combat their disease. *Journal of Mind-Body Health, 7*(3), 41–56.

Daste, B. (1989). Designing cancer groups for maximum effectiveness. *Groupwork, 2*(1), 58–69.

Daste, B. (1990). Important considerations in group work with cancer patients. *Social Work with Groups, 13*(2), 69–81.

Davidson, K. W. (1985). Social work with cancer patients: Stresses and coping patterns. *Social Work in Health Care, 10*(4), 73–82.

Epstein, R. M. (1999). Mindful practice. *JAMA: Journal of the American Medical Association, 282*(9), 833-839.

Evans, C. A., Stevens, M., Cushway, D., & Houghton, J. (1992). Sibling response to childhood cancer: A new approach. *Child Care, Health and Development, 18,* 229–244.

Fawzy, F., Fawzy, N. W., Hyun, C. S., & Wheeler, J. G. (1997). Brief, coping-oriented therapy for patients with malignant melanoma. In J. L. Spira (ed.), *Group therapy for medically ill patients* (pp. 133–164). New York: Guilford.

Ferlic, M., Goldman, A. & Kennedy, B. (1979). Group counseling with adult patients with advanced cancer. *Cancer, 43,* 760–766.

Firestone, R. & Catlett, J. (2009). *Beyond death anxiety: Achieving life-affirming death awareness.* New York: Springer.

Fobair, P. (1997). Cancer support groups and group therapies: Part I. Historical and theoretical background and research on effectiveness. *Journal of Psychosocial Oncology, 15*(1), 63–81.

Forester, B., Kornfeld, D. S., Fleiss, J. L., & Thompson, S. (1993). Group psychotherapy during radiotherapy: Effects on emotional and physical distress. *American Journal of Psychiatry, 150*(11), 1700–1706.

Gansler, T., Kaw, C., Crammer, C., & Smith, T. (2008). A population-based study of prevalence of complementary methods use by cancer survivors: a report from the American Cancer Society's studies of cancer survivors. *Cancer, 113*(5), 1048–1057.

Gelgeson, V. S., Cohen, S., Schulz, R., & Yasko, J. (2000). Group support interventions for women with breast cancer: Who benefits from what? *Health Psychology, 19*(2), 107–114.

Gilbar, O. (1991). Model for crisis intervention through group therapy for women with breast cancer. *Clinical Social Work Journal, 19*(3), 293–304.

Gilbar, O. & Groisman, L. (1991). A training model of self-help groups for patients with cancer of the colon. *Journal of Oncology, 9*(4), 57–69.

Goodwin, P. J., Leszcz, M., Ennis, M., Koopmans, J., Vincent, L., Guther, H., Drysdale, E., Hundleby, M., Chochinov, H. M., Navarro, M., Speca, M., & Hunter, J. (2001). The effect of group psychosocial support on survival in metastatic breast cancer. *The New England Journal of Medicine, 345*(24), 1719–1726.

Gottlieb, B. H. & Wachala, E. D. (2007). Cancer support groups: a critical review of empirical studies. *Psycho-Oncology, 16*(5), 379–400.

Gray, R. E. & Fitch, M. (2001). Cancer self-help groups are here to stay: Issues and challenges for health professionals. *Journal of Palliative Care, 17*(1), 53–58.

Groopman, J. G. (2007). *How doctors think*. Boston: Houghton Mifflin.

Harmon, M. (1991). The use of group psychotherapy with cancer patients: A review of recent literature. *Journal for Specialists in Group Work, 16*(1), 56–61.

Helgeson, V. S., Cohen, S., Schulz, R., & Yasko, J. (2000). Group support interventions for women with breast cancer: Who benefits from what? *Health Psychology, 19*(2), 107–114.

Kaufman, K. L., Harbeck, C., Olson, R., & Nitschke, R. (1992). The availability of psychosocial interventions to children with cancer and their families. *Children's Health Care, 21*(1), 21–25.

Kriss, R. T. & Kraemer, H. C. (1986). Efficacy of group therapy for problems with post-mastectomy self-perception, body image, and sexuality. *Journal of Sex Research, 22*(4), 438–451.

Lieberman, M. A. (1988). The role of self-help groups in helping patients and families cope with cancer. *Ca–A Cancer Journal for Clinicians, 38*(3), 162–168.

Montazeri, A., Jarvande, S., Haghighat, S., Vadhami, M., Sajadian, A., Elrahimi, M., & Haji-Mahmoodi, M. (2001). Anxiety and depression in breast cancer patients before and after participation in a cancer support group. *Patient Education and Counseling, 45*(3), 195–198.

Nessim, S. & Ellis, J. (2000). *Can survive: Reclaiming your life after cancer*. Boston, MA: Houghton Mifflin.

Oktay, J. S. (2002). Standards for qualitative research with exemplars. In A. R. Roberts & G. J. Greene (eds.), *Social workers' desk reference* (pp. 781–786). Oxford, UK: Oxford University Press.

Oliffe, J. L., Ogrodniczuk, J., Bottorff, J. L., Hislop, T. G., & Halpin, M. (2009). Connecting humor, health, and masculinities at prostate cancer support groups. *Psycho-Oncology, 18*(9), 916–926.

Palmer, L., Erickson, S., Shaffer, T., Coopman, C., Amylon, M., & Steiner, H. (2000). Themes arising in group therapy for adolescents with cancer and their parents. *International Journal of Rehabilitation and Health*, *5*(1), 43–54.

Price, K. (1992). Quality of life for terminally ill children. *Social Work*, *34*(1), 53–54.

Roberts, C. S., Piper, L., Denny, J., & Cuttleback, G. (1997). A support group intervention to facilitate young adults' adjustment to cancer. *Health and Social Work*, *22*(2), 133–141.

Sherman, A. C., Pennington, J., Simonton, S., Latif, U., Arent, L., & Farley, H. (2008). Determinants of participation in cancer support groups: The role of health beliefs. *International Journal of Behavioral Medicine*, *15*(2). 92–100.

Simonton, S. & Sherman, A. (2000). An integrated model of group treatment for cancer patients. *International Journal of Group Psychotherapy*, *50*(4), 487–506.

Spiegel, D. (1992). Effects of psychosocial support on patients with metastatic breast cancer. *Journal of Psychosocial Oncology*, *10*(2), 113–120.

Spiegel, D., Bloom, J. R., & Yalom, I. D. (1981). Group support for patients with metastatic cancer: A randomized outcome study. *Archives of General Psychiatry*, *38*(5), 527–533.

Spiegel, D. & Yalom, I. D. (1978). A support group for dying patients. *International Journal of Group Psychotherapy*, *28*(2), 233–245.

Stevens, M. M. & Dunsmore, J. C. (1996). Adolescents who are living with a life-threatening illness. In C. A. Corr & D. E. Balk (eds.), *Handbook of adolescent death and bereavement* (pp. 107–135). New York: Springer.

Taylor, S., Falke, R., Shoptaw, S., & Lichtman, R. (1986). Social support, support groups, and the cancer patient. *Journal of Consulting and Clinical Psychology*, *54*(5), 608–615.

Telch, E. G. & Telch, M. J. (1986). Group coping skills instruction and supportive group therapy for cancer patients: A comparison of strategies. *Journal of Consulting and Clinical Psychology*, *54*(6), 802–808.

Ussher, J. M., Kirsten, L., Butow, P., & Sandoval, M. (2008). A qualitative analysis of reasons for leaving, or not attending, a cancer support group. *Social Work in Health Care*, *47*(1), 14–29.

Vugia, H. D. (1991). Support groups in oncology: Building hope through the human bond. *Journal of Psychosocial Oncology*, *9*(3), 89–107.

Yalom, I. D. & Greaves, C. (1977). Group therapy with the terminally ill. *American Journal of Psychiatry*, *134*(4), 396–400.

Chapter Two

Group Work With People Who Suffer from Serious Mental Illness

Charles Garvin

This chapter describes ways of providing group services to people who suffer from serious mental illness. The term sometimes used is *chronic mental illness*, although many practitioners do not use the word *chronic* because of the negative connotation about recovery. This term applies to "mental disorders that interfere with some area of social functioning. SMI (serious mental illness) includes bi-polar disorders, severe forms of depression, obsessive-compulsive disorder, panic disorder, and schizophrenia" (Dulmus & Roberts, 2008, p. 237). Garvin and Tropman (1998, p. 277) present a different definition of someone with this condition as "an individual who suffers from a major psychiatric disorder such as psychosis, who is so disabled as to have partial or total impairment of social functioning (such as vocational and homemaking activities), and who has had a long or a number of short stays in a mental hospital."

STATISTICS RELEVANT TO THIS POPULATION

Many Americans suffer from severe mental illness; a recent estimate is almost 12 million (Statemaster Health Statistics, 2009). Until the mid 1950s, many people with these diagnoses were confined in mental hospitals. At that time, however, a movement referred to as *deinstitutionalization* became a major determinant of mental health policy. This movement was propelled by the discovery of psychotropic drugs allowing for amelioration of many of the behaviors of mentally ill people that led to their confinement. These behaviors and symptoms include hallucinations, delusions, and actions seen by others as bizarre, as well as mood swings or severe depression.

Other forces that promoted the declining use of institutional care were humane concerns for the civil liberties of patients and fiscal crises related to the greater costs of institutional compared with the costs of community care. Deinstitution-alization was facilitated by the increasing number of community mental health centers designated to care for mentally disabled individuals in the community.

Statistics, which are unfortunately from the previous decade, indicate that about 150,000 of the seriously mentally ill persons were in institutions, about 750,000 were in nursing homes (including about 400,000 who have behavior changes sometimes found in older adults), and between 800,000 and 1.5 million resided in the community and were likely to receive some form of care through community mental health centers (Garvin & Tropman, 1998, p. 277). Hospital stays are likely to be short, due not only to the use of medications and the provi-sion of community-based services but also to the action of insurance providers who limit the amount of hospital care for which they will pay. Social workers are very likely to be the providers of service, and this service is often in the form of groups. Increased resources have been allocated for research and program develop-ment in this field, but much more support is required to realize the aims of the deinstitutionalization movement.

People who suffer from serious mental illness are likely to have other problems as a consequence of their illness. According to Solomon (2008), these people char-acteristically tend to be unemployed and unmarried and to have difficulty with interpersonal relationships. Given their lack of employment, they tend to be eco-nomically disadvantaged and are often financially supported by federal disability benefit programs. In addition, this population is extremely vulnerable to a variety of psychological, medical, and social problems, including cognitive deficits, poor health status, and having relatively high rates of substance abuse, physical and psychological trauma, homelessness, criminal justice involvement, and loss of cus-tody of their children (p. 233).

Recent studies have sought to identify differences among men and women and among people of different ethnic backgrounds with respect to serious mental illness. According to Gerhart (1990, pp. 30–31):

It has been suggested that men tend to develop classic schizophrenic conditions at a slightly higher rate than women, while the latter are more prone to develop schizophreniform conditions. Stressors that cause males to relapse seem to have some connection with their role performance as men, such as criticism of their physical strength or lack of a job, being turned down for a date, and the like. On the other hand, women seem more sensitive to events in their interpersonal relationships.... There is evidence that women are signifi-cantly more prone to depressive disorders than men.... Subsequent investigations con-cluded that it was not women's roles that caused their depression, but rather the uneven distribution of power between husbands and wives.

The U.S. Surgeon General (U.S. Department of Health and Human Services, 2009) reported that the U.S. mental health system is "not well equipped to meet the needs of racial and ethnic minority populations (p. 1). This report indicates that barriers "deter such ethnic and racial minority group members from seeking treatment, and if individual members of groups succeed in accessing services, their treatment may be inappropriate to meet their needs" (p. 1). The aforementioned report links this latter point to differences in coping styles, cultural differences in how individuals experience discomfort, and the likelihood of somatization in many groups, which is the expression of mental distress in terms of physical suffering (p. 5). An additional factor is the use of community and family as resources.

The surgeon general's report discusses the prevalence of mental disorders among members of different ethnic groups. The incidence among African Americans is higher than that among whites but the report attributes this to socio-economic differences "because when these are taken into account, the prevalence difference disappears" (p. 8). African Americans are also overrepresented in inpatient psychiatric care, being about twice that of whites.

The surgeon general's report indicates that it is difficult to provide estimates of mental illness among Asian Americans because of the difficulty of applying standard diagnostic classifications to this population. Asian Americans are, moreover, less likely than other ethnic groups to seek care for mental health problems. According to this report, "One national sample revealed that Asian-Americans were only a quarter as likely as whites, and half as likely as African-Americans and Hispanic Americans, to have sought outpatient treatment" (p. 10). This was attributed by the report to "the stigma and loss of face over mental health problems, limited English proficiency among Asian immigrants, different cultural explanations for the problems, and the inability to find culturally competent services" (p. 10).

The surgeon general's report further indicates that "several epidemiological studies revealed few differences between Hispanic Americans in lifetime rates of mental illness" (p. 10). There were, however, some differences within these groups with respect to specific mental health problems. The incidence of depressive symptomatology among Hispanic women was greater than that among Hispanic men. Also, both Puerto Rican and Mexican American women are underrepresented in mental health services and overrepresented in general medical services.

With respect to American Indian/Alaskan Native communities, according to the surgeon general's report, depression is a significant problem. Alcohol abuse is also a major concern, as is the suicide rate. Posttraumatic stress disorder is especially prevalent among American Indian/Alaskan Native veterans compared with white veterans. Members of these groups are also overrepresented in public inpatient care facilities.

CAUSAL FACTORS

Much is unknown about the causes of serious mental illness. Nevertheless, the current consensus is that it is a condition produced by the interaction of biological and social circumstances with the evolving personality of the individual. Thus, it is often referred to as a *biopsychosocial phenomenon*. The basis of the biological input is concluded from the genetic, biochemical changes in the brain, as well as from heredity and twin studies. The social basis is determined from studies of the family, peer group, and other socialization circumstances of the individual. The developmental circumstances are elucidated by examining the life history of the individual in relation to coping patterns (Gerhart, 1990, pp. 17–20).

PRACTICE PRINCIPLES

A number of practice principles are typically applied when working with people with severe mental illness in light of the characteristics of this client group. While individual (Bentley, 2002), family (Sands, 2001, pp. 312–320), and group approaches are all used, the last are especially prominent. One reason is that with respect to the deficits in social skills found among these clients, groups provide an excellent way to learn to relate to others by observing and practicing social behaviors. Groups can also be used to simulate a variety of social circumstances such as those found in job, recreational, and family settings. Groups offer the client an opportunity to learn how others in similar circumstances have coped with a wide range of real-life situations. In addition, groups allow clients to participate at their current level of readiness: some may be highly active socially, while others are passive participants. This makes a group less stressful for some clients than one-on-one encounters in which they feel a strong expectation to participate actively. On the other hand, some clients may act in ways that other members see as highly inappropriate, express delusions that upset others, or be so stressed by the presence of others that they would be highly disruptive if invited to a group session.

A major practice principle for group work with seriously mentally ill clients is to have a good deal of program structure, because an unstructured group may be experienced at best as a waste of time and at worst as highly stressful. Despite this, we have observed many groups led by social workers for these clients in whom the only structure is the opening query, "What would you like to talk about today?" Some members may prefer this experience to the loneliness and boredom of having no social interaction, but this unstructured approach is an invitation to not participate at all, to engage in unfocused complaints about the "system," or to talk in a disorganized manner. A more structured approach involves such actions as presenting information, introducing structured exercises, identifying problems to be solved, and posing useful questions.

Another practice principle is to use a psychosocial rehabilitation approach more than a psychotherapeutic one (Taintor, 2008). According to Sands (2001), psychosocial rehabilitation encourages people who suffer from severe mental illness to develop to their fullest capacities through learning new skills and through acquiring environmental supports. She states that for the social worker, "this means working with the client and community resources to promote the client's physical, psychiatric, and social functioning to the extent possible" (p. 242). She goes on to say that

> *Programs of intervention target the individual, family, group, and the social environment. Individual, group, family, or milieu therapy can be utilized to teach individuals skills in activities in daily living (self-care, transportation, laundry), interpersonal behaviors, employment, and problem solving through skills training based on social learning theory (p. 242).*

A traditional psychotherapeutic approach, defined as using psychological interpretations and "depth"-oriented questions to enable the client to examine unconscious mechanisms, is not recommended for use with most seriously mentally ill people, either individually or in groups. As Rapp (1985) states, "Psychotherapy and psychosocial services without drugs may be harmful to the chronically mentally ill, not benign. The most prevalent hypothesis is that they overstimulate the client and lead to tension, anxiety, and exacerbation of symptoms" (p. 36). It is possible that some of these clients might benefit from this type of therapy, individually or in groups, after they have recovered sufficiently from their illness and have developed stronger coping abilities, but these will not be the majority. Some clients, however, who are defined as having borderline personality disorder might benefit from psychotherapy because of their greater ability to reflect on their circumstances.

Earlier social workers who thought of severe mental illness as a psychological manifestation produced by traumatic childhood experiences may have favored forms of psychotherapy for these clients. This, however, is not the view of most social workers today, who understand the biological factors in severe mental illness. A significant consequence of this increased biological understanding is a rejection of approaches that blamed mothers for acting in ways that promoted such illness or that blamed the family for engaging in communication patterns that "drove some family members crazy."

Another practice principle is to find ways to make each group session a rewarding one. This is because these clients are likely to find sessions anxiety provoking; they also have to make a considerable effort to attend, given the lethargy produced in some individuals by their illness. They have to look forward with pleasure to attending, especially when they are living in the community. Even hospitalized clients may resist attending group sessions and, when pressured to do so by hospital personnel, may enter meetings with a feeling of anger.

A major way of rewarding members for attending sessions is to use program activities during at least part of each session. Such activities might include the following:

- A game, especially one designed to teach a useful skill. Some workers have invented board games, for example, that help members to formulate individual goals or identify obstacles to obtaining goals.

- A dramatic activity, such as a role play, in which members practice a social skill.
- A musical or craft activity that helps members work together, experience a sense of accomplishment, or express themselves creatively.

Another way of rewarding members for coming to meetings is to ensure that they gain a sense of having accomplished something useful at each meeting. This requires the social workers to think in terms of concrete, short-term goals for each session. Examples of such goals are learning a specific social skill, solving an immediate problem, or creating a tangible product such as through a craft activity.

Another type of practice principle is to respond to a psychotic symptom in ways that help the member to cope with it while protecting other members from some of the anxiety produced by the symptom. One way to help individuals cope with psychotic symptoms is by educating them about such symptoms and labeling symptoms as such. Thus, seriously mentally ill members can be taught that hallucinations, for example, can be produced by their illness and that they can use this understanding when experiencing such hallucinations to tell themselves that they are experiencing something unreal. They also can be taught that some people can be told about symptoms (e.g., the social worker), while other people should not be told because they may be upset. The worker can also empathize with the fact that hearing voices or seeing strange images can be frightening. At the same time, the worker can reassure other members that he or she understands and is able to deal with psychotic symptoms, and will help them to understand and respond helpfully when a member is experiencing such symptoms.

Groups for the seriously mentally ill are often time limited and have specific purposes and goals. The length of time varies from one or two sessions while a client is in the hospital to several months for those in the community. However, because recovery from mental illness may be slow and because there may be periods of illness for many years, some groups members find useful are self-help and support groups in which membership may continue indefinitely, such as Schizophrenics Anonymous and some Alcoholics Anonymous groups attuned to the needs of mentally ill people. Clubhouse-type programs for mentally ill people may sponsor ongoing social activity groups, lunch clubs, and special interest groups.

COMMON THEMES

The above discussion of services to people with serious mental illnesses should suggest to social workers that a number of themes frequently arise in such groups. The following are those that we have encountered.[1]

Stigma

These clients are often avoided, persecuted, and denied their rights by others who become aware of their illness. Actions include being fired from jobs, denied housing, refused entry to educational programs, and other serious consequences of having the label "mentally ill." Members of groups will look for help in deciding how and when to explain their illness, how to pursue their rights in an appropriately assertive manner, and how to find advocates to help them obtain things to which they are entitled.

Coping with Symptoms

The terms *positive symptoms* and *negative symptoms* are often used. Positive symptoms are direct consequences of the illness, such as hallucinations, mania, depression, and confused thought processes. Negative symptoms are behavior deficits due to lack of adequate socialization experiences, such as lack of skill in handling social interactions. Group members will ask for help in coping with positive symptoms and in acquiring the skills to eliminate negative ones.

Housing

As indicated earlier, a lack of adequate low-cost housing severely affects this population. Housing is especially a problem to these clients because they may need support to maintain it once they find it, such as learning to care for an apartment, getting along with a landlord, or locating roommates.

Employment

Many of these clients lack employment or employment for which they are adequately compensated. This may be because they have educational deficits, because they cannot tolerate the stresses of jobs for which they were trained, or because of the stigma factor. They may not be aware of vocational rehabilitation services or these may be lacking. They may also require employment in a setting that offers them some form of support or even a so-called sheltered workshop program. Thus, members may ask help from each other in identifying and utilizing employment resources.

Education

Many of these clients have had their education interrupted by episodes of illness. Despite this, they are as likely to be as capable intellectually of acquiring an education as anyone else. The group is a medium in which they can explore educational opportunities, discover how to cope with school, and learn how to use resources to maintain themselves in an educational program.

Medication Effects

Clients are likely to bring up issues related to the medications they are taking to control their illness. They may not be compliant with their regimen because of a fear of dependence on medication. They may also experience unpleasant side effects of the medication. The medication itself may not be helpful, and the client may be unsure of how to assess this situation and what to do about it. At times, the social workers and other group members may provide useful information. At other times, the social worker will invite medical experts to attend one or more group sessions.

Two family issues are often brought up in these groups. One has to do with parents and siblings with whom the members have conflicts. Some of these conflicts occur because these family members are severely stressed by the client's symptoms. The other issue has to do with the nuclear families that these clients have created and seek to create. They may, for example, have difficulty acting as a spouse and parent. For these reasons, many programs form groups for family members of persons with mental illness and/or refer them to a major self-help organization such as the Alliance for the Mentally Ill (AMI).[2]

Leisure Time

Many of these clients are unemployed and are not attending an educational program; therefore, time hangs heavily on them. Their solution is often to spend a lot of time watching television or "hanging out" in a public place such as the library or park. A major service that can be provided by the group is to help such clients identify interests that can be satisfied, such as engaging in musical activities, attending sports events, or taking courses that further such interests at places such as the local "Y" or adult education program facility. The group can also provide a context for engaging in recreational activities that can then be extended outside of the group.

Problems with the Treatment System

These clients are likely to complain about the way the system reacts to them. Sometimes this is because of the real inadequacies in the system and sometimes it is because of the challenges these clients provide. An additional factor is that these clients may lack the skill to make their needs known. These complaints may concern difficulty in arranging for appointments with professionals, denial of services, frequent changes in professionals, and various forms of prejudice against them. These issues contribute to low self-confidence and self-esteem. The group can help the members come to terms with situations that cannot be changed while seeking changes that are appropriate and possible. On some occasions, group members can join together to engage in social action to change the system.

RECOMMENDED WAYS OF WORKING

Several different approaches to group work with these clients have emerged in response to the needs of different agency contexts and client themes. We will briefly discuss each of these approaches in terms of these conditions.

Group Work: Mutual Aid

Social workers have used traditional group work methods with the seriously mentally ill and have reported successful outcomes. Poynter-Berg (1994) reports one such group whose members lived in an institution and were identified as schizophrenic. A major theme of this group was coping with issues of intimacy and loss. The members approached the first session hostile to or suspicious of the group experience. The social worker was not as direct as she thought she should have been in establishing a contract with the members in which the purposes of the group and the anticipated activities were clearly enunciated. Nevertheless, the social worker sought to relate to members' feelings as they acted in hostile or disruptive ways. She also sought to introduce activities that were familiar to the women in the group, particularly craft projects. This led to a greater degree of security based on trust of the social worker and each other. A consequence of this was that as a holiday approached, the members talked with each other about painful feelings the holiday evoked, as indicated in the following record excerpt:

> The group members slowly came into the meeting room. Beverly sat with her back to the rest of the group, muttering an occasional "fuckin' mishugana." … The women made their instant coffee and drank it, all silently. They were much quieter and still today than usual; they appeared depressed and showed it by their slouched postures and lowered heads. I felt it might have something to do with feelings about Thanksgiving. I said everyone looked quite sad and wondered if they might want to talk about it. Rhoda furrowed her brows and moved her lips. I asked her if she wanted to say something. She shook her head. Another pause. All kept their heads lowered and Arlene, who usually talks to herself, was silent. I said they may all be having thoughts and feelings that the rest of the group might share with them. Silence. I finally said that sometimes it's hard to talk about things that are painful, like being in the hospital on holidays and maybe feeling lonely. Most of the members reacted to this by moving around in their chairs a little. I said I wondered if they did feel sad about tomorrow being a holiday. Rhoda nodded very slightly to herself, but kept her head lowered and didn't speak. Another lengthy pause, with all the ladies looking up at me briefly but not speaking.
>
> When it was time for the group to end, I commented that sometimes it's very hard to talk, like today—and especially when they might be feeling sad. I said I thought next week would be easier. They all looked up at me, and Rhoda smiled, saying, "have a nice Thanksgiving" (Poynter-Berg, 1994, p. 324).

Task-Centered Group Work

Task-centered group work, like traditional group work, models the process of helping the group to become a mutual aid system in which the members are committed to helping one another. The major difference is that in task-centered work, each member is assisted by other members to define a personal goal, choose activities (tasks) to reach the goal, and carry out these tasks (Tolson et al., 2002). While members are helped to express and cope with feelings, this is done in the context of defining and accomplishing tasks. This is accomplished in a limited time, typically about 12 sessions.

Garvin (1992) reported excellent outcomes in using this model in a community mental health setting serving the seriously mentally ill. He tested this approach with four groups composed of members who wished to enhance their use of leisure time. One group was composed of low-functioning clients, another of somewhat higher-functioning schizophrenic clients, a third of women who were trapped in highly dysfunctional family situations, and a fourth of clients who were also chemically dependent.

The plan for the 12 sessions was as follows:

Meeting 1	Get-acquainted activities
	Orientation to task-centered work
	Clarification of group purpose
Meetings 2 and 3	Determining members' goals
	Discussion of the idea of tasks
Meetings 4 and 5	Selection of member tasks
Meetings 6–11	Working on tasks
	Learning to overcome barriers to accomplishing tasks
Last meeting	Termination and evaluation

During these meetings, the social workers used a variety of program tools to help the members maintain their interest in the group and sustain their motivation to participate. One example was a series of board games devised by the staff. Each game taught members how to accomplish some aspect of the process, such as formulating goals or tasks. In a goal game, for example, members moved their "pieces" around a board and "landed" on a problem area for which they had to formulate a goal.

Social Skills Training

A great deal of development, as well as research on effectiveness, has been devoted to create models of social skills training for seriously mentally ill clients. According to Burlingame, Kenzie, and Strauss (2004), the underlying premise of this approach is that deficits in social functioning lead to social isolation, which in turn can exacerbate symptoms and disease management. The modal social skills approach breaks complex interpersonal skills into discrete modules and trains patients in each with behavioral techniques (p. 664).

This approach involves groups, and excellent materials that the social worker can use, such as detailed manuals for practitioners, workbooks for group members, and audiovisual tapes that present models of the skills to be acquired, have been prepared.[3] Liberman et al. (1989) developed separate modules for a variety of social skills, such as recreation for leisure and medication management. Information on teaching friendship and dating skills is also contained in their text *Social Skills Training for Psychiatric Patients* (Liberman et al., 1989). These authors suggest the following steps for the group facilitator to use in planning a social skills session:

1. Give introduction to social skills training.
2. Introduce new patients.
3. Solicit orientation from experienced patients who can explain social skills training to new patients.
4. Reward patients for their contribution to the orientation.
5. Check homework assignments.
6. Help each patient pinpoint an interpersonal problem, goal, and scene for this session.
7. Target scene and interpersonal situation for dry run role play.
8. "Set up" the scene.
9. Give instructions for the scene.
10. Run the scene as a dry run.
11. Give positive feedback.
12. Assess receiving, processing, and sending skills.
13. Use a model.
14. Ensure that the patient has assimilated the demonstrated skills.
15. Use another model.
16. Give instructions to the patient for next rehearsal or rerun.
17. Rerun scene.
18. Provide summary positive feedback.
19. Give real-life assignment.
20. Choose another patient for the training sequence and return to step 1.

The following is a brief excerpt of a social skills session reported by Liberman et al. (1989):

(Karen, at the invitation of the therapist, has been explaining to a new member, Mark, what the members do in social skills training group. The therapist then turns to Ted, who has been in the group for a week, and asks him to add to what Karen has said.)

Therapist: Great, Karen! Ted, would you add to what Karen said?

(Ted has only been in the group for a week. He often gets angry and upset with other people. He decided to seek social skills training because he recently lost his third roommate in 6 months and has begun to realize that he alienates other people, including his coworkers. His boss has told him to improve his relations with workmates or else risk being fired.)

Ted: I don't know, Karen described it.

Therapist: Well, can you think of some of the other things we can focus on?

Ted: You mean like solving our problems by looking at alternatives for communicating? And whether or not we look mad?

Therapist: Right, Ted. We concentrate on facial expression and problem-solving, too. When you talk to someone, that person gets a lot of information from seeing the kind of expression on your face. How loud we talk and our tone of voice are really important, too. Ted, how is voice tone different from voice loudness?

Ted: Why don't you pick on someone else?

Therapist: Because you're doing really well. You've only been here a short time, and you've learned a lot. (pp. 84–85)

Inpatient Group Psychotherapy

A major feature of contemporary hospitalization of patients with serious mental illness is that is it likely to be short—perhaps for only a week or two while the patient becomes stabilized after an acute episode. While in the hospital, patients may attend groups on a daily basis. These groups may be very unstructured, and our experience is that they are of limited usefulness. Yalom and Leszcz (2005) have developed and tested an approach they term *inpatient group psychotherapy*. This approach has two variations—one for high-functioning and one for low-functioning patients. The high-functioning patients are able to make a conscious decision to enter the group, can sustain conversations with other patients that focus on interpersonal behaviors, and can remain in the group for approximately 1 hour. The low-functioning patients are unable to sustain that much verbal inter-action. The structure of groups for the latter patients, therefore, includes more nonverbal activity such as physical exercise.

In the group for higher-functioning patients, the workers ask each member in turn to select a concern (referred to as an *agenda*) that can be worked on in a single session. Examples include telling another group member something about oneself or finding a way of coping with another member's angry response. After social workers have helped each member to choose an agenda for the session, the work-ers promote group interactions that will allow each member to work on her or his agenda for at least part of the session. Workers must have a good deal of skill in helping members choose a workable agenda and then pursue the agenda as part of the subsequent stage of the group's process.

After the interactional period, workers give feedback to members on how they have worked on their agendas. Yalom and Leszcz (2005) also often invite observers (such as interns) to attend and to comment toward the end of the session on the group's process. Members also are given a brief opportunity to react to this feed-back on group processes.

EVALUATION APPROACHES

A great deal of research has been conducted to evaluate services to people with severe mental illness; this had to lead to the development and testing of a variety of instruments to measure client outcomes. The following are some that can readily be used by social workers:

1. Scale for the Assessment of Negative Symptoms; Scale for the Assessment of Positive Symptoms (Fischer & Corcoran, 2007, pp. 650–657). These scales are used by practitioners primarily to assess the symptomatology of schizophrenia.
2. Symptoms Checklist (Fischer & Corcoran, 2007, pp. 823–826). This instrument is designed to measure the frequency of such psychiatric symptoms as tenseness, depressed mood, and difficulty sleeping.
3. Cognitive Slippage Scale (Fischer & Corcoran, 2007, pp. 172–173). This scale is designed to measure the cognitive distortion that is a primary characteristic of schizophrenia.
4. Social Adjustment Scale-Self Report (Fischer & Corcoran, 2007, pp. 752–762). This instrument helps the social worker to assess how adequate the client is in such areas as housework; employment; dealing with salespeople, neighbors, and friends; schooling; and family relations.

CONCLUSION

Group approaches have a great deal to offer to people suffering from serious mental illnesses. These approaches provide experiences in dealing with relationships through group activities, the possibility for mutual aid as members discover the support they can give and receive, and the opportunity for members to learn vicariously when they are not ready to take a more active role. With the large number of investigations currently under way, the future is bright for the creation of even more useful ways of offering group opportunity to these clients.

RESOURCES

National Alliance on Mental Illness
2107 Wilson Boulevard, Suite 300
Arlington, VA 22201
(800) 950-NAMI
www.nami.org

Center for Psychiatric Rehabilitation
Boston University

Sargent College of Health and Rehabilitation Sciences
940 Commonwealth Avenue West
Boston, MA 02215
(617) 353-3549
www.bu.edu/cpr

REFERENCES

Bentley, K. J. (ed.). (2002). *Social work practice in mental health: Contemporary roles, tasks, and techniques.* Pacific Grove, CA: Brooks/Cole.

Burlingame, G.M., MacKenzie, K.R. & Strauss, B. (2004). Small-group treatment: Evidence for effectiveness and mechanisms of change. In M.J. Lambert. (ed.), *Bergin and Garfield's Handbook of Psychotherapy and Behavior Change,* 5th ed (pp. 647–696). New York: Wiley.

Corrigan, P. W., Schade, M. L. & Liberman, R. P. (1992). Social skills training. In R. P. Liberman (ed.), *Handbook of psychiatric rehabilitation* (pp. 95–126). New York: Macmillan.

Fischer, J. & Corcoran, K. (2007). *Measures for Clinical Practice and Research: A Sourcebook.* New York: Oxford.

Dulmus, C.N. & Roberts, A.R. (2008). Mental Illness. In T. Mizrahi & L.E. Davis (eds.), *Encyclopedia of Social Work,* Vol. 3 (p. 238). New York: Oxford.

Federal Interagency Task Force on Homelessness and Mental Illness. (1999). *Report of the Surgeon General.* http://www.surgeongeneral.gov/library/mentalhealth/toc

Garvin, C. (1992). A task-centered group approach to work with the chronically mentally ill. In J. A. Garland (ed.), *Group work reaching out: People, places, and power* (pp. 67–80). New York: Haworth Press.

Garvin, C. & Tropman, J. (1998). *Social work in contemporary society* (2nd ed.) Boston: Allyn & Bacon.

Gerhart, U. C. (1990). *Caring for the chronic mentally ill.* Itasca, IL: Peacock.

Liberman, R. P., DeRisi, W. J., & Mueser, K. T. (1989). *Social skills training for psychiatric patients.* New York: Pergamon Press.

U.S. Department of Health and Human Services, Office of the Surgeon General. (2009). Mental health: A report of the surgeon general. http://surgeongeneral.gov/library/mentalhealth/chapter2/sec6.html

Moxley, D.P. & Finch, J.R. (2003). *Sourcebook of Rehabilitation and Mental Health Practice.* New York: Kluwer Academic & Plenum Publishers.

Poynter-Berg, D. (1994). Getting connected: Institutionalized schizophrenic women. In A. Gitterman & L. Shulman (eds.), *Mutual aid groups, vulnerable populations, and the life cycle* (2nd ed., pp. 315–334). New York: Columbia University Press.

Rapp, C. (1985). Research on the chronically mentally ill: Curriculum implications. In J. P. Bowker (ed.), *Education for practice with the chronically mentally ill: What works?* (pp. 32–49). Washington, DC: Council on Social Work Education.

Robins, L. N., Locke, B. Z., & Regier, D. A. (1991). An overview of psychiatric disorders in America. In L. N. Robins & D. Regier (eds.), *Psychiatric disorders in America* (pp. 328–386). New York: Free Press.

Sands, R. G. (2001). *Clinical social work practice in behavioral mental health: A postmodern approach to practice with adults* (2nd ed.). Boston: Allyn & Bacon.

Solomon, P. (2008). Mental Health: Practice Interventions. In T. Mizrahi & L.E. Davis (eds.), *Encyclopedia of Social Work*, Vol. 3 (pp. 233–237). New York: Oxford University Press.

Statemaster Health Statistics (n.d.) Found in http://www.statemaster.com/graph/

Taintor, Z.C. (2008). Psychosocial and Psychiatric Rehabilitation. In T. Mizrahi & L.E. Davis (eds.), *Encyclopedia of Social Work* (Vol. 3, pp 458–462). New York: Oxford University Press.

Tolson, E. R., Reid, W. J., & Garvin, C. D. (2002). *Generalist practice: A task centered approach* (2nd ed.). New York: Columbia University Press.

Yalom, I. D. with Lesccz, M. (2005). *The theory and practice of group psychotherapy* (5th ed.). New York: Basic Books.

NOTES

1 Many of these themes as well as helpful approaches for each may be found in an excellent sourcebook on rehabilitation and mental health practice edited by Moxley and Finch (2003).

2 The address of AMI is provided at the end of this chapter.

3 These materials can be obtained from Dissemination Coordinator, Camarillo-UCLA Clinical Research Center, Box A, Camarillo, CA 93011.

Chapter Three

Group Work Services to People Living With HIV/AIDS during a Changing Pandemic

George S. Getzel and Phillip Osteen

G roup work and the acquired immune deficiency syndrome (AIDS) have been closely associated in the first efforts, beginning in the early 1980s, to help people living with the human immunodeficiency virus (HIV)/AIDS (PLWHAs). The model of group work for PLWHAs developed then reflected the desperate need to gain social support and to reduce societal isolation.

This chapter reviews the development of group work services to PLWHAs and suggests a reconsideration of the design and implementation of such services in light of the significant changes that have occurred in the treatment of HIV/AIDS and in the sociopolitical and cultural meanings of the disease. An overview of the biopsychosocial factors that surround HIV/AIDS is presented and is related to the core themes that emerge in a support group's interaction and content. The benefits of the group work experience for PLWHAs are identified.

Special attention is given to strategies for pregroup planning, the functional characteristics of groups, and the problem-solving process underlying group themes addressed by the group. Guidelines for the social worker's interventions are detailed. Finally, evaluation criteria are suggested.

OVERVIEW

In the more than 20 years since the appearance of AIDS as a major public health problem and the subsequent discovery of HIV, these conditions have significantly entered the everyday lives of people in far-reaching ways (Cox, 1990; Shilts, 1988; Wright, 2000). Although we may tend to avoid thinking about AIDS and its deadly consequences, growing numbers of people throughout the world are denied that option because their kin, friends, and neighbors who are infected by HIV become irreversibly ill with AIDS-related symptoms and diseases (Mann, Tarantola, & Netter, 1992; Stine, 2001). Although an exact count is impossible to establish due to inconsistencies in reporting laws and the number of undiagnosed cases of HIV/AIDS, the Centers for Disease Control and Prevention (CDC) estimated that in 2007, there were more than 56,000 new cases of HIV/AIDS and more than 1 million people living with HIV/AIDS in the United States.

The AIDS pandemic has produced creative and humane efforts to prevent the spread of HIV and to care for PLWHAs with serious illness and functional impairments. The use of groups with PLWHAs and with kin, friends, and volunteers caring for them has become an integral aspect of many social service and health care programs (Ball, 1998; Danilos, 1994; Dean, 1995; Edell, 1998; Foster et al., 1994; Hayes et al., 1998; Getzel, 1991a; Lopez & Getzel, 1984, 1987). Beginning with the discovery of the first AIDS cases in New York City, group approaches quickly were picked up by newly developing AIDS community-based organizations in other cities.

No longer can people, even in the most sophisticated developed countries, conceive of AIDS as a disease largely of gay men and intravenous drug users, as was the case when the pandemic was first recognized in the early 1980s (Cahill, 1984). The 1990s has been a period with a significant increase worldwide in the proportion of women, children, and men diagnosed with AIDS where infection is attributed directly or indirectly to heterosexual contact (Mann et al., 1992; Stine, 2001). The CDC (2009) estimated that 31% of newly reported HIV/AIDS cases in the United States involved high-risk heterosexual contact. In 2007, there were approximately 10,000 newly reported HIV/AIDS cases among women, with the total HIV/AIDS cases among women surpassing 200,000. All sexually active persons and their offspring throughout the world are at risk of developing HIV infection and the breakdown of bodily immune protection.

HIV infection and AIDS have a profound cultural and economic impact on whole societies (Bateson & Goldsby, 1988; Mann et al., 1992; Smith, 2001; Stine, 2001). The HIV disease sequence has a welter of emotional and practical effects on the lives of all involved (Christ et al., 1988; Getzel, 1991b; Getzel & Willroth, 2001). The psychosocial consequences of HIV/AIDS in many respects resemble the reactions of other categories of persons to life-threatening disease. For example, the prospect of being infected with HIV or the knowledge of being HIV positive may be met with denial, which is dangerous if a person has unprotected sex.

All major illnesses with disabling and disfiguring consequences can result in depression and agitation; it is very common for sick persons to feel shame and guilt about becoming sick, resulting in bouts of anger, isolation, and self-loathing. Sontag (1978) noted that historically, serious diseases like cancer and tuberculosis have had complex metaphorical content and values connotations; this has been strongly demonstrated in the case of AIDS. Because the first identified victims of HIV/AIDS were gay men, drug addicts, and poor persons of color in large cities, the stigma attached to persons with the disease has been insidious, resulting in incidents of withdrawal of care by professionals, violation of human rights, and violence against PLWHAs and their families (Altman, 1986; Bayer, 1989;

Smith, 2001; Gant, 2000). The societal problems of homophobia, classism, racism, and sexism are exposed and magnified in the presence of HIV/AIDS.

As we begin the third decade of the AIDS pandemic, knowledge about AIDS and HIV has greatly expanded. In 2009, results for the first HIV vaccine study to indicate modest effects were reported following a large-scale, randomized trial in Thailand (Rerks-Ngarm et al., 2009). Although scientists have been unable to create a vaccine to completely prevent the spread of the virus or to find methods to eradicate it in the human body (Bartlett & Finkbeiner, 2001), it is hoped that continued medical research will yield promising solutions. A number of useful halfway medical technologies have been developed to temporarily prevent the replication of HIV in infected persons; these antiviral medications have significantly extended longevity but have not altered the disabling course of disease. Antiviral medications also present significant quality-of-life concerns because of side effects and the uncertain benefits for some individuals (Bartlett & Finkbeiner, 2001).

The extension of life for persons with both HIV and AIDS has increased the prevalence of complications from opportunistic infections. The longer persons live with HIV or AIDS, the more apt they are to develop chronic, persistent, disabling, disorienting, and disfiguring conditions (Bartlett & Finkbeiner, 2001). In addition to the physical and medical challenges faced by long-term survivors, increased attention is being given to the unique experiences and psychosocial needs of aging PLWHAs (Nokes, Chew, & Altman, 2003; Robinson, Petty, Patton, & Kang, 2008). According to the most current CDC (2009) surveillance report, 10% of newly reported HIV/AIDS cases occurred in individuals over the age of 50, and more than 150,000 individuals over the age of 50 are currently living with HIV/AIDS.

In contrast, there has also been a marked increase in rates of HIV infection in young adults. Based on the CDC's (2007) most recent surveillance report, 34% of newly reported HIV cases occurred in individuals between the ages of 13 and 29 years. In 2004, it was estimated that nearly 8000 young people were living with AIDS, a 42% increase since 2000 (CDC, 2006), with the number climbing to approximately 23,000 in 2007.

A reconfiguration of group work services is required to respond more effectively to PLWHAs and the evolution of their biomedical treatment. These changes will be described next.

Review of the Literature

From the start of the first AIDS service organizations, support groups were recognized as important normalizing experiences for PLWHAs and for kin and friends caring for them (Hayes et al., 1994; Lopez & Getzel, 1984; Maasen, 1998) and for volunteers in these organizations (Lopez & Getzel, 1984, 1987; Meier et al., 1995; Moore, 1998; Weiner, 1998). Support groups for professionals working with PLWHAs were recognized as a necessary resource later (Cushman et al., 1995;

Garside, 1993; Gladstone & Reynolds, 1997; Grossman & Silverstein, 1993). The use of groups to teach HIV prevention has been extensively reported. Peer education is widely used to teach safer sexual techniques to gay men, women, adolescents, and other populations (Duke & Omi, 1991; Kelly & St. Lawrence, 1990; Palacios-Jimenez & Shernoff, 1986; Ponton et al., 1991; Redman, 1990; Roffman et al., 1997; Subramanian et al., 1995; Yoakum, 1999). The literature on group work with PLWHAs and caregivers, while not large, does point to the widespread use of support groups for special populations in a variety of contexts. Group work models for gay men in community-based organizations have been described in some detail (Gambe & Getzel, 1989; Getzel, 1991a, 1991b; Getzel & Mahony, 1990; Livingston, 1996; Sandstrom, 1996).

Child and Getzel (1989) describe a support group model for poor people in an urban hospital setting that is crisis oriented and capable of serving hospitalized and recently released patients with AIDS, including those with drug histories, women, and gay men of color. PLWHAs who are intravenous drug users can benefit from group support programs that emphasize harm reduction strategies to curtail the use of drugs while providing social support and guidance about the disease process (Bataki, 1990; Greene et al., 1993; Junturem et al., 1999; O'Dowd et al., 1991). Ongoing attention is being given to PLWHAs living in rural areas who are limited in their ability to attend support groups at distant community-based organizations. Telephone support group work models have been developed for both PLWHAs and caregivers to break down the isolation of PLWHAs in rural areas as well as to protect their anonymity (Rounds et al., 1991). Telephone support groups have also been used for parents of children with AIDS (Heckman et al., 1999; Weiner et al., 1993) and for PLWHAs who are older and/or disabled in the terminal phase of the disease process (Nokes et al., 2003; Ritter & Hammons, 1992). Group work approaches for special populations with AIDS and their caregivers are an increasing source of interest: the homeless (Conanan et al., 2003), family members in rural areas (Anderson & Shaw, 1994), parents with HIV/AIDS (Mason & Vazquez, 2007), parents of children with AIDS (Mayers & Spiegel, 1992; Weiner, 1998), gay partners of PLWHAs (Land & Harangody, 1990), women (Wood, 2007), and prisoners (Grinstead, Zach, & Faigeles, 2001; Pomeroy et al., 1997; Richey et al., 1997).

Gambe and Getzel (1989) emphasize that groups provide substitutes for weakened or absent social supports in PLWHAs' lives created by life-threatening disease, the unpredictability of the disease process, and the stigma associated with AIDS. In a similar vein, Getzel and Mahony (1990) identify the themes of loss and human finitude as causing crises in the group and forcing members to confront their personal sense of mortality. The group becomes a context in which to face painful and inchoate feelings of dread, helplessness, shame, and guilt. The social worker's acceptance of members' expressions of vulnerability and the group's constancy permit a sense of security and solidarity when members explore these themes.

PRACTICE PRINCIPLES

Work with PLWHAs entails a clear understanding of the functions of a support group. Critical to the use of group work with PLWHAs is effective pregroup planning and formation.

Pregroup Planning

The capacity of groups to meet the needs of PLWHAs must be clearly understood by the social worker before a group is begun. Groups have the following identified functions for PLWHAs:

1. Assisting members to find support from peers as a way of accepting their new status as PLWHAs
2. Helping members explore ways in which family, friends, and others respond to them differently as PLWHAs and how to handle issues of intimacy, receiving help, and gaining acceptance
3. Assisting members to find safe ways to express the sadness, anger, guilt, helplessness, and shame associated with the problem of living with AIDS
4. Providing opportunities for members to find ways to counter the fright and feeling of powerlessness about death and dying
5. Helping members examine quality-of-life options (how they want to live and die) prompted by serious illness and a likely death from complication from AIDS
6. Assisting members with their personal belief systems about being diagnosed with AIDS and facing an uncertain future in a world that is not sympathetic to their plight

Group Formation and the AIDS Pandemic

Early in the AIDS pandemic, support groups for PLWHAs consisted of members who had recently become aware of their AIDS diagnosis by becoming seriously ill with *Pneumocystis carinii* pneumonia (PCP), discovering a Kaposi sarcoma (KS) lesion, or developing some other symptom associated with an opportunistic infection. Prior to the development of more effective treatments for these diseases and antiviral medication for HIV, most of the initial cohort joining a group died from complications from AIDS over 1 to 2 years (Gambe & Getzel, 1989). There was a brief early period "of quiet before the storm," soon followed by multiple hospitalizations, near-death experiences, and the appearance of other opportunistic infections such as taxoplasmosis, cytomegalovirus (CMV) infections, tuberculosis, and so forth. All of these illnesses can result in death but not before causing extreme body wasting, incontinence, mental confusion, blindness, disfigurement, profound neurological impairments, and other dire consequences.

PLWHAs entering a formed group could see themselves in contrast to very sick members and could be in the group as members died in rapid succession. While this situation was intrinsically frightening and overwhelming, a basis for dropping out of the group, it also provided an opportunity to understand and prepare for the likely biopsychosocial crises to come. Other group members served as models of forbearance and coping. A member could deal with prospective and current quality-of-life issues while providing help to peers. Group members were seen to be in the same lifeboat "until death do them part."

Reconfiguring Group Work Services

While this early model of group support services is still relevant in many respects, it must be adjusted and refined in view of PLWHAs' increased longevity and the highly variegated cohorts of persons now affected by AIDS in many settings. What was once a single model of group work service has become a series of specialized models that reflect with more precision the disease sequence and medical treatment advances.

In an extensive review of literature, Sherman et al. (2004) noted that group work with PLWHAs tended to incorporate one or more of the following treatment goals: (1) altering risky health behaviors, (2) enhancing adjustment and managing stress and/or reducing psychosocial morbidity, and (3) improving health-promoting behaviors and self-care. In addition, Sherman et al. noted that effective group practices matched content, structure, and goals in accordance with the changing needs of clients across different stages in the progression of the illness. Three general types of support groups are recommended and principles for intervention specified.

Orientation Support Group

This group's primary focus is assisting members to cope with the issue of recognizing themselves as persons with AIDS. This may also mean coming out of the closet as a gay person or a person with a history of drug abuse.

Understanding the practical and emotional consequences of the disease for the person's future orientation and management of different aspects of everyday life becomes important. Women with children have to consider custody after they die. All persons must consider how they will manage their income and health care now and if they become unemployed or disabled in the future. Guidance about available health and social services and how to use them is an important aspect of group activities.

Depression, guilt, shame, and powerlessness are reduced as group members gain understanding about the similarity of their reactions and their different coping strategies. The orientation support group is composed of newly diagnosed PLWHAs; it is time limited (six to eight sessions) and focuses on getting on with life after an AIDS diagnosis. These groups are most effective when sponsored by community-based organizations.

Group homogeneity is an important consideration in the design of orientation support groups. Gay men, male intravenous drug users, women who are nondrug abusers and are infected by men, women using intravenous drugs, and age-oriented groups of younger and older clients may benefit from homogeneous group composition that allows for more in-depth discussions of members' diagnosis, needed services, and coping strategies. Linguistic barriers and disabling conditions may necessitate special groups led in a foreign language or American Sign Language. Increased sophistication in developing specialized groups also applies to the two support group models that will now be discussed.

Relationship Support Group

This group is needed after the initial shock of the diagnosis has been handled. This model of group support focuses on the significant changes in the quantity and quality of interpersonal relationships that ensue for PLWHAs after they and other persons in their lives contemplate the current and prospective consequences of the disease. PLWHAs may see themselves as tainted or, as some PLWHAs have described it, as "soiled goods." The stigma attached to PLWHAs is reinforced when other persons, who were previously close, begin to disengage or abandon them. PLWHAs and others close to them may be troubled by the HIV/AIDS diagnosis and by the disclosure of homosexuality, bisexuality, drug use, or marital infidelity.

Just as PLWHAs become preoccupied with recurrent death anxiety, persons close to them must contemplate hospitalizations, new symptoms, and dying. Relatives and others may experience feelings of rage and emotional conflict.

Needless to say, if the PLWHA is presumed to have infected family members, the emotional turmoil and conflict are magnified enormously. Consider the following situation of Mr. A., a 35-year-old man, and his wife of 5 years.

Mrs. A. has been previously married. While she is pregnant with their second child, she and Mr. A. discover that Mrs. A's first husband died of AIDs (related to a hidden history of drug abuse). HIV tests are given to Mr. and Mrs. A. and their first child; the results for each of them are positive. Mrs. A. has been recently diagnosed with disseminated tuberculosis and AIDS; it will take over a year of testing to determine if the newborn is HIV infected because the mother's and the child's antibody production must be distinguished.

The need for a variety of health and social services for this family now and in the future is apparent. Part of a case plan for Mr. and Mrs. A. can be a relationship support group to address the welter of interpersonal problems they may face. Among the possibilities are a couples support group composed of others in a comparable situation, a women's PLWHA group composed of women infected by spouses, and a caregiver support group of men caring for women with AIDS.

Issues surrounding intimacy and sexual activity are important considerations when addressing interpersonal relationships for PLWHA. Substantial emphasis has been given to the notion of "prevention with positives" in which psychoeducational, biomedical, and social support services are targeted at helping PLWHA reduce the risk of transmitting HIV to current and/or future partners. Depending on agency contexts and funding sources, social workers may be expected, if not required, to incorporate prevention efforts into their group practice. Kalichman, Rompa, and Cage (2005) worked closely with a community advisory group to develop a model for incorporating prevention messages into support groups. HIV-positive community leaders recommended that group leaders approach the issue of prevention within a framework of status disclosure, noting that disclosure of HIV status represents "a nearly universal stressor" for PLWHA (p. 265). Social workers face the daunting challenge of addressing important public health considerations while simultaneously avoiding adding to and compounding feelings of guilt, shame, and anger.

Relationship support groups explore the current stresses in interpersonal relationships arising from being a PLWHA or a caregiver. These groups are time limited, with a focus on providing emotional and practical assistance in working out interpersonal conflicts and finding additional sources of support as the mounting demands of self-care and caregiving create stresses for group members. One objective of these groups is to maximize the autonomy and self-determination of the members as they make choices between the demands originating from the disease and those arising from day-to-day living. A group meeting for 8 to 12 weeks is introduced by the social workers, who state that group members will develop the understanding and skills needed to get on with their lives. Throughout this group experience, the social workers reinforce examples of members' resourcefulness in handling AIDS-related problems and making life plans. The social workers state that they believe that living with AIDS means that members get on with their lives, which includes work, friendship, intimacy, and new experiences.

Co-leadership should be considered as a way of modeling roles and providing continuity when a facilitator is absent. The group members may recontract for an extension of the group as needed and as resources permit. Emphasis should be placed on enhancing group members' capacity to understand and to manage HIV/AIDS-related problems that typically arise within their kinship and friendship systems. Problems at work may also be discussed.

Relationship support groups require careful intake. The social worker helps the potential group member or couple identify possible interpersonal issues to be addressed in the group. The intake process is expedited when group candidates have first explored interpersonal concerns in an orientation support group. This model of group support can be based in AIDS community-based organizations, mental health settings, family services agencies, child care agencies, and other settings used by and accessible to PLWHAs, their kin, and others associated with informal caregiving.

Quality-of-Life Support Group

This group is appropriate during periods of serious illness and the end stage of the disease process. It may not address many PLWHAs' needs until a few years after diagnosis. Life-threatening diseases tend to occur later. PLWHAs frequently experience an asymptomatic period or a period of less dramatic symptomatic display when AIDs and its life-threatening potential need not occupy exclusively PLWHAs' cognitive and emotional lives.

A quality-of-life support group provides PLWHAs with a safe location to discuss their reactions to shortened life. A process of life review, more typically associated with older adults, occurs in the group. It is occasioned by serial losses in the form of disfiguring symptoms, social isolation and abandonment, deaths of others, mental disorganization, and other disabling conditions. The group gives support and guidance as members confront humiliating, severe symptoms. For example, the group allows members to exchange opinions about undergoing experimental treatments that may cause irreversible side effects. Members can openly discuss issues like HIV-related dementia symptoms and even use humor to face the affront of baldness caused by chemotherapy treatments.

Particular symptoms of opportunistic diseases may warrant special efforts to develop homogeneous groups. Groups may be composed of PLWHAs with visual impairments resulting from the activity of a persistent, chronic CMV infection that destroys the retina of the eye, or they may consist of members with rapidly progressing and disfiguring lesions of KS, a form of skin cancer. In such groups, members can provide empathetic support and exchange useful information about resources: how to obtain cosmetics to disguise lesions or community resources for mobility training at home. Quality-of-life support groups are found in AIDS community-based organizations, hospitals, long-term care programs, hospices, religious organizations, and local health and social service agencies. Parallel groups of this nature for caregivers are also very useful. Co-leadership is strongly recommended to provide continuity of facilitation and emotional support to leaders in these very demanding groups. This support group model is usually opened-end in time. Careful consideration and preparation must be given to the introduction of a new member (Gambe & Getzel, 1989).

COMMON THEMES

Recurrent themes emerge in group discussion and interaction that present the social worker and members with rich opportunities to work together.

An Uncertain Conditioning

Uncertainty occurs in all support groups during different phases of group development. For example, in the beginning phase of the group, members may express deep ambivalence about being in a group for PLWHAs because they do not understand what AIDS represents to them. Rather than confront the uncertainty of their life course, they protect themselves against death anxiety through simple denial—maybe they really do not have AIDS or perhaps they are not suited for a group of PLWHAs.

Approach-avoidance behaviors appear in the group. Members join subgroups that are in conflict. Some members only want to talk about cures and treatments for HIV/AIDS and castigate others who want to discuss their fear of becoming sick or the recent deaths of friends from complications of AIDS.

Recommended Ways of Working

There is a great temptation to side with one subgroup; this tendency should be avoided. The social worker should make group conflicts a problem for group members to solve. The social worker should assist group members to explore solutions that might simultaneously address the need to accept the uncertainties of disease sequence and treatment while approaching life without a morbid outlook. Group members share thoughts and problem-solve together. The social workers must walk a fine line, carefully accepting different perspectives offered by conflicting subgroups.

If the social worker is not a PLWHA or does not have a background similar to that of the members, he or she may become a target of group members' anger for not having to deal with the same life issues.

The following incident occurred at an early meeting of gay men with AIDS when Robert returns to the group after his lover dies from an opportunistic infection:

> Members are engaged in an intense discussion of the benefits of combining antiviral medications to halt HIV replication when Robert asks, in an off-handed way, if this discussion is boring to the social worker, since he does not have AIDS. Other group members stop and stare at the social worker, who begins to flush. Looking at Robert and the other group members, the social worker says, "The group seems to be reacting to Robert's important question to me."
>
> In defense of the social worker, another member, John, says that you do not need to have AIDS to lead a group of PLWHAs. The social worker indicates that this might be so but wonders if Robert and some other group members might feel differently. An intense group discussion ensues in which Robert talks about his anger about the death of his lover and his

distrust of anyone who does not have AIDS and has not suffered. Some group members, while defending the social worker, acknowledge their jealousy in their lives toward people who do not have AIDS. Group members, with the help of the social worker, go on to discuss their concerns about how Robert is managing after the death of his lover. The discussion slowly edges back to new treatments as the session ends.

Crisis Situations

Recurrent biopsychosocial crisis situations arise in the PLWHAs' interpersonal systems that necessitate in-depth attention by the group members. Previous patterns of adaptation and problem solving may no longer be available to PLWHAs in crisis. Acceptance of powerful emotional displays occurs in the support group. Other members can display a sense of mastery by using their learning from undergoing similar crises to help a peer in active crises.

Recommended Ways of Working

The social worker must see the group members as capable of accepting crisis situations that arise among members, avoiding an overprotective stance. To the extent that the social worker encourages members to discuss how they have handled similar situations, mutual aid will be encouraged, in contrast to flight behavior, in which members give facile advice on a one-on-one basis. It is important to point out themes that reflect emotions and ideas shared by the members. The social worker may also help members reach out to each other as crisis situations arise between sessions, assuming that members agree to this type of support during the group's deliberations.

A crisis situation was revealed in a women's PLWHA group when Mary, in a tearful, agitated manner, told the other members that she had been diagnosed with cervical cancer and would be hospitalized the next day. Mary told the group that she did not care if she lived or died but felt shame for what would happen to her two young children. Shaking convulsively, May wept, saying that she had not planned for guardianship after her husband had died 6 months ago.

Joan held Mary and the group began telling Mary that they were very worried about her. Tanya said that she used a lawyer from the social work agency when she panicked about going into the hospital. The social worker told the group that it seemed very hard to make a will and guardian provisions. Joan said that you just don't want to think about dying but that you have to be realistic, concluding, "Better late than never." The group then began a discussion about how, after being diagnosed, they had grown more responsible in thinking about their children.

A Changed Identity

A very strong theme that emerges in groups of PLWHAs is participants' change of self-image linked to AIDS. For example, receiving an AIDS diagnosis can be seen as a rite of passage. Normalizing an AIDS identity is a way of coping with an otherwise unacceptable condition that others readily see as a death sentence.

Support groups simultaneously normalize the PLWHA status and provide guidance in understanding this status when representing oneself to outsiders. Strongly associated with a shift of self-definition is a greater capacity to look at the question of mortality and the meaning of a life threatened by AIDS.

Erikson (1964) notes that all stages of the life cycle place demands on the individual to find meaning in life in order to cope with the stresses of existence and reminders of death. Human individuality finds its ultimate challenge when a human being confronts mortality. Identity questions may become exquisitely transparent in the face of death.

Recommended Ways of Working

The group becomes a safe context to discuss concerns and express feelings about the inequity of a life ending too early, unfulfilled goals, unfinished projects, and taking leave of loved ones. With the death of a member, surviving members bear witness to the meaning of the loss and the significance of their own lives. Clearly, the social worker must be prepared to listen and not to quickly reassure. The social worker's guilt and helplessness as a survivor necessitate the presence of supervisory and peer supervision.

> After the group discusses the recent death of a member, Greg says to the social workers, "It is your job to remember us after we all die." The social worker, after some hesitation, replies that the deaths of group members sadden him greatly and he feels the heavy burden of loss, yet his is grateful to be part of the group, where he has met so many wonderful men. He can never forget them.
>
> The social worker asks the group members if they have reactions to his outliving them. Some members joke, saying that he had better enjoy himself when they are gone. Paul says that he is jealous of the social worker. Gradually, the subject is adroitly changed by Paul.

EVALUATION APPROACHES

Although difficult, the evaluation of group support models for different population is very much needed. Consumer feedback about short-term support groups is a good way to begin. Measurements of consumer satisfaction, knowledge gained about resources, and the actual use of services and entitlements should be investigated. More traditional measurements of clinical outcomes can be obtained from relationship support groups.

Quality-of-life support groups present serious concerns, and ethnographic approaches should be considered because of the likelihood of physical fragility and HIV-related dementia among members. Because PLWHAs feel stigmatized and may have histories of stigma, respect for the integrity of their personal boundaries, confidentiality, and autonomy is critical. PLWHAs should be allowed to tell their stories without prejudice, coercion, or prior interpretation. Telling their stories may represent the human need to be remembered.

RESOURCES

American Foundation for AIDS Research (AmFar)
120 Wall Street (13th Floor)
New York, NY 10005-3902
(800) 39-amfar
www.amfar.org

Gay Men's Health Crisis
119 West 24th Street
New York, NY 10011
GMHC Hotline (800) 243-7692
hotline@gmhc.org www.gmhc.org

National AIDS Hotline
(800) 342-2437 (English)
(800) 344-7432 (Spanish)
(800) 243-7889 (TSS)
www.ashastd.org/nah

National Association of People with AIDS
8401 Colesville Road, No. 505
Silver Spring, MD 20910
(202) 434-8090
www.nastad.org

Health Resources and Services Administration
HIV/AIDS Bureau
(301) 443-6652
www.aids.gov

San Francisco AIDS Foundation
995 Market Street
San Francisco, CA 94103
California Hotline: (800) 367-AIDS
feedback@sfaf.org www.sfaf.org

REFERENCES

Altman, D (1986). *AIDS in the mind of America.* New York: Anchor Books.

Anderson, D. B. & Shaw, S. L. (1994). Starting a support group for families and partners of people with HIV/AIDS in a rural setting. *Social Work, 39,* 135–138.

Ball, S. (1998). A time-limited group model for HIV-negative gay men. *Journal of Gay & Lesbian Social Services, 8,* 23–42.

Bataki, S. L. (1990). Substance abuse and AIDS: The need for mental health services. *New Directions in Mental Health Services, 48,* 55–67.

Bateson, M. C. & Goldsby, B. (1988). *Thinking AIDS: The social response to the biological threat.* Reading, MA: Addison-Wesley.

Bayer, R. (1989). *Private act, social consequences: AIDS and politics of public health.* New York: Free Press.

Cahill, K. M. (1984). Preface: The evolution of an epidemic. In Cahill, K. M. (ed.), *The AIDS epidemic* (pp. 2–6). New York: St. Martin's Press.

Child, R. & Getzel, G. S. (1989). Group work with inner city people with AIDS. *Social Work with Groups. 12,* 65–80.

Centers for Disease Control and Prevention. (2006). HIV/AIDS among youth. *CDC HIV/AIDS Fact Sheet.* www.cdc.gov/hiv. Revised August 2008.

Centers for Disease Control and Prevention. (2009). *HIV/AIDS surveillance report: Vol. 19.* www.cdc.gov/hiv

Christ, G., Weiner, L., & Moynihan, R. (1988). Psychosocial issues in AIDS. *Psychiatric Annals, 16,* 173–179.

Cox, E. (1990). *Thanksgiving: An AIDS journal.* New York: Harper & Row.

Conanan, B., London, K. J., Martinez, L., Modersbach, D., O'Connell, J. J., Sullivan, M. J., Raffanti, S., Ridolfo, A. J., Rabe, M. S., Song, J. Y., & Treherne, L. L. (2003). *Adapting your practice: Recommendations for homeless patients with HIV/AIDS.* Nashville, TN: Health Care for the Homeless Clinicians' Network, National Health Care for the Homeless Council, Inc.

Cushman, L. F., Evans, P., & Namerow, P. B. (1995). Occupational stress among AIDS social service providers. *Social Work in Health Care, 21,* 115–131.

Daniolos, P. T. (1994). House calls: A support group for individuals with AIDS in a community residential setting. *International Journal of Group Psychotherapy, 44,* 133–153.

Dean, R. G. (1995). Stories of AIDS: The use of narrative as an approach to understanding in an AIDS support group. *Clinical Social Work Journal, 23,* 287–304.

Duke, S. I. & Omi, J. (1991). Development of AIDS education and prevention materials for women by health department staff and community focus groups. *AIDS Education and Prevention. 3,* 90–99.

Edell, M. (1998). Replacing community: Establishing linkages for women living with HIV/AIDS—a group work approach. *Social Work with Groups, 21,* 49–62.

Erickson, E. H. (1964). *Insight and responsibility.* New York: Norton.

Foster, S. B., Stevens, P. E., & Hall, J. M. (1994). Offering support group services for lesbians living with HIV. *Women & Therapy, 15,* 69–83.

Gambe, R. & Getzel, G. S. (1989). Group work with gay men with AIDS. *Social Casework, 70,* 172–179.

Gant, L. M. (2000). Advocacy and social policy issues. In V. J. Lynch (ed.), *HIV/AIDS at year 2000: A sourcebook for social workers* (pp. 197–210). Boston: Allyn & Bacon.

Garside, B. (1993). Physicians mutual aid group: A response to AIDS-related burnout. *Health and Social Work, 18,* 259–267.

Getzel, G. S. (1991a). AIDS. In A. Gitterman (ed.), *Handbook of social work with vulnerable populations* (pp. 35–64). New York: Columbia University Press.

Getzel, G. S. (1991b). Survival modes of people with AIDS in groups. *Social Work, 36,* 7–11.

Getzel, G. S. & Willroth, S. (2001). Acquired immune deficiency syndrome (AIDS). In A. Gitterman (ed.), *Handbook of social practice with vulnerable resilient populations* (2nd ed., pp. 39–63). New York: Columbia University Press.

Getzel, G. S. & Mahony, K. (1990). Confronting human finitude: Group work with people with AIDS. *Journal of Gay and Lesbian Psychotherapy, 1,* 105–120.

Gladstone, J. & Reynolds, T. (1997). Single session group work intervention in response to employee stress during workforce transition. *Social Work with Groups, 20,* 33–51.

Goldfinger, S. M. (1990). *Psychiatric aspects of AIDS and HIV infection.* New York: Jossey-Bass.

Grant, D. (1988). Support groups for youth with the AIDS virus. *International Journal of Group Psychotherapy, 38,* 237–251.

Greene, D. C., McVinney, L. D., & Addams, S. (1993). Strengths in transition: Professionally facilitated HIV support groups and the development of client symptomatology. *Social Work with Groups, 16,* 41–54.

Grinstead, O., Zack, B., & Faigeles, B. (2001). Reducing postrelease risk behavior among HIV seropositive prison inmates: The health promotion program. *AIDS Education and Prevention, 13*(2), 109–119.

Grossman, A. H. & Silverstein, C. (1993). Facilitating support groups for professionals working with people with AIDS. *Social Work, 38,* 144–151.

Hackl, K. L., Somlai, A. M., Kelly, J. A., & Kalichman, S. C. (1997). Women living with HIV/AIDS: The dual challenge of being a patient and a caregiver. *Health and Social Work, 22,* 53–62.

Hayes, M. A., McConnell, S. C., Nardozzi, J. A., & Mullican, R. J. (1998). Family and friends of people with HIV/AIDS support group. *Social Work with Groups, 21,* 35–47.

Heckman, T. G., Kalichman, S. C., Roffman, R. R., Sikkema, K. J., Heckman, B. D., Somali, A. M., et al. (1999). A telephone-delivered coping improvement intervention for persons living with HIV/AIDS in rural areas. *Social Work with Groups, 21,* 49–61.

Juntunen, A., Hwalek, M., & Neale, A. V. (1999). Tracking and interviewing clients at risk for HIV and substance abuse in a Latino community. *Evaluation and Program Planning, 22,* 305–312.

Kalimach, S. C., Rompa, D., & Cage, M. (2005). Group intervention to reduce HIV transition risk behavior among personal living with HIV/AIDS. *Behavior Modification, 29*(2), 256–285.

Kelly, J. A. & St. Lawrence, J. S. (1990). The impact of community-based groups to help persons reduce HIV infection risk behaviors, *AIDS-Care, 2,* 25–35.

King, M. B. (1993). *AIDS, HIV, and mental health.* Cambridge: Cambridge University Press.

Land, H. & Harangody, G. (1990). A support group for partners of persons with AIDS. *Families in Society, 71*, 471–482.

Lopez, D. J. & Getzel, G. S. (1984). Helping gay patients in crisis. *Social Casework, 65*, 387–394.

Lopez, D. J. & Getzel, G. S. (1987). Strategies for volunteers caring for persons with AIDS. *Social Casework, 68*, 47–53.

Maasen, T. (1998). Counseling gay men with multiple loss and survival problems: The bereavement group as a transitional object. *AIDS Care, 10*, 57–64.

Mann, J., Tarantola, D. J. M., & Netter, T. W. (1992). *A global report: AIDS in the world.* Cambridge, MA: Harvard University Press.

Mason, S. & Vazquez, D. (2007). Making positive changes: A psychoeducation group for parents with HIV/AIDS. *Social Work with Groups, 30*(2), 27–40.

Mayers, A. & Spiegel, L. (1992). A parental support group in a pediatric AIDS clinic: Its usefulness and limitations. *Health and Social Work, 17*, 183–193.

Meier, A., Galinsky, M. J., & Rounds, K. A. (1995). Telephone support groups for caregivers of persons with AIDS. *Social Work with Groups, 18*, 99–108.

Moore, P. J. (1998). AIDS bereavement supports in an African American church: A model for facilitator training. *Illness, Crisis & Loss, 7*, 390–401.

Livingston, D. (1996). A systems approach to AIDS counseling for gay couples, *Journal of Gay & Lesbian Social Services, 4*, 83–93.

Nokes, K. M., Chew, L., & Altman, C. (2003). Using a telephone support group for HIV-positive persons aged 50+ to increase social support and health-related knowledge. *AIDS Patient Care and STDs, 17*(3), 345–351.

O'Dowd, M. A., Natalie, C., Orr, D., & McKegney, F. (1991). Characteristics of patients attending an HIV-related psychiatric outpatient clinic. *Hospital and Community Psychiatry, 42*, 615–619.

Palacios-Jimeniz, L. & Shernoff, M. (1986). *Eroticizing safer sex.* New York: Gay Men's Health Crisis.

Pomeroy, E. C., Rubin, A., Van Laningham, L. & Walker, R. J. (1997). "Straight Talk": The effectiveness of a psychoeducational group intervention for heterosexuals with HIV/AIDS. *Research on Social Work Practice, 7*, 149–163.

Ponton, K. E., DeClemente, F. J., & McKenna, S. (1991). An AIDS education and prevention program for hospitalized adolescents. *Journal of the American Academy of Children and Adolescent Psychiatry, 30*, 729–734.

Redman, J. M. (1990). *Women and AIDS: What we need to know.* A workshop manual on educating women about AIDS and safer sex. New Orleans: Planned Parenthood.

Rerks-Ngarm, S., et al. (2009). Vaccination with ALVAC and AIDSVAX to prevent HIV-1 infection in Thailand. *New England Journal of Medicine.* www.nejm.org, October 20, 2009.

Richey, C. A., Gillmore, M. R., Balassone, M. L., Gutierrez, L., & Hartway, J. (1997). Developing and implementing a group skill training intervention to reduce HIVAIDS risk among sexually active adolescents in detention. *Journal of HIV/AIDS Prevention & Education for Adolescents & Children, 1*, 71–101.

Rittner, B. & Hammons, K. (1992). Telephone group work with people with end stage AIDS. *Social Work with Groups, 15*, 59–72.

Robinson, W. A., Petty, M. S., Patton, C., & Kang, H. (2008). Aging with HIV: Historical and intra-community difference in experience of aging with HIV. *Journal of Gay & Lesbian Social Services, 20*(1/2), 111–128.

Roffman, R. A., Downey, L., Beadnell, B., Gordon, J. R., Craver, J. N., & Stephens, R. S. (1997). Cognitive-behavioral group counseling to prevent HIV transmission in gay and bisexual men: Factors contributing to successful risk reduction. *Research on Social Work Practice, 7*, 165–186.

Rounds, K. A., Galinsky, M. J., & Stevens, L. S. (1991). Linking people with AIDS in rural communities: The telephone group. *Social Work, 36*, 13–18.

Sandstrom, K. L. (1996). Searching for information, understanding, and self-value: The utilization of peer support groups by gay men with HIV/AIDS. *Social Work in Health Care, 23*, 51–74.

Sherman, A. C., Mosier, J., Leszcz, M., Burlingame, G. M., Ulman, K. H., Cleary, T., Simonton, S., Latif, U., Hazelton, L., & Strauss, B. (2004). Group interventions for patients with cancer and HIV disease: Part I: Effects on psychosocial and functional outcomes at different phases of illness. *International Journal of Group Psychotherapy, 54*(1), 29–82.

Shilts, R. (1988). *The band played on: Politics, people and AIDS.* New York: St. Martin's Press.

Smith, R. A. (2001). *Encyclopedia of AIDS: A social, political, cultural and scientific record of the HIV epidemic.* New York: Penguin Books.

Sontag, S. (1978). *Illness as metaphor.* New York: Vintage Books.

Stine, G. J. (2001). *AIDS update.* Upper Saddle River, NJ: Prentice Hall.

Subramanian, K., Hernandez, S., & Martinez, A. (1995). Psychoeducational group work for low-income Latina mothers with HIV infection. *Social Work with Groups, 18*, 53–64.

Wiener, L. S. (1998). Telephone support groups for HIV-positive mothers whose children have died of AIDS. *Social Work, 43*, 279–285.

Weiner, L. S., Spencer, E. D., Davidson, R., & Fair, C. (1993). National telephone support groups: A new avenue toward psychosocial support for HIV-infected children and their families. *Social Work with Groups, 16*, 55–71.

Wood, S. A. (2007). The analysis of an innovative HIV-positive women's support group. *Social Work with Groups, 30*(3), 9–28.

Wright, E. M. (2000). The psychosocial context. In V. J. Lynch (ed.), *HIV/AIDS at year 2000: A sourcebook for social workers* (pp. 18–32). Boston: Allyn & Bacon.

Wyatt-Morley, C. (1997). *AIDS memoir: Journal of an HIV-positive mother.* West Hartford, CT: Kumarian Press.

Yoakam, J. R. (1999). The youth and AID projects: School and community outreach for gay, lesbian, bisexual, and transgender youth. *Journal of Gay & Lesbian Social Services, 9*, 99–114.

Chapter Four

Group Work in the Prevention of Adolescent Alcohol and Other Drug Abuse

Andrew Malekoff

The problematic use of alcohol, drugs, and tobacco is unquestionably the nation's number one health problem. While all segments of society are affected, the future of young people is most severely compromised by this epidemic.

Although there have been cumulative declines of illicit drug use, particularly marijuana and various stimulants such as methamphetamine and crystal methamphetamine, among adolescents (grades 8 through 12) between 1997 and 2006, there is a troubling rise in the abuse of prescription painkillers such as OcyContin and Vicodin in this group (Johnston et al., 2007). Misconceptions about the safety of these drugs, coupled with ease of access, have contributed to a dramatic increase in teen prescription drug use (Califano, 2009).

According to the U.S. Office of National Drug Control Policy (2007), more "teens are using prescription drugs because they believe the myth that these drugs provide a medically safe high" (p. 1). In addition, they acquire these drugs for free from the medicine cabinets of friends or relatives.

Another disturbing trend is the increase of heroin use among adolescents in the United States. National and statewide surveys suggest that heroin is more readily available, cheaper to purchase, and easier to use than it was a generation ago. The increase in the quality of heroin offers the option of snorting this substance, thereby reducing the stigma associated with needles (Schwartz, 1998).

The increase in heroin use among teens is not exclusively an inner city problem as some might suspect. For example in the suburbs of Long Island, New York, just east of New York City, heroin is easy to get and can be bought for as little as $5 a bag, less than the cost of six-pack of beer (Bolger, 2008).

Alcohol use among eighth-graders has declined by more than one-third since its peak level in the mid 1990s. Alcohol use among twelfth-graders has also declined by one-seventh during the same period of time (Johnston et al., 1998, 2007).

Despite the promising decline in alcohol use, when teens drink it is likely to excess. According to a report by Joseph A. Califano (2009), founder of the National

Center on Addiction and Substance Abuse at Columbia University, about 20% of 17-year-olds partake in binge drinking in any given month (p. 59).

A national survey (CASA, 2008) on teen and parent substance abuse attitudes found that underaged boys and girls prefer sweetened liquor. This is followed in popularity by beer for boys and wine for girls. Naturally, advertisers spend multi-millions of dollars to develop marketing strategies to target teen preferences (Centers for Disease Control and Prevention, 2007) at the same time that public health education campaigns are devised to prevent alcohol and substance abuse.

Although there have been declines in cigarette use for those in grades 8, 10, and 12, the older adolescent group showed the largest decline among the three grades. The drop in tobacco use among teens offers some evidence of the success of a three-decade–long, and counting, cultural shift that has included increased taxes, bans on smoking in public places, and public health education campaigns (Califano, 2009).

Research analysts (Males, 1999) have consistently pointed out that prevalence rates for teenage alcohol and other drug abuse are at record low levels and that young people are in the greatest danger from their parents' addictions.

There are millions of children who grow up in homes with alcohol- and other drug–abusing parents (Hosang, 1995). It has been estimated that approximately one in four children in the United States is exposed to alcohol abuse and/or drug dependence in the family at some point before age 18 (Grant, 2000). These young people are likely to become alcohol or drug abusers themselves without intervention. Parental alcoholism and drug addiction influence the use of alcohol and other drugs in several ways, including increased stress and decreased parental monitoring. Impaired parental monitoring contributes to adolescents' joining peer groups that support drug use. There is a need for an integrated service approach to enhance the lives of these children (Committee on Child Health Financing, 2001).

Any discussion of drug abuse and prevention today must include the use of anabolic steroids by adolescents to improve athletic performance and body image and to increase physical strength, muscle mass, muscle definition, and endurance (National Institute on Drug Abuse, 2006). Prevention requires that pediatricians inquire about anabolic steroid use during routine health maintenance visits given the health risks to the population at risk (American Academy of Pediatrics, Committee on Sports Medicine and Fitness, 1997).

Promising efforts to prevent steroid use include the ATLAS (Adolescents Training and Learning to Avoid Steroids) prevention program that is geared toward high school football players. In the program, coaches and team leaders offer information on the harmful effects of steroids and other substances and teach refusal skills. ATHENA (Athletes Targeting Healthy Exercise and Nutrition Alternatives) is another program that has proved to be successful. It is patterned on ATLAS and focused on adolescent girls who are active in athletic competition. Such prevention efforts are typically geared toward adolescents involved in team sports (National Institute on Drug Abuse, 2006). Good grounding in group work in implementing programs like ATLAS and ATHENA will only serve to strengthen prevention efforts.

The pervasiveness of the alcohol and other drug abuse and addiction extends well beyond the individual. Alcohol and drug abuse play a major role in "destroying families, crippling U.S. businesses, terrorizing entire neighborhoods, and choking the educational criminal justice and social service systems" (Brandeis University, 1993, summary, p. 1). As social workers committed to youth, and to the families and communities that they live, we cannot escape the need to address the problems of alcohol and drug abuse, regardless of the setting of our work. Where there are people, there is alcohol and drug abuse. Where there are youth, there are youth at risk. The purpose of this chapter is to highlight group work as a protective factor, a powerful preventive tool for youth who show early signs of alcohol and other drug abuse and who are at risk for alcoholism and drug addiction.

REVIEW OF THE LITERATURE

What differentiates people with negative outcomes from those who grow up in similar circumstances and bounce back from great adversity? This question has stimulated much speculation and a dramatic growth of the literature on vulnerability, resiliency and risk, and protective factors (Garmezy, 1991, Garmezy & Rutter, 1983; Glantz, 1995; Goleman, 1987; Landy & Tam, 1998; Rutter, 1979, 1995; Sameroff, 1988; Schorr, 1989; Selekman, 2006, 2009; Werner, 1989, 1990; Werner & Smith, 2001; Werner et al., 1998). What differentiates youth who become alcohol and drug abusers from their contemporaries from similar backgrounds who do not? This question illustrates the special concern of those interested in understanding the relationship between risk reduction strategies and substance abuse prevention (Bernard, 1991; Centers for Disease Control and Prevention, 2009; Griffin et al., 2001; Hawkins, Catalano & Associates, 1992; Hawkins et al., 1992; Vega et al., 1993; Werner, 1986).

Risk factors include constitutional (i.e., physiological) deficits and contextual realities (i.e., the physical, cultural, social, political, and economic environments). Examples of risk factors for youth include a history of alcohol and drug abuse/addiction in the family, neighborhood disorganization, being a victim of child abuse, becoming pregnant, having a chronic history of school failure, being economically disadvantaged, having attempted suicide, and associating with alcohol- and drug-abusing peers.

Protective factors are the individual's constitutional assets (i.e., intelligence, temperament) and family and environmental supports (i.e., a close, lifelong bond with an adult relative or mentor) that have the potential to reduce risk.

Hawkins, Catalano, and Associates (1992) emphasize the importance of bonding as a key protective factor:

Antidrug attitudes are strengthened by promoting adolescents' bonds, including relationships with non–drug users, commitment to the various social groups in which they are involved (families, schools, community, prosocial peer groups), and values and beliefs regarding what is healthy and ethical behavior (p. 27).

Selekman (2005, p. 235) offers a summary of some additional resilience protective factors, which include caring and supportive parents, strong social skills, effective and creative problem-solving abilities, pronounced self-sufficiency, good management of emotions, and low levels of family conflict.

Some of the settings in which group approaches have been used to address and/or study the preventive needs of youth at risk include the school (Bilides, 1992; Brown, 1993; Centers for Disease Control and Prevention, 2009; Hanson, 1992; Kantor et al., 1992; Klem & Connell, 2004; Perry et al., 2002; St. Pierre et al., 2001; St. Pierre & Kaltreider, 2001; Shields, 1986; Sussman et al., 1997; Taylor et al., 1999), the public housing development (Schinke et al., 1992), the community mental health center (Malekoff, 1994a), the criminal justice system (Freidman & Utada, 1992; Smith, 1985), and street youth (Unger et al., 1998). Comprehensive approaches have been described by Hawkins et al. (1992) and by Felner, Silverman, and Adix (1991).

Beyond the physical setting of the service are the cultural context of substance abuse (Bachman et al., 1991; Belgrave et al., 2000; Bilides, 1990; Catalano et al., 1992; De La Rosa & Andrados, 1993; Delgado, 1997; Forgey, 1994; Harachi et al., 2001; Hogue et al., 2002; Myers, 2002; Rich, 2001; Taylor, 2000; Vega et al., 1993; Wallace, 1993) and the family context (Black, 1979; Deckman & Downs, 1982; Efron, 1987; Emshoff, 1989; Gross & McCane, 1992; Johnson et al., 1998; Knight et al., 1992; Treadway, 1989).

A protective network of supports has the potential to increase the individual's resistance to risk, placing him or her in a better position to avoid alcohol and other drug problems. Group work can be an important part of constructing such a network.

PRACTICE PRINCIPLES

Beginning group work with at-risk adolescents requires careful planning, thoughtful programming, and attention to helping the group members to become a system of mutual aid. When combined, these principles set the tone for an experience that provides a sense of order and an opportunity for role flexibility, something often missing in the lives of youth at risk.

Planning

The planning model, as formulated by Kurland (1980, 1982) and further expli-
cated by Northen and Kurland (2001) and Malekoff (2004a), identifies seven
variables necessary for the formation of successful groups. Careful preparation can
make the difference between groups that thrive and groups that fail. The seven
variables are:

Needs:	What are the needs of prospective members?
Purpose:	What are the tentative goals and objectives of the group?
Composition:	Who are the potential members?
Structure:	What concrete arrangements are necessary to proceed?
Content:	What means will be used to enable the group to achieve its purpose?
Pregroup contact:	How will prospective members be recruited?
Agency and social context:	What obstacles exist and how might they be overcome?

Good planning is invaluable when working with youth who live in disorganized families or communities, or both. Consistency, predictability, and structure
elude them in their day-to-day lives. *A well-planned group experience serves as a
counterforce to living in a capricious environment.* What begins as a counterforce
can become a protective factor, mitigating against risk and stimulating healthy
development.

Programming

Redl and Wineman (1952) describe *programming* as "activities which require
a certain amount of definite planning, on the part of the children themselves, of
the adults, or both" (p. 76). Breton (1990) asserts that "the way we structure
groups is all-important, for a group can be structured so that the whole person
in each member is invited to participate, or it can be structured so that only
the troubled, or broken, or hurt parts of the person [are] invited to participate"
(p. 27).

Programming is the activity that the group does to achieve its purpose. How
programming is determined and implemented can make the difference between a
group in which members' strengths are supported (Malekoff, 2004b, 2001) and
one in which deficits (i.e., pathology) are highlighted. In the case of adolescents at
risk, it is important for the social worker to structure the group to invite the whole
person, to blend discussion and activity with an eye toward promoting competency (Malekoff, 2004a).

Mutual Aid

A critical question for all social workers working with groups is, "Am I the central helping person here or do I enable others to help one another?" The latter stance, "the valuation of members as helpers" (Middleman & Wood, 1990, p. 11), distinguishes social work with groups from other group treatments (with the notable exception of self-help groups, such as Alcoholics Anonymous, Narcotics Anonymous, Alanon, and Naranon, which are self-help mutual aid groups). The practice of promoting mutual aid implies faith in the group and its potential to function autonomously. Furthermore, it suggests the social worker's commitment to "learn not only *about* but *from* group members" (Breton, 1990, p. 23). Attention to planning, programming, and mutual aid can lead to the creation of a healthy group environment in which trust is established, various roles are practiced in safety, and reliance on self is broadened to include reliance on others. To structure the group "to invite the whole person," the social worker must have a good understanding of normal adolescent development, the adolescent in the group, the social worker in the group, and the group in context. The following practice principles will address these issues.

1. *Alliance formation with parents and other involved persons and systems is a prerequisite to establishing an engaged group membership* (Malekoff, 2004a).

   Adolescents cannot be seen in a vacuum. Sanction from parents and cooperation with related systems (e.g., school) are necessary for ongoing work with the group. By establishing working alliances with these significant others, the social worker models collaboration and establishes the groundwork for mediating with the various systems. Working relationships with parents help to reduce the guilt that children often feel about betraying the family. Working relationships with all involved persons and systems help to reduce the possibility that dysfunctional interactions will be extended to the helping system.

   In the Youth of Culture Drug Free Club, an after-school program for youth at risk located in Long Island, New York (Malekoff, 1994a; Walthrust, 1992), a well-planned and organized dance for local youth was marred by a postdance fight in which a youngster was slashed with a razor. The staff team worked closely with parents in the aftermath of the incident. This collaboration, in light of a chaotic and potentially tragic situation, enabled the group members to work through the crisis in a thoughtful manner despite their fear that the club might be terminated.

2. *An appreciation for paradox and an ability to differentiate the words from the music is essential to working with adolescents in groups* (Malekoff, 1994b).

Just below the surface of the strident facade or apathetic veneer that many adolescents project are the deeper meanings that not many adults are privileged to discover. Often the familiar refrain "Leave me alone!" carefully conceals the cry for help. It is not always easy to hang around to hear the music underneath the static of the words. Yet to work with adolescents, one must hang in there. Too many adults have already bailed out.

3. *Cultural awareness and sensitivity are essential for practicing social work with groups in a society of ever-increasing diversity.*

Social workers must be aware of racism, sexism, and homophobia, as well as other cultural issues and values, as well as how they impact on group members and how they have affected their own lives. Bilides (1990) suggests some guidelines for putting one's multicultural awareness into practice with groups. These include the following: "discuss stereotypes at all levels (personal, familial and societal) ... point out commonalities ... explore the meanings of words and language ... recognize and acknowledge your own discomfort about race, color, ethnicity, and class issues" (pp. 51–56).

The Youth of Culture Drug Free Club reflects some of the values just suggested in their choice of club name. A predominantly African American group, they planned and presented a communitywide "international cultural day" in which they modeled traditional clothing from various cultures. This was a step in the direction of opening the club to members of other groups, including growing immigrant populations from Central America, Mexico, and Haiti.

4. *Use the self and access to childhood memories.*

Awareness of what the group experience evokes in one is invaluable, especially with a population in motion. This includes conscious memories of the social worker's earlier years and struggles during adolescence (e.g., personal and/or familial experiences with alcohol and drugs). The feelings that inevitably bubble up in the lively context of the adolescent group must not be ignored. Feelings and experiences can be disclosed at times, using good judgment. For example, the purpose of disclosure should never be to gain the acceptance of the group or to tacitly encourage acting-out behavior for a vicarious thrill. This is where good supervision enters the picture.

5. *Boldly address the resistance of involuntary or mandated group members*

Involuntary or mandated group members are a staple for group workers who work with adolescents with problems of drug and alcohol abuse (Malekoff, 2004a). Typically, a mandating force is their "motivation" for attending a group. This might include the threat of a court order, legal action, or pressure from parents or other adults in positions of authority.

Resistance may present itself through denial of the problem (i.e., regarding drug use), superficial compliance, testing the limits, silence, externalizing the problem (i.e., blaming others), minimizing, and devaluation of the group worker or group.

Overcoming resistance among involuntary group members requires worker authenticity and a sense of trust and safety in the group. Clarity of purpose and developing a clear and explicit contract make a difference, especially when feedback from group members is welcomed and important issues such as confidentiality are discussed openly.

When involuntary group members feel in control of their fate, their motivation increases. Although it was not their choice to join the group, it can be their choice to participate freely once there. Motivating involuntary group members is a subtle process of locating the resistance, setting manageable goals, demanding work, being sympathetic, using humor, holding group members to imposed sanctions, and building a culture of mutual aid that fosters playfulness, a sense of safety, and movement toward taking risks (Duffy & Farina, 1992).

For adolescents with dual diagnoses, more commonly known today as co-occurring disorders, motivational interviewing offers an integrated and nonconfrontational approach (Miller & Rollnick, 1991; Sciacca, 1996, 2007) that can be helpful in reducing resistance. This combined approach uses "acceptance, nonconfrontation and recognition of the client's readiness levels and assesses change incrementally" (Sciacca, 2007). Fields (2004) offers a curriculum-based motivational interviewing group that is organized into five sessions and will offer readers a clear approach to using this model in group work.

6. *Do not go it alone.*
   Social workers working with at-risk adolescents in groups need support from colleagues. Too many adults (professional or otherwise) disapprove of the group modality when adolescents are involved. They question the efficacy of the work when confronted with the noise, action, and attitudes that seem absent in the adult group. Colleagues with a track record and an inclination to work with youth can be invaluable partners. This includes good supervision from peers or adults and opportunities for teamwork. Co-leadership of groups is an approach that requires adequate time for planning and reflection. Too many human services workers without adequate group training operate under the false assumption that co-leadership is better, easier, or less stressful than one-person leadership. Maybe it is, but this depends entirely on the match and on the commitment and honesty that develop in the partnership. Simply throwing workers together to lead groups is to be avoided at all costs.

COMMON THEMES

Groups may be formed specifically for children living in families with a present or past history of alcohol or drug abuse. Other groups may be composed of youth who evidence a variety of related risk factors. Substance abuse prevalence rates (and practice experience) suggest that in either case the social workers must have knowledge of the impact of alcohol and drug abuse (including alcoholism and addiction) on the individual in the family.

What are the implications of growing up in a dysfunctional family? How might these issues influence the individual in the group? How might they affect the group as a whole? (Although the attention there is to substance abuse, these questions may also apply to families in which there is child abuse, domestic violence, or severe mental illness.) The following six themes will address these questions.

1. *Children who grow up in families with alcohol and drug abuse/addiction learn to distrust to survive.*
   Attention to the beginning phase of group development is critical in building trust. By exercising anticipatory empathy, the social worker tunes into the experience of the group members, taking an important step in helping to build a safe environment for mutual exchange. At the beginning, the social worker allows and supports distance, searches for common ground, invites trust gently, establishes group purpose, facilitates exploration, begins to set norms, and provides program structure (Garland et al., 1965; Malekoff, 2004a).

2. *Children growing up in alcohol- or drug-abusing/addicted families become uncomfortably accustomed to living with chaos, uncertainty, unpredictability, and inconsistency.*
   It has been said that children growing up under these conditions have to "guess at what normal is." The group experience must provide a clear structure with norms and reasonable limits. Issues of membership (Is it an open or closed group? If it is open, how do new members enter? How do members exit?), space (Is there a consistent meeting place?), and time (Does the group meet at a regular time for a prescribed period?) are all important considerations. Group rituals might be considered to reinforce a sense of order and to establish value-based traditions. For example, in the Youth of Culture Drug Free Club referred to earlier, the members all recite a drug-free pledge at the beginning and end of each meeting.

3. *Denial, secrecy, embarrassment, and shame are common experiences of children who live in alcoholic or addicted families.*
   Joining a group of outsiders might in itself be felt as an act of betrayal, a step toward revealing the "family secret." Awareness at this juncture allows the social worker to invite trust gently while paying careful

attention to questions of trust and confidentiality throughout the life of the group.

4. *Growing up with the ever-present threat of violence (verbal and physical) contributes to a pervasive sense of fearfulness, hypervigilance, and despair.*
   The group can become a place where differences can be safely expressed and where conflicts need not be a matter of life and death. Conflicts can be resolved and differences respected in a thoughtful and increasingly mature manner in the group. The group is a place where members can practice putting a reflective pause between impulse and action and where despair can be transformed into hope.

   In response to another violent incident, an interracial murder in the community, the Youth of Culture Drug Free Club organized the largest youth contingent in a March for Unity. Again they acted to replace despair with hope, and an anticipated riot was averted.

5. *Children, who grow up in alcohol- and drug-abusing/addicted families become rigidly attached to roles.*
   Many of those growing up in alcohol- and drug-abusing/addicted systems construct a wall of defenses and repressed feelings by adopting rigid family roles (Wegscheider, 1981, pp. 86–149). Accompanying these roles are stultifying family rules, unspoken mandates, such as *don't talk, don't trust, don't feel.* A group experience can provide members accustomed to assuming rigid roles with an opportunity to practice role flexibility, broaden their intrapersonal and interpersonal repertoires, and gain competence in coping with the environment.

   In the Youth of Culture Drug Free Club, the members planned a holiday party for themselves and organized a trip to a local nursing home, offering gifts and spending time with an isolated population of patients with AIDS. Both activities, the party and the visit, required careful preparation, enabling the members to assume diverse roles and to work in partnership to accomplish the group's goals.

6. *Growing up in an alcoholic or addicted family system leaves youths with little hope that things will ever change.*
   The group is a social system that develops a life of its own, marked by a developing history of events and relationships. As in any system, there are decisions to be made, problems to solve, and crises to surmount. If a dysfunctional family system is the primary frame of reference for a young person, he or she may have little experience in successfully resolving conflicts or overcoming obstacles. The group can provide members with a growing sense of confidence that difficult and frustrating circumstances can be overcome. The group worker must be tuned in to the sense of hopelessness that such members bring to the group so as not to become easily discouraged. It cannot be emphasized strongly enough that group

work with this population requires hanging in for the long haul and modeling a sense of hope.

One of the activities of the Youth of Culture Drug Free Club is wilderness outings (hiking, canoeing, camping), providing members with multiple obstacles (frustration, fatigue, fear) to confront and overcome. The members learn quickly that surviving in the wilderness requires more than self-sufficiency. They must come to trust and rely on one another to navigate a current or climb a mountain, powerful metaphors for what they face daily. With each trip they experience change as they stretch their limits together, and with each successful journey they increase their appreciation of themselves and their fellow group members. In time the group itself becomes a valuable frame of reference.

RECOMMENDED WAYS OF WORKING

The agency context of the service being offered is a key determinant of the success or failure of the endeavor. In other words, do the values of the agency lead to policies and practices that allow the group to work toward its purpose in a hospitable environment? The answer to this question becomes obvious when arrangements for staffing, space, time, and materials are negotiated. To work effectively with at-risk adolescents, the host agency must sanction the activity in word and deed. The social worker's responsibility is to see to it that the work of the group reflects the stake that the agency and group members have in one another. It is not enough to be available to work with a group. Good planning and sound social work practice often require mediation and advocacy. Although there is a growing body of evidence regarding the efficacy of diverse group treatments for adolescents, researchers believe that aggregation of youths who display problem behavior into group interventions may, under some conditions, produce iatrogenic effects on all participants.

The Leeds Family Place of North Shore Child and Family Guidance Center (The Place) is an alcohol and drug treatment and prevention program for youth and their families. Located in a low-income minority community in Nassau County, New York, The Place's clientele and staff represent a multicultural mix that reflects a growing number of suburban communities. The services of The Place include an intensive after-school program that is a comprehensive blend of group-, family-, and individual-oriented activities. The group program includes services for adults, children, and adolescents; alcoholics and drug addicts; nonaddicted substance abusers; and at-risk, non–substance-abusing significant others (youths and adults).

Some adolescents are seen as referred clients who are admitted to the program following a formal evaluation and case disposition. Others are seen in a variety of after-school programs that do not require a formal clinical evaluation. The Youth

of Culture Drug Free Club is an example of the latter. Many adolescents participate in both programs as clients and as community members.

In her landmark work on "breaking the cycle of disadvantage," Schorr (1989)
asserts that "most successful programs find that interventions cannot be routinized
or applied uniformly. Staff members and program structures are fundamentally
flexible and *see the child in the context of family and the family in the context of its
surroundings*" (p. 257).

Groups at The Place vary in composition, length, and purpose. Content
includes psychoeducation, socialization, discussion, counseling, therapy, outings,
arts and crafts, cultural awareness activities, and community service. Staff members work in teams. This enables program participants to become engaged with
the agency as well as with an individual social worker or counselor. Regularly
scheduled team meetings are held for the purposes of case assignment and management, program development, supervision, and skill development.

Family involvement is an important value at The Place. All incoming families
with adolescents are assigned to an 8-week multiple-family group program. There
are generally four to seven families per group, ranging from 8 to 20+ people. The
group's purposes include helping families with drug and alcohol problems to learn
from one another, to decrease isolation, and to address the shame that children
carry as a secret. These issues are addressed in the service of prevention. The content includes a combination of alcohol and drug education, discussion, role play,
and psychodrama. The first two sessions are structured to allow time for the adults
and youth to meet briefly in separate groups to identify needs and make connections. The groups are co-led by two or three social workers. The number of workers is determined by group size and by the presence of younger (school-age)
children. When the group divides, one of the three workers meets with the children. The different age groups tend to ally, early on, with different workers, who
are tuned in to the importance of modeling collaboration as differences arise. The
cultural diversity of the staff enriches this process as group members see people of
different racial and ethnic backgrounds working together with mutual respect.

The fifth session of one multifamily group series began with a staff presentation of normal development in the latency and adolescent periods and its relationship to the family life cycle. (Psychoeducation on normal development is of great
value for families in which the members have grown accustomed to uncertainty
and consequently must guess at what is "normal.") In the group this process serves
to provide support, encourage dialogue, and reduce isolation. When the theme of
separation was presented, one of the group members, a Hispanic mother who
understands and speaks English but prefers Spanish, addressed the bilingual
worker:

If I may I want to respond to something that the other workers said about
separation. In my country [Colombia], it is different. The kids are expected to
stay with their families until they marry. If they go to college they stay home.

This [discussion] is a problem for us [motioning to her husband, a practicing alcoholic] and upsetting that the children are encouraged to leave.

Once this statement was translated, a lively discussion ensued as the group, consisting of four families of various cultural origins (Columbian, African, Yugoslavian, and Italian), exchanged their feelings about separation. At one point the Hispanic mother's 17-year-old son, who was referred to The Place following a single incident of binge drinking, spoke:

"I didn't know this." He spoke in short, choppy sentences and was encouraged to elaborate. "Well, now that I know [what she thinks], I'll think about looking into colleges close to home, but I'm not staying there until I got married." Everyone laughed, including the boy's parents. One of the social workers summed up, turning to the boy. "It sounds like you're willing to negotiate with your parents." He acknowledged her comment with a smile.

In this interchange, the group was warming up to the meeting, testing the waters, and reestablishing trust. (Remember that distrust is more often than not the norm in these families.) An emotionally charged issue surfaced. Differences along cultural and generational lines were drawn. Respect for differences was modeled by the social worker, who encouraged discussion. Four different cultural groups (one bilingual), four sets of parents (and one grandparent), and four sets of adolescents produced no dire consequences.

All of the adolescents had abused alcohol and/or had tried other drugs on at least one occasion. In all four families, the fathers, only one of whom was present, were alcoholic or drug addicted. As is often the case, the adolescents and their presenting problems were the key to getting help. As the session proceeded, separation issues gave way to issues of limits, boundaries, and private space. The adolescents and parents began to draw battle lines as parents revealed their suspicions.

The group was now heated as the adolescents referred to their parents as "nuts," "stupid," "crazy," and "ridiculous." A 14-year-old girl who had verbally assaulted her mother last week took the offensive again. When one of the social workers reminded her of the rule of not attacking and allowing others to finish speaking, she smiled and said, "Okay, okay." The social workers then asked what a parent should do if she suspects that her child is using drugs. The parents discussed various issues, including the circumstances under which they would search their children's rooms. The mother of the 14-year-old girl then said, somewhat defensively, "People don't know what they would do until it really affects them. I never thought I'd be going through my daughter's room, but I had a feeling and it was right. It was a good thing I followed my instinct because now I can get help." Then for the first time in five meetings, the Hispanic mother spoke in English and directly to the other mother. She exclaimed, "You did right! You did the right thing and I would too, to help my child." This was a moving moment in which a mother who was struggling with an aggressive 14-year-old who abused her in the group setting was supported by others in the presence of her daughter. Returning to Spanish, the Hispanic mother made an impassioned request of the worker: "Please tell her [the girl] if she didn't love her she wouldn't have done this. It is an act of caring, and her daughter is so aggressive. "When this was translated, the 14-year-old girl asked: "What's 'aggressive' mean?" It was described as "hostile." By this time, the group was becoming very intense as the adolescents were beginning to bond in anger against the parents. As angry glances were exchanged across the generational dividing line, one social worker acknowledged the feeling and suggested an activity to promote empathy. Addressing the 14-year-old but speaking to the group, she explained what a role reversal is and said, "I find it helpful to try this when parents and children are in conflict." She then asked the 14-year-old to "put yourself in your mother's shoes. If you thought your child was in danger, that she might have weapons or drugs in her room, would you search it?" The girl became pensive and clearly thought deeply about this, as did the others, judging from their facial expressions and body language. She finally responded, "Yes, I think I would." It was with this reflection, as the other soaked in her response, that the group moved to an ending. One social worker concluded with a brief restatement of the rules regarding confidentially and repeated that there would be no consequences for what was shared in the group. The 14-year-old girl seemed more relieved than offended by the definition of her behavior as aggressive and hostile. A limit was being set that perhaps she had been seeking all along.

The illustration of the multifamily group can be considered in light of the specific group process described or from a metaphorical perspective. In the latter case, the reader might consider the ways in which the family can be brought into the group when it is not part of the group. In either instance, what is clear is that the establishment of trust over time and in each session is essential. While this is true for any group, it is particularly so when distrust becomes the norm for the individual struggling with personal or familial substance abuse/addiction or both. In such families, feelings are often not valued or tolerated, and poor identification and labeling of feelings are a consequence of having little or no practice. The group provides an opportunity to practice these skills with the knowledge that no one will be physically or emotionally destroyed by violent or impulsive acts.

Group work provides people with places in which diversity is tolerated, difference is understood and respected, problems are universalized, and people depend on one another and not only on the experts. To the extent that this occurs, group work becomes a protective factor in the lives of adolescents at risk.

EVALUATION

According to Muraskin (1993), evaluation for drug and alcohol prevention and treatment programs can be conducted for the following purposes:

> To determine the effectiveness of programs for the participants
> To document that program objectives have been met
> To provide information about service delivery that will be useful to program staff and other audiences
> To enable program staff to make changes that improve program effectiveness

Categories of outcome measurement for individuals may include the following variables: use of alcohol and drugs, knowledge of alcohol and drugs, attitudes regarding the use of alcohol and drugs, and ability to refuse using alcohol and drugs in the face of peer pressure, self-esteem, and a sense of hope. Pretests and posttests can be given to determine changes in attitude and habits. Surveys can be developed for this purpose (see Muraskin, 1993, for several examples). In the case of drug and alcohol use, many programs (e.g., in treatment-oriented and criminal justice settings) use the Breathalyzer and urine analysis to test for use. Changes in risk and protective status and in level of functioning over time are also variables that can be used to assess change.

Observations of the group members over time, reports from parents and school personnel, and monitoring of academic, social, and extracurricular progress are all important in the process of evaluation. Not to be underestimated is the self-evaluation of the individual, members' evaluations of one another, and the group's evaluation of itself, a standard part of the ending phase of group work.

The DARE (Drug Abuse Resistance Education) program has been one of the more common school-based programs that target substance use by providing information about drugs. Evaluation studies indicate that DARE has not been effective in reducing drug use. Programs that have been evaluated as effective and that can use group work are those that promote interaction among peers to develop norms and build resistance and other social skills (Silver & Eddy, 2006).

According to Dryfoos (1993), "Prevention programs seem to work best when they address the total life of the young person and focus on the factors that place him or her at risk" (p. 3). In this era of categorical funding for human services, it is not always easy to provide comprehensive services; therefore, collaboration between the various systems that serve youth is essential.

RESOURCES

Al-Anon Family Group Headquarters, Inc.
1600 Corporate Landing Parkway

Virginia Beach, VA 23454-5617
(757) 563-1600
(757) 563-1655
www.al-anon.org

Alcoholics Anonymous (AA)
Mailing address
A.A. World Services, Inc.
P.O. Box 459
New York, NY 10163
(212) 870-3400
www.aa.org

Location
A.A. World Services, Inc.
475 Riverside Drive
at West 120th Street, 11th Floor
New York, NY 10115

Basic Guide to Program Evaluation by Carter McNamara
www.managementhelp.org/evaluatn/fnl_eval.htm

Centers for Disease Control and Prevention
http://www.cdc.gov/

Center for Substance Abuse Prevention (CSAP)
(240) 276-2420
www.prevention.samhsa.gov

Community Anti-Drug Coalitions of America
625 Slaters Lane, Suite 300
Alexandria, VA 22314
(800) 54-CADCA
(703) 706-0565
http://www.cadca.org/

Drug Enforcement Administration (DEA)
http://www.usdoj.gov/dea/

Higher Education Center For Alcohol and Drug Prevention
A program from the U.S. Department of Education
http://www.edc.org/hec/

Institute on Black Chemical Abuse
African American Family Services
2616 Nicollet Avenue South
Minneapolis, MN 55498
(612) 871-7878
www.aafs.net

Join Together
580 Harrison Avenue, 3rd Floor
Boston, MA 02118
(617) 437-1500
(617) 437-9394
www.jointogether.org

Leadership to Keep Children Alcohol Free Foundation
184 Salem Avenue
Dayton OH 45406
(937) 862-9905
http://www.alcoholfreechildren.org/

MADD (Mothers Against Drunk Drivers)
National Office
511 E. John Carpenter Freeway, Suite 700
Irving, TX 75062
(800) GET-MADD
Victim services 24-hour help line:
(877) MADD-HELP
Fax: (972) 869-2206/07
http://www.madd.org/

Nar-Anon Family Group Headquarters, Inc.
22527 Crenshaw Boulevard, No. 200B
Torrance, CA 90505
(310) 534-8188
(800) 477-6291
Fax: (310) 534-8688
www.nar-anon.org
(310) 547-5800
www.onlinerecovery.org

Narcotics Anonymous (NA)
P.O. Box 9999
Van Nuys, CA 91409

(818) 773-9999
www.na.org

National Association for Children
of Alcoholics (NACOA)
11426 Rockville Pike, No. 100
Rockville, MD 20852
(301) 468-0985
www.nacoa.org

National Black Alcoholism and Addiction Council, Inc.
5104 N. Orange Blossom Trail, Suite 111
Orlando, FL 32810
(407) 532-2747
(877) 622-2674
Fax: (407) 532-2815
www.nbacinc.org

National Center on Addiction and Substance Abuse at Columbia University
633 Third Avenue, 19th Floor
New York, NY 10017-6706
(212) 841-5200
http://www.casacolumbia.org

National Clearinghouse for Alcohol and Drug Information (NCADI)
http://www.health.org/

National Council on Alcoholism and Drug Dependence, Inc.
244 E. 58th Street, 4th Floor
New York, NY 10022
(212) 269-7797
Fax: (212) 269-7510
www.ncadd.org

Office of National Drug Control Policy (ONDCP)
http://www.whitehousedrugpolicy.gov/

National Institute on Drug Abuse
www.nida.nih.gov

National Institute on Alcohol Abuse and Alcoholism (NIAAA)
5635 Fishers Lane, MSC 9304
Bethesda, MD 20892-9304

http://www.niaaa.nih.gov
http://www.collegedrinkingprevention.gov

Parents Helping Parents
Sobrato Center for Nonprofits, San Jose
1400 Parkmoor Avenue, Suite 100
San Jose, CA 95126
(408) 727-5775
Fax: (408) 286-1116
http://www.php.com/

SAMHSA's National Clearinghouse for Alcohol and Drug Information
P.O. Box 2345
Rockville, MD 20847-2345
(877) 726-4727
Fax: (240) 221-4292
www.ncadi.samhsa.gov

SAMHSA Referral Hotline
1-800-662-HELP
www.findtreatment.samhsa.gov

Substance Abuse Treatment Facility Locator
http://www.findtreatment.samhsa.gov/

U.S. Department of Education Safe and Drug-Free Schools Program
http://www.ed.gov/offices/OESE/SDFS/index.html

Working Partners for an Alcohol- and Drug-Free American Workplace
http://www.dol.gov/dol/workingpartners.htm

REFERENCES

Bachman, J. G., Wallace, J. M., Jr., Kurth, C. L., Johnston, L. D., & O'Malley, P. M. (1991). *Drug use among black, white, Hispanic, Native American and Asian American high school seniors (1976–1989): Prevalence, trends and correlates* (pp. 1–63). Ann Arbor: Institute for Social Research, University of Michigan.

Belgrave, E., Van Oss Marin, B., & Chambers, D. (2000). Cultural, contextual and intrapersonal predictors of risky sexual attitudes among urban African American girls in early adolescence. *Cultural Diversity and Ethnic Minority Psychology, 6*(3), 309–322.

Bernard, B. (1991). *Fostering resiliency in kids: Protective factors in the family, school and community* (pp. 1–27). Portland, OR: Northwest Regional Training Laboratories.

Bilides, D. (1990). Race, color, ethnicity and class in school-based adolescent counseling groups. *Social Work with Groups, 13*(4), 43–58.

Bilides, D. (1992). Reaching inner city children: A group work program model for a public middle school. *Social Work with Groups, 15*(2/3), 129–144.

Black, C. (1979). Children of alcoholics. *Alcohol, Health and Research World, 1*(1), 23.

American Academy of Pediatrics, Committee on Sports Medicine and Fitness (1997). *Adolescents and Anabolic Steroids: A Subject Review. Pediatrics, 99*(6), 904–908.

Brandeis University, Institute for Health Policy. (1993). *Substance abuse: The nation's number one health problem; Key indicators for policy*. Princeton, NJ: Robert Wood Johnson Foundation.

Breton, M. (1990). Learning from social group work traditions. *Social Work with Groups, 13*(1), 21–34.

Brown, M. E. (1993). Successful components of community and school prevention programs. *National Prevention Evaluation Research Collection, 1*(1), 3–5.

Bolger, T. (2008, December 18-24). Natalie's law: Long Island press series on heroin use prompts new legislation, *Long Island Press, 6* (50), 8–12.

Califano, J. (2009). *How to raise a drug-free kid*. New York: Fireside.

CASA. (2008). *National survey of American attitudes on substance abuse: Teens and parents*. New York: National Center on Addiction and Substance Abuse at Columbia University.

Catalano, R. F., Morrison, D. M., Wells, E. A., Gillmore, M. R., Iritani, B., & Hawkins, D. J. (1992). Ethnic differences in family factors related to early drug initiation. *Journal of Studies on Alcohol, 55*(3), 208–217.

Centers for Disease Control and Prevention. (2009). *School connectedness: Strategies for increasing protective factors among youth*. Atlanta, GA: U.S. Department of Health and Human Services.

Center for Disease Control and Prevention. (2007). Youth exposure to alcohol advertising in magazines—United States, 2001–2005. *Morbidity & Mortality Weekly Report, 56*(30), 763–767.

Committee on Child Health Financing. (2001). Improving substance abuse prevention, assessment, and treatment financing for children and adolescents. *Pediatrics, 108*, 1025–1029.

Deckman, J. & Downs, D. (1982). A group treatment approach for adolescent children of alcoholic parents. *Social Work with Groups, 5*(1), 73–77.

De La Rosa, M. R. & Adrados, J. (1993). *Drug abuse among minority youth; advances in research and methodology*. NIDA Research Monograph 130. Washington, DC: U.S. Department of Health and Human Services.

Delgado, M. (1997). Strengths-based practice with Puerto Rican adolescents: Lessons from a substance abuse prevention project. *Social Work in Education, 19*(2), 101–112.

Dryfoos, J. (1993). Lessons from evaluation of prevention programs. *National Prevention Evaluation Research Collection, 1*(1), 2–4.

Duffy, T. & Farina, T. (1992). *Notes on resistance in groups* (class notes). Boston: Boston University School of Social Work.

Erfon, D. (1987). Videotaping groups for children of substance abusers: A strategy for emotionally disturbed acting out children. *Alcoholism Treatment Quarterly, 4*(2), 71–85.

Emshoff, J. G. (1989). A preventive intervention with children of alcoholics. *Prevention in Human Services, 17*(1), 225–253.

Fields, A. (2004). *Curriculum-based motivation group.* Vancouver, WA: Hollifield Associates.

Felner, R. D., Silverman, M. M., & Adix, R. (1991). Prevention of substance abuse and related disorders in childhood and adolescence: A developmental based, comprehensive ecological approach. *Family and Community Health, 14*(3), 12–22.

Friedman, A. S. & Utada, A. T. (1992). Effects of two group interaction models on substance using adjudicated adolescent males. *Journal of Community Psychology* (Special issue: Programs for Change, Office of Substance Abuse Prevention), 106–117.

Garland, J., Jones, H., & Kolodny, R. (1965). A model for stages of development in social work with groups. In S. Bernstein (ed.), *Explorations in group work: Essays in theory and practice* (pp. 21–30). Boston: Boston University School of Social Work.

Garmezy, N. (1991). Resiliency and vulnerability to adverse development outcomes associated with poverty. *American Behavioral Scientist. 34*(4), 416–430.

Garmezy, N. & Rutter, M. (1983). *Stress, coping and development in children.* New York: McGraw-Hill.

Glantz, M. (1995). *The application of resiliency and risk research to the development of preventive interventions.* Bethesda, MD: National Institute on Drug Abuse.

Goleman, D. (1987, October 13). Thriving despite hardship: Key childhood traits identified. *New York Times,* pp. C1, C11.

Griffin, K., Scheier, L., Botvin, G., & Diaz, T. (2001). Protective role of personal competence skills in adolescent substance use: Psychological well being as a mediating factor. *Psychology of additive behaviors, 15*(3), 194–203.

Gross, J. & McCane, M. (1992). An evaluation of a psychoeducational and substance abuse risk reduction intervention for children of substance abusers. *Journal of Community Psychology* (OSAP Special Issue), 75–87.

Grant, B. F. (2000). Estimates of U.S. children exposed to alcohol abuse and dependence in the family. *American Journal of Public Health, 90*(1), 112–115.

Hansen, W. B. (1992). School based substance abuse prevention: A review of the state of the art in curriculum, 1980–1990. *Health and Education Research: Theory and Practice, 7*(3), 403–430.

Harachi, T., Catalano, R., Kim, S., & Choi, Y. (2001). Etiology and prevention of substance use among Asian American youth. *Prevention Science, 2*(1), 57–65.

Hawkins, J. D., Catalano, R. F., Jr., & et al. (1992). *Communities that care: Action for drug abuse prevention.* San Francisco: Jossey-Bass.

Hawkins, D., Catalano, R., & Miller, J. (1992). Risk and protective factors for alcohol and other drug problems in adolescence and early adulthood: Implications for substance abuse prevention. *Psychological Bulletin, 112*(1), 64–105.

Hogue, A., Liddle, H., Becker, D., & Johnson-Leckrone, J. (2002). Family-based prevention counseling for high risk young adolescents: Immediate outcomes. *Journal of Community Psychology, 30*(1), 1–22.

Hosang, M. (1995). Group work with children of substance abusers: Beyond the basics. In M. Feit, J. Ramey, J. Wodarski, & A. Mann (eds.), *Capturing the power of diversity* (pp. 109–114). New York: Haworth.

Johnson, K., Bryant, D., Collins, D., Noe, T., Strader, T., & Berbaum, M. (1998). Preventing and reducing alcohol and other drug use among high-risk youths by increasing family resilience. *Social Work, 43*(4), 297–308.

Johnston, L. D., O'Malley, P. M., Bachman, J. G., & Schulenberg, J. E. (2007). *Monitoring the future, national results on adolescent drug use: Overview of key findings.* Bethesda, MD: National Institute on Drug Abuse.

Kaminer, Y. (2005). Challenges and opportunities of group therapy for adolescent substance abuse: A critical review. *Addictive Behaviors, 30*(9), 1765–1774.

Kantor, G., Candill, B. & Ungerleider, S. (1992). Project Impact: Teaching the teachers to intervene in student substance abuse problems. *Journal of Alcohol and Drug Education, 38*(1), 11–29.

Klem A., Connell J. (2004). Relationships matter: linking teacher support to student engagement and achievement. *Journal of School Health, 74*(7), 262–273.

Knight, A., Vail-Smith, K., & Barnes, A. (1992). Children of alcoholics in the classroom: A survey of teacher perceptions and training needs. *Journal of School of Health, 62*(8), 367–371.

Kurland, R. (1980). Planning—The neglected component of group development. *Social Work with Groups, 1*(2), 173–178.

Kurland, R. (1982). *Group formation: A guide to the development of successful groups.* Albany, NY: Continuing Education Program, School of Social Welfare, State University of New York at Albany and United Neighborhood Centers of America.

Landy, S. & Tam, K. K. (1998). *Understanding the contribution of multiple risk factors on child development at various ages.* Quebec, Canada: Hull: Applied Research Branch, Strategic Policy, Human Resources Development.

Malekoff, A. (1994a). Action research: An approach to preventing substance abuse and promoting social competency. *Health and Social Work, 19*(1), 46–53.

Malekoff, A. (1994b). A guideline for group work with adolescents. *Social Work with Groups, 17*(1/2), 5–19.

Malekoff, A. (2004a). *Group work with adolescents: Principles and practice* (2nd ed.). New York: Guilford.

Malekoff, A. (2004b). Strengths-based group work with children and adolescents. In C. Garvin, L. Guttierrez, and M. Galinsky (eds.), *Handbook of social work with groups* (pp. 227–245). New York: Guilford.

Malekoff, A. (2001). The power of group work with kids: A practitioner's reflection on strength-based practice. *Families in Society, 82*(3), 243–249.

Males, M. A. (1999). *Framing youth: 10 Myths about the next generation.* Monroe, MN: Common Courage Press.

Middleman, R. & Wood, G. G. (1990). From social group work to social work with groups. *Social Work with Groups, 13*(1), 3–20.

Miller, W. & Rollnick, S. (1991). *Motivational interviewing: Preparing people to change addictive behavior.* New York: Guilford.

Muraskin, L. D. (1993). *Understanding evaluation: The way to better prevention programs.* Washington, DC: U.S. Department of Education.

Myers, P. (2002). Pain, poverty, and hope. *Journal of Ethnicity in Substance Abuse, 1*(1), 1–5.

National Institute on Drug Abuse Research Report Series. (2006). *Anabolic steroid abuse.* Bethesda, MD: U.S. Department of Health and Human Services, National Institutes of Health.

Northen, H. & Kurland, R. (2001). *Social work with groups* (3rd ed.). New York: Columbia University Press.

Perry, C., Williams, C. L., Komro, K., Veblen-Mortenson, S., Stigler, M., Munson, K., Farbakhsh, K., Jones, R. M., & Forster, J. (2002). Project Northland: Long-term outcomes of community action to reduce adolescent alcohol use. *Health Education Research, 17*(1), 117–132.

Office of the National Drug Control Policy, Executive Office of the President. (2007, February). *Teens and prescription drugs: An analysis of recent trends on the emerging drug threat.* Washington, DC: Author.

Prothrow-Stith, D. & Weissman, M. (1991). *Deadly consequences.* New York: Harper Collins.

Redl, F. & Wineman, D. (1952). *Controls from within: Techniques for the treatment of the aggressive child.* New York: Free Press.

Rich, J. A. (2001). Primary care for young African American men. *Journal of American College Health, 49*(4), 183–186.

Rutter, M. (1979). Protective factors in children's responses to stress and disadvantage. In M. W. Kent & J. E. Rolf (eds.), *Primary prevention psychology: Social competence in children,* Vol. 3. Hanover, NH: University Press of New England.

Rutter, M. (1984, March). Resilient children. *Psychology Today,* 57–65.

Rutter, M. (ed.). (1995). *Psychosocial disturbances in young people: Challenges for prevention.* New York: Cambridge University Press.

Sameroff, A. (1988, June). *The concept of the environtype: Integrating risk and protective factors in early development.* Keynote address for North Shore Child and Family Guidance Center Conferences, Garden City, NY.

Schinke, S. P., Orlandi, M. A., & Cole, K. C. (1992). Boys' and girls' clubs in public housing developments: Prevention services for youth at risk. *Journal of Community Psychology* (OASP Special Issue), 118–128.

Schorr, L. B. (1989). *Within our reach: Breaking the cycle of disadvantage.* New York: Doubleday.

Sciacca, K. (2007). Dual diagnosis treatment and motivational interviewing for co-occurring disorders. *National Council Magazine, 2,* 22–23.

Sciacca, K. (1996, July 3). On co-occurring addictive and mental disorders: A brief history of the origins of dual diagnosis treatment and program development [published and invited letter to the editor]. *American Journal of Orthopsychiatry, 66*(3). http://users.erols.com/ksciacca/brifhst.htm

Selekman, M. (2005). *Pathways to change: Brief therapy with difficult adolescents.* New York: Guilford.

Selekman, M. (2006). *Working with self-harming adolescents: A collaborative strengths-based therapy approach.* New York: Norton.

Selekman, M. (2009). *The adolescent and young adult self-harming treatment manual.* New York: Norton.

Shields, S. (1986). Busted and branded: Group work with substance abusing adolescents in schools. *Social Work with Groups, 8*(4), 61–81.

Silver, R. & Eddy, J. (2006). Research-based prevention programs and practice for delivery in schools that decrease the risk of deviant peer influences. In K. Dodge, T. Dishion, & J. Lansford (eds.), *Deviant peer influences in programs for youth* (pp. 253–277). New York: Guilford.

Smith, T. E. (1985). Group work with adolescent drug abusers. *Social work with Groups, 8*(1), 55–64.

St. Pierre, T., Mark, M., Kaltreider, D., & Campbell, B. (2001). Boys' and girls' clubs and school collaborations: A longitudinal study of a multicomponent substance abuse prevention program for high-risk elementary school children. *Journal of Community Psychology, 29*(2), 87–106.

St. Pierre, T. & Kaltreider, D. (2001). Reflections on implementing a community agency–school prevention program. *Journal of Community Psychology, 29*(2), 107–116.

Taylor, A. S., LoSciuto, L., Fox, M., Hilbert, S., & Sonkowsky, M. (1999). The mentoring factor: Evaluation of the across ages' intergenerational approach to drug abuse prevention. *Child and Youth Services, 20*(1/2), 77–99.

Taylor, M. (2000). The influence of self efficacy on alcohol use among American Indians. *Cultural Diversity and Ethnic Minority Psychology, 6*(2), 152–167.

Treadway, D. C. (1989). *Before it's too late: Working with substance abuse in the family.* New York: W. W. Norton.

Unger, J., Simon, T., Newman, T., Montgomery, S., Kipke, M., & Albornoz, M. (1998). Early adolescent street youth: An overlooked population with unique problems and service needs. *The Journal of Early Adolescence, 18*(4), 325–348.

Vega, W. A., Zimmerman, R. S., Warheit, G. J., Apospori, E., & Gil, A. C. (1993). Risk factors for early adolescent drug use in four ethnic and racial groups. *American Journal of Public Health, 83*(2), 185–189.

Wallace, B. C. (1993). Cross-cultural counseling with the chemically dependent: Preparing for service delivery within a culture of violence. *Journal of Psychoactive Drugs, 25*(1), 9–20.

Wegscheider, S. (1981). *Another chance: Hope and health for alcoholic family.* Palo Alto, CA: Science and Behavior Books.

Werner, E. (1986). Resilient offspring of alcoholics: A longitudinal study from birth to age 18. *Journal of Studies on Alcohol, 44*(1), 34–44.

Werner, E. (1989). High-risk children in young adulthood: A longitudinal study from birth to 32 years. *American Journal of Orthopsychiatry, 59*, 72–81.

Werner, E. (1990). Protective factors and individual resilience. In S. Meisels & J. Shonkoff (eds.), *Handbook of early childhood intervention* (pp. 97–116). New York: Cambridge University Press.

Werner, E., Smith, R. S., & Garmezy, N. (1998). *Vulnerable but invincible: A longitudinal study of resilient children and youth.* New York: Adams, Bannaster, Cox Publishers.

Werner, E. & Smith, R. S. (2001). *Journeys from childhood to midlife: Risk, resiliency and recovery.* Ithaca, NY: Cornell University Press.

Part Two

Adjusting to Change

Chapter Five

Children of Divorce Groups

Janice L. DeLucia-Waack

In the United States, only 7% of all children actually live in traditional families (Crespi & Howe, 2002), and 46.2% of those who marry will divorce (U.S. Census Bureau, 2005, Table 3). Furthermore, it is projected that 40% of all U.S. children will be affected by parental divorce by the time they reach the age of 18 (Barker, Brinkman, & Deardoff, 1995). Divorce and remarriage are a series of transition and family reorganizations that modify the lives of children and parents (Pedro-Carroll, Nakhnikian, & Montes, 2001). Psychoeducational groups for children of divorce (COD) convey knowledge and teach skills to help COD cope with current realities and future situations. Pedro-Carroll (2005) suggested that the development of active and effective coping skills (e.g., problem solving and positive thinking), accurate attributions, hope for the future, and realistic appraisal of control contribute to resiliency in COD. This chapter discusses key issues relevant to the planning, execution, common themes, and evaluation of COD groups.

REVIEW OF THE LITERATURE

Amato (2001), based on a meta-analysis of 67 studies published between 1990 and 1999 of COD, concluded that those from divorced homes struggle more than did children from intact families in the areas of academic achievement, psychological adjustment, self-concept, social relations, and conduct problems. While Wallerstein (2004) suggested that parental divorce is a "*life-transforming experience for the child*" (p. 367), others have argued that the negative effects of marital disruption have been exaggerated (Hetherington & Kelly, 2002). They suggest that 25% of COD have serious problems compared to 10% of those from continuously married parents. The true percentage probably lies somewhere in the middle. However, the act of parental separation and/or divorce creates change in the family in both the short term and long term that needs attention. Amato and Cheadle (2005) concluded that "marital disruption is not uniformly harmful to children, and most offspring with divorced parents develop into well-adjusted adults. Nevertheless, the increase in risk associated with parental divorce is not trivial, and for some outcomes (such as poor father-child relationships), the estimated effects of parent divorce are quite strong" (p. 191). Booth and Amato (2002) suggested that "children appear to benefit from divorce of parents in high-conflict marriages. On the other hand, children appear to suffer from the divorce of parents in low-conflict marriages" (p. 197). Regardless of the conflict and stress prior to separation and/or divorce, "the disruption process typically sets into motion numerous events that most children experience as stressful. For example, divorce sometimes results in less effective parenting from the custodial parent, exposure to continuing interpersonal discord, a decline in economic resources, and other disruptive life events such as moving and changing schools" (Booth & Amato, 2002, p. 198).

Pomrenke (2007) reported those COD with the most resilience received emotional support from multiple sources: parents, grandparents, stepparents, friends, or school counselors or a combination. Brown and Portes (2006) suggested that boys and girls may react to divorce differently and, thus, have different needs for treatment. Hetherington, Bridges, and Insabella (1998) suggested that adolescent boys were more likely to exhibit conduct disorders while adolescent girls were more likely to exhibit increased depression at the time of divorce.

Group Counseling Is the Treatment of Choice for COD

Group work emphasizes helping children to feel less isolated, connect with and learn from others, receive peer validation and support, and normalize experiences (DeLucia-Waack, 2006; Gladding, 2005). Psychoeducational and counseling groups in schools and community agencies have been a popular and efficient method of providing treatment for COD (Crespi, Gustafson, & Borges, 2005; Riva & Haub, 2004). Banana Splits (Nugent, 1990) is a common school-based group program, and the three programs most systematically developed and empirically evaluated for COD are (a) the Children's Support Group (Stolberg & Cullen, 1983), (b) the Children of Divorce Intervention Program (Pedro-Carroll & Cowen, 1985), and (c) the Developmental Facilitation Model (Kalter, Pickar, & Lesowitz, 1984). DeLucia-Waack (2001) also designed a group protocol for COD using music, with preliminary results (DeLucia-Waack & Gellman, 2007). Durlak and Well's (1997) meta-analysis indicated that prevention programs for COD were moderately effective, whereas Stathakos and Roehrle's (2003) more recent meta-analysis yielded positive but cautious support. Group size, focus, duration of sessions, and leadership experience all affected COD group effectiveness.

Creative Arts Are Effective Interventions with COD

It is important to acknowledge the differences in working with children versus adults, particularly in group work. Children have shorter attention spans, they are more likely to project their feelings onto others, and they have much less control over their situation and their environment. Thus, different techniques must be used to ensure participation and developmental appropriateness.

Creativity in activities, particularly singing, dancing, and music, is a way for children to identify and express feelings, brainstorm, and practice new behaviors and coping skills (DeLucia-Waack, 2001; Gladding, 2005). Gladding suggested that creative arts, such as music, in counseling are beneficial for a number of reasons: (a) to experience the connectedness between mind and body, (b) to increase energy flow, (c) to focus on goals, (d) to increase creativity, (e) to establish a new sense of self, (f) to provide concrete interventions that are beneficial, (g) to provide insight, and (h) to promote socialization and cooperation. Traditional methods of talk therapy do not work for children and adolescents. Children in particular often respond better to nonverbal techniques, such as music or drawing, because of their limited vocabularies. Gladding also noted additional benefits of creative arts in groups, including that they are multicultural, energize, communicate messages on multiple levels, are playful and nonthreatening, and open up options (p. 8).

Irrational Beliefs as a Mediator of Depression

Kurdek and Berg (1987) suggested that children with superior cognitive capacity who "make personal sense" of the divorce assess their own role in the divorce and, thus, are able to take control over their behavior and emotions and suffer less negative consequences. Others (DeLucia-Waack, 2001; McConnell & Sim, 1999) have also suggested that children often hold certain detrimental irrational beliefs (e.g., they caused the divorce, their parents will reunite). McConnell and Sim reported that individual counseling reduced the level of dysfunctional beliefs that children held about their parents' divorce, while Jupp and Purcell (1992) found that irrational beliefs about divorce were decreased as a result of participation in a COD group. Many children report lingering hopes for reconciliation (DeLucia-Waack & Gellman, 2007). Those children who placed blame for the divorce on themselves tended to be more poorly adjusted (Bussell, 1995; Healy, Stewart, & Copeland, 1993)

Zubernis, Cassidy, Gilham, Reivich, and Jaycox (1999) reported that a 12-week Depression Prevention Program was successful in preventing depressive symptoms in both COD and children from intact families. DeLucia-Waack and Gellman (2007), in their study of 134 elementary school children in 16 COD groups, found that anxiety, depression, and irrational beliefs about divorce decreased as a result of the 8-week group treatment. In addition, irrational beliefs about divorce mediated between pretreatment and posttreatment depression scores.

PRINCIPLES THAT GUIDE PRACTICE

This section is organized around the Association for Specialists in Group Work (ASGW, 2007) Best Practice Guidelines that emphasize planning, performing, and processing.

Planning

Group Goals

The general goals for the COD must be decided prior to selection of group members. Then specific content can be tailored after group members are identified. All activities should be based on the specific goals. As a general guideline, at least one session should be spent on each goal or area of concern. For example, reasonable goals for a 6-week COD group for second- and third-graders include gaining an accurate picture of the divorce process, normalizing common experiences and feelings related to divorce, and providing a safe and supportive place to talk about divorce-related concerns.

Gender Mix and Group Size

Ideal group size varies according to the age of the children, beginning with three to six children in younger age groups, five to seven children between ages 6 and 9, and up to eight children in older age groups. It is ultimately up to the style and experience of the social worker or counselor as to whether to lead mixed- or single-gender groups. Crespi et al. (2005) suggest mixed groups "offers opportunities to clarify and teach students about gender and relational dynamics" (p. 73). Some leaders report the diversity in emotions and reactions in mixed groups enhances their effectiveness (Kalter, 1998). Others lead same-gender groups in middle school to lessen the self-consciousness and decreased self-disclosure that may result from boys and girls being in the same group.

Length and Number of Sessions

The ideal length of the group sessions also varies according to the age of the children: 20 to 30 minutes is optimal with children 6 years or younger, 30 to 40 minutes is optimal with children between 6 and 9 years old, and 40 to 75 minutes is optimal with children 9 years or older.

Although standard programs suggest 12 to 14 sessions (e.g., Stolberg & Cullen, 1985; Pedro-Caroll & Cowen, 1985), most groups in the schools last 6 to 8 weeks (DeLucia-Waack, 2001). To counter the limited number of sessions, school counselors report students may participate in a COD group at different ages. This format is also useful in that it allows children to address the same issues at different developmental stages and as they encounter issues. It also encourages and supports the idea that it is normal for kids to "repeat" group. Mental health agencies may be able to sustain longer groups. An ideal length would be 12 to 16 sessions, allowing time to deal with more complex issues such as parental dating and remarriage, communication with new siblings and stepparents, and adaptation to the new family setting. Court-referred groups most likely will be short term (e.g., one 4- or 8-hour session or four 2-hour sessions).

Group Structure

Structure is essential to providing safety and continuity to the children. Structure is also necessary to manage time efficiently and to focus on relevant issues

(DeLucia-Waack, 2001, 2006). Depending on the type of group and the age of the children, the level of structure may vary. The younger the children, the more structure is necessary.

To provide structure, each group session includes the following: Review and Check-In or Warm-Up, Working Activities, Processing, and Closing. Possible ways to begin sessions include check-ins or go-rounds that focus members on what they want to talk about and work on that day, review of homework from previous sessions, or reading a poem or paragraph related to the issues previously discussed in the group. The working part of the session is focused on issues and skill building based on the goals of the group. Teaching and practicing specific skills such as assertiveness, expression of feelings, and communication may be helpful for COD. Some ways to end sessions include summaries (by the leader, by one member, or briefly by all), go-rounds of what each person has learned today and/or was most helpful, brief written reactions given to the leader, rating sheets, discussion of homework or things to work on or think about over the next week, or a poem or thought to inspire the week.

Recruitment of Group Members

Recruitment efforts should focus on children who would like to participate in a COD group and those who are identified by professionals (i.e., counselors, teachers, physicians) and family members as having difficulty adjusting to the divorce.

Selection Criteria

The following general selection criteria are suggested for groups for COD:

a. All children in the group must be within 2 years in age of each other (Crespi et al., 2005; Kalter, 1998);
b. Siblings should not be in the same group because of conflict of loyalty and the difficulty of the group in acknowledging two perspectives on the same family;
c. Children must be willing to disclose about their family situation in a group and explore new solutions to problems;
d. There should be a mixture of family situations among the children, with variation in the time since divorce, living situation, parental dating, and remarriage.

These differences serve to promote peer role models, generate alternative solutions to problems, and instill hope. Any one child should not be so different in terms of family situation that he or she feels isolated or scapegoated by the group. Although it is impossible to prevent scapegoating, a conscious effort to select and link members on the basis of their similarities (e.g., feelings, experiences) may help group members to make connections and increase cohesiveness among members. It is important that children are able to connect with other children around the issues related to divorce. Each child must have one other child in the group with whom he or she can initially connect and one child who will be able to serve as a role model. In addition, the gender and ethnicity of group members should be taken into consideration when trying to prevent scapegoating.

Screening Interview

All students should be interviewed to assess their ability to participate in and benefit from a COD group. An interview, for a maximum of 30 minutes, should be sufficient to assess (a) the child's willingness to participate, (b) any issues or concerns the child has that are related to the divorce and his or her current living situation, (c) the child's willingness and ability to verbally and nonverbally disclose thoughts and feelings, and (d) the child's ability to follow directions and answer questions asked of him or her. Prior to beginning the group, it is important to collect the following information from parents: age and gender of all siblings of the child, amount of time since parental separation, current marital status of both parents, custodial situation, and frequency and regularity of visitation with the noncustodial parent.

Informed Consent for Parents and Children

In recent divorces, custody (and who can consent for counseling services) is often an explosive issue for parents. Therefore, it is recommended that regardless of the official policy, leaders of the COD groups make an effort to inform all adults involved with the child (including noncustodial parents and family members) of the goals and focus of the group.

To make an informed decision about participation in a COD group, parents and children must be given information verbally and in writing about goals; format, structure, and typical interventions; and leadership style and credentials of the group leader(s). Ritchie and Huss's (2000) article is a valuable reference with regard to how to make decisions related to selection, screening, and recruitment of minors in a way that protects confidentiality and addresses issues of informed consent, particularly how to secure parental consent without violating confidentiality. Wilcoxon and Magnuson (1999) also provide specific suggestions about how to balance the needs and demands of custodial and noncustodial parents and, most important, the child while taking into consideration each individual situation and ethical and legal issues. For children, it is important to ensure that they are informed about the group at a level that they can understand. Leaders should choose words that are appropriate to the children's grade level and should use examples whenever possible. It is helpful to explain to children the goals, kinds of activities that may occur in group, and ground rules before they enter the group, to ensure that they understand and are ready to participate in group. DeLucia-Waack (2001) provides sample letters to parents and information for children.

Performing

Beginning and Ending Sessions

Regardless of the length of the group, the first session must be devoted to the establishment of ground rules and goals for the group, the introduction of members to each other, and an explanation of the purpose of the group. At the end of the group, at least one session, if not two, must be devoted to termination, with the goals of helping the children (a) summarize what they have learned, (b) express their feelings about the group and the group members, and (c) discuss how they will use what they learned in their families and outside situations. Termination of the group often brings up abandonment and loss issues related to the divorce; thus, this is an excellent time to intervene through modeling, expression of feeling, and development of coping plans. DeLucia-Waack (2001), Pedro-Carroll, Gillis, Sutton, and Black (1999), DeLucia-Waack, Bridbord, Kleiner, and Nitza (2006), Foss, Green, Wolfe-Stiltner, and DeLucia-Waack (2008), and Smead (1994) include session outlines for beginning and termination sessions.

Choosing the Content of Sessions

Depending on the individual needs of the children, the content sessions in the middle of the group might focus on the following:

- Discussion of the family situation (e.g., living arrangements, custody, visitation, extended family, other support); definition of important legal terms (e.g., *separation, divorce, custody, courts*) and information about divorce
- Identification and evaluation of worries and beliefs, specifically magical thinking and irrational beliefs about the divorce (e.g., "I'll never see my father again," "I can get my parents back together again," "We'll be homeless," "My Dad left me so my Mom may leave me, too," "It is my fault that they got divorced")
- Expression of feelings about the divorce (e.g., anger, sadness, grief, loneliness, relief)
- Solutions to problems generated by problem solving around difficult situations (e.g., visitation, new parental relationships, parental fighting, parental dating, blended families, stepparents, stepsiblings)
- Development of skills to deal with difficult situations (e.g., communication, conflict resolution, anger management, expression of feelings).

The Initial Assessment Instrument (Beech Acres Aring Institute, 1993, in DeLucia-Waack, 2001) assesses potential concerns in the following areas: the divorce experience, parental fighting, legal aspects of the divorce, feelings of being caught in the middle, how to maintain parental relationships, changes since the divorce, parents' new partners, stepfamilies, traditions and holidays, and future family plans. The Children's Beliefs about Parental Divorce Scale (Kurdek & Berg, 1987) assesses irrational beliefs related to the divorce: fear of peer ridicule, avoidance, paternal blame, fear of abandonment, hope of reunification, and self-blame. Smead (1994) includes a pretest to assess potential areas of focus.

Group Leader Preparation

Co-leadership for a COD group is preferable. The benefits of co-leadership are that there are two role models, two leaders who can cooperate and work together, and two sets of eyes and ears to observe the content and process of the group. In addition, for COD groups, a male-female co-leadership team can model collaboration between men and women and can provide contact with supportive and caring adults of both genders. A male presence in the group is particularly important because many of the children may not have much contact with a male adult, especially if they are in an elementary school setting (Kalter, 1998).

Processing

Supervision and Planning

Regardless of skill and experience, group leaders must commit to weekly planning and supervision sessions to prepare for their group and to process what has happened (ASGW, 2007). A dedicated hour each week is essential to working cooperatively with a co-leader, planning individual strategies for each child, reviewing session events and group process, and planning for future sessions. When co-leadership is not possible, a leader should still set aside an hour a week to plan and process for the group. DeLucia-Waack (2006) includes examples of planning and processing forms.

To prepare for the group, leaders need to think about it from several different perspectives. How will they personally and professionally prepare for the group? How will they prepare others for the group, specifically their school or agency (including administrators), parents, and children? As leaders begin to get ready for a COD group, they need to have a sense of their beliefs about divorce, the needs of COD, and how a group can best help these children. To do this, they first must examine their own personal values and experiences with divorce and separation. Second, they must examine current literature about what is most effective with COD in terms of themes, interventions, structure, and so forth. To begin to establish trust and cooperation with their co-leader, they should meet regularly before the group starts to discuss theoretical orientation, leadership style, and goals and interventions for the group. Each co-leader should assess his or her strengths and weaknesses as a leader of the particular COD group that he or she is planning. The ASGW Best Practice Guidelines (2007), ASGW Professional Standards for the Training of Group Workers (2000), and ASGW Principles for Diversity-Competent Group Workers (1999) also provide guidelines for group leader training, practice, and supervision.

Evaluation

ASGW (2007) suggests assessment of group process and dynamics, outcome, and group leader impact. What follows is a brief description of measures that may be appropriate by topic.

The Critical Incidents Questionnaire (Kivlighan & Goldfine, 1991) assesses the most important therapeutic factor for each group member during a specific group session and has been used with minimal rewording with elementary school children (DeLucia-Waack, 2001). Group members can respond verbally or in writing: *Of all the things that happened in our group today, which was the most helpful for you? Describe what happened and tell why it was important to you.* Leaders can then assess what therapeutic factor is described. Rich, Molloy, Hart, Ginsberg, and Mulvey (2007) operationally defined the therapeutic factors as they relate to COD.

COD often exhibit symptoms of anxiety, depression, and low self-esteem (Amato, 2001). Thus, it is important to include measures to assess the initial circumstances and impact of the group. The Child Behavior Checklist (Achenbach, 2001) is completed by parents and teachers to assess the child's level of functioning. The Revised Children's Manifest Anxiety Scale (Reynolds & Richmond, 1985) assesses physiological symptoms, worry/oversensitivity, and concentration. The Children's Depression Inventory (Kovacs, 1992) assesses psychomotor, cognitive, and effective dimensions of depression (normed specifically on COD). The Perceived Competence Scale for Children (Harter, 1982) assesses children's perception of competence on physical, cognitive, social, and general self-worth.

Common Themes and Goals for COD Groups

Goal 1: *To help children gain an accurate picture of the divorce process through discussion and information.* It is important to provide COD with information about separation, divorce, custody, visitation, parental fighting, parental dating, stepparents, blended families, and remarriage (Campbell, 2008; Neale, 2002; Pedro-Carroll, 1995). Early sessions focus on definitions of words such as *separation, divorce,* and *custody.* Wilcoxon and Magnusom (1999) is a good resource with specific definitions of these and related terms. Campbell (2008) suggests the importance of understanding the concepts of "children's best interests." Later sessions may focus on how families deal with issues of visitation, parental dating, and blended families.

Goal 2: *To normalize the common experiences and feelings around divorce.* Children need a safe place to talk about their thoughts, feelings, and experiences with others, both adults and children, who are not involved in the divorce of their family (Pedro-Carroll, 1985; Rich et al., 2007; Stolberg & Mahler, 1994; Ziffer, Crawford, & Penney-Wietor, 2007). Pedro-Carroll et al. (2001) suggested normalizing

the common feelings: "sadness, anxiety, anger, resentment, confusion, loyalty, conflict, guilt" (p. 377). It is important that children
learn that their situation is not unique and that others also live with
one parent (or other family members) and have parents who do not
get along (Barker et al., 1995). COD "may need help with feelings
that overwhelm them" (Brown & Portes, 2006, p. 15). They also
need to share their experiences related to divorce, such as how they
found out about the divorce and what their visits are like with the
noncustodial parents, in a nonjudgmental environment. Groups
create a place where children can receive peer support and validation for what they experience and feel.

Goal 3:   *To provide a safe and supportive place to talk about divorce-related
concerns.* Creating a safe place to talk is essential in COD groups.
"One of the most comforting aspects of the group for children
comes from mutual support for shared experiences and learning
that they are not alone at a time when they feel that everything in
their life is changing" (Pedro-Carroll, 2005, p. 56). It is helpful in
early sessions to have children draw pictures of what their families
look like. This process helps children share about the divorce and
also connect with each other on similarities (Pedro-Carroll, 1995,
1997; Rich et al., 2007; Stolberg & Mahler, 1994). "It is critical to
help them identify peers who can help them through this difficult
period in their lives and assist them to form groups where they can
express their pain to one another. It is most important to teach girls
to get support from one another as a way of caring for themselves"
(Brown & Portes, 2006, p. 16). Sentence completion exercises such
as "The most frustrating part of divorce for me is ...," "I would like
Dad (Mom) to ...," and "One thing that has changed for the better
is ..." also help to begin and structure discussions about concerns
related to the divorce.

Goal 4:   *To help children label, understand, and express feelings about the divorce.*
Young children may often deny their feelings of loss over the separation. Discussion of these feelings, particularly about the loss of a
parent through divorce, is very important (Pedro-Carroll, Sutton, &
Wyman, 1999; Ziffer et al., 2007). Children need to be able to
express the anger, fear, and sadness that they may be experiencing
(Pedro-Carroll, 1997; Rich et al., 2007; Stolberg & Mahler, 1994).
Because the divorce or separation has significantly changed the constellation of their family, they need to mourn the loss of their family
of origin as it was or the way they would like it to be (Bernstein,
2006). They also need help focusing on their feelings of guilt; children often feel responsible for the divorce in some way. Disloyalty is
another feeling that arises for COD; they may feel that they are

being asked to choose one parent over another or that, if they make certain choices, then the other parent will be angry or hurt or will leave them. Early exercises in group focus on the identification of feelings through the use of aids such as feeling charts and feeling charades. Later, activities that act out feelings behaviorally are useful to help children learn about and focus on their feelings, normalize expression of both positive and negative emotions, and practice expressing feelings in different situations and to different people. Art therapy, music therapy, and play therapy are useful to help children identify and express their feelings. Puppets may also be useful for younger children as a model of how to express feelings.

Goal 5: *To assist children in developing new coping skills to deal with the feelings and situation experienced as a result of the divorce.* The skills that children already know may be too limited or overtaxed to deal with the multitude of issues surrounding the divorce. Techniques that may be useful in this process include teaching and practicing communication, problem solving, anger management, and conflict resolution skills (Brown & Portes, 2006; Pedro-Carroll, 1997, 2005; Stolberg & Mahler, 1994). Communication and conflict resolution skills may be particularly useful to help with stepfamily problems, parental and sibling conflicts, and divided parental loyalty. Role-playing of relevant situations such as parental arguing, custody, and court scenarios helps children to understand difficulties, gain perspective, see others' viewpoints, and express their fears about potential situations, enabling them to identify new ways of coping (Pedro-Carroll, 2005).

Goal 6: *To use reality testing as an important focus of COD groups.* Children, particularly young children, often have unrealistic fears and beliefs about what will happen as a result of the divorce (Pedro-Carroll, 1997). They may fear that both parents will stop loving them or will abandon them or that they have in some way caused the divorce by wishful thinking or something they did. Some of the irrational fears and thoughts can be dispelled through exercises in which a possible situation is described and the group is then asked to decide how likely it is that that situation could happen. DeLucia-Waack and Gellman (2007) reported that several irrational beliefs related to divorce significantly decreased as a result of participation in COD groups—specifically, fear of peer ridicule, avoidance, paternal blame, fear of abandonment, and self-blame. The one irrational belief examined in the study not impacted by group treatment was hope of reunification.

Goal 7: *To help children gain realistic and attainable dreams about their family life for the future.* They also need to gain a realistic perspective about how relationships work and what to expect in a relationship. Groups for COD instill hope for the future when children see others changing and adapting to and even enjoying their new situation. Wallerstein (2004) suggested "engendering hope, creating good images of man-woman relationships, and teaching young people to choose appropriate partners and create relationships that will hold" (p. 368).

Goal 8: *To help the children focus on the positive aspects of their new family structure.* Positives may include spending more time with the mother or father, less arguing between parents, seeing grandparents more often, and being closer to siblings. Eaves and Sheperis (2010) believe children "must be encouraged not only to mourn their loss but also consider the positive aspects of their new family structure" (p. 247).

Intervention Methods

It is important to provide children with a concrete reminder of what they have learned. Songs reverberate in their head while banners and note cards can be displayed in public (in their locker, on the mirror at home) and in private places (inside their planner, in their wallet) to remind them of their strengths, their new skills, and new positive thoughts. Eaves and Sheperis (2010) identified the most used techniques for COD groups as bibliotherapy, movies, board games, drawings, brainstorming, role-playing, and puppets.

Bibliotherapy

The use of books and films helps children and adolescents express their feelings and concerns and learn new skills. Children can deal with their feelings indirectly through the use of books and films. For example, after reading a book about a family whose parents get divorced, the group leader might begin a discussion with questions such as, How did the children in the book feel? How did they express their feelings? Verbally? Behaviorally? Nonverbally? In later sessions, group members may be encouraged to write their own books to suggest to other children how to express their feelings and then actively prescribe ways to cope with the feelings and the situations that they have encountered.

Music

Music is particularly important when trying to help children to express their feelings. Music also helps to link people and gives them a common basis for discussion. The words to a song may provide children with a way to express themselves. For adolescents, connecting to the words of a song helps them feel understood and not so alone.

Songs are useful in terms of helping COD to identify potential thoughts and feelings through the concept of displacement. Children are able to listen to a song and then discuss what the person who wrote it might have been feeling or thinking. This "one step removed" technique identifies potential feelings and thoughts without attaching them to a specific group member, something that can be threatening for a child. Such a technique also helps to normalize some of the children's experiences as they realize that others have similar thoughts and feelings about divorce. For example, the song "Divorce" by Dan Conley (1994) leads into an activity in which the group can list all the people they know whose parents are divorced, including celebrities, TV and movie characters, and their friends and family, to normalize the experience of divorce (DeLucia-Waack, 2001). Dan Conley (1994)'s CD "If You Believe in You" focuses on self-esteem, coping skills, communications skills, and the pain of divorce (DeLucia-Waack, 2001; DeLucia-Waack & Gellman, 2007). At home, children may listen to songs as a way to cope with distressing feelings or remind them of strategies that they have discussed in group. Vines (2004, pp. 12-13) suggested several questions used to stimulate discussion after students listen to a specific song: What is the meaning of the song? What did the author mean when he said XXXX? What feelings did you experience when he repeated the chorus? Why do you think he sang those words over and over?

Group members may write verses to a song to identify their own experiences, or they may want to choose a song (and bring it to group) that exemplifies their feelings, thoughts, and experiences. It is also helpful to have group members choose a song that is motivational and inspirational for them that they can listen to for guidance and support.

Visual Arts

Gladding (2005) suggested that visual arts activities tap into the unconscious, help individuals express a multitude of emotions, and assist people in picturing themselves and their situations in a concrete manner. Because they are often perceived as nonthreatening, they may overcome resistance to self-disclosure and self-exploration.

In most COD groups, it is helpful to ask group members to draw a picture of their family and typical activities that they do together. Group members use the pictures as a starting point to self-disclose a little bit about their family and what kinds of things they like to do together. This activity gives group leaders some sense of strengths and potential problems within the family.

Writing

Wenz and McWhirter (1990, p. 38) suggested that "creating and sharing writing seems to improve and increase self-disclosure, self-actualizing behaviors, and self-acceptance of feelings and experience ... the function of writing as a way to express ideas, attitudes, and feelings in an indirect manner as though they are abstract or belonging to someone else ... may elicit new and significant insights that may not surface through other therapeutic modalities." Group leaders may present a poem to introduce a topic and then ask members to react to it indirectly or directly. Group members may use poetry as a way to "focus their attention on images, thoughts, and emotions ... to encourage a deeper expression of hidden information that can stimulate the group interaction" (Wenz & McWhirter, p. 38) either as an icebreaker to facilitate trust, affiliation, and self-disclosure or as an assessment of perceptions of group process and stage.

Group members may be asked to journal in group or as a homework assignment to focus them on what is helpful in group sessions, what progress they are making toward group goals, and the identification of potential situations that they may want a discuss or role-play to practice coping skills or new behaviors. Sometimes it may be helpful to assign a specific theme that group members write about in their journal, and sometimes a format may be suggested. Cognitive interventions often use a thought diary where specific situations are recorded that trigger negative thoughts along with what the thoughts are, how realistic they are, and eventually how they can be disputed. In "Autobiography" (Bridbord, 2002) asks group members, based on their life, to create a title, define the type of book it would be (e.g., fiction, romance, etc.), and identify events that have happened along with events that are expected to occur in an effort to recognize the uniqueness of each group member and to connect group members as well.

Drama and Role-Playing

Other creative arts interventions include the use of puppets, drama, and role-plays. Because young children are often unable to express their feelings directly, using puppets may help to express their feelings, thoughts, and potential fears. Used along with music and bibliotherapy, puppets help take the information and situations in the songs and books and make it real for children. After listening to a song or reading a book, the group leader may say to the children. "Let's act out that story now."

For instance, children may listen to a song or read a book about how children find out that their parents are getting a divorce. The children may then act out the situation, with each child choosing a puppet to portray a specific person: mother, father, children, and other important figures in the situation. The group leader can act as a facilitator of the puppet show, instructing the parents to disclose certain information (i.e., reasons for the divorce, that they will still see them every week) and encouraging the children to express feelings or ask certain questions, or to back up and replay a situation in a different way (now reacting with anger or sadness instead of saying everything is OK).

Role-plays are essential activities in psychoeducational groups for children and adolescents. They can be structured in that the group leaders provide scenarios and roles for group members and includes coaching to practice new behaviors. It is also useful to ask group members to identify situations in writing anonymously that they would like to work on. Role-plays can also re-enact a current situation to identify relevant issues and feelings, and practice new behaviors and skills.

Gestalt techniques may also be used to clarify thoughts and feelings and to practice new behaviors. An empty chair technique may be used for the child who is angry at a parent because the parents are getting divorced. The group member may be urged to say whatever he wants to say to the parent. It may then be helpful to process the activity focusing on how he felt, what it was like to say this, and then realistically how he can express his anger to the parent in a way that invites discussion rather than offends the parent. Whenever role-plays involve only one or two group members, it is helpful to ask the rest of the group to discuss their reactions as much vicarious learning may occur. Group members may support and validate the group member's feelings, or they may suggest a different perspective or way to communicate. Observing group members may also notice emotional reactions or new behaviors that they want to discuss or practice in future group sessions or activities.

Games

Games are often helpful in teaching rules of interaction, such as turntaking, listening, speaking directly to another person, and following directions. Carlson (1999) suggested that group leaders "break from traditional, therapeutic rituals, habits, and routines and learn to encompass a spectrum of multi-modal strategies such as games and exercise" (p. 231). He suggested cooperative games, which are non-competitive physical activities that incorporate exercise, movement, and coordination. The benefits of cooperative games include health, expression of feelings, relaxation, fun and enjoyment, learning physical skills, forming positive peer relationships, increasing positive self-image, developing problem-solving and goal-setting skills, and learning self-control behavior (p. 232). Carlson suggested the adaptation of many commonly known games such as tag, telephone, hot potato, and red rover to emphasize cooperation, inclusion, and friendship skills.

In addition, some games have been designed to be therapeutic. In the UnGame (1987), there is no competition, no way to win, and no time limit. Group members move around the UnGame board, landing on squares that ask the participant to describe experiences related to specific feelings. Group members can make comments or ask questions of other members but only at specified times.

CONCLUSIONS

The outlook for interventions for children of divorce is hopeful. Pedro-Carroll, Sandler, and Wolchik (2005) commented, "Children's problems are *not* inevitable. While almost all children experience considerable distress, the majority do not suffer serious long-term adjustments problems following their parents' divorce. Much depends on the extent to which children's needs are kept a top priority by the parents and the powerful systems (legal, judicial, educational, family, community) that affect their lives" (p. 18). COD groups using creative arts techniques to identify feelings and teach communication and coping skills appear to be the most promising interventions for children and adolescents.

In addition, the research suggests that interventions for parents are also helpful for helping children cope with divorce. Programs such as Assisting Children through Transition (A.C.T).–For the Children Program model (Pedro-Carroll et al., 2001), the New Beginnings Program for residential parents (Wolchik, Sandler, Winslow, & Smith-Daniels, 2005; Zhou, Sandler, Millsap, Wolchik, & Dawson-McClure, 2008), DADS for Life with nonresidential fathers (Braver, Griffin, & Cookston, 2005), and the Boomerang Bunch (Ziffer et al., 2007) have all been shown to be effective. Pedro-Carroll (2005) stressed the importance of early intervention for COD as well as the need for child custody courts to make education programs available to all separating parents, ease the stress of break-up, and protect them from ongoing conflict (e.g., the Collaborative Divorce Project; Pruett, Insabella, & Gustafson, 2005).

RESOURCES

For Parents

Beyer, R., & Winchester, K. (2001). *Speaking of divorce: How to talk with your kids and help them cope.* Minneapolis, MN: Free Spirit Publishing.

Gardner, R. (1991). *The parents' book about divorce.* New York: Bantam.

Kalter, N. (1990). *Growing up with divorce: Helping your child avoid immediate and later emotional problems.* New York: Free Press.

Sommers-Flanagan, R., Elander, C., & Sommers-Flanagan, J. (2000). *Don't divorce us! Kids' advice to divorcing parents.* Alexandria, VA: American Counseling Association.

Stahl, P. M. (2000). *Parenting after divorce: A guide to resolve conflicts and meeting your children's needs.* Atascadero, CA: Impact Publishers.

Wallerstein, J. S. (2005). *What about the kids: Raising your children before, during, and after the divorce.* New York: Hyperion.

Books

Beyer, R., & Winchester, K. (2001). *What in the world do you do when your parents divorce? A survival guide for kids.* Minneapolis, MN: Free Spirit Publishing.

Blume, J. (1972). *It's not the end of the world.* New York: Bradbury Press.

Boelts, M. (1992). *With my Mom, with my Dad.* New York: Pacific Press.

Brown, L. K., & Brown, M. (1986). *Dinosaurs' divorce.* Boston: Little, Brown.

Field, M., & Shore, H. (1994). *My life turned upside down, but I turned it rightside up: A self-esteem book about dealing with shared custody.* New York: Center for Applied Psychology.

Hoffman, E. (1995). *Kids can cope with divorce.* Marco Products.

Lash, M. (1990). *My kind of family: A book for kids in single-parent homes.* Burlington, VT; Waterfront Books.

MacGregor, C. (2004). *The divorce helpbook for teens.* Atascadero, CA: Impact Publishers.

MacGregor, C. (2001). *The divorce helpbook for kids*. Atascadero, CA: Impact Publishers.

Mayle, P. (1988). *Why are we getting a divorce?* New York: Harmony.

Rogers, F. (1996). *Let's talk about it: Stepfamilies*. New York: Putnam.

Rogers, F. (1997). *Let's talk about it: Divorce*. New York: Putnam.

Swan-Jackson, A. (1998). *When your parents split up...How to keep yourself together*. New York: Penguin Putnam Books.

Videos and Audio Tapes

Cambridge Educational Media. (Producer). *Divorce: A survival guide for kids*. [Video]. Princeton, NJ: Films for the Humanities and Sciences.

Cooper, J., & Martenz, A. (1993a). *Divorce I*. Warminster, PA: Mar*co Products.

Cooper, J., & Martenz, A. (1993c). *Stepfamilies I*. Warminster, PA: Mar*co Products.

Kids Rights. (1995a). *No fault kids: A focus on kids with divorced parents* [Video]. Charlotte, NC: Author.

Kids Rights. (1995b). *When Mom and Dad break up* [Video]. Charlotte, NC: Author.

Sunburst Communications. (1997). *If your parents break up...* [Video]. Pleasantview, NY: Author.

(1988). *Yours, mine, and ours*. [Video]. New York: Insight Media.

Group Activities.

Banks, A. (1990). *When your parents get a divorce: A kid's journal*. New York: Viking Press.

Beyer, R. *The mom and dad pad: A divorce communication tool*. [Activity]. Minneapolis, MN: Free Spirit Publishing.

Deaton, W. (1994). *A separation in my family: A child's workbook about parental separation and divorce*. New York: Hunter House.

DeLucia-Waack, J. L. (1996). Children of divorce group work in the schools. In S. T. Gladding (ed.), *Group process and group counseling* (pp. 27–28), Greensboro, NC: ERIC/CASS.

DeLucia-Waack, J. L. (2001). Effective children of divorce groups for elementary school children. *The Family Journal, 9*, 273–284.

DeLucia-Waack, J. L. (2001). *Using music in children of divorce groups: A session-by-session manual for counselors*. Alexandria, VA: American Counseling Association.

Epstein, Y. M., & Borduin, C. M. (1985). Could this happen? A game for children of divorce. *Psychotherapy, 22*, 770–773.

Games, T. (1997). *The divorce game*. Pleasantville, NY: Sunburst Communications.

Garigan, E., & Urbanski, M. (1991b). *Living with divorce—primary grades: Activities to help children cope with difficult situations*. New York: Good Apple.

Hage, S. M., & Nosanow, M. (2000). Becoming stronger at broken places: A model for group work with young adolescents from divorced families. *The Journal for Specialists in Group Work, 25*, 50–66.

Ives, S. (1985). *The divorce workbook: A guide for kids and families*. New York: Waterfront Books.

Margolin, S. (1996). *Complete group counseling program for children of divorce: Ready-to-use plans and materials for small and large divorce groups, 1-6*. Indianapolis, IN: Wiley.

Pedro-Carroll, J. L. (1985). *The Children of Divorce Intervention program: A procedures manual for facilitating a divorce support group for 4th-6th grade children*. Rochester, NY: University of Rochester Center for Community Study.

Pedro-Carroll, J. L., & Cowen E. L. (1987). The Children of Divorce Intervention program: Implementation and evaluation of a time-limited group approach. In J. P. Vincent (ed.), *Advances in family intervention, assessment and theory* (Vol. *4*, pp. 281–307) Greenwich, CT: JAI Press.

Rose, S. R. (1998). Applications of group work: Parental divorce. In S. R. Rose, *Group work with children and adolescents: Prevention and intervention in school and community systems* (pp. 87-105). Thousand Oaks, CA: Sage Publishing.

Worthen, T. (ed.) (2001). Broken hearts...healing: Young poets speak out on divorce. Poet Tree Press.

Materials for Children (Books, Games, Puppets, etc.).

Clawson, C. (1995). *Self-within: therapeutic puppets designed for professional use.* West Lafayette, IN: Aughor. (765-477-6193).

Cooper, J., &Martenz, A. (1993a). *Divorce I.* Warminster, PA: Mar*co Products.

Cooper, J., & Martenz, A. (1993b). *Divorce II.* Warminster, PA: Mar*co Products.

Cooper, J., & Martenz, A. (1993c). *Stepfamilies I.* Warminster, PA: Mar*co Products.

Cooper, J., & Martenz, A. (1993d). *Stepfamilies II.* Warminster, PA: Mar*co Products.

Erford, B. (n.d). *Therapeutic Dinosaur Games.* Alexandria, VA: American Counseling Association. www.counseling.org

Erford, B. (n.d). *Mutual Storytelling Technique Game* (CD). Alexandria, VA: American Counseling Association. www.counseling.org

Epstein, Y.M., & Borduin, C.M. (1985). Could this happen? A game for children of divorce. *Psychotherapy, 22,* 770–773.

Games, T. (1997). *The divorce game.* Pleasantville, NY: sunburst Communications. (www.sunburst.com)

Hudgins, M. (1993). *Feelings bingo game.* Warminster, PA: Mar*co Products.

The Ungame Company (1987). *The ungame game.* Anaheim, CA: Author.

Related Information About Children's Groups.

Kids Rights. (1994). Movin'on [Game]. Charlotte, NC: Author. (1-800-892-KIDS).

Information on the Internet

American Coalition for Fathers and Children. www.acfc.org.

Center for Divorce Education. www.divorce-education.com/mainbar.htm, www.divorce-education.com/banner2.htm.

Childrenanddivorce.com.http://www.childrenanddivorce.com/

Children and Divorce. www.aacap.org/factsfam/divorce.htm.

Children of Divorce: All Kinds of Problems. www.divorceform.org/all.html.

Children of Divorce Intervention Project. www.childrensinstitute.net/CODIP/.

Children's Rights Council. www.vix.com/crc/home.html.

Divorce Central. www.divorcentral.com

DivorceSource.Com.http://www.divorcesource.com/info/children/children.shtml

Divorce Course: A Parenting Course for Divorcing Couples.
www.unimind.com/index.htm.

Divorce Doesn't Go Away. www.4children.org/news/198divo.htm.

Divorce Info. www.divorceinfo.com

Divorce Reality. www.4children.org/news/198ccon.htm.

Divorce Source: A Legal Resource for Divorce, Custody, Alimony, and Support.
www.divorcesource.com.

Kid'sTurnCentral.http://www.kidsturncentral.com/topics/issues/divorce.htm

Healing the Broken Heart: Children of Divorce. www.childrenofdivorce.com/index.html.

How Divorce Affects Children. www.vix.com/men/mitch/needless.html.

Neumann, G. The Sandcastles Program: Helping Children of Divorce Rebuild.
www.sandcastlesprogram.com/index.html.

For a complete list, see DeLucia-Waack (2001).

REFERENCES

Association for Specialists in Group Work. (1999). Association for Specialists in Group Work principles for diversity-competent group workers. Retrieved June 22, 2009, from www.asgw.org

Association for Specialists in Group Work. (2000). Association for Specialists in Group Work professional standards for the training of group workers (revised). Retrieved June 22, 2009, from www.asgw.org

Association for Specialists in Group Work. (2007). Association for Specialists in Group Work best practice guidelines (revised). Retrieved June 22, 2009, from www.asgw.org

Amato, P. R. (2001). Children of divorce in the 1990s: An update of the Amato and Keith (1991) meta-analysis. *Journal of Family Psychology, 15*, 355–370.

Amato, P. & Cheadle, J. (2005). The long reach of divorce: Divorce and child well-being across three generations. *Journal of Marriage and Family, 67*, 191–206.

Achenbach, T. M. (2001). *Teacher's report form for ages 6–18 (6-01-01 edition–301).* Burlington, VT: University of Vermont, Research Center for Children, Youth and Families.

Barker, J., Brinkman, L., & Deardoff, M. (1995). Computer interventions for adolescent COD. *Journal of Divorce and Remarriage, 23*, 197–213.

Bernstein, A. (2006). Re-visioning, restructuring, and reconciliation: Clinical practice with complex postdivorce families. *Family Process, 46*, 67–78.

Booth, A. & Amato, P. R. (2001). Parental predivorce relations and offspring postdivorce well-being. *Journal of Marriage and Family, 63*, 197–212.

Braver, S. L., Griffin, W. A., & Cookston, J. T. (2005) Prevention programs for divorced nonresidential fathers. *Family Court Review, 43*, 81–96.

Bridbord, K. H. (2002). Autobiography. In J. L. DeLucia-Waack, K. H. Bridbord, & J. S. Kleiner (eds.), *Group work experts share their favorite activities: A guide to choosing, planning, conducting, and processing* (pp. 26–27). Thousand Oaks, CA: Sage.

Brown, J. & Portes, P. R. (2006). Understanding gender differences in children's adjustment to divorce: Implications for school counselors. *Journal of School Counseling, 4*(7). Retrieved June 15, 2009, from http://www.jsc.montana.edu/v4n7.pdf

Bussell, D. A. (1995). A pilot study of African American children's cognitive and emotional reactions to parental separation. *Journal of Divorce and Remarriage, 25,* 1995.

Campbell, A. (2008). The right to be heard: Australian children's views about their involvement in decision-making following parental separation. *Child Care in Practice, 14,* 237–255.

Carlson, J. M. (1999). Cooperative games: A pathway for improving health. *Professional School Counseling, 2,* 230–236.

Conley, D. (1994). *If you believe in you.* New City, NY: Treehouse Music.

Crespi, T. D., Gustafson, A. L., & Borges, S. M. (2005). Group counseling in the schools: Considerations for child and family issues. *Journal of Applied School Psychology, 22,* 67–85.

Crespi, T. D. & Howe, E. A. (2002). Families in crisis: Considerations for special service providers in school. *Special Services in the Schools, 18,* 43–54.

DeLucia-Waack, J.L. (2001). *Using music in COD groups: A session by session manual for counselors.* Alexandria, VA: American Counseling Association.

DeLucia-Waack, J. L. (2006). *Leading psychoeducational groups for children and adolescents.* Thousand Oaks, CA: Sage Publications.

DeLucia-Waack, J. L., Bridbord, K. H., Kleiner, J. S., & Nitza, A. (eds.). (2006). *Group work experts share their favorite activities: A guide to choosing, planning, conducting, and processing* (revised). Alexandria, VA: Association for Specialists in Group Work.

DeLucia-Waack, J. L. & Gellman, R. A (2007). The efficacy of using music in children of divorce groups: Impact on anxiety, depression, and irrational beliefs about divorce. *Group Dynamics: Theory, Research, and Practice, 11,* 272–282.

Durlak, J. A. & Wells, A. M. (1997). Primary prevention mental health programs for children and adolescents: A meta-analytic review. *American Journal of Community Psychology, 25,* 115–152.

Eaves, S. H. & Sheperis, C. J. (2010). Special issues in group work in the schools. In B. T. Erford (ed.), *Group work in the schools* (pp. 237–258). Boston: Pearson.

Foss, L. L., Green, J., Wolfe-Stiltner, K., & DeLucia-Waack, J. L. (eds.). (2008). *School counselors share their share their favorite activities: A guide to choosing, planning, conducting, and processing.* Alexandria, VA: Association for Specialists in Group Work.

Gladding, S. T. (2005). *Counseling as an art: The creative arts in counseling* (3rd ed.). Alexandria, VA: American Counseling Association.

Harter, S. (1982). The Perceived Competence Scale for Children. *Child Development, 53,* 87–97.

Healy, J. M., Stewart, A. J., & Copeland, A. P. (1993). The role of self-blame in children's adjustment to parental separation. *Personality and Social Psychology Bulletin, 19,* 279–289.

Hetherington, E. M. & Kelly, J. (2002). *For better or worse: Divorce reconsidered.* New York: Norton.

Hetherington, E. M., Bridges, M., & Insabella, G. M. (1998). What matters? What does not? Five perspectives on the association between marital transitions and children's adjustment. *American Psychologist, 53,* 167–188.

Jupp, J. J. & Purcell, I. P. (1992). A school-based group programme to uncover and change the problematic beliefs of children from divorce families. *School Psychology International, 13,* 17–29.

Kalter, N. (1998). Group interventions for children of divorce. In K. C. Stoiber & T. R. Kratochwill (eds.), *Handbook of group intervention for children and families* (pp. 120–140). Boston: Allyn & Bacon.

Kalter, N., Pickar, J., & Lesowitz, M. (1984). School-based developmental facilitation groups for children of divorce: A preventive intervention. *American Journal of Orthopsychiatry, 54,* 613–623.

Kivlighan, D. M., Jr. & Goldefine, D. C. (1991). Endorsement of therapeutic factors as a function of stage of group development and participant interpersonal attitudes. *Journal of Counseling Psychology, 38,* 150–158.

Kovacs, M. (1992). *The Children's Depression Inventory manual.* North Tonawanda, NY: Multi-Health Systems, Inc.

Kurdek, L. A. & Berg, B. (1987). Children's Beliefs about Parental Divorce scale: Psychometric characteristics and concurrent validity. *Journal of Consulting & Clinical Psychology, 55,* 712–718.

McConnell, R. A. & Sim, A. J. (1999). Adjustment to parental divorce: An examination of the difference between counselled and non-counselled children. *British Journal of Guidance & Counseling, 27,* 245–257.

Neale, B. (2002). Dialogues with children: The same or different from research with adults? *Childhood, 9*(3), 321–341.

Nugent, P. (1990). Children of divorce. *American School Board Journal, 177*(5), 31.

Pedro-Carroll, J. L. (1995). *The Children of Divorce Intervention program: A procedures manual for facilitating a divorce support for 4th-6th grade children.* Rochester, NY: University of Rochester Center for Community Study.

Pedro-Carroll, J. L. (2005). Fostering resilience in the aftermath of divorce: The role of evidence-based programs for children. *Family Court Review, 43,* 52–64.

Pedro-Carroll, J. L. & Cowen, E. L. (1985). The Children of Divorce Intervention project: An investigation of the efficacy of a school-based prevention program. *Journal of Consulting and Clinical Psychology, 53,* 603–611.

Pedro-Carroll, J. L., Gillis, S. S., Sutton, S. E., & Black, A. E. (1999). Children of Divorce Intervention Project (CODIP): Procedures manuals for conducting support groups. www.childrensinstitute.net/programs/CODIP

Pedro-Carroll, J. L., Nakhnikian, E., & Montes, G. (2001). Assisting children through transition: Helping parents protect their children from the toxic effects of ongoing conflict in the aftermath of divorce. *Family Court Review, 39,* 377–392.

Pedro-Carroll, J. L., Sandler, I. N., & Wolchik, S. A. (2005). Forging interdisciplinary partnerships in the courts to promote prevention initiatives for children and families. *Family Court Review, 43,* 18–21.

Pedro-Carroll, J. L., Sutton, S. E., & Wyman, P. A. (1999). A two-year follow-up evaluation of a preventive intervention for young COD. *School Psychology Review, 28,* 467–476.

Pomrenke, M. (2007). Using grounded theory to understand resiliency in pre-teen children of high-conflict families. *The Qualitative Report, 12,* 356–374.

Pruett, M. K., Insabella, G. M., & Gustafson, K. (2005). The Collaborative Divorce Project: A court-based intervention for separating parents with young children. *Family Court Review, 43,* 38–51.

Reynolds, C. R. & Richmond, B. O. (1985). *Revised Children's Manifest Anxiety Scale.* Los Angeles, CA: Western Psychological Services.

Rich, B. W., Molloy, P., Hart, B., Ginsberg, S., & Mulvey, T. (2007). Conducting a children's divorce group: One approach. *Journal of Child and Adolescent Psychiatric Nursing, 20,* 163–175.

Ritchie, M. & Huss, S. N. (2000). Recruitment and screening of minors for group counseling. *Journal for Specialists in Group Work,* 25, 146–156.

Riva, M. & Haub, A. (2004). Group counseling in the schools. In J. DeLucia-Waack, D. Gerrity, C. Kalodner, & M. Riva (eds.), *Handbook of group counseling and psychotherapy* (pp. 309–321). Thousand Oaks, CA: Sage Publications.

Smead, R. (1994). *Skills for living: Group counseling activities for elementary school students.* Champaign, IL: Research Press.

Stathakos, P. & Roehrle, B. (2003). The Effectiveness of intervention programmes for COD: A meta-analysis. *International Journal of Mental Health Promotion,* 5, 31–37.

Stolberg, A. L. & Cullen, P. M. (1983). Preventive psychopathology in children of divorce: The divorce adjustment process. In L. Kurdek (ed.), *New directions for child development: Children and divorce* (pp. 71–81). San Francisco: Jossey-Bass.

Stolberg, A. L. & Mahler, J. (1994). Enhancing treatment gains in a school-based intervention for children of divorce through skill training, parental involvement, and transfer procedures. *Journal of Consulting and Clinical Psychology,* 62, 147–156.

The Ungame Company. (1987). *The ungame.* Anaheim, CA: Author.

U. S. Bureau of the Census. (2005). Detailed tables—number, timing, and duration of marriages—2004. Retrieved June 23, 2009, from www.census.gov/population/socdemo/marri-div/2004detailed_tables.html

Vines, G. (2004). Turn on the music. *ASCA School Counselor* (newsletter), 41, 10–13.

Wallerstein, J. (2004). The unexpected legacy of divorce: Report of a 25-year study. *Psychoanalytic Psychology,* 21, 353–370.

Wenz, K. & McWhirter, J. J. (1990). Enhancing the group experience: Creative writing Exercises. *Journal for Specialists in Group Work,* 15, 37–42.

Wilcoxon, S. A. & Magnusom, S. (1999). Considerations for school counselors serving noncustodial parents: Premises and suggestions. *Professional School Counseling,* 2, 275–279.

Wolchik, S. A., Sandler, I., Winslow, E., & Smith-Daniels, V. (2005). Programs for promoting parenting of residential parents: Moving from efficacy to effectiveness. *Family Court Review,* 43, 65–80.

Zhou, Q., Sandler, I. N., Millsap, R. E., Wolchik, S.A., & Dawson-McClure, S. R. (2008). Mother-child relationship quality and effective discipline as mediators of the 6-year effects of the New Beginnings Program for children from divorced families. *Journal of Counseling Psychology,* 76, 579–594.

Ziffer, J. M., Crawford, E., & Penney-Wietor, J. (2007). The Boomerang bunch: A school-based multifamily group approach for students and their families recovering from parental separation and divorce. *Journal for Specialists in Group Work,* 32, 154–164.

Zubernis, L. S., Cassidy, K. W., Gilham, J. E., Reivich, K.J., & Jaycox, L. H. (1999). Prevention of depressive symptoms in preadolescent children of divorce. *Journal of Divorce and Remarriage,* 30, 11–36.

Chapter Six

Group Work With Older Adults

Steve Wilson and Susan Rice

The purpose of this chapter is to provide the beginning group worker with an understanding of conducting social group work with older adult clients. The demographics of the older adult population in this country and others dramatically demonstrate that the aging population is growing and will potentially need not only more gerontological social workers but also improved service programming by group workers. Therefore, a compelling need exists to provide effective, user-friendly group work services to older adults to enhance both the quality and the span of their lives.

There is a second important need for social workers to provide effective group work for the older adult population: One of the primary problems of older adults is isolation. Isolation has been identified as a chronically stressful condition to which individuals who are undergoing multiple transitions in older adulthood are particularly vulnerable. Further, interventions that enhance the level of social involvement may buffer the effects of stressful events experienced among older adults (Wethington, Moen, Glasgow, & Pillemer, 2000). It has been well documented that group work with older adults can improve psychological, physiological, and social well-being because groups can work to reduce isolation and facilitate sharing of feelings and other issues surrounding later adulthood (Goelitz, 2001, 2003; Gore-Felton & Spiegel, 1999). Thus, what better method is there than working with older adults in group settings to help them address their daily dilemmas?

REVIEW OF THE LITERATURE

What defines an "older adult" population? A variety of definitions have been used, focusing on the difference between the "young-old" and the "old-old" (Neugarten, 1975). Adults between ages 55 and 74 are considered "young-old," adults between 75 and 84 are deemed "old-old," and those over the age of 85 are classified as the "oldest-old" (Harrigan & Farmer, 2000). All groups are different, yet they all face the same unrelenting biology of aging.

The aging process apparently involves failure of the surveillance, repair, and replacement process typical of a young body (McInnis-Dittrich, 2005). The body loses the ability to replace cells that compose most of its tissues. The immune system often loses the ability to eliminate cancerous cells. Tissues that are damaged in daily life can no longer be repaired. When all of these processes occur, senescence appears, causing the organism to deteriorate and eventually die. This accounts for the physical and mental deterioration that occurs in old age, although for many people it does not happen fast enough to cause severe functional problems before some dramatic disease or occurrence causes immediate death.

The term "senescence" (or "senility") is a common term used to describe the changes that cause a progressive decline in functioning and cognitive abilities (Beers & Berkow, 2000). Many of these declines are attributed to aging itself; in other words, they are considered normal and not disease related. However, people age very differently. Some older adults acquire diseases and impairments in their young-old age, while others seem to live disease free and later are identified as having died of "old age." *Successful* or *healthy aging* refers to a process by which harmful effects of aging are minimized as much as possible, preserving function until senescence takes hold. Adults who age successfully typically avoid experiencing many of the undesirable features of aging and strive to remain both physically and mentally active throughout their later years.

It is important for new group workers to reflect on their personal beliefs and attitudes about aging and older adulthood. Later life can be associated with positive connotations such as increased wisdom or valued expertise. However, just as often there are many negative connotations such as physical and mental health impairment, disease, and death. These stereotypes have been contradicted in countless books and scholarly journals, but distorted media representations of later life can influence people about perceptions of senility, crankiness, and slowness of movement and thought as we enter old age. Just as significant as the real changes that take place in an older adult are the perceived changes, those largely due to the ageism that permeates our society.

Ageism refers to the negative stereotyping of older adults based on their age (Salzman, 2006). This term was initially coined by Robert Butler in 1969, who thereafter became the founding director of the National Institute on Aging (Alliance for Aging Research, 2003). Ageism has the potential to lead to ageist discrimination. While ageism is the negative attitude toward older adults, ageist discrimination is the negative behavior directed to them. Stereotypes of older adults are usually derogatory and convey an attitude that older adults are less valuable as human beings, thus justifying inferior or unequal treatment of them. For example, the typically negative ways in which older adults are portrayed in commercials and television shows that reach millions of people on a daily basis reinforce stereotypical ageist attitudes. That message is even reinforced by the medical profession as biases against older adults have been reported to be prevalent among health care professionals (Alliance for Aging Research, 2003; Kane & Kane, 2005).

Typically, this is seen in extremely brief medical office visits and a disregard for the physical complaints presented by an older patient.

Many older adults can begin to believe that they are not capable of rehabilitation as their body is something that he or she no longer controls. For instance, when a person forgets the house keys and says "I must be getting senile" and the reply is "It happens to everyone over 60," the individual believes that her memory is failing and that there is nothing she can do about it. Consequently, the stereotype becomes self-fulfilling with the individual believing her own time of life is a period of mental and physical frailty. It is apparent how easily older adults, and often families around them, can slip into a mindset that allows deterioration to occur without being concerned that unusual biological changes contribute to a delay in seeking the necessary professional care. Thus, as health symptoms or concerns among older adults are dismissed as typical "aging," conditions can go undiagnosed and, consequently, undertreated (Salzman, 2006).

GROUP WORK INTERVENTIONS

One method of assisting older adults is to provide social support, which has been documented repeatedly in the literature as benefiting both mental and physical health (Eng, Rimm, Fitzmaurice, & Kawachi, 2002; Jacobs, Masson, & Harvil, 2002; Seeman, Lusignolo, & Albert, 2001). Moreover, findings from the gerontological literature show that merely having knowledge that support from others is available if necessary (such as perceived or anticipated support) may be even more beneficial to an older adult's well-being than receiving the support itself or having a large social group (Krause, 1997). These findings suggest that pertinent to well-being and overall successful aging are perceptions among older adults of the strength of their own "social safety net" and not merely increasing the size or contact frequency of their social network (Krause, 2001). Such a "social safety net," in which the individual is aware that others are available to help, provides encouragement for the individual to solve problems autonomously, which in turn allows for healthy feelings of personal control, self-worth, and independence (Krause, 2001).

Social support groups are an effective way of providing this support. Berkman and Glass (2000), in their extensive literature review, detail several benefits of social support that reduce the consequences of stress—namely, access to useful information, instrumental help, and emotional support. Further, social support groups can "normalize" the concerns of the members, which is central to mutual aid. Community-based senior centers, in which older adults often find a network of peers with whom they can share common ground, are a frequent source of these groups, which provide a great range of social support. Senior centers are a resource that provides an array of services that includes social, nutritional, health and educational services, as well as recreational activities that promote social interaction

(Gelfand, 2006). Senior centers have offered essential services to older adults since 1947, such as health, social, and educational services. There are currently approximately 15,000 senior centers that serve 10 million older Americans annually (National Council on Aging, 2006). Studies have indicated that program participants among senior centers have reported greater psychological well-being (Mehta & Ching Ee, 2008), as well as perceived physical and emotional well-being, suggesting that senior centers serve as a protector and buffer of the negative consequences of stress in older adulthood (Fitzpatrick, Gitelson, Andereck, & Mesur, 2004). This chapter uses a mutual aid model to explore the practice principles, themes, and ways of working with older adults to help improve their quality of life.

PRACTICE PRINCIPLES

Group work practice has been defined in a number of ways. In working with older adults, the large majority of support groups function most effectively using the mutual aid model of practice, first described by Schwartz (1961) and developed and elaborated on by Gitterman and Shulman (1994). The mutual aid model states that clients have difficulties that arise from three interrelated problems of living: life transitions, environmental pressures, and maladaptive interpersonal processes. Using the mutual aid process to address these problems gives each member of a group the ability to help every other member through a naturally occurring process. Self-help mutual aid groups are typically peer-led, address a common problem or condition, and are voluntary in their enrollment. The purpose and role of a professional or leader in such a group is to be a mediator, facilitating the engagement of individual members within the group as a whole. Through the mutual aid process, group cohesion is developed (Goelitz, 2004). The mutual aid model allows older adults to function in a way that draws on their strengths and allows them maximum freedom in determining the scope and course of the group.

How do these general practice principles coincide with group work with older clients? Most social work practitioners envision a model of social work practice (individual or group) that includes a focus on assessment, planning, contracting, building rapport, direct action, indirect action, evaluation, and then termination (Toseland & Rivas, 2008). Each phase needs to be modified to accommodate the needs of groups composed of older clients. In all phases of practice, the level of the social worker's activity with older adults in a group setting is high, perhaps higher than in working with younger clients. The reasons for this are numerous. Many older clients have had minimal exposure to the world of social work. They have, more or less, adequately resolved their problems throughout their lives, counting on informal support systems to help them through hard times. As adults reach later life, such as in their 80s and 90s, those informal systems often disappear.

The individual is left to struggle on his own and often seeks social work services perhaps for the first time, without really knowing what to expect. The worker's job is then to model what a group member may do by being active in the group from the very beginning. For example, in assessment, the social worker is often trying to understand the degree to which group members are willing to provide mutual aid and to share their solutions to a problem. The worker needs to demonstrate actively how the mutual aid process takes place. The worker does this by drawing on his or her knowledge of each member's experience and encouraging that member to share that experience with others in the group. The worker also encourages all members to see the similarities among them and tries to help each client understand the source of his or her discomfort.

Contracting is often done on an informal basis in support groups for older adults because the themes of groups are so amorphous. In general, when a younger client or a client with a concrete need contracts for services (or a worker offers services), there is a fairly clear understanding of what the agency is prepared to offer and what the client wants to receive. Groups with clear contracts include those where clients want to learn to be better parents (see Chapter 19) or where older people are learning to deal with insulin-dependent diabetes to manage their illness effectively. However, social support groups for older adults are often seen as a forum for members to adjust to losses or changing life situations. That rubric could fit almost everyone, and so, in practice, the contract becomes a statement of allowing members to decide, as they participate in the group, what the benefits might be and what they might want to focus on. Thus, treatment goals can be established by the group, for the group. Some goals will be universal for all group members, while others will be individual. Such informality also provides a safety net that allows fearful, timid clients to "try out" the group without being committed to one specific goal for change in their lives. Informality does not necessarily mean lack of clarity. Shulman (1999) describes contracting as clarifying the worker's purpose and role. He stresses the importance of eliminating jargon in contracting and urges workers to state clearly what they can offer. For example, in a group that has been formed to help frail older clients to continue living independently in the community, a leader might say, "This group will be a place where you can explore the feelings you have about living alone or feeling isolated some of the time." Each client is then free to pick up on that theme in whatever way seems appropriate.

There is a general belief (Corey & Corey, 2002) that older adults need support and encouragement more than they need confrontation. The goal of group work with older adults is less oriented toward radical personality change than it is toward making quality of life in the present more meaningful and enjoyable, such as by alleviating some of the negative aspects of the older adults' life through addressing their struggles with increased dependency (Kivnick & Murray, 2001) and facilitating the need for vital involvement with ideas, materials, activities, people, and institutions (Erikson, Erikson, & Kivnick, 1986). The social worker, for example, is more likely to be an advocate for the group that needs help with transportation (indirect intervention) than he or she is to empower the members to either work out the transportation problem as a way of building strength or advocate for themselves (direct intervention). However, this is a fine distinction because sometimes one does want older people to see the extent to which they can remain powerful (Kivnick & Stoffel, 2005). Often, however, workers try to make it easier to attend the group as part of the goal of offering a service that will enhance the quality of members' lives.

The theme of learning to resolve conflict is related to this goal. Many theorists agree that conflict is an integral part of group development, and allows members to become intimate and work together more beneficially (e.g. Kottler, 2001; Wallach, 2004). For older people, however, conflict is often seen as threatening to the relationships they are taking significant risks to build (Bergstrom & Nussbaum, 1996). Still, learning skills of conflict resolution can allow true intimacy to develop in groups, facilitating the mutual aid process.

Termination is another area that needs to be planned carefully in groups with older people. Termination is important both in the here and now, and because of the memories the experience evokes for clients in relation to past terminations in their lives (Shulman, 1999). For people who are seeing friends, family members, and acquaintances die on a regular basis, all endings take on an especially poignant meaning. In fact, many older adult clients will bluntly say that they do not want to become close to other group members "because they're only going to die anyway." However, group endings can serve as a vehicle for the discussion of end-of-life talk and for relating group termination to the many losses experienced by older adults at the end-of-life stage (Goelitz, 2004; Toseland & Rizzo, 2004). Thus, many group workers, and those who attend groups, believe that the benefits of forming close relationships with others in mutual support to improve their quality of life outweigh the pain associated with separations and endings.

To effectively use the termination stage as a tool for assisting older adults with end-of-life issues, social workers need to make group endings positive and honest, allowing the expression of a wide range of feelings. This may require the discussion of termination early in the group process and continuously readdressing the topic despite potential resistance from members (Goelitz, 2004). Or, similarly, when a group ends, the members need to be helped to express the importance that it has had in their lives, as well as frustrations about what was not accomplished in the group. Toseland and Rizzo (2004) have suggested ending groups gradually, even extending the time between meetings and encouraging follow-up meetings with participants to ease the separation.

Finally, social workers need to facilitate an open and comfortable environment during any incidences of early termination of individuals who leave the group. For example, when a person drops out of a group because he or she is too ill to attend, it is useful to encourage the others in the group to write to the member or pay a visit to the member's home or the hospital to provide closure. This is not only helpful to the individual who has left but also provides a reassuring message to the older adult participants in the group: *My absence is important, and people care about what happens to me.* Overall, it is imperative that social workers be aware of their own feelings about endings and the termination process so as to effectively implement the discussed strategies and allow for open expression and exploration among group members. That said, it is also important to suggest that open-ended groups that *do not* terminate can be valuable in a mutual aid context as well. Recognizing the need for an ongoing group social support for older adults with common life problems may be a treatment goal in and of itself.

COMMON THEMES

The most common themes encountered in groups for older adults are loneliness, social isolation, loss, poverty, the feeling of rejection, the struggle to find meaning in life, dependency, feelings of uselessness, hopelessness, and despair, fears of death and dying, grief over losses, sadness over physical and mental deterioration, depression, and regrets over past events (Corey & Corey, 2002). If this seems like a list of negative, depressing concerns, one can turn to an emphasis on the wellness model of aging (Crowther, Parker, Achenbaum, Larimore, & Koenig, 2002; Rowe & Kahn, 1998; Sheehy, 1995), which says that the norm is very different from that of people who are struggling. However, as discussed, it is difficult to age without struggling. By definition, *older adulthood* includes multiple and sequential losses.

We need to keep the wellness model of aging in mind so that we do not stereotype all older adults as invalids with persistent mental and physical health problems. However, we also need to recognize and appreciate the degree to which physical changes affect mental status and emotional involvement in different situations. A balance needs to be achieved between focusing on positive and negative themes.

Some groups can be used to promote activities that emphasize the positive, while others can use activities that allow for the safe expression of negative feelings. For example, music can be used to enhance the psychological, emotional, and physical well-being of older participants (Blank, 2009; Bright, 1997; Grobman, 2009), as studies have shown that it can facilitate in the engagement of social activities, allows people to feel accepted, valued, and needed (Hays, 2006), assists people in the understanding of the society in which they live (DeNora, 2000), and can serve as a vehicle for self-expression, mood enhancement, and spiritual awareness (Sloboda & O'Neill, 2001). More specifically, when used with older adults, music has even been shown to foster communication among people with Alzheimer disease and other dementias by serving as a link between the past and present (Koger, Chapin, & Brotons, 1999) and has been found to stimulate frail older adults in residential care into participating in physical movement and exercise (Johnson, Otto, & Clair, 2001). Moreover, a recent study examined the importance of music in enhancing well-being among older adults and found that it served to assist in feelings of competence, feeling less isolated, connecting with others, and encouraging the maintenance of good health (Hays, 2006).

Nonetheless, the efficiency of the human body does decline gradually with age, as older adulthood can be marked by a variety of physical and cognitive changes (Nelson-Becker, 2004), such as depression (National Institutes of Health, 2007), and a variety of chronic health conditions and co-morbidities (Fillenbaum, Pieper, Cohen, Cornoni-Huntley, & Guralnik, 2000). Ironically, what people are most aware of first are the cosmetic changes associated with aging, such as gray hair, wrinkles, and a widening pelvis. These are the changes that cause many people to *feel* that they are getting old, although these conditions do not relate to physical functioning at all.

Mental health functioning is perhaps the essence of who we are, and when one sees one's functioning deteriorating, or sees it in others, the effects are devastating. Alzheimer disease causes cruel changes in a person's personality and cognitive abilities that effectively isolate the person from everyone. It is estimated that 5.1 million people aged 65 and older suffer from Alzheimer disease, a number that is expected to increase to 7.7 million by 2030 and to between 11 and 16 million by 2050 (Hebert, Scherr, Bienias, Bennett, & Evans, 2003). Group work services to such clients can have a number of beneficial effects (Clare, 2002; Goldsliver & Gruneir, 2001) including a chance to foster peer experiences and emotional support, stimulating and encouraging the functioning of all remaining intellectual and social capacities, affirming a sense of individual identity, eliminating frustrating expectations, and replacing them with supportive social and group controls. While this chapter focuses on older adults as clients, it is important to note that groups for family caregivers can also help relieve the tension and strain that tear families apart as they watch a loved one, previously capable, competent, and intelligent, deteriorate. A national study of caregivers to persons over the age of 50 revealed that support groups were ranked among the top six outside services used by caregivers (National Alliance for Caregiving and AARP, 2004).

Loneliness and Social Isolation

Loneliness, social isolation, and poverty are familiar themes in groups composed of older clients. As the population enters older adulthood, the male-to-female ratio changes drastically. In 2008, men in the 55- to 64-year-old age group totaled 11% of the population and, comparatively, women in the 55- to 64-year-old age group totaled 11.3%. However, in the 80+ age group, men totaled only 2.4%, while women accounted for 4.1%, nearly twice the number of men (U.S. Census Bureau, 2009a).

Among people who were older than 75 years, only 38% of women were married; for women aged 85 and over, just 15% are married (Federal Interagency Forum on Aging-Related Statistics, 2008). Ethnic differences also exist. In 2006, non-Hispanic whites accounted for 81% of the population aged 65 and older, while blacks accounted for 9%, Hispanics totaled 6%, and Asians accounted for 3% (Federal Interagency Forum on Aging-Related Statistics, 2008).

Income also changes with gender, age, and living arrangements. In 2007, 8.8% of older adults aged 65 to 74 years were below the poverty line. This number increases to 9.8% of those aged 75 to 84 years, and increases yet again to 13% of those 85 years and older (U.S. Census Bureau, 2009b). Older women, in general, have a higher poverty rate than older men; 12% of women aged 65 and older were under the poverty line in 2007, while only 6.6% of men were at that level (U.S. Census Bureau, 2009b). African American and Hispanic women may be at particular risk for poverty (Stanford & Usita, 2002; U.S. Census Bureau, 2006).

Social isolation is known to contribute to higher rates of substance abuse and suicide (DeSpelder & Strickland, 2009). Moreover, rates of substance abuse are high among older adults, with reports of alcohol abuse being as high as 15% (Blow, Oslin, & Barry, 2002), as well as reports of the intentional or accidental misuse and abuse of prescription drugs by older adults (Sadock & Sadock, 2003). In addition, suicide has been reported as a problem among older adults, particularly among older men (Bartels & Smyer, 2002). Group work interventions can directly address this phenomenon and impact the populations involved (McInnis-Dittrich, 2005). More specifically, group interventions have been found to be effective in reducing social isolation among older adults (Cattan, White, Bond, & Learmouth, 2005). Feelings of uselessness, hopelessness, despair, and regrets over past events are also the foci of many discussions in social support groups. Moreover, retirement represents a significant milestone for older adults. Research has identified a variety of experiences and consequential issues among those transitioning into retirement (Kim & Moen, 2002; Marshall, Clark & Ballantyne, 2001; Szinovacs & Davey, 2005). Particularly for men in our society, there can be a loss of meaningful job roles, income, productivity, and even their identity, because these work relationships have been central throughout adult life (Carter & McGoldrick, 1999).

One way to conceptualize these feelings is through the work of Erik Erikson. Erikson (1963) describes the last two developmental stages of life—generativity versus stagnation and ego integrity versus despair—as two sides of a coin. *Generativity* refers to the concern about establishing and guiding the next generation. When one feels that one has not been instrumental in this process, either through one's own children or by giving to society in a larger way, a pervasive sense of stagnation occurs. *Ego integrity* is the sense that one has accepted "one's one and only life cycle as something that had to be and that, by necessity, permitted of no substitutions" (Erikson, 1963, p. 268). If one cannot feel that way about one's life, despair is the result. If one looks back at one's life and blames oneself for the paths not taken, the overall feeling is one of making wrong choices. Older adults often struggle with issues of regret in groups.

Death, Dying, and Grief

Death and dying remain taboo subjects in our society. Many people of all ages cannot (or will not) openly discuss these significant issues, although they secretly harbor strong feelings about them. Elizabeth Kubler-Ross (1975) has described America as a "death denying society," as we typically evade issues surrounding death and our own finiteness out of fear. It has been postulated that this is due to the anxiety that death and dying elicits, causing discomfort among people otherwise surrounded by a pleasure-driven and narcissistic American culture (Johnson & McGee, 2004). However, talking about death is emotionally laden as it activates our own sense of mortality and fears of loss and separation.

In a youth-oriented society, the impact of multiple losses in later life, including the loss of meaningful employment, loss of financial income, loss of friends and support systems to death, family transitions, and loss of physical functioning in the case of chronic illnesses, coupled with ageist societal attitudes toward older adults can cause many older adults to feel depressed and depreciate their own sense of worth. Unfortunately, this can also lead to a medicalization of their bereavement-related feelings (Garaviglia, 2006). In an attempt to find a quick remedy to pervasive sadness often associated with personal losses, many older adults turn to pharmacological interventions to relieve these feelings of grief-related sadness. Medications can temporarily ease the symptoms of grief; however, a psychosocial grief group intervention might be the best treatment for this type of condition. Allowing the open expression of grief, the support of others in similar situations and experiencing the universality of feelings can produce profound results for those facing life losses.

Meanwhile, the controversy continues about how death should occur and how much control we should have over it. Hospice care allows a terminally ill person to die with palliative interventions. Essentially, hospice care provides continuous pain and symptom management for the patient until such time as death occurs. However, end-of-life care has also led to bioethical decisions regarding the moral distinction between "ordinary" versus "extraordinary" care (DeSpelder & Strickland, 2009). When is artificial nutrition or artificial hydration or breathing equipment considered "ordinary" care with conventional and proved outcomes, as opposed to "extraordinary" care that has life-sustaining interventions with an uncertain outcome and may even be considered intrusive to the patient? The withdrawal of these interventions can cause even more moral ambiguity for patients and families. These circumstances can lead to discussions in groups beyond hospice and palliative care to end-of-life issues involving physician-assisted suicide or euthanasia. The theme of death, dying, and loss recurs in groups, although it is rarely brought up unless the group worker is willing to facilitate the sharing of painful and risky feelings related to the topic.

RECOMMENDED WAYS OF WORKING

First, to work with clients, we need to reach them. A sobering fact is that for most types of social work services, including group work, minorities are served less often—not because there are fewer potential clients for a given service but because of perceived and actual barriers to receiving that service (Palinkas et al., 2007). For example, many concrete services specifically developed for older adults (e.g., homemaker services, home health care, congregate meals) are used primarily by older white adults, despite the fact that older persons of color have been reported to have greater needs, as studies have found that older minority groups have an increased risk for disease and dysfunction in activities of daily living (Hayward & Heron, 1999; Williams & Wilson, 2001), have a higher amount of functional disabilities, and have greater prevalence of disease (Wallace & Villa, 2003) than their white counterparts. Older adults belonging to minority groups have been repeatedly reported in the literature to delay use of professional assistance or abstain from accessing formal support (Hinton, 2002; Ho, Weitzman, Cui, & Levkoff, 2000; Markides, Eschbach, Ray, & Peek, 2007). Successful attempts to increase minority representation in client groups include efforts to increase the cultural competence of the workers. This is seen in speaking in the client's own language or having workers with cultural similarity interact with the client, which makes the act of accepting help much easier (Min, 2005; Valle, 1998). Because in our country ethnic minority status is often tied to lower income, accessibility issues need to be addressed, too, including transportation, cost of services, and flexibility of hours.

Second, in developing groups of clients, it is important to pay attention to issues of homogeneity and heterogeneity (Corey & Corey, 2002). In general, groups need to have maximum homogeneity in terms of degree of vulnerability and capacity to tolerate anxiety. In other words, the ego strength of all members needs to be at similar levels. On the other hand, maximum heterogeneity in participants' conflict areas and patterns of coping allows input of new ideas and perspectives on the situations that clients face. Regardless of the themes discussed, this balancing rule between difference and similarity will allow participants to use the mutual aid model to share with each other. These themes can be incorporated in most groups that allow clients to determine the focus of the discussion.

An example of this is that for 5 years, one of the authors directed a weekly support group for members of a retirement community. Pairs of undergraduate students facilitated weekly support groups that lasted for a full academic year and combined small-group discussions and programs with occasional large-group workshops and potluck dinners (Black, Kelly, & Rice, 2005). These groups were ongoing, in the sense that many members stayed with the groups from year to year, but the student workers changed every September. As people grew older and frailer, there was a fairly high degree of turnover among the group members, and ways of working with them needed to change while maintaining the initial purposes of the group.

An example of this was the potluck dinners, which were initially a wonderful opportunity for members to demonstrate their culinary skills and to "give," in a concrete way, to their friends and to the student workers. Over time, the participants' cooking abilities faltered as their vision, hearing, and health deteriorated. It was decided to cater the main dish for the potluck dinners, and the members brought desserts to share. Even with dessert, however, we saw a gradual change from the "famous homemade recipe for brownies" to boxes of cookies that were store bought. This change saddened those staff who had been with the group from the beginning. However, it was a richly expressive example of changing the parameters of the situation so that the members could still enjoy the essence of the program. Most recently, the potluck dinners were changed to potluck luncheons because more members were having trouble getting out at night even within their gated community. Workers must be sensitive to the environmental changes that need to be made to allow the substantive work of the group to continue. The purpose of the potluck dinners has remained constant: They combat the social isolation and loneliness of the members (about 70% of whom live alone) and allow them to feel part of a community and a family.

In addition, workshops held twice each semester gave members specific skills to improve their ability to function within the group. For example, one of the authors held a 3-hour workshop on conflict resolution skills, including teaching "I-messages," discussing innate styles of conflict ("turtles" or "sharks"), and demonstrating skills of negotiation and mediation. A presentation of these skills coupled with an opportunity to discuss the feelings attached to them primed members to use them outside of the group.

In addition to retirement communities, groups for older adults can be located in institutions. In contrast to retirement communities, where residents live independently in whatever manner they choose, institutions provide the assistance needed for their residents to perform the tasks of daily living at the cost of lessened freedom. In an examination of institutions, Schmidt (1990) begins by describing people's feelings about them. "Most elderly persons entering a home for the aged view this move as their last one. But, whatever sense of loss they may feel, they are concerned also with the life they can make there. Thus, homes for the aged become laboratories of human behavior as residents deal with change on a scale for which their previous lives have not prepared them" (p. 1).

Reminiscence Therapy in Groups

Reminiscence storytelling is another form of group work therapy that focuses on increasing social interaction to decrease depressive symptoms, such as feelings of loneliness and sadness (Bohlmeijer, Smit, & Cuijpers, 2003). Reminiscence work has also been shown to strengthen confidence and enhance social contacts of older adults with depressive symptoms and certain forms of dementia (Van Puyenbroeck & Maes, 2008). The literature identifies several forms of reminiscence therapy. Two key forms are instrumental reminiscence and integrative reminiscence (Watt & Cappeliez, 2000). Instrumental reminiscence uses memories to recall past positive coping strategies, which can possibly be used during stressful life events in the present. The other form, integrative reminiscence, uses a cognitive-behavioral model whereby the participant uses constructive reappraisal of emotions and interpretations of his or her central life events. Both forms of reminiscence work well with older adults who are experiencing depressive symptoms or life challenges (Watt & Cappeliez, 2000).

Reminiscence can stimulate memories that can be used as part of a participant's narrative and autobiography. This can be done through use of all the senses. It can be done visually through use of historical photographs or video clips from past events (such as USO shows or celebrities from earlier generations). Reminiscence can also be auditory through music, such as using familiar radio shows or early television shows, CDs of historically famous performers, or even making their own music with various musical instruments. It can include olfactory senses such as using smell kits of spices and scents such as cinnamon, cedar, or different foods. It can be tactile though the touching of objects, feeling fabric textures, painting, and even pottery work.

For younger group workers, reminiscence can be a way to learn about the past and gain a deeper understanding of the group members as they hear about the experiences that brought their clients to the present. Group members feel an increased sense of understanding and support for each other as they witness the commonality of their experiences.

Grief Support Groups

Grief counseling is a form of group work with older adults that focuses on the participants' intense feelings of loss, most often after a death. Grief counseling works well in group settings because peer support and relationships with others who can empathize with one's loss can help reduce feelings of isolation caused by grief. In some cases a grief counselor may facilitate the grief group, but it can be a mutual aid format as well. The facilitator or counselor is not the expert; instead "the grief counselor acts as a fellow traveler rather than consultant, sharing the uncertainties of the journey, and walking alongside, rather than leading the grieving individual along the unpredictable road toward a new adaptation" (Neimeyer, 1998, p. 200). Essentially, the role of the facilitator is to be "present" for the bereaved, helping the group best by simply actively listening and demonstrating empathy.

While much has been written about stage and task models of grief therapy (Kübler-Ross, 1969; Rando, 1993; Worden, 2002), contemporary grief work models follow a more integrative method similar to reminiscence by allowing the person to recollect and reexperience her life with the deceased in order to cherish old attachments. This allows the bereaved to make sense of her loss with the aim adapting to life without that person.

Group Work Activities

Programming (using an activity to further a treatment goal for the group) can also be used in beneficial ways. In one group session of the support group program described earlier, the worker brought in the game "Trivial Pursuit" (immensely popular at the time). The game consists of a board, dice, and cards with questions on them, asking for answers about different topics including science, nature, history, entertainment, arts and leisure, and sports. The usual game rules were modified for this group by abandoning the board, the dice, and the competitive aspect of the game. Instead, the worker read a question and all group members tried to answer it, often asking each other questions about their personal circumstances during the event in question. For example, to the question of when a baseball player broke a major league record, the answer came via a path that included deciding if it was before or after World War II, where each group member had been during those years, and what they were doing. Again, this became a form of reminiscence therapy. There was no score keeping and no winner or loser. The group spent as much time as they wanted on one question, and it ended when the right answer was given or the group as a whole gave up. The entire session used only four or five cards from the game, but the group emerged with a sense of closeness and cohesiveness that had not been present previously.

Evaluating Success

How does one know when a group is successful? If the treatment goals have been met? Much has been written about single-subject design and about the importance of every practitioner's evaluation of his or her own practice (Bloom et al., 2003; Nugent, Sieppert, & Hudson, 2001). This emphasis exists because we need to know if the money spent on a resource is effective and if the interventions we are using are helpful. To evaluate social support groups for older adults, one of the most effective ways is to go to the source—the consumer.

In many groups, sessions end with a 1-minute evaluation. This evaluation consists of three questions: (1) What was the most helpful thing that happened for you here today? (2) What was the least helpful thing that happened for you here today? (3) What would you suggest that we do differently next time? If the clients are able to write, this can be done on a sheet that is handed to each member. If writing is too burdensome, the clients can answer these questions quickly in a round-robin format.

More formal evaluations can be done at the midpoint and/or endpoint of a time-limited group. Clients can be asked about their overall satisfaction, about the effectiveness of specific techniques or sessions, and about how the enjoyment of their group is related to the goals they wanted to reach. This can be done via mail to increase the objectivity or verbally by a colleague (e.g., a worker at an agency or center) who the participants may recognize but is not affiliated with the group.

As with all evaluations, the introduction of the evaluation is crucial to its success. If the worker asks for feedback with leading questions that implies that only positive feedback is welcome, then that may be what he or she will get. If the members think that the continuation of the program is riding on their feedback, the responses may be greatly distorted. Allowing time for objective and subjective critique sends a welcome message to participants. It puts them in control of their group and enables them to make it the best it can be through their feedback. With groups of older adults, as with other groups, evaluation should be an ongoing part of group work that contributes to the group's overall effectiveness.

CONCLUSION

The primary reason that group work with older adults is so effective is that human beings are programmed to connect with others. Older age becomes a time when natural, informal connections falter due to illness, deaths, difficulties in mobility, and exhaustion. Providing ways to bolster human connection, through use of mutual aid groups, is one of the most valuable services that group workers can offer at this important time in an adult's lives.

RESOURCES

Administration on Aging
Center for Communication and
Consumer Services
330 Independence Avenue SW, Room 4656
Washington, DC 20201
(202) 619-7501
www.aoa.gov/NAIC/

Alzheimer's Association
225 N. Michigan Avenue, Floor 17
Chicago, IL 60601
(800) 272-3900
www.alz.org

American Association for Retired Persons
601 "E" Street NW

Washington, DC 20049
(800) 424-3410
www.aarp.org

Association for the Advancement of Social Work with Groups
2303 Winfield Street
Rahway, NJ 07065-3620
(732) 669-7852
www.aaswg.org

National Institute on Aging
Building 31, Room 5C27
31 Center Drive, MSC 2292
Bethesda, MD 20892
(301) 496-1752
www.nia.nih.gov

GriefShare
P.O. Box 1739
Wake Forest, NC 27588
(800) 395-5755
www.griefshare.org

REFERENCES

Alliance for Aging Research. (2003). Ageism: How healthcare fails the elderly. Retrieved from http://www.agingresearch.org/content/article/detail/694/
Bartels, S. J. & Smyer, M. A. (2002). Mental disorders of aging: An emerging public health crisis? *Generations, 26*, 14–20.
Beers, M. H. & Berkow, R. (eds.). (2000). *The Merck manual of geriatrics* (3rd ed.). Rahway, NJ: MERCK Publishing.
Bergstrom, M. J. & Nussbaum, J. F. (1996). Cohort differences in interpersonal conflict: Implications for the older patient-younger care provider interaction. *Health Communication, 8*, 233–248.
Berkman, L. F. & Glass, T. (2000). Social integration, social networks, social support, and health. In L. F. Berkman & I. Kawachi (eds.), *Social epidemiology*. New York: Oxford University Press.
Black, J., Kelly, J., & Rice, S. (2005). A model of group work in retirement communities. In B. Haight and F. Gibson (eds.), *Burnside's Working with older adults: Group processes and techniques* (4th ed., pp. 273–285). Boston: Jones and Bartlett.
Blank, B. T. (2009). David's harp: Bringing healing through music. *The New Social Worker, 16*(1). Retrieved July 15, 2009, from http://www.socialworker.com/home/component/remository/showdown/14/

Bloom, M., Fischer, J., & Orme, J. (2003). *Evaluating practice: Guidelines for the accountable professional.* Boston: Allyn and Bacon.

Blow, F. C., Oslin, D. W., & Barry, K. L. (2002). Use and abuse of alcohol, illicit drugs, and psychoactive medication among older people. *Generations, 25,* 50–54.

Bohlmeijer, E., Smit, F., & Cuijpers, P. (2003). Effects of reminiscence and life review on late-life depression: A meta-analysis. *International Journal of Geriatric Psychiatry, 18,* 1088–1094.

Bright R. (1997). *Wholeness in later life.* London: Jessica Kingsley.

Carter, B. & McGoldrick, M. (1999). *The expanded family life cycle: Individual, family, and social perspectives* (3rd ed.). Boston: Allyn and Bacon.

Cattan, M., White, M., Bond, J., & Learmouth, A. (2005). Preventing social isolation and loneliness among older people: A systematic review of health promotion interventions. *Ageing & Society, 25,* 41–67.

Clare, L. (2002). We'll fight it as long as we can: Coping with the onset of Alzheimer's disease. *Aging and Mental Health, 6,* 139–148.

Corey, G. & Corey, M. (2002). *Groups: Process and practice* (6th ed.) Monterey, CA: Brooks/Cole.

Crowther, M. R., Parker, M. W., Achenbaum, W. A., Larimore, W. L., & Koenig, H. G., (2002). Rowe and Kahn's model of successful aging revisited: Positive spirituality: The forgotten factor. *The Gerontologist, 42,* 613–620.

Denora, T. (2000). *Music in Everyday Life.* Cambridge, MA: Cambridge University Press.

DeSpelder, L. A. & Strickland, A. L. (2009). *The last dance: Encountering death and dying* (8th ed). New York: McGraw-Hill.

Eng, P. M., Rimm, E. B., Fitzmaurice, G., & Kawachi, I. (2002). Social ties and change in social ties in relation to subsequent total and cause-specific mortality and coronary heart disease incidence in men. *American Journal of Epidemiology, 155,* 700–709.

Erikson, E. (1963). *Childhood and society.* New York: W. W. Norton.

Gallagher-Thompson, D. (1994). Direct services and interventions for caregivers. In M. H. Cantor (ed.), *Family caregiving: Agenda for the future* (pp. 102–122). San Francisco: American Society on Aging.

Erikson, E. H., Erickson, J. M., & Kivnick, H. Q. (1986). *Vital involvement in old age.* New York: W. W. Norton & Company, Inc.

Federal Interagency Forum on Aging-Related Statistics. (2008). *Older Americans 2008: Key indicators of well-being. Federal Interagency Forum on Aging-Related Statistics.* Washington, DC: U.S. Government Printing Office.

Fillenbaum, G. G., Pieper, C. F., Cohen, H. J., Cornoni-Huntley, J. C., & Guralnik, J. M. (2000). Comorbidity of five chronic health conditions in elderly community residents: Determinants and impact on mortality. *Journal of Gerontology: Medical Sciences, 55A,* 84–89.

Fitzpatrick, T. R., Gitelson, R., Andereck, K. L., & Mesbur, F. S. (2005). Social support factors and health among a senior center population in Southern Ontario, Canada. *Social Work in Health Care, 40*(3), 15–37.

Garavaglia, B. (2006). Avoiding the tendency to medicalize the grieving process: Reconciliation rather than resolution. *The New Social Worker Online.* Retrieved from http://www.socialworker.com/home/component/magazine/edition/Summer-2006-Edition/

Gelfand, D. (2006). *The aging network: Programs and services* (6th ed.). New York: Springer Publishing Co.

Gitterman, A. & Shulman, L. (eds.). (1994). *Mutual aid groups and the life cycle* (2nd ed). New York: Columbia University Press.

Goelitz, A. (2001). Dreaming their way into life: A group experience with oncology patients. *Social Work with Groups, 24,* 53–67.

Goelitz, A. (2003). When accessibility is an issue: Telephone support groups for caregivers. *Smith College Studies in Social Work, 73,* 385–394.

Goelitz, A. (2004). Using the end of groups as an intervention at the end-of-life. *Journal of Gerontological Social Work, 44*(1/2), 211–221.

Goldsilver, P. M. & Gruneir, M. R. (2001). Early stage dementia group: An innovative model of support for individuals in the early stages of dementia. *American Journal of Alzheimer's Disease, 16,* 109–114.

Gore-Felton, C. & Spiegel, D. (1999). Enhancing women's lives: The role of support groups among breast cancer patients. *Journal for Specialists in Group Work, 24,* 274–287.

Harrigan, M. P. & Farmer, R. L. (2000). The myths and facts of aging. In R. L. Schneider, N. P. Kropf & A. J. Kisor (eds.), *Gerontological social work: Knowledge, service settings and special populations* (2nd ed., pp. 26–64). Belmont, CA: Brooks/Cole.

Hays, T. (2006). Facilitating well-being through music for older people with special needs. *Home Healthcare Services Quarterly, 25*(3/4), 55–73.

Hayward, M. & Heron, M. (1999). Racial inequality in active life among adult Americans. *Demography, 36,* 77–92.

Hebert, L. E., Scherr, P. A., Bienias, J. L., Bennett, D. A., & Evans, D. A. (2003). Alzheimer's disease in the U.S. population: Prevalence estimates using the 2000 census. *Archives of Neurology, 60,* 1119–1122.

Hinton, L. (2002). Improving care for ethnic minority elderly and their family caregivers across the spectrum of dementia severity. *Alzheimer's Disease & Associated Disorders, 16*(2), 50-55.

Ho, C., Weitzman, P. F., Cui, X., & Levkoff, S.E. (2000). Stress and service use among minority caregivers to elders with dementia. *Journal of Gerontological Social Work, 33,* 67–88.

Jacobs, E., Masson, R., & Harvil, R. (2002). *Group counseling: Strategies and skills* (4th ed.). Monterey, CA: Brooks/Cole/Thomson Learning.

Johnson, C. J. & McGee, M. (2004). Psychosocial aspects of death and dying, *Gerontologist, 44*(5), 719–722.

Johnson, G., Otto, D., & Clair, A. (2001). The effect of instrumental and vocal music on adherence to a physical rehabilitation exercise program with persons who are elderly. *Journal of Music Therapy, 38*(2), 82–96.

Kane, R. L. & Kane, R. A. (2005). Ageism in healthcare and long-term care. *Generations, 29*(3), 49–54.

Kim, J. & Moen, P. (2002). Retirement transitions, gender and psychological well-being: A life-course, ecological model. *The Journals of Gerontology Series B: Psychological Sciences and Social Sciences, 57,* 212–222.

Kivnick, H. Q. & Murray, S. V. (2001). Life strengths interview guide: Assessing elder clients' strengths. *Journal of Gerontological Social Work, 34*(4), 7–32.

Kivnick, H. Q. & Stoffel, S. A. (2005). Vital involvement practice: Strengths as more than tools for solving problems. *Journal of Gerontological Social Work, 46,* 85–116.

Koger, S., Chapin, K., & Brotons, M. (1999). Is music therapy an effective intervention for dementia? A meta-analytic review of literature. *Journal of Music Therapy, 26,* 2–15.

Kottler, J. (2001). *Learning group leadership: An experiential approach.* Boston: Allyn and Bacon.

Krause, N. (1997). Anticipated support, received support, and economic stress among older adults. *Journal of Gerontology: Psychological Sciences, 52,* 284–293.

Krause, N. (2001). Social support. In R. H. Binstock & L. K. George (eds.), *Handbook of aging and the social sciences* (pp. 272–294). San Diego, CA: Academic Press.

Kübler-Ross, E. (1969). *On death and dying.* New York: Macmillan.

Kubler-Ross, E. (1975). *Death: The final stage of growth.* New York: Simon and Schuster.

Markides K. S., Eschbach K., Ray, L. A., & Peek, M. K. (2007). Census disability rates among older people by race/ethnicity and type of Hispanic origin. In J. L. Angel & K. E. Whitfield (eds.), *The health of aging Hispanics: The Mexican-origin population* (pp. 26–39). New York: Springer Publishing Co.

Marshall, V. W., Clarke, P. J., & Ballantyne, P. J. (2001). Instability in the retirement transition: Effects on health and well-being in a Canadian Study. *Research on Aging, 23,* 379–409.

Mehta, K. K. & Ching Ee, J. C. (2008). Effects of good life program on Singaporean older adults' psychological well-being. *Activities, Adaptation & Aging, 32*(3/4), 214–237.

McInnis-Dittrich, K. (2005). *Social work with elders: A biopsychosocial approach to assessment and intervention.* Boston: Allyn and Bacon.

Min, J. W. (2005). Cultural competency: A key to effective future social work with racially and ethnically diverse elders. *Families in Society, 86,* 347–358.

National Alliance for Caregiving & AARP. (2004). *Caregiving in the U.S.* Bethesda, MD: Author.

National Council on Aging. (2006). *Fact sheet: Senior centers.* Retrieved from http://www.ncoa.org/content.cfm?sectionID=103&detail=2741

National Institutes of Mental Health. (2007). *Older adults: Depression and suicide facts* (fact sheet). Retrieved from http://www.nimh.nih.gov/health/publications/older-adults-depression-and-suicide-facts-fact-sheet/index.shtml

Neimeyer, R. A. (1998). *Lessons of loss: A guide to coping.* New York: McGraw-Hill.

Nelson-Becker, H. B. (2004). Meeting life challenges: A hierarchy of coping styles in African American and Jewish American older adults. *Journal of Human Behavior in the Social Environment, 10*(1), 155–174.

Neugarten, B. (1975). The future and the young-old. *The Gerontologist, 15,* 4–9.

Nugent, W., Sieppert, J., & Hudson, W. (2001). *Practice evaluation for the 21st century.* Monterey, CA: Brooks/Cole (Wadsworth Press).

Palinkas, L. A., Criado, V., Fuentes, D., Shepherd, S., Milian, H., Folsom, D., & Jeste, D. (2007). Unmet needs for services for older adults with mental illness: comparison of views of different stakeholder groups. *American Journal of Geriatric Psychiatry, 15,* 530–540.

Pillemer, K., Moen, P., Wethington, E., & Glasgow, N. (2000). *Social integration in the second half of life.* Baltimore, MD: John Hopkins University Press.

Rando, T. (1993). *Treatment of complicated mourning.* Champaign, IL: Research Press.

Rowe, J. & Kahn, R. (1998). *Successful aging*. New York: Pantheon Books.

Sadock, B. J. & Sadock, V. A. (2003). *Kaplan & Sadock's Synopsis of psychiatry* (9th ed.). Philadelphia, PA: Lippincott Williams & Wilkins.

Salzman, B. (2006). Myths and realities of aging. *Care Management Journal, 7*(3), 141–150.

Schmidt, M. G. (1990). *Negotiating a good old age: Challenges of residential living in late life*. San Francisco: Jossey-Bass.

Schwartz, W. (1961). The social worker in the group. *The Social Welfare Forum*. New York: Columbia University Press.

Seeman, T. E., Lusignolo, T. M., & Albert, M. (2001). Social relationships, social support, and patterns of cognitive aging in healthy, high-functioning older adults: MacArthur studies of successful aging. *Health Psychology, 20,* 243–255.

Sheehy, G. (1995). *New passages: Mapping your life across time*. New York: Random House.

Shulman, L. (1999). *The skills of helping individuals, families and groups* (4th ed.). Itasca, IL: F. E. Peacock.

Sloboda, J. & O'Neill, S. (2001). *Music and emotion: Theory and research*. Oxford: Oxford University Press.

Stanford, E. P. & Usita, P. M. (2002). Retirement: Who is at risk? *Generations, 26*(11), 45–48.

Szinovacs, M. E. & Davey, A. (2005). Predictors of perceptions of involuntary retirement. *The Gerontologist, 45,* 36–47.

Toseland, R. & Rivas, R. (2008). *An introduction to group work practice* (6th ed.). Boston: Allyn and Bacon.

Toseland, R. W. & Rizzo, V. M. (2004). What's different about working with older people in groups? *Journal of Gerontological Social Work, 44,* 5–23.

U.S. Census Bureau, Current Population Reports. (2005). 65+ in the United States: 2005. Retrieved July 8, 2009, from http://www.metlife.com/assets/cao/mmi/publications/studies/mmi-studies-65-profile-20041010.pdf

U.S. Census Bureau. (2006). Income, poverty and health insurance coverage in the U.S., 2005. Retrieved July 13, 2009, from http://www.census.gov/prod/2006pubs/p60-231.pdf.

U.S. Census Bureau: Population Division. (2009a). Current population survey, annual social and economic supplement, 2008. Retrieved July 8, 2009, from http://www.census.gov/population/www/socdemo/age/age_sex_2008.html

U.S. Census Bureau. (2009b). Poverty status of the population 55 years and over by sex and age: 2007. Current population, annual social and economic supplement, 2008. Retrieved July 13, 2009, from http://www.census.gov/population/www/socdemo/age/older_2008.html

Valle, R. (1998). *Caregiving across cultures: Working with dementing illness and ethnically diverse populations*. Washington, DC: Taylor & Francis.

Van Puyenbroeck, J. & Maes, B. (2008). A review of critical, person-centered and clinical approaches to reminiscence work for people with intellectual disabilities. *International Journal of Disability, Development and Education, 55,* 43–60.

Wallach, T. (2004). Transforming conflict: A group relations perspective. *Peace and Conflict Studies, 11,* 76–95.

Wallace, S. & Villa, V. (2003). Equitable health systems: Cultural and structural issues for Latino elders. *American Journal of Law and Medicine, 29,* 247–267.

Watt, L. & Cappeliez, P. (2000). Integrative and instrumental reminiscence therapies for depression in older adults: Intervention strategies and treatment effectiveness. *Aging and Mental Health 4*, 166–177.

Wethington, E., Moen, P., Glasgow, N., & Pillemer, K. (2000). Multiple roles, social integration, and health. In K. Pillemer, P. Moen, E. Wethington, & N. Glasgow (eds.), *Social integration in the second half of life* (pp. 48–74). Baltimore, MD: Johns Hopkins University Press.

Williams, D. & Wilson, C. (2001). Race, ethnicity, and aging. In R. H. Binstock & L. K. George (eds.), *Handbook of aging and the social sciences* (4th ed., pp. 160–178). San Diego: Academic Press.

Worden, J. W. (2002). *Grief counseling and grief therapy: A handbook for the mental health practitioner* (3rd ed.) New York, NY: Springer.

Chapter Seven

En Dos Culturas: Group Work With Latino Immigrants and Refugees

Luz M. López and Erika M. Vargas

The experience of being a member of a Latino group in the United States or being the only Latino in a treatment group can mirror or reflect the experience of adapting to a new culture and a new environment. It may be helpful for group leaders to think of these as a parallel process. Just as leaving one's homeland in search of work or a "better life" can simultaneously be an exciting and frightening experience, joining a group can stimulate such mixed feelings. When most immigrants arrive in the United States, they face many challenges requiring adaptation to a different culture and set of values. Similarly, a group member's ethnic identity and culture of origin impact the development of group dynamics, the level of cohesiveness, and the group members' interactions and relationship building with one another.

Every ethnic population has its own set of characteristics that influences a practitioner's approach to social work with that particular group. Working in groups with Latinos means understanding what it is like for members to be in two cultures—sometimes in two cultures with opposing values (i.e., individualism versus collectivism) while adapting to a new culture, language, and lifestyle in the United States.

This chapter will focus on the experiences particular to Latino immigrants and refugees. An understanding of the Latino immigration process, including the process of acculturation, can contribute to a practitioner's cultural competence (Bacallao & Smokowski, 2005). This chapter will help group work practitioners to increase their understanding of biculturalism, learn concepts related to Latino cultural values, improve their multicultural competency, become familiar with transnational family communications, and learn the differences between working with Latinos who are immigrants and those who are refugees. In addition, the chapter will explore limitations in evidence-based group work curricula with Latinos, highlight strengths in group work practice, and identify ways for resiliency building in working with Latinos. The first section will offer a review of the literature; the next section will provide an overview of the acculturation process and other Latino immigration issues, followed by guidelines for the group leader and case study illustrations. The chapter ends with a section on evaluation and resources that could be used with Latino immigrants and refugee groups.

REVIEW OF THE LITERATURE: DESCRIPTION OF LATINO POPULATIONS AND CULTURAL PATTERNS

According to the U.S. Census Bureau (2009a), as of 2008, there were an estimated 46.9 million Latinos living in the United States. At 15% of the total population, Latinos are the largest racial/ethnic minority. Latinos are also the fastest growing minority group, with a 3.2% population increase between 2007 and 2008. By the year 2050, it is estimated that there will be 132.8 million Latinos, which will account for 30% of the total U.S. population (U.S. Census Bureau, 2009a). Latinos also are spreading out across the nation. Sixteen states have at least 500,000 Hispanic residents, with clusters in large metropolitan areas like Metro-Dade County in Florida, New York City, Los Angeles County, and areas along the Mexican border (U.S. Census Bureau, 2009b). The rapid increase and spread of Latinos across the nation indicate a growing need for culturally sensitive and bilingual social workers in all 50 states who are proficient in culturally specific group interventions.

Latinos represent a multicultural and a multiracial group with diverse Spanish language use and expressions, migration patterns, social and economic conditions, and educational backgrounds (Padilla & Pérez, 2003). Yet, Latinos are also a single unit, in the sense that many have a common legacy evident in a shared language and cultural values. The sense of oneness is, of course, defined by context (Falicov, 1998). For example, belonging to a Latino social group can create the sense of oneness because everyone in the room values the central role of family in the same way; however, there may be differences in communication styles and belief systems within each family or among group members.

Culture, according to Lu, Lum, and Chen (2001), represents the language, religious ideals, habits of thinking, patterns of social and interpersonal relationships, prescribed ways of behaving, and norms of conduct that are passed on from generation to generation. The process of *acculturation* involves adjusting to a new environment, which holds different cultural norms, behaviors, and values from one's own (Robbins, Chatterjee, & Canda, 2006). The acculturation process is the cornerstone to understanding and addressing the intercultural differences, distress, or conflict in points of views experienced by the Latino immigrant coming to a new culture (Furman et al., 2009)—in this case, the United States. Research indicates that how an individual resolves the point of conflict or differences between two cultures is indicative of his or her emotional, mental, physical, and social well-being (Bacallao & Smokowski, 2005; Feliciano, 2001; Furman et al., 2009;

Gil, Vega, & Dimas, 1994). There are two ways of resolving the conflict: *assimilation* and *biculturalism*. When the exchange between the two cultures results in an individual giving up his or her way of life and taking on the customs and beliefs of the dominant culture, this is assimilation. Assimilation has been identified as a risk factor for increased negative health behaviors and mental health problems (Bacallao & Smokowski, 2005). Latinos who are highly assimilated struggle with identity. They drop their cultural identity and adopt the identity of the host culture to gain a sense of belonging within the dominant culture. High levels of assimilation are also associated with an increase in risky behavior (e.g., drinking, marijuana use, dropping out of high school). Therefore, assimilation is the least desired form of acculturation.

On the other hand, biculturalism, or being able to navigate both cultures comfortably without losing the culture of origin (Robbins at al., 2006), has been found to be a protective factor against the stress of acculturation (Bacallao & Smokowski, 2005). Recent waves of Latin American immigrants are living in two cultures (deAnda, 1984; Feliciano, 2001); they retain their values, beliefs, language, and behaviors while adapting to different values, beliefs, language, and behaviors of the American culture. In doing so, Latino immigrants maintain strong ties to their homeland.

Feliciano (2001) uses alternation theory—that is, fluid movement between two cultures while retaining the primary cultural identity—to explain this recent phenomenon and further points out that there are many benefits to retaining one's primary cultural identity by becoming bicultural. For instance, bicultural Latinos suffer less from acculturation stress, report stronger family pride, experience fewer occurrences of depression, and have stronger bilingual abilities (Feliciano, 2001). In addition, bicultural Latinos, in comparison to highly assimilated Latinos, reach higher levels of quality of life and better psychological adjustment (Lang, Muñoz, Bernal, & Sorenson, 1982). Therefore, by these measures, biculturalism is the optimal achievement of the acculturation process.

IMMIGRATION AND ACCULTURATION PROCESSES AND CHALLENGES

The immigration and acculturation process is accompanied by changes and stressors as one adapts to the mainstream culture of the United States. It is important for group facilitators to explore the different catalysts behind the reasons for immigration. Latinos are not a homogeneous group. Each Latino country has diverse cultures, ethnic backgrounds, and sociopolitical climates. For instance, Puerto Ricans are a mixture of Taíno Indian, Spaniards, and West Africans from the slave trade. More recently, Dominican Republican immigrants and visiting/migrating Americans from the United States who live in Puerto Rico have added to the Puerto Rican culture. The sociopolitical climate also varies from one Latino country to another. For example, Costa Rica does not have an army, while in Mexico it is common to see the military armed with automatic rifles standing among civilians on street corners.

It is essential for the group facilitator to conduct a cultural assessment of the individual group members and of the group as a whole. The clinician should ask about each individual's country of origin, length of time in the United States, and reasons for immigration (was it voluntary or did the person arrive as a refugee?). The clinician will also want to inquire about the generation status of each group member (i.e., first- or second-generation immigrant), first language learned, and dominant language spoken at home.

For group leaders interviewing prospective Latino clients for participation in group treatment, there are a number of appropriate questions that could be asked related to country of origin, conditions of migration, level of acculturation, and cultural identity. Therefore, the typical question, "What brings you here today" should go beyond the reasons for coming to that particular group and further explore the reasons for coming to the United States. One of the authors finds the following go-around technique useful when starting a group, "Before we start, let's go around; say your name, which country you are from, and how long you've been in the United States. Does everyone speak English or do some prefer Spanish?" These questions will provide the context for future discussion on acculturation, conditions of migration, and cultural identity.

Another important aspect to explore within the group is long-distance relationships with family members who remained in the country of origin. The increased access to transnational communication in the homeland affects the psychological adjustment of Latino immigrants (Falicov, 2007). For instance, the separation of various family members from one another is common in the immigration experience. One or both parents may emigrate first, leaving the children behind with a grandmother or other family members. In other situations, it is parents, siblings, aunts, and uncles who are left behind. The group leader should be aware of the impact of long distance familial relationships on individual group members. Such awareness allows the group leader to highlight the resources, strengths, and values in each group member and identify how such strengths can help with adjusting to the changes of being in the United States. Falicov (2007) identifies relational stress as being at the center of a new immigrant's experience. Alternatively, the widespread use of technology (i.e., phone cards, email, cell phones, and video conferencing) enables families to maintain emotional and economic connections across continents. These connections make it possible for immigrants to continue to feel connected and share developmental milestones with the family.

For second-generation or later-generation Latinos and those who arrive at a very young age, the challenge may not be in adapting to a new environment but, rather, in meeting family expectations that may be different from the cultural norm in the United States. For instance, in the United States, it is typical for an 18-year-old to leave home for college or work and is viewed as part of the process of individuation and independence for these young adults. However, for Latino parents and their children, leaving home can become a point of contention. The expectation in traditional Latino culture is to uphold *colectivismo* and *familismo* by maintaining close contact (i.e., attending family events and celebrating holidays together) and fulfilling responsibilities to assist other family members (Falicov, 2007). The young adult may feel torn between fulfilling his or her own desires (i.e., going on a ski trip with friends over the holidays) and upholding *colectivismo* (i.e., going home for the holidays to spend time with the family).

Another challenge later-generation Latinos may encounter is that various family members have differing levels of linguistic ability in Spanish and English. Children who stop speaking Spanish may have difficulty communicating with their grandparents. They may also be unable to read history books or sing *poesías* and songs in Spanish, which keep their country's written and oral histories alive. The significance of detaching from cultural traditions and losing the ability to read in Spanish and sing folkloric songs is that it may result in a loss of understanding and identification with one's ethnic roots and cultural history. An individual's identity is tied to his or her country's rich cultural history; therefore, cultural history influences one's worldview and cultural pride.

Additional challenges may include having family members with different levels of acculturation and exposure to institutional racism, oppression, and economic disparities. Many Latino immigrants and refugees experience the stress of poverty, a different pace of life, and social isolation (Gurman & Becker, 2008; Sorensen, López, & Andersen, 2001). The assumption that all Latinos are the same further limits the individual's growth within a cultural context. Often, there are expectations on the individual in the United States to provide financial support for family members who remain in the homeland. Further, such individuals have to learn to navigate through the immigration process to obtain a visa or permanent residency in the United States.

DIFFERENCES IN WORKING WITH IMMIGRANTS VERSUS REFUGEES

Immigration refers to those Latinos who come into the United Sates and stay. *Emigration* refers to people who leave their homeland. The term *migration* is often used to refer to one of these types of travel from one country to the next. *Refugees* are those who flee in search of refuge from war, political oppression, religious persecution, violence, or a combination. Sometimes they are forced to be in exile and are unable to have contact with family members in their country of origin.

Refugees have a particular set of experiences (i.e., escaping from political turmoil, violence, or war and applying for political asylum) that is unique to their country and that may influence group dynamics. Leaving their homeland under these circumstances may be painful and not necessarily a voluntary choice. Aside from having to adapt to a new culture and new language, Latino refugees may also be dealing with significant trauma histories, which may not be the presenting problem or the focus of the group. A group discussion may reveal diverse reasons for immigration and the hardships encountered by refugees. The facilitator of a group with Latino immigrants and refugees should not be afraid to ask about previous experiences of oppression, trauma histories, and other topics that may be taboo in their countries and in the United States. This is shown in the following excerpt from a mixed group of immigrant and refugee parents who are working on bridging cultural generational gaps with their teenage children:

Facilitator: As Latinos from diverse countries, some of us may have experienced violence, political persecution, or trauma. And in this group we're going to build up trust so that we can talk about these topics and eventually look at the strengths you have in coping and surviving these difficult situations. We may also find some commonalities between our experiences.

The above scenario was not with a trauma-focused group, yet it was important to examine how the members' immigration history may have affected their current relationships with their teenage children. Opening such a discussion can lead to group cohesion and mutuality among group members. The group then becomes a vehicle for an appropriate intervention that assists immigrants and refugees during their transition to a new country as they navigate through the acculturation process.

It is important to keep in mind the diversity of Latino immigrants, who come from 20 different Spanish-speaking countries (Bernal, Rodriguez, & Domenech, 2009). The group facilitator must be able to demonstrate skills in responding to the complex histories of group members and promote an environment of respect and acceptance of multiple worldviews; this would affirm and promote a culturally competent and responsive group intervention.

Puerto Ricans have a distinctive pattern of circular migration. They also may have an assortment of reasons for leaving the island and moving to the U.S. mainland; however, they are in a unique situation because they are U.S. citizens and passport holders. Their travel to and from Puerto Rico is done with relative ease in comparison to other immigrants, who are restricted by immigration laws limiting international movement to the United States due to visa requirements, national quotas, and financial obstacles (Deren et al., 2003). For Puerto Ricans, "circular migration" is a common pattern of movement that paints a picture of the "revolving door" relationship that often exists for many between the island and the mainland United States (Duany, 2002; López, Zerden, Fitzgerald, & Lundgren, 2008). When considering this group, it is necessary to distinguish between:

> The "one way migrants" who move permanently to the U.S. mainland; the "return migrants" who migrate to the U.S. mainland but after many years return to the Island and reestablish residence; and the "circular migrants" who migrate back and forth between the Island and the United States mainland spending substantial periods of residence in both places (Acevedo, 2004, p. 69).

Duany (2002) uses a "flying bus" metaphor, whereas Deren et al. (2003) refer to another term commonly used, an "air bridge," to illustrate the migration patterns of Puerto Ricans from the Island to the mainland, particularly in the northeast corridor.

An increasing number of recent immigrants maintain intense connections with their home countries and extended families that live there. The complexity of relationships that arise from transnational connections calls into question dominant discourses about family bonds and requires that we adopt new theory and social work treatment considerations. Falicov (2007) proposes new approaches in family therapy by focusing on three crucial contexts for work with immigrants: the relational, the community, and the cultural-sociopolitical. A relational context looks at the family system and reframes relationships and roles of family members. A community context examines the relationship between immigrants, their homelands, and the new environment and finds ways to rebuild their social capital. In a cultural-sociopolitical context, the focus is on approaches to social justice and overcoming the racism and discrimination experienced by immigrants. The group facilitator can highlight the intersection of the three contexts as members relay their stories.

MULTICULTURAL COMPETENCY AND EVIDENCE-BASED PRACTICE IN GROUP WORK WITH LATINOS

The Latino experience of immigration, adaptations, motives, challenges, and resiliency are important to understand with particular attention to how cultural changes and transitions vary within and across group membership (Falicov, 2007). The rich diversity among Latinos brings a unique perceptive to social work practice and group work. Each Latin American country, with its unique sociopolitical history, develops its own way of responding to situations that influences the way inhabitants behave within that social framework. For instance, every country has unique phrases used to express joy or concern that may be particular to that country and may not carry the same meaning in another Spanish-speaking country. Therefore, when transnational Latinos share their ideas in a group setting in the United States, the facilitators have an additional task of encouraging openness and understanding of these unique cultural identities and diverse reasons for immigration. Thus, knowledge of the social context, meanings, and consequences of those immigration patterns is essential if the group facilitator is to provide culturally competent services and support.

Cultural competency in social work practice is defined by Lu, Lum, and Chen (2001) as a "clinician's acceptance and respect for cultural differences, self analysis of one's own cultural identity and biases, awareness of the dynamics of differences in ethnic diverse groups and the need for additional knowledge research" (p. 3). The dynamics of culture are constantly changing based on the introduction of new technologies, methods of communication, and influences from outside forces, thus creating a need for new knowledge and research. Falicov (2007) emphasizes an awareness of current trends in multiculturalism as pivotal for clinicians in establishing a relationship with Latinos. Falicov also suggests that the future trend of multiculturalism will define *culture* as dynamic and *cultural identities* as fluid. Therefore, cultural competency is something that is never mastered but something that one strives for and constantly reevaluates.

In recent years, the emphasis has shifted from implementing multicultural competency models to initiating evidence-based group interventions. Evidence-based practice (EBP) is concerned with promoting effective practice through integration of the best available research with clinical expertise in the context of client characteristics (i.e., values, religious beliefs, worldviews, goals, and treatment preferences) and sociocultural factors (American Psychological Association, 2006). However, there are some limitations of EBP that every group worker should be aware of when working with Latinos.

One consideration posed by Chen, Kakkad, and Balzano (2008) is how to develop and maintain multicultural practice, on the one hand, and incorporate EBP, on the other. Similar to Falicov (2007), Chen et al. (2008) also emphasize that multicultural competence is not static but rather varies according to the specific composition of the group as well as the attributes of the group facilitator. Any discussion of developing evidence-based interventions with multicultural competence should take into account the visible or invisible diversity in the group membership, as well as the cultural background of the group facilitator. Race/ethnicity matters, and having multicultural competency will make a difference in group dynamics.

Furthermore, there are a limited number of group interventions that have been tested specifically with Latinos. This may be because, except in geographic areas where the Latino population has reached some level of critical mass, Hispanics/ Latinos present for social work services and group work in relatively small numbers compared with other Americans. Therefore, the issue of identifying best practices for Latinos has not been a pressing matter for researchers or practitioners, at least at the national level (Ortiz & Aranda, 2009). Often, when using scales or instruments, substantial psychometric work is needed before the study (Bernal & Rodriguez, 2009) to ensure linguistic and cultural accuracy. Competence to lead research efforts with ethnic minority samples requires the usual set of scientific and scholarly skills as well as added multicultural competencies. The latter may also include translations and cultural adaptations, as well as the development of bilingual instruments or measures to test the effectiveness of these interventions (Bernal et al., 2009). As the number of Latinos continues to increase, more research in this area will be needed that combines multicultural competence and EBP.

STRATEGIES AND TECHNIQUES FOR DELIVERING CULTURALLY COMPETENT GROUP INTERVENTIONS FOR LATINOS

In the group work service delivery arena, many strategies can be implemented to facilitate a program's cultural sensitivity. Ensuring that recruiting materials and group curricula are translated into Spanish, having bilingual staff available, and addressing client accessibility concerns (i.e., location of the group, transportation to group, and group meeting times) are some measures that increase a program's cultural sensitivity. It is essential to also include cultural adaptations. The term *cultural adaptation* (Whaley & Davis, 2007) refers to changes in the approach to providing services, in the nature or expression of the therapeutic relationship, or in components of the treatment itself to accommodate the cultural beliefs, attitudes, and behaviors of the target group member.

In a culturally diverse group, assessment of acculturation level, conceptualizations of health and mental health, and the experience of physical or emotional symptoms within different contexts (i.e., school, family, and work) should be considered for each individual member and for the group as a whole. Groups are most successful when both the facilitator and individual members agree on the treatment goals and form a strong therapeutic alliance (Chen et al., 2008); consequently, cultural differences, roles, and alliances will need to be examined.

Specific Techniques

- Story circles/storytelling in groups creates a space for members to listen and share personal migration experiences, relationship building across cultural lines, collective problem solving, and social action.
- Group work enhances opportunities for learning about one's ethnic heritage through creative artistic expressions, with special formats such as theatre groups, video making, art work, and/or paintings. This is also effective when English is not the first language of the group members.
- Integrating culturally specific and/or culturally adapted curricula for structured, time-limited psychoeducational groups also strengthens and increases the effectiveness of group work with Latinos.

THEMES AND CONCEPTS IN WORKING WITH LATINOS

There are different concepts that express cultural values that are particular to the Latino community. Different authors have defined these concepts as follows:

1. *Collectivism and individualism*—often focusing on family traditions and rituals, emphasizing "close nurturing and supportive interpersonal relationships." It is valued in most Latino cultures over *individualism*, which is a more prominent value in mainstream U.S. culture (Acevedo, 2008; Mason, Marks, Simoni, Ruiz, & Richardson, 1995, p. 7). *Collectivism* points to Latinos' tendency to think of collective well-being (i.e., that of the family) over one's individual needs.
2. *Familismo/familism*—a deeply ingrained sense of being rooted in the family. The term refers to attitudes, behaviors, and family structures within an extended family system (Acevedo, 2008). The family is the primary unit within Latino culture. Sometimes it also involves a sense of responsibility or obligation to support the family emotionally and materially (Mason et al., 1995, p. 7).
3. *Personalismo*—a cultural concept that guides interpersonal relationships, highlighting Latinos' desire for intimate, personal relationships, and individualized attention (Galanti, 2003).
4. *Simpatía*—refers to the desire for Latinos to maintain harmony, politeness, and respect in relationships (Mason et al., 1995). Members of a group may disagree with a point of view but avoid verbalizing their concern for fear of conflict or being disrespectful to others. *Simpatía* is a cultural concept that can be applied to familial or nonfamilial interpersonal relationships and emphasizes the need for promoting behaviors that result in pleasant social interactions and harmony in interpersonal relationships (Varela, Sanchez-Sosa, Biggs, & Luis, 2008).
5. *Respeto*—Respect for individuals, especially for figures of authority or older adults. Participants may not raise questions or express different point of views to a social worker, group leader, or a person in authority to avoid being disrespectful (Gurman & Becker, 2008).

These concepts are part of a Latino's cultural identity, but they vary according to acculturation level, age, gender, national origin, sexual orientation, geographic region and rural-versu-urban focus, and other related factors (Delgado, 2001, 2007). Research on help-seeking behaviors has shown that Latinos most often turn to community members, and particularly indigenous leaders, before contacting formal helping networks (Delgado, 2007). Group recruitment strategies may incorporate community leaders in a participatory process. As trusted members of the community, the community leader accompanies the group facilitator in his/her outreach and recruitment efforts. They can help identify potential members and promote the group.

Case Examples: Latino Groups

The following two scenarios illustrate the application of the above cultural concepts and multicultural competencies.

Scenario 1: This group consists of 10 Latino members from various Central American countries and a Latino facilitator, a seemingly homogeneous group. However, is any group truly homogeneous? Each member brought his or her past and present experiences into the group, such as different age of entry into the United States, length of residence in the state or region, exposure to racism, and perception of acceptance into their new community. In this group, there were also differing socioeconomic levels and retention of cultural traditions in the home. About five members retained cultural traditions, three kept very few traditions, and two did not celebrate any cultural traditions. The members' relationship with family members who remained in the home country also followed diverse patterns of long distance communication.

How is the topic of diversity and openness to different points of view encouraged in this group? How do these differences impact group dynamics?

The first task for the group leader is to foster a safe environment by establishing guidelines for expressing different ideas and beliefs without making assumptions—for instance, stating that members may have different levels of comfort speaking Spanish or English. The group facilitator may initiate a discussion about the preferred language to be used in the group. Would only Spanish be spoken or both Spanish and English? There may be different levels of fluency among group members, which can affect group dynamics. What if the group agrees to speak in Spanish yet there are a few second-generation Latinos who have a lower level of fluency? There are also many sayings, or *dichos*, that are particular to certain Spanish-speaking countries. There is the potential for a group member to misinterpret another member because the *dicho* means something different to him or her. On the other hand, some people may be more comfortable expressing feelings in Spanish and they may not be able to express themselves as easily in English. Group facilitators or group members should offer to translate in these situations.

Scenario 2: The group members are all Latinos and the facilitator is white but speaks Spanish fluently. What kind of dynamics could occur in this type of group? There can be a certain level of acceptance of the facilitator as "one of us." She or he has learned the language and is open to the Latino culture, although, at the same time, some members may feel the facilitator cannot understand everyone's perspective because she or he did not grow up in a

Latino family. The facilitator may be open but may also miss a cultural reference mentioned in the group. In this case, it would be important for the group leader to encourage the members to be open about this. It is not the sole responsibility of the facilitator to bring attention to something that was missed in the group. All the members can participate and assist in this process. Relationship building is important in all groups, but especially in Latino groups because of their collective-oriented culture. Emphasis on developing trust and openness in the group would encourage the sharing of each member's individual ideas.

In addition, the use of self is a key element for the group facilitator. The facilitator may share personal experiences more openly if they are related to the purpose and goals for the group. Self-disclosure may also convey to the group that the facilitator has a sense of respect toward the group's values and goals (Camacho, 2001). A Latino facilitator may share more openly about his or her own migratory experience, while a member of a different ethnic group may share their experiences as a non-Latino who is open to learning more about the Latino culture.

RECOMMENDATIONS FOR GROUP PRACTICE WITH LATINOS

To work effectively with the Latino population today, social workers must be able to acknowledge and value their diversity (Camacho, 2001). A goal of conducting culturally diverse groups is that the facilitator will embrace differences among members because Latino groups will rarely be homogeneous. Further, members can learn different ways of relating to each other and develop effective problem-solving strategies—the diversity of membership can be used as group strength if the leader highlights this in an effective way.

Groups are microcosms of communities. Understanding why the members came to a particular group and what expectations they hold is part of assessing the appropriateness of the member for group participation and possible differences among group members. Some members join groups with individuals from the same cultural or ethnic group because they feel they will find support and understanding from individuals who have had similar experiences, yet they may not be prepared to handle the diversity they discover within a group of people with similar identities (Camacho, 2001).

Members in diverse groups worry about their sense of belonging and their capacity to influence the group's purpose. According to Schiller (2007), groups are characterized by the members' need for inclusion during the beginning phase and by the development of a relational model, where there is intimacy, interdependence, and separation among members, during later stages. Members who identify strongly with a subgroup or subgraoups may feel in the minority despite being a part of the group's majority. For example, "a member whose country of origin is Colombia may feel that he or she does not have the same degree of influence in a group of mostly Puerto Rican or Mexican members" (Camacho, 2001, p. 137). Helping the group develop trust and acceptance of each member's cultural assets could make a significant difference in the success of the group.

BENEFITS OF GROUP WORK AND RESILIENCY BUILDING WITH LATINOS

- Group work provides a source of social networking and social support and decreases isolation for immigrants and refugees.
- Groups are mechanisms for addressing intergenerational gaps within Latino families.
- Support groups highlight the member's inner strengths in the process of leaving his or her country of origin and adapting to a new culture and new environments.
- Group work offers a medium for interpersonal learning where experienced immigrants share their knowledge, with those with less time residing in the United States.
- Participation in groups increases knowledge of and access to local health services, education, job training programs, and housing and employment opportunities.
- Group work connects members of similar backgrounds and affirms one's ethnic self-concept in the United States.

EVALUATION

A very limited number of evaluation tools have been developed specifically for Latinos. Often, validated English tools are translated into Spanish. However, these translations have to take into account the linguistic level of the group members. Such tools may also have to incorporate specific cultural terminology or less academic language; some words may also be added that are from a particular country or region. For example, in a psychoeducational group, when asked about level of knowledge of HIV transmission, a Spanish translation may use the words *propagar*, *transmitir*, or *pasar el virus*. *Pasar* is a more common or familiar term than *propagar*. All these terms could be included in a questionnaire. For recent immigrants, the use of symbols or drawings may be another mechanism that could be helpful in an evaluation tool. For example, on a questionnaire assessing the level of satisfaction with the group process, drawings that represent being happy, satisfied, sad, or frustrated could be included to ensure that the respondent understands the concept.

The drawings might also reflect the ethnicity of the group members.

The use of some clinical terms may also carry some stigma. For example, in the following question, "Have you felt depressed in the last 30 days?" there may be cultural taboos and stigma in the disclosure of depression and the phrasing of the question may not capture accurate responses. Asking the question with more focus on somatic symptoms, such as, "Have you felt down, very sad, or without energy?" may yield more accurate results.

Despite limited tools, evaluation is an important component of group practice. Members may need to be reassured that the tools are only going to be used for the group leader's benefit in understanding the success of the group and that their responses will not affect the service they receive from the agency in any way.

RESOURCES

The following are web resources on evidence-based group curriculums that may be helpful in working with Latinos.

http://www.cdc.gov/hiv/topics/prev_prog/rep/packages/!cuidate!.htm
¡*Cuídate!* is a six-session psychoeducation group aimed at increasing Latino youth's HIV/AIDS knowledge. Topics (i.e., condom negotiation, refusal of sex, and correct condom use skills) are introduced through the use of interactive games, group discussion, role-plays, video, music, and mini-lectures.

http://www.effectiveinterventions.org/go/interventions/voices-/-voces
Voices/Voces is a single-session group curriculum that targets African American and Latino men and women. The purpose of the group is to increase condom use. The video is available in English and Spanish.

http://www.seekingsafety.org/3-03-06/aboutSS.html
En Busca de la Seguridad (Seeking Safety, by Lisa Najavitz, PhD) is a trauma/ PTSD and substance abuse group cognitive/behavioral group that has been translated into Spanish. It covers 25 topics on how to seek safety in your life. The group can be used with female, male, and mixed-gender groups.

http://www.eric.ed.gov/ERICWebPortal/custom/portlets/recordDetails/detailmini. jsp?_nfpb=true&_&ERICExtSearch_SearchValue_0=ED303541&ERICExtS earch_SearchType_0=no&accno=ED303541

This is a teaching unit composed of 11 lessons that can be easily adapted to develop a psychoeducation group. It emphasizes a strengths based approach to developing self-esteem in youths in grades 5 through 8.

http://www.ncbi.nlm.nih.gov/sites/entrez?Db=pubmed&Cmd=Search&Term=%22Aviera%20A%22%5BAuthor%5D&itool=EntrezSystem2.PEntrez.Pubmed.Pubmed_ResultsPanel.Pubmed_DiscoveryPanel.Pubmed_RVAbstractPlus

Dichos is a therapy group that provided therapeutic use of the Spanish language. *Dichos*, or sayings, are used to engage participants in discussing a wide range of issues through the use of cultural and familial relevance, vivid imagery, and flexibility, to build rapport and decrease defensiveness.

http://www.cdc.gov/hiv/hispanics/index.htm

The latest information on Hispanics/Latinos and HIV/AIDS from the Centers for Disease Control and Prevention, this site also links to other useful resources and information on the composition of Hispanics/Latinos in the United States and Puerto Rico.

REFERENCES

Acevedo, G. (2004). Neither here nor there: Puerto Rican circular migration. In D. Drachman, & A. Paulino (eds.), *Immigrants and social work: Thinking beyond the borders of the United States* (pp. 69–85). New York: The Haworth Social Work Practice Press.

Acevedo, V. (2008) Cultural competence in a group intervention designed for Latino patients living with HIV/AIDS. *Health & Social Work, 33*(2), 111–120.

American Psychological Association Presidential Task Force on Evidence-Based Practice. (2006). Evidence-based practice in psychology. *American Psychologist, 61*, 271–285.

Bacallao, M. L. & Smokowski, P. R. (2005). "Entre dos mundos" (between two worlds): Bicultural skills training with Latino immigrant families. *The Journal of Primary Prevention, 26*(6), 485–509.

Bernal, G. & Rodriguez, M. (2009). Advances in Latino family research: Cultural adaptations of evidence-based interventions. *Family Process, 48*(2), 169–178.

Bernal, G., Rodriguez, M., & Domenech, M. (2009). Advances in Latino family research: Cultural adaptations of evidence-based interventions. *Family Process, 48*, 169–178.

Camacho, S. (2001) Addressing conflict rooted in diversity: The role of the facilitator. *Social Work with Groups, 24*(3/4) 135–152.

Centers for Disease Control and Prevention. (2004). HIV/AIDS among Hispanics. Retrieved February 19, 2006, from http://www.cdc.gov/hiv/pubs/facts/hispanic.htm

Chen, E., Kakkad, D., & Balzano, J. (2008). Multicultural competence and evidence-based practice in group therapy. *Journal of Clinical Psychology, 64*(11), 1261–1278.

deAnda, D. (1984). Bicultural socialization: Factors affecting the minority experience. *Social Work, 29*(2), 101–107.

Delgado, M. (2001). *Where are all the young men and women of color? Capacity enhancement practice and the criminal justice system.* New York: Columbia University Press.

Delgado, M. (2007). *Social work with Latinos: A cultural assets paradigm.* New York: Oxford University Press.

Deren, S., Oliver-Vélez, D., Finlinson, A., Robles, R., Andia, J., Colón, H., et al. (2003). Integrating qualitative and quantitative methods: Comparing HIV-related risk behaviors among Puerto Rican drug users in Puerto Rico and New York. *Substance Use and Misuse, 38*(1), 1–24.

Duany, J. (2002). *Puerto Rican nation on the move: Identities on the Island and in the United States.* Chapel Hill, NC: University of North Carolina Press.

Falicov, C. (2007). Working with transnational immigrants: Expanding meanings of family, community, and culture. *Family Process 46*:157–171.

Falicov, C. (1998). *Latino families in therapy: A guide to multicultural practice.* Guilford: New York.

Feliciano, C. (2001). The benefits of biculturalism: Exposure to immigrant culture and dropping out of school among Asian and Latino youths. *Social Science Quarterly, 82*(4), 865–879.

Furman, R., Negi, N. J., Iwamoto, D. K., Rowan, D., Shukraft, A., & Graff, J. (2009). Social work practice with Latinos: Key issues for social workers. *Journal of Social Work, 54*(2), 167–174.

Galanti, G. (2003). The Hispanic family and male-female relationships: An overview. *Journal of Transcultural Nursing, 14*{3), 180–185.

Gil, A. G., Vega, W. A., & Dimas, J. M. (1994). Acculturative stress and personal adjustment among Hispanic adolescent boys. *Journal of Community Psychology, 22*(1), 43–54.

Gurman, T. & Becker, D. (2008). Factors affecting Latina immigrants' perceptions of maternal health care: Findings from a qualitative study. *Health Care for Women International, 29*, 507–526.

Lang, J. G., Muñoz, R., Bernal, G., & Sorensen, J. (1982). Quality of life and psychological well-being in a bicultural Latino community. *Hispanic Journal of Behavioral Sciences, 4*, 433–450.

López, L., Zerden, L. Fitzgerald, T., & Lundgren, L. (2008). Capacity enhancement prevention model for Puerto Rican injection drug users in Massachusetts and Puerto Rico. *Evaluation and Program and Planning Journal, 31*, 64–73.

Lu, Y. E., Lum, D., & Chen, S. (2001). Cultural competency and achieving styles in clinical social work practice: A conceptual and empirical exploration. *Journal of Ethnic and Cultural Diversity in Social Work, 9*(3/4), 1–32.

Mason, H. R. C., Marks, G., Simoni, J. M., Ruiz, M. S., & Richardson, J. L. (1995). Culturally sanctioned secrets? Latino men's nondisclosure of HIV infection to family, friends, and lovers. *Health Psychology, 14*(1), 6–12.

Ortiz, L. & Aranda, M. (2009). Guest editorial for special issue on "Intervention outcome research with Latinos: Social work's contributions." *Research on Social Work Practice, 19*(2); 149–151.

Padilla, A. & Perez, W. (2003). Acculturation, social identity and social cognition: A new perspective. *Hispanic Journal of Behavioral Sciences, 25*(1), 35–55.

Robbins, S. P., Chatterjee, P., & Canda, E. R. (2006). *Contemporary human behavior theory: A clinical perspective for social work.* Boston: Pearson.

Schiller, L. Y. (2007). Not for women only: Applying the Relational Model of group development with vulnerable populations. *Social Work with Groups, 30*(2), 11–26.

Sorensen, W., Lopez, L., & Anderson, P. (2001). Latino AIDS immigrants in the Western Gulf States: A different population and the need for innovative prevention strategies. *Journal of Health & Social Policy, 13*(1), 1–19.

U.S. Census Bureau. (2009a). Census Bureau estimates nearly half of children under age 5 are minorities: Estimates find nation's population growing older, more diverse [Press Release]. Retrieved July 30, 2009, from http://www.census.gov/Press-Release/www/releases/archives/population/013733.html

U.S. Census Bureau. (2009b). Census Bureau releases state and county data depicting nation's population ahead of 2010 census: Orange, Fla., joins the growing list of 'majority-minority' counties [Press Release]. Retrieved July 30, 2009, from http://www.census.gov/PressRelease/www/releases/archives/population/013734.html

Varela, E., Sanchez-Sosa, J., Biggs, B., & Luis, T. (2009). Parenting strategies and sociocultural influences in childhood anxiety: Mexican, Latin American descent, and European American families. *Journal of Anxiety Disorders, 23*(5), 609–616.

Whaley, A. L. & Davis, K. E. (2007). Cultural competence and evidence-based practice in mental health services: A complementary perspective. *American Psychologist, 62*, 563–574.

Chapter Eight

Group Work With Operation Enduring Freedom and Operation Iraqi Freedom Combat Veterans[1]

Julie A. Ellis and Matt Camardese

Nearly 1.64 million service members have been deployed in the Operation Enduring Freedom and Operation Iraqi Freedom (OEF/OIF) conflicts since 2001. Many of these men and women have been exposed to prolonged periods of combat, leading to combat stress and multiple exposures to traumatic events (The Rand Corporation, 2008). Veterans returning home from war must make many adjustments to reintegrate into their families, communities, and work environments. Based on initial research studies, data from the U.S. Department of Defense (DoD), and information available through the U.S. Department of Veterans Affairs (DVA), we know that "over 29,000 of those deployed have been physically wounded, but many more return from deployments with mental health symptoms" (Batten & Pollack, 2008). These mental health symptoms can manifest in a variety of ways and may emerge immediately or several years after deployment. Intervention through the use of groups can help reduce the impact of these potentially chronic symptoms in new veterans (Hoge et al., 2004). We first discuss some of the issues returning veterans experience and then describe a group designed to assist veterans with these issues.

WHO ARE VETERANS OF TWENTIETH CENTURY WARS, AND WHAT DO THEY EXPERIENCE?

Veterans can be categorized into three main groups: Active Duty (AD), United States National Guard (USNG) and Individual Ready Reserves (IRR). During peacetime, the AD component secures our land and our seas by working in their respective roles in the military. During peacetime, those in the USNG and IRR serve on active duty status one weekend a month and 1 weeks a year, while the rest of their time is spent as civilians. "Up to 30% serving in OEF/OIF are USNG and

IRR troops" (Waterhouse & Bryant, 2008). The wars in Afghanistan and Iraq are relying heavily on USNG and IRR personnel to maintain appropriate combat power in the overseas operations. Many of these troops have experienced multiple deployments; some are currently participating in their fourth or fifth combat tour. The experience of the USNG/IRR veterans varies from the AD service member. The USNG/IRR leave their home, civilian employment, and family to fulfill their commitment and duty to the country for a specified period of time. These individuals are brought together from different geographic locations. After their tour of active duty, they return to their life and often have difficulty reacculturating. They can feel isolated because they are not surrounded by the men and women with whom they spent the past several months and who understand what they have experienced. The AD component has a somewhat different experience, whereby the military member returns from war still surrounded by his or her battle buddies. The people the AD service member served with during deployment are the same men and women with whom they work on a day-to-day basis. They all have had similar experiences and have a clearer understanding of the adversities that have been faced while at war. The AD component faces the difficulties of readjustment together when returning home. All combat veterans are returning to their home communities typically with a sense of "meaning and gratification in their helper roles in Iraq and Afghanistan" (Litz, 2009, p. 2) but often to an environment that is no longer familiar. Repeat deployments increase stress and strain on the service member and family exponentially (The Rand Corporation, 2008). These individuals typically have changed views of themselves, others, and their world.

This changed world view is not a surprise. These men and women have survived in a war zone from 6 to 18 months at a time with little or no break or relief. "There is no safe place and no safe role. Soldiers are required to maintain an unprecedented degree of vigilance and to respond cautiously to threats" (Litz, 2009, p. 1). While at war, these men and women develop "battlemind." Battlemind consists of combat skills and a battle mindset that sustains survival in the combat zone (Walter Reed Army Institute of Research, 2006). War/combat skills are necessary to remain safe and to accomplish the mission. These war skills must be transitioned into skills for home once the service member returns from battle to avoid their taking a toll on social and behavioral health (Walter Reed Army Institute of Research 2006). Once the service member returns home, the battlemind mentality typically remains for a period of time while the war skills are transitioned into productive home skills. For example, battlemind keeps the service member alert, surveying the area for threats such as sniper fire or mortar attacks. She or he is trained to be unpredictable and to avoid open exposure unless necessary. This skill once returning home may make the service member feel keyed up or anxious in large groups or situations where he or she may feel confined. The service member may find herself continually scanning her surroundings (e.g., home, mall, etc.) for possible threats. The act of continual scanning and alertness is known as tactical awareness; should this skill remain highly intact after returning from the battlefield, it may result in hypervigilance at home. Battlemind can be controlled over time by learning how to relax, by monitoring tendencies toward escalation, and by evaluating the reactions to minor events.

A case example of the battlemind mentality is represented by "Mr. Smith." Mr. Smith has returned home from deployment and is back at work. He and his family are attempting to return to normal, which, for most families, includes predictability in their routines. Mr. Smith works 10 minutes from his home. His wife has noticed that he returns from work anywhere from 10 minutes to 90 minutes late each night but knows he does not work over-time. After a few weeks, she approached Mr. Smith, who answered that he takes one of several routes home from work on a given night; he does this so that his patterns are not predictable or easily tracked. Mr. Smith explained that taking different routes home made him and his family less of a target, keeping them safe. Ms. Smith was initially relieved to hear this explanation but later became concerned that Mr. Smith's fears and actions might be prob-lematic. She was able to share her concerns with him. Through additional time and reflection, Mr. Smith was able to understand his wife's concern and recognize that continued use of this skill over time at home might not be healthy. Mr. Smith and his wife agreed to seek readjustment counseling.

In *Courage after Fire: Coping Strategies for Troops Returning from Iraq and Afghanistan and Their Families*, Armstrong, Best, and Domenici (2006) review the positive and negative effects of war and outline common reactions when transi-tioning from combat to home. These issues may include anxiety, hyperarousal, anger, and isolation. During deployment, adrenalin levels are much higher than normal to keep the service member battle ready. These increased adrenalin levels may partly speak to why many returning veterans partake in thrill-seeking and risk-taking behaviors. Clinicians and family members may notice that the veteran has an increased desire for immediate gratification, perhaps stemming from anxi-ety and hypervigilance. These symptoms have implications for treatment regi-mens, as the veteran may not stick with traditional treatment programs or the services that he or she sought. Returning veterans may have difficulty going back to work and with reintegration processes as a result.

While research suggests that most trauma survivors experience some posttrau-matic stress disorder (PTSD) symptoms soon after a traumatic event, these symp-toms abate after a few months at home (Blanchard, Jones-Alexander, Buckley, & Forneris, 1996: Riggs, Rothbaum, & Foa, 1995). It is important to assist these service members in making sense of their experiences, providing validation and education, and normalizing some of the symptoms they are experiencing. Social workers have the opportunity to support these men and women in their reintegra-tion by allowing each time to process their experiences, exploring their battlemind skills, and assisting them in finding equilibrium in their "new normal." Consideration must be made regarding the support system for these returning veterans and inclu-sion of them in their treatment. Their recovery and reintegration to "normal" must encompass not only their trauma issues but also their relationship and work issues. "Problems with family relationships, relationships with other people or day-to-day life should not be overlooked" (National Center for Posttraumatic Stress Disorder, 2006, p. 4). With the family being the primary source of support for the returning soldier, there is risk of disengagement from the family at time of return from a war zone.

Roles and responsibilities within the family have changed. Children have grown up and developed new social skills. The spouse has taken on more responsibilities and control of the family while the veteran is away. The service member has changed as well. A challenge for everyone in the family is learning how to reconnect and establish a new normal. When the veteran returns home, the spouse might be eager to return many responsibilities to the veteran, and the veteran may not be ready to accept them. Conversely, the veteran may desire to take over their previous roles/responsibilities and the home spouse may want change the way tasks were done prior to the veteran's deployment. Children become used to the "home" parent disciplining and caring for them; when the returning veteran attempts to discipline them, it may be met with resistance. The returning veteran may feel very isolated when at home and may wish to spend time with battle buddies rather than with family and friends. Everyone in the family needs to acclimate to a new family pattern that works for all involved (National Center for Posttraumatic Stress Disorder, 2006). Problems with acute stress disorder and PTSD can cause difficulty with the competency and comfort the returning solder experiences as a parent and partner (Ruzek et al., 2004). Returning service members need to relearn how to feel safe and trusting, and family members need to feel they can connect with and are important to the service member. Screening for problematic behaviors when working with these men and women and their families is important (Hankin et al., 1999). Consider extending treatment to spouses, children, parents, or whoever is included in their immediate support system. "Support for the veteran and family can increase the potential for the veteran's smooth immediate or eventual reintegration back into family life, and reduce the likelihood of future more damaging problems (Ruzek et al., 2004, p. 8).

As the Iraq and Afghanistan conflicts continue, returning service members seeking care will benefit from a holistic and integrated system of services. OEF/OIF service members are sustaining traditional battle injuries and being exposed to new challenges and conditions due to intense blast exposures, urban warfare, and multiple and prolonged deployments. "Current battlefields produce a wide variety of injuries ranging from dermatological irritants to penetrating wounds, burns, complex fractures, and severe musculoskeletal strains" (Brown, 2008, p. 344.) In addition to these physical wounds, psychological and traumatic brain injuries are to be considered. The physical injuries of war such as amputations, burns, and fractures are easily seen and treated. The others are not. Some data suggest that the psychological toll of the deployments may be significantly higher than the toll of physical injuries (The Rand Corporation, 2008.) Nearly one-third of OEF/OIF veterans treated at the VA between the years 2001 and 2005 were diagnosed with mental health and/or psychosocial problems. In addition, one-fifth were diagnosed with a substance use disorder (National Survey on Drug Use and Health, 2005).

Multiple studies have evaluated OEF/OIF veterans and the effects of combat. Up to 42% of the Iraq veterans are estimated to need mental health care (Miliken, Auchterlonie, & Hoge, 2007). In 2007, the White House formed the President's Commission on Care for America's returning Wounded Warriors. The Commission's best estimates are that PTSD of varying degrees of severity affects 12% to 20% of returnees from Iraq and 6% to 11% of returnees from Afghanistan. There is increasing concern about the incidence of suicide attempts and suicide (Kang & Bullman, 2008), as well as concern about increased rates of depression (The Rand Corporation, 2008.)

The military branches have instituted suicide-prevention programs in the hope of educating service members about the warning signs and broadening the discussion regarding resources available to assist them or their battle buddy. Additionally, the VA has expanded their mental health services and outreach to all veterans. The VA has developed a program specifically for the returning combat veteran. Staff members provide screening, treatment, and education for veterans and their families. Outreach is provided through multiple contacts by the VA staff as the service member is leaving active duty. Additionally, VA staff offer workshops and classes in the community, partner with local organizations and groups, and participate in local events in the hope of reaching the returning veterans where they live and work.

Many service members never seek mental health services because of numerous stigmatic barriers and the impact that diagnosis may have on their career. Service members believe that mental health care or a diagnosis may affect their future security clearance, which is essential in remaining in the service. They may also worry that peers will question their reliability in future combat situations and that family members will see mental health issues as a weakness rather than an injury. The Department of Defense recognizes these issues and the resistance many service members have toward mental health services. Although stigma deters many soldiers from accessing mental health care, studies show that spouses are often more willing to seek care for themselves or their soldier-partner, making them important in early intervention strategies (Miliken, Auchterlonie, & Hoge, 2007). There is growing research evaluating the effects of deployment on familial relationships and the effects that social supports can have in mitigating negative consequences of war. The Department of Defense and the Department of Veterans Affairs have partnered to develop a program for returning veterans, where they and their fellow service members, as well as their family members, participate in reintegration and reunion workshops. These reintegration seminars provide a great deal of education to the service member and family, to raise awareness, provide information and resources, as well as to initiate discussions regarding historically difficult issues such as PTSD, financial difficulties, and others. The Department of Defense is committed to transforming its culture by emphasizing that seeking treatment is an act of courage and strength. The Marines, for example, have begun embedding a mental health professional in combat units before, during, and after service in Iraq and Afghanistan. The goal is to build trust and rapport of the clinician among the Marines, by providing continuity and familiarity.

OEF/OIF veterans have some unique characteristics in comparison to veterans from prior wars—OEF/OIF service members are generally younger, more likely to be female, less likely to be married or divorced, and more often are working (Fontana & Rosenheck, 2008). Fontana and Rosenheck (2008) also describe this new group of veterans as being more socially integrated than their veteran predecessors, and they also report higher levels of violence, alcohol abuse, and drug abuse. Identification of all these characteristics becomes important in identifying new treatment strategies for work with this group.

Returning veterans present with a myriad of issues that typically encompass relationship and familial issues, difficulties returning to and maintaining gainful employment, questions regarding their identity and self view, and struggles with anger, rage, and the legal consequences that sometimes stem from these struggles. These and countless other issues provide opportunities in group work to focus on their strengths and challenges. Returning veterans do not want the symptoms or the diagnosis to define them. They may recognize that their rage, anger, or inability to connect with others is problematic but are often unable to commit to consistent treatment, a hallmark symptom of PTSD. It is not unusual for a clinician to hear, "I wish there was just a pill to make all of this better." The goals of treatment should be aimed at helping veterans gain meaning and an understanding of what has occurred, aiding them in learning new coping strategies. Additionally, treatment should help to foster strengths and a focus on the positive aspects of life, while also helping them to accept limitations and minimize destructive behaviors. To help connect veterans and their families to services, treatments may have to be available during nonconventional hours.

Deployments are difficult at best; veterans' families are faced with adjusting to the deployment of a loved one, as well as with the readjustment of that person returning to home and attempting to again find his or her place in the relationship. Often readjustment groups are a meaningful and productive way to assist these returning veterans while also providing them an opportunity to come together in a space where others speak their common language, hear their common themes and issues, and understand the code and honor of the military.

PRACTICE PRINCIPLES

The group discussed in the following pages takes place at the Baltimore VA Medical Center. The group, "Courage After Fire," is open to most OEF/OIF veterans who are enrolled in the VA Maryland Health Care System. Group participants may be self-referred but are most often referred after a thorough psychosocial intake assessment by a trained clinician, which is sometimes the second author (to be referred to as the leader). If the veteran did not receive his intake from the leader, then the intake notes are reviewed for each referral by the leader to ensure that it is an appropriate referral. Veterans with active substance abuse disorders are encouraged to address their substance abuse before attending the group or to come after some considerable progress in treatment. Those with a serious mental illness, such as schizophrenia, may not be a good fit for the group. Considerations, though, are made on a case-by-case basis.

The Courage After Fire group follows a seven-session cycle where each session aims to address a common readjustment issue. In order, the seven sessions are: 1) Readjusting to Civilian Life, 2) Strengthening Your Mind and Body, 3) Coping Strategies, 4) Grief and Loss, 5) Changed Views of Self, Others and the World, 6) Returning to Civilian Life, and 7) Restoring Family Roles and Relationships. After the seventh session, the cycle repeats. It is an open group so members may enter at any point during the cycle. This works well because the sessions do not necessarily build on each other. The group provides both psychoeducation and mutual support. While the topic of each session frames the discussion, other topics may be raised.

There is no formalized contracting, as with closed groups, just a brief recap of the rules when a new member starts. Clear instructions and information are given to the veteran at the intake and prior to attendance at the first group. In this manner, the veteran has a sense of what the group may be able to offer and what topics will be discussed. Potential referrals are typically given flyers on the group, or the intake clinician may see if the leader is available for a brief screening with the veteran to prepare the veteran for the group. The leader's contact information is also on the flyer and potential members are free to call with any questions or concerns. Educating staff is a critical element in the process, so they are able to refer and educate potential members appropriately. The leader of the group is not a veteran. This distinction is offered at the outset of the group, while also highlighting 3 years of experience working with the OEF/OIF population. The purpose of this is to communicate some degree of familiarity with the population, while pointing out that only the members can really "know" what it is like to be deployed to a war zone. Just as with any population at risk, a good group leader does not need to be part of the population receiving services as long as the leader acknowledges this and comes from a place of wanting to help and to understand. Those leaders without substantial experience working with the population must become familiar with military culture and the specifics of current military engagements. This can be done by interviewing nonclient veterans and using good sources on the Internet or in professional journals. The point is to demonstrate a working knowledge that reflects a stance of caring about the issues faced by the population, while not mistaking researched knowledge with experience.

Even within the group, experiences vary. Some members may have been exposed to heavy combat during an invasion campaign, while others may have served their time onboard a ship near Kuwait. Still others may have been treating injured service members on the battlefield or in a nearby medical facility. The variety of experiences and differences adds value to the group.

While many assume that the group would be composed mainly of men in their 20s, the group members on a given day are an accurate snapshot of the population based on several demographics. Usually there are one or two officers, while the rest served as enlisted personnel. Several women with exposure to combat are apt to attend. Group members range in age from the early 20s to the late 50s, and the veterans may have been on one deployment or several. Some members appear to have some degree of affluence, while others have been referred by the Homeless program. Some members will head to jobs or to their families after the group, while others will spend the rest of the day at the VA attending to their other needs. The common bond among all group members is that each individual is currently experiencing some sort of difficulty readjusting to civilian life.

The leader and other clinicians at the VA noted that it was increasingly difficult to keep members of this population engaged in mental or behavioral health treatment for extended periods of time. Yet the demand for services within the population is increasing, perhaps due to greater societal awareness of common readjustment issues and reduced stigma about seeking mental health services.

The group meets for 1.5 hours once a week from 8:30 AM to 10:00 AM each Monday. This time was chosen due to staff and meeting room availability and after carefully considering data collected through client surveys, needs assessments, and anecdotal evidence that suggested early morning appointment times were most likely to be kept. The group leader begins with a brief self-introduction, highlighting the leader's nonveteran status and experience working with the population. After this, group rules and confidentiality requirements are outlined by the leader. The leader explains that he must breach confidentiality for certain client reports, such as threatening harm to self or other. Members are encouraged to be "respectful" of others in the room. The leader asks the members to take turns making introductions and to share what brought them to the group that day. It may be easier to ask one of the members of the group who has previously presented and appeared to benefit from the group, so that he or she can perhaps serve as a model to newer members. The author has found that being somewhat vague about expected deportment allows space for each member to genuinely express thoughts and feelings about experiences that only a fellow veteran can come close to understanding. In this sense, rules are enforced only to ensure safety, comfort, and some degree of order, without intimating that the members will be unruly or act as "crazy veterans," which is a message many members report receiving frequently. The members are all familiar with the expectations of proper deportment from their military days, so making excessive rules for group behavior may serve to limit a member's willingness to enter more taboo areas, where they may need the most support or constructive feedback from a peer. By setting a respectful tone as the group leader and generally being warm and open, the members will tend to follow this lead. A mutual respect exists among the members that crosses racial, gender, age, and service branch differences to allow for less formalized rule setting. The members often report that civilians cannot "understand" what it is like to have served in a combat zone. The leader can use this point to direct questions back to the group and reenforce the group's importance, because the experts on their situation are in the room. Often, the group leader begins by introducing a vignette and then assumes a peripheral position and only offers a few "hmmms" and questions for the remainder of the session. At the end of the group, members are asked to check out and share what they liked or did not like about the group. This leader has noted that members will typically mingle for several minutes after the group in a hallway. This time of engaging is neither discouraged nor encouraged and has occurred naturally from the inception of the group. Typically, lighter subjects are discussed, or a more experienced group member will assist a newer client in navigating the VA system or by offering support in another way. Some members request time individually with the leader to discuss a certain aspect of their care. If the leader has the time, the issue can be addressed then, or another time may be offered. Some members will complete the cycle and continue into another cycle, while others may come once or twice a month. Additional services, such as an appointment with a medication provider or referral to another treatment program, are offered on an as-needed basis.

COMMON THEMES

Feeling Alone

Perhaps the most common theme reported at intake, and in the group, is a sense of feeling alone or that nobody understands them, not even their loved ones. The group offers a place for the veteran to gain a sense of being understood and not alone in the world with his or her readjustment issues. The leader attempts to foster openness in the group and typically will verbalize at the beginning of group that this sense of aloneness, or isolation, is common to make the members aware that they are all in the same boat. Often, members will report that the group is the only place they feel they can open up about their issues and frustrations. Once an issue is opened up in group discussion, many members can relate on some level, through either their own experiences or the experiences of a close friend in the military. By stating this common theme of "aloneness" upfront, the leader is attempting to quickly connect with the group and reassure members that others have similar feelings, thoughts, or experiences.

Renegotiating Roles in Families and Relationships

Time apart presents many challenges for the deployed soldier and the support system that is left behind. Some veterans may have been able to keep in constant contact with their families, especially when the Internet is available. Other veterans may not have been as fortunate, with some unable to make firm commitments as to when they could talk, based on the availability of communication devices and time. Each veteran presents a unique situation. Family members may have taken on new roles or duties, and the veteran may have missed important family milestones through no fault of his or her own. Often veterans report some degree of tension negotiating their place in the system, which has functioned, often very well, without them for some time. The veteran may feel as if he or she is not as needed as he or she thought or, conversely, that his or her absence may have been a major contributor to family disruption during deployment. They may feel guilty and some members have reported being blamed for family problems that occurred during their time away. Family tension is not unusual and can be couched in terms that make this issue more universal and less of an issue about the veteran. The leader can point out that it is not unusual to experience difficulty during any adjustment period, such as entering a new grade in school or moving to a new area and finding a first job. This can shift thinking from an emotionally loaded area (family disruption) to a more pragmatic area, where the veteran has succeeded in the past with similar skills. Members are often asked to think of times they have gone through changes before and reflect on strengths they have used during previous adjustment periods in their life. Members have reported complicating factors such as new illnesses, loss of financial stability (many Reserve and Guard members take significant pay cuts or do not have time to devote to finances while deployed), a death or loss in the family, children acting out while the veteran is deployed, and partners who have left the relationship or engaged in extramarital affairs during a deployment. Equipping the members with a set of skills, working around rigid and inflexible patterns of thinking and focusing on strengths can be helpful. Again, the leader should be allowing space for members to safely discuss their frustrations or issues with their family, to gain support and a sense that they are not unique in having a difficult time readjusting to a support system or lamenting the loss of one. Once the issues are discussed, the leader can attempt to guide members into exploring their feelings and thoughts they may have difficulty expressing in a meaningful way to their support system. Vignettes used to illustrate common readjustment issues are often helpful in getting this topic going in a constructive way, as they can de-personalize an issue and lower defenses. During one group, a younger member, who left his hometown several hundred miles away to get away from family and a girlfriend he perceived as intrusive and not understanding, brought in a book that was mailed to him by his family about becoming "un-broken." Many members related to this type of treatment by family members and offered that it was no wonder why the veteran left home, as his behavior was interpreted as dysfunctional. The member who received the book looked on the book as humorous, as did many other members. Ways of interpreting family behavior in this sense were explored. Member opinions tended to be critical of the family at first, perhaps due to similar experiences or feelings. After members spent several minutes exploring how the family erred, an older female veteran spoke up to state that while she understood the veteran being put off by this, she also indicated that as a mother, she saw the sending of the book as an attempt to genuinely help the veteran and offer a message that the family cared about his well-being. While the leader was thinking along the same lines as the female veteran, the message was more powerfully delivered by a member who was a veteran and a mother, with children about the same age as the veteran. The issue was explored further to help veterans look at family behavior and their behavior in the family system more flexibly and realistically.

"Crazy" Veterans

Some members will state that their families, friends, peers, and colleagues are convinced, or will assume, that their time away at war has made them "crazy." Depending on knowledge about their service or their news sources, those who the veterans leave behind may develop preconceived notions of what the returning veteran may be like upon return and attempt to fit the veteran into their expectations. Often, members report a polarized reaction upon return, where the member is either praised as a hero or condemned as a "crazy" veteran. Both reactions can elicit strong emotions. Getting members to discuss ways they have been received is helpful, as well as ways they have found helpful in dealing with this adjustment. Sometimes this may take the form of the leader offering the members educational materials to take home or reliable literature on websites, so the family can receive more realistic and less sensationalized news about the readjustment process.

Often members discuss how some civilians can ask questions, such as "Did you kill anyone?" or "Did you see anyone get blown up by an IED?" These types of questions can, and often do, provoke an angry response. When this topic is brought up, most members will have stories to share. The veteran cannot control the well-meaning civilian who asks a stupid question but can exercise control in his or her response. Recognizing that the civilian does not understand can often deescalate a situation, as does having stock answers to insensitive questions that the veteran can offer without much thought. Here the goal is to avoid acting out of anger after being triggered to perhaps relive a painful situation. Sometimes humor can be interjected into this often stressful component of the readjustment process. One veteran reported that a "preppy kid" attending the same introductory-level college class asked the veteran: "What's it like over there?" Not wanting to go into details with a person he just met, the veteran responded with humor, telling the civilian that if he really wanted to know what it was like, "Go home. Stick your head in the oven at 200 degrees and have someone nearby continually throw sand all over your body." Here, the veteran used humor to deescalate and move forward, rather than discussing his difficult times in combat or becoming angry and combative. As a side note, the veteran and "preppy kid" got along well during the class from that point on and found they had some common interests.

How different this member's college experience would have been if he had acted on his initial impulse to physically lash out.

Arousal and Alertness

The veteran may be transitioning from a war zone where trash/debris along the side of the road (a typical way to hide IEDs) is a threat. Enemies in the combat zone are typically unknown to the veteran, so, for protection, the veteran may have developed a constant state of alertness. While this type of alertness is part of the normal human response to promote survival, always being on guard and treating others as potential threats can pose problems in a civilian context. Group members report having difficulty tolerating large crowds, traffic, or unfamiliar areas. Sometimes members report acting on their feelings and engaging in defensive measures when they felt threatened, as in Mr. Smith's case. The leader continually reassures members that remaining vigilant and on guard was helpful during the deployment and must be hard to let down. Here, the goal of the leader is to shift focus away from the members' feelings of guilt or dysfunction, to a more normalized approach, suggesting that their reactions are part of human nature. Working from this perspective, the members may be allowed to share experiences where they have acted on their feelings of being threatened and develop ways to check-in the next time they have those feelings. Mindfulness and relaxation exercises can be introduced during the group to help veterans focus on the moment, while reducing tension. Introducing the exercises in the group serves two distinct functions. For starters, the members are taught ways to self-soothe in a safe environment and they can use and practice the exercises they have found to be helpful. Second, by modeling these exercises where the veteran is asked to "pay attention to the way his feet feel in his shoes," among other things, the leader can use himself and the power of the group to help veterans engage in these activities and build skills, where they may otherwise have been resistant. When angered or threatened, veterans can engage in grounding exercises to offer them some time to decide about the appropriateness of the array of choices available in a given context. Being supportive and understanding the member's situation destigmatizes a common response style adopted during the uncommon conditions of a war zone.

Isolation

Often, tension will exist between veterans wanting to reengage in previously enjoyable activities and concern that they may display anxiety or act out on perceived threats if they are caught off guard or triggered by stimuli in the environment beyond their control. Sometimes this worry can lead to isolation. Normalizing these reactions by talking about them serves an important function for the group.

Isolation may also be a sign of intense sadness or guilt and, in this case, the veteran may need to feel very comfortable to discuss particulars. One veteran recounted how, during a pregame ceremony to baseball game, fireworks unexpectedly went off by his section where he was with several friends and a new love interest. The veteran responded to the fireworks by "hitting the ground." He reported feeling intense embarrassment and felt that his behavior demonstrated to his friends and love interest that he was a "weak" person. For several weeks, the veteran reported that he had a hard time giving up the controlled environment of his room for an unpredictable environment outside. He was sure that he had ruined his chances with this woman and he was also sure that he never wanted to appear so "weak" again. Upon hearing this, many members recalled how they, too, have "hit the deck" after hearing a car backfire, etc. One member, who was also a Gulf War veteran, indicated that after the "hundredth time," he started to laugh at this survival behavior and his friends and wife would even tease him a bit. Previously, out of regard for the member's sensitivity to this matter, his friends and wife pretended they had not seen him, or ignored it, although the member knew they saw him and surely thought he was "nuts." The new and humorous response, the member admitted, had taken him many years to develop and choosing to view his response with some humor has made ducking less embarrassing. Here the member took the approach that he would probably respond to loud and sudden noises for the rest of his life in some way, due to being injured by an explosion. After many years fighting against it, he had accepted his response and chose to laugh at himself and be open to it, rather than becoming angry, embarrassed, or sad. He offered hope to other members and espoused greater flexibility and less self-criticism. He also encouraged the other member not to be embarrassed and to go after his love interest, with a new sense that his response was not unusual given his experiences.

EVALUATION

Evaluation in the group has focused on decreasing symptoms and improving social functioning. During the initial intake, the veteran receives a thorough psychosocial assessment which includes screenings for depression, PTSD, substance abuse, and a suicide risk assessment. This particular group is designed to target returning veterans who are having adjustment issues and is a part of adjunctive treatment. Evaluation tools have included a needs assessment where veterans identify what has been helpful about the group as well as what might be added or changed to improve the group. From the needs assessments, 96% of the returning veterans indicated they would prefer individual treatment over group work. Despite the high percentage, this particular group has had consistent attendance and continues to grow. The group is viewed as a success as veterans continue to return and refer their other veteran friends. This group receives six to eight new combat veteran referrals per week; many of these are self-referrals and referrals through other veterans.

Research evaluating the effectiveness of group and individual treatment for the OEF/OIF population is scarce at this time. It is unclear if the OEF/OIF population is similar enough to combat veterans from other wars to adapt or use existing treatments with good efficacy. Current research projects are under way evaluating the use of trauma-focused cognitive-behavioral therapies with exposure therapy, cognitive processing therapy, early interventions and screening, as well as the impact of psychopharmacology, physical injuries, women veterans, and dual diagnosis. Efforts are under way to find the most effective treatment options and care.

CONCLUSION

"Veterans surviving combat deployments possess a tremendous number of strengths and the intensity of caring for them are balanced by the value of working with someone to transform his or her life following the trauma of combat" (Batten & Pollack, 2008, p. 938). Returning veterans may present themselves for care through a number of avenues. It is important that clinicians be prepared to meet them in a way that is engaging, focused, and respectful. These men and women have taken a risk by entering treatment given the perceived and sometimes real cost to their promotion potential in the military and loss of esteem from some of their battle buddies who stigmatize mental health services.

Each of these men and women has strengths that need to be emphasized. Their treatment needs to be succinct and meaningful to them as individuals and allow them to serve others as this is part of their military training. Clinicians must be aware of the myriad issues that this population brings and be prepared to provide referrals and services as needed. Additionally, clinicians should be mindful that these men and women have access to multiple health care systems, which creates a unique situation in which veterans can, and often do, seek care from providers who may not communicate to coordinate their care (Shen, Hendricks, Zhang, & Kazisl, 2003). While access to care and options are important, these veterans may be receiving care through multiple systems where the providers do not communicate or know that the veteran receives care elsewhere. Such issues may need to be addressed during the course of clinical work. It is essential that the clinician's skill set is expanded and updated to manage the complex needs of the returning veteran population. Additional research is needed to identify the most appropriate and effective treatment strategies for the various groups within the OEF/OIF population. Group work, with all it has to offer this population, should be included in these strategies.

RESOURCES

American Psychiatric Association
www.psych.org

100 Wilson Boulevard, Suite 1825
Arlington, VA 22209

American Psychological Association
www.apa.org
750 First Street NE
Washington, DC 20002

Anxiety Disorders Association of America
www.adaa.org
8730 Georgia Avenue, Suite 200
Silver Spring, MD 20910

Association for Behavioral and Cognitive Therapies
www.aabt.org
305 Seventh Ave, 16th Floor
New York, NY
(800) 789-2647

Department of Veterans Affairs
www.va.gov

Institute of Medicine: Veterans
www.veterans.iom.edu
500 Fifth Street NW
Washington, DC 20001
(800) 374-2721

International Society for Traumatic Stress Studies
www.istss.org
111 Deer Lake Road, Suite 100
Deerfield, IL 60015
847-480-9028

National Center for PTSD
www.ncptsd.va.gav
PTSD Info Line: 802-296-6300

National Institute of Mental Health
www.nimhinfo@nih.gov
6001 Executive Boulevard
Bethesda, MD 20892
(703) 907-7308

National Mental Health Organization
www.nmha.org

SAMHSA's National Mental Health Information Center
www.mentalhealth.samhsa.gov
P.O. Box 2345
Rockville, MD 20847

The Center for Study of Traumatic Stress
University Health Services
www.usuhs.mil
4301 Jones Bridge Road
Bethesda, MD 20814

VA National Suicide Hotline: (800) 273-TALK (8255)

REFERENCES

Armstrong, K., Best, S., & Domenici, P. (2006). *Courage after fire: Coping strategies for troops returning from Iraq, Afghanistan and their families.* Berkeley, CA: Ulysses Press.

Batten, S. V. & Pollack, S. J. (2008). Integrative outpatient treatment for returning service members. *Journal of Clinical Psychology, 64,* 928–939.

Blanchard, E. B., Jones-Alexander, J., Buckley, T. C., & Forneris, C. A. (1996). Psychometric properties of PTSD Checklist (PCL). *Behavior Research Therapy, 34,* 669–673.

Brown, N. D. (2008). Transition from the Afghanistan and Iraqi battlefields to home: An overview of selected war wounds and the federal agencies assisting soldiers regain their health. *Journal of American Association of Occupational Health Nurses, 56,* 343–346.

Fontana, A. M. & Rosenheck, R. (2008). Treatment-seeking veterans of Iraq and Afghanistan: Comparison with veterans of pervious wars. *Journal of Nervous and Mental Disease, 196,* 513–521.

Hankin, C. S., Spiro, A., Miller, D., & Kazis, L. (1999). Mental disorders and mental health treatment among U. S. Department of Veterans Affairs outpatients: The Veterans Health Study. *American Journal of Psychiatry, 156,* 1924–1930.

Hoge, C. W., Castro, C. A., Messer, S. C., McGurk, D., Cotting, D., & Koffman, R. L. (2004). Combat duty in Iraq and Afghanistan, mental health problems, and barriers to care. *New England Journal of Medicine, 351,* 13–22.

Kang, H. K. & Bullman, T. A. (2008). Risk of suicide among US veterans after returning from the Iraq or Afghanistan war zones. *Journal of American Medical Association, 300,* 652–653.

Litz, B. (2009). *A brief primer on the mental health impact of the wars in Afghanistan and Iraq.* Washington, DC: National Center for Post Traumatic Stress Disorder.

Litz, B. T., Gray, M. J., Bryant, R. A., & Adler, A. B. (2002). Early intervention for trauma: Current status and future directions. *Clinical Psychology: Science and Practice, 9*(2), 112–134.

Miliken, C. S., Auchterlonie, J. L., & Hoge, C. W. (2007). Longitudinal assessment of mental health problems among active and reserve component soldiers returning from the Iraq War. *Journal of American Medical Association, 298,* 2141–2148.

Substance Abuse and Mental Health Services. (2005). *National Survey on Drug Use and Health*. Washington, DC: Substance Abuse and Mental Health Services.

President's Commission on Care for America's Returning Wounded Warriors. (2007). *Serve, support, simplify: Report for the President's Commission on Care for America's Returning Wounded Warriors*. Washington, DC: U.S. Congress, House Committee on Veterans Affairs, U.S. Government Printing Office.

National Center for Posttraumatic Stress Disorder. (2006). *Returning from the war zone: A guide for families of military members*. Washington, DC: National Center for Posttraumatic Stress Disorder.

Riggs, D., Rothbaum, B. O., & Foa, E. B. (1995). *A prospective examination of symptoms of post traumatic stress disorder in victims of nonsexual assault. Journal of Interpersonal Violence*, *10*, 201–214.

Ruzek, J. I., Curran, E., Friedman, M. J., Gusman, F. D., Southwick, S. M., Swales, P., Walser, R. D., Watson, P. J., & Whealin, J. (2004). *Treatment of the returning Iraq War veteran*. Washington, DC, National Center for Posttraumatic Stress Disorder.

Shen, Y., Hendricks, A., Zhang, S. I., & Kazis, L. E. (2003). VHA enrollees' health care coverage and use of care. *Medical Research and Review*, *60*, 253–267.

The Rand Corporation. (2008). Invisible wounds of war; Psychological and cognitive injuries, their consequences, and services to assist recovery. http://www.rand.org/multi/military/veterans/

Walter Reed Army Institute of Research (WRAIR). (2006). WRAIR Land Mind Combat Study Team. *Battlemind training: Transitioning from combat to home*. Washington, DC: Walter Reed Army Institute of Research.

Waterhouse, M., & O'Bryant, J. (2008). *National guard personnel and deployments: Fact sheet*. Congressional Research Service. Washington, DC: Library of Congress.

NOTE

1 We dedicate this chapter to our colleague, Lt. Col. Juanita Warman, who was killed at Fort Hood in November 2009.

Chapter Nine

Integrating In-person Counseling and Internet Support Communities: "E-volving" Practice Models for Social Group Work With At-Risk Populations

Andrea Meier

> *For people confronted with challenging life-changing situations, the Internet can be a valuable gateway to information and self-help resources to help them cope. Social workers can help their clients benefit from the social support and social learning that Internet self-help groups offer. When they help clients learn how to use these online support resources effectively, social workers are writing new chapters in the profession's history of using the mutual aid of groups for individual growth and collective empowerment (Association for the Advancement of Social Work with Groups, 1999).*

This quote was published in the second edition of this book in 2005. While the statements are still true, what a difference 5 years makes! The contexts for technology-mediated (TM) social support have changed dramatically. In 2005, Internet users were communicating primarily through text-based channels (e-mail, Web discussion forums, and IRC chat). Clinicians, including social workers, were leery about using the Internet to communicate with clients. When social services organizations had their own websites, they were usually digital analogs of the paper pamphlets they used to inform the public about their services. Social workers and agencies viewed TM groups as beyond their capacity because they lacked the clinical expertise, technological sophistication, and support to implement and sustain them.

Once a technological innovation has been widely adopted in a society, it is almost impossible to remember what life was like before its introduction. In the case of the Internet, it is astounding to realize that commercial Internet services were introduced only 20 years ago. (Figure 9.1 shows a timeline of Internet-based innovations since 1989.) Today, Internet-mediated (IM) communication systems have permeated U.S. society profoundly, *if unevenly*, through all socioeconomic classes, ages,

Diminishing Cost, Increasing Speed, Access, Portability, individualization and Choice

1989	1993–94	2000–01	2004–05	2006
Computer Mediated Communication (CMC)	Instant messaging (IM) 1-1 short messages 160 char	High speed internet services ("broadband")	Web 2.0 "Participatory web" Non-professional users able to create their own interactive websites	Introduction of Twitter (mass microblogging "140 chars per tweet")
Text-based internet communication: Email, IRC chat	Web 1.0 Static websites with content controlled by site owners	Wireless Mobile Devices Laptops Cell phones, PDAs	Participate in producing multimedia content, gather feedback using e-surveys, comment sections	
Usenet, bulletin board and listerv groups	Multi-functional websites with access to listservs and chat rooms with graphical interfaces		Internet social mediasites	
	Weblogs (Blogs)		Smart phones	
	Introduction of Digital TV		Internet Telephony (VOIP)	
			Internet teleconferencing	
			Internet videoconferencing	

*The first electronic message was transmitted over the ARPAnet in 1969

Figure 9-1. Twenty years of innovations in technology-mediated communication.*

and cultural and ethnic groups. We are all now embedded in IM networks. For most, our use of them seems as normal—and necessary—as breathing.

Text-based IM communication channels continue to be widely used but, now, Web-based audio and video communication is becoming increasingly popular. Technical boundaries between different types of digital technologies have begun to blur as in the implementation of new kinds of channels such as telephony (VOIP), which transmit telephone call data over the Internet, making it easy and economical to conduct group teleconferences and videoconferences. Where e-groups used to be limited to technically sophisticated users, new Web 2.0 technologies make it easy for almost anyone to implement and run an online community or social media site of practically any size.

THE SOCIAL WORK PROFESSION AND SUPPORT E-COMMUNITY RESOURCES: FACILITATORS AND BARRIERS TO ADOPTION

To date, social workers have not been major participants in the development of support e-community (SeC) resources. To provide the highest quality services to their clients, workers need to acknowledge the expanding role of IM communication in their clients' social environments. Further, they need to understand how these technologies can be used as supportive and potentially empowering resources.

Recognizing the growing importance of information technologies and their impact on the roles of individual workers and agencies, the National Association of Social Workers and the Association of Social Work Boards collaborated to produce updated *Standards for Technology and Social Work Practice* (National Association of Social Workers & Association of Social Work Boards, 2005). The two associations defined technology and social work practice as "any electronically mediated activity used in the conduct of competent and ethical delivery of social work services" (National Association of Social Workers & Association of Social Work Boards, 2005, p. 6).

The standards offer a comprehensive view of the new professional expectations for social workers in their use of these technologies and the ways traditional practice protocols need to be adapted to ensure competent and ethical practice. These standards emphasize the need to insure that workers and clients have appropriate access to IM resources. Further, the use of IM practices must be attuned to cultural differences and responsive to the needs of vulnerable populations. They emphasize the importance of training social workers so they will enter the profession competent in IM practices applicable to clinical and community practice and to advocacy and social action. The standards also require social workers to seek appropriate training and consultation to stay current with the risks and benefits of emerging technologies.

Following on these new standards, NASW has taken an important step of sponsoring a practitioners' portal linked *to* the Association's website "Help Starts Here" (see http://helpstartshere.org/PortalHome/tabid/128/language/en-US/Default. aspx) The portal provides a searchable Web directory to help clients find licensed social workers who practice near where they live. More specifically, clients can also search for workers who offer face-to-face therapy and support groups.

It is difficult to determine the extent to which social workers are engaged in facilitating therapeutic online groups. We know that there are still many deterrents to their engagement in this area, first among them being lack of training. Many schools have dropped their group work-specific courses (Knight, 1999) and so students are less likely to be prepared with in-person group work skills, much less the skills needed to organize and manage IM groups. A content analysis of group work course syllabi of the top 10 MSW programs in the United States (U.S. News & World Report, 2008) conducted in preparation for this chapter found that only three listed any readings on virtual groups. (Paradoxically, these same schools now all have their own Facebook pages with "walls" where students actively post messages to their schools' eCs.).

Lack of reimbursement has been another major barrier. Over the past decade, opportunities for reimbursement for telehealth services for have been increasing for health care providers. These initiatives have been led by Medicare and Medicaid, with private insurers slowly following suit. The few clinicians in private practice who engage in e-therapy services must do it on a fee-for-service basis; third-party payers do not reimburse for these services (Dunaway, 2000). Across the country, ethical standards and regulations for IM practice are still in flux. The 2005

Standards note that workers are responsible for complying with their licensing board regulations regarding whether delivery of services take places where the consumer is located or where the worker is. NASW Assurance Services, the insurance company that provides professional liability coverage for NASW members, has been proactive in offering online education on best practices and risk management for those interested in technology mediated practice. That said, *at this time* the company will cover e-therapy services but only in states where the worker is licensed (NASW Assurance Services, 2009).

Overview

Since there are so few models of professionally facilitated Internet groups, this chapter describes ways social workers can help their clients benefit from the myriad of self-help eCs that already exist (Meier, 2000). In face-to-face counseling sessions, practitioners can help their clients identify online self-help that might meet their needs, and then work with them to integrate their group experiences with the rest of their lives. (The discussion that follows assumes that readers have at least some experience with e-mail and the World Wide Web.)

Given all the demands on social workers' time, it is probably unrealistic to assume that many social workers will be facilitating SeCs. But workers can serve their clients in helping them benefit from SeC resources in three important ways. First, they can help clients understand the potential benefits of eC support. Second, workers can educate clients about where to look for credible SeCs and how to recognize well-functioning ones. Finally, in individual face-to-face counseling sessions, they can work *with* clients who are members of such SeCs to maximize the benefits of eC participation and minimize the risks.

With these aims in mind this chapter is divided into four parts. The first section describes the sociodemographics of Internet users and trends in Internet access. The second section addresses two psychoecological issues related to Internet user–technology interactions. How do the characteristics of IM communication channels affect users' internal awareness and their relationships with the people they interact with online? At the collective level, how do SeCs function and provide support? The third section summarizes the growing body of research evidence on the benefits and limitations of these emergent variants in group social support. The last section presents a practice model that can guide social workers when they work in-person with clients who are already involved with Internet self-help groups or would like to join one.

POPULATING THE CYBERFRONTIER: WHO GOES THERE?

To avoid stereotypical assumptions about who among their clients are Internet users, social workers must understand how far Internet technology has penetrated in the U.S. population. Since 2000, the Pew Internet and American Life Project has been conducting systematic surveys to track how Internet technology is being used and its social impacts in the United States (Pew Internet and American Life Project, 2009a). Based on those surveys, Pew estimates indicate there are nearly 172 million adult Internet users (79% of the adult population) who have one or more ways to access the Internet.

Internet User Characteristics

Over the past decade, the profile of the typical Internet user has changed. Until about 2000, typical users were college-educated white men between the ages of 30 and 65, living in urban areas, who were fully employed, with incomes over $50,000. In 2001, the Pew surveys began to detect important changes in Internet user demographics. More women, children, and minorities, and people with incomes under $30,000 were gaining access at an increasing rate (Rainie & Packel, 2001).

This trend has continued. In 2009, Pew tracking surveys (Pew Internet and American Life Project, 2009a) found that there was rough parity between men and women (81%/77%) Internet users in the United States. Internet use among English-speaking minorities has grown substantially, with proportional use rates similar to—or greater than—white, non-Hispanic users. Seventy-nine percent of white non-Hispanics surveyed now go online, compared to 84% of Hispanics and 67% of African Americans. Among all age groups in the general population, younger adults (ages 18–29) continue to be most likely to be using the Internet.

Another minority group, the gay, lesbian, bisexual, and transgender (GLBT) communities, has enthusiastically adopted Internet technologies (Researchand Markets.com, 2007). In 2007, there were an estimated 12.1 million adult GLBT Internet users in the United States (7.9% of the adult Internet user population). According to market researchers, this population segment has more disposable income and discretionary time than its heterosexual counterpart. Gay and lesbian Internet users are very active on social networking sites and blogs.

Trends in Internet Access

Historical differences in Internet access among population groups related to income, age, and geographic location persist, but they are rapidly diminishing (Pew Internet and American Life Project, 2009a). Although people with incomes above $50,000 are much more likely to have access (95%), those with incomes less than $30,000 represent the most rapidly growing group of new Internet users. There has also been substantial growth in the number of adults in the 50-to-64 age group with Internet access. Older adults, aged 65 years and older, were the least likely to report using the Internet. That said, over 40% reported that they went online. Of these, the greatest increase in Internet use since 2005 has been in the 70- to 75-year-old age group.

In 2000, Internet penetration was relatively shallower in rural areas compared with that in urban centers, largely because fewer people in rural areas used computers (Lenhart, 2000). As of 2009, approximately three-quarters of adults in urban and suburban communities accessed the Internet compared with two thirds of rural residents (Pew Internet and American Life Project, 2009a).

In 2003, the Pew survey estimated that about 40% of adults do not currently use the Internet (Horrigan et al., 2003). This finding does not necessarily mean that they did not have access or lacked the skills to use it if they had access. About a fifth of these nonusers lived in households where someone else was an Internet user who could retrieve the nonuser's e-mail messages or information from the Web when needed. Seventeen percent of nonusers were users in the past but dropped off the networks due to problems with their computers or their Internet service providers.

Only a quarter of Americans had no direct or indirect access to or experience with the Internet. The subgroup of nonusers who believe that they will never go online (56%) tend to be the poorer, older segment and are more likely to be white, female, retired, and living in rural areas.

INTERNET USE PATTERNS

Pew's recent surveys (Pew Internet and American Life Project, 2009b) have found that most Internet users (90%) continue to use it most often to read and send e-mail. More than 88% of users report that they use Internet search engines (such as Google, Yahoo!, and MSN.com) to find information.

"Always On": Ubiquitous Internet Access

Among the myriad changes wrought by widespread adoption of the Internet are transformations in the physical and social contexts of IM interactions. The direction of these transformations has enabled users to have access to TM communication resources more economically, with faster transmission speeds, at more locations, with enhanced portability, individuality, and choices about what they can do online.

When the second edition of this book came out, IM communication was referred to as "computer-mediated communication," because access was generally limited to stationary desktop computers in users' offices, homes, libraries, and community centers. Now, widespread adoption of Internet-enabled wireless technologies (laptop computers, cell phones, and other mobile devices) has made it possible to access the Internet from almost anywhere. A 2009 survey by the Pew Internet and American Life Project found that 56% of American adults have accessed the Internet using wireless means (Horrigan, 2009). The same survey found increasing use of mobile handsets to access the Internet; nearly one third

(32%) have used using these e-devices to access the Internet for e-mailing, instant-messaging, or information-seeking.

INTERNET COMMUNICATION CHANNEL EFFECTS

People do more than coexist with their physical environments; they interact with them. In the case of IM self-help groups, the Internet is the medium through which all member interactions take place. Social psychologists have studied how IM communication can affect the ways Internet users function in their online social networks and the subnetworks that they use for social support.

This section will be devoted to a brief "psychoecological" description of these human and e-technological interactions (Fig. 9.2). Underlying all aspects of these systems, there must be two elements: paired message senders and receivers and a medium through which messages are sent. Senders are the sources of the messages; receivers act to reconstruct senders' signals. The medium can be any technology-mediated communications channel used to transmit electronic signals (Shannon, 1948). Electronic communication channels vary in the amount of data that can be transmitted per unit time. This characteristic is called *bandwidth*. The more data transmitted, the greater is the bandwidth needed. In IM communication,

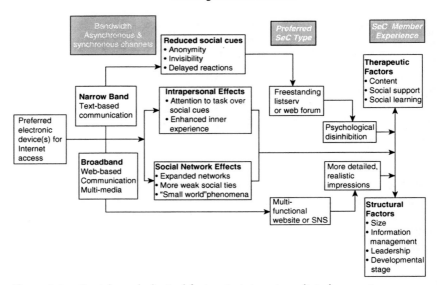

Figure 9-2. Social psychological factors in Internet-mediated support e-communities.

different types of messages require different amounts of bandwidth. Messages containing numbers and text require the least. Messages containing audio or video data require much more; multimedia communication, as used on IM social network sites (SNSs) requires the greatest amount of bandwidth. Widespread adoption of broadband services has enabled users to have many more choices about what they can do while online, including more choices about the kinds of SeCs they can form.

Communication is also affected by the timing of message sending and receiving. When message senders and receivers do not have to be present at the same time, this is called *asynchronous communication*. On the Internet, e-mail communication, usenet and listserv groups, and Web discussion forums are familiar examples of *asynchronous* communication in which messages are stored in a dedicated computer for recipients to retrieve at their convenience. As in face-to-face communication, *synchronous* e-communication (chat, instant messaging, and video) requires message senders and receivers to be present at the same time,

Once they log on, users' intrapersonal and interpersonal behaviors are influenced by the Internet channel they use. Social workers need to understand these effects so they can understand clients' online experiences, to help them be good "cyber-citizens," and reduce their risks for Internet abuse.

Intrapersonal Effects

Computer monitors are similar to television screens; both have low-level stimuli and "light-through" effects that can be mesmerizing (Hill, 2002). With text-based communication channels (e.g., e-mail and chat), users can remain anonymous and invisible to each other. In combination, the effects of the computer monitor and Internet-related reductions in social cues cause deindividualization (Siegel, Dubrovsky, Kiesler, & McGuire, 1986). Computer use can have psychoactive effects that enhance users' awareness of their thoughts and feelings and alter their moods (Greenfield, 1999). Users can become intensely engaged in their online transactions, tuning out cues and stimuli from their local, "real world" environments.

Interpersonal Effects

People who participate in text-based SeCs are invisible to each other. Members must construct mental images of others in their eCs based on incomplete information and come to terms with the fact that they may never meet them in person. Reduced social cues also affect how Internet users interact with one another and how they behave in groups. Invisibility and anonymity can reduce users' presentation anxiety, especially for those living with stigma (Mickelson, 1997). Internet users can control how much information they reveal about themselves and the timing of those disclosures. When in states of Internet-induced "boundarylessness," users are more likely to idealize or project onto the people they communicate with

(Colon, 1996; Walther, 1996). Incomplete information and delayed feedback can make it harder to develop realistic impressions.

SNSs are still too new for researchers to have completed much research on their interpersonal effects. One important difference between traditional text-based eCs and SNSs is that SN members must assume that they are *not* anonymous. A lot of their background information is public or obtainable by any other member who wants to search for it using Google. These conditions can enhance members' social presence, enabling them to have more realistic impressions of each other.

Psychological Disinhibition

Social psychologists have argued that Internet-induced weak social ties and reduced social cues can combine to produce disinhibition, the constellation of behaviors associated with Internet use. These include emotional regression, projection, weakened boundaries, and feelings of safety due to anonymity and invisibility. These conditions prompt some users to disclose sensitive details about their lives much sooner than they would in face-to-face transactions. The same factors elicit emotional regression in its creative and destructive forms. As a creative state, regression enables people to be playful (including experiments in gender and other identity shifts), nonconformist, and altruistic. As a destructive state, it can lead to impulsive and hostile acts, such as rapidly escalating verbal attacks ("flaming") or gender and other forms of harassment (Alonzo & Alken, 2004). Flaming is related to personality types. Overall, individuals who have a high level of disinhibition seeking and assertiveness tend to flame as a pastime. More specifically, disinhibition-seeking men are more likely to engage in flaming for entertainment. Highly anxious people may try to diffuse tension by flaming for escape and relaxation.

THE EMERGENCE OF E-COMMUNITIES

Soon after the introduction of the Internet in 1974, users soon recognized that this new technology could be used to facilitate group communication (Kristula, 1997) and eliminate geographic barriers that prevent people from coalescing around shared concerns (Meier, 2000). By 2002, a quarter of all Internet users reported that they had participated in chat or text-based eCs. Of these who had ever been in an eC member, 23 million described themselves as currently "very active" in the eCs where they were members. There is no central directory of these groups and no researchers have attempted a census of groups since the 2002 Pew survey.

INTERNET SOCIAL NETWORK STRUCTURES: E-GROUPS OR NETWORKED E-COMMUNITIES?

When people participate in eCs of any kind, they extend their social networks. Internet researchers have debated whether these electronic social networks constitute electronic groups (e-groups) or electronically networked communities (eCs). As small e-networks grow in size, they also become more internally differentiated, enabling members to take on different roles and have more different needs met. e-Networks that are successful in attracting and retaining members can evolve over time into multipurpose, virtual communities that serve as "networks of interpersonal ties that provide sociability, support, information, a sense of belonging and social identity" (Wellman, Boase, & Chen, 2002, p. 153).

More recently, social network theorist have concluded that eCs behave like "small world" networks (Milgram, 1967; Watts, 1999). According to this view, smaller networks with strong ties and shared interests are embedded in larger more loosely linked networks. On the Internet, these small e-networks behave more like conventional offline groups. Within those groups, a few members are the most active contributors to the ongoing discussions. These more active members are also more likely to engage in boundary-spanning activities by staying in touch with other equivalent members of other online communities. Because of the wide variation in sizes and structural complexity in these new forms of social networks, for simplicity's sake, all e-groups and social networks will be referred to generically here as eCs.

Participation in e-Communities

Innovations in eC technologies are continually being introduced and widely adopted. Pew tracking surveys estimate that the share of adult Internet users who have a profile on an SNS has more than quadrupled in the past 4 years—from 8% in 2005 to 35% in 2008 (Lenhart, 2009). Although there is substantial variability in the characteristics of SNS website owners, studies have found that SNS members are typically young adults who tend to be open minded but also somewhat more shy than their peers in the general population. Confidence in their job-related and professional skills compensates for other weaknesses in self-esteem, motivating them to spend time setting up and elaborating their SNS pages, leaving less time for face-to-face social interactions (Marcus, Machilek, & Schutz, 2006).

The newest of Internet networking tools, Twitter, enables users to "microblog" about the small details of their lives by exchanging short, 140-character messages over the Web or instant messaging software on their mobile devices. This kind of "always on" connectivity can generate a "sense of presence" and "ambient intimacy" that is now being used to extend the supportiveness of support eC SNSs.

To some degree, participation in social networks appears to be supplanting involvement in older, single-function e-group sources of social support. In May 2009, the major social media sites, Facebook and MySpace, had a total 146 million unique visitors (82.9 million and 69 million unique visitors, respectively) by U.S. subscribers. Facebook participation has increased faster than MySpace, doubling every year. By comparison, in 2009. rates of e-support group participation had dropped to 6% of all Internet users (Pew Internet and American Life Project, 2009b). While participation in online support groups is now less common than many other Internet uses, nonetheless, 6% of the Internet-using public in the United States still constitutes a substantial number of participants, 12 million people, who have had experience with text-based SeCs (Bernstein, 2009).

MATCHING SUPPORT NEEDS TO E-COMMUNITY RESOURCES

In an ideal world, everyone would have supportive families and friends and live in communities where social support services were adequate to meet local needs. Unfortunately, for many this is not the case. Where there are gaps in social systems, SeCs can be key in providing alternative resources for people who need them (Fogel, Ribsl, Morgan, Humphreys, & Lyons, 2008).

What factors prompt some people to choose SeCs to help them cope with stress instead of—or in addition to—their local support resources? Social psychologists have described such support-seeking behaviors as attempts at "optimal matching," so that the type of support is appropriate to the perceived controllability, duration, and intensity of stressors (Cutrona, 1990). Optimal matching theory (OMT) differentiates between emotional support from informational and instrumental support, hypothesizing that their relative importance as social resources depends on the controllability of a stressor. Thus, when facing an uncontrollable stressor, such as death, unemployment, or illness, OMT suggests that emotional support will prove most important, promoting healthy adjustment. On the other hand, when an individual faces a stressor over which he or she has relatively more control, such as marriage or smoking, informational and instrumental support are more important in facilitating healthy adjustment. In the OMT framework, acute and early stage stressors are events for which instrumental and informational support will be more important than emotional support. For stressful situations in which outcomes are highly uncertain or involve chronic problems, emotional support may be more helpful for adaptive coping.

In-person social network members provide different kinds of support, based on their life experiences, their resources, and their history of interaction with support recipients. In many ways, people who participate in SeCs are similar to those in face-to-face support groups. Both seek support for conditions that are embarrassing, socially stigmatizing or disfiguring (Davidson, Pennebaker, & Dickerson, 2000). Structurally, however, SeCs differ significantly from their face-to-face equivalents. In-person support groups tend to be small, composed of 10 to 12 members (Schopler, Abell, & Galinsky, 1998). By contrast, support eCs can range in size from three or four members to several thousand (for an example of a very large text-based SeC, see the Chronic Lymphocytic Leukemia listserv at http://listserv.acor.org/archives/cll.html).

Because their communities are larger and not constrained by geography, SeC members can establish "weak ties" to others beyond their intimate or local social networks. These weaker ties offer support seekers access to a more diverse set of potential sources of support than they might find among members of their intimate or local support networks (Walther & Boyd, 2002).

SeCs organized to address health-related problems have tended to attract members for two reasons. Around the time of a diagnosis of a significant illness, such as cancer, patients or their caregivers may join an SeC to get information to that will enable them to better understand a condition and its prognosis (Rimer et al., 2005). Those who are coping with chronic, rare, or poorly understood conditions may join SeCs to obtain emotional support needed to adjust to the prospect of an uncertain and less controllable future (Davidson et al., 2000).

Many people who seek out SeCs never participate in face-to-face individual therapy or therapeutic groups because they are unwilling or unable to do so (Suler, 1999). Others may seek out support online if their needs are so intense that they are unable to find the support they need from their intimate social networks and therapeutic services (Fiegelman, Gorman, Beal, & Jordan, 2008). There have not been any systematic surveys to estimate the total number of people who have received face-to-face counseling or group services while also participating in online self-help groups. However, in his survey of parent survivors of suicide, Fiegelman and colleagues found that intensely traumatized parents used both e- and face-to-face support groups, sometimes alternating between them, sometimes concurrently (Fiegelman et al., 2008).

SUPPORT E-COMMUNITY TYPES

The increasing diversity and dynamism of the population of U.S. Internet users mean that social workers are likely to have clients who use the Internet. What are the implications of these circumstances for social work practice? Workers must know which types of SeCs are available and how to find them on the Web.

Listservs and Web Forums

The widespread adoption of broadband Internet services has enabled Web-hosting services, such as Yahoo.com (Yahoo.com, n.d.) and Google.com (Google.com, n.d.), to integrate text-based group communication features into websites. Now participants can opt for the convenience of having messages from their eC's websites "pushed" to their e-mail inboxes, where they are most likely to see them. Or, if they prefer, they can reduce their e-mail volume and have messages "reside" on the group's website where they are available for review when the member has time to visit the site.

Web group–hosting services, Google Groups and Yahoo! Groups provide free services that enable users to create their own freestanding, asynchronous Web forums quickly and easily. Anyone who wishes can start *her or his* own eC whenever they are moved to do so. These eCs vary dramatically in technical sophistication and complexity. Until recently, most were simple listserv-based networks.

eCs with Web forums, however, may also maintain separate public information Web portals with links to their discussion forum sites. (For example, see the Web portal for family survivors of suicide: http://www.pos-ffos.com/, which links to separate discussion forums for parents of children who died by suicide and other bereaved relatives and friends.) As Internet users have become more adept with Web 2.0 features that enable them to produce their own multimedia content, an increasing number of multifunctional websites now include other components, such as member-created Web pages, uploaded documents and photographs, calendars of community events, links to other websites, and other kinds of digital graphical displays. Members can also obtain site metadata that allow them to track the number of subscribers and number of messages posted each month.

Chat Groups

Chat groups use synchronous Internet communication technologies to communicate. Because they take place in "real time" (e.g., all members must be online at the same time to participate), chat groups are more like in-person groups. They have scheduled sessions and usually have less than 20 members. Many chat groups are text-based and use Internet relay chat (IRC) to host the groups. The texts of member comments scroll up the screen as they are added and disappear after successive messages fill the screen behind them. Because members have to type quickly to participate, comment texts are usually telegraphic, using short phrases, abbreviations and emoticon symbols to communicate emotions. Many SeCs offer both asynchronous lists and scheduled chat groups (see, for example, the www. ParentsofSuicide support eC; Jones & Meier, in press). Chat groups attract participants who like the immediacy and conversational quality of member interactions (Domestic Violence Resource Center, 2009).

Weblogs

Weblogs ("blogs") are another important Web-based innovation for multiuser communication. Blogs are websites that enable individual users to create online journals. On a successful blog, the blogger makes regular entries of commentary, descriptions of events or other materials such as graphics or videos. Blog commentaries can be of any length. A typical blog combines texts, images, and links to other blogs, Web pages, and other media related to its focal topic. An important feature of blog sites is their interactivity. Internet users who come to the site can leave comments for the blogger. When a blog is successful, it stimulates "group-like" interactions among readers who begin to comment on each other's comments as well as those of the blogger.

Social Network Sites

SNS formats exploit Web 2.0 technologies that encourage users to interact with each other in new ways, as well as to produce and share content. They have been widely adopted by businesses and to attract online customers and by nonprofit organizations promote their causes (Fritz, 2009). Where Google Groups and Yahoo! Groups offer primarily asynchronous group interactions, a social media site can integrate a bewildering array technologies including Web forums, text-based and video blogs, wall-postings, e-mail, instant messaging, and picture and music sharing, to name a few. One of the newest health support social media sites is a shared video site that enables patients to post YouTube videos of themselves describing illness and treatment experiences (Icyou.com, 2009; Kahanna, 2008).

Individuals who want to access an SNS must be asked to join by another member of that network. The procedure for joining involves two steps: registering with the network and establishing a "personal page." The registration process collects basic profile information (age, sex, location, and "about me" details). This information is published on the site and is searchable by other network members. When users create their personal pages, they "type themselves into being" (Sudén, 2003, p. 3). Once a personal page is established, the owner can e-mail others in their personal and professional networks and invite them individually to become their "friend" by joining the social media site and linking their personal pages. Members can create different categories of "friends" and control what parts of their personal pages each type of friend can view

Beyond the basic information required by the system, owners of these personal pages can customize them by adding content and blogging. Each interaction within between members in these personal networks takes several steps. When the page owner adds a blog comment on a website or a "friend" responds, all "friends" in the network with the appropriate level of access are notified by e-mail that a change has been made on the blog. To view the new information, however, "friends" must go back to the website. Kramer and Winter's exploratory study of comparing SNS participants according to three stable personality traits (introversion, self-esteem, and self-efficacy) found that that higher extraversion and self-efficacy in being able to create a positive impression were related to the number of personal details disclosed on their personal pages and inclusion of self-portrait photographs and the number of virtual friends listed in their networks (Kramer & Winter, 2008).

Members of Facebook and MySpace can also create group pages. The major difference between these group and personal pages is that the owner of a group page can send out "bulk" invitations to join the network, while personal page owners must do their invitations one at a time. This means that the rates of network member interactions can increase much more quickly than they do on personal pages.

FINDING A SUPPORT E-COMMUNITY

People form eCs so they can overcome the barriers of geographic distance or time and interact with others who share their interests and concerns. But these eCs do not have physical locations, so how do support seekers find SeCs that would best meet their needs? In this context, support seekers must decide whether they want to find a freestanding text-based SeC or one that uses Web 2.0 channels.

Freestanding Support e-Communities

Both Google and Yahoo! host thousands of SeCs organized to address a myriad of health and social problems. To find a group for a specific problem, users perform keyword searches combining the term "social support" with other descriptors such as problem type, age group, geographic region, and language. These searchers result in lists of links to SeCs along with brief descriptions of the purpose of each community, whether it has open or closed membership and whether it has a moderator who monitors members' message content. Googling for SeCs may also lead to discoveries of "portal" websites that organize links to text-based SeCs that address related problems. Two of the most well-known and well-organized portals are Association of Cancer Online Resources (www.acor.com) and BrainTalk Communities (file://localhost/(http/::brain.hastypastry.net:forums:index.php) for patients living with neurological diseases.

These SeC listings also provide information to decide whether the group is large enough to be functional. Each listing includes the date the group was formed, the number of subscribers, and the number of messages posted in the past month. Because only a small proportion of members consistently contribute, these groups need to achieve a "critical mass" to ensure that the online discussions are substantive and supportive enough to attract and retain members whenever they log in. Researchers disagree on the critical mass of subscribers needed to keep an e-group viable; Shirkey (2008) found that such groups typically need to have 100 to 150 members to be sustainable. In another study, CHESS researchers found that when groups get too big they become less intimate (e.g., are experienced as less supportive). Those that purposefully limit their size can be viable with a critical mass of 50 members, of which about half will participate regularly (Shaw & Kling, 1999).

To know how well any eC is functioning, seekers must join and participate. New members are required to subscribe to the group by completing an online registration process if they want to join. Open membership groups use an automated procedures. Closed membership groups require applicants to obtain the list owner's approval before they can read or exchange messages with other members.

Support Social Networking Sites

Social networking differ significantly form freestanding listservs and Web forums in one important respect. Where free-standing eSs seek to capitalize on weak ties, social media sites "articulate and make visible members' existing social networks" and to strengthen ties with those whom they already have some kind of offline connection (Boyd & Ellison, 2007, p. 2). One consequence of this recruitment process is that the social media groups are likely to be more homogeneous in terms of their members' characteristics than other kinds of eCs (Boyd & Ellison, 2007). This differentiation also persists at the macro-level within social media networks. For example, MySpace was founded to help artists and musicians disseminate their work. It soon became popular with a younger and more racially and ethnically diverse membership. Facebook was originally created by college students as a virtual yearbook and continues to attract more highly educated and older members.

Although social media network members are typically recruited by other members, unaffiliated Internet users can find networks to affiliate with using Google searches. For example, a cancer patient can find cancer support networks on Facebook using the search terms "Facebook," "cancer," and "social support." Once at that site, the patient can sign up to be a Facebook member and connect with as many other sites as are of interest.

Information Management

While members of traditional listservs can sort their messages by sender, date, and keywords, all members are exposed to all the messages in their e-mail inboxes. Even if they do not read them all, this message delivery format gives the entire community an overall impression of who are the most active members, who is in distress, and which topics are "hot." Web forums differ from listservs in messages displayed on the website are "threaded," automatically sorted by topic. It takes an extra step to click open a new window displaying all the messages on a given topic. The result is a fragmentation of the group. Members who prefer the Web forum format to interact with their eCs will not see all the posts but are able to "drill down" on a topic and follow discussions that most interest them more easily.

As with Web forums, Facebook and MySpace interactions do not fill up members' e-mail boxes with floods of messages. Members are notified periodically by e-mail when new comments have been added to a blog on the personal page of one of their network members but each member must make a conscious choice to go to the site to see it.

Because of all of the website features and applications available to social media site members, these sites tend to be much more individualized in their format and complicated to navigate. This means that learning how to be a competent participant in social media sites can take longer than with other kinds of SeCs. Newcomers to social media networks must expect to spend considerable time discovering how to work with different page features if they are going to make best use of them. Much of the information about how to use social media is conveyed through blogs on this subject. So, apart from finding a friend who is an experienced social media site user to help, new users may need to do Google searches for these blogs using queries such as "How do I [topic] on [Facebook/MySpace]?"

LEADERSHIP ROLES IN SUPPORT E-COMMUNITIES

In eCs, there are two kinds of leaders: technical administrators and facilitators. In some eCs, one person carries out these two roles. Regardless of whether the tasks are done by one individual or a team, for an eC to thrive, two key functions of eC management must be routinely accomplished. First, someone must decide on what type of eC technology to use and manage members' access to the community's resources. Effective technical administration ensures that the network is reliable and that the communication channels over which of an eC interacts match the skills and needs of its members (Jones & Meier, in press; Ley, 2007). Second, someone must establish and communicate group norms and promote positive interactions between members. Effective eC leadership involves many of the same responsibilities as in face-to-face groups and communities: setting, communicating and enforcing appropriate group norms; promoting positive interactions between members, promoting the development of individual capacities, group cohesiveness, and collective capacities (Ley, 2007; Toseland & Rivas, 1995).

It is easier to assess group leadership in freestanding listervs and Web forums than in SNSs. Yahoo! Groups and Google Groups indicate whether a group is moderated, indicating that there is an individual or a team responsible for monitoring technology reliability and member interactions. In these kinds of groups, new members will typically receive subscription confirmation and an automatic welcome message with information about the group's purpose and norms. A content analysis of Facebook and MySpace e-support network sites conducted in preparation for this chapter suggests that it can be difficult to determine who, if anyone, is recognized as being in leadership roles. There are rarely documents on sites that specify group norms.

One important consequence of the technical ease of eC formation is that SeCs do not require formal organizational support (Shirkey, 2008) and so are less likely to have professional leadership. Support eCs are often started by individuals who are coping with problems but are unsuccessful in finding a satisfactory local face-to-face support group they could join. Others may have been motivated to form their own support SeCs after having joined face-to-face support groups and then discovered that they needed ongoing support between meetings. Still others may have been members of one SeC and then decided to form a new one because of conflicts with the leaders of their original group (Ley, 2007). This means that eC founders may not have group facilitation experience and must acquire their e-group facilitation and organizational skills by trial and error as their communities grow (Jones & Meier, in press; Meier, Lyons, & Frydman, 2007; Meier, Lyons, Frydman, Forlenza, & Rimer, 2007).

Effective eC leaders stay actively involved in overseeing and encouraging member interactions, promoting harmonious member interactions, and asking questions to promote discussions (Jones & Meier, in press). They participate in ongoing discussions, recognizing members' unique contributions and promoting group cohesion by acknowledging member similarities (Ludford, Cosley, Frankowsky, & Terveen, 2004). When persistent conflicts between members arise, they use their eC technologies to create specialized groups within the portal of the larger community (GriefNet.org, 2009; Jones & Meier, in press; Ley, 2007). In some cases, such as SeCs for bereaved people, SeC organizers may arrange for professional clinicians to supervise volunteer leaders (GriefNet.org, 2009).

Keeping a successful SeC going is time and labor intensive. Effective eC leaders nurture informal leaders from among their members and recruit them to become members of leadership teams who collaborate in serving the community's many leadership functions (Cosley, Frankowsky, Kiesler, Terveen, & Riedll, 2005; Jameson, 2009; Jones & Meier, in press). They publicly acknowledge the contributions of members who do research on the community's focal problem and report back on their discoveries of new resources and interventions. These members become known as local experts. Some help to prevent information overload and repetitive discussions by compiling and updating periodically posted "Frequently Asked Questions" messages (Meier et al., 2007). In some SeCs, members acquire their leadership skills through informal apprenticeships (Meier et al., 2007). Community leaders may also help members develop skills by encouraging them to take on projects that extend the technical resources for the community (Jones & Meier, in press; Meier et al., 2007). Members who have shown themselves to be fairly active, constructive participants may be recruited to assist more experienced members with group management tasks.

To thrive, SeCs have to work on capacity building at the organizational level. For example, as freestanding SeCs become more internally complex, leadership teams may establish their own specialized listserves as forums to discuss community management issues apart from the ongoing discussions of the larger community (Jones & Meier, in press). In the better-organized portals for freestanding SeCs addressing related problems, SeC leaders have organized their own eCs to discuss how to manage problems common to all their communities (Meier et al., 2007).

COMMUNITY DEVELOPMENTAL PROCESSES

Optimal matching theory only addresses the factors influencing whether an individual will seek social support online. However, the experience of support is also affected by its accessibility and timeliness. In addition to basic computer skills (e.g., keyboarding and accessing the Internet), SNS members need to know how to "navigate" the Web to get to their community's websites, and, once there, know how to access the resources those sites. Clearly, the e-support networks described here vary in their accessibility and required "navigation" skillfulness.

As in face-to-face groups, the supportive potential of an SeC depends on how many members there are and how many actively they participate. Rates of growth in listserv and Web forum eCs tend to grow slowly, depending on how intense the interest is in the group's focal concern and how easy it is to find the group online. SNSs can grow much faster because individual members take the initiative of informing their network members about a group's formation and invite them to join. As other social media network members join the group, they too can send out bulk initiations to members in their own networks (Smarty, 2009).

Face-to-face group sessions are time-limited, and members know who is in the group because they can see each other. In eCs, relatively few members carry on the work of the group. Most members "lurk"—reading messages but contributing only rarely (Nonnecke & Preece, 2000). In their study of health support listservs, Nonnecke and Preece (2000) found that, on average, only 45% of members post more than once every 3 months. This pattern of participation is significant because it means that eCs must achieve a critical mass to ensure that there will be sufficient levels of activity to keep members engaged. The listserv groups and Web forum can grow to have thousands of members, but only about 1% will be active. This is not necessarily a bad situation. If all members were active contributors all the time, then the community would be crushed under the deluge of messages. Too many messages can make it difficult for members to decide whom to respond to and so they stop posting entirely (Meier, 1999).

Whether or not they participate actively, all SeC members can benefit. Other members' posts can be important sources of informational support. They can learn about new treatments, support services, advocacy organizations, and policy changes that could affect their wellbeing. By observing other members' interactions online, members have opportunities for social learning (Bandura, 1977; Meier et al., 2007). Members can read about or (sometimes) watch videos about other members' strategies for solving problems that are similar to their own. They can learn to think critically about the information they are receiving from health care and other professional advisors (Eysenbach, 2007). They are exposed to role models for effective self-advocacy in dealing with health care and other professional service providers (Eysenbach, 2007). In all types of these eC systems, posts are archived. Members can use keyword searches of message contents to find information on specific topics without having to ask for it (Meier et al., 2007).

If they are successful in recruiting and retaining members, SeCs can evolve to the point where some members have had their support needs met and want to go beyond simply helping each other. As the eC becomes more cohesive and informal leaders emerge, some may initiate projects (Jones & Meier, in press; Meier, Lyons, & Forlenza, 2006; Meier et al., 2007). For example, Parents of Suicide eC members have commemorated the lives of their children by creating cloth and "virtual" quilts (see http://www.parentsofsuicide.com/Mem_quilt.htm), showing pictures and other memorabilia, and a cookbook with their favorite recipes (see http://www.parentsofsuicide.com/cookbook_home.html).

If their internal projects succeed, some SeC members may begin to be interested in addressing macro sociostructural issues that contribute to their individual challenges. They may decide to expand their corporate missions beyond member support to the alleviation of social injustices—in this case, unmet needs for social support and resources (Durning, 1989; Fisher, 1997). At this stage, these eCs may begin to function like grassroots organizations. As with their offline grassroots advocacy groups, e-advocacy groups are usually volunteers from subgroups of larger SeCs who share similar concerns and who come together in small, informally organized groups. The Internet makes it convenient for members of all kinds of advocacy groups to communicate easily and mobilize quickly to respond to emerging opportunities and crises (Andrews, 2002; Shirkey, 2008).

Listserv-based support groups usually begin with the mission to provide information and emotional support. They only take on projects when there are enough volunteers among their members to engage in advocacy action. With support SNSs, the move to advocacy activities can happen much sooner. An SNS group may immediately set up two sites, one a portal for member information and support and another for fundraising (Bender, Marroquin, & Jadad, 2009).

RESEARCH ON THE BENEFITS AND LIMITATIONS OF SUPPORT E-COMMUNITIES

As the number and variety of eCs as burgeoned over the past decade, so have the number of social scientists who have taken up the challenge of studying their social network structures and dynamics—and especially those of e-social networks. One notable recent study in this area was Christakis and Fowler's research of social contagion. They demonstrated how behavior by one person in a social network can significantly affect the norms and behavior of groups at distant points in that network (Christakis & Fowler, 2009). While such studies may appear in almost any journal that accepts studies of e-network and eC research, some have specialized in reporting studies of in eC behavior: *The Journal of Computer Mediated Communication*, *The Journal of Media Psychology*, and the *ACM Conference Proceedings on Human Factors in Computing Systems*.

Intervention researchers have explored how the Internet can be used to deliver interventions and social support. However, the process of generating the evidence base for SeCs lags far behind the capacity of Internet users to create them (Potts, 2006). A few journals specialize in publishing e-intervention research studies, notably, the *Journal of Medical Internet Research*, *Cyberpsychology and Behavior*, and *Cybertherapy and Rehabilitation*. Regrettably, very few social work researchers have conducted studies in this area. Instead, they have tended to focus on the use of communications technology in social work education (Beaulaurier & Haffey, 2005). One peer-reviewed social work journal, *Journal of Technology in Human Services*, periodically includes articles describing Internet-delivered programs, but its focus is also more on the use of technology in education.

Ethical and Methodological Factors in Research on Support e-Communities

Before describing the state of the art of research on the benefits and limitations of SeCs, it is important to consider factors that have shaped research activities in this area. In earlier stages of eC development, researchers viewed the enormous archives of messages generated by eC members as a potential treasure trove of observational data. However, getting access to these data has proved difficult for ethical reasons. Researchers studying eCs have debated whether mailing lists and other online groups are "public spaces or private rooms" (Eysenbach, 2001; Kraut et al., 2004). Electronic community members are more likely than researchers to view the eCs as "private spaces" when they have to go through some kind of registration procedure to participate and the groups are smaller (<100 members). Because Web 2.0 makes it easy to conduct surveys and create databases, SeCs are becoming increasingly interested in surveying members, compiling data on member characteristics and concerns, and making these data available to researchers for analysis. For text-based SeCs, community leaders and members have been less willing to have their mailing lists or Web forums used as conduits for recruiting research participants. Many have been unwilling to release their message archives to researchers out of concern for member confidentiality. Some Web forums have created specialized "Research Project" threads to post recruitment invitations to those members who are interested in participating in studies. In this way, they have used eC technologies to create opportunities for researchers and members to communicate directly with each other, while shielding other members from irrelevant messages.

Even when researchers are given access to SeC message archives, there are major methodological challenges to conducting qualitative research with these eCs related to their internal variability in leadership roles and participation rates. For example, it is difficult to know how to sample members' messages because they are highly variable in their timing and frequency (Meier et al., 2007). Text-based SeCs usually do not collect background information about their members, so it is difficult to know how heterogeneous the groups are in their composition, making comparisons between SeCs difficult. For within-SeC studies, mailing list hosting services collect metadata on member participation rates, but since the timing and frequency of member posts are unpredictable, there has been no consensus on the most reliable ways to sample them (Meier et al., 2007).

Analyzing SeC message texts is challenging because members use informal language (e.g., slang, incomplete sentences, writing about several topics in one post). This communication characteristic coupled with the mass of textual data collected in these kinds of qualitative studies of eCs pushes the limits of conventional qualitative data analysis methods. Many researchers have adapted to these constraints on data collection and data quality by collecting indirect data on SeCs using Web surveys, in-depth interviews, and/or focus groups (Eysenbach & Kohler, 2002). Even when researchers use computerized qualitative data analysis programs, progress on their analyses is time and labor intensive, contrasting dramatically with the speed of the production of messages produced within these communities.

Information and social scientists (Arguello et al., 2006; Pennebaker, Francis, & Booth, 2001; Seale, Ziebland, & Charteris-Black, 2006) have been working to develop efficient text data mining procedures that will work with semistructured textual data, such as e-mail messages (Dorre, Gerstl, & Seifert, 1999). These innovative tools will be critical for rapidly gaining insights into the processes and discussion content of SeC member interactions. These emerging analytical techniques will make it feasible for researchers to use mixed methods—qualitative methods to explore the depth and richness of qualitative data and quantitative methods to achieve the potential precision and generalizability of quantitative data.

Focal Populations and Issues

Over the past two decades, research on SeCs has focused on two different areas. In the first, formal intervention studies incorporate short-term SeCs, formed by systematic recruitment of members, as components of multimodal interventions that also include psychoeducational components (Ritterband et al., 2003). The second area of research has investigated members' experiences and satisfaction with self-forming SeCs. It is this body of research that is the focus of the following discussion.

Intervention researchers have studied text-based SeCs for people who were living with chronic or life-threatening physical conditions. Listserv-based SeCs for cancer survivors have been among the most intensely studied (Han et al., 2008; Meier et al., 2007; Rimer et al., 2005; Shaw, DuBenske, Han, Cofta-Woerpel, Bush, & Gustafson, 2008; Shaw et al., 2007; Winzelberg et al., 2003).

Fogel and colleagues have examined differences in minority participation in SeCs for cancer (Fogel, Albert, Schnabel, Ditkfoff, & Neugut, 2002; Fogel et al., 2008). Other investigators have studied different aspects of text-based SeCs for a wide range of other chronic conditions including amyotrophic lateral sclerosis (Feenberg, Licht, Kane, Moran, & Smakith, 1996) and diabetes (Loader, Muncer, Burrows, Pleace, & Nettleton, 2002; Zrebiec & Jacobson, 2001). Other studies have examined the appropriateness of SeCs for people living with mental health challenges, including obsessive-compulsive disorders (Stein, 1997), depression (Salem, Bogat, & Reid, 1997), eating disorders (North, 1998), or sexual abuse (Finn & Lavitt, 1994); alcoholics (Van Lear, Sheehan, Withers, & Walker, 2005); survivors of alcoholic families (Phillips, 1996); recovering drug addicts (King, 1994); and self-injuring adolescents (Whitlock, Powers, & Eckenrode, 2006). There have also been studies of support groups for older adults (Wright, 2000) and caregivers of people with mental illness (Peron, 2002). Some studies have explored differences in participation rates in SeCs across racial and ethnic groups (Case et al., 2009; Fogel et al., 2008).

Other researchers have compared how problem themes were discussed in different kinds of groups. McKenna and Bargh surveyed members of mailing list–based support groups that addressed concerns about marginalized identities. Some discussed visible stigmas (obesity, stuttering, cerebral palsy, and baldness) and others discussed drugs, homosexuality, and sexual bondage (McKenna & Bargh, 1998). Miller and Gergan (1998) explored how suicidality was discussed in groups for recovering alcoholics, child abuse survivors, and parents.

Intervention researchers have studied text-based SeCs for people who were living with chronic or life-threatening physical conditions. Listserv-based SeCs for cancer survivors have been among the most intensely studied (Han et al., 2008; Meier et al., 2007; Rimer et al., 2005; Shaw et al., 2007, 2008; Winzelberg et al., 2003).

Text-based SeCs have been around for much longer than Web-based communities, so research on their benefits has been much more extensive. Many of the benefits of these SeCs identified early on are still true today. Support eCs are convenient and accessible to members around-the-clock and through wired and wireless channels (Finn & Lavitt, 1994; Phillips, 1996; Van Lear et al., 2005). These technologies enable people who are unable or unwilling to attend a face-to-face group to interact with each other. Thus, geographically distant from each other, people who suffer from rare diseases, or who are homebound due to illness or caregiving obligations, can now benefit from group support. In text-based SeCs, members are invisible and can choose how much to disclose to each other. People who suffer from stigmas may be attracted to these groups because of the control they have over their self-presentation (King, 1994; Kummervold et al., 2002; Radin, 2006)

Because SNS-based SeCs are so much newer, research on them is less extensive. In many respects, the social support that SNS members receive appears to be similar to that derived by members of text-based SeCs. SNS members benefit by contributing to blogs on their communities' site, enhancing their ability to cope with distress by being in community with empathic others (Baker & Fortune, 2008; Pennebaker, 1990; Whitlock, 2006).

Participants in text-based SeCs may seek out communities in which they can maintain their invisibility and anonymity. By contrast, SNS participants may be attracted to the ways that these multimedia portals can provide them very rich impressions of each other's circumstances so they can judge how similar their circumstances are and, therefore, how valid their opinions might be. For example, the PatientsLikeMe eC is a portal for SeCs for people living with chronic conditions. Included in this site is a searchable database of members' personal health information. The database allows members to discover and contact others in the network who are experiencing problems similar to their own (Frost & Massagili, 2008; Patientslikeme.com, 2009).

SeCs can be important sources of informational support. Members frequently offer each other information and advice about the practicalities of daily living that enhance coping (Braithwaite, Waldron, & Finn, 1999; Fogel et al., 2002; Kerr, Murray, Stevenson, Gore, & Nazareth, 2006; Loader et al., 2002; Peron, 2002).

When sharing health information, SeC members' online discussions can enhance their understanding of the substance, and apply their collective critical processes to correct misinformation and misapprehensions (Hoch & Ferguson, 2005). One benefit of this informal mutual education process may be improved treatment adherence (Kirshner, 2003)

These eCs are also important sources of emotional support. Members can vent about their problems and have their feelings validated by others (Loader et al., 2002; McKenna & Green, 2002; Meier et al., 2007). Many members who participate in these groups feel less isolated and more hopeful (Clifford, 2009; Loader et al., 2002; Meier, 2007; North, 1998). Sometimes, the support members receive from the group may spur them to social action (Jones & Meier, in press; Kummervold et al., 2002; Meier et al., 2007).

Limitations

There are five main types of limitations ascribed to SeCs. The first category includes problems arising out of the need to rely on telecommunications technology to communicate. Participation in SeCs is limited to people who can afford Internet services and are competent in using their desktop computers or other mobile electronic devices to access the Internet. They must also be able use their technology to express themselves. With the advent of Web 2.0, users may feel pressure to be to be able to more than read and write. They may need to learn specialized communication skills like texting and create audio, photographic, or video content. Broadband Internet is fast and amazingly reliable, but when it crashes, users must be able to weather the frustration and confusion of disrupted or delayed transmissions.

The informality of SeCs can also affect the quality of the informational support that members receive. Because SeC membership is heterogeneous, new members may have very different information needs than more seasoned members who have become more experienced in managing their life challenges. More experienced members who want more in-depth scientific information and specific treatments may become frustrated with repeated requests by "newbies" for basic information (Kerr et al., 2006). Collectively, the information members exchange may be reliable, but individual members may communicate incorrect or biased information (Finfgeld, 2000; Hoch & Ferguson, 2005).

Most SeCs have open membership and are ongoing; consequently, there can be a high level of turnover among members (Cummings, Butler, & Kraut, 2002). Unless leaders actively work to keep discussions on topic, discussions can be superficial (Finn & Lavitt, 1994; Meier et al., 2007). In SeCs, members who have unrealistic expectations about the group may feel frustrated because they are unable to get their needs met for emotional support.

Because text-based e-communication promotes psychological deindividualization and disinhibition, social controls in those kinds of SeCs can be weaker than in face-to-face groups. SeCs are not necessarily safe places to air divergent views. Debates on controversial issues can be harsh, as opinion leaders attempt to force members to have conforming opinions (Rier, 2007). In such conflicted situations, some members may express hostility or become verbally abusive ("flame"), wounding other emotionally fragile members (Finn & Lavitt, 1994). In most cases, leadership in SeCs is unsupervised and unregulated. Members may have unrealistic expectations about the leader's role and skills (Holmes, 1997). Volunteer SeC leaders with little experience in group facilitation may not know how to intervene if problems arise. Finally, because many SeCs are run by volunteers, they may dissolve with little warning if the SeCs owner decides that it takes too much time and energy (K. Beal, Founder, ParentsofSuicide SeC, personal communication, September 30, 2009). If this happens, group members who have come to rely on it for companionship and other support may feel bereft.

A third type of limitation includes problems that can arise when members' lives in the "virtual world" are not well integrated with their lives in the "real world" (Suler, 2000). In a few cases, users who compulsively overuse the Internet can create problems in their relationships, family life, and work because they spend so much time online (Young, 1999). When this occurs, those Internet users may develop cyber-relationship addictions in which they experience their online relationships as more rewarding than their in-person relationships (Young, 1999). Or, they may spend so much time online participating in their cyberspace communities that they reduce their participation in their face-to-face social networks (Young, 1999). Some clinicians have expressed concern that people may become so dependent on the support of their online communities that they delay seeking professional help when they need it (Finn, 1996).

A fourth type of limitation is the risk of being exposed to disruptions caused by individual members (Meier et al., 2007). Some may be "trolls" who make intentionally disruptive or offensive comments simply for the attention gained by causing a commotion in the community. Another form of SeC deviance is misrepresentation of self. This type of destructive behavior can take several forms: falsely claiming to have the same illness as other members (Munchausen by Internet?) or posing as several different members using multiple online identities. In rare instances, a member will write such inconsistent comments that he or she raises suspicions that he or she has a multiple personality disorder. Finally, someone may post to SeC claiming to be a friend or relative of a community member, reporting falsely that the member has died. Often these reports are accompanied by requests to raise money for the deceased's bereaved family. Members' personal stresses combined with Internet-related psychological disinhibition and members' genuine concern for each other result in their feeling intense anger, foolish, betrayed, or frightened because the situation is so far beyond the range of their normal SeC experience.

A fifth category of limitation for participation is the risk of member exposure to individual members or the group as a whole who endorse self-destructive behaviors or recruit members for socially deviant eCs. For example, in the Pro-Anorexia mailing list, SeC members endorse anorexia as a positive lifestyle and share tips for dieting and how to hide weight loss from parents or physicians (Lyons, Mehl, & Pennebaker, 2006). Other examples include members in SeCs for depression who encourage others in the community to commit suicide (Biddle, Donovan, Hawton, Kapur, & Gunnell, 2008; Sandler, 2009). Unmoderated groups are vulnerable to hackers who post offensive or pornographic messages. Another more serious risk associated with eC participation—and, to some degree, SeCs—is their growing use by hate groups to target alienated members for recruitment into hate groups (Weisenthal Center, 2009).

Despite these potential risks, surveys and SeC participation rates consistently document that these Internet users believe that the advantages outweigh the risks. They continue to "vote with their fingers" when they seek out information and emotional support from text-based and social media SeCs.

COMBINING INDIVIDUAL COUNSELING AND SUPPORT E-COMMUNITIES: A NEW PRACTICE MODEL

Currently, there are no evidence-based practice guidelines for combining Internet self-help groups and face-to-face individual treatment. Even the most recent NASW/ASWB *Standards for Technology and Social Work Practice* (National Association of Social Workers & Association of Social Work Boards, 2005) presents separate standards for technology-mediated individual clinical and community practice with no recommendations about how to integrate in-person services with SeC resources. The practice model is described here based on best practices for individual and group interventions and communication theory. It maps out what social workers should do at each phase of treatment, starting from the initial assessment through termination and posttreatment client empowerment (Figure 9.3).

Assessment

Social workers are not trained to ask clients about their Internet use and experiences as part of the initial assessment process. As a result, they may only learn about clients' Internet experiences or their interest in using the Internet after treatment is well under way. Given the statistics on Internet penetration in the United States, social workers should not be surprised to discover their clients have access somewhere to the Internet.

The Internet demographic trends described previously signal to social workers that they should assume that their clients are using the Internet or, at least, rule it out. If they learn that their clients are already going online, practitioners need to explore with them how their Internet experiences fit in with their other life

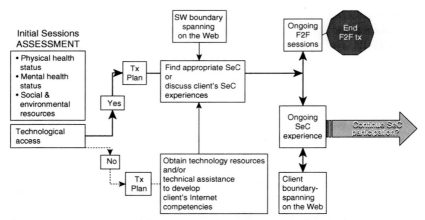

Figure 9-3. Practice model: Integrating in-person counseling and support e-community participation.

domains. Even if clients do not have access to the technology, many may like help to obtain it. Such situations offer social workers opportunities to strengthen their clients' connections to a virtual universe of potentially helpful information and resources.

To obtain this information, social workers need to modify their biopsychosocial assessment routine. They will need to probe further to discover whether clients have the physical, cognitive, expressive, and interpersonal capacities to interact competently on the Internet. Mental health assessments should assess whether and how the psychoactive effects of Internet use might strengthen or weaken clients hold on reality, as well as identify SeCs that match their technical competencies and support needs.

When clients do have Internet access, technological assessments should determine the extent of their access and their experience with it. In these cases, the assessment would also determine the number and kinds of devices they use (desktop computers or wireless laptops, cell phones, or other mobile devices) and who is available to provide technical assistance when they go online. For clients with Internet access, this stage of the assessment would also explore their patterns of Internet use (e-mail and Web), their experiences establishing and maintaining relationships via e-mail and the Web, and their experiences with and preferences for different kinds of eCs.

Where clients do not have access but do want it, social workers' case management efforts could focus on locating community access sites and volunteers who could provide training and technical assistance. Alternatively, the social worker could seek donors who could supply computers and modems, and, if needed, subsidized Internet services. Once clients who are new users go online, social workers need to monitor their use patterns and how they are coping with technological problems.

Finding a Good Support e-Community

If clients are new to the Internet, they may need help finding an SeC. As part of their ongoing resource-seeking strategies, social workers who specialize in specific at-risk populations may want to scan the Internet periodically for SeCs addressing those problems. Workers should promote clients' resourcefulness by teaching them how to find these groups for themselves. Practitioners should discuss with clients what their goals are for joining an SeC and also inform them about local face-to-face groups that address the same issues.

Using Google or other Web search engines, it is relatively easy to find information about SeCs on any topic. For text-based SeCs, the resulting lists also include metadata about community size and structure. eCs can be implemented technologically but never attract a sufficient number of members to be viable. Workers need to alert clients that the number of subscribers is not a reliable indicator of group functioning. Some groups have an Internet "presence" and a long list of subscribers, with only a few who post regularly. New members who sign on may discover that the groups are moribund and there is very little activity. Unfortunately, there is no good way to assess group functioning without joining.

When referring clients to 12-step and other face-to-face self-help groups, social workers would offer information about how a self-help group works before clients join. Likewise, social workers need to help clients understand how SeCs work. For clients experiencing a lot of strain, it may be wise to recommend joining a text-based SeC that does not require them to acquire as many Web navigation skills to participate.

Workers should discuss with clients how to learn about community norms. In text-based SeCs, these may be posted automatically to new members in "Frequently Asked Questions (FAQ)" texts. If the SeC has a website (or is an SNC) as with a listserv or Web forum, its norms may be posted as a page on those sites. Having explicit norms and active leadership makes it more likely that members will adhere to them. Workers can discuss with clients whether and how member interactions are facilitate and help them understand the characteristics of a well-functioning eC. Clients need to know the steps for withdrawing from the group if they decide it is not helpful.

Protecting Confidentiality

Technology-mediated disinhibition can prompt Internet users to take risks that they would not do otherwise. The intense attentional focus generated by TM interactions can lead to users to disregard environmental hazards. Clients may believe that messages sent to their eCs are private and will be kept confidential (American Association for the Advancement of Science, 1999). While the sheer volume of transmissions would appear to protect Internet user privacy, posts to publicly accessible eCs remain as records in virtual archives indefinitely and are searchable by Web search engines. Social workers are ethically obliged to inform clients of the risks to confidentiality when they communicate online (National Association of Social Workers & Association of Social Work Boards, 2005). For example, systems operators at any computer node in the Internet telecommunications system can intercept messages. Employers have the right to review all messages sent through their worksite computers or Internet systems. Members of SeCs may forward messages without permission to people outside the group. Given all these opportunities for violations of privacy, clients should be forewarned, and periodically reminded, that they should absolutely not write anything in an online communication that they do not want others to know.

Treatment Plans

When social workers negotiate treatment plans with Internet-using clients in face-to-face sessions, they should also contract when and how they will discuss those clients' experiences with the Internet and eCs. These discussions should be seen as part of a larger exploration of the clients' engagement in their social networks. Here the treatment model would be roughly similar to working with clients who are in one-to-one counseling along with a face-to-face self-help group (Nowinski et al., 1992). In their face-to-face sessions, discussions should cover information clients have received from their eCs, what they are learning from their eC's process, and how they are applying the information or suggestions received through those interactions to their "real world" lives.

Storm King, a clinical psychologist and researcher, has proposed using client participation strategically by moving clients through more than one group. A client who is socially phobic, for example, could be encouraged to join an online group that discussed a hobby or other safe topic as a way of learning how to carry on a conversation (King & Moreggi, 1998). When the client has become comfortable with IM communication and desensitized to presentation anxiety with this type of interaction, he or she could then be encouraged to join a self-help group on social phobias. Although no systematic research has been done on this kind of intervention strategy, it is a good example of the variety of ways SeCs could be used as interventions.

Middle Stage

Once a client has been successful in getting online and is regularly participating an SeC, those experiences become part of the ongoing therapeutic discussion. Clients may ask the worker to clarify information offered by other SeC members or want to discuss how to apply it to their situations. Sometimes the clients may wonder whether information they receive through their SeCs is accurate and need the worker's help in confirming or disconfirming it (Finfgeld, 2000; Hoch & Ferguson, 2005; Winzelberg, 1997). In-person sessions can be used as opportunities to identify and correct errors as they arise.

Social workers can inquire about their clients' positive and negative experiences in the group or those that were particularly meaningful or troubling (King & Moreggi, 1998). Clients can also bring in the texts of salient messages to review and discuss. They may wish to consult about alternative ways to respond to messages or their feelings about messages that they composed before posting them.

Well-functioning SeCs offer members opportunities to develop and share expertise and to take on informal leadership roles in the community. Social workers can discuss with clients whether there are issues that they would like to learn more about and how best to share what they find with other members. Workers can also explore with clients how leadership roles are enacted in their SeCs, which ones they find attractive, and develop strategies for discovering how they could obtain the benefits of playing those roles, too.

Social workers also need to monitor whether and how clients' Internet use patterns change significantly over time. Have other family members begun to criticize them about their Internet use? Do clients discuss their Internet group experiences with their families and friends? Do they discuss their families and work experiences with other members in their Internet groups (Greenfield, 1999; Grohol, 1998)? If clients begin to show signs of compulsive Internet use, social workers should explore the reasons for these behaviors and suggest shifting to offline sources of support.

Termination

Ideally, clients leave their self-help groups because they decide they no longer need them. Internet groups, however, can also dissolve because the list owner or other key members withdraw. Alternatively, clients may decide to drop out because their groups do not address their needs or have become dysfunctional. Social workers should discuss with clients whether they want to join other SeCs, such as those with a more activist orientation. Alternatively, clients may want to think about how to apply what they learned through their SeC experiences to a face-to-face group. If clients are reaching the end of their face-to-face sessions, social workers can help them examine how their participation in the SeC can serve as a source of continuing support.

Evaluation

Because social workers are not running these SeCs, they cannot evaluate them directly. What they can do is help their clients assess group cohesion, the accuracy of information exchanged, and the extent to which they are able to draw on group experience to become more resourceful in the real world.

NATIONAL RESOURCES

The national support organization websites listed at the end of this chapter are a sampling of the resources available to social workers. These sites offer up-to-date, evidence-based information about physical and behavioral health problems, current treatments, and other support resources. Almost all have Facebook sites that are linked to Twitter feeds. These websites usually include organizational contact information and e-mail links for users to interact with the sponsors, their Web masters, and list owners. Social workers can contact these website staff members to determine the extent to which sponsors monitor their groups. Practitioners may want to join particular groups for a while to learn about participants' concerns and strengths before advising clients to do so. Technically, anyone can join publicly accessible Internet groups, but group members may object to having "outsiders" (people without the shared problem) in the group. As a professional courtesy, social workers should contact Web masters/list owners of a group they are interested in to find out if the eC has policies governing professional observers.

CONCLUSION

This description of combined in-person counseling and SeCs takes advantage of existing free information and support resources and builds social worker and client capacity. As with all social work practice, readers should continue to draw on their own practice wisdom, seek client feedback, and consult with other experienced social workers when they apply these ideas and models in their own work settings. My hope is that readers will come away appreciating how the Internet is transforming the helping professions and motivated to discover about how they could use this abundance of SeC resources to help their clients.

RESOURCES

The 15 organizations listed here all sponsor one or more kind of text-based SeC (listserv, Web forum, or chat groups). Thirteen have Facebook support and fundraising sites, and nine have Twitter feeds as of this writing. This information was found by Googling the name of each organization to see whether they listed links to one or more SeCs (listserv, discussion group, forum, or chat groups). Facebook sites were found by doing Google searches using the organization's name and Facebook as search terms. Information about Twitter feeds was found using a similar Google search strategy but replacing "Facebook" with the search term "Twitter." This list documents how support organizations are rapidly adopting multiple Internet channels to deliver information and support. This means that organizations serving at-risk groups that are not listed below are likely to implement SeCs soon.

Using these Internet search strategies will make it efficient to look for them.

Arthritis Foundation
http://www.arthritis.org

Attention Deficit Disorder Association
ADDA
http://www.add.org/

Online Alanon Outreach
http://www.ola-is.org/

Alcoholics Anonymous
http://aa-intergroup.org

American Cancer Society
http://www/cancer.org

American Pain Foundation
http://painid.painfoundation.org/

Association for the Advancement of Retired People
http://www.aarp.org

Asthma & Allergy Foundation of America
http://www.aafa.org

Child and Adolescent Bipolar Foundation
http://www.bpkids.org

Council for Equal Rights in Adoption
http://www.adoptioncrossroads.org

Family Caregiver Alliance
http://www.caregiver.org/caregiver/jsp/home.jsp

GrandsPlace
http://grandsplace.org/

Multiple Sclerosis Foundation
http://www.msfocus.org/ms-community.aspx

Narcotics Anonymous
http://www.12stepforums.net/na/

Parents, Family & Friends of Suicides
http://www.pos-ffos.com/

REFERENCES

Alonzo, M. & Alken, M. (2004). Flaming in electronic communication. *Decision Support Systems, 36*(3), 205–213.

Andrews, D. C. (2002). Audience-specific online community design. *Communications of the ACM, 45*(4), 64–68.

Arguello, J., Butler, B. S., Joyce, E., Kraut, R., Ling, K. S., & Wang, X. (2006, April 24-27). *Talk to me: Foundations for successful individual-group interactions in online communities.* Paper presented at the In CHI 2006: Proceedings of the ACM Conference on Human-Factors in Computing Systems, Quebec.

Association for the Advancement of Social Work with Groups, I. (1999). Standards for social work practice with groups. Retrieved August 2, 2000, from http://www.aaswg.org/standards.htm

Baker, D. & Fortune, S. (2008). Understanding self-harm and suicide websites. *Crisis, 29*(3), 118–122.

Bandura, A. (1977). *Social learning theory.* Englewood Cliffs, NJ: Prentice Hall.

Beaulaurier, R. L. & Haffey, M. (eds.). (2005). *Technology and social work education and curriculum: The high tech, high touch social work educator.* New York: Haworth Press.

Bender, J. L., Marroquin, C. J., & Jadad, A. R. (2009). *Facebook: Awareness-raising, fund-raising and support for people affected by breast cancer.* Paper presented at the Medicine 2.0 Conference, Toronto, Canada.

Bernstein, R. (2009). Census Bureau estimates number of adults, older people and school-age children in states. *US Census Bureau News.* Retrieved October 10, 2009, from http://www.census.gov/Press-Release/www/releases/archives/population/001703.html

Biddle, L., Donovan, J., Hawton, K., Kapur, N., & Gunnell, D. (2008, Suicide and the Internet [800–802]. http://www.bmj.com/cgi/content/full/336/7648/800?eletter.

Boyd, D. M. & Ellison, N. B. (2007). Social network sites: Definition, history and scholar-ship. *Journal of Computer Mediated Communication, 13*(1), Article 11. jcmc.indiana.edu/vol13/issue1/boyd.ellison.html

Braithwaite, D. O., Waldron, V. R., & Finn, J. (1999). Communication of social support in computer-mediated groups for persons with disabilities. *Health Communication, 11*, 123–151.

Case, S., Jernigan, V., Gardner, A., Ritter, P., Heanery, C. A., & Lorig, K. R. (2009). Content and frequency of writing on diabetes bulletin boards: Does race make a dif-ference. *Journal of Medical Internet Research, 11*(2), e22.

Christakis, N. A. & Fowler, J. H. (2009). *Connected: The surprising power of our social Networks and how they shape our lives.* New York: Little, Brown & Company.

Clifford, S. (2009). Online, "a reason to keep on going." Retrieved September 6, 2009, from http://www.nytimes.com/2009/06/02/health/02face.html?_r=1&pagew

Colon, Y. (1996). Chattering through the fingertips: Doing group therapy online. *Women and Performance: A Journal of Feminist Theory, 9*, 205–215.

Cosley, D., Frankowsky, D., Kiesler, S., Terveen, L., & Riedll, J. (2005). *How oversight improves member-maintained communities.* Paper presented at the Conference on Human Factors in Computing Systems: Proceedings of the SIGCHI conference on Human factors in computing systems, Vienna, Austria.

Cummings, J. N., Butler, B., & Kraut, R. (2002). The quality of online social relationships. *Communications of the ACM, 45*(7), 103–108.

Cutrona, C. E. (1990). Stress and social support: In search of optimal matching. *Journal of Social and Clinical Psychology, 9*(1), 3–13.

Davidson, K. P., Pennebaker, J. W., & Dickerson, S. S. (2000). Who talks: The social psychology of illness support groups. *American Psychologist, 55*(2), 205–217.

Domestic Violence Resource Center. (2009). Support groups, message boards and chatrooms for survivors of abuse. Retrieved October 29, 2009, from http://www.dvirc.org.au/LibraryHub/SupportGroups.htm

Dorre, J., Gerstl, P., & Seifert, R. (1999). Text data mining: Finding nuggets in mountains of textual data. In M. A. Bramer (ed.), *Knowledge discovery and data mining* (pp. 398–401). London: The Institution of Electrical Engineers.

Durning, A. B. (1989). Action at the grassroots: Fighting poverty and environmental decline. *WorldWatch Paper, 88*(January), 1–70.

Eysenbach, G. (2001). Ethical issues in qualitative research on Internet communities. *British Medical Journal, 323*, 1103–1105.

Eysenbach, G. (2007, August 20–24). *From intermediation to disintermediation and apomediation: New models for consumers to access and assess the credibility of health information in the Age of Web 2.0.* Paper presented at the In: Medinfo 2007: Proceedings of the 12th World Congress on Health (Medical) Informatics; Building Sustainable Health Systems; pages 162–166, Brisbane, Australia.

Eysenbach, G. & Kohler, C. (2002). How do consumers search for and appraise health information on the World Wide Web? Qualitative study using focus groups, usability tests, and in-depth interviews. *British Medical Journal, 324*, 573–576.

Feenberg, A. L., Licht, J. M., Kane, K. P., Moran, K., & Smakith, R. A. (1996). The online patient meeting. *Journal of Neurological Sciences, 139*(Suppl.), 129–131.

Fiegelman, W., Gorman, B. S., Beal, K. C., & Jordan, J. R. (2008). Internet support groups for suicide survivors: A new mode for gaining bereavement assistance. *Omega: Journal of Death and Dying, 57*(3), 217–243.

Finfgeld, D. L. (2000). Therapeutic groups online: The good, the bad and the unknown. *Issues in Mental Health Nursing, 21*, 241–255.

Finn, J. (1999). An exploration of helping processes in an online self-help group focussing on issues of disability. *Health and Social Work, 24*, 220–231.

Finn, J. & Lavitt, M. (1994). Computer-based self-help for survivors of sexual abuse. *Social Work with Groups, 17*(1), 21–46.

Fisher, R. (1997). Social action community organization: Proliferation, persistence, roots, and prospects. In M. Minkler (ed.), *Community organizing & community building for health* (pp. 53–65). New Brunswick, NJ: Rutgers University Press.

Fogel, J., Albert, S. M., Schnabel, F., Ditkfoff, B. A., & Neugut, A. I. (2002). Racial/ethnic differences and potential psychological benefits in the use of the Internet by women with breast cancer. *Psycho-Oncology, 12,* 107–117.

Fogel, J., Ribsl, K. M., Morgan, P. D., Humphreys, K., & Lyons, E. J. (2008). The under-representation of African Americans in online cancer support groups. *Journal of the National Medical Association, 100*(5), 705–712.

Fritz, J. (2009). The young are wired for social media: Is your nonprofit? *Nonprofit Charitable Orgs.* Retrieved October 24, 2009, from http://nonprofit.about.com/od/fundraising/a/wiredyoung.htm

Frost, J. H. & Massagili, M. P. (2008). Social uses of personal health information within PatientsLikeMe, an online patient community: What can happen when patients have access to one another date. *Journal of Medical Internet Resarch, 10*(3), e3. Retrieved from http://www.jmir.org/2008/3/e15/.

Google.com. (n.d.). Google groups. Retrieved October 10, 2009, from http://groups.google.com/

Greenfield, D. N. (1999, August 20). *The nature of Internet addiction: Psychological factors in compulsive Internet use.* Paper presented at the American Psychological association, Boston, MA.

GriefNet.org. (2009). GriefNet.org: e-mail support groups. Retrieved October 26, 2009, from http://griefnet.org/support/sg2.html

Grohol, J. M. (1998). Future clinical directions: Professional development, pathology and psychotherapy on-line. In J. Gackenbach (ed.), *Psychology and the Internet, intrapersonal, interpersonal and transpersonal implicaitons* (pp. 111–140). San Diego, CA: Academic Press.

Han, J. Y., Shaw, B. R., Hawkins, R. P., Pingree, S., McTavish, F. M., & Gustafson, D. H. (2008). Expressing positive emotions within online support groups by women with breast cancer. *Journal of Health Psychology, 13*(8), 1002–1007.

Hill, D. (2002). Computer-mediated therapy: Possibilities and possible limitations. Retrieved August 23, 2002, from http://www.psybc.com/library_cyber.html

Hoch, D. & Ferguson, T. (2005). What I learned from e-patients. *PLoS Medicine, 2*(8), e206. Retrieved from http://www.plosmedicine.org/article/info:doi/10.1371/journal.pmed.0020206

Holmes, L. (1997). The pros and cons of support groups for trauma survivors: Part 2 Retrieved April 4, 2002, from http://mentalhealth.about.com/library/weekly/aa092297.htm

Horrigan, J. (2009). Wireless Internet use. Retrieved October 10, 2009, from http://www.pewinternet.org/Reports/2009/12-Wireless-Internet-Use.aspx

Horrigan, J., Rainie, L., Allen, K., Boyce, A., Madden, M., & O'Grady, E. (2003). *The ever-shifting Internet population: A new look at Internet access and the digital divide*: Pew Internet and American Life Project.

Icyou.com. (2009). Homepage: Icyou.com: intensive content for your health. Retrieved October 23, 2009, from http://www.icyou.com/

Jameson, J. (2009). Distributed leadership, trust and online communities. *Online communities and social computing* (pp. 226–235). Berlin: Springer.

Jones, A. & Meier, A. (in press). Growing www.ParentsofSuicide: A case study. *Journal of Computer Mediated Communication.*

Kahanna, P. M. (2008). Icyou: How social media is the new resource for online health information. *The Medscape Journal of Medicine, 10*(5). http://www.medscape.com/viewarticle/573272

Kerr, C., Murray, E., Stevenson, F., Gore, C., & Nazareth, I. (2006). Internet interventions for long-term conditions: Patient and caregiver quality criteria. *Journal of Medical Internet Research, 8*(3), e13.

King, S. (1994). Analysis of electronic support groups for recovering addicts. *Interpersonal Computing and Technology, 2*(3), 47–56.

King, S. & Moreggi, D. (1998). Internet therapy and self-help groups--the pros and cons. In J. Gackenbach (ed.), *Psychology and the Internet: Intrapersonal, interpersonal and transpersonal implications*, Vol. 1998 (pp. 77–106). New York: Academic Press.

Kirshner, M. (2003). *Preliminary exploration of online social support among adults with asthma.* Paper presented at the American Medical Informatics Association Annual Symposium. Retrieved October 26, 2009, from http://www.pubmedcentral.nih.gov/articlerender.fcgi?artid=1480016

Knight, C. (1999). BSW and MSW students' perceptions of their academic preparation for group work. *Journal of Teaching in Social Work, 18*, 133–148.

Kramer, N. C. & Winter, S. (2008). Impression management 2.0: The relationship of self-esteem, extraversion, self-efficacy, and self-presentation within social networking sites. *Journal of Media Psychology, 20*(3), 106–116.

Kraut, R., Olson, J., Banji, M., Bruckman, A., Cohen, J., & Couper, M. (2004). Psychological research online: Report of Scientific Affairs' Advisory Group on the Conduct of Research on the Internet. *American Psychologist, 59*(2), 105–117.

Kristula, D. (1997, August 2001). The history of the Internet. Retrieved February 28, 2008, from http://www.davesite.com/webstation/net-history.shtml

Kummervold, P. E., Gammon, D., Bergvik, S., Johnson, J. A., Hasvold, T., & Rosenvinge, J. H. (2002). Social support in a wired world: Use of online mental health forums in Norway. *Nordic Journal of Psychiatry, 56*(1), 59–65.

Lenhart, A. (2000). Report: Who's not online: 57% of those without Internet access say they do not plan to log on. Retrieved October 15, 2009, from http://www.pewinternet.org/Reports/2000/Whos-Not-Online.aspx

Lenhart, A. (2009). Data Memo: Adults and social network websites. Retrieved October 10, 2009, from http://www.pewinternet.org/Reports/2009/Adults-and-Social-Network-Websites.aspx

Ley, B. (2007). Vive les roses! The architecture of commitment in an online pregnancy and mothering group. *Journal of Computer-Mediated Communication, 12*(4), article 12. http://jcmc.indiana.edu/vol12/issue4/ley.html

Loader, B., Muncer, S., Burrows, R., Pleace, N., & Nettleton, S. (2002). Medicine on the line? Computer-mediated social support and advice for people with diabetes. *International Journal of Social Welfare, 11*(1), 53–65.

Ludford, P. J., Cosley, D., Frankowsky, D., & Terveen, L. (2004). Think different: Increasing online community participation using uniqueness and group dissimilarity. Paper presented at the Conference on Human Factors in Computing Systems: Proceedings of the SIGCHI Conference on Human Factors in Computing Systems, Vienna, Austria.

Lyons, E. J., Mehl, M. R., & Pennebaker, J. W. (2006). Pro-anorexics and recovering anorexics differ in their linguistic Internet self-presentation. *Journal of Psychosomatic Research, 60*(3), 253–256.

Marcus, B., Machilek, F., & Schutz, A. (2006). Personality in cyberspace: Personal web sites as media for personality expressions and impressions. *Journal of Personality and Social Psychology, 90*(6), 1014–1031.

McKenna, K. Y. A. & Bargh, J. A. (1998). Coming out in the age of the Internet: Identity "demarginalization" through virtual group participation. *Journal of Personality and Social Psychology, 75*(3), 681–694.

McKenna, K. Y. A. & Green, A. S. (2002). Virtual group dynamics. *Group Dynamics, 6*(1), 116-127.

Meier, A. (1999). A multi-method evaluation of a computer-mediated, stress management support group for social workers: Feasibility, process, and effectiveness. Unpublished Dissertation, University of North Carolina, Chapel Hill.

Meier, A. (2000). Offering social support via the Internet: A case study of an online support group for social workers. In J. Finn & G. Holden (eds.), *Human services online: A new arena for service delivery* (pp. 237–266). New York: Haworth Press.

Meier, A., Lyons, E. J., & Forlenza, M. (2006). The Health e-Communities Project: Exploring how cancer survivors use Internet groups for support and empowerment. Paper presented at the 28th International Symposium on Social Work with Groups, San Diego.

Meier, A., Lyons, E. J., & Frydman, G. (2007). Patient-centered wikis: Cancer health e-communities. Retrieved October 23, 2007, from http://lo-wiki.acor.org/index.php/Cancer_Health_e-Communities

Meier, A., Lyons, E. J., Frydman, G., Forlenza, M., & Rimer, B. K. (2007). How cancer survivors provide support on cancer-related Internet mailing lists. *Journal of Medical Internet Research, 9*(2), e12. http://www.jmir.org/2007/2/e12.doi:10.2196/jmir.9.2.e12

Mickelson, K. D. (1997). Seeking social support: Parents in electronic support groups. In S. Kiesler (ed.), *Culture of the Internet.* Mahwah, NJ: Laurence Erlbaum Associates.

Milgram, S. (1967). The small world problem. *Psychology Today, 2*, 60–67.

Miller, J. K. & Gergan, K. J. (1998). Life on the line: The therapeutic potentials of computer-mediated conversation. *Journal of Marital and Family Therapy, 24*(2), 189–202.

NASW Assurance Services (2009). ASI Education Center: An important caution for social workers practicing online therapy. Retrieved October 11, 2009, from http://www.naswassurance.org/online_therapy.php?page_id=6

National Association of Social Workers & Association of Social Work Boards (2005). Standards for technology and social work practice. Retrieved October 11, 2009, from www.aswb.org/pdfs/TechnologySWPractice.pdf

Nonnecke, B. & Preece, J. (2000, April 1–6). *Lurker demographics: Counting the silent.* Paper presented at the Proceedings of CHI 2000, The Hague, Netherlands.

North, C. L. (1998). Computer-mediated communication and social support among eating disordered individuals: An analysis of the alt.support.eating-disord news group. *Dissertation Abstracts International Section A: Humanities and Social Sciences., 58*(12-A), 4496.

Patientslikeme.com. (2009). Patientslikeme.com Home Page. Retrieved October 27, 2009, from http://www.patientslikeme.com/

Pennebaker, J. W. (1990). *Opening up: The healing power of expressing emotions.* New York: The Guilford Press.

Pennebaker, J. W., Francis, M. E., & Booth, R. J. (2001). *Linguistic Inquiry and Word Count (LIWC): A computerized text analysis program.* Mahwah, NJ: Lawrence Erlbaum Associates.

Peron, B. (2002). Online support for caregivers of people with a mental illness. *Psychiatric Rehabilitation Journal, 26*(1), 70–77.

Pew Internet and American Life Project. (2009a). Demographics of Internet users. Retrieved October 10, 2009, from http://www.pewinternet.org/Static-Pages/Trend-Data/Whos-Online.aspx

Pew Internet and American Life Project. (2009b). Trend data: Internet activities. Retrieved October 10, 2009, from http://www.pewinternet.org/Trend-Data/Online-Activites-Total.aspx

Phillips, W. (1996). A comparison of online, e-mail and in-person self-help groups using Adult Children of Alcoholics as a model. Retrieved April 29, 1999, from www.rider.edu/users/suler/psycyber/acoa.html

Potts, H. W. W. (2006). Is E-health progressing faster than e-health researchers? *Journal of Medical Internet Research, 8*(3), e24. Retrieved from http://www.jmir.org/2006/3/e24/

Radin, P. A. (2006). "To me, it's my life": Medical communication, trust and activism in cyberspace. *Social Science & Medicine, 62,* 591–601.

Rainie, L. & Packel, D. (2001). More online, doing more: 16 million newcomers gain Internet access in the last half of 2000 as women, minorities and families with modest incomes continue to surge online. Retrieved May 19, 2001, from http://www.pewtrusts.com/pdf/vf_pew_Internet_population_report.pdf

ResearchandMarkets.com. (2007, November, 2007). Gay and Lesbian Internet users: The GLBT community. http://www.researchandmarkets.com/.../gay_and_lesbian_Internet_users_the_glbt.pdf

Rier, D. A. (2007). Internet social support groups as moral agents: The ethical dynamics of HIV+ status disclosure. *Sociology of Health and Illness, 29*(7), 1043–1058.

Rimer, B. K., Lyons, E. J., Ribsl, K. M., Bowling, J. M., Golin, M. J., & Meier, A. (2005). How new subscribers use cancer-related online mailing lists. http://www.jmir.org/2005/3/e32/.doi:10.2196/jmir.7.3.e32

Ritterband, L. M., Gonder-Frederick, L. A., Cox, D. J., Clifton, A. D., West, R. W., & Borowitz, S. M. (2003). Internet interventions: In review, in use and into the future. *Professional Psychology, Research and Practice, 34*(5), 527–534.

Salem, D. A., Bogat, G. A., & Reid, C. (1997). Mutual help goes on-line. *Journal of Community Psychology, 25*:(2), 189–207.

Sandler, E. P. (2009, October 27). Blog entry: Can social media help prevent suicide? http://www.psychologytoday.com/node/4184.

Schopler, J. H., Abell, M. D., & Galinsky, M. J. (1998). Technology-based groups: A review and conceptual framework for practice. *Social Work, 43*(3), 254–267.

Seale, C., Ziebland, S., & Charteris-Black, J. (2006). Gender, cancer experience and Internet use: A comparative keyword analysis of interviews and online cancer support groups. *Social Science & Medicine., 62*(10), 2570–2577.

Shannon, C. E. (1948). A mathematical theory of communication. *Bell System Technical Journal, 27*, 379–423 and 623–656.

Shaw, B. R., DuBenske, L., Han, J. Y., Cofta-Woerpel, L., Bush, N., & Gustafson, D. H. (2008). Communicating about self and others within an online support group for women with breast cancer and subsequent outcomes. *Journal of Health Psychology, 14*, 930–939.

Shaw, B. R., DuBenske, L., Han, J. Y., Cofta-Woerpel, L., Bush, N., Gustafson, D. H., et al. (2008). Antecedent characteristics of online cancer information seeking behaviors among rural cancer patients: An application of the Cognitive-Social Health Information Processing (C-SHIP) model. *Journal of Health Communication, 13*, 389–408.

Shaw, B. R., Han, J. Y., Baker, T., Witherly, J., Hawkins, R., McTavish, F. M., et al. (2007). How women with breast cancer learn using interactive cancer communication systems. *Health Education Research, 22*, 108–119.

Shaw, R. A. & Kling, N. D. (1999). The use of technology based groups for idea generation. *Journal of Rehabilitation Administration, 23*(1), 5–18.

Shirkey, C. (2008). *Here comes everybody: The power of organizing without organizations.* New York: Penguin Press.

Siegel, J., Dubrovsky, V., Kiesler, S., & McGuire, T. W. (1986). Group process in computer mediated communication. *Organizational Behavior and Human Decision Processes, 37*, 157–187.

Smarty, A. (2009). Facebook group vs Facebook fan page: What's better. *Search Engine Journal* Retrieved October 23, 2009, from http://www.searchenginejournal.com/facebook-group-vs-facebook-fan-page-whats-better/7761/

Stein, D. J. (1997). Psychiatry on the Internet: Survey of an OCD mailing list. *Psychiatric Bulletin, 21*, 95–98.

Sudén, J. (2003). *Material virtualities.* New York: Peter Lang.

Suler, J. (1999, January 2001). Psychotherapy in cyberspace: A 5-dimensional model of online and computer-mediated psychotherapy 2. Retrieved October 10, 2009, from http://www-usr.rider.edu/ suler/psycyber/therapy.html.

Toseland, R. W. & Rivas, R. F. (1995). *An introduction to group work practice* (2nd ed.). Boston: Allyn and Bacon.

U.S. News & World Report (2008). Schools of social work ranked in 2008. Retrieved October 11, 2009, from http://grad-schools.usnews.rankingsandreviews.com/best-graduate-schools/top-social-work-schools/rankings

Van Lear, C. A., Sheehan, M., Withers, L. A., & Walker, R. A. (2005). AA online: The enactment of supportive computer mediated communication. *Western Journal of Communication, 69*(1), 5–26.

Walther, J. B. (1996). Computer-mediated communication: Impersonal, interpersonal and hyper-personal interaction. *Communication Research, 23*, 3–43.

Walther, J. B. & Boyd, S. (2002). Attraction to computer-mediated social support. In C. A. Lin & D. Atkin (eds.), *Communication technology and society: Audience adoption and uses* (pp. 153–188). Cresskill, NJ: Hampton Press.

Watts, D. J. (1999). *Small worlds: The dynamics of networks between order and randomness.* Princeton, NJ: Princeton University Press.

Weisenthal Center (2009). Report: Facebook, YouTube +: How social media outlets impact digital terrorism and hate (Interactive CD-ROM). Available from http://fswc.ca/digital_terrorism_hate.aspx

Wellman, B., Boase, J., & Chen, W. (2002). The networked nature of community: Online and offline. *IT & Society, 1*(1), 151–165.

Whitlock, J. L., Powers, J. L., & Eckenrode, J. (2006). The virtual cutting edge: The Internet and adolescent self-injury. *Developmental Psychology, 42*(3), 407–417.

Winzelberg, A. (1997). The analysis of an electronic support group for individuals with eating disorders. *Computers in Human Behavior, 13*(3), 393–407.

Winzelberg, A. J., Classen, C., Alpers, G. W., Roberts, H., Koopman, C., Adams, R. E., et al. (2003). Evaluation of an Internet support group for women with primary breast cancer. *Cancer, 97*(5), 1164–1173.

Wright, K. (2000). Computer-mediated social support, older adults, and coping. *Journal of Communication, 50*(3), 100–118.

Yahoo.com. (n.d). http://groups.yahoo.com/. Retrieved October 10, 2009, from http://groups.yahoo.com/

Young, K. S. (1999). Internet addiction: Evaluation and treatment. *Student British Medical Journal Archive*. http://archive.student.bmj.com/issues/99/10/editorials/351.php

Zrebiec, J. F. & Jacobson, A. M. (2001). What attracts patients with diabetes to an Internet support group? A 21-month longitudinal website study. *Diabetes UK, 18*, 154–158.

Part Three

Violence: Victims and Perpetrators

Chapter Ten

Group Work With Adult Survivors of Childhood Sexual Abuse[1]

Carolyn Knight

exual abuse is defined as sexual contact between a child or adolescent and a person in a position of power and authority. It includes, but is not limited to, vaginal and anal penetration, oral sex, masturbation, and exposure to or participation in pornography. The prevalence of sexual abuse in the general population is difficult to determine due to a lack of a uniform definition and victims' unwillingness or inability to disclose. But, conservative estimates suggest that one-third of adult women and one-quarter of adult men may have experienced some form of sexual abuse prior to reaching age eighteen (Finkelhor, Ormrod, Turner, & Hamby, 2005). Research also indicates that a majority of individuals seeking treatment voluntarily or involuntarily in a range of clinical settings are likely to be survivors (Arata & Lindman, 2002; Breslau, 2002).

REVIEW OF THE LITERATURE

Long-term Consequences of Sexual Abuse

Survivors of sexual abuse experience a range of emotional problems including low self-esteem, guilt, shame, fear, social isolation, and depression. Substance abuse, self-injury, sexual dysfunction, eating disorders, and posttraumatic stress disorder (PTSD) symptoms, such as flashbacks, also are common (P..own, Schrag, & Trimble, 2005; Soloman & Heide, 2005; Weichelt, Lutz, Smyth, & Sims, 2005). Survivors are likely to develop core beliefs about themselves and their social world that are characterized by mistrust, powerlessness, and a lack of safety, security, and control (McCann & Pearlman, 1990). Survivors also tend to lack "self-capacities" (McCann & Pearlman, 1990), which include, among others, the ability to self-soothe, regulate affect, and handle disagreements and conflict.

More fundamentally, sexual abuse can rob the individual of a stable sense of self (Janoff-Bulman, 1992).

Differences in how men and women respond to sexual abuse have been observed and can be attributed to the nature of the victimization and the sociocultural context (Alaggia & Millington, 2008). Men typically have been sexually abused by men and struggle with what they perceive to be the homosexual nature of their abuse. A common sentiment I hear from male group members is, "I *must* be gay if I 'had sex' with another guy." This sentiment tends to be especially strong in those instances where the victim was sexually aroused. Sexual arousal is not uncommon, but it is more likely to occur among boys, thus intensifying feelings of shame and confusion (Hunter, 1990).

Self-blame, although common for both men and women, tends to be more problematic for men. Male survivors must reconcile their victimization with what they perceive to be expected of them as men. A member of one of my groups, Nick, stated, "I'm the man. I'm supposed to be the one who comes in and protects others from harm. I'm not supposed to be the helpless victim." Nick was 8 when he was sodomized and forced to perform oral sex on his camp counselor during a weekend camping trip. Nick tried to escape but the counselor threatened to leave him in the woods and to harm him and his family if he told anyone.

Male survivors also may experience more extreme feelings of isolation and inadequacy than women as well as greater difficulty managing anger (O'Leary & Barber, 2008). Most males who were sexually abused in childhood do *not* go on to molest children, yet there is evidence that male survivors are at greater risk for sexually abusing others, perhaps as a way of managing these feelings (Connolly & Woollons, 2008).

Memory loss and dissociation can provide victims with valuable ways of coping, when few other resources are available. There is debate about the validity of "recovered memories" (Barber, 1997), but there is ample evidence that male and female survivors of sexual abuse often have limited or incomplete memory of their victimization and may recall aspects of it years later (Alison, Kebbell, & Lewis, 2006; McNally, 2003; Nemeroff, 2004).

Almost all survivors exhibit the mildest form of dissociation, in which feelings are split off from experiences. For example, the survivor can recount her or his "story" devoid of any affect. With dissociative identity disorder (DID), the most extreme manifestation of dissociation, feelings, memories, and experiences may be housed in separate parts of the self. There may be little awareness among these parts of one another. Debate centers on the legitimacy of DID (Piper & Merskey, 2004), though evidence suggests that when survivors have experienced ritualistic sexual abuse, they are particularly likely to develop separate and distinct parts of the self (Simeon, Guralnick, Schmeidler, Sirof, & Knutelska, 2001). Women are more likely to be diagnosed with DID, but it is not clear whether this reflects differences between men's and women's responses to sexual abuse, the nature of their victimization, or how they are assessed.

Advantages of Group Membership for Adult Survivors

A fundamental advantage of group membership for survivors is that the experience of being with others with a similar history normalizes their experiences, as well as their current challenges. Second, as a result of discovering they are all in the "same boat" (Shulman, 2008), survivors' feelings of being alone and different are lessened. Third, group membership affords survivors the opportunity to develop connections to one another, which is inherently therapeutic, since it provides them with a corrective emotional experience (Yalom, 1995). Members' relationships with one another enhance their worth and esteem and challenge directly their distortions in thinking about self and others. Finally, participation in a group provides members with the opportunity to develop their self-capacities as they learn from and provide support to one another.

Research supports the efficacy of groups for survivors of childhood sexual abuse (Wright, Woo, Muller, Fernandes, & Kraftcheck, 2003). A more structured group that has a psychoeducational component and focuses on present-day challenges and normalization of members' experiences is a necessary starting point for many survivors (Klein & Schermer, 2000). A group with a focus on members' relationships in the here-and-now and in which members are encouraged to disclose their victimization and confront their feelings is often more appropriate with individuals who are more stable in their functioning and have achieved some basic insight into their difficulties (Spiegel, Classen, Thurston, & Butler, 2004).

Groups for survivors of sexual abuse typically are small, six to eight members, to encourage intimacy and honest discussion. Groups can be open-ended or time-limited. However, time-limited groups, in which members start and finish together have the advantage of promoting intimacy and have been found to enhance client motivation and attendance (Budman, Cooley, Demby, & Koppenaal, 1996).

Given survivors' tendency toward isolation and feeling different, the worker must attend to composition issues. At the very least, we should adhere as much as possible to the "not the only one" principle (Gitterman, 2005). No one member should stand out in a way that isolates her or him from others in the group. A complementary principle is "Noah's Ark," which suggests that each member should share with at least one other member characteristics that are central to or relevant for the group's focus (Yalom, 1995). Survivors' sense of urgency tends to mitigate the potentially disruptive effects of racial and cultural differences. Yet, in a group that includes men and women, only one man or one woman in the group would be ill-advised, since she or he would stand out in a way that is significant to the group's purpose.

PRACTICE PRINCIPLES

The first practice principle lays the foundation for five others and is that group intervention should enhance members' self-capacities. A second principle is the need to foster *mutual* aid in the group. Survivors of sexual abuse struggle with multiple problems in living and their (and our) sense of urgency may lead us to engage in "casework in the group" (Kurland & Salmon, 2005) rather than group work. When we devote too much attention to individual members, we deny them the support of other members and deny members the satisfaction and sense of esteem that comes from helping others, which is know as altruism (Yalom, 1995).

A third principle is that the group should adopt an appropriate treatment focus so that members' self-capacities are enhanced. There is nothing inherently thera-peutic about encouraging survivors to talk about their past victimization (Courtois, 2001; Wright et al., 2003). A trauma-focused orientation on members' sexual abuse and their feelings about and reactions to it can be retraumatizing and under-mine the development of self-capacities. For most clients, stabilization and pres-ent focused treatment must precede trauma-focused work. This explains the research finding that structured groups that focused on members' current prob-lems have been found to be a necessary starting point for most survivors.

A fourth practice principle is closely related and is the need for the worker to maintain a trauma-sensitive orientation in her or his work. This means under-standing the ways in which members' current problems in living, as well as their relationships with one another and with us as helpers, reflect their experiences as victims of sexual abuse.

A fifth principle is that the group worker must remain mindful of boundaries, given survivors lack self-capacities and an integrated sense of self. Individual mem-bers may need assistance in distinguishing their feelings and experiences from others in the group. One of the benefits of group membership is that hearing the stories and experiences of others is validating. Yet, the social worker must look for signs of what is referred to as *group contagion* (Alonso & Rutan, 1996).

A final principle addresses the impact that working with survivors of sexual abuse has on us. We must recognize that when we work with survivors of sexual abuse, we will be indirectly traumatized (Knight, 2009). Therefore, we need to be proactive in taking care of ourselves and develop ways of minimizing the impact of our work (Clemans, 2004; Cunningham, 2004). This includes giving voice to our feelings and reactions, seeking out supervisory support, and maintaining and deepening our personal relationships.

Survivors can be difficult to engage in a working relationship. The range and depth of problems in living they experience can be overwhelming, and their sto-ries of exploitation can be painful to hear. We can experience intrusive symptoms analogous to those associated with PTSD, known as secondary traumatic stress (Figley & Kleber, 1995), and distortions in thinking about self and others, known as *vicarious traumatization* (Pearlman & Saakvitne, 1995). Indirect trauma also can be manifested in a diminished capacity to empathize, known as *compassion fatigue* (Figley & Kleber, 1995).

Indirect trauma is not countertransference, which involves our reactions to particular clients, often in response to our own personal issues (Pearlman &

Saakvitne, 1995). However, our efforts to protect ourselves from being indirectly traumatized can lead to countertransference reactions like denial, avoidance, and overidentification (Cramer, 2002; Pearlman & Saakvitne, 1995).

COMMON THEMES

Themes in the Beginning Phase

In any group, new members want to know, "Who are these people?"and "How can this group help me?"(Shulman, 2008). These questions can be especially pressing for survivors of sexual abuse, given their mistrust of self and others. Since survivors of sexual abuse may have had numerous experiences with helping professionals that weren't helpful, they may be particularly likely to question the value of group membership (Palmer, Brown, Rae-Grant, & Loughlin, 2001).

Survivors' feelings of being alone and different tend to dominate early sessions. Members are likely to assume that they were somehow to blame for their sexual abuse and adhere to the "everyone but me" perspective, convinced that everyone but them is a victim who did not deserve the abuse and warrants the concern and support of the group (Knight, 2009). This belief is often manifested through members' reluctance to disclose sensitive information out of fear that they will be rejected.

The following excerpt comes from the first session of Laura's group for female survivors who also have problems with substance abuse. As the leader, she is able to effectively use the "problem swap" (Shulman, 2008) to encourage members to share sensitive information with one another. She then uses these disclosures to point out underlying commonalities. In so doing, she challenges members' beliefs that they are somehow different.

Laura: I want to give each of you a chance to introduce yourself. So let's take some time and go around the room. Please share your name, of course, and what brought you to the program—a little bit about your addiction, what your drugs of choice were, how long you have been clean, whether you've been able to be clean in the past. It also would be helpful to share a little about your childhood—just whatever you are comfortable with—because, again, the group can be helpful by giving you a place to talk about those experiences and to find ways other than drugs and alcohol to deal with them. You might also let us know a little bit about your family if you want—whether or not you have kids, are in a relationship, that sort of thing—and what you would like to get out of the group. I know this isn't easy to do, so just say as much or as little as you feel comfortable with to begin. [*Laura turns to the*

	member who happens to be seated to her right.] Sherrell, would you be willing to start the ball rolling?
Sherrell:	Oh, lord. Do I have to go first? [*She giggles nervously.*] Well, I'm Sherrell. I'm 25, and I have two babies—Darren and Marlene. They're living with my mother right now on account of I lost custody—you know, 'cause of I'm addicted to cocaine. [*She looks down and fidgets with the hem of her blouse.*] I feel so bad that I can't even keep my own children with me—I don't know if I can ever get them back, I'm so afraid I won't. I really want to get clean and bring 'em home where they belong, but I just don't know if I can do it...
	[*Sherrell went on to disclose additional experiences with sexual abuse and domestic violence. The following exchange then occurred.*]
Laura:	Thank you, Sherrell, for being so honest. It's never easy to go first, but you did just fine. I noticed while Sherrell was talking, some of you were nodding your heads and it seemed like you were feeling some of the sadness and regret that Sherrell talked about. It's like you not only have to deal with what happened to you when you were children, but then the drugs just took control of your lives and now you also have to deal with the consequences of the choices you made as a result. Does that ring a bell with some of you? [*Several members nod their heads.*] I suspect that's something we'll talk about a lot in this group— what you've all lost and the poor choices you made, sometimes because you simply didn't know you had a choice. [*Laura pauses.*] Nakita, how about you? Can you tell us a little bit about yourself?
Nakita:	Well, my name's Nakita, I'm 25, and I don't have no children— well, at least none that lives with me. I had a son—I guess he be 'bout 10 now. I got pregnant when I was 15, and my grand-mother made me give up my baby. I was living with her 'cause my daddy was in jail and my momma had died of AIDS. The man that got me pregnant? He raped me—but I never told my grand-mother that. She thinks I'm no-good anyway. Fact is, he was my friend's daddy, and he used to get both of us drunk and then he have his way with us. Make us do all sorts of filthy shit to each other and to him. That's when I started using—anything I could get my hands on—and I been doing it ever since. I tried getting clean a couple of times, but it don't last. Really, I don't do much hard shit anymore—but I do like my beer and some reefer now and again. I want to get my shit together, maybe even find out what happened to my baby—but it just seems so hard, and it's been so long ...

Laura: Wow, Nakita. Again, thank you so much for your honesty. I know it's not easy to talk about this stuff—but it's so important that you do. Nakita, you described a lot of hurt in your life. Being raped, having a baby, losing your mother, not having your father around. It makes sense that you would escape into drugs and alcohol. I think that's a common theme for each of you, isn't it? Using drugs to numb out and escape the pain? [*Laura turns her attention to Monica, who is seated opposite.*] Monica, I noticed you were really listening intently to what Nakita was saying. What was going on for you while she was talking?

Monica: I was thinking about what happened to me when I was around the same age. Nobody ever messed with me, so I guess that's good, but I remember when my daddy got shot and killed. In a drive-by. I was 16, and me and Daddy was sitting out front on our steps. This car come speeding down the street, and he got shot in the head. There was blood and brains all over me, and I was holding him and crying and screaming. They never caught who did it. My dad was selling drugs, so the police thought that it was related to that. Maybe it was. They didn't really pay too much attention or try to solve the case. We was black and poor, he was a drug dealer. So nobody much cared—except me and my brothers.

Laura: Oh, Monica, how horrible for you. [*Laura pauses for a moment before continuing.*] It sounds like, even though the specifics are different for Nakita, Monica, and Sherrell, the pain was the same—the pain that comes from such terrible experiences. I suspect that this is true for all of you, isn't it? [*Several members nod. Then Laura turns to Karen who is seated next to Nakita.*] Karen, how about if we hear from you next? Can you tell us a little bit about you?

Survivors' distortions in thinking about self and others may cause them to approach others in the group with a mixture of hostility and resentment. In groups that include men and women, this hostility is likely to be particularly strong, since sexual abuse distorts survivors' views of gender, sex, and sexuality. Core beliefs about others, including the group worker, are likely to be apparent from the beginning and manifested through transference reactions (Ziegler & McAvoy, 2000).

Themes in the Middle Phase

In groups that are more structured and maintain a present focus, the following themes may be less apparent. Yet, in any group for survivors, the worker should anticipate that as members develop greater comfort with one another, they will be able to talk more openly about their abuse which can lead to strong emotional reactions. Members may experience some relief and sense of validation, but this is likely to be tempered by fears about being overwhelmed.

As members hear the stories and witness the distress of others, they may adopt the "that's not me!" perspective (Knight, 2009). They seek to distance themselves from others as a way of protecting themselves from the feelings being expressed. The following example comes from a more trauma-focused group for female survivors with eating disorders. In the previous sessions, members have talked more openly and graphically about their sexual abuse as children. One member, Paula, struggles with the group's focus on such painful content and questions the need for this.

> Becky: I thought about what Vanessa [another group member] said last week about how when we purge, we're punishing ourselves. That makes sense to me. The more we talk about what happened when we were kids, the more I feel ashamed of myself and dirty. And when I feel like that I want to purge. It's like I just want to get that shit out of me.
>
> Lynn: I realized that same thing. What my dad [her abuser] did to me made me feel so ashamed and embarrassed. I never talked about it. I thought I was the only one. He told me we had this special relationship, that I was his favorite. I knew it wasn't right, but I kept the secret. I just feel so ashamed of myself *(starts crying)*.
>
> Andrea: When I was nine, my Sunday school teacher took a bunch of us on a picnic. I remember he took me into the bathroom and started touching me. He told me I was beautiful—that I could be a model. I was so scared, and I knew that what he was doing was wrong, but I just felt like I was frozen in place. I was stuck or something. This happened a lot, and he would be like, "I can't help myself, you're just so beautiful. I can't help myself." That really messed me up. I just felt like it had to be my fault—Somehow, when I don't eat, I feel more in control and more powerful. I know it sounds weird, but that's how it feels to me.
>
> Pam (co-leader): It seems like many of you are now really seeing the connection between what happened to you as children and the eating problems you have now. Sometimes it's about punishing yourself, sometimes it's about feeling more in control, sometimes it's about covering up your femininity, and sometimes it's all those things.

> What I sense is that all of you are becoming aware of feeling shame and humiliation.
>
> Paula: I am not sure why we have to talk about this. When I joined this group, I thought it was going to be a place where I could learn how to eat healthier and manage my eating disorder. What's the point of dredging up the past? How's that going to help us now?
>
> Marcus (co-leader): Paula, you seem angry. It is hard to talk about this, isn't it? When you hear others talking about what happened to them as children, it is painful—especially since there's not much you can do about it now, right?
>
> Paula: My brother raped me for years, and his friends paid him so they could rape me, too. There's not a day goes by that I don't think about what happened to me. What good does it do to talk about this now? They [*referring to other members of the group*] just need to get on with their lives.
>
> Pam: I'm wondering, Paula, if you're talking as much to yourself as you are to others in the group. It would be nice, wouldn't it, if you all could just forget about it and move on? It just isn't that easy, I'm afraid. This group can help each of you put the past behind you so that it doesn't control you. It can also help you gain control of your eating disorder so that it doesn't control you either.

Cautious optimism about the group can give way in the middle phase to a second theme which is disillusionment with the group. This may be manifested by members desiring to quit or missing sessions. Dissociation, either by individual members or by the group as a whole, also may occur. Absences and dissociation reflect additional ways that members distance themselves from the work of the group. The group worker should be prepared to directly discuss both of these dynamics with members and, in the case of dissociation, help members understand the protective role that it serves.

A third theme in the middle phase reflects members' growing realization that they were, in fact, victims as children, which results in anger at perpetrators and at those who did not protect them. A related theme is anger at the unfairness of the victimization, which can lead to the question, "Why me?" This may take the form of anger at God and anger at the group worker, since she or he is not "in the same boat" as the members.

The following excerpt comes from a group for men and women that I facilitated. Members have been meeting for about sixteen weeks, and the exchange occurred in response to Paul's disclosure that his mother had recently died. A number of members expressed anger at Paul's mother.

Carolyn: So it seems like some of you believe that the passing of Paul's mother is a good thing. That he is better off without her, since she wasn't much of a mother to him anyway.

Peter: Right! Like he told her what happened when she was a kid, and all she does is say, 'That happened years ago, get over it!'? What kind of shit is that?!

Lucy: My parents are still alive, but I stay as far away from them as possible. They continue to treat me like I'm the black sheep. Ain't that a bitch? My grandfather and my uncle molest me, and it's my fault- I'm the one with the problem!

Melinda: My father died several years ago. I was glad to see him go. He was a son of a bitch until the day that he died. [*Starts to cry.*]

Silence. Paul is teary-eyed as are several other members.

Carolyn: I see some of you crying. I am wondering what's going on for you all. There was all this anger, and now, it seems to be something else.

Silence.

Melinda: Why did this have to happen? Why?! What did I do to deserve what happened.

Lucy: I'm angry at my parents, sure. But somehow it's not enough to be angry at them. It's like I get angry at the world! At everyone and everything for what happened to me.

Susan: Right! What was so wrong with us that we could be hurt like this? Why didn't it happen to you [*pointing at me*]? Oops...I'm sorry, I shouldn't have said that.

Carolyn: No need to apologize. That is the question, isn't it? Why you and not me? Why you at all? I wish I could give you an answer that would satisfy you all. But I really can't. Bottom line is that it wasn't fair, and you didn't deserve it.

Paul: Right now, I am not even angry, I'm not even asking myself 'Why me?' I have, I guess, but not now. Now, all I feel is lost and alone. My mother- my mom- is dead.

Members are silent and crying.

Carolyn: It seems like you all go back and forth in your feelings- one is the flipside of the others. It's the anger at the abusers and at others who didn't care or protect you, the sense of unfairness and injustice. But, beneath that, it seems, there's the loss. And for Paul, there's the realization that with his mom dead, he'll never have the relationship with her that he wanted. It's like the dream of having a mom- a real mom- dies when his mom died.

Members are silent and continue to cry.

Paul: I know it's stupid. I'm 55 years old! My mother was never a mother to me! But I guess I sort of held on to this belief that maybe she would be some day. Maybe I would have a real mom. (*Cries harder*).

I didn't have to reach for members' resentment toward me, since Susan put this into words directly. Group leaders should anticipate, though, that members are often not able to express negative feelings openly, particularly if these involve the leader. In this example, members were able to handle their emotional responses, but group workers also should be prepared to assist members in managing their feelings as a way to enhance self-capacities, as well as process members' reactions to the pain and distress of others.

Another theme, regret, reflects members' attempts to reconcile behaviors and choices they made as adults. While members may come to accept that they were, in fact, victims as children, they have difficulty reconciling behaviors they have engaged in as adults such as addiction and prostitution. Feelings of guilt, embarrassment, and shame can surface. Regret also can reflect members' realization of all that they have lost as a result of their victimization.

Finally, members' increasing comfort with one another will allow them to interact more genuinely. Manifestations of transference may be quite powerful, since members' comfort with one another will encourage honest expression of feelings. Mutual acceptance also will lead to feelings of affection, which can be both affirming and disconcerting, since they are in such contrast to members' previous relationships and their resulting views of others.

In the following case example, transference is evident, as are members' underlying feelings of connectedness. This example comes from Laura's group for substance abusing women who are survivors of sexual abuse. One of the members, Dawn, has missed two sessions without explanation.

Laura: So, let me start this session by reminding you all that it's important that everyone attend, since when you aren't here you are missed, and you miss a lot. Dawn, we've noticed that you have missed and I'm wondering if everything is okay?

Dawn: Yeah, everything's fine. I'm not using or nothing. I just have had a lot on my plate. I am sorry, y'all [*to the group*]. I'll be here from now on.

Sarah: It's fine by me, I know how that is. Shit happens, right? [*Smiles.*]

Laura: Well, that's true. Shit does happen [*smiles*]. But, I have to wonder whether some of you might be just a little bit pissed that Dawn missed? Even just a little bit?

Mona: Well, I have to admit, I was, like, if I have to be here, why doesn't she [*pointing to Dawn*]. [*Turning to Dawn*] I mean, I really am not angry, but I did miss you, and I did sort of think you were ditching us. And that sort of bothered me.

Dawn: I am sorry, I didn't mean anything by it. It's not you guys, I love you guys. You are there for me, and I really mean that. It's just life, you know? It's gets too overwhelming sometimes.

Silence

Laura: I am thinking that some of you might be feeling a bit guilty for being upset with Dawn? Since you can relate to what she is saying? Life does get overwhelming for all of you.

Debra: Speaking for me, I am used to this shit. People say they're going to be there for you and they aren't. It ain't no big deal to me.

Sarah: Right, I got enough problems of my own, I don't need to be worrying about Dawn and her shit.

Laura: I sense some real anger here? At Dawn? Maybe at others who have let you all down and not been there when you needed them?

Dawn: I really am sorry! You all are like my family- more than like family. I didn't mean to let you down.

Mona: I feel the same way, Dawn. But I was worried about you. I really thought maybe you were using again or something.

Laura: What I am sensing is that you all have come to care about one another a lot.

Members nodded their heads.

Sarah: I'm sorry, Dawn, I shouldn't have gotten pissed. You all are like my sisters. My family. I just got pissed, thinking you were like everybody else.

Laura: So, even though you care about one another, sometimes you get angry, which is part of any relationship. And sometimes that anger is really about other people in your lives.

Themes in the Ending Phase

The ending of the group can be difficult for survivors of sexual abuse (Knight, 2009). Members have developed a level of comfort with one another that provides affirmation and validation. Therefore, denial of the group's ending can be a prominent theme. A related theme is members' concern that any positive changes that have occurred in themselves or their lives are due to the group. They worry that they will "fall apart" or "go backwards" once the group ends. This reflects members' underlying and longstanding beliefs about themselves as worthless.

The group worker will need to assist members in talking about their work together and their fears about going on without the support of the group. The group worker also should help members identify the gains they have made. In cases where a member leaves an ongoing group, the worker will need to help the member end with the group and the group to end with her or him, thus minimizing feelings of abandonment, guilt, and anger.

RECOMMENDED WAYS OF WORKING

A strategy that is critical to reducing survivors' sense of isolation is the worker's ability to connect the individual to the group and the group to the individual. This requires that we reframe individual members' experiences and reactions so that they resonate with others. Cognitive behavioral techniques are especially helpful (McDonagh et al., 2005; Messman-Moore & Resick, 2002). The uniqueness of members' experiences aren't ignored, as discussed, but it is the underlying commonality of members' experience that is emphasized.

Working in the here and now is a second strategy that can be especially useful. Working with transference affords members the opportunity to examine directly how their beliefs about others get in the way of their relationships. The worker can help individual members see the impact that their actions and reactions have on others. In the following excerpt from one of my groups, it actually is another group member who suggests that Bob's anger at Denise was really a reflection of his anger at his mother.

> In the twelfth session, Denise was again saying that she was never going to get hurt again: "I'm going to live my life as I see fit, fuck everybody else." Bob refused to look at Denise, and played nervously with his hands. One of the other women said, "Come on Bob, you look upset. What's up? Is it Denise?" Bob acknowledged, "As soon as she opens her mouth, I get pissed off at her. I'm sick of her bullshit. This 'I don't care' shit gets on my nerves big time." Such an outburst from Bob was very uncharacteristic. However, he openly struggled with his feelings about his mother, whom he described as uncaring and as never having hugged or touched him. In a previous session, he had tearfully exclaimed, "I am fifty-five years old. In my whole entire life, I never remember- ever- my mother kissing me or touching me. I don't really remember her ever even really looking at me. Even now, when she talks to me, she doesn't really look at me." In response to Bob's anger at Denise, another member of the group observed, "Denise really stirred up something for you, didn't she? Who does she remind you of? Isn't that how you think of your mother, like she's cold and hard?"

Working in the here and now also is necessary, given members' tendency to dissociate. The group worker needs to look for signs of dissociation among individual members and the group as a whole and be prepared to process this directly. We can't compel survivors to explore their feelings, but we can alert them when they have "taken off" and assist them in identifying what triggered this reaction. As survivors do this, they are learning to be more affectively present.

A third strategy is that we must be prepared to use our feelings and reactions as a way to validate and normalize members' feelings. There will be times when the worker will need to put into words his or her reactions to members' disclosures, since members, themselves may be unable to do so. Sharing one's feelings and reactions is an example of what is more widely known as use of self and therapist "transparency" (Shulman, 2008; Smolar, 2003). The following example comes from a 20-session group that I led that included four women and three men, all of whom were survivors of sexual abuse. This excerpt occurred in the twelfth session.

Bill:	I've been thinking a lot more about what happened to me. It just keeps coming up, even though I don't want it to.
Carolyn:	So, maybe it's time to talk about it? Let the group know? Just get it out?
Bill:	So, in middle school, I was a walker. Had about a half mile or so walk home from school. These guys- they were like in high school, I think. They and this older man would all hang out at the man's house, and I'd have to walk by on my way home. One day they grabbed me and hauled me into the garage. They each took turns with me. Raped me. Sodomized me. Made me suck on them. This happened a lot all through middle school. They'd just wait for me to come by, laugh and make fun of me and then grab me.

Silence. Some members are teary-eyed.

Carolyn:	Wow, Bill. How awful for you...
Bill (interrupting):	I'd go home and my clothes would be all messed up. I'd have semen on me, and I'd be limping and stuff. What they did to me, when they sodomized me, it would be so painful. I could hardly walk.
Peter:	Oh man, Bill. That's fucking awful. That is sick stuff.
Lucy (crying):	I'm so sorry for you, Bill. What about your parents? Did you tell your parents?

Bill: I never said anything. To anyone. For two fucking years, these assholes did this shit to me. And I didn't say anything. I tried to once, but it wasn't any use. I remember coming home and my mother telling me, 'You stink.' Making me go take a shower, telling me that I was too old to go around smelling like a 'cesspool'. She'd say this a lot, but she'd never ask me what happened or act like anything was wrong.

Silence.

Carolyn: So, what's going on with you all? Bill's disclosures seem to have hit people really hard.

Silence. Some members are teary-eyed, others are rocking back and forth or clenching their fists.

Carolyn: What Bill has shared with us is incredibly painful. Very powerful. I am finding myself going between feeling sick to my stomach and totally disgusted with what these guys did to him to feeling such hurt for what Bill had to endure to being enraged-ENRAGED—at his mother for not seeing what was right in front of her face.

Silence.

Carolyn: I am thinking that others of you are feeling the same sorts of things I am feeling, and these feelings are incredibly powerful, and scary. And that you all would like to just run from them. Shut down and just run.

Bill (crying): I sometimes find myself asking myself why I didn't tell my mother. Or my father. But, who am I kidding? They wouldn't have done anything anyway. My father was always working, avoiding being with my mom and us. My mother? She spent her day watching TV and playing bingo and drinking. I was just an inconvenience...

Denise (interrupting): These fucking people! It's bad enough that we had these weirdos molesting us, but then we had parents who just didn't give a shit. No one gave a shit about us! No one!

In previous sessions, Bill had characterized his parents as cold and distant and had described incidents that suggested he experienced a great deal of emotional and physical neglect. Other group members described similar experiences, but prior to this session, members had "danced around" the intense pain that was associated with their abuse. Bill's honesty signaled his—and the group's—readiness to confront their feelings. Yet, his disclosures initially were met with silence and little, if any affect. Members resorted to the ways of coping with feelings that had allowed them to survive their abuse—they dissociated. Thus, it was necessary for me to share my own feelings of anger—rage, really—and sadness.

A fourth practice approach requires that the group worker be prepared to balance the expression of feelings with the containment of feelings. Anytime we encourage members to express feelings, we also must be ready to help them contain them, so their self-capacities are not undermined. Guided imagery, journaling, art, and other nonverbal techniques have been found to be helpful for adult survivors and can be used for expression or containment (Avrahami, 2005; Naparstek, 2004; Nelson & Loomis, 2005; Park & Blumberg, 2002; Pizarro, 2004). For example, I often ask members to bring in photographs of themselves as children. Showing the photographs in group inevitably leads to the expression of strong feelings of sadness, loss, and anger. However, members' feelings can become so intense that they need help in containing them. When this happens, I suggest that I keep the photographs and the feelings they generate. I inform members that I'll bring the photographs in each week, and we can take them out and examine them and the feelings that they evoke. Turning the photographs and the feelings over to me enhances members' self-capacities.

A final way of working reflects the controversy that surrounds recovered memories and DID. It is important to maintain a position of neutrality and *work with* members' memories and fragmented sense of self rather than engaging in "memory work" or "self-work." Critics of memory recall and the DID diagnosis correctly note that if we *assume* that the survivor has repressed memories of sexual abuse, she or he may very well recall such memories. If we *assume* she or he has different parts of the self, these are likely to surface. In the course of group treatment, members may dissociate, and they may spontaneously recall aspects of their abuse. If these phenomena occur, we can normalize and reframe them as coping mechanisms. However, we should avoid seeking them out, assuming they are there, or creating a group for this purpose.

EVALUATION

Ironically, an indicator of a successful group experience can be members' difficulties ending with one another, given their struggles with intimacy. More objective measures of the group's success will reflect the group's purpose. At minimum, however, it can be helpful to ascertain whether group participation has altered members' views of themselves and others. A rapid assessment instrument that can be used pre- and post-group to accomplish this is the Beliefs Associated with Childhood Sexual Abuse (BACSA) (Jehu, Klassen, & Gazan, 1986).

Generally, survivors of sexual abuse will participate in groups at least in part because of problems in living they are experiencing in the present. Therefore, it would be important for the group worker to assess whether participation in the group had any effect on the difficulties that necessitated the group in the first place. Members can provide a self-anchored rating of their progress or can be asked to complete one of the many rapid assessment instruments available to measure behavioral and emotional problems such as depression, substance abuse, eating disorders, and low self-esteem.

RESOURCES

Sidran Institute
200 East Joppa Road, Suite 207
Baltimore, MD 21286-3107
http://www.sidran.org/

National Institutes of Health
MEDLINE Plus
http://www.nlm.nih.gov/medlineplus/childsexualabuse.html

REFERENCES

Alaggia, R. & Millington, G. (2008). Male child sexual abuse: A phenomenology or betrayal. *Clinical Social Work Journal, 36*, 265–275.

Alison, L., Kebbell, M., & Lewis, P. (2006). Considerations for experts in assessing the credibility of recovered memories of child sexual abuse: The importance of maintaining a case-specific focus. *Psychology, Public Policy, and Law, 12*, 419–441.

Alonso, A. & Rutan, S. (1996). Separation and individuation in the group leader. *International Journal of Group Psychotherapy, 46*, 149–162.

Arata, C. & Lindman, L. (2002). Marriage, child abuse, and sexual revictimization. *Journal of Interpersonal Violence, 17*, 953–971.

Avrahami, D. (2005). Visual art therapy's unique contribution in the treatment of post-traumatic stress disorders. *Journal of Trauma and Dissociation, 6*, 5–38.

Barber, J. (1997). Hypnosis and memory: A hazardous connection. *Journal of Mental Health Counseling, 19*, 305–317.

Brown, R., Schrag, A., & Trimble, M. (2005). Dissociation, childhood interpersonal trauma, and family functioning in patients with somatization disorder. *American Journal of Psychiatry, 162*, 899–905.

Budman, S., Cooley, S., Demby, A., & Koppenaal, G. (1996). A model of time-effective group psychotherapy for patients with personality disorders: The clinical model. *International Journal of Group Psychotherapy, 46,* 329–355.

Breslau, N. (2002). Epidemiological studies of trauma, posttraumatic stress disorder, and other psychiatric disorders. *Canadian Journal of Psychiatry, 47,* 923–929.

Clemans, S. (2004). Recognizing vicarious traumatization: A single session group model for trauma workers. *Social Work with Groups, 27,* 55–74.

Connolly, M. & Woollons, R. (2008). Childhood sexual experience and adult offending: an exploratory comparison of three criminal groups. *Child Abuse Review, 17,* 119–132.

Courtois, C. (2001). Healing the incest wound: A treatment update with attention to recovered-memory issues. *American Journal of Psychotherapy, 51,* 464–496.

Cramer, M. (2002). Under the influence of unconscious process: Countertransference in the treatment of PTSD and substance abuse in women. *American Journal of Psychotherapy, 56,* 194–210.

Cunningham, M. (2004). Avoiding vicarious traumatization: Support, spirituality, and self-care. In N. Boyd Webb (ed.), *Mass trauma and violence: Helping families and children cope* (pp. 327–346). New York, NY: Guilford Press.

Figley, C. & Kleber, R. (1995). Beyond "victim": Secondary traumatic stress. In R. Kleber, C. Figley, & B. Gersons (eds.), *Beyond trauma: Cultural and societal dynamics* (pp. 75–98). New York: Plenum.

Finkelhor, D., Ormrod, R., Turner, H., & Hamby, S. (2005). The victimization of children and youth: A comprehensive national survey. *Child Maltreatment, 10,* 5–25.

Gitterman, A. (2005). Group formation: Tasks, methods, and skills. In A. Gitterman & L. Shulman (eds.), *Mutual aid groups, vulnerable and resilient populations, and the life cycle* (3rd ed., pp. 73–110). New York: Columbia University Press.

Hunter, M. (1990). *Abused boys: The neglected victims of sexual abuse.* Lexington, MA: Lexington Books.

Janoff-Bulman, R. (1992). *Shattered assumptions: Towards a new psychology of trauma.* New York: The Free Press.

Jehu, D., Klassen, C., & Gazan, M. (1986). Cognitive restructuring of distorted beliefs associated with childhood sexual abuse. *Journal of Social Work and Human Sexuality, 4,* 49–69.

Klein, R. & Schermer, V. (2000). Introduction and overview: Creating a healing matrix. In R. Klein & V. Schermer (eds.), *Group psychotherapy for psychological trauma* (pp. 3–46). New York: The Guilford Press.

Knight, C. (2009). *Introduction to working with adult survivors of childhood trauma: Techniques and strategies.* CA: Thomson Brooks/Cole.

Kurland, R. & Salmon, R. (2005). Group work versus casework in a group: Principles and implications for teaching and practice. *Social Work with Groups, 28*(3/4), 121–132.

McCann, I. & Pearlman, L. (1990). *Psychological trauma and the adult survivor.* New York: Brunner/Mazel.

McDonagh, A., Friedman, M., McHugo, G., Ford, J., Sengupta, A., Mueser, K., Demment, C., Fournier, D., Schnurr, P., & Descamps, M. (2005). Randomized trial of cognitive-behavioral therapy for chronic posttraumatic stress disorder in adult female survivors of childhood sexual abuse. *Journal of Consulting and Clinical Psychology, 73,* 515–524.

McNally, R. (2003). Recovering memories of trauma: A view from the laboratory. *Current Directions in Psychological Science, 12,* 32–35.

Messman-Moore, T. & Resick, P. (2002). Brief treatment of complicated PTSD and peri-traumatic response in a client with repeated sexual victimization. *Cognitive And Behavioral Practice, 9,* 89–95.

Naparstek, B. (2004). *Invisible heroes: Survivors of trauma and how they heal.* New York: Bantam Dell.

Nelson, G. & Loomis, C. (2005). Review: Self-help interventions improve anxiety and mood disorders. *Evidence-based Mental Health, 8,* 44.

Nemeroff, C. (2004). Neurobiological consequences of childhood trauma. *Clinical Psychiatry, 65,* 18–28.

O'Leary, P. & Barber, J. (2008). Gender differences in silencing following childhood sexual abuse. *Journal of Child Sexual Abuse, 17,* 133–143.

Palmer, S., Brown, R., Rae-Grant, N., & Loughlin, M. (2001). Survivors of childhood abuse: Their reported experiences with professional help. *Social Work, 46,* 136–145.

Park, C. & Blumberg, C. (2002). Disclosing trauma through writing: Testing the meaning-making hypothesis. *Cognitive Therapy and Research, 26,* 597–616.

Pearlman, L. & Saakvitne, K. (1995). *Trauma and the therapist: Countertransference and vicarious traumatization in psychotherapy with incest survivors.* New York: W. W. Norton.

Piper, A. & Merskey, H. (2004). The persistence of folly: A critical examination of dissociative identity disorder. Part I. The excesses of an improbable concept. *Canadian Journal of Psychiatry, 49,* 592–600.

Pizarro, J. (2004). The efficacy of art and writing therapy: Increasing positive mental health outcomes and participant retention after exposure to traumatic experience. *Art Therapy, 21,* 5–12.

Shulman, L. (2008). *The skills of helping individuals, families, groups, and communities* (6th ed.) CA: Thomson Brooks/Cole.

Simeon, D., Guralnik, O., Schmeidler, J., Sirof, B., & Knutelska, M. (2001). The role of childhood interpersonal trauma in depersonalization disorder. *American Journal of Psychiatry, 158,* 1027–1033.

Smolar, A. (2003). When we give more: Reflections on intangible gifts from therapist to patient. *American Journal of Psychotherapy, 57,* 300–323.

Solomon, E. & Heide, K. (2005). The biology of trauma. *Journal of Interpersonal Violence, 20,* 51–60.

Spiegel, D., Classen, C., Thurston, E., & Butler, L., (2004). Trauma-focused versus present-focused models for women sexually abused in childhood. In L. Koenig & L. Doll (eds.), *From child sexual abuse to adult sexual risk: Trauma, revictimization, and intervention* (pp. 251–268). Washington, DC: American Psychological Association.

Weichelt, S., Lutz, W., Smyth, N., & Syms, C. (2005). Integrating research and practice: A collaborative model for addressing trauma and addiction. *Stress, Trauma, and Crisis, 8,* 179–193.

Wright, D., Woo, W., Muller, R., Fernandes, C., & Kraftcheck, E. (2003). An investigation of trauma-centered inpatient treatment for adult survivors of abuse. *Child Abuse and Neglect, 27,* 393–411.

Yalom, I. (1995). *The theory and practice of group psychotherapy* (4th ed.). New York: Basic Books.

Ziegler, M. & McAvoy, M. (2000). Hazardous terrain: Countertransference reactions in trauma groups. In R. Klein & V. Schermer (eds.), *Group psychotherapy for psychological trauma* (pp. 116–137). New York: Guilford Press.

NOTE

1 Some of the case examples in this chapter first appeared in Knight, C. *Introduction to working with adult survivors of childhood trauma: Techniques and strategies*, CA: Thomson Brooks/Cole, 2009.

Chapter Eleven

Group Work With Victims of Hate Crimes

Joan C. Weiss and Jack McDevitt

Incidents of harassment, intimidation, assault, or vandalism can be particularly traumatic and have long-lasting effects when directed against people because of their race, ethnicity, religion, sexual orientation, or disability.[1] The terms *hate crime, bias crime*, and *ethnoviolence* are used interchangeably to describe such incidents. This chapter will provide social workers with an understanding of the nature of such incidents and their effects on victims.

Knowledge of the character and impact of hate crimes is critical for all group work, because any group may contain members whose experiences of hate crimes may affect their reactions and behaviors to a wide range of issues and actions, as well as to other people, both in and out of the group who may be similarly affected. In communities dealing with intergroup tensions and incidents, there may be a clear need for a group for victims of hate crimes. Hate crimes can occur in neighborhoods or workplaces, such as when an individual or family is the first of a minority group to appear on the block or in the office; in houses of worship, schools, or other public places; or when someone is attacked just walking down a street. Often these incidents are not reported to officials because victims fear retaliation.

A group format is particularly suited to this population for several reasons. All members of a family are affected when one member has been victimized, so group work with one or more families may be indicated. Also, when one person in a community has been targeted, based upon race or religion for example, there are frequently others who have had similar experiences or fear becoming the next victim. Furthermore, seldom is there only one isolated incident; victims often have experienced numerous incidents over time. Perhaps most important, being a victim of ethnoviolence stigmatizes and isolates individuals.

Sharing the experiences and ways of coping in a group format can be cathartic and healing, and can provide a support network for the future. In addition, being able to air grievances with others, such as anger toward police or public officials, can serve to both validate the feelings and help dissipate the impact for the victim.

REVIEW OF THE LITERATURE

Although victimization based on someone's race, ethnicity, religion, or sexual orientation is not a new phenomenon, it is only during the past 30 years or so that social workers have worked with groups whose primary characteristic is their members' experiences of hate crimes. Prior to that, people who were victimized because of their group identity, rather than for any act they committed, turned to institutions representative of these groups for support. African Americans could count on support from the NAACP or local churches; Jews turned to the Anti-Defamation League or the American Jewish Committee, and so on. Informal support often came from family members and neighbors but seldom did discussions of these incidents occur outside of the affected groups.

In 1979, police departments began keeping records of "bias crimes" or "hate crimes." The Boston and New York City departments were two of the first in the country to designate specific units to handle such crimes; others soon followed. In Maryland, Montgomery and Baltimore counties were two jurisdictions whose police departments began keeping such records early. Each assigned specially trained community relations officers to deal with the problems of investigating hate crimes and their impact both on the victims and on the communities involved.

Local and state human rights agencies began working with victims of hate crimes and began formal efforts to provide support to victims. Programs that agencies developed included those designed to train citizens to respond to victims in their communities. The "Network of Neighbors" and "Network of Teens," created by the Commission on Human Relations in Montgomery County, Maryland, to provide support to adults and youth who are victimized, are examples of programs that have been replicated in other jurisdictions. Training on issues of victimization and in basic skills of support is available to people who join the groups. The Los Angeles County Human Rights commission is another example of an agency that for the past 20 years has developed and led programs to engage in community dialogue about race relations and to target hate crime educations program toward high school students.

National organizations that tracked racially and religiously motivated incidents as well as neo-Nazi, Ku Klux Klan, and other hate group activity included the Southern Poverty Law Center and its affiliate, Klanwatch, in Alabama, and the Anti-Defamation League (ADL) in New York. The ADL was the first national organization to regularly report hate crimes in its Annual Audit of Anti-Semitic Incidents. The ADL also developed the first model hate crime statues in 1981 and continues to be a national leader in programming to increase awareness of hate crimes in a variety of programs most notable their "World of Difference Campaign." In 1985, the first national organization devoted exclusively to research, education, and training on the problem of hate crimes, the National Institute Against Prejudice and Violence, was established in Baltimore. The Institute, which used the term *ethnoviolence* rather than *hate crime* to highlight the fact that incidents are directed at victims because of animus toward a group they belong to but many incidents of ethnoviolence do not meet the definition of a crime, conducted the first nationwide study of incidents and their effects on victims.[2]

National attention to the problem of hate crimes, and the efforts of a coalition of many organizations representing a wide range of minority populations and civil rights groups, led to the passage of the Hate Crime Statistics Act of 1990 (Public Law 101–275). The law required the attorney general of the United States to compile data and publish a summary of crimes that "manifest evidence of prejudice based on race, religion, sexual orientation or ethnicity" for 5 years, beginning in 1990. Bias against persons with disability was added to the Hate Crime Statistics Act in 1994, and in 1996, the sunset clause was removed from the original statute, mandating the permanent collection of hate crime data.

While the nationwide data on hate crimes do not accurately represent the prevalence of the problem, they do reveal a widespread phenomenon that warrants serious attention. The Uniform Crime Reporting Program of the FBI is responsible for maintaining the data collected under the Hate Crime Statistics Act, and began collecting national data on hate crimes in 1991. In its report *Hate Crime Statistics 2008*, the FBI indicated that 2145 law enforcement agencies (of almost 17,000 that report to the FBI), representing 46 states and the District of Columbia and approximately 58% of the U.S. population, had reported 7783 bias-motivated criminal incidents. These incidents involved 9691 victims and 9168 total offenses. Fully 60% of the offenses were crimes against individuals; the rest targeted businesses, religious organizations, and other institutions. Racial bias was the motivation in 51% of the incidents, and religion in 17%. Sexual orientation was the motivation in an additional 17% of the incidents. Of the rest, 12% were motivated by the ethnicity or national origin of the victim, the majority of whom were Hispanic. Incidents based on disability, first reported in the FBI report for 1997, constituted 1%. Of the racial incidents, 73% were antiblack; 17% were antiwhite. The rest were directed against Asians/Pacific Islanders, American Indians/Alaskan natives, or multiracial groups. The majority of the incidents motivated by religious bias were directed against Jews (66%); anti-Islamic bias accounted for 8%. There were 7 murders, 11 forcible rapes, 1025 aggravated assaults, 1778 simple assaults, and 2704 acts of intimidation, as well as 3576 property crimes (FBI, 2008).

Official statistics understate the problem of hate crimes, because many victims of hate crimes do not report their experiences to police. In 2005, the Bureau of Justice Statistics reported on hate crimes identified as part of the National Crime Victimization Survey (Harlow 2005). This is a national survey of households that identifies crime which may or may not have been reported to the police. In this survey, which identified an annual average of 210,000 hate crime nationally, only 44% of the hate crimes were reported to the police.

Reasons for not reporting vary. For immigrant groups, there is often a language barrier and, for some, a fear of police. In some communities, victims do not trust the police. For other victims, the level of frustration with the inability of police to apprehend perpetrators convinces them that reporting an incident will not accomplish anything. In many cases, victims, witnesses, and even the broader community may perceive hate as the motivation for a crime, but perpetrators may not be charged with a hate crime for a variety of reasons (Shively & Mulford, 2007). Fear of having their privacy compromised inhibits some victims, including many gays and lesbians. In the National Crime Victimization Survey, victims reported that the primary reason they did not report the crime to the police was that it was dealt with another way, often by reporting to another official. Some examples of this might be reporting to a supervisor at work or reporting to a member of the clergy or a local advocacy organization such as the ADL or NAACP. Additionally, in cases of assault where the perpetrator is known, there is frequently fear of retaliation. In addition to nonreporting by victims, official statistics are low because police do not always accurately identify or record the motivation in a bias incident.

Information from organizations that represent victimized populations further illuminates the problem. The ADL, which documents anti-Semitism, publishes an annual audit of incidents reported to its offices around the country. In 2004, they recorded 954 incidents against Jews across the nation (ADL, 2009). The American-Arab Anti-Discrimination Committee, in its report of hate crimes against Arab Americans for 1998–2000, notes that such incidents are not distinguishable in the FBI reports of hate crimes. The Committee documents several dozen incidents of physical and psychological attacks for the period reported, which does not include incidents experienced by Arab Americans in the wake of the terrorist acts of September 11, 2001. In fact, the incidents counted as anti-Islamic in the FBI report cited above represented an increase from 28 in 2000 to 481 in 2001 (FBI, 2000, 2001).

The National Coalition of Anti-Violence Programs published a report, "Anti-Lesbian, Gay, Bisexual and Transgender Violence in 2009," based on incidents monitored by a network of 35 antiviolence organizations in 25 states across the country. For 2008, 1677 incidents directed at 2424 victims were reported. They included 29 murders (the highest since 1999), 138 sexual assaults/rape, and 492 assaults or attempted assaults; the majority of the rest were intimidation or verbal harassment (National Coalition of Anti-Violence Programs, 2009).

In its tenth annual report of violence directed at Asian Pacific Americans, the National Asian Pacific American Legal Consortium documented 275 reported anti-Asian incidents, fully 29% of which involved aggravated or simple assaults. In the report, the Consortium states that underreporting of hate crimes continues to be a serious problem, which is compounded by the fact that community groups that collect information from victims who are reluctant to report to the police were forced to scale back their efforts due to insufficient resources (National Asian Pacific American Legal Consortium, 2002).

Little research has been conducted on victims of hate crimes—their responses to incidents and the impact of victimization on their lives. Advocacy organizations, such as those mentioned earlier, collect anecdotal reports. In addition, the National Crime Victimization Survey has included some questions on experiences with hate crimes. What is evident from both anecdotes and the quantitative research is that the reactions to being targets of hate crimes are both similar to and different from those of victims of random acts of violence. On the one hand, the feelings of victims of hate crimes are common to victims of crime in general: anger, fear, vulnerability. Many crime victims experience psychosocial adjustment problems, including disorientation, fear, helplessness, anger, and depression (Davis, 1987; Office for Victims of Crime, 1994; Resick, 1987). Furthermore, being victimized by crime sparks fear of further victimization, often resulting in changes in behavior (Skogan, 1987).

As with other crime victims, the seriousness of the crime does not necessarily determine the extent of reactions of a victim of ethnoviolence (Ehrlich, Larcom & Purvis, 1994). That is, someone who is the victim of repeated harassment where there is no physical injury may take longer to recover emotionally and return to a normal pattern of activities than would someone who is the victim of a serious physical assault. The duration of reactions and level of life disruption depend on a host of factors, including the social context of the incident, the meaning of the incident to the victim, the availability of a network of support, and the individual's coping mechanisms.

On the other hand, being targeted for who one is rather than for something one has done creates fears and feelings that separate victims of hate crimes from victims of random violence. Research findings indicate that victims of ethnoviolence do suffer more in response to incidents of comparable violence than do victims of random crimes (Dunbar, 2006; Ehrlich et al., 1994; Iganski, 2001; McDevitt et al., 2001). If one is convinced that being a victim was a coincidence of time and place, at least one can try to avoid those circumstances. But correctly believing that one is being attacked for how one looks, or for one's identity in a given group, can create an ongoing level of fear that one is forever at risk.

Another characteristic of hate crimes is that they are often committed by strangers (Harlow, 2005; Levin & McDevitt, 2003). Recent research in England concludes that even in crimes where the victim and offender know each other, the relationship is very casual, often a neighbor or co-worker (Mason, 2005). Attacks by strangers tend to raise the anxiety of the victim and, in the case of hate crimes, all those who share characteristics with the victim. When victims believe that any stranger may attack them, their level of concern and anxiousness can be further heightened.

In 1986, the National Institute Against Prejudice and Violence conducted a pilot study of the effects of hate crimes on minority group members. Ten focus groups were convened around the country, and victims, identified through police departments, human rights organizations, and community leaders, were interviewed using open-ended questions. Crimes the victims had experienced included physical assault; harassment and threats by mail, telephone, and in person; vandalism of their homes; and symbols or slogans of hate on their property. The costs to victims can be emotional, physical, and financial, and the effects can be long lasting. The most prevalent reaction was one of anger toward the perpetrator (68%), followed by fear for the safety of their families (51%). Over one-third indicated feelings of sadness. Behavioral changes were also reported by one-third of the victims. Actions taken by victims included moving, reducing social interactions, taking security measures, and purchasing guns, both for increased safety and in preparation for retaliation if attacked again. Almost one-third of the victims never reported their experiences to the police (Barnes & Ephross, 1994; Ephross, 1994; Ephross et al., 1986; Weiss, 1990).

The first national study designed to assess the prevalence and impact of eth-noviolence and other forms of victimization was also conducted by the National Institute Against Prejudice and Violence in 1989. Telephone interviews, using a stratified random sample, were completed with 2078 respondents. To determine how the experience of being victimized in general compared with being victimized because of prejudice, interviewers asked subjects about symptoms they experienced that are associated with stress. A comparison of four groups of respondents—nonvictims, victims of group defamation, victims of random crimes, and victims of hate crimes—revealed that victims of ethnoviolence experienced the greatest number of negative psychophysiological symptoms as well as the most social and behavioral changes of any group. (Examples of psychological and psychophysiological symptoms included feeling depressed or sad, feeling more nervous than usual, having trouble sleeping, and feeling very angry. Social and behavioral changes included items such as, "moved to another neighborhood"; "tried to be less visible"; "bought or started carrying a gun"; "took a self-defense class.") The study concluded that victims of ethnoviolence exhibited more symptoms with greater frequency than did victims of random violence (Ehrlich et al., 1994).

A more recent study was conducted in Boston from 1992 to 1997, to compare the impact of aggravated assault in bias-motivated cases and non–bias-motivated cases. The researchers found that bias crime victims were more likely to be attacked by a group of attackers than non-bias victims, and bias crime victims were significantly less likely to have a prior relationship with the offender. Nearly all bias assaults were committed by strangers, and most of those victims reported that the assault was an unprovoked attack. Whereas the victims of non-bias assaults could foresee how they could prevent such crimes in the future by changing their behavior, bias crime victims expressed feelings of frustration and felt powerless to protect themselves in the future. On measures of postevent stress, bias victims had a higher incidence of adverse psychological sequelae than the non-bias control group on all 19 of the items measured. Bias victims also felt less safe after the crime and suffered more health problems (McDevitt et al., 2001).

PRACTICE PRINCIPLES

Maintain Objectivity and Balance

In working with victims of hate crimes in groups, it is critical that social workers be in touch with (1) their own personal experiences with hate crimes that might affect the way they view others' experiences and (2) prejudices that might interfere with working with such victims. While this principle applies under all circumstances, working with victims of hate crimes calls for a particular combination of skills:

> A worker must be empathic and sensitive to the pain, yet maintain sufficient detachment to be effective.... Maintaining this delicate balance can cause a worker considerable stress. Additional strain often derives from the inherent limits of the situation: legal remedies are often infeasible or unenforceable. The perpetrator is nameless and faceless, official response sometimes denigrates the experience, and the ultimate enemy—the conditions and institutions that breed the isms in society— seem undefeatable (Weiss & Ephross, 1986, p. 134).

Understand Intergroup Relations

It is important that the social worker not only have a general understanding of the history of minority groups and their interactions with each other but also to have a clear sense of the intergroup factors that exist in the community in which one is working. This is true in general, but particularly so for those dealing with hate crimes. Isolated incidents can lead to widespread intergroup conflict, and lower levels of harassment can escalate into more violent acts (Iganski, 2001; Levin & Rabrenovic, 2001; McDevitt et al., 2001; Wessler & Moss, 2001). The stereotypes minority groups have about each other, and the possibility of competition between victim groups, can interfere with the goals of the group. The social worker must understand the history and current state of black–Jewish relations, for example, or the feelings of other minority groups regarding the apparent success of Asian American immigrants.

Current events also have an impact. Events like the terrorist acts of September 11, 2001, created thousands of victims and also had a ripple effect, resulting in crimes directed at those perceived as Muslim and Arab American and, hence, connected somehow to the terrorism. Other factors that exist in the group, often as silent contributors to tension, are race/ethnicity and social class, the interplay of which influences reactions such as resentment and lack of empathy and must be understood.

Group workers must also keep abreast of legislative and political events that affect members of the group and attitudes of others. For example, recent and rapid changes in laws pertaining to the gay and lesbian community can have a dramatic impact. While legal sanctions such as the 2008 law in Massachusetts legalizing gay marriage and the 2009 Act in the District of Columbia recognizing such marriages from other jurisdictions are a reflection of changes in community norms, they also inflame preexisting prejudices and can lead to an increase in hate crimes against the subject group.

Focus on the Present and on the Individual

The issues surrounding intergroup relations and the historical factors affecting victims' feelings demand that the social worker acknowledge the impact of the past. Racial/ethnic group histories can become a major force to be contended with in victim groups and can be used by group members to avoid dealing with the current victimization issues. Victims may want to talk about historical events that affected their families and are recalled by the current incidents. Without minimizing the impact of history, the social worker must help the individual and the group stay focused on the effects of recent events and how they affected the victim. It is important that group members be helped to see the costs and benefits of identifying themselves as victims, and the positive results that could result from their gaining a feeling of empowerment.

COMMON THEMES

Fear

The fear connected with hate crimes often affects not only the individual victim but the family and community as well. An underestimated aspect of hate crimes is the ripple effect on the community. One case one of the authors dealt with involved a black family who had a cross burned on their lawn. They had a young daughter and, after the incident, were very fearful that the unknown perpetrator would attack again. Overly cautious behavior began to govern their lives. They would no longer allow their daughter to walk alone to her friends' houses on the same block, for fear that she might be in danger. Worse, families in the neighborhood—well-meaning and supportive on the surface—would not let their children visit the home of the victim family, for fear that their children might be in danger if another, more serious, incident occurred while they were visiting.

Fear associated with having been targeted for attack can manifest itself in the group. Individuals may be highly suspicious of others and be reluctant to trust the social worker, or, if it was a racial incident, any members of another race, for example. A primary focus of initial stages of the group should be to help members feel safe in the group so acute symptoms can be addressed.

Anger

Many victims of hate crimes are angry. The anger is directed not just toward the perpetrator, whether known or unknown. Frequently, there is a great deal of anger toward the police. The rate of arrest for crime is low to begin with, and extremely low in cases of property crime where the perpetrator acted under cover of darkness, without witnesses. Victims often feel frustrated by the lack of resolution and afraid of the nameless, faceless enemy, about whom they can do nothing. That frustration is often directed at the police and other aspects of the criminal justice system, and can extend to others in the school or other site of attack, because victims often aren't sure who sympathizes with them, and who with the enemy. Anger and frustration may also be directed at the social worker and other members of the group.

Members must be given an opportunity to vent their feelings and have them validated by others in the group, lest they turn the anger toward themselves. A major goal of the group is to help the victims move beyond their anger so that they can deal with the aftermath of incidents constructively and have their daily routines return to normalcy.

Physical and Psychological Symptoms and Behaviors

Like other types of victimization, hate crimes can result in a wide range of physical and psychological symptoms. Examples of physical symptoms are changes in sleep patterns (difficulty falling asleep, waking frequently during the night), weight loss or gain, onset or exacerbation of back pain or other ailments, and development of nervous tics. Psychological symptoms may include fear of all strangers who look like the perpetrator (or imagined perpetrator), being particularly jumpy in response to unexpected noise, or acting suspicious of everyone, including friends and acquaintances if the act was committed by a stranger ("How do I know whom I can trust?") or having intrusive thoughts about the incident. Changes in behaviors include resuming or increasing smoking or drinking, changing routes walked or driven to work, changing jobs, moving, staying home, or becoming particularly protective of children. Some symptoms may manifest themselves in ways victims may be unaware of. Conversely, victims can blame their victimization for things that occur in their lives that may or may not be connected to the victimization. A critical role for the social worker in working with groups of victims of hate crimes is to facilitate discussions of symptoms and behaviors that are problematic for the group members, and help them separate the ones related to the victimization from the ones that need other types of attention. Because of the wide-ranging nature of symptoms that need to be addressed in the wake of hate crime experiences, effective treatment often requires the integration of behavioral, cognitive and multicultural counseling modalities (Dunbar, 2001).

Dealing with Legal Issues and the Criminal Justice System

It is important that the social worker be able to serve as an advocate for the victim, and make appropriate referrals to legal resources, while maintaining clear boundaries. Hate crimes may crimes by legal definition but can affect the victim in significant ways nonetheless. Some victims, for example, may be suffering because of repeated verbal harassment where there is no legal recourse because the incidents did not qualify as crimes. In some cases, the victim may be working with the police to identify perpetrators; in others, there may be no leads to the perpetrators. In still other cases, the victims may be loath to report the victimization to police either because of fear (as in the case of illegal aliens who are victims) or because of past experience leading to the conviction that the police cannot do anything (Doerner & Lab, 1995). Issues and concerns frequently arise that are related to working with the criminal justice system. Victims worry, "Will I be in danger if I identify the perpetrator or testify at a trial? Will my family? Can the police protect me? What will happen during the trial? Who will pay for the damage to my property?"

As with all groups, members can benefit a great deal from each other's experiences. Social workers should be knowledgeable about the laws that apply both in the state and the local jurisdiction in which they work, and be able to answer basic questions. While it is appropriate for social workers to be advocates, and identify appropriate resources and information within the criminal justice system that might be helpful to clients, they should not give advice on whether to press charges or take particular actions that the police or others might recommend; instead, they should facilitate group members' own decision-making processes.

Continued Interaction with an Offender/Perpetrator

When the incidents have occurred in the workplace or when the perpetrator is someone the victim comes into contact with regularly, such as a next-door neighbor, victims need guidance on how to handle unavoidable interactions and how to avoid confrontations. These incidents often take the form of persistent harassment, sometimes in subtle ways over a long period, and are designed to force the victim of such acts to quit a job or move. Victims need help in assessing the possible ramifications of taking formal actions to stop the perpetrators. Discussion of the pros and cons of such actions, and of how best to handle interactions with the perpetrators, often forms a significant part of group's content and consciousness.

RECOMMENDED WAYS OF WORKING

Agency Context

One type of agency particularly well suited for groups of victims of hate crimes is a local human rights (or human relations) agency that traditionally deals with cases of discrimination in housing, employment, and public accommodations. Some human-relations commissions have a community relations component that specializes in intergroup conflict in the community. Certain school systems, those used to dealing with intergroup tension, can also provide the official context for such groups, particularly when juveniles are involved, either as victims or perpetrators. Mental health associations or interfaith organizations often have programs designed to promote positive intergroup relations and can provide a setting for groups of hate crime victims.

Time Frame

Groups of hate crime victims need immediate crisis counseling and help in dealing with the initial aftermath of the incident. It is important to provide assistance within a few days so that the immediate fear of danger can be addressed. Although there is no reason that groups of victims should not meet for a long period (12 months or more), and the group members could certainly provide support for each other through the often grueling aspects of arrest and trial, if they occur, the most critical time is the first few weeks following an incident. A short-term group (8 to 10 weeks) can frequently address the most critical issues.

Open versus Closed Groups

While either type can be used, there are several advantages to an open group when working with victims. One never knows when support for victims will be needed, and it is better for a victim to have immediate access to an ongoing group, and deal problems of acceptance and entry, than to have to wait until a new group starts. Incidents, with or without physical harm, should be treated as crises initially. Also, victims at different stages can help each other, not only with emotional support but also with practical advice (such as dealing with the police and other aspects of the justice system).

Co-Leadership Involving a Team with Different Races, Ethnicities, or Orientations

Victims of hate crimes are often more wary of other groups after an incident. While a co-leadership team can represent only a few categories, it is frequently advantageous for such a team to work with a victim group. Co-leaders can diffuse the fear and distrust that might exist toward a particular person who might look like the perpetrator. Also, co-leaders can model openness about racial or other sensitive issues. Because white social workers can feel less successful when working with minority group members than do minority social workers (Davis & Gelsomino, 1994), and groups of hate crime victims may be composed entirely or primarily of members of minority groups, a co-leadership team may contribute to the success of the group.

WORKING WITH THE ENTIRE FAMILY WHEN THE VICTIM IS A CHILD

Sometimes the group consists simply of the family. An important issue when a child is attacked, either in the neighborhood or in school, is that of parents becoming overprotective. In some cases, the children want to return to normal routines, which may make parents uneasy. Parents sometimes want the child to change schools or stop walking to school, when the child is worried more about the stigma attached to those behaviors than to any danger. In other cases a child who has been harassed or intimidated is too ashamed to tell parents and is worried about their reaction, particularly if the parents have shared stories of their own experiences. The social worker can help family members separate the realities from the fears, and help the parents and child sort out what is relevant from the past and what needs to be addressed now.

DEALING WITH LANGUAGE BARRIERS

An inadequate command of the English language coupled with cultural differences may prevent some victims of hate crimes from reporting incidents or participating in programs of support. Studies by service providers have pointed to the language barrier as one factor that makes access to services difficult for some minority groups (Browne & Broderick, 1994). Provision of service may be complicated by relationships within a family where children are fluent in English and serve as interpreters for parents. In such cases, the children may be more comfortable dealing with the authorities and the justice system, while the parents are distrustful and anxious. There are several ways to address the language barriers. One is for materials providing helpful information and resources to be printed in as many languages as possible for a given community. Another is to limit some groups to a particular victim population and arrange for an interpreter to work with the social worker if a social worker who speaks the language of the victims is not available or trained to work with groups. In addition, social workers can train bilingual members of the victim community to serve as facilitators in self-help groups. Of course, attempts by the worker to gain even minimal command of other languages are helpful and appreciated by group members.

MEDIATION BETWEEN THE VICTIM AND THE OFFENDER

Ad hoc short-term groups can be an important tool of social workers dealing with hate crimes. Mediating the conflict between the victim and the offender can be the purpose of such a group, particularly when there is continued interaction between the victim and the offender through work, school, or neighborhood contact. Critical group work skills are required for effective mediation. Following is a case study of a successful use of mediation:

> A 16-year-old white youth assaulted a black youth the same age on a basketball court during an informal after-school game, calling him names such as "dirty nigger." The fight was stopped by a school official. Police were not called because there were no serious injuries and no weapon was involved. Because a racial epithet had been used, however, and officials learned that the white youth had been harassing the black youth for some time, they

contacted the local human-relations commission and asked for assistance. There was fear that the tension between the youths would spill over to other students and become more violent. The community relations specialist, a white female social worker, had the school arrange a meeting with both youths at the school one evening. Each student was required to bring one parent. The social worker brought a black male police officer experienced in community relations work. No school official was permitted to participate. Over the course of two sessions of 2 hours each, the black student had a chance to talk about his feelings about being called racist names and being attacked. The white student expressed no remorse at first, only anger toward the black student, who had teased him for months because he was very small in stature. When the black student realized how painful the white youth's experience of being small was for him, and had been for years, he was able to forgive the assault. The mediation was followed up by periodic contacts for the rest of the school year; the intervention was successful in averting what could have been an explosive situation.

EVALUATION APPROACHES

There have been no rigorous evaluations of work with groups of hate crime victims. It is not difficult to evaluate their impact, however. The primary purpose of such groups is to help victims express and work through the psychological and psychophysiological symptoms they experience, and empower them to make critical decisions relevant to the criminal justice system if that is relevant, and about choices they need to make (such as whether to move, change jobs, etc.).

One way to evaluate the effectiveness of the group experience is to have members fill out questionnaires at the inception regarding the nature of the incident, symptoms they are experiencing, concerns they have, and decisions they would like to make. They could then complete another questionnaire at the termination of their time in the group, and possibly also at a point in the future, to measure changes in attitudes and experiences and to determine how much they felt they had accomplished. A somewhat stronger research design might compare these responses to other groups of hate crime victims who did not engage in post-incident group therapy.

With juveniles, both they and their parents could fill out relevant questionnaires. Follow-up could be done with them as well as with their teachers, if the victimization was affecting classroom performance and/or behavior.

CONCLUSION

Groups offer particular advantages for work with victims of hate crimes. Working with such groups calls for sophisticated knowledge both of the issues involved and of group work skills. Social workers must have a clear understanding of the manifestations of victimization based on race, religion, ethnicity, sexual orientation, or disability in order to determine whether crises in the group are related to group process, the stage of development, or to individuals' experiences of trauma.

Knowledge about hate crimes is also valuable for social workers called on to work with other types of groups. Interorganizational task groups or committees created to address the issue of violence in schools, workplaces, or communities would benefit from social workers' knowledge of hate crimes and the ways it affects both individuals and the groups to which they belong. Additional information about hate crimes or ethnoviolence could be obtained from a local police department or human rights agency or from the resources listed below.

RESOURCES

American-Arab Anti-Discrimination Committee
1732 Wisconsin Avenue, NW
Washington, DC 20007
(202) 244-2990
www.adc.org

Anti-Defamation League
823 United Nations Plaza
New York, NY 10017
(202) 885-7700
www.adl.org

Asian American Legal Defense and Education Fund
99 Hudson Street, 12th Floor
New York, NY 10013
(212) 966-5932
www.aaldef.org

LAMBDA GLBT Community Services
216 South Ochoa Street
El Paso, TX 79901
(206) 350-HATE
www.grd.org

Leadership Conference on Civil Rights
1629 K Street NW, 10th Floor
Washington, DC 20006
(202) 466-3311
www.civilrights.org

NAACP National Headquarters
4805 Mt. Hope Drive
Baltimore, MD 21215
(877) NCCAP-98
www.naacp.org

National Coalition of Anti-Violence Programs
240 West 35th Street, Suite 200
New York, NY 10001
(212) 714-1184
www.ncavp.org

Southern Poverty Law Center
400 Washington Avenue
Montgomery, AL 36104
(334) 956-8200
www.splcenter.org

U. S. Department of Justice Community Relations Service
600 E Street, NW, Suite 6000
Washington, DC 20530
(202) 305-2935
www.usdoj.gov/crs

REFERENCES

American-Arab Anti-Discrimination Committee. (2001). *1998–2000 Report on hate crimes and discrimination against Arab Americans.* Washington, DC: Author.

Anti-Defamation League. (2001). *2000 Audit of anti-Semitic incidents.* New York: Author.

Barnes, A. J. & Ephross, P. H. (1994). The impact of hate violence on victims: Emotional and behavioral responses to attacks. *Social Work, 39*(3), 247–251.

Browne, C. & Broderick, A. (1994). Asian and Pacific Island elders: Issues for social work practice and education. *Social Work, 39*(3), 252–259.

Community Relations Service, U.S. Department of Justice. (2001). *CRS Bulletin—Hate crime: The violence of intolerance.* Washington, DC: Author.

Davis, L. E. & Gelsomino, J. (1994). An assessment of practitioner cross-racial treatment experiences. *Social Work, 39*(1), 116–123.

Davis, R. C. (1987). Studying the effects of services for victims in crisis. *Crime and Delinquency, 33*(4), 520–531.

Doerner, W. G. & Lab, S. P. (1995). *Victimology.* Cincinnati: Anderson Publishing Co.

Dunbar, E. (2001). Counseling practices to ameliorate the effects of discrimination and hate events. *The Counseling Psychologist, 29*(2), 279–307.

Dunbar, E. (2006). The importance of race and gender membership in sexual orientation hate crime victimization and reportage: identity politics or identity risk? *Violence and Victims*, *21*(3), 323–337.

Ehrlich, H. J. (1990). *Campus ethnoviolence and the policy options* (Report No. 4). Baltimore, MD: National Institute Against Prejudice and Violence.

Ehrlich, H. J. (1992). *Campus ethnoviolence: A research review* (Report No. 5). Baltimore, MD: National Institute Against Prejudice and Violence.

Ehrlich, H. J., Larcom, B. E. K., & Purvis, R. D. (1994). *The traumatic effects of ethnoviolence*. Baltimore, MD: The Prejudice Institute.

Ephross, P. H., Barnes, A. J., Ehrlich, H. J., Sandnes, K. R., & Weiss, J. C. (1986). *The Ethnoviolence Project Pilot Study*. Baltimore, MD: National Institute Against Prejudice and Violence.

Federal Bureau of Investigation, U.S. Department of Justice. (1991). *Training guide for hate crime data collection*. Washington, DC: Author.

Federal Bureau of Investigation, U.S. Department of Justice. (2009). *Hate crime statistics, 2008*. Washington, DC: Author.

Federal Bureau of Investigation, U.S. Department of Justice. (2002). *Hate crime statistics, 2001*. Washington, DC: AUthor.

Harlow, C.H. (2005). *Hate crimes reported by victims and police* special report Bureau of Justice Statistics, U.S. Department of Justice. Washington D.C.

Herek, G. M. & Berrill, K. T. (eds.). (1992). *Hate crimes: Confronting violence against lesbians and gay men*. Newbury Park, CA: Sage Publications.

Iganski, P. (2001). Hate crimes hurt more. *American Behavioral Scientist*, *45*(4), 626–638.

International Association of Chiefs of Police. (2000). *Responding to hate crimes: A police officer's guide to investigation and prevention*. Alexandria, VA: AUthor.

Levin, J. & Rabrenovic, G. (2001). Hate crimes and ethnic conflict. *American Behavioral Scientist*, *45*(4), 574–587.

Mason G. (2005). Hate crime and the image of the stranger. *British Journal of Criminology*, *45*, 837–859.

McDevitt, J., Balboni, J., Garcia, L., & Gu, J. (2001). Consequences for victims: A comparison of bias- and non–bias-motivated assaults. *American Behavioral Scientist*, *45*(4), 697–713.

National Asian Pacific American Legal Consortium. (1999). *1998 Audit of violence against Asian Pacific Americans: Sixth Annual Report*. Washington, DC: Author.

National Coalition of Anti-Violence Programs. (2002). *Anti-lesbian, gay, bisexual and transgender violence in 2001*. New York: Author.

Pincus, F. L. & Ehrlich, H. J. (1994). *Race and ethnic conflict: Contending views on prejudice, discrimination and ethnoviolence*. Boulder, CO: Westview Press.

Shively, M. & Mulford, C.F. (2007). Hate crime in America: The debate continues. *National Institute of Justice Journal*, *257*, 8–13.

Strom, K. (2001). *Hate crimes reported in NIBRS, 1997–1999*. Washington, DC: Bureau of Justice Statistics, U.S. Department of Justice.

Weiss, J. C. (1990) Violence motivated by bigotry: "Ethnoviolence." In *Encyclopedia of social work* (18th ed., 1990 supplement, pp. 307–319).

Weiss, J. C., Ehrlich, H. J., & Larcom, B. E. K. (1991–1992). Ethnoviolence at work. *Journal of Intergroup Relations*, *18*(4), 21–33.

Weiss, J. C. & Ephross, P. H. (1986). Group work approaches to hate/violence incidents. *Social Work, 31*(2), 132–136.

Wessler, S. & Moss, M. (2001). *Hate crimes on campus: The problem and efforts to confront it*. Washington, DC: Bureau of Justice Assistance, U.S. Department of Justice.

NOTES

1 Legislation in some jurisdictions has expanded the reach of protected classes. For example, In May 2009, Maryland became the first state to extend hate crime protection to homeless people. While the information contained in this chapter is relevant to persons victimized because of any group affiliation, the focus is on race, religion, ethnicity and sexual orientation, only because far less information is available about working with other populations in a hate crimes context.

2 The National Institute Against Prejudice and Violence closed in 1995. Some of its work was continued by The Prejudice Institute.

Chapter Twelve

Group Work With Women Who Have Experienced Abuse

Margot Breton and Anna Nosko

This chapter discusses specific aspects of group practice with women who have experienced abuse in their relationships with male partners. This practice is based on a recognition of the women's strengths and of their competence to identify what they want and what they need, as well as the competence of practitioners to activate the mutual aid dynamics of groups (see Glassman, 2009 on mutual participation groups, and Steinberg 2004 on mutual aid groups). One mutual aid group is used to illustrate various points: it is sponsored by Family Service Toronto (which has sponsored such groups for over a decade) and will be referred to as the *FST group*. It meets in a multiservice center that has a full health clinic, a full legal clinic, and a counseling unit; the coleaders of the group are in the counseling unit. Working out of a multiservice center helps the group leaders maintain a broad perspective on the context of the group and on the members' issues and needs, as well as on their cultural differences. It also allows them to keep in mind that, when dealing with a social problem such as violence against women, interdisciplinary cooperation is essential to providing effective services, as research findings indicate (see, e.g., Horton & Johnson, 1993; Edelson & Eisikovits, 1996).

The female coleaders of the FST group have worked for 10 years with women who have experienced abuse. They have learned that it is best if the decision on whether the group should remain open or closed is not predetermined before the group begins to meet but rather is made by the coleaders and the group members together. Although the FST group has a limit of 12 members, the group may be closed when, after several weeks, there is a core of seven or eight members, and both the workers, and the members agree that the size is right for a productive group. If the membership drops off, then the members can be asked how they feel about allowing more women into the group. Their answer has always been that they want more women in their position to benefit from the group experience. Whether the group is short- or long-term is negotiated between the women and the agency—the number of women awaiting entry into the group being one of the most important determining factors for reopening the group.

Even though the cost of having two workers exceeds that of having only one, experience has shown that the increment in benefits of having a coleader is greater than the increment in costs because coleadership *(1)* provides the women with a model of a relationship based on equality, respect, and caring; *(2)* demonstrates to the women that two people can be different and yet can accept their differences, work together, accommodate, and adapt to each other; *(3)* offers the workers the opportunity to debrief after the sessions, which lessens the probability of burnout, always high in work with this population, as studies have shown (see, e.g., Horton & Johnson, 1993); and *(4)* becomes a support system for the workers (Chataway & Nosko, 1989).

The major reasons for working with the women *in a group* are that *(1)* groups offer a warm, accepting, and caring milieu in which the women can feel secure and appreciated—the tendency of professionals in responding to the plight of women who have experienced abuse is to consider them *deviant* for staying with the abusers (Saunders, 1993; Pollio, 2000): other women "in the same boat" do not have that tendency; *(2)* groups provide the ideal structure for consciousness raising, that is, for dispelling a number of false perceptions (including that of being alone with the particular problem and/or that of being somehow responsible for the violence they experience), as well as for instilling new perceptions (such as that of connecting their personal situations with the structural/political conditions that affect them collectively) (see Profitt, 2000; Mok et al., 2006; and Morales-Campos et al., 2009); and *(3)* groups are the most efficient venue for accessing information on how other women handle their situations and on what they have done or are doing to change these situations. Sharing such information is one of the aspects of mutual aid groups most highly valued by the women. As Killilea (1976, p. 72) noted: "what constitutes 'help' is often a new definition of the problem and specific information about practicalities learned through experience and shared with others because it 'works'."

REVIEW OF THE LITERATURE

Knowledge of wife assault is evolving, and perhaps because this is a relatively new field of study, many myths still abound (Saunders, 1993; Pollio, 2000). Compounding the problem, the etiology of female battering is difficult to explore, for the privacy of the family, traditionally paramount in most societies, is respected both legally and socially. This hampers the work of researchers who wish to conduct empirical studies of spouse abuse (Horton & Johnson, 1993). Furthermore, some of the earlier work in the field is being challenged, if not discredited. For example:

> *Clinical lore of a decade ago presented similar profiles of the offender and victim. They were both said to be from violent homes, to be isolated, to be deficient in communication*

skills, and to have low self-esteem. Recent reviews of empirical studies make it clear that it is the offender who differs most from the norm. Hotaling and Sugarman (1986) reviewed controlled studies of husband-to-wife violence. Out of 15 risk factors reviewed, the men had nine, including nonassertiveness, alcohol abuse, and a propensity to abuse their children. The women, on the other hand, had only one risk factor: a greater likelihood of having witnessed violence between their parents. (Saunders, 1993, pp. 209–210; see also Holtzworth-Munroe et al., 1997b).

The early literature on female spouse abuse presents issues from a psychological/victim perspective, viewing the women as pathological; for example, the concept of masochism assumes that women enjoy suffering (see Gelles, 1979, on this point). The literature then moves from pathology to social and structural issues; for example, social learning theories postulate that one learns to be a victim first through intergenerational transmission of violence and then through rigid sex role definitions (Eisikovits et al., 1998). This theory of learned helplessness assumes that women do not learn the skills necessary to leave abusive situations (see Mahoney, 1994). Social interaction theory views men as attempting to gain control over their spouses through various means, including the use of violence; this is deemed particularly relevant where there is a threat from female competence (Holtzworth-Munroe et al., 1997b). Resource theories connect abuse to economic issues, surmising that a woman's greater status and resources undermine the man's traditional role as breadwinner, with violence seen as a way to regain control (Holtzworth-Munroe et al., 1997b). Sociocultural theories view violence as endemic to society and therefore as normal (Straus, 1980). The structural/political approach (Holtzworth-Munroe et al., 1997a; Pahl, 1985), adopting a historic overview, examines how social institutions, over the millennia and in all societies, condone a husband's authority over his wife and support laws such as the "rule of thumb" in England, whereby a husband could hit his wife with a stick no wider than his thumb. (For an excellent and comprehensive review of the early literature, see Health and Welfare Canada, 1989.)

More recent studies focus on women who cope with abusive situations (Baker, 1997; Lampert, 1996; Nurius et al., 1992) or have successfully ended them. For example, Horton and Johnson (1993), and Baker (1997) document the tremendous investments women make to end the abuse in their lives. This new research recognizes women's strengths and resourcefulness. Building on this research, it is important to look for new solutions. Until recently, one of the most common approaches to the problem of spouse abuse was to enjoin women to leave their spouses. Yet research indicates that the majority of women return to their partners (Bell et al., 2009; Holtzworth-Munroe et al., 1997a; Horton & Johnson, 1993). This information challenges the field to find out from the women themselves what it is they want changed. It also indicates that it is time to develop practice principles that build on the strengths and resourcefulness of women who have experienced abuse (Edelson & Eisikovits, 1996; Goldberg, Wood, & Roche, 2001; Pollio, 2000).

Before discussing these principles, we want to make a point about the use of theories in the kind of group practice we advocate. Practitioners should not focus on theories that purport to explain wife assault or women battering but should listen to the women themselves as *they* explain their reality. In other words, it is essential to stop looking at the women through the lenses of theories. A change of theoretical lenses does not suffice, for these lenses always distort. It is not a question of adopting a particular clinical or political stance or theoretical perspective, whether it represents the latest research or the latest fad, because the women and their experiences (recognized as diverse; see, e.g., Nurius et al., 1992) simply do not fit neatly within any one theory. The leaders of the FST group, instead of teaching the women, as they used to do, about the theory of learned helplessness for example, now ask them if that theory applies to them. Some say yes and others no, and the leaders, willing to learn from the women, treat the answers as information that becomes a learning tool for everyone in the group. This in no way implies that practitioners do not have a very important leadership role to play in a group, nor that they can ignore the latest research and theories. It simply emphasizes that they need to subordinate the theories to what the women identify as their reality.

PRACTICE PRINCIPLES

The practice principles that should guide social workers beginning with a group of women who have experienced abuse are essentially the same as those principles guiding all practice that is focused on strengths and competence and is empowerment oriented (see, e.g., Breton, 1994, 2002; Brun & Rapp, 2001; Mok et al., 2000; Saleebey, 1997). Such practice demands that from the outset the workers *demonstrate respect for the women.* This first principle is operationalized through the following actions and attitudes: *(1) let each woman tell her story* and encourage her to use her new-found voice to "name [her] world" (Freire, 1993, p. 159); *(2) believe the women*, their stories, and what they understand as the facts. In other words, accept their representation of their situation as "legitimate knowledge" (Weick, 1997, p. 23), and do not assume that the women have low self-esteem (Saunders, 1993). A rather telling and funny dialogue took place in the group one day:

Woman: I have no self-esteem. *Worker:* What does self-esteem mean to you?
Woman: I don't know, really. *Worker:* Well then, maybe you have some.
Woman: Well, yeah ...

This interchange emphasizes the need for workers to have a sense of humor, which, as Malekoff (1994, p. 7) points out, refers to "the ability to see the humor in a situation or exchange and the capacity not to take oneself too seriously." This "in no way refers to making light of deadly subjects as an end in itself. What it implies is a flexibility of mind and spirit and the faith and trust that the group can and will, with a little assistance, move through the humor in a growth inducing way" (p. 8); *(3) facilitate the process of consciousness raising:* (a) affirm the actual and potential competence and strengths of the women, emphasizing "how they have survived thus far" (Goldstein, 1997, p. 32) and using their stories and their "own knowledge of their lives ... as a natural resource" (Weick, 1997, p. 24); (b) confront the oppressor within (Freire, 1993) and challenge negative self-images and self-evaluations, stressing that "they were capable of solving their problems" (Morales-Campos et al., 2009, p. 61); (c) help the women to identify, as they become aware of the patterns in their stories, the common social, political, economic, and cultural contexts of their situations. This last guideline should not be construed as a license to proselytize and to impose the workers' belief system or values on the members. On the contrary, it is up to the women themselves to choose what to do with the awareness they develop of the interconnection of issues. The workers should inform them of various alternatives, including some form of social action, but the choice remains the women's.

Thus the second principle, which flows from the first, is that workers *base all interventions on member self-determination.* It is important for workers to acknowledge that self-determination is a concept long-accepted in the western world, whereas collectivism represents a value held in many other parts of the world, where the emphasis is on relationship, connection, and community. This emphasis can mean that being a wife and mother is more important than being an individual (see Singh & Hays, 2008). To make this second principle operational requires that the workers *trust the members.* In a group, one major manifestation of the workers' trust is the emergence of a mutual aid system, for this happens when workers trust the members to help one another. From the very beginning of the group, as the women tell their stories, each woman realizes that hearing the stories of others makes her feel less alone and better about herself. When the workers acknowledge that the women are indeed the experts at helping each other, the process of mobilizing and supporting their competence and strengths can begin.

Self-determination also requires that workers *identify what the women want.* As Rapp (1997, p. 48) states unequivocally: "if client self-determination is to be taken seriously, the client's desires must be given absolute primacy." This may cause problems for workers when a group member chooses to stay with an abusive partner, but it is *not* the workers' prerogative to dictate what another person should want. Challenging, discussing, confronting—those behaviors are in the workers' rightful domain; pretending to know what is best for other people is not. It is important to signal here that the notion of contracting, as a formal mechanism to ensure self-determination and to establish the specific conditions under which the group will operate, may not always be relevant to work with a group of women who have experienced abuse; it may have to be abandoned if the women interpret it as a constraint that locks them into a situation and once again makes them feel controlled. What is essential is to be accountable to the women; how this accountability plays itself out will vary, depending on a number of factors, including the cultural background of the women and their individual motivations, including their distrust of would-be helpers, their fear of failure, and their aversion to risk taking (Breton, 1985).

To be accountable and to base interventions on self-determination means that workers are guided by a third principle, that of *individualization.* Pray (1991) makes a strong case that this principle is given lip service more than genuinely honored in traditional problem-focused and pathology-centered social work approaches. A renewed and vigorous interpretation of the principle, one that is congruent with a focus on strengths, competence, and empowerment, demands that workers *(1) eschew preconceived plans and solutions,* generic goals, and all other forms of "homogenization of clients" (Rapp, 1997, pp. 51–52)—*and of groups,* we hasten to add. This suggests a flexible approach to group structure. As indicated above, choosing an open or closed format, for example, will depend on the needs of the group at various points in its evolution. Individualization also suggests that the process of termination be left to the women to determine and be individually tailored; each member's termination should occur when she has achieved the goals she has set for herself and does not believe the group can be of further help.

Individualization further requires that workers *(2) reject labels,* such as "abused women" and "abused women's group"; this implies seeing the women as whole persons, not just as victims. The idea is to reject the connotation of passivity that pervades the label of "victim" without rejecting the fact of victimization/oppression. The intention is to always put the accent on the women as active subjects, not as passive objects. Thus the reference to the members of the FST group as "women who have experienced abuse" provides them an opportunity to take back some control over their lives by identifying the abuse as something *they* experienced, and not primarily as something *others* perpetrated against them. Workers who forget that women who have been victimized "above all are whole human beings with the same potential and aspirations as anyone else … further victimize them" (Breton, 1990, p. 26; see also Saleebey, 2001).

Seeing the women as whole persons demands that workers *(3) promote a group context and encourage group programs in which the women can demonstrate and share their specific strengths,* showcase their talents, and acknowledge their abilities, including their ability to empathize, nurture, and comfort each other, and practice and develop their skills. The group should enable the women to translate into action their changing ways of thinking and feeling about themselves (see Pollio, 2000).

However, like all human beings, the women need ongoing support networks, not only to sustain their present strengths and to maintain changes already achieved, but also to develop potential strengths and continue to make changes, a condition of survival and growth in this world. Although women who have experienced abuse usually need the support of a professionally led mutual aid group for a relatively long period of time, their relationship with the group and the workers eventually ends. The workers, knowing that the group's support is time limited, have the responsibility to ensure postgroup support that will endure over time.

Therefore, the last principle is that workers *make maximum use of natural supports in the community.* This entails that workers *(1) perceive the community as a resource* (Sullivan, 1997), identifying natural helpers and natural resources such as recreation centers, libraries, and Ys, informing women about these people and resources, and connecting them to each other if the women so wish. The principle also demands that workers *(2) maximize the potential support in the women's environment,* modifying existing structures or creating new ones to meet the members' needs (Wood & Middleman, 1989). Where personal natural support networks are nonexistent, workers encourage group members to see themselves as the first links in a new natural support system, one that exists outside of the group and will continue to exist once they leave the group (Breton, 1985; Morales-Campos et al., 2009). Finally, workers will be required to *(3) create partnerships in the community* (Breton, 1994; 2004). By acknowledging community strengths, and by accepting collaboration as partners with natural helpers and with normal community services and institutions, workers facilitate the women's perception of being not only members of a group but also members of a community, and thus facilitate their integration into that community.

COMMON THEMES AND HOW TO DEAL WITH THEM

Workers need to be prepared (tuned in) to pick up on themes that regularly come up in groups of women who have experienced abuse. An important one to emphasize from the very beginning is that of *power.* For example, assuming that the members cope with their situations, and expecting that they will share how they cope, harnesses the positive interactional energy of the group. "The concept of *social capital* offers a useful framework to describe how participation is linked to personal empowerment and how personal empowerment brings about benefits in the forms of social support, coping skills and information" that the women use to solve their problems (Mok et al., 2006, p. 91; see also Laurance et al., 2004). The workers presume that each woman has some power and that together the women have greater power. Starting from a proactive position (namely, a position that postulates that the women already have strengths) lays a foundation for them to acknowledge the choices they make and to move toward different choices. This proactive stance is illustrated when workers ask "What are you doing to keep yourself safe?" instead of "Are you keeping yourself safe?"

Assuming that the women have *choices* creates an atmosphere of respect and encourages the women to see themselves as capable and open to yet other choices:

> *Barbara:*   You know, I really don't want to leave my husband because I love him. I've invested too much for too many years to go—

Tina: Me too. For thirty years I looked after him and raised my children so they would have a mother and father, but my job is done
and I don't need to take it anymore.

Karen: I have left many men, and I still haven't learned how to find a
good man; do they exist?

Heddy: If they abuse you, get rid of them, find someone else.

Many significant themes emerge from each interchange among the members.
The workers keep a list of these individual "strands" and rethread them through
the discussions. The women themselves then weave these strands into a coherent
and resilient tapestry in which they are highlighted and from which radiates the
support they get from and give each other.

One of these other significant themes is *safety*. It needs to be kept in the fore-
ground of the group. The workers approach it from the perspective that each
woman is responsible for her safety and that of her children, which again presumes
that each woman is capable and competent. The concern for their children often
motivates the women to do something about the violence they experience:

Jan: I won't let my child suffer like I did.

Heddy: It's not fair to the children. They shouldn't have to suffer from
seeing all this abuse. I worry about how it is affecting them.

This concern is well founded; a Canadian national survey indicates that children witnessed violence against their mothers in almost 40% of marriages with
violence (Rodgers, 1994; see also Holtzworth-Munroe et al., 1997c). The theme
of safety thus expands into the theme of *love for their children*, and the women
move from considering their own experiences to reflecting on the different experiences they want their children to have (Morales-Campos et al.,2009). Workers
who trust that it is the members who know best what will help them to reach their
goals support the transformations or evolutions of themes.

The theme of safety also involves a consideration of *violence* per se and an
examination of its possible sources. This often leads to exploring the *resources
available* to do something about violence. These resources include knowledge of
the legal system and of various social agencies, the role of the police and of one's
physician, and so on. At this point, the women have an opportunity to share their
experiences about resources and to pursue the themes of their *right to protection
under the law* and their *right to access community resources*, the themes of the *ade-
quacy of services* offered and of the *cultural and societal biases* influencing the reactions of police and physicians, as well as other related themes. As research indicates
(Horton & Johnson, 1993, p. 490), "Clinicians' advocacy and educational roles
are important factors in stopping the cycle of abuse."

It can be argued that *mutual aid* with its "strength in us" dynamic, constitutes
the leitmotif or dominant theme that recurs throughout the duration of the group.

For example, Miller (1991, p. 199) believes that one of the strengths women possess is being relational, that is, being adept at "using one's power to help another ... increasing the other's resources, capabilities, effectiveness and ability to act." The mutual aid system of the group encourages and buttresses this relational strength or competence. As members explore themes important to them, they experience positive human relations:

> *Susan:* I feel so comfortable talking about how I feel. If I'm disappointed with myself, I don't fear being judged or put down here, like I do by my husband.

The sense of acceptance and of respect is also achieved through another mutual aid dynamic; the dialectical process that recognizes diversity and differences along with the common ground:

> *Tina:* You young women should save yourselves, don't wait till you are old like me.
> *Susan:* Tina, you give me hope that it is never too late to change.
> *Worker:* Each one of you has much to share; you can help each other in different ways.

Themes provide a "mirror" in which each woman sees part of herself or her issue (Alonso & Rutan, 1988). For example, as Mary tells Jane to stand up for herself (the theme of *assertiveness*), she also sees this advice reflected back to her. In this way, many topics that are perceived as threatening or painful to broach are made safe because they are accessed indirectly. When the theme of abuse is activated and women *choose* to talk about their experience, or even when only one woman, at a particular point, chooses to talk, all the women become part of the disclosure; each woman need not directly disclose all the specific details of her situation because it is captured in the stories of others—hence the group mirror.

Any time the group discusses one of the themes, new knowledge is gained. The group workers' role is to monitor these themes, label them, reintroduce them when appropriate, add information that may be helpful, expand, and connect them. For example, when the women talk about how they have been trying hard to get their husbands to change, the workers raise the point that they are presently focusing on changing the other, yet earlier they had agreed that one can only change oneself. This comment connects the discussion to earlier themes (those of *responsibility* and *change*) and challenges the women to look in a direction in *which they have more control and choice.*

EVALUATION APPROACHES

Evaluating the progress made by the abused women in the group would enhance the process through which they acquire a voice, as suggested by all empowerment research (Bartle et al., 2002). This demands that the women participate in planning the evaluation, that is, in deciding what will be evaluated and how. Indeed, if the purpose of research is to provide useful information, "not just for professionals, but for their clients" (Holmes, 1997, p. 159), then the participation of the women as partners in the evaluation is imperative. In a collaborative approach to the evaluation process, the members become research participants whose stake in the research is fully recognized (see, e.g., Lee, 2001).

As early as possible, therefore, and with the encouragement and help of the workers, the members should consider how the evaluation could "authenticate the resources and transformation capacities" that they have as individuals and as a group (Saleebey, 1997, p. 178) and how it could help them "to redefine their experience of the world, [and] to act within it from a position of greater human potential and power" (Holmes, 1997, p. 164). Empowerment research challenges the traditional assumption that what is important in the evaluation process is how the *professional* judges if there is change. In their study of women who have ended abuse, Horton and Johnson (1993, p. 491) recognize the inherent limitations of self-reporting but conclude that "Nevertheless, the women … were 'experts' on wife abuse. Researchers' tasks are to summarize the data victims provide, explore their strategies for ending abuse, and report what works and does not work" (see also Edelson & Eisikovits, 1996).

In the FST group, the workers gather qualitative data every group session from each woman's own assessment of how she believes she is progressing towards her goal of improving her situation. For example, as she arrived one day, Lisa told the workers that her exboyfriend had been phoning her frequently during the past week, and she didn't know if she should let him come back. Her dilemma was brought up in the group, and as she discussed with other women what she should do, she evaluated the changes she had made thus far. She then admitted that to maintain the progress she had made, she would have to be very careful about not being enticed back into the relationship by her expartner's sweet words. To help her chart her progress, she employed an unorthodox but effective measure of progress used repeatedly in the group: "the garbage collection day" metaphor. The women had decided that each week, in the group, they have the opportunity to throw out old, useless ideas and behaviors to make room for new ones. As they help each other to discard their "garbage," they are conscious of making choices, making progress, and moving forward. This is, for them, a meaningful and valuable evaluation process. The more garbage they throw out, the more progress they make.

Evaluation of progress is essential in groups of women who have experienced abuse, but it is more significant *for the women* and more supportive of the changes *they* want when it is incorporated in the group's life and becomes a natural feature of the work that goes on in the group. An ongoing parallel process of evaluation must take place between the workers, not only for them to fully understand what is happening in the group, but so that the group never suffers from unresolved issues arising within the coleaders subgroup (Nosko & Wallace, 1992).

CONCLUSION

The group practice presented in this chapter is driven not by the preferred ideologies and theories of professionals, but rather by what the group members say they need and want. The principles discussed above should help practitioners who work with women who have experienced abuse to listen to what the women say and pay heed to their voices. This, as pointed out earlier, does not mean that workers cannot challenge the women, or cannot plan or prepare for the group, but simply that they should not pre-determine what the work of the group will be or what changes the women will seek in the way they conduct their lives and/or in the way social systems limit their lives. When practitioners believe in, and take into account, the strengths that individuals bring to groups and further develop in and through groups, the possibilities for all kinds of changes are as vast as the human spirit that characterizes women who have experienced abuse and are willing to work together in a group to overcome these experiences.

RESOURCES

Sources of information for social workers who wish to begin a group of women who have experienced abuse exist at the national, provincial/state, regional, and local levels. A good place to start is the local Family Services Association, where a list of other relevant resources may be available. Municipal libraries are also a good source of information, though in some rural areas, women's shelters may be the best resource.

Canada National Clearinghouse on Family Violence
Family Violence Prevention Division
Health and Welfare Canada
Government of Canada
Ottawa, Ontario, K1A 1B5
(613) 957-2938 or 800-267-1291
Telephone Devices for the Deaf (613) 952-6396 or 800-561-5643
www.hc-sc.gc.ca/hppb/family violence/index.html

United States National Coalition Against Domestic
Violence and National Domestic Hotline
(800) 799-7233
www.ncadv.org

REFERENCES

Alonso, A. & Rutan, S. (1988). The experience of shame and restoration of self-respect in group therapy. *International Journal of Group Psychotherapy, 38*(1), 3–14.

Baker, P. L. (1997). And I went back—Battered women's negotiations of choice. *Journal of Contemporary Ethnography, 26,* 55–74.

Bartle, E. E., Couchonnal, G., Canda, E. R., & Staker, M. D. (2002). Empowerment as a dynamically developing concept for practice: Lessons learned from organizational ethnography. *Social Work, 47*(1), 32–43.

Bell, M. E., Goodman, L. A., & Dutton, M. A. (2009). Variations in health-seeking, battered women's relationship course, emotional well-being and experiences of abuse over time. *Psychology of Women's Quarterly, 33*(2), 149–161.

Breton, M. (1985). Reaching and engaging people: Issues and practice principles. *Social Work with Groups, 8*(3), 7–21.

Breton, M. (1990). Learning from social group work traditions. *Social Work with Groups, 13*(3), 21–34.

Breton, M. (1994). Relating competence-promotion and empowerment. *Journal of Progressive Human Services, 5*(1), 27–44.

Breton, M. (2002). Empowerment practice in Canada and the United States: Restoring policy issues at the center of social work. *Social Policy Journal, 1*(1), 19–34.

Breton, M. (2004). An empowerment perspective. In C. D. Garvin, L. M. Gutiérrez, & M. J. Galinsky (eds.), *Handbook of social work with groups* (pp. 58–75). New York: The Guilford Press.

Chataway, C. & Nosko, A. (1989). Group work with abused women. Paper presented at the 11th Annual Symposium of the Association for the Advancement of Social Work with Groups. Montreal, October.

Edelson, J. L. & Eisikovits, Z. C. (eds.). (1996). *Future intervention with battered women and their families.* Thousand Oaks, CA: Sage Publications.

Eisikovits, Z., Buchbinder, E., & Mor, M. (1998). What it was won't be anymore: Reaching the turning point in coping with intimate violence. *Affilia: Journal of Women and Social Work, 13,* 411–434.

Freire, P. (1993). *Pedagogy of the oppressed* (20th anniversary ed.). New York: Continuum.

Gelles, R. J. (1979). *Family violence.* Beverly Hills, CA: Sage Publications.

Goldstein, H. (1997). Victors or victims: Contrasting views of clients in social work practice. In D. Saleebey (ed.), *The strengths perspective in social work practice* (pp. 27–38). New York: Longman.

Health and Welfare Canada. (1989). *Family violence: A review of theoretical and clinical literature.* Catalogue No.: H21-103/1989E.

Holmes, G. E. (1997). Social work research and the empowerment paradigm. In D. Saleebey (ed.), *The strengths perspective in social work practice* (pp. 158–168). New York: Longman.

Holtzworth-Munroe, A., Bates, L., Smutzler, N., & Sandin, E. (1997a). A brief review of research on husband violence: Part 1. Maritally violent versus nonviolent men. *Aggression and Violent Behavior, 3,* 65–99.

Holtzworth-Munroe, A., Smutzler, N., & Bates, L. (1997b). A brief review of research on husband violence: Part 3. Sociodemographic factors, relationship factors, and differing consequences of husband and wife violence. *Aggression and Violent Behavior, 3,* 285–307.

Holtzworth-Munroe, A., Smutzler, N., & Sandin, E. (1997c). A brief review of research on husband violence: Part 2. Psychological effects of husband violence on battered women and their children. *Aggression and Violent Behavior, 3,* 179–213.

Horton, A. L. & Johnson, B. L. (1993). Profile and strategies of women who have ended abuse. *Families in Society: The Journal of Contemporary Human Services, 74*, 481–492.

Killilea, M. (1976). Mutual help organizations: Interpretations in the literature. In G. Caplan and M. Killilea (eds.), *Support systems and mutual help: Multidisciplinary explorations.* New York: Grune and Stratton.

Lampert, L. B. (1996). Women's strategies for survival: Developing agency in abusive relationships. *Journal of Family Violence, 11,* 268–289.

Laurance, L. Y. & Porter, M. L. (2004). Observations from practice: Support group membership as a process of social capital formation among female survivors of domestic violence. *Journal of Interpersonal Violence, 19*(6), 676–689.

Lee, J. A. B. (2001). *The empowerment approach to social work: Building the beloved community.* New York: Columbia University Press.

Mahoney, M. R. (1994). Victimization or oppression: Women's lives, violence and agency. In M. A. Fineman & B. Mykitiuk (eds.), *The public nature of private violence* (pp. 59–92). New York: Routledge.

Malekoff, A. (1994). A guideline for group work with adolescents. *Social Work with Groups, 17*(1/2), 5–19.

Miller, J. B. (1991). The development of women's sense of self. In J. V. Jordan, A. C. Kaplan, J. Baker Miller, J. P. Stiver, & J. L. Surfey (eds.), *Women's growth in connection: Writings from the Stone Center* (pp. 11–26). New York: Guilford Press.

Mok, B.-H., Cheung, Y. W., & Cheung, T.-S. (2006). Empowerment effect of self-help group participation in a Chinese context. *Journal of Social Service Research, 32*(3), 87–102.

Nosko, A. & Wallace, R. (1992). Female and male coleadership. Paper presented at the 14th Annual Symposium of the Association for the Advancement of Social Work with Groups, Atlanta.

Nurius, P. S., Furrey, J., & Berliner, L. (1992). Coping capacity among women with abusive partners. *Violence and Victims, 7*(3), 229–243.

Pahl, J. (ed.). (1985). *Private violence and public policy.* London: Routledge & Kegan Paul.

Pollio, D. E. (2000). Reconstructing feminist group work. *Social Work with Groups, 23*(2), 3–18.

Pray, J. E. (1991). Respecting the uniqueness of the individual: Social work practice within a reflexive model. *Social Work, 36,* 80–85.

Profitt, N. J. (2000). Survivors of woman abuse: Compassionate fires inspire collective action for social change. *Journal of Progressive Human Services, 11*(2), 77–102.

Rapp, C. A. (1997). The strengths perspective of case management with persons suffering from severe mental illness. In D. Saleebey (ed.), *The strengths perspective in social work practice.* New York: Longman.

Rodgers, K. (1994). Wife assault: The findings of a national survey. *Juristat: Service Bulletin, 14*(9). Ottawa: Statistics Canada. Catalogue No. 85-002 ISSN 0715-271X.

Saleebey, D. (ed.). (1997). *The strengths perspective in social work practice.* New York: Longman.

Saleebey, D. (2001). The diagnostic strengths manual. *Social Work, 46*(2), 183–187.

Saunders, D. G. (1993). Woman battering. In R. T. Ammerman & M. Hersen (eds.), *Assessment of family violence. A clinical and legal sourcebook* (pp. 208–234). New York: Wiley.

Steinberg, D. S. (2004). *The mutual-aid approach to working with groups: Helping people to help each other* (2nd ed.). Northvale, NJ: Aronson.

Sullivan, W. P. (1997). Reconsidering the environment as a helping resource. In D. Saleebey (ed.), *The strengths perspective in social work practice* (pp. 148-157). New York: Longman.

Weick, A. (1997). Building a strengths perspective for social work. In D. Saleebey (ed.), *The strengths perspective in social work practice* (pp. 18-26). New York: Longman.

Wood, G. & Middleman, R. (1989). *The structural approach to direct practice in social work.* New York: Columbia University Press.

Wood, G. G. & Roche, S. E. (2001). Representing selves, reconstructing lives: Feminist group work with women survivors of male violence. *Social Work with Groups, 23*(4), 5–23.

Chapter Thirteen

Group Work With African American Youth in the Criminal Justice System: A Culturally Competent Model

Aminifu R. Harvey

There is no wealth where there are no children.
—African proverb

I first wrote this chapter in 1997. More than a decade later, the plight of African American males in the United States has not significantly improved (Harvey & Hill, 2004). Twenty years ago, Gibbs (1989) was so alarmed at the plight of African American males that she raised the possibility of this population's extinction. Kunjufu (2001) wrote that the plight of the African American is so serious that America is faced with a state of emergency. Also 20 years ago, Wilson (1990) stated his concern about the large number of male African American adolescents who endanger their lives or their prospects for a physically, mentally, spiritually, and economically healthy life by their involvement in criminal activities. In addition, these young men endanger the health and well-being of the African American community. The community violence has killed other young men (Butterfield, 2004) and innocent bystanders (Erdley, 2009). The violence reduces the value of private residences, raises insurance costs for homes and autos, and eliminates the interest of businesses coming into the community. This violence also reduces the availability of employment and forces community residents to travel great distances for employment, shrinking the time necessary to raise and demonstrate necessary values to their children. Gilbert, Harvey and Belgrave (2009) contend that a significant cause of the latter "are rooted in impoverished living conditions and stressful life events resulting from historical oppression and loss of culture and identity" (p. 250). Bent-Goodley (2003) speaks to the fact that crime increases in poor communities when unemployment rises and job prospects are bleak. She also discusses the disproportionality of sentencing for young African American males. Exacerbating this problem is that, in the nation's largest cities where most African

American youths live, the high school graduation rate is less than 50% (Reuters, 2009).

African American boys between 14 and 18 years of age are a significant percentage of the youths involved in the juvenile justice system (Wilson, 1994). Their offenses include selling drugs, rape, armed robbery, auto theft, burglary, and a host of other crimes (Black Americans, 2008). These crimes are destructive to the boys, their families, and their communities. Yet, these male youths cannot be held totally responsible for their behaviors as change in family structure can have a direct effect on antisocial behavior and drug involvement (Krohn, Hall, Penly, & Lizotte, 2009). Additionally, living in a partner-violent home can increase the potential for aggressive and antisocial behavior in youths (Ireland & Smith, 2009).

The youths are either sentenced to serve time in institutions or are put on probation. A disproportionate number of African American youths are sentenced to institutions (Black Americans, 2008). Because of this discriminatory practice, the juvenile justice system is exploring alternative methods of intervention and supervision. The Child Welfare League of America recognizes the need for a new framework for improved outcomes in this area and the need for more coordination between juvenile justice and child welfare (Wiig & Tuell, 2008).

The purpose of this chapter is to address issues of working with groups of African American boys involved in the juvenile justice system. One effective program based on small groups of African American boys 14 to 18 years of age who are on probation will be described.

REVIEW OF THE LITERATURE

There is a scarcity of social work literature on group work with African American youths. Two articles were located (Franklin, 1989; Lee, 1989). Franklin points out that the issue of respect is significant in the lives of African American youths and must be addressed in the context of the group. He also states that the group can serve as an "alternative peer reference group" (p. 330) to counteract negative peer influences and provide support in the face of adversity. Lee (1989) presents a group work model that is school based but has applicability to other settings. This model reinforces the approach for working with African American males presented later in this chapter. Lee's model is not gender specific; it can be generalized to males or females. He contends that a concentrated effort is needed to develop comprehensive interventions that reflect the needs and contemporary realities of black youths. He further states that it is important to create methods of incorporating African American culture into the helping process because culture-specific approaches have the potential to transform basic aspects of African American life generally ignored or perceived as negative into positive psychoeducational experiences. Lee contends that "in order to maximize the effectiveness of cultural specificity in the helping process, emphasis should be placed on group approaches to guidance and counseling with Black youth" (p. 294). Harvey and Coleman (1997) present an agency's comprehensive program from an Africentric perspective based upon one author's work with African American youth. Harvey and Rauch (1997) present another description of this same agency's group work with this population.

Non–social work publications contain material on risk factors, resiliency factors, and concepts for interventions pertaining to African American male youths. Kunjufu (1985) identifies the following factors that enable African American youths to overcome the negative influences of inner-city life: strong family background, positive peer pressure, social survival skills, participation on athletic teams, high teacher expectations, low student-teacher ratio, and religious participation. Similarly, Lewis and Lewis (1984) identify effective mental health prevention programs for African American families and children as those that help them in developing satisfying relationships, acquiring effective cognitive problem-solving skills, managing personal stress, and maintaining positive self-concepts. Hill (1972), in his seminal work on the strengths of African American families, identifies the following resiliency factors: strong achievement orientation, strong work orientation, flexible family roles, strong kinship bonds, and strong religious participation.

It is recognized that high-risk behaviors are significantly interrelated, especially among youths (Penkower et al., 1991). According to Dryfoos (1990), one in four young people in America "do it all" and are in jeopardy of not growing into responsible adults unless immediate interventions occur. This is more likely to happen among those with low self-esteem, low educational aspiration, low social skills, and low social approval (Botvin & McAlister, 1981; Millman & Botvin, 1983). Many of these children are being negatively stereotyped, culturally misunderstood, and misdiagnosed (Fusick & Bordeau, 2004).

Through a complex system of formal and informal networks rooted in family life and ongoing socialization processes, families, adult relatives, and communities traditionally maintained effective social control and instilled common values in their members (Kornhauser, 1978; Sampson, 1987). Marital and family disruption, predominance of street corner peer groups, and decline of formal and informal social controls have all contributed to the demise of traditional constraints on the behavior of adolescents (Krohn, 1986). By the 1980s, as children approached adolescence, there appeared to be a progressive decline in the influence of parents and adults and a corresponding increase in the impact of peer networks (Glynn, 1981; Hare & Hare, 1985). Seventy percent of African American children are born to unwed mothers (Pleasant-Immanuel, 2009). Winbush (2001) tries to counter these phenomena with his guide for parents for raising healthy black boys. Kunjufu (2001) also provides a list of what he calls solutions to the problem.

While parents and adult networks tend to hold values, norms, and attitudes that discourage criminal behavior (Wills & Vaughan, 1984), street peer groups that are prone to antisocial behavior may encourage criminal behavior (Skogan, 1986).

Due to what has been characterized as "adolescent egocentrism" (Elkind, 1978), adolescents tend to have a heightened sense of self-consciousness concerning their appearance, personal qualities, and abilities. The combination of adolescent ego-centrism and the increased influence of street gangs tends to promote substance abuse and other criminal behaviors among many inner-city youths. This is particu-larly true among inner-city African American boys, for whom the "street culture" is a major institution comparable to the family, the school, and the church (Perkins, 1986). Majors and Mancini (1992), in their classic work, discuss the importance for African American of being "cool," which fosters a certain cultural life style which brings public attention by civil authorities to their presence. The more such traditional institutions in the African American community abdicate their respon-sibility for socialization of their children, the greater is the influence of the street gangs (Harvey, 1988).

Research reveals that several problem behaviors appear to be caused by the same underlying factors (Jessor, 1982). For this reason, it is suggested that prevention programs be developed that target the underlying determinants of several theo-retically and empirically related problem behaviors (Botvin, 1982; Swisher, 1979; Wiig & Tuell, 2008). This assumes that an effective treatment program should aim at promoting youths' general personal needs, social competences, vocational aspi-rations, self-esteem, and cultural integrity (Smokowsk & Bacallao, 2009), thereby affecting the factors that underlie many types of delinquent behaviors.

Perkins (1986) states that an Africentric cultural approach is needed to deal effectively with the antisocial behavior of high-risk African American youths and to outline a youth rites-of-passage program. Warfield-Coppock and Harvey (1989) describe various rites-of-passage programs across the nation targeted at African American boys and girls. According to them, the rites-of-passage approach is based on African and African American cultures, which seek to restore traditional social constraints on the behaviors of African American youths, help them to develop their emotional and cognitive abilities in a constructive fashion, and prepare them to become responsible members of society.

AN AFRICENTRIC APPROACH

An Africentric approach according to Gibert, Harvey, and Belgrave (2009):

> ... stems from the premise that African Americans, for the most part, survived historically because of values such as interdependence, collectivism, transformation and spirituality that can be traced to African principles for living (p. 243).

An Africentric approach to the delivery of psychosocial educational treatment services is based on a humanistic and naturalistic orientation. An Africentric view recognizes that African American culture is a nexus between Western culture and traditional African culture. It is within the African culture—a holistic and naturalistic orientation to the world—that the value system and behavioral patterns of African Americans have their roots. The philosophical concepts work in conjunction with the natural order, working toward such principles as balance in one's environment; family/personal life, and a multifunctional, discretionary, harmonious approach to life rather than a one-dimensional, predetermined, conflictual approach. The Africentric approach incorporates the individual, the family, and the community as an interconnected unit, so that any intervention must include interactions with all three entities. This approach recognizes the presence of spirituality (Pinkett, 1993) and interconnectedness (Richards, 1989) in the African American community and that these characteristics are key in understanding the psychosocial dynamics of the African American community, family, and individual in order to develop and implement appropriate, effective interventions.

The goal of the Africentric approach is to facilitate the development of persons who are aware and who can operationalize their sense of unity or collective, extended selves (Nobles, 1976). The desired outcome is to influence families and persons to cooperate, to understand and respect the sameness of self and of other persons, and to have a strong sense of responsibility for the well-being and harmonious interconnection between self and others (Nobles, 1976). In summary, an Africentric intervention approach is "based on reinstilling traditional African and African American cultural values in people of African descent" (Gilbert, Harvey, & Belgrave, 2009, p. 243).

The Nguzo Saba ("Seven Principles" in Kiswahili) are employed as a value system to foster and evaluate these outcomes. The Nguzo Saba created by Karenga (1965) are as follows:

Umoja/Unity. To strive and maintain unity in the family, community, nation, and race

Kujichagulia/Self-Determination. To define ourselves, name ourselves, and speak for ourselves instead of being defined and spoken for by others

Ujima/Collective Work and Responsibility. To build and maintain our community together, and to make our brothers' and sisters' problems our problems and to solve them together

Ujamaa/Cooperative Economics. To build and own stores, shops, and other businesses and to profit from them

Nia/Purpose. To make our collective vocation the building and developing of our community in order to restore our people to their traditional greatness

Kuumba/Creativity. To do always as much as we can, in the way we can, to restore our people to their traditional greatness

Imani/Faith. To believe in our parents, our teachers, our leaders, our people, and ourselves, and in the righteousness and victory of our struggle

Another goal of an Africentric psychosocial program is to provide principles (Harvey, 1988) (and to assist in their internalization) by which youths and families can become constructive contributors to their community through appreciation of themselves and their culture.

PRINCIPLES OF AFRICENTRICISM

The principles of Africentricism (called RIPSO) are the seven Rs: responsibility, reciprocity, respect, realness, restraint, reason, and reconciliation; three Is: interconnectedness, interdependence, and inclusivity; three Ps: participatory, patience, and perseverance; three Ss: sharing, sacrifice, and spirituality; and three Others: cooperation, discipline, and unconditional love. These principles are universal principles of successful Africentric people.

PRACTICE PRINCIPLES

The philosophical orientation of the social worker is critical. The social worker should view the youths as being misdirected and victims of a system that discriminates and has intentionally denied African Americans access to their cultural identity (Akbar, 1991; McRoy, 1990; Polite & Davis, 1999) and are victims of dysfunctional families and communities and, in many cases, have been abused and neglected. It is important for the social worker to hold the belief that the youths are capable of change when involved in a program designed to reduce the factors that place them at risk (Harvey & Hill, 2004). These programs should be formulated from a group work perspective since African American youths move through adolescence in peer groups. For these youths, group interventions must provide a positive perspective on African and African American culture, assist them in developing their own African American group identity (Lambert & Smith, 2009), and provide them with tools to deal with the oppressiveness of white supremacy (Welsing, 1991; Wilson, 1990; Winbush, 2001; Wright, 1984).

To establish rapport and connectedness, it is important for the youths to believe that the social worker is truly interested in them and is not working with them only because required to do so. The youths will usually state the latter belief directly or indirectly. It has been effective to employ the analogy of Kobe Bryant, who enjoys playing basketball but at the same time is paid to do so. We explain that this is similar to why we choose this work: that we work with them both out of a concern for their well-being and because we enjoy it. Social workers must be cognizant of the origins of the concept of healthy "cultural paranoia" (Fusick & Bordeau, 2004).

With African American youth, it is necessary to place the group within the program rather than label the program a "group." Many youths have been placed in psychotherapeutic groups in institutions and believe that being involved in a group implies that something is innately wrong with them or that they are crazy.

If the service is being provided by an agency contracted with the court system, it is important to establish a referral process that connects the youth, the group leaders, the youth's parents (guardian or another family member), and the probation officer. This process enables the youth to experience connectedness between the agencies and to know from the very beginning that the probation officer and the social worker will be in contact with each other and are working together as a team. Connecting with the family early in the referral process demonstrates respect for the rights of the family and establishes a cooperative relationship. Many families have control and influence over the behavior of their children and want to work with the social worker to promote the wellbeing of their children.

There are issues that African Americans will not raise but will discuss if the group leaders introduce them. These include issues of skin color (Harvey, 1995), body type, sexual identity, and inter/intraracial identification (Smokowski & Bacallao, 2009). The latter include the negative perceptions that white supremacy promulgates about African American youths.

In working with African American youths, it is critical for the social worker to respect their opinions and their right to voice their opinions, even when these differ from the opinions of the social worker. This does not mean agreeing with their opinions but rather giving them the opportunity to develop and express their ideas. It also means that it is the worker's responsibility to challenge their opinions but not to use the authority of the worker's position to impose views.

The worker gains respect by skillfully handling differences that arise. The youths will assess whether the social worker remains "cool" (Majors & Billson, 1992) or is easily intimidated. The youths give respect based on the social worker's ability to handle situations, not because of the social worker's professional degree or authority provided by the job title.

Structure is important, and each session needs to be planned. Nevertheless, the social worker must be flexible enough to focus on the concerns the youths might have during each session, such as a friend's being shot either by another youth or by the police.

These youths want the group leaders to be "real." Thus, it is critical that the group leaders self-disclose appropriately (Yalom, 1995) in a manner that demonstrates familiarity with the African American culture and community.

The transformational process is greatly enhanced when the group leaders are African American adults (Brody, Kogan, Chen, & Murry (2008), as they act as positive same-race role models (Richardson, 2009). The lack of positive African American role models is one factor in African American youths being at risk. This lack of same-race role models has been critical in fostering a sense of hopelessness in African American boys.

COMMON THEMES

The following questions and themes are consistently raised by African American youths:

- "Why should I change my behavior when I see adults involved in illegal activities?" Youths state that the only thing wrong with their behavior is that they were caught. The task is to help them respect moral and upright behavior.
- "What are the alternatives to violence?" Youths state, "If I don't fight back, my peers will think I am a punk and abuse me on a regular basis." Also, people respect you on the street only if you "kick their ass." People think you are a punk if you try to work out conflicts verbally.
- "How do I maintain my self-respect and moral upbringing without being a social isolate and without being perceived as vulnerable to the violence of other youths?" This is important, as many of the youths' parents stress morality, a characteristic of African American culture. There is a tension between the morality and materialism of American society that creates conflicts in family values.
- A reputation for being "cool" is important (Majors & Billson, 1992) for self-protection. If you do not display any affect or emotion, people cannot read you and thus hesitate to challenge you physically or mentally. Being cool also attracts females to you because it implies that you are street smart and not a nerd.
- Issues pertaining to male-female relationships: sex and respect for females and nonviolent behavior toward females. Many youths perceive male-female relationships from a superior-inferior paradigm rather than a harmonizing, diunital paradigm (T'Shaka, 1995).
- Issues of respect from police officers whom youths perceive as harassing them, being dishonest, and violating the law. Police are perceived as the enemy (Wilkinson, Beaty, & Lurry, 2009). A dilemma for these youths is how to interact with police, who at times do harass them, so that they do not become victims of police brutality.
- Critical to this population are issues of racism: how to deal with the reactions of white people to them in stores and on public transportation, as well as the racism of teachers and school administrators.
- Lack of cultural identification and racial appreciation, and lack of knowledge of the African and African American heritage. Central to this issue is how to be successful, yet remain connected to the African American community (Hines, Gracia-Preto, McGoldrick, Almeida, & Weltman, 1993; Lambert & Smith, 2009) and not "become white." Sometimes "being white" erroneously means being a good student, speaking proper English, or pursuing activities such as tennis.

RECOMMENDED WAYS OF WORKING

The MAATIAN Youth Group Model

Given a social environment where children are physically violent to other children (Wilson, 1991) and are seduced or forced into selling and taking drugs, it is essential for children to be involved with a group that operates out of a positive frame of reference, with guidance from well-trained social workers. The goal of the group is to assist youth in developing the emotional strength to become self and community advocates guided by the MAATIAN principles of truth, justice, and righteousness (Obenga, 1995). This is accomplished by providing youth with higher values to employ as life guidelines (Nguzo Saba) and a support group of peers who can assist each other in self-evaluation and provide emotional and physical support to do the right thing.

The group helps youth develop interpersonal skills, fostering new relationships and building a positive self-concept. The emphasis is on youths interacting with youths to develop constructive lifestyles and positive solutions to life problems, as well as to recognize their personal and cultural strengths and abilities. The small-group model employed is a youth rites-of-passage model, a group model many African American practitioners advocate (Hare & Hare, 1985; Harvey & Hill, 2004; Long, 1993; Perkins, 1986; Warfield-Coppock, 1990; Warfield-Coppock & Harvey, 1989).

When a referral for the rites-of-passage program is received from the court, the probation officer and the group leaders coordinate a meeting with the youth and a parent/guardian. At this meeting the program is explained, including the parent's/guardian's participation in a parenting skills group.

The youths participate in an orientation entitled "Brotherhood Training," which lasts for 8 weeks. This prepares them for the sacredness of the transformation of the rites of passage. During this phase, the youths are oriented to the group process, the Nguzo Saba, and the Africentric principles; at this time, the group is accepting new members while others are dropping out. At the end of this 8-week period the youths, who are called *pre-initiates*, participate in a weekend retreat focusing on cultural and personal survival and enhancement of the community. At the end of the weekend, 15 youth are selected to become initiates based on an evaluation conducted by the co-leaders and a group of older male adults called *Elders*. Youths who pass the evaluation are called *Initiates*. *Initiates* are required to take an Initiates' Code of Conduct Oath and to participate in a sacred initiation ritual in which they pledge to uphold the Nguzo Saba, receive an African name based on the day of the week on which they were born (Assem & Dodson, 1994), and are given a special identifying symbol to be worn at all group sessions. At this point in the group process, membership is closed. The group develops a sense of we-ness; its members are integrated into the group, trust each other, and are ready to work.

The group meets once a week for 90 minutes. Each participant is expected to participate in a unity circle as part of the opening group ritual. All members hold each other's hands, and one member reads a spiritually oriented text followed by the pouring of a libation (respect for the community of ancestors). Water, a symbol of life, is poured into a group-owned plant, a symbol of growth and transformation, as names of ancestors are called out loud by the members.

Each group is co-led. The leaders have included social workers, as well as a person with a master's degree in African American studies, an artist, and a person with expertise in music and the theater. Group meetings are supplemented by follow-up home visits with the family, focusing on the impact of the program on the youths' overall development. The group incorporates creative intervention techniques such as music (use of rap songs to analyze life or create songs as a project), films, videos, and audiotapes. African American guest presenters are invited to conduct meetings on specific topics, called *modules*. All aspects of the group are structured to develop an appreciation for African and African American culture. The following is a list of possible modules: Principles and Guides for Living, Win-Win Relationships, Entrepreneurial Development, Personal Development and Self-Control, Mental Health Issues (Skin Color, Negative Names, Body Type), Meditation for Self-Development and Self-Control, African American Culture and Heritage, African Culture and Heritage, Male-Female Relations, Fatherhood, Motherhood and Marriage, Male and Female Health Issues, Teenage Pregnancy, HIV/AIDS and Sexually Transmitted Diseases, Oppression and Racism, Alcohol Abuse, Tobacco and Other Drug Use, Date Rape and Incest, and Family Violence.

Each module consists of four to six sessions. The first session includes a presentation by a person of African descent who is knowledgeable concerning the topic area. The second session consists of a discussion of the information contained in the topic and how it relates to the youth's life. In the remaining sessions, the youths develop a project related to the topic to demonstrate transformation on the cognitive, emotional, spiritual, and behavioral planes. The variation in sessions allows flexibility in creating the project. Adolescents receive a certificate for the completion of the module at a small ceremony. A youth who misses a session has a follow-up meeting with the probation officer, a home visit, and a letter mailed to the parent/guardian. If an Initiate is consistently disruptive or noncooperative, he is presented to his peers, who recommend how he should reconcile with the group.

At the completion of all the modules, each youth conducts a self-evaluation and is evaluated by his peers, the group leaders, and the elders in order to pass into the final phase: a transformational weekend. During this experience, the Initiates are expected to demonstrate all they have learned and prepare for their rites ceremony.

On successful completion of the transformational weekend, Initiates participate in a final transformation ceremony. It is at this ceremony, to be witnessed by family, friends, court personnel, agency staff, its board of directors, and the general community, that the youths demonstrate specific knowledge, attitudes, and skills indicative of maturation. They announce their sacred name (based on their personality) received at the transformational weekend, to the public, and receive a symbol and a certificate of sacred transformation. Each family who participates in the program will also receive a certificate of transformation. The Initiates, in conjunction with the group leaders, plan and implement the ceremony, allowing the adolescents to experience kuumba (creativity), ujima (collective work and responsibility), and other principles of the Nguzo Saba.

Case Studies: Approaches to Dealing with Common Themes

Case 1

The issue of respect for females is critical in the development of African American males, especially since there has been an influx of antifemale rap videos, T-shirts and HIV/AIDS targeted to the African American community. In this particular session, an African American transit policewoman was invited as a guest. The youths discussed how they handled relationships with their female peers. One youth stated that if a woman doesn't do as you say or dates someone else, you should "kick her ass." The officer asked how the group members would feel if someone "kicked their sister's or their mother's ass." The youths reacted angrily, stating they probably would retaliate. Then the worker asked if they should not respect every woman as their mother or sister. Some youths agreed and others tried to explain the difference, but it was evident that they were now beginning to question their value system.

The session continued, with the group leaders raising the issue of spirituality. Emphasizing that each person is unique, has a special reason to be here, and is a reflection of the Creative Force, the leaders asked how one could justify oppression against a woman. This helped the youths to consider alternative methods of dealing with confrontational situations. It also allowed the group leaders to pursue the emotions the youths were experiencing. They reported being angry because they had been treated with disrespect. When probed, they acknowledged that they were hurt emotionally. They also stated that if they did not respond physically, their friends would think they were punks. At that point, the group leaders had them participate in a role play to experience alternative behaviors, thoughts, and emotions.

The role play had the participants take on the role of the plantation master during slavery and act the brutality imposed on the enslaved African female. This scenario was processed in terms of behaviors and emotions. Then the participants were requested to act the hero and save the female from such brutality. Then we correlate this with their role in present day America.

Case 2

White (1984) contends that the issue of racial identity in African American youth is crucial to the development of a positive self concept that includes appreciation of and identification with African American culture. A number of Afri-centric techniques are employed to facilitate this development. For example, youths are provided with biographies of African American personalities and are asked to select a person they admire. Each youth is presented with a challenging situation and is asked to think, feel, and behave like the African American personality he admires in order to resolve the problem. The purpose of this exercise is to enhance the Initiate's ability to employ high-level principles in his thought process, to feel the emotions of a constructive African American, and to behave in a positive manner in challenging situations.

Some youths react to the infusion of African and African American culture by stating that they are not African. The group leaders take this opportunity to explain the importance of the rituals, their history, and the role Africa has played with its well developed cultures, such as the Mali and Songhai (deGraft-Johnson, 1986), in world development. The group leaders show videos and films concerning the culture. Many African American youth use the word *nigger* as both an affective and a derogatory term when addressing their peers. Harvey (1995) explains this as the "paradox of blackness": The oppressor's definition is employed to define one's culture in both positive and negative terms simultaneously because the oppressed culture has not defined itself based on its own world view. In this situation, the history of the term is provided and the paradox is explained. Then the youths are guided through a relaxation exercise to allow them to "feel" their physiological reaction to the world. The youths almost always state that the word creates funny feelings in their stomachs. Then they ask them to use the term *brother* affectionately. They respond that the new term "feels good."

OUTCOMES

Following group participation, it is anticipated the youths will experience:

- Increased appreciation of the African and African American heritage and culture
- Reduction in repeated criminal activity
- Enhanced positive engagement with their family and community
- Increased school attendance
- Improvement in school grades
- Increase in employment for youth of appropriate age
- Increased sense of self-worth

- Increased sense of respect for self, family, and community and an increase respect for females

EVALUATION

The participants are evaluated through a process evaluation and a final evaluation. Their degree of participation and transformation while in the program are evaluated. The seven principles of African life (Nguzo Saba) Assessment Scale is employed by the Council of Elders in evaluating the development of the youths. Each youth must score at least a 3 of 5 points on each dimension of the Likert-type scale in order to graduate from the program.

Preliminary results indicate that over 80% of the youths who complete the orientation phase of the program complete the entire program. Family members report an increase in school attendance, in obeying curfews, in performing household chores, and in showing respect. When the youths are asked what they learned from the program, all of them report that they learned to respect themselves and appreciate their heritage.

RESOURCES

African-American Males Leadership Institute, Inc.
P.O. Box 32025
Baltimore, MD 21208
(410) 602-8058
AAMLI@aol.com

Juvenile Justice Institute
Criminal Justice Department
208 Whiting Criminal Justice Building
North Carolina Central University
Durham, NC 27707
(919) 530-7092

State Relations and Assistance Division
OJJDP
810 7th Street, NW
Washington, DC 20531
(202) 514-1319
(202) 307-2819 (fax)
www.ojjdp.ncjrs.gov/dmc/

The Urban Institute
2100 M Street NW
Washington, DC 20037
(202) 833-7200
www.urban.org

U.S. Department of Health and Human Services
Public Health Services
Substance Abuse and Mental Health Services
Administration Center for Substance Abuse Prevention
5600 Fishers Lane, Rockwall II
Rockville, MD 20857
(301) 443-0353
www.us.dhhs.gov

Joint Center for Political and Economic Studies
1090 Vermont Ave., NW
Suite 1100
Washington, DC 20005
www.jointcenter.org
Report: "A Way Out: Creating Partners for Our Nation's Prosperity by
    Expanding Life
Paths of Young Men of Color"

Institute for the Advanced Study of Black Family Life and Culture 1012
    Linden St.
Oakland, CA 94607
(510) 836-3245

Office of Juvenile Justice and Delinquency Prevention
1810 7 Street NW
Washington, DC 20531
(202) 307-5911
www.ojjdp.nejrs.org

National Cares Mentoring Movement
230 Peachtree Street, Suite 530
Atlanta, GA. 30303
(404) 584-2744
(404) 525-6226
www.caresmentoring.com

Think Tank for African American Progress
www.thinktankforprogress.org

Open Society Justice Institute–DC
1120 19th Street, NW, 8th Floor
Washington, DC 20036
(202) 721-5600
www.soros.org/initial
Report: "Moving Toward a More Integrative Approach to Justice Reform,"
    February 2008

Juvenile Justice Planner
North Carolina Governor's Crime Commission
Committee on Minority Disproportionality
1201 Front Street, Suite 200
Raleigh, NC 27609
(919) 733-4564, ext. 244
bdolby@ncgccd.org

REFERENCES

Akbar, N. (1991). *Visions for black men*. Tallahassee, FL: Mind Productions and Associates.

Assem, K. & Dodson, J. (1994). Strengthening the African-American family: The birth to re-birth life cycle. In G. R. Preudhomme & K. Assem (eds.), *National public policy institute* (pp. 6–15). Detroit: National Association of Black Social Workers.

Bent-Goodley T. B. (2003). Policy implications of the criminal justice system for African-American families and communities. In T. B. Bent-Goodley (ed.), *African-American social workers and social policy* (pp. 167–161). New York: The Social Work Practice Press.

Black Americans: A statistical sourcebook & guide to government data (2008). Woodside, CA: Information Publications.

Botvin, G. J. (1982). Broadening the focus of smoking prevention strategies. In T. Cotes, A. C. Petersen, & C. Perry (eds.), *Promoting adolescent health: A dialog on research and practice* (pp. 137–148). New York: Academic Press.

Botvin, G. J. & McAlister, A. (1981). Cigarette smoking among children and adolescents: Causes and prevention. In C. B. Arnold (ed.), *Annual review of disease prevention* (pp. 222–249). New York: Springer.

Brody, G. H., Kogan, S. M., Chen, Y-f, & Murry, V. M. (2008). Long-term effects of the African American families program on youths' conduct problems. *Journal of Adolescent Health Care*, 43, 474–481.

Butterfield, F. (2004, January 17). Rise in killings spurs new steps to fight crime. *The New York Times*, p. A1.

deGraft-Johnson, J. C. (1986). *African glory*. Baltimore: Black Classic Press.

Dryfoos, J. (1990). *Adolescents at risk: Prevalence and prevention*. New York: Oxford University Press.

Elkind, D. (1978). Understanding the young adolescent. *Adolescent*. 49, 127–134.

Erdley, D. (2009). Drive-by shootings in Pittsburg claim two victims. *Pittsburgh Tribune Review*, p. B-1.

Franklin, A. J. (1989). Therapeutic interventions with black adolescents. In R. L. Jones (ed.), *Black adolescents* (pp. 309–337). Berkeley, CA: Cobb & Henry.

Fusick, L. & Bordeau, W. C. (2004). Counseling at-risk Afri-American youth: an examination of contemporary issues and effective school-based strategies. *Professional School Counseling*, 8, 109–115.

Gibbs, J. T. (1989). Black adolescents and youth: An update on an endangered species. In *Black adolescents* (pp. 3–27). Berkeley, CA: Cobb & Henry.

Gilbert, D. J., Harvey, A. R., & Belgrave, F. Z. (2009). Advancing the Africenric paradigm shift discourse: Building toward evidence-based Africentric interventions in social work practice with African Americans. *Social Work*, 54, 243–252.

Glynn, T. J. (1981). From family to peer: Transitions of influence among drug-using youth. In D. Lettieri & J. Ludford (eds.), *Drug abuse and the American adolescent* (pp. 57–81). Washington, DC: National Institute on Drug Abuse. DHHS Publication No. (ADM) 81–1166.

Hare, H. & Hare, J. (1985). *Bringing the black boy to manhood: The passage*. San Francisco: Black Think Tank.

Harvey, A. R. (1988). Extended family: A universal and naturalistic salvation for African Americans (pp. 11–19). In *Proceedings of the Black Task Force on Child Abuse and Neglect*. New York: Black Task Force on Child Abuse and Neglect.

Harvey, A. R. (1995). The issue of skin color in psychotherapy with African Americans. *Families in Society: The Journal of Contemporary Human Services*, 76, 3–10.

Harvey, A. R. & Coleman, A. A. (1997). An Africentric program for African-American males in the juvenile justice system. *Child Welfare: Journal of Policy, Practice and Program*, 76(1), 197–211.

Harvey, A. R. & Hill, R. B. (2004). Africentric youth and family rites of passage program: Promoting resilience among at-risk African American youths. *Social Work*, 49, 65–74.

Harvey, A. R. & Rauch, J. B. (1997). A comprehensive Africentric rites of passage program for black male adolescents. *Health & Social Work*, 22(1), 30–37.

Hill, R. B. (1972). *The strength of black families*. New York: Emerson Hall Publishers, Inc.

Hines, P. M., Gracia-Preto, N., McGoldrick, M., Almeida, R., & Weltman, S. (1993). Intergenerational relationships across cultures. In J. B. Rauch (ed.), *Assessment: A sourcebook for social work practice* (pp. 371–394). Milwaukee: Families International.

Ireland, T. O. & Smith, C. A. (2009). Living in partner-violent families: Developmental links to antisocial behavior and relationship violence. *Journal of Youth and Adolescence*, 38, 323–339.

Jessor, R. (1982). Critical issues in research on adolescent health promotion. In T. Coates, A. C. Petersen, & C. Perry (eds.), *Promotion of adolescent health: A dialog on research and practice* (pp. 447–465). New York: Academic Press.

Karenga, M. (1965). *Kwanzaa: Origin, concepts and practice*. Los Angeles: Kawaida Publications.

Kornhauser, R. (1978). *Social sources of delinquency*. Chicago: University of Chicago Press.

Krohn, M. (1986). The web of conformity: A network approach to the explanation of delinquent behavior. *Social Problems, 33*, 81–93.

Krohn, M. D., Hall, G. P., & Lizotte, A. J. (2009). Family transactions and later delinquency and drug use. *Journal of Youth and Adolescents, 38*, 466–480.

Kunjufu, J. (1985). *Countering the conspiracy to destroy black boys*, Vol. II. Chicago: African American Images.

Kunjufu, J. (2001). *State of emergency: We must save African American males*. Chicago: African American Images.

Lee, C. C. (1989). Counseling black adolescents: Critical roles and functions for counseling professionals. In R. L. Jones (ed.), *Black adolescents* (pp. 293–308). Berkeley, CA: Cobb & Henry.

Lewis, J. & Lewis, F. (1984). Prevention programs in action. *Personnel and Guidance Journal, 62*, 550–553.

Lambert, M. C. & Smith, W. K. (2009). Behavioral and emotional strengths in people of African heritage: Theory, research, methodology and intervention. In H. A. Neville, B. M. Tynes, & S. O. Utsey (eds.), *Handbook of African American psychology* (pp. 385–399). Thousands Oaks, CA: Sage Publications

Long, L. C. (1993). An Africentric intervention strategy. In L. L. Goddard (ed.), *An African-centered model of prevention for African-American youth at high risk* (pp. 87–92). CSAP Technical Report No. 6. Rockville, MD: U.S. Department of Health and Human Services.

Majors, R. & Billson, J. M. (1992). *Cool pose: The dilemma of black manhood in America*. New York: Lexington Books.

McRoy, R. G. (1990). A historical overview of black families. In S. M. L. Logan, E. M. Freeman, & R. G. McRoy (eds.), *Social work practice with black families: A culturally specific perspective* (pp. 3–17). New York: Longman.

Millman, R. B. & Botvin, G. J. (1983). Substance use, abuse, and dependence. In M. D. Levine, W. B. Carey, & A. C. Crocker (eds.), *Developmental-behavioral pediatrics* (pp. 683–708). Philadelphia: W.B. Saunders.

Nobles, W. W. (1976). African consciousness and black research: The consciousness of self. In L. M. King, V. Dixon, & W. Nobles (eds.), *African philosophy: Assumption and paradigms for research on black persons* (pp. 163–174). Los Angeles: Fanon Center.

Obenga, T. (1995). *A lost tradition: African philosophy in world history*. Philadelphia: Source Editions.

Penkower, L., Dew, M. A., Kingsley, L., Becker, J. T., Satz, P., Scherf, F. W., & Sheridan, K. (1991). Behavioral, health, and psychosocial factors and risk for HIV infection among sexually active homosexual men: The multi-center AIDS cohort study. *American Journal of Public Health, 81*, 194–196.

Perkins, U. E. (1986). *Harvesting new generations: The positive development of black youth*. Chicago: Third World Press.

Pinkett, J. (1993). Spirituality in the African-American community. In L. L. Goddard (ed.), *An African-centered model of prevention for African-American youth at high risk* (pp. 79–86). Rockville, MD: U.S. Department of Health and Human Services. CSAP Technical Report No. 6.

Polite, V. C. & Davis, J. E. (eds.). *African American males in school and society: Practices and policies for effective education*. New York: Columbia University: Teachers College Press.

Richards, D. M. (1989). *Let the circle be unbroken*. Trenton, NJ: Red Sea Press.

Richardson, J. B. (2009). Men do matter: Ethnographic insights on the socially supportive role of the African American uncle in the lives of inner-city African American male youth. *Journal of Family Issues, 30*, 1041–1069.

Reuters. (2009). http://www.reuters.com/article/pressRelease/idUS39830+22PRN20090422

Sampson, R. J. (1987). Urban black violence: The effect of male joblessness and family disruption. *American Journal of Sociology, 93*, 348–382.

Skogan, W. (1986). Fear of crime and neighborhood change. In A. J. Reiss & M. Tonry (eds.), *Communities and crime* (pp. 203–229). Chicago: University of Chicago Press.

Smokowski, P. R. & Bacallao, M. (2009). Entre dosmundos/between two worlds youth prevention: Comparing psychodramatic and support group delivery formats. *Small Group Research, 40*, 3–26.

Swisher, J. D. (1979). Prevention issues. In R. L. Dupont, A. Goldstein, & J. A. O'Donnell (eds.), *Handbook on drug abuse* (pp. 423–435). Washington, DC: National Institute of Drug Abuse.

T'Shaka, O. (1995). *Return to the African mother principle of male and female equality*, Vol. 1. Oakland, CA: Pan African Publishers and Distributors.

Warfield-Coppock, N. (1990). *Africentric theory and applications: Adolescence rites of passage*, Vol. I. Washington, DC: Baobob Associates.

Warfield-Coppock, N. & Harvey, A. R. (1989). *Teenage pregnancy prevention: A rites of passage resource manual*. Washington, DC: MAAT Institute for Human and Organizational Enhancement.

Welsing, F. C. (1991). *The Isis papers: The keys to the colors*. Chicago: Third World Press.

White, J. L. (1984). *The psychology of blacks: An Afri-American perspective*. Englewood Cliffs, NJ: Prentice Hall.

Wilkinson, D. L., Beaty C. C., & Lurry, R. M. (2009). Youth, violence, crime or self-help? Marginalized urban males' perspectives on the limited efficacy of the juvenile justice system to stop youth violence. *The Annals of the American Academy of Political and Social Science*, 25–38.

Wiig, J. K. & Tuell, J. A. (2008). *Guidebook for juvenile justice & child welfare system coordination and integration* (rev. ed.). Arlington, VA: Child Welfare League of America.

Wills, T. A. & Vaughan, R. (1984). *Social support and smoking in middle adolescence*. New York: Academic Press.

Wilson, A. N. (1990). *Black-on-black violence: The psychodynamics of black self-annihilation in service of white domination*. Bronx, NY: Afrikan World Infosystems.

Wilson, A. N. (1991). *Understanding black adolescent male violence: Its remediation and prevention*. Bronx, NY: Afrikan World Infosystems.

Wilson, A. N. (1992). *Awakening natural genius of black children*. Bronx, NY: Afrikan World Infosystems.

Wilson, J. J. (1994). Disproportionate minority representation. *Juvenile Justice, 2*(1), 21–23.

Winbush, R. A. (2001). *The warrior method: A parent's guide to rearing healthy black boys.* New York: Harper Collins Publishers.

Wright, B. E. (1984). *The psychopathic racial personality and other essays.* Chicago: Third World Press.

Yalom, I. D. (1995). *The theory and practice of group psychotherapy* (4th ed.). New York: Basic Books.

Chapter Fourteen

Group Work With People Who Sexually Offend

Paul H. Ephross

Social workers are frequently called on to provide group treatment to change the behavior of sex offenders. One can acquire the label of sex offender in a variety of ways: most commonly, one is found guilty in court of violating a law against a particular sexual behavior. These prohibitions are of several types. One, often viewed as archaic by social workers but still on the books in many jurisdictions, prohibits a particular form of sexual expression, without regard for the consenting nature of the act or the relationship between the adult partners. The fact that laws banning normative behaviors—oral sex, in private, between adult partners married to each other, for example—are still on the books makes for rueful comments on late-night television programs and produces cartoons of the "believe it or not" genre. Less amusing is the fact that selective prosecution, or the threat of it, is sometimes used to discredit persons who express and promulgate views seen as undesirable by people in politically or socially powerful positions.

In this chapter, however, the term *sex offender* refers to two other types of persons: (1) those who have coerced others into participating in sexual activities through either force or the threat of force and (2) those who have engaged in sexual activities with partners who are incapable of giving informed consent. Children and adolescents under the legal age of consent and persons of diminished capacity, regardless of age—such as mentally retarded people and mentally ill people—illustrate categories of forbidden partners, while rapists and perpetrators of child sex abuse form part of the coercive cohort. In recent years, there has been a growing awareness of adolescents as sexual abusers of younger children and as perpetrators of sexual coercion on other adolescents.

While technically one must be adjudicated as such in order to be known as a sex offender, in fact there may be as many persons unknown as known who have carried out or perpetrated the same destructive and illegal behaviors. Judging from studies of the prevalence of rape and the behaviors of rape victims, for example, even today only about one-half—in the past, even fewer—of rapes committed in this country are reported to the police or to any other official agency (Bureau of Justice Statistics, 2002). The true prevalence rates of sexual coercion and abuse are unknown, in part because of the peculiar and confusing mixture of attitudes toward (1) sex and sexuality in general and (2) deviant, coercive, and illegal sexual activities that characterize American culture and its various subcultures at the end of the twentieth century. It is important to try to understand these attitudes and perceptions before we can analyze in any depth the issues involved in group treatment of sex offenders.

"THAT SUBJECT"

One of the world's most distinguished, if often controversial, scholars of human sexuality, writing in 1994, bluntly characterized contemporary American culture as "taboo-ridden [and] antisexual." In the same discussion, he characterized sexual identities that differ in any way from society's prescriptive norms as "unspeakable monsters." He notes, "Being literally unspeakable, an unspeakable monster is not spoken of" (Money, 1994, p. ix). Many writers have commented on how difficult it is for Americans to talk about sex in general and their own sexuality in particular. Although some may think that men find it easier to talk about sex than women, a noted authority on male sexuality states, "men have been, and to a large extent still are, extremely secretive about their sexuality … other than … bits of bravado, most men simply don't talk about sex to anyone" (Zilbergeld, 1999, p. 4). Allgeier et al. (1999) point out that our cultural norm of segregating the "sexual" from the rest of our experience begins to be taught in infancy. Some observers find the roots of widespread inability to communicate about sex even with a partner in common childhood experiences:

> As children, most of us were discouraged from saying much about sex and many never learned the terminology to describe their sexual anatomy…. So, part of the hesitancy people have in talking about sex … is actually a carryover from these childhood taboos (Masters et al., 1986, p. 259).

One can relate the difficulties of talking about sex to the ambivalence about sexual experience that is reflected in the culture of our society. Carole Vance has noted, with regard to women's experiences:

> The tension between sexual danger and sexual pleasure is a powerful one, in women's lives. Sexuality is simultaneously a domain of restriction, repression and danger as well as a domain of exploration, pleasure, and agency (1984, p. 1).

Small wonder, then, that discussions about sex, especially about feelings, experiences, fears, perceptions, doubts, and joys, are viewed as potentially dangerous.

In addition, to the extent that they are pleasurable, that very pleasure may be experienced as illicit.

Sex is difficult to talk about even for people whose sexual behavior and identities have been labeled as normal. How much more difficult, then, is it for people whose sexual behavior has been labeled as actually or potentially criminal? The stigmas associated with being labeled abnormal, criminal, evil, and, if the victim is a child, unnatural as a man or woman (Scaveo, 1989) combine for a convicted sex offender. Few identities are as universally despised as that of a sexual abuser of children. In prison, the known abuser of children is often at risk of being physically attacked, or worse, by other inmates. Neither murder nor treason, robbery nor criminal conspiracy carries the perceived loathsomeness that attaches to sexual abuse of children and certain other sexual offenses. The sex offender, then, faces a difficult task while carrying multiple stigmas: to admit to oneself and others the nature of the offense and to participate in discussion of feelings, alternatives, reasons, cognitive and emotional triggers, related to sex—a subject difficult and dangerous to discuss at best.

Difficulty communicating about sex is not restricted to people of lower educational or social classes. The title of this section, "That Subject," was the term used by a senior, highly regarded female educator to characterize the topic of a graduate student's thesis research in a school of social work. The student, a gifted researcher, was studying women's experiences of orgasm: "that subject," as the professor described it. The student produced a study that made a genuine contribution to the research literature on an important topic. In general, and with apologies to a few exceptional people within the profession, one cannot describe social work as having distinguished itself in the front rank of the sexual revolution, nor even in promoting healthy and open discourse on sexual subjects. At times, social workers have been willing to discuss sexual pathology but not sexual normality—sexual harassment, for example, rather than the sexuality of organizational life. For the most part, one looks in vain for positive, affirmative discussions of sexual expression in the literature of our profession.

Smith and Farolo (2005) have pointed out the difficulty of communicating directly and accurately about topics that involve not only sexual behavior but sexual misbehavior to and from people in our society who often do not have the benefits of the best educations and even with those who do. Catalano (2009) refers to the difficulties involved in tracing trends accurately over recent U.S. history about sexual and often illicit and illegal behaviors in various social strata, ethnicities, and traditions of taboo. Anyone who has attempted to engage either in sex education or to gather information about American intimate behavior in either a scientific or a literary way is familiar with the problem. Yet both legal and behavioral professional behavior in this area are dependent on basing one's perceptions and behaviors on scientifically valid data rather than on personal or class-linked prejudices and prejudgments.

While the dominant culture of the United States has historically been ambivalent about sexuality at best and antisexual at worst, there is great variation among various American subcultures, whether defined by religion, national origin, or race. It is a curious fact, remarked on by behavioral scientists for many decades, that there is generally a sexual aspect to racism (Bettelheim & Janowitz, 1964, pp. 287–288). Sexual superiority is attributed to the oppressed group, and this attribution plays a part in the self-justifying ideology of the dominant group. It is partly for this illogical reason, perhaps, that minorities of color and certain immigrants have at times been viewed as sexual athletes, and thus simultaneously as both desirable and fearsome. Sexuality is one of the topics about which it is often difficult to communicate across ethnic/racial/cultural barriers of difference.

Another factor that makes sexual discussion, and especially discussion about paraphilias, difficult is the issue of countertransference. Sensitivity and strong feelings about sex, sexual behavior patterns, paraphilias, and punishments for unusual sexual activities are widespread in our society. Feelings of both repulsion and attraction can easily be mobilized by working with sex offenders. The group setting, as always, provides a measure of protection, but only a measure.

One of the factors that make communicating about sex difficult, both in groups and in other interpersonal settings, is the choice of vocabulary. There is an uncommonly wide range of terms available for English speakers to use about sex, virtually all of them unacceptable for some people for various reasons. Professionals often escape to the use of multisyllabic medical terms of ancient Latin or Greek heritage. Besides communicating a vague sense of disapproval, such words are often unknown to ordinary people. For example, the word *coitus*, a more or less standard medicolegal term, is hardly ever heard in spoken English and is therefore unknown to many people. The word *fuck*, which is known to everyone, is unacceptable to offensive to virtually everyone. Social workers are often concerned about "lowering" themselves by using street language to describe sexual activities. This is a legitimate concern, as is the fear that clients simply do not understand the language that social workers feel is more appropriate. Given this question of words and its importance in relation to communication, I suggest here three guiding principles:

1. Ask group members which terms they use and feel comfortable with. Either use their terms or explain why you prefer to use other terms. Let them practice using the new ones together with you. The object is effective communication; there are no *good* or *bad* terms.
2. Be sure that you (and *group members*) understand the meaning of terms. There is probably no subject on which more deliberate obfuscation is employed in the choice of words. Be sure, to the point of being boring, if necessary, that you understand the behaviors to which words refer. "We ... you know ... did it ... we had relations" sounds behaviorally specific. Sometimes it is not. Ask questions. Men who have sex with

other men may or may not identify themselves as homosexual, depending on the specific roles taken during particular sexual activities and on ethnocultural definitions (Doll et al., 1992; see also Chapter 20).

3. Watch out for your own assumptions that may get in the way of your understanding the words that others are using. This is especially true when (a) group members' age- or sex-specific expectations are different from the social worker's or (b) when the abusive, coercive, or paraphilic behaviors are so distasteful to the worker that a sensation of horror replaces a desire for effective listening. This aspect of working with sex offenders in groups will be discussed below under "Practice Principles."

Sexual fantasies, sometimes bizarre, often accompany racist perceptions and attitudes, as has been noted. These aside, several subcultures and cultural groups in American society are less sex negative, or erotophobic, than is the culture as a whole. Among these are communities defined by race, by culture and language, by being foreign born or native born of foreign parents, and by ethnic identity. There is also abundant evidence that views on the nature of male and female sexuality, and on the nature and origins of heterosexuality and homosexuality, vary by social class and have varied over time, reflecting and responding to other societal changes (D'Emilio & Freedman, 1988). To take just one example, living quarters and standards of past generations and past centuries allowed for, or required, much less privacy for most Americans than is thought necessary by contemporary middle- or even working-class standards. Not only birth and death, but also many other behaviors, including sexual behavior, were more visible to others in the household simply because people lived closer together.

At present, communicating about sex has been made more difficult by the imposition in some professional settings of political limits to discourse focusing on the "discomfort" of anyone present. Certain words and concepts, in this view, are so offensive that they should be banned from civilized discourse. Since sexual topics, almost by definition, can be guaranteed to make someone uncomfortable in a social context that is ambivalent about sex, these topics become doubly taboo because of the possibility that whoever introduces them will be viewed as a harasser by those who experience discomfort. Certainly whatever discomfort is introduced into a treatment group for sex offenders by a discussion of sexual subjects and specific sexual behaviors should be recognized, but this should hardly serve as a justification for avoiding such charged and supercharged topics.

We have been discussing difficulties in communicating about sex, especially about deviant sexual behaviors. By now, the reader may wish to protest that contemporary American society is obsessed with sex—that sexuality, sometimes of the most primitive and evident sort, is displayed daily and nightly on television and in other mass media, on advertising billboards, and in the lyrics of popular songs. This obsession should not be viewed as a sign of growing openness and greater comfort with communicating about sex, but rather as the opposite. It is precisely the potential titillation and inherent discomfort accompanying sexual display and images that give TV images and billboard illustrations dramatic power. Sex as tenderness, as communication, as love, as communication and closeness between two people can be difficult to portray or to discuss. The concomitants of sexual activity, such as pregnancy, sexually transmitted diseases, sexual dysfunction, variations of sexual identity and various other aspects of human sexual behavior are just now becoming visible in the mass media in the first decade of the twenty-first century. In their own way, the mass media of our society are just now beginning to stop treating sex as an "unspeakable monster."

COMMON GROUP THEMES

What makes these observations relevant to the task of treating sex offenders in groups? First, not only the group but also the worker(s) is doing something that is relatively deviant in our society, namely, legitimating group members' talking about their own sexual behaviors, sometimes in an explicit and detailed way. The worker needs to anticipate and develop comfort with the fact that *resistance in such groups takes many forms*, often including intense fantasizing in all possible directions about the worker. The worker's own sexual experience, motivation for working with a group of sex offenders, and feelings toward the group members may become, for a time, common topics of conversation both inside the group and in the group's interstices— before and after meetings, for example. Some of these issues may be projections of group members' discomfort, guilt, shame, and fears elicited by being in an offenders' group and the process that brought them there. Other comments and discussions may be part of the process of *testing the worker*, a process that is universal in such groups, in this writer's experience.

There are various theories about the origins of destructive sexual behaviors that violate laws and the rights and needs of other people. Regardless of their theoretical orientation, however, a wide range of researchers and practitioners, from a variety of professional backgrounds, agree on the importance of group experience and group treatment for sex offenders (Haugaard & Reppucci, 1988; Ingersoll & Patton, 1990; Maletzky & McGovern, 1990; O'Donahue & Letourneau, 1993). Writers differ as to *whether group treatment should be the primary treatment of choice*, long-term, supplemented by individual therapy on a diminishing frequency basis, which would be the first choice of this writer. Some treatment programs employ two forms of group treatment: one for offenders only and one for couples or, in some cases, entire families formed into groups.

There are biases built into most social workers' education, and perhaps into our culture in a broader way, that tend to prejudice therapists and, through them, clients in favor of individual therapy as being deeper and more effective—in short, better. Such an assumption, often unexamined, characterizes many treatment programs. Assertions are blithely made about readiness for group treatment, who can and who cannot be treated in groups, the issue of confidentiality, the unbearable strains supposedly placed not only on group members but also on group therapists, and other reasons why group treatment can work as a supplement to individual therapy but not as the primary modality for service delivery. The suggestion here is that if a reader is faced with some of the projective rationalizations cited, an appropriate response is to smile and ask calmly for the research findings that support such antigroup treatment views. None will be cited, for there are none that support such views. A good follow-up for social workers of the individualistic heresy is to prescribe a careful reading of Falck (1988). An alternative suggestion, readily available to all readers of this book, is to read its other chapters.

Most sex offenders have violated both the legal codes and the civilized norms of sexual interaction. They have also demonstrated an inability to understand the concepts of individual boundaries and rights. *These represent failures of learning, either from socialization in general or from interpersonal and group experiences in particular. Group experience is the primary setting in which such failures can be remedied through new learnings.* As one participates as a social worker in treatment groups with sex offenders, one is frequently struck by the lack of empathic ability, in the literal sense of being unable to take or understand others' roles that many group members display. One may also observe a woodenness and lack of skill in understanding any aspect of others' communications beyond the literal.

As mentioned above, there are two routes to membership in sex offenders' groups. The first is adjudication. In effect, those found guilty of sexual offenses are given the "choice" of attending a treatment program or going to prison. For such group members, and for groups composed entirely of such (actually) involuntary members, the *fact that membership is involuntary is a major issue with which the group must deal if it is to form in any genuine sense.* Confidentiality, at least within the group, is less of an issue since the facts of the members' deviant sexual activity are known, at least to the court and, often, the correctional system. With regard to the outside world, *confidentiality is a major issue, especially if reports of group attendance and/or participation need to be made to a court, a parole officer, or another official.*

Nor are issues of authority resolved by one discussion, even an extensive one. Issues of authority, the involuntary nature of the group, and the power that the court or social agency has over members in terms of compelling attendance tend to resurface repeatedly. If the group is having the desired effect, each resurfacing of this concern will be a bit less intense and the group members themselves will be able to reassert the group's purpose and the group's contract progressively more easily as time goes on.

The second route to membership is a voluntary one, undertaken by the group member without the coercion of a court, even though fear of being arrested and prosecuted is often a strong motivating factor for seeking treatment. For such members, confidentiality is an overwhelming concern. The sexual behaviors involved may have been hidden—may still be, for that matter—from significant others in the group member's life. Often, such *group members express such an intense terror of exposure* that one cannot help wondering whether this "coming out" is something that some people both fear and want, even though the latter desire may well be unconscious.

There is no lack of evidence that victims of sex offenders can suffer serious, long-term harm. Lives can be blighted and sexual activity turned from the natural route to connectedness with a loving partner and expression of one's deepest impulses, as it should be, to an area of life poisoned by fear and degradation. Nonetheless, *denial remains a prominent theme for many sessions of many sex offenders' groups.* This denial takes several forms. One is that the person has been wrongly accused and wrongly charged. Either the act of which the member is accused did not take place or it did not take place in the manner described. The group member is, according to this pattern, the real victim: being set up by a vengeful spouse, being persecuted by the police, wrongly accused in an atmosphere of hysteria.

Another variation is that the offender has not done anything that others do not do. The main difference is that the offender got caught. Group members will sometimes seek to get confirmation by going around the group and interrogating others—sometimes including the worker—about their sexual activities. Again, often there is said to be a villain in the piece: the spouse, a relative of the victim, a misunderstanding and unsympathetic bystander, a nosy neighbor, or some other person who butted in.

One of the most disturbing versions of denial places the major blame on the victim. The rape victim was seductively clothed and "was just asking for it." The stepdaughter was flirtatious: "The kid just came over and sat right down on my lap." Without in any way questioning the fact that children, especially adolescents, can be seductive, and that some victims of sexual assault wear short skirts, it is very important that these behaviors be reinterpreted in the group as *not* being invitations to coercive, illegal, and destructive sexual activity. "I couldn't help myself" is an avoidance of responsibility and a copout. It is often a false, *post facto* rationalization.

Substance abuse and dependence and their role in the offending behaviors are often the "uninvited guests" in offenders' treatment groups. Patterns of dealing with this content vary widely. The substance use may be part of what is denied. Alternatively, it may be used as a justification and explanation for the behavior. "I was really stoned out of my mind and barely remember what happened" is a characteristic presentation from this stance. The message of the group needs to emphasize the issue of responsibility with regard to the substance use as well as the sexual behavior. Experience has taught this writer of the truth of the position generally taken by experts in substance abuse: unless the abuse/addiction is being treated effectively, by whatever means, treatment for other pathologies is usually wasted. Gains dissolve into the pattern of abuse or addiction.

"I/a man/someone like me/a person of my background/she gotta have it" is another characteristic theme. Often this is combined with accusing the worker—or other members—of not being able to understand because they are so different from the

group member talking. The essence of the group's message, and the worker's, should be that sexual drives, urges, and appetites are strong, real, and natural, but need to be and can be under the conscious control of their owners. A great deal is yet to be learned about what Money (1986) has called *lovemaps*, the patterns of sexual attraction that each person develops. The *DSM-IV-TR*, the *Diagnostic and Statistical Manual, Edition 4, Text Revision* (2000), of the American Psychiatric Association clearly identifies various paraphilias as disorders. The culture of victimhood, however, is not helpful for sex offenders, whether individually or in groups, since it relieves one of responsibility for one's actions. In the short run, such a stance is countertherapeutic. In the long run, it holds out only the "hopes" of death or incarceration for life, since it denies the possibility of change that is, at least partly, under the individual's control.

Several of these themes are alternative forms of a presentation for self as *helpless* in the face of internal and external sexual cues. Altering and reversing this view of one's own sexuality and sexual appetites is the major task of these treatment groups. Support, skill teaching, learning alternative ways of structuring time, and, strangely enough, legitimating a healthy frequency and intensity of sexual activities with an appropriate and consenting partner are other positive outputs of treatment groups. Why is legitimating sexual activity needed? Although one should always be aware of the dangers of stereotyping, a surprising proportion of sex offenders view sexual activity as illicit, as needing to be imposed on others by force or other coercive means. The concept of their being viewed as sexually desirable is mind-boggling.

Neal was attending the group as part of a plan worked out with the state's attorney's office after having admitted to an incestuous relationship with his daughter, who had been in his custody, from ages 11 to 14. (The daughter had been removed to another state by her grandparents, with whom she now was living.) Neal told the group that something unexpected had happened to him this past week. He had been advertising a room in his house since he needed the money and had three extra bedrooms. About two months ago, a woman named Sybil had rented the room. She seemed a pleasant enough person who paid her rent on time, but conversation between the two of them had been limited to brief inquiries about using the washing machine and where to get one's shoes fixed. The other night, Sybil, who is 28, knocked on his bedroom door and asked whether he would like some company. This led, the following night, to the two of them going out to dinner and then "'making love,' as she likes to call it." In the group discussion, Neal revealed that he had never before had a sexual experience with a woman older than 18, the age his wife had been when she left him. Group members interrogated Neal thoroughly to make sure that the activity had been voluntary, and combined congratulating him with sympathy and warnings about how he needed to learn to treat Sybil.

PRACTICE PRINCIPLES

In working with sex offenders, it is particularly important to avoid going to extremes: being seduced into accepting the group members' views of the world or viewing the group members as loathsome and less than human. Either set of perceptions and attitudes on the part of the worker is both unhelpful to the group and poses a serious danger of burnout for the worker. One worker said that working with groups of offenders had the danger of turning her into a "prohibitionist," an antisex erotophobe.

Worker boundaries need to be kept. Testing of the worker may include inquiries about the worker's own sexual past and present. One needs to be both transparent as to one's feelings and responses in the group and reserved with regard to a sphere of privacy in one's own life. Perhaps most difficult, one needs to feel legitimated in both spheres as a worker.

It is useful to provide some structure for group meetings. For long-term, open-ended groups, one fruitful technique is to "bridge" from one meeting to another. This involves using some time—say, the last 5 or 10 minutes of a meeting—to summarize learnings from this meeting and to plan together the content, or at least the starting points, of the next meeting.

Shorter-term groups and groups with fixed life spans—say, 12 meetings over 12 weeks—can be problematic in treating sex offenders. These groups often move slowly for quite a while. Members need to get involved in looking at attitudes and behaviors they may have learned over a long period of time or even an entire lifetime. Genuine change is rarely dramatic but needs to be processed over time. Sometimes membership is not under the worker's control.

In a group that meets within a correctional facility, for example, a person may have completed the term of a sentence, or may have been released on parole, and may leave the group as a result. Generally, however, it is good practice to contract with members for participation in the group as a relatively long-term commitment that will pay long-term rewards to the member and to the group as a whole.

As a worker/therapist, one should mistrust sudden conversions, protestations of "seeing the light," and professions of virtue. There is what may be called a *culture of conning* that surrounds many inpatient and outpatient correctional processes, and those noted here are among the classic signs that this culture is at work.

Violence is absolutely antithetical to group work and group process. As a worker, you should share with the group what your response will be should any violence be threatened or undertaken. You should make the necessary administrative and logistical arrangements to act on your statements and should do so at the first hint that interpersonal violence is even being seriously contemplated.

Co-therapy is sometimes very productive, as with a mixed-sex co-leadership team with sexually assaultive men. However, co-working takes careful thought, attention, and follow-through. Unless you have a positive reason for co-working (see Introduction, this volume), a solo worker format is recommended.

Do not, under any circumstances, make "deals" with group members, no matter how innocent they may appear. Subgroups or entire groups may participate in a "splitting" process in which an attempt is made to split the worker from the sponsoring organization. Do not be seduced into doing this. If you have tensions or problems with the organization, find productive means for dealing with them but leave them outside of the group.

Do be creative with program techniques, discussion starters, and ways of posing problems for the group to consider. Often newspaper articles, television stories, or readily available video clips do well and introduce a productive note. As noted above, sex is often hard to talk about, and deviant and criminal sex harder yet.

EVALUATION

Groups for the treatment of sex offenders have objectives that are unique to groups of this type, objectives shared with some other types of groups, and objectives shared with groups in general. The evaluation plan should be discussed and requisite permissions obtained at the time a member joins the group, if it is an open-ended group, or at the time the group begins, if it is a closed-ended group.

The unique objective is the prevention of repeat offenses, and every treatment group should be evaluated in terms of success in achieving this objective. It will generally be necessary to obtain information from other sources in addition to group members' reports. Permission to get this information from, for example, police records will need to be obtained from voluntary group members; those adjudicated are generally viewed as having waived their right to privacy with regard to criminal conduct or have signed such a waiver as a condition of having been released on parole or placed on probation. Family members, those sharing living quarters, and friends may also serve as sources of information, although discretion must be used and permission obtained, in most cases, to use these sources.

As with other types of treatment groups, pre-during-post measurements may be sought in an attempt to accomplish two purposes. The first is evaluation of the effectiveness of the group. The second is the stimulus it provides to members to reflect on their experiences in the group and on their meaning.

This writer is committed to the value of feedback *during* the sessions because it can be useful to the worker and the group members in modifying the content, process, or time allocations of the group. All too often, the post measurements provide feedback that, were there time to act on it, would have made the group more meaningful, effective, or satisfying to its members. When these data are available in an organized way only when the group has finished or is about to finish its life span, the most one can do is seek to apply the knowledge gained to future group experiences.

Experience with both structured and precoded questionnaires, on the one hand, and with less structured one-page questionnaires with four to five questions and space for comments, on the other, have demonstrated both that each kind can furnish valuable information and that each kind can be sabotaged. Clearly there are situations—when one is taking part in a study involving many groups, for example—in which structured instruments, tested for validity and reliability, are preferred. What is most important, however, is the willingness of the worker— and, where appropriate, the group—to *listen to and hear* the data and the feedback they provide.

RESOURCES

Justice Research and Statistics Association
www.JRSA.org
Provides links to resources including state agencies that conduct programs for juvenile sex offenders.

Peace and Healing
www.peaceandhealing.com

State of Colorado
See North Cottage Program for Sex Offenders
www.doc.state.co.us

REFERENCES

Allgeier, R., Allgeier, A. R., & Allgeier, E. R. (1999). *Sexual interactions* (5th ed.). Lexington, MA: D.C. Heath.

Barnard, G. W., Fuller, A. K., Robbins, L., & Shaw, T. (1989). *The child molester: An integrated approach to evaluation and treatment.* New York: Brunner/Mazel.

Bettelheim, B. & Janowitz, M. (1964). *Social change and prejudice, including dynamics of prejudice.* New York: Free Press.

Bureau of Justice Statistics, US Dept. of Justice. (2002). *Crime and the nation's households, with trends, 1994–2000.* Washington, DC: Government Printing Office, Sept. (NCJ 194107).

Bureau of Justice Statistics, US Dept. of Justice (2000). *Sexual assault of young children as reported to law enforcement: Victim, incident and offender characteristics.* Washington: Government Printing Office, July.

Catalano, S. (2009). Intimate partner violence in the United States, 1993-2005. Bureau of Justice Statistics. www.ojp.usdoj.gov; see www.ncjrs.gov, click on "sex offenders, sexual assault, and domestic violence"

Conrad, P. & Schneider, J. W. (1992). *Deviance and medicalization: From badness to sickness* (expanded ed.). Philadelphia: Temple University Press.

D'Emiio, J. & Freedman, E. G. (1988). *Intimate matters: A history of sexuality in America.* New York: Harper & Row.

Diagnostic and statistical manual of mental disorders (4th ed., text revision) (DSMIV). (2000). Washington, DC: American Psychiatric Press.

Doll, L. S., Petersen, L. R., White, C. R., Johnson, E. S., Ward, E. W., & the Blood Donor Study Group. (1992). Homosexually and nonhomosexually identified men who have sex with men: A behavioral comparison. *Journal of Sex Research, 29,* 1–14.

Donaldson, M. A. & Cordes-Green, S. (1994). *Group treatment of adult incest survivors.* Thousand Oaks, CA: Sage.

Falck, H. S. (1988). *Social work practice: The membership approach.* New York: Springer.

Haugaard, J. J. & Reppucci, N. D. (1988). *The sexual abuse of children.* San Francisco: Jossey-Bass.

Horton, A. L., Johnson, B. L., Roundy, L. M., & Williams, D. (eds.). (1990). *The incest perpetrator: A family member no one wants to treat.* Newbury Park, CA: Sage.

Ingersoll, S. L. & Patton, S. O. (1990). *Treating perpetrators of sexual abuse.* Lexington, MA: D.C. Heath.

Maletzky, B. & McGovern, K. B. (1990). *Treating the sexual offender.* Newbury Park, CA: Sage.

Masters, W. H., Johnson V. E., & Kolodny, R. C. (1986). *Sex and human loving.* Boston: Little, Brown.

Money, J. (1986). *Lovemaps: Clinical concepts of sexual/erotic health and pathology, paraphilia, and gender transposition in childhood, adolescence and maturity.* New York: Irvington.

Money, J. (1994). *Reinterpreting the unspeakable: Human sexuality 2000.* New York: Continuum.

O'Donohue, W. & Letourneau, E. (1993). A brief group treatment for the modification of denial in child sexual abuses: Outcome and follow-up. *Child Abuse and Neglect, 17,* 299–304.

Pithers, W. D., Kashima, K. M., Cumming, G. F., & Beal, L. S. (1988). Relapse prevention: A method of enhancing maintenance of change in sex offenders. In A. Salter (ed.), *Treating child sex offenders and victims: A practical guide.* Newbury Park, CA: Sage.

Roth, N. (1993). *Integrating the shattered self: Psychotherapy with adult incest survivors.* Northvale, NJ: Jason Aronson.

Rutan, J. S. & Stone, W. N. (1993). *Psychodynamic group psychotherapy* (2nd ed.). New York: Guilford Press.

Salter, A. C. (ed.). (1988). *Treating child sex offenders and victims: A practical guide.* Newbury Park, CA: Sage.

Scaveo, R. R. (1989). Female adolescent sex offenders: A neglected treatment group. *Social Casework, 70,* 114–117.

Shaffer, J. & Galinsky, M. D. (1989). *Models of group therapy* (2nd ed.). Englewood Cliffs, NJ: Prentice-Hall.

Smith, E. & Farolo, D., Jr. (2009, October). *Profile of intimate partner violence cases in large urban counties.* Washington, DC: Bureau of Justice Statistics.

Vance, C. S. (ed.). (1984). *Pleasure and danger: Exploring female sexuality*. Boston: Routledge & Kegan Paul.

Whitaker, D. L. & Wodarski, J. S. (1988). Treatment of sexual offenders in a community mental health center: An evaluation. *Journal of Social Work and Human Sexuality, 7*, 49–68.

Zilbergeld, B. (1999). *The new male sexuality* (Rev. ed.). New York: Bantam Books.

Chapter Fifteen

Group Work With Children Impacted by Sexual Abuse

Kay Martel Connors, Jessica Lertora, and Kyla Liggett-Creel

Research indicates that child maltreatment such as child sexual abuse (CSA) causes changes in the developing brain and its functioning and alters a child's developmental trajectory, including the ability to be resilient and adjust later in life (Cohen, Perel, DeBellis, Friedman, & Putnam, 2002). Social workers can strengthen children's and their families' efforts to recover and cope with the aftermath of CSA and work to reduce future victimization through psychoeducation, social support, and trauma-focused group work.

Although not all children and adults who were sexually abused develop behavioral or mental health disorders, most would benefit from treatment that focuses on managing posttraumatic stress reactions as well as the familial, psychological, and social aftermath of this widespread childhood trauma. Group work has been widely used for treating children affected by CSA. However, studies indicate mixed efficacy for some group approaches largely due to the lack of specificity in group format, recruitment criteria, and availability of control groups (England & Connors, 2005; Knight, 2006; Smith & Kelly, 2008). In this chapter, the authors report on the current research on CSA and highlight evidence-based treatments, core components, and practice approaches associated with effective group therapy for sexually traumatized children and their families.

DEFINING CHILD SEXUAL ABUSE AND ITS PREVALENCE

Each year it is estimated that 90,000 children are victims of CSA or assault (Finkelhor, Ormrod, Turner, & Hamby, 2005). While this estimate is based on investigated reports of CSA, data from other sources, such as lifetime prevalence reports, indicate that CSA occurs at a higher rate than is reported to child protection agencies (Finkelhor et al., 2005). CSA is the sexual victimization of a child by an adult or older child (most often a male acquaintance or member of the family), and it is frequently accompanied by coercion, threats, and force. The National Child Abuse and Neglect Data System defines CSA as a range of sexual acts that may include oral, genital, or anal penetration, as well as sexual touching, exposure, exploitation, and voyeurism. Legal definitions vary by state.

According to the National Child Abuse and Neglect Data System's Child Maltreatment Report for 2007, substantiated reports of CSA were highest among children between the ages of 12 and 15 (at 35.2%), followed by children aged 8 to 11 (23.8%) and 4 to 7 (23.2%). After the age of 6, girls are sexually abused at a higher rate than boys (Finkelhor et al., 2005). Although CSA, as a single event or a pattern of abuse, occurs in all communities and regardless of racial background, ethnicity, or socioeconomic status, children living in poverty and exposed to multiple traumatic events, such as community and domestic violence, are at higher risk of sexual victimization (Finkelhor et al., 2005).

Due to the secrecy surrounding CSA and children's understandable reluctance to report it, social workers need to be aware and educate parents, teachers, and community organizations about the signs of CSA. Signs include children exhibiting increased nightmares, high levels of distress and fearfulness, withdrawn behaviors, anger or aggressive outbursts, unusual sexualized behaviors, and knowledge of sexual information not consistent with what is age appropriate. Social workers should also be alert to signs in adults who, when interacting with children, display or have a history of inappropriate behaviors. These behaviors can include making sexually provocative or degrading comments or jokes, hugging or kissing too often, patting others on the buttocks, initiating intimate/romantic/sexual contact, using corporal punishment on children they are supervising, allowing or encouraging youth to go to Internet sites with sexual content, using electronic communication to send youth sexually oriented photographs or messages, showing pornography, involving youth in pornographic activities, and/or having a known history of sexual perpetration.

Social workers can help others better understand why children are reluctant to disclose CSA, so that they can help stop the abuse and the healing process can begin. Parents, teachers and providers need to understand that children who have been sexually abused often feel shame and guilt. They fear the perpetrator will hurt them or their family. Children also fear that they will be not be believed if they disclose the abuse and that they may be removed from their homes.

REVIEW OF THE CSA LITERATURE

Effective treatments are essential tools in reducing the long-term negative effects of CSA. Multiple studies indicate that children who have been sexually abused are at high risk of serious mental and behavioral health disorders and poor social and emotional outcomes (Kendall-Tackett, Williams, & Finkelhor, 1993; Trickett & Putnam, 1993). CSA can result in posttraumatic stress disorder (PTSD), ranging from acute to chronic in nature. Symptoms of PTSD include numbing, avoidance, hyperarousal, and reexperiencing the abuse (American Psychiatric Association, 1995). Victims of CSA report four times as many self-harm or suicide attempts and twice as many episodes of revictimization, including sexual abuse, rape or assault, domestic violence, and physical affronts (Noll, Horowitz, Bonanno, Tricket, & Putnam, 2003). A hallmark longitudinal study on CSA provided evidence of the biopsychosocial impact of CSA on 82 females across developmental stages (Putnam, 2003). Although the findings identify the resilience of these young women, they also highlight the toll CSA has had on their physical and psychological health and social development. When compared with their peers, these women had lower social competence; lower academic performance; higher school avoidance; more depression; increased self-harm and suicidal behaviors; more dissociation; more sexual acting-out behaviors; more behavior problems and delinquency; lower self-esteem; higher rates of teen sexual activity and pregnancy; higher rates of substance abuse; poorer physical health, including obesity, hormonal disruption, and gastrointestinal complaints; lower rates of health care utilization; and more sleep disturbances (Noll et al., 2003; Noll, Trickett, & Putnam, 2003)

In attempting to explain the complexities of CSA and its sequelae, researchers have investigated risk and protective factors, such as abuse (e.g., duration, severity), family (e.g., maternal mental illness and substance abuse; parental history of victimization; family communication, functioning and ability to protect its members), socioeconomic risk factors (e.g., poverty, homelessness, access to services), and child characteristics (e.g., age, gender, intelligence, temperament). Child outcomes are mediated by parent and family responses to their sexual trauma. In order to support child adjustment, family members need to nurture and protect their child as they learn about the impact of CSA and to apply consistent parenting practices that help children stay on their developmental trajectory (Cohen & Mannarino, 2000). Another major factor influencing adjustment is children's cognitions, including attributions associated with the abuse and use of coping strategies (Valle & Silovsky, 2002). Children may attribute sexual abuse to internal or external factors; for instance, they may blame themselves or the dangerousness of the world. Children who recognize that the abuser is responsible for their actions fare better later in life than do children who assume some blame (Lev-Wiesel, 2000).

In an effort to negate long-term mental health and adjustment problems, group therapy can have a positive impact on these cognitive factors by setting forth treatment goals to correct cognitive misattributions, increase self-esteem, reduce isolation, strengthen coping skills, and promote prosocial behaviors (Connors & Schamess, 1999; Hetzel-Riggins, Brausch, & Montgomery, 2007; Silverman et al., 2008). Increasing access to resources and strengthening the child and family's capacity for resiliency are essential protective factors in the recovery process (Wilcox, Richards, & O'Keefe, 2004).

PRACTICE PRINCIPLES AND EVIDENCE-BASED PRACTICES

Social workers in the mental health and child welfare fields are increasingly challenged to effectively apply research findings to their complex daily work with children and families affected by CSA. Social work group practice focusing on mutual aid, strengths, and empowerment is well suited for children and families affected by trauma, including CSA (Knight, 2006). Therapeutic groups offer opportunities to reduce the isolation that often accompanies CSA as well as support coping and resilience through educating clients on the impact of CSA and teaching effective psychological and prosocial skills (Knight, 2006). The following sections detail the practice guidelines for social workers conducting groups aimed at reducing risks and supporting growth and recovery among children and families impacted by CSA. The sections include information on the impact of culture on CSA, screening/assessment, core components, and available group treatments for CSA. Tips for successful implementation and common themes observed in groups are included.

PRACTICE GUIDELINES

Impact of Culture

Respect for clients' cultural, geographical, religious, spiritual, and ethnic identities are core social work values, and effective practitioners seek to understand and mobilize cultural resources to help the child and family recover from CSA. Cultural perceptions about healing and the helpfulness of mental health services impact the treatment process and vary based on experience with mental health care and the child welfare system, racial/ethnic discrimination or cultural isolation, and the family's cultural and spiritual beliefs and traditions (U.S. Department of Health and Human Services, 2007). The following example illustrates how spiritual and cultural values can affect the course of CSA treatment:

> A mother brought her 11-year-old daughter for treatment after she had disclosed that her father had sexually abused her on multiple occasions. The mother reported that she was reluctant to have her daughter participate in therapy that encouraged her daughter to talk about what happened and she did not want to testify against the father in court. She reported that she had talked with her family and pastor about her doubts and they advised her to focus on forgiving the father (a central theme in Christian religions) rather than prosecuting him for the crime of CSA. During this time, a family had been murdered in the community for informing the police of neighborhood drug dealing activities and citizens were being threatened to "Stop Snitching." The mother and daughter felt frightened and conflicted by their

cultural context and spiritual beliefs. The therapist asked the mother to invite her family to treatment and offered information on CSA to the pastor. Eventually, the mother and daughter participated in trauma-focused cognitive behavioral therapy and completed the trauma narrative. They testified in court and the father pled guilty and was sentenced to jail.

Cultural norms and beliefs often determine the family's views on sexuality, nudity, discipline practices, family boundaries, respect for elders, personal and familial privacy, family roles, and acceptance of strangers (Saunders, Berliner, & Hanson, 2004). One study indicates that ethnicity may play a role in the development of posttraumatic stress symptoms; it found that Asian American children who have been sexually abused reported more suicidal thoughts but less anger and sexual acting out than their white and African American peers (Cohen, Deblinger, Mannarino, & DeArellano, 2001). Although more research is needed to understand how sociocultural factors affect CSA, it is clear families' and caregivers' responses to CSA and the cultural context have a powerful effect on outcomes for children (Cohen & Mannarino, 2000; Kiser & Black, 2005; Saunders et al., 2004). Culturally relevant, trauma informed engagement strategies that research indicates are effective in groups include addressing stigma associated with CSA and mental health service usage; understanding the acceptable range of emotional expressions and attitudes regarding the "telling of family business" and other cultural considerations related to CSA; attending to concrete barriers to services, such as lack of insurance, transportation, and child care; conducting structured intakes and follow-up telephone calls; offering social support and multifamily groups; partnering with families to develop a treatment plan that best fits their preference; supporting parents' and caregivers' efforts to understand the impact of CSA on their child's development and in advocating for needed services; and offering groups in settings that are more accessible to families such as, pediatricians' offices, schools, and faith-based or community organizations (Cohen et al., 2001; McKay, Hibbert, Hoagwood, et al., 2004; Snell-Johns, Mendez, & Smith, 2004). Building on the inherent strengths of the family and their community, combined with identifying group interventions that are effective and congruent with the families' cultural values and norms, increases the likelihood that children will get the care they need.

Screening and Assessment

Social workers preparing to start group therapy with this population should conduct comprehensive biopsychosocial assessments to better understand the impact of each child's symptoms on the child and his or her family. The National Child Traumatic Stress Network defines *trauma informed care* as including trauma-specific, developmentally relevant screening, assessment, and treatment (www.nctsn.org). Although the tools for forensic assessment have improved, standardized

CSA clinical assessment are rare (Lev-Wiesel, 2008). Social workers must be cautious to avoid misdiagnosing children who have been sexually abused. For example, many behavioral symptoms are indicators of more than one mental health diagnosis; children with trauma symptoms can be misdiagnosed as having attention-deficit/hyperactivity disorder (ADHD) (Cohen & Mannarino, 2000).

In addition to assessing a child's individual strengths and needs, effective assessment practices emphasize focusing on family relationships, as well as environmental and cultural contexts. Structured interviews and standardized measures guide the process of gathering information to design a treatment plan that fits the families' needs and allows the family and social worker to monitor change over time. The overall goal of treatment is to reduce symptoms and increase child and family safety, health, and well-being (de Arellano & Danielson, 2008).

Group Treatments

Group work is frequently used in the treatment of CSA. Clinical services research is advancing the field's efforts to identify the most effective group treatment for victims of CSA (Hetzel-Riggin et al., 2007; Tourigny & Hebert, 2007). The Institute of Medicine and California Evidence-based Clearinghouse for Child Welfare define "evidence-based practice" (EBP) as interventions that are theoretically sound; consistent with practice principles and values; acceptable and applicable to clients; effective and has no or low risks associated with it; manualized and supported by at least two randomized controlled treatment outcome studies that indicate the treatment is superior to the comparison treatment (Institute of Medicine, 2001).

Multiple studies and systematic reviews indicate that cognitive-behavioral therapy (CBT) is highly effective for the treatment of PTSD symptoms, including CSA (Avinger & Jones, 2007; Hetzel-Riggin et al., 2007; MacDonald, Higgins, & Ramchandani, 2009; Silverman et al., 2008; Tourigny & Hebert, 2007)

In preparing for group work with sexually abused children, social workers should incorporate a developmental approach that includes cognitive-behavioral interventions that focus on the impact of the traumatic experience(s) (understanding the trauma story, correcting misattributions and cognitive distortions). Such an approach should also include the management of stress reactions and distressing emotions (e.g., coping with traumatic memories and reminders, stress inoculation techniques) and should support adjustment to secondary adversities (e.g., removal from home, court testimony, maternal response, etc.) (McFarlane, 1996).

Group work can be effective for early latency aged children up to adolescents. For example, group CBT has been found to decrease future sexual acting out and offenses in children who have experienced sexual abuse (Carpentier, Silovsky, & Chaffin, 2006). There is some evidence that treatment of young sexual abuse victims helps reduce symptoms, as well as prevent potential negative outcomes (Deblinger, Stauffer, & Steer, 2001). School-aged children who are familiar with classroom formats and enjoy peer interaction feel comfortable in groups. They can benefit from the interactive format of CBT groups focusing on action-oriented planning and coping. Group therapies using CBT techniques are also highly effective for adolescents as peer identification and interactions are a developmental priority. Tourigny, Hébert, Daigneault, and Simoneau (2005) found that adolescent girls who had been sexually abused and participate in group therapy had an increased sense of empowerment, better relationships with their mothers, and a decrease in symptoms of PTSD after group therapy. Another study with adolescent girls found group participation helped decrease depressive and PTSD symptoms (Smith & Kelly, 2008). Connecting with peers facing similar problems reduces the shame and isolation surrounding CSA for all age groups (Avinger & Jones, 2007). Children and adults can benefit from the unique experience groups offer to give and receive help from others (Knight, 2006).

Several trauma-specific group therapies (beyond the scope of this chapter to describe in depth) have been developed through collaborations between researchers and clinicians. These include trauma-focused cognitive-behavioral therapy (TF-CBT) (Silverman et al., 2008); cognitive behavioral interventions for trauma in schools (CBITS) (Jaycox, 2004); structured psychotherapy for adolescents responding to chronic stress (SPARCS; www.nctsnet.org); safety, mentoring, advocacy, recovery, and treatment (SMART) (Belcher, Johnson, Johnson-Brooks, & Offermann, 2008); and trauma adaptive recovery group education and therapy (TARGET) for adolescents and preadolescents (Avinger & Jones, 2007; Hetzel-Riggin et al., 2007).

Therapeutic Stance

Despite the enormous needs of this population, Friedrich (1991) reports that much of the treatment of CSA "is frequently relegated to a continually changing group of novice therapists" (p. 277). Beginning group leaders need training and supervision to conduct groups or any other type of treatment with sexually abused children. Social workers planning to conduct such groups must be creative and consistent in setting limits and managing challenging behaviors in the group. Empathy and acceptance are key elements in creating a safe space for child victims to discuss the thoughts, feelings, and memories. Social workers are challenged to develop the capacity to feel deeply for what the children are feeling without losing their own perspective (Compton & Galaway, 1989).

Tips for Successful Implementation

Getting Started

Group treatment offers an economic option when resources are limited and demand is high (Tourigny & Hebert, 2007). However, it requires adequate space, supplies, and support for successful implementation. In addition to receiving training and adhering to evidence-based or promising group therapy models, organizational support is critical to successful implementation (Fixsen, Naoom, Blasé, & Friedman, 2005). The availability of a regular group room to promote privacy and consistency, as well as access to art and play supplies to encourage group interaction and communications, is important in promoting rapport and trust among the members (Strieder, Schamess, & Martel-Connors, 1996). Unfortunately, such resources and supplies are often difficult to obtain in agencies with budget and space limitations. Social workers' initiative and ingenuity are essential to overcoming these obstacles.

> In one urban agency, group leaders effectively advocated for the conversion of a staff room into a child's play room. They negotiated for the exclusive use of the room for evening group sessions, while agency social workers were given daily access to conduct child interviews. Another group leader got several donations from community toy and art stores. The result: an exceptionally well-stocked playroom well beyond the agency's limited budget.

Group Structure

The group's structure is largely determined by the model, but here are some general considerations:

1. *Open- vs. closed-ended group:* Research indicates that participants can benefit from both types of groups and participants have demonstrated increased use of problem solving and coping skills as well as social support seeking behaviors (Tourginey & Hebert, 2007). The fluid membership of an open-ended group can be a challenge for the leader who has to prepare the space and supplies each week.
2. *Group composition:* Age, development, and gender are important factors in composing a CSA group. Younger children's groups should be smaller, with four to six children. Adolescent groups can be larger, with 10 members being the upper limit. Leaders must carefully distinguish between children's chronological age and developmental age.

> Yvonne, a physically mature 12-year-old, had been sexually abused by her mother's boyfriend and sexually active with neighborhood boys for over a year. Her placement in a latency-aged group was fraught with difficulties. Yvonne wanted to discuss her sexual experiences with her boyfriend, while the other members could not comprehend why anyone would engage in sex willingly. Group leaders suggested an early graduation for Yvonne and transferred her to the older adolescent group

Due to the sexual content of CSA groups, groups should be single sex so that children can feel more comfortable discussing sexual content. Trauma groups not solely focused on discussing CSA can be coed.

3. *Co-leaders:* There are advantages and disadvantages to co-leadership in CSA groups. Co-leaders can give each other support and encouragement and an opportunity to talk over the group process with another colleague. Continuity problems are reduced when one leader is absent. Also, having two observers reduces the likelihood of missing important interchanges among the members. Disadvantages include cost and inter-leader conflict. Dissension or personality conflicts between group leaders will be readily apparent to members and can dramatically impair group effectiveness. Yet if the group leaders are aware of possible conflicts and willing to examine them constructively, they can provide excellent opportunities to model conflict resolution behavior for the group members. Group leaders should be prepared for the children's tendency to sexualize the relationship between the leaders.

When setting the table for a snack, the group members consistently seated the two group leaders together. When asked why, the children said they thought the leaders would want to be together since they were married or boyfriend and girlfriend.

Common Themes

Developmental Considerations
Some sexually abused children experience significant delays in their social-emotional development (Friedrich, 1991, p. 25; Mandel & Damon, 1989). Group structure (i.e., schedules, behavior incentives, etc.) and activities should match the developmental needs of the child or adolescent and support the development of age-appropriate skills (Mandel & Damon, 1989). Group workers must strike a delicate balance between doing too much or too little when helping children overcome these developmental delays and acquiring appropriate socialization skills. Intervention must be structured without denying group members opportunities to work out conflicts and to learn cooperative play and negotiation skills.

Emotional Regulation
Children experience a range of feelings related to CSA, including, fear, anger, pleasure, shame, guilt, and sadness (Berliner, 1991; Finklehor, 1986). Effective groups normalize these emotional responses and teach new coping skills to manage them. Typically, children fear repeated abuse, the consequences of sexual activity, and retaliation and separation from their families (Johnson, 1991; Sturkie, 1992). Therapists and caregivers help children distinguish between realistic and unrealistic fears. Children's fears are reasonable when the perpetrator has continued access to the child, the child is not believed or supported by a caretaker, or the child is exposed to unsafe situations. If these conditions exist, social workers must collaborate with the child welfare system and advocate for changes in the children's environment. Trauma symptoms will not improve until a child is safe.

Children often express anger toward the caretaker who did not protect them from the abuse or who did not respond protectively after the abuse was revealed. Guilt or shame accompanies perceptions that they are responsible for the sexual abuse, its disclosure, and the resulting family disruption. The following examples illustrate the complexity of these emotional responses:

> Vicki's father forced her to adopt her deceased mother's parental and marital role. Disclosure occurred when neighborhood children saw Vicki's father raping her through the bedroom window. Eight-year-old Vicki believed herself to be an "unfit parent" who caused her five siblings to be placed in three different foster homes.
>
> Cindy, age 10, felt shame for experiencing pleasure during oral sex with her aunt.

Depression and Self-harm

Depression, suicide, and self-mutilation have been observed in both sexually abused children and adults (Noll et al., 2003; Pisaruk, Shawchuck, & Hoier, 1992). Young (1992) hypothesizes that self-abuse may occur when survivors believe they cannot trust their own bodies because they feel vulnerable or ashamed or because they felt some pleasure while the abuse was occurring. Social workers should evaluate all children in CSA treatment for possible depression and suicidal ideation and listen during group for overt or covert references to self-harm.

> Sarah, 11, who was forced to perform oral sex on her mother, slashed at her wrist with a pen knife, put broken glass in her mouth and threatened to swallow the pieces, and kept several physicians, nurses, and social workers at bay before she was finally hospitalized.
>
> Eight-year-old Michah, who was sexually abused by her mother's three boyfriends, reported to her group that she planned to jump out of her second-story window onto the concrete pavement below.

Setting Limits

Offenders have often used and abused their position of authority to gain control over and sexually assault children (Groth, 1982). In the authors' experience, children will generalize this misuse of authority to their social workers and expect them, too, to abuse their authority. This can result in avoidant or oppositional behaviors. Social workers should anticipate this testing of authority as an opportunity for children to experience authority in a more appropriate manner. It is the group leaders' responsibility to set and adhere to clear, consistent rules, routines and schedules. At a minimum, children should be told that they will not be permitted to hurt themselves or another group member, nor will they be permitted to break or destroy any of the toys or equipment in the playroom. Group members require a high degree of trust and comfort to discuss their sexual abuse experiences. Limits and clear expectations build a foundation of trust and help reduce anxiety.

Confidentiality

It is unrealistic and erroneous to tell children that everything they say is confidential. It is important, however, for children to know which information will be shared with their caretakers and other professionals. Group leaders should tell participants that if they say anything indicating that they may be or have been abused or hurt again, either by themselves or by others, their group leaders will take action to protect them. This statement should be made in the initial interview and reiterated throughout the life of the group. In the authors' experience, this message does not inhibit children's discussion or revelations. Children will continue to reveal important information, counting on social workers to act responsibly and to take protective action on their behalf. When social workers give unrealistic assurances of confidentiality or fail to take protective action, children can be harmed and their trust irrevocably broken. If a child's statement must be revealed, group leaders should inform the child of the decision and the reasons (Koverola, Murtaugh, Connors, Reeves, & Papas, 2007).

Legal and Court Intervention

Social workers working with sexually abused children must understand both the criminal and civil legal systems. Often children will require assistance in understanding both the purpose and the outcome of legal intervention. Children may experience fear or anxiety about testifying in court, retaliation by the perpetrator, not being believed, being on trial themselves, or embarrassing questions on the witness stand (O'Donohue & Geer, 1992). By contrast, some children demand to have "their day in court" and become angry if they are not allowed to testify at trial or at sentencing. Green (1992) reports that testifying in court has potential advantages, including giving children an active role in mastering the trauma, offering children a chance to be believed and to see justice work, and providing children a constructive outlet for their anger (p. 298). Last, children may feel dejected after completion of the court process as social workers, investigators, police, and prosecutors may discontinue or curtail their services to children, thus leaving the children to cope with the aftermath of court intervention alone. Having the opportunity to talk about legal experiences in the group can normalize these experiences for group members.

Managing Therapist's Reaction to Traumatic Stories

Group work with children affected by CSA is very intense. Social workers have to manage their own reactions to the stories of trauma, as well as their own stress and feelings related to this challenging work. Therapists are at risk of vicarious traumatization that can cause "fundamental shifts in their views of themselves and their social world" (Knight, 2006, p. 25) and a decreased sense of safety and increased feelings of hopelessness. Reflective supervision and stress reducing and pleasurable activities are core self care plans (Pearlman & Saakvitne, 1995).

Group Techniques

The agenda and activities are determined by the model and its weekly goals or lesson plans. In general, activities should be safe, relevant and fun. Below are some general group techniques that help build rapport, trust and cohesion and have relevance in many settings:

Ice-breakers

These help build rapport in the first group. Young children especially enjoy name games that make the chore of learning new names fun. Older children respond well to activities designed to ease their anxiety about the group in more sophisticated and direct ways. Using "getting to know you" activities that promote discussion about favorite movies, music or video games, as well as things they don't like, eases anxiety and helps them find common ground.

Creative Activities

There is a long tradition of using expressive therapies or techniques to promote emotional expression (Hetzel-Riggin et al., 2007). Making collages, drawing, writing poetry, and song writing are excellent ways for children to express feelings, tell their story, and build relationships within the group.

> Eight-year-old Danny compared his obviously distorted and depressed first self-portrait with his happier and smiling second portrait and said, "Oh, that one [the first portrait] was because of what happened to me [sexual abuse] and how sad I was; the other [second portrait] was because I was happier, cause I was in group and I got to talk about everything."
>
> Nine-year-old Lea was drawn with 2 mouths in one group member's picture, with an extra-large mouth in another's, and with no mouth in a third's. When the children were asked why this was so, they readily pointed out that Lea talked too much. A constructive discussion then followed on how Lea's monopolizing of the meeting prevented the other members from talking. The discussion concluded with Lea asking the other girls to tell her when she talks too much.

Letter writing is a common technique used in groups to help children integrate thoughts and feelings about their trauma story. Members can write letters to their perpetrators or nonsupportive caretakers and express their feeling about their abuse. The children can then read their letters aloud, have another member read them silently or aloud, send them to their perpetrators, share them with the caregiver or destroy them. In the following example, it is clear that this 9-year girl learned what sexual abuse is, is placing blame with her father, and is able to think about the future.

Dear Dad,
　　I do not want to see you no more. I am glad the judge put you in jail. You should not have done that to a child (put your privacy in my butt, that is called sexual abuse of a child). I hope you stay in jail a long time. You cannot come to my graduation from 5th grade. I will tell you if you can come to high school graduation.

Role-Playing
Techniques that are well suited for cognitive behavioral interventions can help children of all ages to practice coping and problem-solving skills. Participants role-play interpersonal dilemmas with which they are struggling and can practice talking with someone about a difficult topic or personal feelings (Beidel, Turner, & Morris, 2000).

Bibliotherapy
Reading books or short stories on CSA or other problems can be very helpful. Books that focus on sex education and CSA prevention are also beneficial, as many children experiencing CSA are at high risk of future abuse. Books or stories that provide metaphors for abuse (or loss of control) but do not specifically address it can be helpful to older children who can then connect the experiences of those in the book to their own experiences without having to specifically read about abuse. A short bibliography is provided at the end of this chapter.

Skill in Group Termination
Saying goodbye is an opportunity to celebrate accomplishments and practice coping with difficult feelings, such as sadness, anger, and anxiety. Group leaders must not only pay attention to the structured activities planned for the end of group, but to the process as well (Heiman & Ettin, 2001). Sexually abused children often have experienced many abrupt and traumatic endings in their lives. Their own separation or family member's removal leaves little or no opportunity to say goodbye to family members or neighborhood friends. The reality of these traumatic, abrupt endings in these children's lives should be considered in determining guidelines for group termination.

In one group consisting of latency-aged sexually abused girls, the group leaders failed to address termination issues. The group was open-ended, with no planned termination. As members grew too old for the group they left, sometimes abruptly. The group leaders failed to address the needs of both the girls departing and those left behind. Members perceived the departures as a rejection. When asked to draw pictures of their group, girls included former group members who had left months earlier while omitting new members. Those girls leaving the group felt no sense of completion. Recognizing that the group was exacerbating the girls' chaotic lives, the group leaders attempted to redefine these endings. But the poorly handled departures proved to have a more lasting impact than the subsequent intervention. Finally, the group leaders closed entry into the group and began to work on termination issues with the remaining members. Eventually, the group was disbanded.

Social workers conducting groups with sexually abused children should provide a well-defined termination process when members enter the group. By making group termination an expected and positive outcome, social workers can help children plan more thoroughly for endings. One successful strategy is to invite the caregivers/families to a graduation party and have the children give a performance, such as a play or puppet show, or display artwork or projects that demonstrate what they learned in the group.

EVALUATION

A review of the literature reveals that many researchers evaluate groups' effectiveness by investigating the amelioration of or reduction in posttraumatic stress symptoms (Deblinger, 2001; Trowell et al., 2002). The following assessment tools measure changes in PTSD symptoms and can be administered at the beginning and end of treatment: UCLA PTSD Index for DSM-IV (Pynoos, Rodriguez, Steinberg, Stuber, & Frederick, 1998) and the Trauma Symptom Checklist for Children (TSCC) (Briere, 1996). These measures are considered valid and reliable in evaluating the posttraumatic symptoms of avoidance, arousal, and reexperiencing.

CONCLUSION

Therapeutic groups offer opportunities to reduce PTSD symptoms and isolation often associated with CSA. Effective group treatments support the development of new coping skills and foster resilience through educating clients on the impact of CSA and teaching effective psychological and prosocial skills (Knight, 2006). The authors have found conducting groups with sexually abused children to be a professionally rewarding experience. Group work using trauma-focused cognitive behavioral interventions is highly effective in reducing posttraumatic stress symptoms and addressing the psychosocial needs of this vulnerable population. In our experience some children who refuse to speak about their abuse and are quiet and reticent in individual therapy disclose their victimization more readily within groups and experience relief on meeting and hearing from other children with similar experiences. The discovery that they are not alone, combined with the opportunity to help other children, promotes prosocial skills and much needed social support. Group therapy is most effective in combination with individual and family therapies, parent training/education and social work interventions such as advocacy, referral, and care coordination (De Luca, Grayston, & Romano, 2000).

RESOURCES

Resources on Defining CSA

Childhood Sexual Abuse Fact sheet
http://www.unh.edu/ccrc/factsheet/pdf/childhoodSexualAbuseFactSheet.pdf

Child Welfare Gateway Information
http://www.childwelfare.gov:80/index.cfm

Centers for Disease Control and Prevention link for preventing child sexual
http://www.cdc.gov/ncipc/dvp/PreventingChildSexualAbuse.pdf.

National Child Traumatic Stress Network Fact Sheets on CSA
http://www.nctsn.org/nccts/nav.do?pid=typ_sa_prom

Resources for Preparing to Work with Children Impacted by CSA

The Promise of Trauma-Focused Therapy for Childhood Sexual Abuse This DVD was developed to provide information on the impact of CSA and highlight critical elements for successful treatment. http://www.nctsnet.org/nccts/nav.do?pid=ctr_top_trmnt

Reading List for Children

Bell, R. (1998). *Changing bodies, changing lives: Expanded 3rd edition: A book for teens on sex and relationships.* New York: Times Books.
Hansen, D. (2007). *Those are MY private parts.* Redondo Beach, CA: Empowerment Productions.
Stauffer, L., & Deblinger, E. (2004). *Let's talk about coping and safety skills: A workbook about taking care of me!* Hatfield, PA: Hope for Families.

REFERENCES

American Psychiatric Association. (1995). *Diagnostic and statistical manual of mental disorders (DSM-IV), fourth edition.* Washington, DC: American Psychiatric Association.

Avinger, K. A. & Jones, R. A. G. (2007). Group treatment of sexually abused adolescent girls: A review of outcome studies. *The American Journal of Family Therapy, 35,* 315–326.

Beidel, D. C., Turner, S. M., & Morris, T. (2000). Behavioral treatment of childhood social phobia. *Journal of Counseling and Clinical Psychology, 63,* 1072–1080.

Belcher, H. M. E., Johnson, E., Johnson-Brooks, S. T., & Offermann, B. J. (2008). Get SMART: Effective treatment for sexually abused children with problematic sexual behavior. *Journal of Child and Adolescent Trauma, 1,* 179–191.

Berliner, L. (1991). Cognitive therapy with a young victim of sexual assault. In W. N. Friedrich (ed.), *Casebook of sexual abuse treatment* (pp. 93–111). New York: W. W. Norton.

Briere, J. (1996). *Manual for the Trauma Symptom Checklist for Children (TSCC).* Lutz, FL: Psychological Assessment Resources.

Carpentier, M. Y., Silovsky, J. F., & Chaffin, M. (2006). Randomized trial of treatment for children with sexual behavior problems: Ten year follow-up. *Journal of Consulting and Clinical Psychology, 74,* 482–488.

Cohen, J. A., Perel, J. M., DeBellis, M. D., Friedman, M. J., & Putnam, F. W. (2002). Treating traumatized children. Clinical implications of the psychobiology of PTSD. *Trauma, Violence and Abuse, 3,* 91–108.

Cohen, J. A., Deblinger, E., Mannarino, A. P., & De Arellano, M. A. (2001). The importance of culture in treating abused and neglected children: An empirical review. *Child Maltreatment, 6,* 148–157.

Cohen, J. A. & Mannarino, A. P. (2000). Predictors of treatment outcome in sexually abused children. *Child Abuse & Neglect, 24,* 983–994.

Compton, B. R. & Galaway, B. (1989). *Social work processes.* Pacific Cove, CA: Brooks/ Cole Publishing Company.

Connors, K. M. & Schamess, G. (1999). Traumatized and neglected children. In C. Schaefer (ed.), *Short-term psychotherapy groups for children: Adapting group processes for specific problems* (pp. 219–248). Northvale, NJ: Jason Aronson.

de Arellano, M. A. & Danielson, C. K. (2008). Assessment of trauma history and trauma-related problems in ethnic minority child populations: An informed approach. *Cognitive & Behavioral Practice, 15,* 53–67.

deLuca, R. V., Grayston, A. D., & Romano, E. (2000). Sexually abused boys. In C. Schaefer (ed.), *Short-term psychotherapy groups for children: Adopting group processes for specific problems* (pp. 183–218). Northvale, NJ: Jason Aronson.

Deblinger, E., Stauffer, L. B., & Steer, R. A. (2001). Comparative efficacies of supportive and cognitive behavioral group therapies for young children who have been sexually abused and their nonoffending mothers. *Child Maltreatment, 6,* 332–343.

Department of Health and Human Services, Administration on Children, Youth, and Families. (2007). Child Maltreatment 2007 [online]. Washington, DC: U.S. Government Printing Office. Retrieved August 20, 2009, from www.acf.hhs.gov

England, S. & Connors, K. M. (2005). Group work with sexually abused children. In G. L. Greif & P. H. Ephross (eds.), *Group work with populations at risk* (pp. 267–286). New York: Oxford University Press.

Finkelhor, D., Ormrod, R. K., Turner, H. A., & Hamby, S. L. (2005). The victimization of children and youth: A comprehensive, national survey. *Child Maltreatment, 10*(1), 5–25.

Fixsen, D. L., Naoom, S. F., Blasé, K. A., & Friedman, R. M. (2005). *Implementation research: A synthesis of the literature.* Tampa, FL: University of South Florida, Louis de la Parte Florida Mental Health Institute, National Implementation Research Network.

Friedrich, W. N. (1990). *Psychotherapy of sexually abused children and their families.* New York: W. W. Norton.

Friedrich, W. N. (ed.). (1991). *Casebook of sexual abuse treatment.* New York: W. W. Norton.

Green, A. H. (1992). Application of psychoanalytic theory in the treatment of the victim and the family. In W. O'Donahue & J. H. Geer (eds.), *The sexual abuse of children* (pp. 285–300). Hillsdale, NJ: Erlbaum.

Groth, N. A. (1982). The incest offender. In S. Sgroi (ed.), *Handbook of clinical intervention in child sexual abuse* (pp. 215–239). Lexington, MA: Lexington Books.

Heiman, M. L. & Ettin, M. F. (2001). Harnessing the power of the group for latency aged sexual abuse victims. *International Journal of Group Psychotherapy, 51,* 265–280.

Hetzel-Riggin, M. D., Brausch, A. M., & Montgomery, B. S. (2007). A meta-analytic investigation of therapy modality outcomes for sexually abuse children and adolescents: An exploratory study. *Child Abuse & Neglect, 31,* 125–141.

Institute of Medicine. (2001). *Crossing the quality chasm: A new health system for the 21st century.* Washington, DC: National Academies Press.

Jaycox, L. (2004). *Cognitive-behavioral intervention for trauma in schools.* Longmont, CO: Sopris West.

Johnson, T. C. (1991). Treatment of a sexually reactive girl. In W. N. Friedrich (ed.), *Casebook of sexual abuse treatment* (pp. 270–290). New York: W. W. Norton.

Kendall-Tackett, K. A., Williams, L. M., & Finkelhor, D. (1993). The Impact of sexual abuse on children: A review and synthesis of recent empirical studies. *Psychological Bulletin, 113,* 164–180.

Kiser, L. J. & Black, M. A. (2005). Family processes in the midst of urban poverty. *Aggression and Violent Behavior, 10,* 715–750.

Knight, C. (2006). Groups for individuals with traumatic histories: Practice considerations for social worker. *Social Work, 51,* 20–30.

Koverola, C., Murtaugh, C., Connors, K., et al. (2007). Children exposed to intra-familial violence: Predictors of attrition and retention in treatment. *Journal of Aggression, Maltreatment and Trauma,* 14, 19–42.

Lev-Wiesel, R. (2008). Child sexual abuse: A critical review of intervention and treatment modalities. *Children and Youth Services Review, 30,* 665–673.

Lev-Wiesel, R. (2000). Quality of life in adult survivors of childhood sexual abuse who have undergone therapy. *Journal of Child Sexual Abuse, 9,* 1–13.

MacDonald, G., Higgins, J. P. T., & Ramchandani, P. (2009). Cognitive-behavioral interventions for children who have been sexually abused. *Cochrane Database of Systematic Reviews, 2006*(4), CD001930.

Mandel, J. G. & Damon, L. (1989). *Group treatment for sexually abused children.* New York: Guilford Press.

McFarlane, A. C. (1996). Traumatic stress in childhood and adolescence: Recent developments and current controversies. In B. van der Kolk, A. C. McFarlane, & L. Weisaeth (eds.), *Traumatic stress: The effects of overwhelming experience on mind, body and society* (pp. 331–358). New York: Guilford Press.

McKay, M., Hibbert, R., Hoagwood, K., Rodriguez, J., Murray, L., Legerski, J., & Fernandez, D. (2004). Integrating evidence-based engagement interventions into 'real world' child mental health settings. *Journal of Brief Treatment and Crisis Intervention*, *4*, 177–186.

Noll, J. G., Horwowitz, L. A., Bonanno, G. A., Tricket, P. K., & Putman, F. W. (2003). Revictimization and self-harm in females who experienced childhood sexual abuse: Results from a prospective study. *Journal of Interpersonal Violence*, *18*, 1452–1471.

Noll, J. G., Trickett, P. K., & Putnam, F. W. (2003). A prospective investigation of the impact of childhood sexual abuse on the development of sexuality. *Journal of Consulting and Clinical Psychology*, *71*(3), 575–586.

O'Donohue, W. & Geer, J. H. (eds.). (1992). *The sexual abuse of children: Clinical issues*, Vols. 1 and 2. Hillsdale, NJ: Erlbaum.

Pearlman, L. & Saakvitne, K. (1995) *Trauma and the therapist: Countertransference and vicarious traumatization in psychotherapy with incest survivors*. New York: W. W. Norton.

Pisaruk, H. I., Shawchuck, C. R., & Hoier, T. S. (1992). Behavioral characteristics of child victims of sexual abuse: A comparison study. *Journal of Clinical Child Psychology*, *21*, 16–17.

Putnam, F.W. (2003). Ten-year research update review: Child sexual abuse. *Journal of American Academy Child and Adolescent Psychiatry*, *42*, 269–279.

Pynoos, R. S., Rodriguez, N., Steinberg, A., Stuber, M., & Frederick, C. (1998). *University of California Los Angeles Post Traumatic Stress Disorder–Reaction Index (UCLA PTSD-RI) Manual*. Los Angeles, CA: UCLA.

Safety, Mentoring, Advocacy, Recovery, and Treatment (SMART). National Child Traumatic Stress network online. Retrieved June 01, 2009, from www.nctsnet.org/nctsn_assets/pdfs/promising_practices/SMART_fact_sheet_3-21-07.pdf

Saunders, B. E., Berliner, L., & Hanson, R. F. (eds.). (2004). Child physical and sexual abuse: Guidelines for treatment (Revised Report: April 26, 2004). Charleston, SC: National Crime Victims Research and Treatment Center.

Silverman, W. K., Ortiz, C. D., Viswesvaran C., Burns, B. J., Kolko, D. J., Putnam, F. W., & Amaya-Jackson L. (2008). Evidence-based psychosocial treatments for children and adolescents exposed to traumatic events. *Journal of Clinical Child and Adolescent Psychiatry*, *37*, 156–183.

Smith, A. P. & Kelly, A. B. (2008). An exploratory study of group therapy for sexually abused adolescents and nonoffending guardians. *Journal of Child Sexual Abuse*, *17*, 101–116.

Snell-Johns, J., Mendez, J. L., & Smith, B. H. (2004). Evidence-based solutions for overcoming access barriers, decreasing attrition, and promoting change with underserved families. *Journal of Family Psychology*, *18*, 19–35.

Strieder, F., Schamess, G., & Martel-Connors, K. (1996). Creating and sustaining a group treatment program for cumulatively and repetitively traumatized children: Administrative principles and systemic considerations. *Journal of Child and Adolescent Group Therapy*, *6*, 61–74.

Sturkie, K. (1992). Group treatment of child sexual abuse victims: A review. In W. O'Donohue & J. H. Geer (eds.), *The sexual abuse of children: Clinical issues*, Vol. 2 (pp. 331–364). Hillsdale, NJ: Erlbaum.

Structured Psychotherapy for Adolescents Responding to Chronic Stress (SPARCS). A guide for trauma focused groups. National Child Traumatic Stress network online. Retrieved June 01, 2009, from http://www.nctsn.org/nctsn_assets/ppt/powerpoints/SPARCS_Hab_DeRosa_7-19-06.ppt

Tourigny, M. & Hebert, M. (2007). Comparison of open versus closed group Interventions for sexually abused adolescent girls. *Violence and Victims, 22,* 334–349.

Tourigny, M., Hébert, M., Daigneault, I., & Simoneau, A. C. (2005). Efficacy of a group therapy for sexually abused adolescent girls. *Journal of Child Sexual Abuse, 14,* 71–93.

Trickett, P. K. & Putnam, F. W. (1993). The impact of sexual abuse on female development towards a developmental, psychobiological integration. *Psychological Science, 4,* 81–87.

Trowell, J., Kolvin, T., Weeramanthri, H., Sadowski, M., Berelowitz, D., Glasser, D., & Leitch, I. (2002). Psychotherapy for sexually abused girls: Psychopathological outcome findings and patterns of change. *The British Journal of Psychiatry, 180,* 234–247.

U.S. Department of Health and Human Services. (2007). *Mental health: Culture, race, and ethnicity—A supplement to mental health: A report of the Surgeon General.* Rockville, MD: U.S. Department of Health and Human Services, Public Health Service, Office of the Surgeon General.

Valle, L. A. & Silovsky, J. F. (2002). Attributions and adjustment following child sexual and physical abuse. *Child Maltreatment, 7,* 9–25.

Wilcox, D. T., Richards, F., & O'Keefe, Z. C. (2004). Resilience and risk factors associated with experiencing childhood sexual abuse. *Child Abuse Review, 13,* 338–352.

Young, L. (1992). Sexual abuse and the problem of embodiment. *Child abuse & neglect, 16,* 89–100.

Chapter Sixteen

Group Work With People Who Offend

Margaret M. Wright

Social work with offender populations is a challenge to the beginning worker. One of the first hurdles that the worker must face is the "lock them up and throw away the key" attitude of some of the most vocal members of the public and the tendency of politicians to take on this theme as their electoral rallying cry and an easy way of garnering votes. This hostile attitude is sometimes present in the institution among staff and administrators. Social workers are often viewed as being naïve and easy prey for manipulative inmates who are looking for ways to increase their privileges and speed up their release. The challenge for the social worker is to demonstrate clearly to all segments of the institution, both staff and inmates, that he or she has a valuable service to provide that does not minimize the inmates' responsibility for their behavior. Some research indicates that prison wardens in the United States are receptive to the rehabilitative ideal within a controlled environment (Cullen et al., 1993). This reflects research into attitudes of the public:

> *Americans favor a balanced approach, one that exacts a measure of justice, protects the public against serious offenders, and makes every effort to change offenders while they are within the grasp of the state. Rehabilitation often is characterized as a "liberal idea" because it endorses "going easy" on offenders. But the public recognizes a canard when it sees one. Here is one liberal idea that citizens embrace because it is eminently rational: Why would we return any offender to the community without making a good faith effort to "save" the person and, in so doing, reduce the collateral threat to public safety? The failure to do so, Americans recognize, makes little sense and, in fact, borders on outright irresponsibility (Cullen, 2007, p. 4).*

The social work service can be seen as credible when presented as a concrete effort to help inmates confront the issues, over which they have control, that resulted in their imprisonment.

The population of offenders in prisons is very difficult to categorize. It is generally accepted that most offenders come from disadvantaged backgrounds and tend to be the poorest citizens of the area in which they reside (U.S. Department of

Justice, 2008). The ethnic or racial composition of offenders reflects the degree of representation of the ethnic and racial groups among the poor in the community from which the offenders originate. Specific population groups, then, differ depending on the area from which the prison derives its catchment. Most inmates are poorly educated and may have not had a stable employment pattern (Adler et al., 2000). One clear characteristic of prison inmates is that most of them are male (Kong & AuCoin, 2008). The management of men and women in prisons differs considerably because of the clearly different issues presented by the gender of the offender.

Male offenders' issues are usually depicted as relating to substance abuse (alcohol and/or drug abuse), aggression and assaultive behavior, impulsivity and poor frustration tolerance, poor education and work skills, and employment record. Problems in relationships with family members or social isolation resulting in the absence of any significant attachment to another person also exist.

Female offenders frequently have issues related to substance abuse as well as poor education and work skills, but one of the primary concerns for many female offenders is the problems related to their role as mothers (Spjeldnes & Goodkind, 2009). Canadian studies of women inmates serving sentences of more than 2 years show that two-thirds of them are mothers and that, of these, two-thirds have been single parents for at least part, if not all, of their children's lives. They are trying to cope with maintaining contact and relationships with children who are in the care of relatives or social agencies and who do not understand why their mothers have left them (Hayman, 2006).

The prison environment has been described by many writers (e.g., Goffman, 1973; Sykes, 1958). It is consistent with Goffman's descriptions of asylums and is similar to other total institutional environments. It is potentially a more oppressive environment for both inmates and staff than some other total institutions because of the traditional focus on the prison as a paramilitary structure in which inmates are kept against their will by the superior physical force of their keepers. This involuntary environment has not traditionally had any component of helping in the way that other total institutions, like hospitals for the mentally ill, have had. While the effect on keeping people against their will may be the same, the message sent to the inmates is different and much more obviously oppressive in the prison context.

One of the major issues/problems in prisons is the violence or the threat of violence that is part of the fabric of prison life. In most judicial jurisdictions, the population of inmates assigned to or choosing to live in protective custody (apart from other inmates and usually alone for up to 23 hours a day) has become a significant management problem because of their increasingly large numbers. Those inmates who do not choose to enter protective custody usually have to accept a lifestyle that involves violence in the conduct of everyday life, an "attack or be attacked" mentality (McCorkle, 1992). Not all prison environments have the same level of inmate subculture and violence or staff control. There is a wide variety of possible prison environments, ranging from relatively open, community focused, minimum security, or halfway house environments to maximum security, closed institutions in which the presence of mechanisms for physical restraint like mace, batons, or other weapons is obvious. Each level of security presents its own challenges and opportunities to the social worker. Work in the most secure institutions presents the greatest number of limitations to the social worker in terms of group programs because mobility and potential interaction among the inmates are severely limited. According to Griffiths (2004), these limitations may be due to the level of acting out of the inmates. This conclusion is questionable because of the custom of putting protective custody offenders who may otherwise present the lowest risk for acting out in maximum security. The inmates' need may be great, but support for social work intervention, particularly in groups, is likely to be low on the list of institutional priorities. Social workers are more likely to work in medium and minimum security institutions simply because the emphasis on physical security is reduced and the opportunities for inmates to interact are greater.

PRACTICE PRINCIPLES

The social worker who hopes to provide a group work service to inmates has to take the environment into account in constructing and operating the group. The environment is the immediate context in which the inmate lives. The staff who work in the prison are also part of the inmate's social context. The social worker cannot work in isolation from other staff in the institution and must attempt to develop positive relationships with custodial/correctional staff, as well as with nurses, teachers, administrators, and as many staff as possible in order to have the greatest possible impact on the environment, which consists of much more than the physical structure of the facility. Social group work (in fact, all social work) should be an authentic experience (Lang, 1978; Papell & Rothman, 1980), and any attempt to ignore the reality of the social context will, at best, result in an artificial attempt to intervene with people for whom the environment is very important[1].

The inmates in correctional institutions usually attempt to construct their own reality in opposition to the one imposed on them by the official institution. As noted earlier, this subculture has a hierarchical form in which the physically strong and the most antisocial are at the top and the physically weak and most intellectually and emotionally vulnerable are at the bottom. The values of this subculture are not compatible with prosocial functioning, but are strongly held and often supported within the prison by the staff, who believe that allowing this system to exist will keep the prison under control. When these values are shared by the inmates and the staff, the result is an understanding that the victims or potential victims of violence will be isolated and the belligerents will have the highest level of privilege. This contradicts the stated purpose of prisons, which is to sanction and/or rehabilitate the aggressor in order to protect the victim and possible future victims. The social worker cannot operate groups or any other programs that support these subcultural values but must recognize and confront their existence on a daily basis. The strength of the subculture in any given institution will affect the social worker's ability to form and guide authentic empowering group experiences for inmates. These prison realities make the contracting process an indispensable part of the social worker's intervention. Inmates must have a clear understanding of what is involved in the group and an awareness of how the group will fit into the institutional milieu. Will membership in the group enhance their lives in the institution or will it put them at risk?

At the point of contracting, it is important to recognize that the members of the group may be quite skeptical about the group's usefulness to them. They may be even more skeptical about the usefulness and trustworthiness of the worker. The worker will have to recognize and address these doubts. What in some settings may be signs of lack of motivation to change in a prison environment may simply be a reflection of the inmate's response to the involuntary nature of the setting and the implications that has for involvement with a social worker (Behroozi, 1992; Howells & Day, 2007).[2]

In beginning a group within a correctional environment, the worker must acknowledge that the activity of the group is taking place in an authority focused setting and that there are limits to what the group can do based on the limits of members as inmates in an institution. The worker must help the members identify the limits imposed by the setting and articulate them explicitly. The worker must also make it clear that although the limits are significant, there is a lot that the group can do. For example, although women inmates cannot be with their children in the community, they can discuss the problems they share as mothers in prison. They can help each other to explore new ways of dealing with the questions their children ask during visits and discuss how to prepare themselves and their children for their return to the community. The focus of the social workers is on what can be done in the present context of the prison to prepare the inmates for the future context of their home community. Part of the purpose of contracting is to let group members know what skills and strengths of the worker will enable the members to explore issues that they need to work on. The members need to decide as a group what their focus will be.

Confidentiality

In order to create a sense of safety, the group worker must state that personal disclosures will not be shared inappropriately with inmates and staff who are not part of the group. Providing this assurance is not easy for the worker in a prison because of the emphasis on security and the inmate's environment. The worker must emphasize to the members of the group, both in pregroup interviews and in the first session, the importance of keeping confidences within the group and the damage that can be done to individuals and to the group as a whole if confidences are violated. The worker's own ability to maintain confidentiality must also be made clear. The worker must make a commitment not to talk about the group to other staff without the inmates' permission but must also admit the responsibility to inform other staff members about disclosures that may signal a potential for suicide in a member, a potential for one member to possibly assault another inmate or a staff member, or to inform other authorities about confessions of child abuse. New workers may be concerned that an admission of limits to the ability of the worker to maintain confidentiality may damage the worker's relationship with the group. In fact, honest acknowledgment of the reality that many inmates are already aware of usually enhances the worker's credibility. In keeping with concerns about confidentiality, the worker should caution group members against sharing areas of vulnerability without thinking and should help them to make careful, informed, and deliberate decisions about sharing this information. The worker should encourage group members to take their time in developing their comfort with and their position in the group. The worker should not tell the members *not* to use or invest in the group but should tell them to go slowly and to develop their relationships as group members gradually, rather than expecting to make disclosures and develop closeness immediately.

Composing the Group

Given the power of the environment discussed above, it is important for the social worker to think carefully about the composition of the group. Klein (1972, chapter 2) discusses some key considerations in the selection of members for a group, and Kurland (2005) talks about the importance of a purposeful approach to planning a group. The emphasis is on balance and compatibility. The group members may not have many things in common, but they must at least have a common goal and some complementary characteristics in terms of similar life experiences or behavioral attributes (Bertcher & Maple, 1985). In a correctional institution, one of the main things that people have in common is their status as inmates. For this reason, it is useful to think about forming the group from the living unit on which the inmates are held. Because of the size of some living units, this may mean that the group would be a subset of the living unit composed of people who have a similar identified need. Groups based on living units ensure that offenders in the group have the same security status and, generally speaking, the same behavioral capacity in terms of their overall relationship to the institution. When the group is composed on this basis, the potential for rivalries based on differing levels of privilege or risk is minimized. In addition, their presence on the same living unit allows the inmates to develop their relationships outside of the group more completely if they choose to do so. They have the opportunity to discuss issues raised in the group outside of meetings without concern about violating the confidentiality of the group. The group is thereby a more real or authentic experience because it is relevant to their lives, rather than existing for 1 or 2 hours a week apart from their other realities.

Even though the residents of the same living unit share similar security issues, they may not share the same desire to make changes in their lives. For this reason, the social worker should screen potential group members closely for their motivation to make use of a group. As mentioned earlier, the issue of motivation to change is complex in the prison environment. The worker must not confuse motivation with level of difficulty; that is, the worker must not assume that the inmates with the best social skills who can easily articulate reasons for being in the group are necessarily more motivated than inmates who experience more difficulty in presenting themselves succinctly and who express more concern about their ability to change. Many inmates who genuinely want to make changes find it difficult to do so without the guidance of a group and may appear at first to be resistant or hesitant because they are unsure about what is possible. The more articulate inmates can sometimes be those who are not interested in change but rather in using the group to improve their chances for parole or to increase their privileges within the institution. The social worker should attempt to determine the level of need of the inmate for the group and should attempt to group inmates accordingly.

Open or Closed Group

Both open- and closed-ended groups are possible and desirable in correctional settings. The group structure will vary depending on the purpose of the group. Some purposes can be met without developing a high level of cohesion among the members and therefore can be carried out in an open-ended format. These tend to be groups in which the social worker is attempting to provide an educational service that also gives the members a chance to become comfortable enough to ask questions and to solicit advice from both the social worker and other group members. In constructing a group on these lines, the social worker should be clear as to what he or she wants to accomplish and in the case of some particularly volatile institutions should not expect a high level of cohesion or intimacy to develop among the members (Lang, 1987; Schopler & Galinsky, 1985, 1990; Sulman, 1987).

If the social worker wants to create a group atmosphere in which the members can safely discuss deeply felt personal struggles and challenges, the worker must recognize that an open-ended group is generally not capable of providing that opportunity. This is particularly true in the correctional institution. The worker needs to develop a climate of safety in order to facilitate successful work at this level. There are some notable exceptions to this general observation, which usually characterize groups that consist of a small number of inmates sharing a common residence (unit or halfway house) where the turnover of inmates is usually low and where the social worker uses the principles of the mainstream model mentioned earlier (Wright, 1993). The worker must determine to what extent a closed-ended group is possible in his or her setting.

Can a group of 10 or 12 inmates meet together regularly for a significant period of time without fear of losing much of the membership to parole, discharge, or transfer to another institution?

The worker will need to be familiar enough with the setting, and with the policies and practices concerning the transfer of inmates, to be able to ensure stability of membership.

COMMON GROUP WORK THEMES

Substance Abuse

Many studies of prisoners indicate that substance abuse is reported by considerably more than half of them (Begin et al., 2006). This may include alcoholism, drug abuse, or both. Some offenders are incarcerated because of drug abuse but many have been convicted of robberies committed to obtain money to buy drugs. Group work with substance abusers can take the form of structured group interaction with education about the risks of drug abuse. However, most prisoners are already experiencing the consequences of drug abuse, and want and need an opportunity to explore alternatives, share their fears, and talk about the lifestyle they have developed around their addiction. While it is not necessary to structure a closed group experience in order to provide education, it may be necessary to ensure a closed-group opportunity for the exploration and integration of the information and in which the difficult concept of changing the drug or alcohol lifestyles can be addressed. Peat and Winfree (1992) studied the progress of drug-addicted inmates and found that they performed better and reported more success in a therapeutic prison community, that is, on a unit devoted to the treatment of such addicts, rather than when worked with in open-ended groups.

They maintain that the closed unit was the only way in which the effects of the subculture could be counteracted or negated. When a therapeutic milieu and even a closed group are not possible, it is important, as noted earlier, to attempt to control the intake and exits from the group so that the opportunity exists to develop a level of trust and openness. This is supported by more recent similar work (Varis et al., 2006).

Relationship Issues

Some offenders have families that they have left behind when they entered prison. Many other offenders have burned their bridges in terms of family and other relationships and are searching for reasons for their failure in this area. Groups dealing with relationship issues should be conducted separately for these two populations. Inmates who are experiencing family and/or marital separations will not have much in common with those who are having problems finding positive relationships nor will they have much tolerance for them. Men, and especially women, who have spouses and children who visit them, frequently experience a great deal of guilt about being incarcerated and fear that they will lose their families as a result. These people need a group to share their experience of this difficult life situation and to gain mutual support.

Those inmates, usually young men, who have difficulty forming and maintaining relationships often exhibit a wider range of difficulties. They are usually more unsocialized and antisocial in a variety of ways, and may require life and social skills training before they can begin to deal with more complex relationship issues. For these men, the worker will need to provide a higher degree of structure than might otherwise be required in group work with inmates. Some individual work may be necessary before group membership is possible. A clear educational format in which a certain degree of didactic instruction and dyadic practice/role-play are provided will be necessary. This is a group in which co-leadership (Wright, 2002) is advisable because of the demanding nature of the inmate client whose unsocialized behavior is demonstrated in an inability to sustain focus in a group. Such groups often resemble groups of latency-age children who require activities as well as opportunities for talk and sharing.

Aggression Management

Some inmates identify themselves as having problems with their tempers and/or are described as being assaultive or explosive by people in the community or in prison. Unfortunately, these offenders have often used their aggression as a method of coping both inside and outside prison. Some of them may be the same inmates who identify themselves as having problems in developing close relationships with others. They will need to explore their use of violence as a means of coping with perceived threats or getting what they want. They need to explore the effects of violence on their own lives and on the lives of those with whom they attempt to become close. Structured anger anger management techniques are important to incorporate into this group, but they will not be sufficient. These inmates need opportunities to share their histories of powerlessness and their own feelings of vulnerability and threat so that they can experience openness without threat and have opportunities to practice anger management and conflict resolution techniques outside of a structured group. As noted above, they may need some individual work prior to being referred to group. This individual work could focus on reducing their anxiety about joining a group by using systematic desensitization techniques through which they can learn to improve their listening skills before becoming group members.

Abuse

Issues of abuse are evident in inmate populations, both perpetrators and victims. Although there is some debate about the long-term effects of abuse on eventual criminality, Widom (1989a, 1989b, 1989c, 1989d, 1999, 2000), McGloin and

Widom (2001), and English, Widom, and Brandford (2002), in a series of studies on the methodological weaknesses in research into the possible link between child abuse and the development of adult pathology, found a higher rate of delinquency and adult criminality in a study of individuals who were abused as children than in a nonabused control group. Dutton and Hart (1992) found that in inmates who reported having been abused as children, there was a significant correlation between the type of crime they committed and the kind of abuse they had experienced. Dutton and Hart recommend that consideration be given to providing treatment for the posttraumatic stress disorder symptoms that these inmates may exhibit. Those who have been abused and have not become abusers should not be put into groups with abusers. Byrd and Davis (2009) studied the traumatic effects of abuse as possible predictors of violent behavior in women. They conclude that "continued research in this area has possible implications for implementing more trauma-focused interventions within correctional centers for women and a stronger trauma-based focus within violence prevention programs" (p. 390). Female survivors of abuse should not be put into co-correctional or coeducational situations with men with whom they may feel at risk. As well, it may be most efficacious to put men who have been abused and are abusers in groups separate from others in order to explore how both of these complex areas interact in their particular circumstances.

Men who are abusive need to discuss their experiences of abuse as children, but the primary focus of any group with this population must be on their responsibility for the abuse and their plans for ensuring that they will not be abusive in the future (Chovanec, 2009; Rooney & Chovanec, 2004). Goldberg-Wood and Middleman (1992) described a process for working with men who batter that incorporates challenges to the men's view of women as chattel and that allows the men to make changes in their perceptual and value systems. Their model is also valuable, with some modifications, for work with men who sexually abuse both women and children. Social workers who are attempting to provide service to male abusers should always have information from sources other than the offender about the nature of the abusive behavior and, if possible, the degree of harm done by him. These men will usually minimize both their responsibility for the abuse and the harm done. Good assessment increases the worker's effectiveness (Evans, 2003).[3]

Several helpful texts focus on relapse prevention (e.g., Witkiewitz & Marlatt, 2007). However, many relapse prevention groups do not allow the group to develop in the way the mainstream model of social work with groups suggests is possible and necessary. These approaches can be useful if the worker incorporates a social group work approach. Caplan and Thomas (2003, 2004) and talk about the drawbacks of structured group formats with this population and the need to work flexibly at the group member's pace so as not to reinforce patriarchal attitudes.

Some education (Roffman, 2004) is necessary with abusive men, especially input that challenges their notions of patriarchy and examines concepts of male socialization. The idea of biology as destiny, and the resultant excuses and sense of entitlement that these ideas foster, must be challenged. But these men must also have the opportunity to develop as a group and to explore the meaning of their behavior to themselves and to others.

Women who have been incarcerated for offenses involving child abuse and neglect need to be approached differently in groups than men who commit similar or other acts of abuse (Breton, 1979; Butler & Vintram, 1991; Home, 1991; Lewis, 1992; Lovell et al., 1992). They have had different socialization and life experiences and react differently to being convicted of child abuse. Breton (1979) describes the ways in which these women need to be "nurtured" in order to be helped to change abusive patterns.

Coping with Stigma

Most inmates raise issues at some point related to the label that they carry as identified criminals. They present this label as an impediment to any change in behavior that they may wish to make regarding both personal relationships and job opportunities. They need group experiences in which they can share their fears and needs in terms of strategies to deal with the label they have earned through deviant behavior in the past. The group experience gives them the chance to talk about common concerns while attempting to achieve a common solution to a problem that inmates have always shared.

Discharge Planning

The issue of stigma may be addressed on its own in a specifically formed group or it may be discussed in groups on discharge planning, one of the most frequently identified needs of prison inmates. Inmates should be encouraged to think about planning for their discharge from the time of their admission, particularly in times of high unemployment, low welfare rates and increasing problems finding housing for marginalized people. However, a group dealing with this discharge, in order to be most effective, should be composed of inmates who are reasonably close to discharge. In this way, the focus of the group can be real and immediate. As well, group members can be encouraged to think about community services or groups that may be helpful in their reintegration. Members can also be supported in efforts to arrange appointments with these resource services prior to their discharge, or supported for temporary absences from the institution close to the time of discharge, or encouraged to arrange appointments soon after their release.

As noted earlier, this group could be either open- or closed-ended. If it is open-ended, the turnover of members should not be so great at any one time that the group repeatedly has to spend a great deal of time dealing with issues of trust.

Identity

Depending on the demographics of the prisoners in the group, the social workers may deal with issues of race and culture in all group interactions. In some institutions, the prisoners may belong to different racial groups and may benefit from specialized services. Usually the racial groups present will consist of several cultural subgroups, so the group should not be considered homogeneous. There will probably be a common ground on which to meet, however, since the experience of oppression and the history of the group may be unifying themes. For example, native inmates in many Canadian prisons come from a range of tribal groups but they have as shared themes of displacement, attempts at cultural genocide, similar understandings of native spirituality, and practices that have a common core, although they may vary. These are self-help groups in terms of their organizational style. Institutional social workers are directly involved in these group programs. The groups are guided by members of Native Sons organizations from the community. The role of the social worker is to develop and maintain links with these community organizations so that they come into the prison to provide the service.

AIDS

AIDS continues to be a significant issue in prison populations because of the significant number of inmates with a history of intravenous drug use. Inmates are at high risk of contracting and/or passing on the human immunodeficiency virus (HIV).through continuing drug use in prison and practices like tattooing with dirty needles.[4] This makes social work intervention important in a number of ways. First, social workers should work with health care professionals and community AIDS organizations to develop and deliver educational programs that help inmates and correctional staff understand how AIDS is transmitted and what precautions they should take with respect to drug use and sexual practices. Second, social workers should work with inmates who are HIV positive to provide both education and support. Groups are useful in both of these situations (Froeror, 2009). Education about AIDS presented in groups allows the group members to discuss their fears and misconceptions and to have them addressed. Group work with inmates who are HIV positive can provide them with mutual support in what is a difficult life circumstance in any environment but one that is further complicated by the fact that the prison environment is even more afraid of and hostile to them than many communities would be. As well, these individuals do not have ready access to AIDS support groups and to supportive family and friends.

Working with Female Offenders[5]

As noted at the beginning of this chapter and as alluded to above, female offenders as a group may have some problems in common with male offenders, but generally the approach to meeting their needs has to be different (Adelberg & Currie, 1993; Axon, 1989; Gelsthorpe & Morris, 1990; Trotter, 2006). Women are frequently attempting to cope with issues related to their children. They are concerned about what is happening to their children while they are incarcerated and about how their children perceive them as inmates or as bad mothers who have deserted them. They are also worried about the staff of the social agencies concerned with their children. They feel powerless and without sufficient resources to cope with the day-to-day reality of prison and the pressures created by their children and other family members. These women need to explore their feelings, to provide support for each other, and to discuss how to cope with and reduce their feeling of powerlessness. Some women who have been abused will display self-mutilating behavior[6] while incarcerated. Both the women and the institutional staff will need considerable help in dealing with this issue positively. Schilller (2007) discusses a relational model of group development that is particularly useful in working with women but that she contends can be productive for all people in vulnerable positions.

Women who have been prostitutes may need to come together in groups to identify and work on the issues that this occupation has created for them. A feminist perspective should be used in work with all women but is imperative in this type of group (Moyer, 1992). Women need to enter groups without feeling that they will be judged as "bad women." They may be especially sensitive to male workers because of their experience with the sexuality of some males. Social workers should take this into account in planning any intervention. Saulnier (2003) describes a feminist social group work approach that enables women to set their own goals and work towards them without judgmental interference from the worker.

RECOMMENDED WAYS OF WORKING

As noted earlier, the social worker must always consider the correctional environment as part of the client "package."

> Male offenders of a correctional center asked for a group to talk about issues concerning relationships with women. In the third group session, one member brought up concerns about his performance in sexual relationships with women. Another member, a leader on the living unit, expressed disapproval about discussing this material in front of the female social worker. The disgruntled member refused to participate and sat in stony silence, nonverbally disapproving of the group members' attempts at discussion. All efforts on the part of group members to address his silent control of the process failed. Finally, he announced that he would not be returning. The social worker met with the inmate alone after the group session. She indicated that there was no possibility of a male worker replacing her and that the group was important to the members. She was careful to discuss the fact that any influence that he brought to bear on the remaining members of the group living on the unit might seriously damage the usefulness of the group.

He agreed to come back for the next session, explain his position, and attempt to reassure the group members that he would not make fun of them or otherwise harass them about their continuing membership. After he did so, the members appeared to be reassured both by the fact that he was no longer there and by his stated intention to respect their group. In the next two sessions, group members dealt directly and indirectly with issues of trust. The worker recognized the need for the group to deal with these basic forming issues and did not push the group. In the third session after the crisis, the members once again began to discuss concerns about sexuality. The remaining sessions were characterized by increasing openness and comfort in dealing with sensitive relationship issues.

The success of the group was determined by the worker's handling of the threat posed by the disgruntled inmate and by her understanding of the importance of the feeling of safety to the members. Safety and competence are primary issues for inmates in groups. Workers must always keep them in mind.

Lee (1994) has developed a useful framework for assessing the client that is particularly appropriate for the correctional setting, which she titles "Assessment for Empowerment" (pp. 143–145). The social work role in correctional facilities is to help the client group to become socialized to the possibility of positive, satisfying, nonexploitive relationships. As noted above, to do this, the worker must overcome the skepticism of both inmates and correctional officers. To be genuinely helpful, the social worker must help clients develop skills that will help them reach their fullest potential. This will involve the use of empowerment approaches summarized as follows: social work practice with groups encompasses both intervention within the group and intervention outside the group, that is, that the group is both a context and an instrument of change involving actions by the group and its members inside group meetings as well as actions by the group and its members in situations outside the group (Moore & Starkes, 1992, p. 183).

However, the worker must use considerable judgment and careful planning in deciding what form that empowerment takes. Advocacy for and empowerment approaches with inmates should not set up the inmates or allow them to set themselves up for failure or punishment. On the other hand, approaches that do not include empowerment treat inmates as incapable of positive and reasonable social action.

Women in a local jail were concerned because the director did not allow many community leaves. They discussed their anger about the difficulty of achieving these privileges, and one particularly angry inmate advocated a hunger strike as a way of "getting back at" the director. Other women jumped on the bandwagon and began to plan the protest. The social worker leading the group asked the members to pause and think about the possible negative consequences to them of this course of action. After they listed several, she guided them into a discussion of what other courses of action might be more effective. They concluded with a general discussion about how to get what they wanted in prison in ways that did not make them more vulnerable.

Training is necessary to help inmates overcome their sense that lawful or traditional ways of trying to solve problems do not work for them. They will need to practice empowerment strategies within institutions, but they must be helped to choose and plan strategies that have a very high probability of success. The social worker must have a very good working knowledge of the particular correctional environment in order to know what these opportunities might be.

Group workers like Lee (1982, 1989, 1994; and in Schwartz, 1978), Breton (1979, 1985, 1989), Jacobs (1964), and Brooks (1978) give graphic examples of the effectiveness of the social group work method in helping people to take an active part in decisions that affect them. Giving inmates the opportunity to experience relationship-building and decision-making successes while they are in the institution helps them to feel better about their chances for achieving similar success in the community when they are released and lifts some of the depression that is a constant reality for them as prisoners. Middleman and Goldberg-Wood's structural model of social work, originally described in 1974 and further developed in subsequent publications (Goldberg-Wood & Middleman, 1989, 1991, 1992; Middleman & Goldberg-Wood, 1991), helps the worker to keep his or her focus on the clients as whole persons who are capable of self-determination while still keeping the reality of their limitations in view.

EVALUATION APPROACHES

Social workers in correctional institutions are always faced with the problem of determining success or failure in their work with clients in almost life-or-death terms. The traditional test of success with offenders is whether or not they offend again. This information may tell the social workers something about the offender's experience of incarceration in general, but the absence of a return to jail does not necessarily entitle the social workers to claim that his or her group was a success. Nor is a return to jail an indication of a group's failure. Research into correctional treatment indicates that many factors have to be taken into consideration (MacKenzie, 2006). The worker must then decide how to judge the utility of the intervention for the members of the group. One way of doing this is through a qualitative study of the life of the group. An analysis of the group's progress may tell the worker whether the group was able to do the work for which it contracted. Did the members use the group in a meaningful way? Did they discuss the issues that they agreed to at the outset of the group? Did all members make use of the group? Was there a high dropout rate? Did the group end prematurely? Did the members express satisfaction with the group while it was meeting? In addition to a qualitative analysis of the group's ongoing functioning, the social worker can conduct exit interviews with the participants to learn about their experience with the group. The worker can also give the group members a written questionnaire before the group begins, asking for their expectations of the group, and another questionnaire at the end asking whether the original expectations were met. The questionnaires may be anonymous so that the fear of consequences can be minimized if members have negative feedback about the group experience. As well, the social worker should ask front-line correctional staff for their impressions of the usefulness of the group, either at the end or while it is still ongoing. Some front-line workers may not support the notion of rehabilitation of inmates and may feel that groups are useless in general, but many correctional officers will provide concrete feedback on whether the inmate's behavior has been influenced by the group experience.

CONCLUSION

When all is said and done, prison inmates are people who have come from a variety of communities and who may have been engaged in social work interventions in other settings. The primary challenge of the social worker in a prison environment is to come to grips with the fact that this environment is a "shadow client" that must be worked with concurrently as the social worker works with the person. There can be no success without a clear acknowledgment of this reality.

ACKNOWLEDGMENT

I would like to thank members of the social work department of the Ontario Correctional Institute for their suggestions about what should be included in this chapter.

RESOURCES

Social workers should use as many local organizations as are available to them. For example, most communities have AIDS organizations that will provide support to inmates who are HIV positive and education to others. The following national organizations may be helpful in providing workers with local city or province/state groups that could be helpful.

Canadian Association of Elizabeth Fry Societies (CAEFS)
Association Canadienne des Sociétés Elizabeth Fry (ACSEF)

701-151 Slater Street
Ottawa, Ontario, Canada K1P 5H3
(613) 238-2422
(613) 232-7130
CAEFS@web.ca
http://www.elizabethfry.ca/

Women's Prison Association
110 Second Avenue
New York, NY 10003
(646) 336-6100
(646) 292-7763
http://www.wpaonline.org/

John Howard Society
809 Blackburn Mews
Kingston, Ontario, Canada K7P 2N6
(613) 384-6272
(613) 384-1847
national@johnhoward.ca
http://www.johnhoward.ca/

National Institute on Drug Abuse
6001 Executive Boulevard, Room 5213
Bethesda, MD 20892-9561
Information@lists.nida.nih.gov
http://www.drugabuse.gov/

National Prison Project
733 15th Street, NW, Suite 620
Washington, DC 20005-2302
(202) 393-4930
(202) 393-4931
http://www.nsvrc.org/organizations/193

REFERENCES

Adelberg, E. & Currie, C. (eds.). (1993). *In conflict with the law: Women and the Canadian justice system.* Vancouver: Press Gang.
Adler, F., Mueller, G. O. W. & Laufer, W. S. (2000). *Criminology.* New York: McGraw-Hill.
Axon L. (1989). *Model and exemplary programs for female inmates: An international review.* Ottawa: Solicitor General of Canada.

Begin, P., Weekes J., & Thomas, G. (2006). The Canadian Addiction Survey: Substance use and misuse among the Canadian population. *Forum on Corrections Research*, *18*(1).

Becker, J. V. & Quinsey, V. L. (1993). Assessing suspected child molesters. *Child Abuse and Neglect*, *17*, 169–174.

Behroozi, C. S. (1992). A model for social work with involuntary applicants in groups. *Social Work with Groups*, *15*, 223–238.

Bertcher, H. J. (1994). *Group participation: Techniques for leaders and members*. Thousand Oaks, CA: Sage.

Bertcher, H. J. & Maple, F. (1985). Elements and issues in group composition. In M. Sundel, P. Glasser, R. Sarri, & R. Vinter (eds.), *Individual change in small groups* (pp. 186–208). New York: Free Press.

Breton, M. (1979). Nurturing abused and abusive mothers: The hairdressing group. *Social Work with Groups*, *2*(2), 161–174.

Breton, M. (1985). Reaching and engaging people: Issues and practice principles. *Social Work with Groups*, *8*(3), 7–21.

Breton, M. (1989). The need for mutual aid groups in a drop-in for homeless women: The sistering case. In J. A. B. Lee (ed.), *Group work with the poor and oppressed* (pp. 47–59). New York: Haworth.

Breton, M. (1991). Toward a model of social groupwork practice with marginalized populations. *Groupwork*, *4*(1), 31–47.

Brooks, A. (1978). Group work in the Bowery. *Social Work with Groups*, *1*(1), 53–63.

Butler, S. & Wintram, C. (1991). *Feminist groupwork*. Newbury Park, CA: Sage.

Byrd, P. M. & Davis, J. L. (2009). Violent behaviour in female inmates: Possible predictors. *Journal of Interpersonal Violence*, *24*(2).

Caplan, T. & Thomas, H. (2004) If we are all in the same canoe, why are we using different paddles? The effective use of common themes in diverse group situations. *Social Work With Groups*, *27*(1), 53–73.

Caplan, T. & Thomas, H. (2003). "If this is week three, we must be doing 'feelings'": An essay on the importance of client-paced group work. *Social Work With Groups*, *26*(3), 5–14.

Chovanec, M. G. (2009). Facilitating change in group work with abusive men: Examining stages of change. *Social Work With Groups*, *32*(1), 125–142.

Cullen, F. T., Latessa, E. J., Burton, V. S., Jr., & Lombardo, L. X. (1993). The correctional orientation of prison wardens: Is the rehabilitative ideal supported? *Criminology*, *31*(1), 69–92.

Cullen, F. T., (2007). Criminology and public policy. *Behavior*, *6*(4), 717–727.

Dutton, D. G. & Hart, S. D. (1992). Evidence of long-term, specific effects of childhood abuse and neglect on criminal behaviour in men. *International Journal of Offender Therapy and Comparative Criminology*, *36*(2), 129–137.

English, D. J., Widom, C. S., & Brandford, C. (2002). Childhood victimization and delinquency, adult criminality, and violent criminal behavior: A Replication and Extension, Final Report. US Department of Justice. http://www.ncjrs.gov/pdffiles1/nij/grants/192291.pdf

Evans, D. (2003). Assessment and management of sexual and violent offenders. *Corrections Today*, *65*(4), 114–116.

Froerer, A. S., Smock, S. A., & Seedall, R. B. (2009). Solution-focused group work: Collaborating with *Clients Diagnosed* with HIV/AIDS. *Journal of Family Psychotherapy, 20*(1), 13–27.

Gelsthorpe, L. & Morris, A.. (eds.). (1990). *Feminist perspectives in criminology.* Philadelphia: Open University Press.

Goffman, E. (1963). *Asylums: Essays on the social situations of mental patients and other inmates.* New York: Doubleday.

Goldberg-Wood, G. & Middleman, R. R. (1989). *The structural approach to direct practice in social work.* New York: Columbia University Press.

Goldberg-Wood, G. & Middleman, R. R. (1991). Advocacy and social action: Key elements in the structural approach to direct practice in social work. *Social Work with Groups, 14,* 53–63.

Goldberg-Wood, G. & Middleman, R. R. (1992). Recasting the die: A small group approach to giving batterers a chance to change. *Social Work with Groups, 15,* 5–18.

Griffiths, C. (2004). *Canadian criminology* (2nd ed.). Vancouver: Nelson Education

Hayman, S. (2006). *Imprisoning our sisters: The new federal women's prison's in Canada.* Montreal: McGill-Queen's University Press.

Home, A. M. (1991). Mobilizing women's strengths of social change: The group connection. *Social Work with Groups, 14,* 153–154.

Howells, K. & Day, A. (2007) Readiness for treatment in high risk offenders with personality disorders. *Psychology, Crime and Law, 13,* 47–56.

Jacobs, J. (1964). Social action as therapy in a mental hospital. *Social Work, 9*(1), 54–61.

Kershaw, A. & Lasovitch, M. (1991). *Rock-a-bye baby: A death behind bars.* Toronto: McClelland & Stewart.

Klein A. F. (1972). *Effective groupwork: An introduction to principle and method.* Bloomfield, CT: Practitioners Press.

Kurland, R. (2005). Planning: The neglected component of group development. *Social Work with Groups, 28*(3/4), 9–16.

Kong, R. & AuCoin, K. (2008). Female offenders in Canada. Juristat. Statistics Canada. Catalogue No. 85-002, Vol. 28, No. 1.

Lang, N. (1988). Social work practice in small social forms: Identifying collectivity. *Social Work with Group, 9*(4), 7–32.

Laws, D. R. (1989). *Relapse prevention with sex offenders.* New York: Guilford Press.

Lee, J. A. B. (1982). The group: A chance at human connection for the mentally impaired older person. *Social Work with Groups, 5*(2), 43–55.

Lee, J. A. B. (1994). *The empowerment approach to social work practice.* New York: Columbia University Press.

Lee, J. A. B. (ed.). (1989). *Group work with the poor and oppressed.* New York: Haworth Press.

Lewis, E. (1992). Regaining promise: Feminist perspectives for social group work practice. *Social Work with Group, 15,* 271–284.

Lovell, M. L., Reid, K., & Richey, C. A. (1992). Social support training for abusive mothers. *Social Work with Groups, 15,* 95–108.

MacKenzie, D. L. 2006. *What works in corrections reducing the criminal activities of offenders and delinquents.* New York: Cambridge University Press.

McCorkle, R. C. (1992). Personal precautions to violence in prison. *Criminal Justice and Behavior, 19*(2), 160–173.

McGloin, J. M. & Widom, C. S. (2001). Resilience among abused and neglected children grown up. *Development and Psychopathology, 13*(4), 1021–1038.

Middleman, R. R. & Goldberg-Wood, G. (1991). *Skills for direct practice social work.* New York: Columbia University Press.

Moore, E. E. & Starkes, A. J. (1992). The group in institution as the unit of attention: Recapturing and refining a social work tradition. *Social Work with Group, 15*, 171–192.

Moyer, I. L. (1992). *The changing roles of women in the criminal justice system.* Prospect Heights, IL: Waveland Press.

Papell, C. P. & Rothman, B. (1980). Social group work models: Possession and heritage. In A. Alissi (ed.), *Perspectives in social groupwork practice* (pp. 66–77). New York: Free Press.

Peat, B. J. & Winfree, L. T. (1992). Reducing the intra-institutional effects of "prisonization": A study of a therapeutic community for drug-using inmates. *Criminal Justice and Behavior, 19*(2), 206–225.

Roffman, R. (2004). Psychoeducational groups. In C. D. Garvin, L. M. Gutierrez, & M. J. Galinsky (eds.), *Handbook of social work with groups* (pp. 160–175). New York: Guilford Press.

Rooney, R. & Chovanec, M. (2004). Group work in involuntary settings. In C. D. Garvin, L. M. Gutierrez, & M. J. Galinsky (eds.), *Handbook of social work with groups* (pp. 212–226). New York: Guilford Press.

Scudder, R. G., Blount, W. R., Heide, K. M., & Silverman, I. J. (1993). Important links between child abuse, neglect and delinquency. *International Journal of Offender Therapy and Comparative Criminology, 37*(4), 315–323.

Schiller, L.Y. (2007). Not for women only: Applying the relational model of group development with vulnerable populations. *Social Work With Groups, 30*(2), 11–26.

Schopler, J. H. & Galinsky, M. J. (1984). Meeting practice needs: Conceptualizing the open-ended group. *Social Work with Groups, 7*(2), 3–21.

Schwartz, W. (1978). Rosalie. *Social Work with Groups, 1*(3), 265–278.

Saulnier, C. F. (2003). Goal setting process: Supporting choice in a feminist group for women with alcohol problems. *Social Work With Groups, 26*(1), 47–68.

Sulman, J. (1987). The worker's role in collectivity. *Social Work with Group, 9*(4), 59–67.

Sykes, G. (1958). *The society of captives: A study of a maximum security prison.* Princeton, NJ: Princeton University Press.

Spjeldnes, S. & Goodkind, S. (2009) Gender differences and offender reentry: A review of the literature. *Journal of Offender Rehabilitation, 48*, 314–335.

Trotter, C. (2006). *What works with women offenders.* Australia: Willan Publishing.

Trotter, C. (2006). *Working with involuntary clients: A guide to practice.* Australia: Allen and Unwin.

U.S. Department of Justice. (2008). Bureau of Justice statistics. http://www.ojp.usdoj.gov/bjs/welcome.html

Varis, D. D., Lefebvre, D., & Grant, B. A. (2006). Intensive support units for federal offenders with substance abuse problems: An impact analysis. *Forum on Corrections, 18*(1).

Widom, C. S. (1989a). Child abuse, neglect and violent criminal behavior. *Criminology, 27*(2), 251–271.

Widom, C. S. (1989b). Child abuse, neglect and adult behavior: Research design and findings on criminality, violence and child abuse. *American Journal of Orthopsychiatry, 59*(3), 355–366.

Widom, C. S. (1989c). Does violence beget violence? A critical examination of the literature. *Psychological Bulletin, 106*(1), 3–28.

Widom, C. S. (1989d). The cycle of violence. *Science, 244*, 160–165.

Widom, C. S. (1999). Posttraumatic stress disorder in abused and neglected children grown
up. *American Journal of Psychiatry, 156*(8), 1223–1229.

Widom, C. S. (2000). Understanding the consequences of childhood victimization. In R.
M. Reece (ed.), *The treatment of child abuse* (pp. 339–361). Baltimore, MD: Johns
Hopkins University Press.

Witkiewitz, K. & Marlatt, G. A. (2007). *Therapist's guide to evidence-based relapse prevention.* Chichester, West Sussex, England/Hoboken, NJ: John Wiley & Sons.

Wright, M. M. (1993). Family-like group in a correctional setting. *Social Work with Group,
16*(4), 125–135.

Wright, M. M. (2002). Co-facilitation: fashion or function? *Social Work with Groups, 25*,
77–93.

NOTES

1 Middleman and Goldberg-Wood's (1991) quadrant model is useful in thinking about
working with clients within this context.

2 See Behroozi (1992) for a schema of pregroup and group behaviors suggested for social
workers dealing with involuntary clients and Trotter (2006) for a text on working with
this population in a variety of settings.

3 For a debate on the currently popular use of risk assessment tools with offenders, see
2007 *Canadian Journal of Criminology and Criminal Justice,49*(4).

4 For a discussion of this issue, see *Evaluation Report: Correctional Service Canada's Safer
Tattooing Practices Pilot Initiative* (http://www.csc-scc.gc.ca/text/pa/ev-tattooing-394-
2-39/ev-tattooing-394-2-39_e.pdf).

5 Judith Lee's (1994) book *The Empowerment Approach to Social Work Practice* (New York:
Columbia University Press) is particularly useful in work with women in these
circumstances.

6 Any social worker dealing with incarcerated women should read the 1991 biography of
Marlene Moore by Anne Kershaw and Mary Lasovitch, *Rock A Bye Baby: A Death Behind
Bars* (Toronto: McClelland and Stewart). This work is particularly helpful in educating
social workers about self-mutilation behaviors.

Part Four

Gay Men and Lesbian Issues

Chapter Seventeen

Group Work With Gay Men

Steven Ball and Benjamin Lipton

Social group work with gay men developed and continues to evolve in response to a history of mental health services that started from a predominantly pathological stance that regarded homosexuals as mentally ill to an affirmative model that assists these men in asserting their equal, healthy, and ethical place in society (Abelove; 1993; Gonsiorek, 1985; Isay, 1996, Ritter & Terndrup, 2002). Since the psychosocial issues facing all gay men are the result of adapting to an environment that still denies them recognition and acceptance, groups serving this population can provide a healing antidote to a lifelong history of second class citizenship. The developmental process of growing up in a world generally hostile to same sex love creates a stigmatized identity for all gay men. Even four decades after the Stonewall Riot signaled gay liberation and ever increasing numbers of gay men began living openly, gay affirmative psychotherapy regards homophobia—antihomosexual attitudes and behaviors (O'Hanlan et al., 1997)—rather than homosexuality as the major pathological variable affecting the mental health of this population (Margolies, Becker, & Jackson-Brewer, 1987; Meyer, 1995). As a result, it is essential that workers understand the overriding psychosocial factors arising from homophobia that inform individual responses to particular environmental stressors and life issues. Societal and internalized homophobia, stigmatization, coming out, familial, work and social relationships, and the powerful impact of HIV are concerns that continue to inform the process of all group work with gay men, regardless of the specific commonalities around which these groups may be organized. While the psychosocial needs and experiences of gay men are as diverse as those of any other minority group, this chapter will provide essential clinical information about the above issues that can inform practice with more specific subgroups of the population in a variety of social service settings.

REVIEW OF THE LITERATURE

Any overview of the social service and mental health literature on gay men must be understood within the rapidly changing social context of the past four decades

(Abelove, 1993; Adamczyck & Pitt, 2009; Duberman, 1991; Miller, 2006; Signorile, 1997; Stein & Cohen, 1986). The response of social workers to those with a same-sex orientation reflects the historical progression from pathology to ambivalence across all mental health professions. Prior to 1973, when the American Psychiatric Association officially declassified homosexuality as pathological, gay men were considered mentally ill or perverse because of their sexual object choice. While a small but dedicated group of influential practitioners to this day remain committed to labeling homosexuality an illness (Cohen, 2000; Nicolosi, 1991), growing numbers of gay and lesbian mental health practitioners, including many social workers (Deyton & Lear, 1988; Getzel, 1998), have united with an increasingly vocal and organized gay community in leading the way toward dismantling homophobic myths and creating a psychosocial model for healthy homosexuality. By openly challenging traditional models of pathology and exposing their lack of empirical support (Friedman & Downey, 1993), these men and women have paved the way toward developing an alternative, affirmative practice base for working with gay and lesbian clients.

Practitioners began developing a significant body of literature on the theory and practice of gay affirmative counseling and psychotherapy prior to the onset of AIDS in the early 1980s (Bell & Weinberg, 1978; Cass, 1979; Coleman, 1982; Gonsiorek, 1977). During this same period, psychotherapy groups for gay men primarily came out of the private practices and agency work of increasing numbers of openly gay mental health practitioners who were responding to the long-suppressed needs of their clients. Reviews of the literature on group psychotherapy with this population in the 1980s by Conlin and Smith (1985) and by Schwartz and Hartstein (1986) revealed that there were few articles of their kind that specifically address the role of group work in fostering psychosexual maturation in gay men rather than focusing on a particular psychosocial stressor affecting this population. Their articles documented the ongoing need of designing groups for gay men whose purpose is to foster disclosure of sexual orientation and sexuality, provide opportunities for emotional intimacy, and confront both external stigmatization and internalized homophobia. Outside of personal websites and gay service organizations there still exists a paucity of new research and documentation on general group work with gay men.

How can we account for the gap in the literature over the past decades? We believe there are at least three related reasons. First, many social workers conventionally think of first contacts as individual, often relegating group treatment to a secondary or auxiliary position in treatment. Initial developments in gay affirmative psychotherapy seem to reflect this pattern. Second, at the historical moment when mental health agencies were beginning to sanction the use of affirmative models for group work with gay men, the biopsychosocial crisis of AIDS necessitated an immediate shift in treatment to this population (Caputo, 1985; de la Vega, 1990; Nichols, 1986; Shernoff, 1991). As clients and workers began to view the ongoing external and internal stressors of being self-identified as a gay man through the lens of the human immunodeficiency virus (HIV), the literature on practice with gay men focused on AIDS-related issues of immediate concern and provided a new context in which to understand gay identity development (Burnham, Cadwell, & Forstein, 1994; Isay, 1989; Odets, 1994). Third, self-help has always been a necessary and essential part of the gay experience in a heterosexist, homophobic environment and consistently filled the gap in social services long before mainstream professionals formally responded by incorporating services into their organizations and documenting their work with contributions to the literature (Eller & King, 1990). The most powerful example of this process was the rapid and comprehensive organization of the gay community in response to AIDS when their needs were not addressed by social service agencies.

While much remains to be written about groups for gay men that do not specifically focus on HIV issues, ongoing resources continue to emerge (Getzel, 1998; Lipton, 2004). Nonetheless, the literature on HIV-related group work provides an invaluable resource not only for understanding HIV issues but also for understanding deeper conflicts about being gay that will inform the process of working with any group of gay men (Tunnell, 1994). Regardless of the particular focus of any group, whether or not related to HIV, what is most crucial is the opportunity to build social supports and interpersonal connections. *Homosocialization*, defined as building relationships with other gay men, is essential to the healthy integration of a gay identity and the discovery of positive role models (Isay, 1989). In their discussions of their work with gay populations, Hetrick and Martin (1987), Conlin and Smith (1985), and Schwartz and Hartstein (1986) all suggest that commonly shared issues arising from stigmatization such as social, cognitive, and emotional isolation—the negative outcomes of stigmatization—can best be coped with by creating opportunities for socialization with peers. Despite increasing visibility of gay people and debates in public law and social policy, recent research continues to uphold these earlier findings (Frable et al., 1997, 1998; Greene, 1996; Igreja et al., 2000; Lambda Legal Defense and Education Fund, 1999; Meyer, 1995). Since gay men are one of the few minorities still denied the opportunity to developmentally identify with others like themselves because of both the absence of identifying factors and the oppression of a homonegative environment, group work with this population takes on ever-increasing importance in the lives of its members.

PRACTICE PRINCIPLES

Based on the pervasive impact of stigmatization and homonegativity on gay male development, as well as the need for homosocialization to mitigate the influence of these factors, the following practice principles and procedures should guide a social worker in beginning group work with the population.

Level of Worker Activity Inside and Outside of the Group

The worker's role in any group for gay men extends far beyond facilitating the group process. When developing a group for gay men, the need for outreach and psychoeducation can be guaranteed. Those most in need of a gay men's group may be the hardest to reach, as they remain unaffiliated with the gay community or unacknowledged within it (adolescence) as in the case of HIV-negative men and gay men living with chronic illnesses other than HIV (Ball, 1998; Lipton, 1998, 2004; Odets, 1994). Outreach to the larger, nonspecifically gay environment away from traditional resources for membership such as community centers, bars, and social clubs may provide new awareness not only to those isolated men who could benefit from a gay group but also to the nongay community at large about issues confronting gay men.

While a secondary gain may be public education about the realities of gay life, an essential task of a social worker leading a gay men's group is to educate the staff of his or her social service agency about gay men. In-service training in addition to individual interactions will increase understanding about gay men and their particular issues as well as the potential for referrals. The combined acknowledgment of the community and the agency positively influences the functioning of the group, as potential members see the group as an acceptable and accepted source of support and a safe place to explore their concerns.

When the group process moves from the stage of pregroup formation to the beginning phase of group work, the social worker's role as an educator continues. Not only must the worker lend a vision and contribute data to the group as it begins to take shape, but throughout the life of the group he or she must continue to provide resources, conceptual frameworks, interpersonal modeling, and general education to counter the cognitive and experiential deficits that result from growing up in an environment void of healthy and varied gay role models and gay affirmative information. Implicit in a social worker's vision of the group must be the awareness that a gay person's stigmatization stems from a society—and a gay community— that often dictate a rigid repertoire of physical and social expressions that may impair healthy psychosocial development.

The Group as a Basic Resource

While the leader is initially responsible for guiding the development of group norms and modeling adaptive interpersonal relating, the goal of these interventions is to help group members see themselves as a source of support for each other and to develop a sense of belonging. Gay men often enter groups with a legacy of isolation. Historically, societal groups have been sources of persecution for this population that reinforce a feeling of powerlessness rather than resources for affiliation and validation. When the group recognizes and employs their communal resources for support, group members can begin to counteract their collective history of disenfranchisement. Groups offer an opportunity to clarify emotional priorities and increase their capacity for building cohesive interpersonal networks. To this end, the social worker must consistently introduce, model, and reinforce group norms that invite the group to join with the leader as a basic resource for answers, empathy, and conflict resolution.

Boundaries and Confidentiality

A powerful effect of homophobia and stigmatization has been the internalization by many in the gay community of a narrow sense of identity organized around sex rather than sexual orientation. This reality makes group contracting around the issues of interacting both within and outside of the group of paramount importance in developing an environment of safety and trust. Often group members initially alternate between expressions of excitement and pleasure resulting from identification among members, and fear that the group will become yet another sexualized experience and lose its credibility as a safe space for exploring feelings. To foster and preserve a safe environment, the role of sex within the group process must be addressed from the outset. While setting limits for socialization may include members' abstaining from having sex with each other, it is particularly important in a group where sexual identity is an essential commonality to help members explore how sexual involvement between them would affect the ability of the group to function successfully. A social worker's initial interventions must reflect and normalize sexualized interactions such as flirting among members while helping the group to identify the role of these interactions in defending against emotional intimacy. Modeling an inquisitive stance toward the role of sexuality in initiating relationships in the group empowers members to begin to question what modes of socializing will best fit their needs and help them to realize their treatment goals.

Since gay men have historically had to respond to rather than determine the social norms, boundaries, and limits established by a heterosexual culture, social workers must recognize the interplay between the opportunity for self-determination and the fear of acquiescing to the restrictive norms of a dominant culture. It is the authors' experience that even in large cities that offer some sense of anonymity within the gay community, members may share some past or present social connection to other members. As a result, restricting socialization to the group may, on the one hand, not meet the needs of isolated gay men who would benefit from outside social support and, on the other hand, fail to mesh with the social reality of men already socialized within the gay community. While the group may recognize the need for guidelines on sexual interactions among members, efforts to restrict outside socialization, a common limit in traditional group therapy, need to be explored, contracted, and recontracted throughout the group process.

All of the principles discussed here must be founded on a firm commitment to the guiding group work principle of confidentiality. The leader must actively address the place of confidentiality in the group process and in outside contacts in order to establish a feeling of safety, particularly for those who have yet to speak openly about their sexual orientation. An ongoing exploration of this principle may provide a powerful opening to discussions of stigmatization and shame.

COMMON THEMES

While the themes discussed in this section will assume varying degrees of priority in groups organized around any number of commonalities, including coming out, substance abuse, sexual abuse, parenting, couples, bereavement, HIV status, aging, and socialization, they may also serve as the target issues for which groups for gay men are developed.

Homophobia

The socialization of every gay man still involves exposure to homophobia. The literature refers to the subsequent internalization of the social animosity that a gay man experiences (Hetrick & Martin, 1987) as *internalized homophobia* and widely supports the view that the external and internal impacts of the resulting stigmatization must be addressed in treatment (Hetrick & Martin, 1987; Isay, 1989; Margolies et al., 1987; Silverstein, 1991; Tunnel, 2003). Homophobia frequently manifests itself alongside heterosexism, the culturally conditioned bias that heterosexuality is superior to other sexual orientations (Gonsiorek, 1985; Sears & Williams, 1997).

Homophobia manifests itself in a variety of ways, blatant and subtle, internal and external, within the gay community and in society at large. It is essential to understand, first that recognizing homophobia is not equal to eradicating it and, second, that one's same-sex orientation does not preclude homophobic beliefs and behaviors. Within the group process, homophobia may present as fear of disclosure in general; fear of disclosing one's sexual orientation; fear of commitment to the group; discomfort with more open group members or leaders; generalized rejection of heterosexuality; and denial of social differences between gay and heterosexual men. While some of these manifestations may on the surface seem far from homophobic, exploration of feelings will most often unearth negative attitudes and beliefs about what it means to be a gay man.

Stigmatization and Shame

As previously noted, stigmatization is the inevitable result of developing within a homophobic environment. Stigma is the precursor to shame in the psychosocial development of every gay man (Cadwell, 1992; Cain, 1991; Cornett, 1993). As members begin to share life histories, whether anecdotally in support groups or more formally in psychotherapy groups, common themes of rejection, isolation, violence, and abuse will often surface. This retelling of the impact of stigmatization will frequently find its complement in the current group process. Isensee (1991) and Cornett (1993) carefully outline the process by which shame interferes with interpersonal relating and fosters the development of a false self. Since the legacy of shame leads gay men to embrace negative stereotypes about their potential for developing lasting and important relationships, members may initiate a self-fulfilling prophecy that often results in treating one another in the same hostile/rejecting ways in which they fear being treated themselves.

Coming Out

As a gay man begins to integrate his sexuality, the impact of homophobia and stigmatization on gay male development necessitates a process that the literature defines as coming out—an ongoing developmental process of gay identity formation organized around revealing and accepting one's sexual orientation. Of seminal importance to the coming-out literature have been Coleman's (1982) five-stage model, which describes a developmental process from before coming out to integration, and Cass's (1979) six-stage model, which leads from identity confusion to identity synthesis as the gay man works to synthesize his sexuality with his self-concept. For a review of the coming-out literature that also provides insight into the impact of HIV on gay male development, see Linde (1994) and Martin and Hunter (2001).

In order to understand the impact of any life crisis or stressor around which a group for gay men has been formulated, it is necessary to recognize the impact of coming out on each of the group members and on the group process as a whole (Cass, 1979). As stereotypes and dormant issues of homophobia, self-definition, and self-acceptance are activated by the diverse psychosocial issues and stages of members, a group organized around any task can offer a powerful experience on the coming-out continuum for those just beginning the process, as well as for those more openly identified as gay. Initial movements toward coming out are often limited to sexual experimentation and sexualized socialization in bars, dance clubs, and parties. There are few opportunities to attend to the powerful emotions that generate and are generated by the coming-out experience. Whether beginning to come out or already identified as gay, gay men often arrive at a group with a lack of knowledge related to the diversity of gay lifestyles, range of social outlets, and ways of relating to others like themselves. A gay men's group can serve not only as an emotional anchor to explore turbulent feelings to self and others in regard to a specific common issue. It can also be a window on the diversity of the gay experience as one begins to identify more openly as a gay man and/or to expand one's understanding of what it means to be gay.

HIV

HIV still remains a consistent and often hidden stressor in the daily lives of all gay men, regardless of their HIV status (Burnham et al., 1994; see also Chapter 3). Living with HIV is not only a long-term health issue; it is a mental health issue that may further exacerbate existing stressors related to family, friends, relationships, life choices, and a sense of the future. Agencies may organize groups for gay men presenting with any number of HIV-related issues: adjustment to new HIV conversion, serodiscordant coupling, risk reduction and prevention, or comorbid substance use and abuse (Tunnel, 1994: Gardner & Kosten, 2008).

Regardless of the particular task around which a social worker organizes a group for gay men, and regardless of whether the group task is itself specific to HIV, this concern will undoubtedly appear as a theme in the group process. Gay men of all ages, particularly younger men unaware of the history and reality of AIDS, need to make sense of their identity in a world where HIV remains a powerful force and growing stigma (Kershaw, 2008). In this era, uncertainty remains a powerful challenge for both HIV-positive and -negative gay men. For HIV-negative men, the threat of infection is often looming. Such anxiety may manifest itself in hypervigilance—a preoccupation with any signs of illness at the expense of more productive and fulfilling activities of daily living. For HIV-positive men, the anxiety regarding prognosis and treatment may manifest as depression and a radical reevaluation of life goals. For men who have lived through the worst of AIDS, anxiety may also manifest itself unconsciously as survivor guilt, a complex process through which one maladaptively manages overwhelming feelings of loss and abandonment by acting out a variety of more or less overtly self-destructive behaviors (Odets, 1994).

As gay men struggle with survivor guilt, internalized homophobia, and denial of the realities associated with HIV, they may play out conflicting feelings in unsafe sexual practices or feelings of fear in abstinence. Additionally, challenges to HIV medication adherence can become entangled in psychological struggles that both predate and relate to one's status as HIV positive. These issues require support and exploration toward empowering men to care for themselves most effectively. In an environment in which the link between sex and survival has been turned upside down for over two decades, groups for gay men may offer invaluable forums for normalizing fears, clarifying values, disseminating information, and building a community of concern to mitigate against overwhelming feelings of confusion and isolation that might otherwise lead to self-destructive behavior. To this end, social workers must be willing to take on a psychoeducational role on the issues of protected sex, drug use, and the latest information on HIV. Workers must not only respond to requests for information and discussion but also initiate them. When necessary, they must be prepared to make empathic, attuned interventions to clarify and address maladaptive defense structures of members and foster effective problem-solving skills.

Family Issues

As in group work with any population, the group process recapitulates for each gay member the family dynamics that he brings to the group (Yalom, 1995). For gay men who have most often grown up hiding their true selves from their families

of origin, this aspect of the group process can prove either particularly traumatizing or extremely empowering. Even in families that appear to function well and
attend to the psychosocial needs of all members, apparent attunement can mask
underlying, unintentional emotional abuse. As the family fails even to consider
the possibility that a son, brother, or father may be gay, the gay member remains
silenced by shame, guilt, and secretiveness. If the group process recreates this experience for its members by failing to reach for and affirm self-disclosure and self-
reflection about being gay, then the group will perpetuate emotional trauma. If,
on the other hand, members are made aware of the dynamic of familial recapitula-
tion in the group process and helped to use it to create new scripts of acceptance
and affirmation, then the group can be an important place for developing and
consolidating feelings of empowerment (Cornett, 1993; Isay, 1996).

For many gay men, particularly those who came of age in the period preceding
public debate about the place of gay men within social structures, their definition
of *family* has been expanded to include families of choice in addition to families
of biological origin. Families of choice often develop during the initial stages of
the coming-out process, as gay men have had to look outside of their families for
acceptance and affirmation, as well as for affiliation with other gay men.
Interdependent groups of gay men develop out of this search and provide each
other with the physical and emotional caring that heterosexuals can usually expect
from their families of origin. For some gay men, families of choice may even
replace their families of origin as the primary reservoirs of emotional security.
When working with gay men, it is essential to value and respect the place of these
families within the lives of group members and to assess the roles that a member
may play within his family of choice. Often these roles coincide with earlier roles
played out in a member's family of origin and provide helpful information toward
understanding the interpersonal dynamics that a member may bring to the group.
With older gay men, social workers must also be alert to the devastating impact of
multiple losses and continual grieving on this system of psychosocial support since
the beginning of the AIDS epidemic.

Gender Roles

Popular gay culture seems to have evolved, at least in part, in reaction to the collective childhood trauma of gender role nonconformity (Friedman, 1988).
Literature on gay male development (Isay, 1989; Schwartz & Hartstein, 1986)
suggests that such trauma may begin with a prehomosexual boy's relationship with
his father. Emotional distance and unavailability of fathers often develop out of
the father's conscious or unconscious homophobia and contribute to poor relations between these men and their gay children. Early negative relationships with
fathers then are reinforced as developing gay men continue to interact with heterosexual males in larger social circles. Teased and ostracized for not taking part in
traditionally masculine social and sexual pursuits, gay adolescents and younger

men often develop feelings of shame and insecurity for failing to fit into heterosexual definitions of masculinity. In keeping with theories of oppressed populations, gay men may defend against these feelings by identifying with the same stereotypical images of traditional masculinity that oppress them. Unfortunately, identification with traditional masculine gender roles creates significant problems with building intimacy, trust, and a willingness to depend on other men.

Since many gay men come to groups with scarred self-images and difficulty relating openly to other men, an important task of any social worker will be to foster interdependence and group cohesion by exploring and normalizing an expansive, inclusive definition of masculinity unimpaired by traditional limitations. The group leader can use basic, supportive social work skills to help members identify their feelings and learn to hear each other in increasingly empathic ways. The particular tasks of any group for gay men may allow members to peel away layers of maladaptive, rigid identifications in search of more fluid, emotionally responsive, true selves.

Relationships and Intimacy

Men who choose membership in a gay men's group desire relationships with other gay men. Often men may want to use the group either to get help in finding a romantic partner or to explore difficulties in their already existing partnerships. While the impulse to fall in love and partner exists for heterosexual as well as gay men, a social worker must be sensitive to the particular difficulties confronting single and coupled group members. Living within a homophobic society excludes gay men from the legal, religious, financial, and social structures that affirm and sanctify heterosexual coupling. Nevertheless, surveys of gay men demonstrate that more than half of them are involved in ongoing partnerships (Peplau, 1991).

To provide help in this area of psychosocial development, social workers must come to understand the ways in which both societal oppression and the characteristics of same-sex relationships impact on gay male couples and on gay men looking for a partner (Greenan & Tunnel, 2002). For example, in contrast to the accepted heterosexual model of monogamy, many male couples in durable, committed relationships distinguish between emotional and sexual fidelity (Johnson & Keren, 1996). As members of a culture steeped in heterosexual norms, social workers must reflect carefully on their heterosexist biases and strive not to assign pathology or dysfunction to gay couples. A group leader must transfer these challenges to group members as well, reinforcing hope by presenting the group as a model for the potential in each member to build intimate relationships. At the same time, the social worker must identify the negative impact of internalized homophobia, heterosexist assumptions, and misleading stereotypes on the process of building intimacy in the group and help the group to reflect on how each of these affects external partnerships or efforts to establish them.

Ethnocultural Diversity

Contrary to prevalent stereotypes, racial, cultural, and ethnic diversity impact on the development and functioning of individual gay men (Fukujama & Ferguson, 2000; Greene, 1996). Just as the white, middle-class male does not represent all of American society, a social worker must recognize that the most easily identifiable gay men do not represent the population in all of its complexity. Since the majority of the literature on gay men is based on samples of white, middle-class men, neither the theory nor research that has resulted is necessarily relevant to all subgroups of the gay population. The marginalized place of ethnic and racial minorities within the literature on gay men parallels the social realities of minority populations not only within society at large but also within the gay community. Being gay does not preclude one from experiencing or fomenting ethnocultural prejudice. It is imperative for a group leader to recognize the additional stigmas of discrimination based on race, gender, age, or ethnicity that many men must carry.

Social workers must help group members to articulate and validate their particular ethnocultural experiences and conflicts in relation to their sexual orientation. For example, African American gay men may experience identity conflicts as they search for a healthy place amid two problematic environments: their homophobic African American heritage, on one hand, and the racist white gay culture, on the other (Adams & Kimmel, 1997; Crisp, 1998; Martinez & Sullivan, 2000). Carballo-Dieguez (1989), Colon (2000), Diaz (1997), Pares-Avila (1994), Rodriguez (1996), and Chan (1989) explore similar difficulties that arise from the interplay of race, ethnicity, and sexual orientation for Latino and Asian American gay men. A group leader can help clients develop effective coping strategies for traversing seemingly exclusive cultures and provide a safe place for ventilating painful feelings of alienation from one or both groups.

In addition to ethnocultural factors, age affects one's identity as a gay man. Since AIDS began to take its toll on the lives of gay men, the concept of longevity has undergone radical redefinition. After the deaths of thousands of gay men from AIDS, men in their 40s and 50s are joining those in their 60s, 70s, and 80s in the developmental tasks of survivorship as they work through issues of loss and strive for regeneration (Rofes, 1996). As they tackle these difficult tasks, middle-aged and older gay men must develop an identity outside of a mainstream gay culture that lauds youth and pays little regard to its older members or to the realities of aging (Adams & Kimmel, 1997; Behney, 1994; Herdt et al., 1997; Kooden & Flowers, 2000; Rosenfeld, 1999). It is ironic that so many younger members in groups for gay men lament the scarcity of role models, while the culture in which these men are trying to find a place continues to marginalize older gay men. These men, the first generation to have had the possibility of living as openly gay for most of their adult lives, are invaluable and overlooked resources for the younger generation.

RECOMMENDED WAYS OF WORKING

The authors' clinical and anecdotal experiences reveal that many gay men continue to mistrust mental health providers, particularly in nongay settings. Such mistrust underscores the marginalized place of gay men within the mental health system, the need for outreach to the gay community, and the ways in which unattuned social work agencies and workers might reinforce injurious feelings of difference, isolation, and invisibility among gay people. To this end, the following section will provide information on effective ways of addressing the needs of this population through group work.

Pregroup Interview

The pregroup interview, an essential procedure for composing all groups, is particularly charged for gay men. It must initiate a process of attunement. For an individual whose identity and way of relating to his environment rest on anticipated rejection, the pregroup interview must set a tone of acceptance as the social worker actively normalizes a gay identity. As social workers attend to the psychosocial assessment of a prospective group member, including a determination of his developmental stage in the coming-out process, the worker must demonstrate real knowledge and awareness of gay issues and the gay community. At the same time, the worker who is less informed about these subjects must acknowledge his ignorance and demonstrate a willingness to learn more about them from sources *outside* of the group so as not to reinforce or repeat negative experiences of members requiring them to confront homophobic misinformation from the group leader (Kus, 1990). Clients must be informed about the diversity of membership and told that the group will not focus on labels or definitions, but instead on their own needs regarding their concerns about being gay and how it may relate to the specific focus of the group.

Member Selection

Groups for gay men must affirm inclusion. As a social worker evaluates an interviewee's appropriateness for group membership, he or she must guard vigilantly against recapitulating a lifelong process of rejection and exclusion from social group participation. Excluding gay men from groups designed specifically for them may not only perpetuate feelings of isolation but may actually leave the client isolated from specific gay services, particularly in geographic areas where there are few alternative resources for this population. Since many agencies do not offer a wide variety of group services to gay men, social workers may find themselves leading groups that must address myriad divergent needs. As a result, the major criteria for membership should be an expressed desire to be a group member and a willingness to commit to the group process. For groups that do not require specific inclusion criteria, only those who are unable to acknowledge consciously that they are attracted primarily to other men to satisfy their sexual and affectional needs, or who are actively psychotic or antisocial in personality, should be excluded (Getzel, 1998). The question of whether to include bisexual clients in groups for gay men often depends on the specific focus and setting of the group. If the group is a more general therapy group, then including bisexual men may prove very helpful in fostering acceptance of diversity and recognition of the complexity of sexual identity. Similarly, in a coming-out group, one could include bisexual men because they share issues with gay men regarding accepting their desire for members of the same sex. In fact, many men who later identify as gay prefer to label themselves bisexual when they first begin to integrate their same-sex object choice (Isay, 1989). If, however, group cohesion is organized around a particular issue or theme not focused on identity formation, then including bisexual men may prove counterproductive to the group task. In an HIV-negative men's group, for example, including bisexual men may create scapegoating and divert the group's process away from the established group focus. At the same time, the limitations of agency provisions and geographic realities may require the group leader to adjust inclusion criteria for the needs of a bisexual client.

Self-Disclosure and Modeling

The social worker's disclosure of his or her own sexual orientation is essential to creating an affirmative environment in which clients can explore their sexuality. Cornett (1993) and Frommer (1994) suggest that clients enter treatment with an inherently nonneutral, heterosexist assumption of a social worker's orientation. As a result, they believe a gay social worker should disclose this information when asked by the client and after a careful exploration to determine its meaning for the client in treatment. They contend that gay leaders provide invaluable opportunities for positive gay role models in a world where too few exist (Isay, 1996). Failure to self-disclose as a gay leader at the beginning of the group experience forsakes an invaluable opportunity to model an affirmative stance toward homosexuality in the service of establishing a trusting environment and building cohesion. Conlin and Smith (1985) believe that gay social workers leading groups for gay men should be in the late stage of their coming-out process. Such leaders may be more able to tolerate the often powerful and ambivalent feelings of those members who remain at earlier stages in the process and reflect to the group more subtle manifestations of homophobia in the group process.

The issue of self-disclosure for heterosexual social workers leading groups for gay men has not been adequately addressed in the literature. Gay affirmative theory seems to be moving toward asserting the value of gay clients receiving treatment from gay practitioners (Ball, 1998; Isay, 1989). However, the reality of human resources within social service agencies requires that heterosexual social workers also provide services to gay clients. The question of self-disclosure remains for heterosexual leaders, but the dynamics are significantly different. Particularly in short-term, problem-focused, and support groups, persistent focusing on the group leader who does not disclose may well sidetrack or derail the necessary tasks of the group and permit the development of maladaptive defenses against group affiliation and intimacy. In any group, a heterosexual social worker must have become a social anthropologist prior to beginning work with the group. He or she must not only identify his or her own homonegative attitudes, beliefs, and behaviors but also develop a firm understanding of and belief in the complexity of gay culture and life experiences.

While self-disclosure is important, how one handles disclosure is as important as the act of disclosing itself. The tension between offering a supportive, positive environment for self-exploration, on the one hand, and impinging on a client's ability to verbalize any and all feelings of shame and self-doubt, on the other, must inform the social worker's process of disclosing his or her sexual orientation to group members. The social worker who does not remain keenly aware of his or her own internalized homophobia may shut the door on more helpful explorations of shame and guilt and the healthy desire of members to identify with the gay group leader as a positive role model or a heterosexual leader as a genuinely informed and nurturing influence.

A heterosexual female social worker experienced in group work with gay men was assigned to lead a coming-out group in the absence of openly gay staff at the university counseling service where she worked. After the second group session, the group fell into several weeks of very little activity despite the worker's skilled efforts to elicit participation. Long periods of silence were followed by occasional bickering and apologies between members. After 5 weeks, two members had dropped out of the group and those remaining began to express feelings of hopelessness. The worker's supervisor stated that these dynamics were not unusual in the beginning stages of group work and focused on processing the worker's anxiety about her difference from group members. Nonetheless, after reviewing the group process of the preceding weeks, the social worker suggested to the group in the next session that their disappointment and difficulty in moving forward was related not only to her gender difference but also to her perceived sexual orientation as heterosexual.

The group immediately responded. Several members finally expressed feelings of mistrust, anger, and disappointment that the leader was not a gay man. The social worker validated their concerns and managed to redirect the group's anger away from each other and toward her. Her ability to remain supportive and empathic during this period in the group process helped move the group to a new level of openness, understanding, and cohesion.

After many weeks, group members expressed idealized feelings toward the social worker and expressed surprise that they could experience her as particularly nurturing. One client joked, "You must be a lesbian." The group immediately picked up on this theme and demanded an answer, which the leader agreed to provide after the group explored their thoughts and fantasies on the subject. When the social worker acknowledged her heterosexuality, the members were able to explore more fully both their heterophobia and their homophobia within a safe environment.

Group Prospectus

A social worker, and sometimes an agency or another sponsoring organization, must decide whether a group should be open or closed and short or long term, based on the group's task and setting. To hasten acceptance within a non–gay-identified agency that has not previously had a gay-related group, a worker should structure the group to imitate the prevailing model for group work in the agency in order to integrate and normalize the group within the agency culture. These efforts not only elicit acceptance by staff and administration but also suggest to gay clients that the agency provides a safe place to discuss and explore their sexual orientation.

An openly gay social worker in a continuing day treatment program recognized the need for a gay men's group after several clients confided feeling isolated and unable to express themselves openly in groups, the primary treatment modality at the agency. The worker confronted agency homophobia by educating the staff about the needs of gay and lesbian clients and documenting clients' concerns. The executive director ultimately overrode the worker's immediate supervisor and sanctioned the group.

Initially, the group was composed of clients who had been attending the treatment program for some time. The group process seemed to parallel longstanding institutional beliefs that the group did not belong in the treatment program. Members projected powerful feelings of internalized homophobia onto each other and prevented group cohesion by verbally attacking each for coming out to community members outside of the group. One member stated, "I didn't come to this place to work on my sexual orientation or identity stuff. I came here to deal with my psychiatric problems."

As some of the more hostile, intensely homophobic clients left the group, new clients who had entered treatment after the gay group had already been integrated into the agency began contributing more to the process. Members developed greater social relatedness as they began to see themselves not only as part of an affirming gay subgroup, but also as people integrated and accepted by the rehabilitative community.

Whether gay, lesbian, bisexual, transgendered, or heterosexual, a social worker leading groups for gay men must be gay affirmative; cognizant of the powerful impact of homophobia on oneself and on one's clients and willing to address the issue directly; sensitive to the diverse experiences of gay and bisexual men; vigilant against subscribing to destructive stereotypes; and open to exploring all sexual identities without permitting personal ideology to contaminate professional explorations. In the authors' experience, coming out professionally not only enhances one's self-esteem and professional identity but also may be a primary step toward helping an agency respond to the emotional needs of its gay, lesbian, transgender, and bisexual clients and staff. Hiring motivated, openly gay social workers may increase interest in and attention to the particular needs of gay men while providing essential role models for an all too often silenced, shamed, and ignored population. Armed with awareness, acceptance, and a genuine desire to be helpful, social workers working with gay men can create precious spaces in which these individuals can work toward developing self-esteem, integrating their sexuality, and building emotionally intimate relationships with their peers.

EVALUATION APPROACHES

Outcome measures for clients in gay men's groups remain anecdotal. To date, no instruments directly addressing the outcomes of work with this population in groups have been developed for public use, although instruments for addressing individual problems such as low self-esteem or homophobia could certainly be incorporated into an outcome study of group work with gay men. As in most group work, eliciting outcome information is an essential component of termination. Statements about improved psychosocial functioning seem to be the best barometer for determining the effectiveness of the group. Desire for continued affiliation with other gay men, a sense of belonging both within the gay community and within the larger social environment, improved social and intimate relationships, and diminished homophobic statements and behaviors all would testify to positive outcomes. As men in these groups learn to celebrate their everyday heroism and hard-earned strengths in living as openly gay, it is hoped that they will carry their resilience outside of their groups, use it to expand on previous roles, and adopt a more affirmative sense of themselves.

RESOURCES

For the most part, mental health services for this population are provided at the local and regional levels. To locate these services in a particular region, we suggest consulting the Gay Yellow Pages (gayyellowpages.com), which can be found online or in libraries.

American Civil Liberties Union
Lesbian and Gay Rights Project

125 Broad Street
New York, NY 10004
(212) 944-9800
www.aclu.org
The ACLU provides legal services aimed at advancing the rights of gay men and
    lesbians and educating the public about discrimination.

Gay Asian Pacific Support Network (GAPSN)
PO Box 461104
Los Angeles, CA 90046
www.gapsn.org
GAPSN is a source of support and information for gay, lesbian, bisexual, and
    transgender people of Asian/Pacific Islander descent.

Gay and Lesbian Alliance Against Defamation (GLAAD)
104 West 29th Street, 4th Floor
New York, NY 10011
(212) 629-3332
www.glaad.org
GLAAD promotes visibility of the gay and lesbian community and organizes
    grassroots responses to homophobia in the media.

Gay, Lesbian and Straight Education Network (GLSEN)
90 Broad Street
New York, NY 10004
(212) 727-0135
www.glsen.org
GLSEN is a national alliance with regional offices and local chapters that
    advocates for the dignity and respect of all students regardless of sexual
    orientation.

Gay Men of African Descent (GMAD)
44 Court Street, Suite 1000
Brooklyn, NY 11201
(718) 222-6300
www.gmad.org
The mission of GMAD is to empower gay men of African descent through
    education, advocacy, health and wellness, prevention, and social support.

The Hetrick Martin Institute
2 Astor Place
New York, NY 10003
(212) 674-2400
www.hmi.org

The Hetrick Martin Institute provides comprehensive social services, high school education, and referrals for gay and lesbian adolescents.

Lambda Legal Defense and Education Fund
120 Wall Street, Suite 1500
New York, NY 10005
www.lambdalegal.org
Lambda is an organization of gay men and lesbians providing political advocacy and legal services to gay men and lesbians.

Llego
PO Box 444483
Washington, DC 20026
(202) 544-0092
www.llego.org
Llego is a national organization whose mission is to effectively address issues of concern to lesbian, gay, bisexual, and transgender Latinas/Latinos at local, state, regional, national, and international levels.

Parents and Friends of Lesbians and Gays (P-FLAG)
1726 M. Street, NW, Suite 400
Washington, DC 20036
(202) 467-8180
www.pflag.org
With chapters throughout the country, P-FLAG is an invaluable resource for gay people, families, and friends, particularly those struggling with coming out.

Pride Institute Hotline
800-54-PRIDE
(612) 934-7554 (within Minnesota)
www.pride-institute.com
The Pride Institute provides residential chemical dependency programs as well as referral to local resources.

Senior Action in a Gay Environment (SAGE)
208 West 13th Street
New York, NY 10011
(212) 741-2247
www.sageusa.org
SAGE provides services and socializing for older gay men and lesbians. The New York office may provide referrals to services throughout the nation.

REFERENCES

Abelove, H. (1993). Freud, male homosexuality and the Americans. In H. Abelove, et al. (eds.), *The lesbian and gay studies reader* (pp. 381–393). New York: Routledge Press.

Adams, C. L. & Kimmel, D. C. (1997). Exploring the lives of older African American gay men. In B. Greene (ed.), *Ethnic and cultural diversity among lesbians and gay men: Psychological perspectives on lesbian and gay issues*, Vol. 3 (pp. 132–151). Thousand Oaks, CA: Sage Publications.

Adamczyk, A. & Pitt, C. (2009). Shaping attitudes about homosexuality: The role of religion and cultural context. *Social Science Research*, *38*(2), 338–351.

Ball, S. (1994). A group model for gay and lesbian clients with chronic mental illness. *Social Work*, *39*(1), 109–115.

Ball, S. (ed.). (1998). *The HIV-negative gay man*. New York: Harrington Park Press.

Behney, R. (1994). The aging network's response to gay and lesbian issues. *Outword*, *Winter*, pp. 2–5.

Bell, A. P. & Weinberg, M. S. (1978). *Homosexualities: A study of diversity among men and women*. New York: Simon & Schuster.

Bieber, I. (1962) *Homosexuality: A psychoanalytic study*. New York: Basic Books.

Burnham, R. A., Cadwell, S. A., & Forstein, M. (eds.), *Therapists on the front line: Psychotherapy with gay men in the age of AIDS* (pp. 453–471). Washington, DC: American Psychiatric Press.

Cadwell, S. (1992). Twice removed: The stigma suffered by gay men with AIDS. *Smith Studies in Social Work*, *61*(3), 236–246.

Cain, R. (1991). Stigma management and gay identity development: *Social Work*, *36*(1), 67–73.

Caputo, L. (1985). Dual diagnosis: AIDS and addiction. *Social Work*, *30*(4), 361–363.

Carballo-Dieguez, A. (1989). Hispanic culture, gay male culture, and AIDS: Counseling implications. *Journal of Counseling and Development*, *68*(1), 26–30.

Cass, V. (1979). Homosexual identity formation: A theoretical model. *Journal of Homosexuality*, *4*, 219–235.

Chan, C. (1989). Issues of identity development among Asian-American lesbians and gay men. *Journal of Counseling and Development*, *68*(1), 16–20.

Coleman, E. (1982). The developmental stages of the coming out process. In J. C. Gonsiorek (ed.), *Homosexuality and psychotherapy: A practitioner's handbook of affirmative models* (pp. 31–43). New York: Haworth Press.

Cohen, R. (2000) Understanding and healing homosexuality. Winchester: Oakhill Press.

Colon, E. (2001). An ethnographic study of six Latino men. *Journal of Gay and Lesbian Social Services*, *12*(3–4), 77–92.

Conlin, D. & Smith, J. (1985). Group psychotherapy for gay men. In J. Gonsiorek (ed.), *A guide to psychotherapy with gay and lesbian clients* (pp. 105–112). New York: Harrington Park Press.

Cornett, C. (ed.). (1993). *Affirmative dynamic psychotherapy with gay men*. Northvale, NJ: Jason Aronson.

Crisp, D. (1998). African American gay men: Developmental issues, choices and self concept. *Family Therapy*, *25*(3), 161–168.

De la Vega, E. (1990). Considerations for reaching the Latino population with sexuality and HIV/AIDS information and education. *SIECUS Report, 18*(3), 1–8.

Deyton, B. & Lear, W. (1988). A brief history of the gay/lesbian health movement in the U.S.A. In M. Shernoff & W. Scott (eds.), *The sourcebook of lesbian/gay healthcare* (2nd ed., pp. 15–19). Washington, DC: National Lesbian/Gay Health Foundation.

Diaz, R. (1997). Latino gay men and psycho-cultural barriers to HIV prevention. In M. Levine & P. Nardi (eds.), *Changing times: Gay men and lesbians encounter HIV/AIDS* (pp. 221–244). Chicago: University of Chicago Press.

Eller, M. & King, D. (1990). Self help groups for gays, lesbians and their loved ones. In R. Kus (ed.), *Keys to caring* (pp. 330–339). Boston: Alyson Publications.

Frable, D. E. S., Platt, L., & Hoey, S. (1998). Concealable stigma and positive self perceptions: Feeling better around similar others. *Journal of Personality and Social Psychology, 24*(4), 909–922.

Frable, D. E. S., Wortman, C., & Joseph, J. (1997). Predicting self-esteem, wellbeing, and distress in a cohort of gay men: The importance of cultural stigma, personal visibility, community networks, and positive identity. *Journal of Personality, 65*(3), 599–624.

Friedman, R. C. & Downey, J. (1993). Psychoanalysis, psychobiology and homosexuality. *Journal of the American Psychoanalytic Association, 41*(4), 1159–1198.

Frommer, M. S. (In press). Homosexuality and psychoanalysis: Technical considerations revisited. *Psychoanalytic Dialogues, 4.*

Fukuyama, M. A. & Ferguson, A. D. (2000). Lesbian, gay and bisexual people of color: Understanding cultural complexity and managing multiple oppressions. In R. Perez & K. DeBord (eds.), *Handbook of counseling and psychotherapy with lesbian, bay and bisexual clients* (pp. 81–105). Washington, DC: American Psychological Association.

Gardner, T. & Kosten, T. (2008). International Implications of HIV and substance younger gay men and HIV abuse. *American Journal of Drug and Alcohol Abuse, 34*(1), 1–3.

Getzel, G. (1998). Group work with gay men and lesbians. In G. Mallon (ed.), *Foundations of social work practice with gay men and lesbian women* (pp. 131–144). New York: Haworth Press.

Gonsiorek, J. (1985) *A guide to psychotherapy with gay and lesbian clients.* New York: Harrington Park Press.

Gonsiorek, J. (1977). Psychological adjustment and homosexuality. *JSAS Catalog of Selected Documents in Psychology, 7,* 45 (MS No. 1478).

Greenan, D. & Tunnel, G. (2002). *Couples therapy with gay men.* New York: Guilford Press.

Greene, B. (1996). Lesbian and gay men of color: The legacy of ethnosexual mythologies in heterosexim and homophobia. In E. D. Rothblum & L. A. Bond (eds.), *Preventing heterosexism and homophobia: Primary prevention of psychopathology,* Vol. 17 (59–70). Thousand Oaks, CA: Sage Publications.

Hays, R. B., Turner, H., & Coates, P. (1992). Social support, AIDS-related symptoms, and depression among gay men. *Journal of Consulting and Clinical Psychology, 60,* 463–469.

Herdt, G., Beeler, J., & Rawls, T. W. (1997). Life course diversity among old lesbians and gay men: A study in Chicago. *Journal of Gay, Lesbian and Bisexual Identity, 2*(3/4), 231–246.

Herek, G. M. (1990). Illness, Stigma and AIDS. In P. T. Costa & G. R. VandenBos (eds.), *Psychological aspects of serious illness: Chronic conditions, fatal diseases, and clinical care* (pp. 107–149). Washington, DC: American Psychological Association.

Hetrick, E. S. & Martin, A. D. (1984). Ego-dystonic homosexuality: A developmental view. In E. S. Hetrick & T. S. Stein (eds.), *Innovations in psychotherapy with homosexuals* (pp. 2–21). Washington, DC: American Psychiatric Association Press.

Hetrick, E. S. & Martin, A. D. (1987). Developmental issues and their resolution for gay and lesbian adolescents. In E. Coleman (ed.), *Integrated identity for gay men and lesbians* (pp. 25–43). New York: Harrington Park Press.

Igreja, I., Zuroff, D., Koestner, R., & Saltaris, C. (2000). Social motives, social support and distress in gay men differing in HIV Status. *Journal of Research in Personality, 34*(3), 287–304.

Isay, R. (1989). *Being homosexual: Gay men and their development.* New York: Farrar, Straus & Giroux.

Isay, R. (1996). *Becoming gay: The journey to self-acceptance.* New York: Pantheon Books.

Isensee, R. (1991). *Growing up gay in a dysfunctional family.* New York: Prentice Hall Press.

Johnson, T. W. & Keren, M. S. (1996). Creating and maintaining boundaries in male couples. In J. Laird & R. Green (eds.), *Lesbians and gays in couples and families: A handbook for therapists* (pp. 231–239). San Francisco: Jossey-Bass Publishers.

Kooden, H. & Flowers, C. (2000). *Golden men: The power of gay midlife.* New York: Avon Books.

Kershaw, S. (2008). New HIV cases drop but rise in young gay men. *New York Times,* January 2, 2008.

Kus, R. (1990). *Keys to caring.* Boston: Alyson Publications.

Lambda Legal Defense and Education Fund. (1999). *State-by-state sodomy law update.* New York: Author.

Lewes, K. (1988). *The psychoanalytic theory of male homosexuality.* New York: Simon & Schuster.

Lewis, J. (1999). Status passages: The experience of HIV-positive gay men. *Journal of Homosexuality, 37*(3), 87–115.

Linde, R. (1994). Impact of AIDS on adult gay male development: Implications for psychotherapy. In R. A. Burnham, S. A. Cadwell, & M. Forstein (eds.), *Therapists on the front line: Psychotherapy with gay men in the age of AIDS* (pp. 453–471). Washington, DC: American Psychiatric Press.

Linn, G. L., Lewis, F. M., Cain, V. A., & Kimgrough, G. A. (1993). HIV-illness, social support, sense of coherence, and psychosocial well-being in a sample of helpseeking adults. *AIDS Education and Prevention, 4*(3), 254–262.

Lipton, B. (2004). Gay men living with chronic illnesses and disabilities: From crisis to crossroads. *Journal of Gay and Lesbian Social Services.* New York: Harrington Park Press.

Margolies, L., Becker, M., & Jackson-Brewer (1987). Internalized homophobia: Identifying and treating the oppressor within. In Boston Lesbian Psychologies Collective, *Lesbian psychologies: Explorations and challenges* (pp. 229–241). Chicago: University of Illinois.

Martin, J. & Hunter, S. (2001). *Lesbian, gay, bisexual and transgender issues in social work: A comprehensive bibliography with annotations.* Alexandria, VA: Council on Social Work Education.

Martinez, D. G. & Sullivan, S. C. (2000). African American gay men and lesbians: Examining the complexity of gay identity development. In L. A. Letha (ed.), *Human behavior in the social environment from an African American perspective* (pp. 243–264). Athens, GA: University of Georgia Press.

Meyer, I. H. (1995). Minority stress and mental health in gay men. *Journal of Health and Social Behavior, 36*(March), 38–56.

Miller, N. (2006). *Out of the past: Gay and lesbian history form 1899 to present.* New York: Alyson Books

Nichols, S. E. (1986). Psychotherapy and AIDS. In T. S. Stein & C. J. Cohen (eds.), *Contemporary perspectives on psychotherapy with lesbians and gay men* (pp. 209–239). New York: Plenum Press.

Nicolosi, J. (1991). *The reparative therapy of male homosexuality: A new clinical approach.* Northvale, NJ: Jason Aronson.

Odets, W. (1994). Survivor guilt in seronegative gay men. In R. A. Burnham, S. A. Cadwell, & M. Forstein (eds.), *Therapists on the front line: Psychotherapy with gay men in the age of AIDS* (pp. 473–491). Washington, DC: American Psychiatric Press.

O'Hanlan, K., Cabaj, R. B., Schatz, B., Lock, J., & Nemrow, P. (1997). A review of the medical consequences of homophobia with suggestions for resolution. *Journal of the Gay and Lesbian Medical Association, 1*(1), 25–40.

Paradis, B. A. (1993). A self-psychological approach to the treatment of gay men with AIDS. *Clinical Social Work Journal, 21*(4), 405–416.

Pares-Avila (1994). Issues in the psychosocial care of Latino gay men with HIV infection. In R. Burnham, S. Cadwell & M. Forstein (eds.), *Therapists on the front line: Psychotherapy with gay men in the age of AIDS* (pp. 339–362). Washington, DC: American Psychiatric Press.

Peplau, L. (1991). Lesbian and gay relationships. In J. Gonsiorek & J. Weinrich (eds.), *Homosexuality: Research implications for public policy* (pp. 177–196). Newbury Park, CA: Sage Publications.

Pillard, R. (1999). The causes of homosexuality are probably genetic. In M. E. Williams (ed.), *Homosexuality: Opposing viewpoints* (pp. 27–34) San Diego, CA: Greenhaven Press.

Ritter, K. & Terndrup, A. (2002). *Handbook of affirmative psychotherapy with lesbians and gay men.* New York. Guildford Press.

Rodriguez, R. (1996). Clinical issues in identity development in gay Latino men. In C. Alexander (ed.), *Gay and lesbian mental health: A sourcebook for practitioners* (pp. 127–157). New York: Haworth Park Press.

Rofes, E. (1996). *Reviving the tribe: Regenerating gay men's sexuality and culture in the ongoing epidemic.* New York: Harrington Park Press.

Rosenfeld, D. (1999). Identity work among the homosexual elderly. *Journal of Aging Studies, 13*(2), 121.

Ross, M. R. (1990). The relationship between life events and mental health in homosexual men. *Journal of Clinical Psychology, 46*(4), 403–411.

Rotheram-Boerus, M., Hunter, J., & Rosario, M. (1994). Suicidal behavior and gayrelated stress among gay and bisexual male adolescents. *Journal of Adolescent Research, 9,* 498–508.

Russell, A. & Winkler, R. (1977). Evaluation of assertiveness training and homosexual guidance service groups designed to improve homosexual functioning. *Journal of Consulting and Clinical Psychology, 45*(1), 1–13.

Sandstrom, K. (1996). Searching for information, understanding, and self-value: The utilization of peer support groups by gay men with HIV/AIDS. *Social Work in Health Care, 23*(4), 51–74.

Savin-Williams, R. (1994). Verbal and physical abuse as stressors in the lives of lesbian, gay male, and bisexual youths. *Journal of Consulting and Clinical Psychology, 62*, 261–269.

Schoenberg, R. & Goldberg, R. S. (eds.). (1985). *With compassion towards some: Homosexuality and social work in America.* New York: Harrington Park Press.

Schwartz, W. (1985). The group work tradition and social work practice. *Social Work with Groups, 8*(4), 7–27.

Schwartz, R. & Hartstein, N. (1986). Group psychotherapy with gay men. In T. Stein & C. Cohen (eds.), *Contemporary perspectives on psychotherapy with lesbians and gay men* (pp. 157–177). New York: Plenum Press.

Sears, J. T. & Williams, W. L. (eds.) (1997). *Overcoming heterosexism and homophobia: Strategies that work.* New York: Columbia University Press.

Shernoff, M. (1991). Eight years of working with people with HIV: The impact upon a therapist. In C. Silverstein (ed.), *Gays, lesbians, and their therapists* (pp. 227–239). New York: W. W. Norton.

Shulman, L. (1984). *The skills of helping individuals and groups.* Itasca, IL: F. E. Peacock.

Signorile, M. (1997). *The Signorile report on gay men: Sex, drugs, muscles and the passages of life.* New York: Harper Collins.

Silverstein, C. (ed.). (1991). *Gays, lesbians, and their therapists.* New York: W. W. Norton.

Socarides, C. (1978). *Homosexuality.* New York: Jason Aronson.

Stall, R. (2002). Access to health care among men who have sex with men: Data from the Urban Men's Health Study. *Advancing gay and lesbian health: A report from the gay and lesbian health roundtable.* Los Angeles, CA: Los Angeles Gay and Lesbian Center.

Stein, T. S. & Cohen, C. J. (eds.). (1986). *Psychotherapy with lesbians and gay men.* New York: Plenum Press.

Tunnel, G. (1994). Special issues in group psychotherapy for gay men with AIDS. In R. A. Burnham, Jr., S. A. Cadwell, & M. Forstein (eds.), *Therapists on the front line: Psychotherapy with gay men in the age of AIDS* (pp. 453–471). Washington, DC: American Psychiatric Press.

Tunnel, G. (2003, Jan/Feb). Social change in working with gay and lesbian clients. *Family Therapy Magazine.*

Wagner, G., Brondolo, E., & Rabkin, J. (1996). Internalized homophobia in a sample of HIV+ gay men, and its relationship to psychological distress, coping, and illness progression. *Journal of Homosexuality, 32*(2), 91–105.

Yalom, I. (1985). *The theory and practice of group psychotherapy* (3rd ed.). New York: Basic Books.

Chapter Eighteen

Group Work With Lesbians

Bonnie J. Engelhardt

The purposes of this chapter are to acquaint social workers with the important socioeconomic and clinical issues facing lesbian women and to promote social group work as the primary modality offered to the lesbian client. Lesbians live in a culture of presumed heterosexuality; they cannot fully participate in our societal institutions without exposure and fear. Because they are frequently denied complete social acceptance and are at risk in our heterosexist, misogynist, homophobic society, it is imperative to include lesbians in a social work textbook focusing on at-risk populations. Dr. Caitlyn Ryan (1998) states:

> One of the greatest challenges facing LGBT [lesbian, gay, bisexual, or transgender] youth and adults has been longstanding—lack of accurate information about sexual orientation and gender identity—among providers, families and policymakers. Many providers and so many families wrongly believe that heterosexual identity is innate and that homosexuality is only acquired later in life. But research shows that children—gay and straight—become aware of sexual attraction, on average, at about age 10. Until accurate education on sexuality and human development is included in schools and professional training, basic misconceptions about human development will continue to restrict the humanity, life chances and civil rights of LGBT people.

SAGE (Services and Advocacy for Gay, Lesbian, Bisexual, and Transgender Elders) was formed to help GLBT older adults manage social isolation and the struggles of finding appropriate affirming resources as they age.

> Despite advances in LGBT civil rights, many senior care providers never stop to consider that their older clients may be lesbian, gay, bisexual, and transgender (LGBT)—and even those who do may not know how to provide services in culturally-sensitive ways. As a result, LGBT seniors often avoid seeking needed services out of fear of discrimination. The tendency for LGBT seniors to go "back in the closet" is particularly pronounced in situations where they are most vulnerable—such as when accessing home health care or residing in assisted living or residential care facilities. One study indicated that LGBT seniors may be as much as five times less likely to access needed health and social services

because of their fear of discrimination from the very people who should be helping them (www.sageusa.org).

Previously, little nonheterosexist material was available for new social workers. *An Annotated Bibliography of Gay and Lesbian Readings* edited by Judith A. B. Lee under the sponsorship of the Commission on Lesbian Women and Gay Men of the Council on Social Work Education (CSWE) was published in 1991. It was developed out of the Council's mandate "to build knowledge about diversity and its commitment to oppressed groups" (p. i). The second edition introduction states, "(it represents approximately a twenty-year survey and review of the literature with an eye toward what is genuinely helpful to minorities of sexual orientation" (p. v), noting that previously articles had been written in "medical language with words like 'deviance,' 'perversion,' 'ego-dystonic homosexuality,' 'developmental arrest,'" and other pejorative terminology. The Commission on Lesbian Women and Gay Men of CSWE is now the Commission for Diversity and Social/Economic Justice under the Council on Sexual Orientation and Gender Expression of CSWE and offers a track on LGBT issues at each CSWE annual program.

As clinical social workers, we cannot support any implication that the primary cause of lesbians' difficulties in adjusting to their sexual identity is intrapsychic. The primary obstacles for any minority group today originate in the dominant culture and interaction with it. Saulnier (2000) provides a practice example of the need "to examine the power of words by analyzing the social production of lesbianism." A group facilitator of a lesbian support group states:

> I wanted us to look at lesbianism not just as a personal phenomenon but as a social phenomenon ... people still deal with stigma and that's a major issue in terms of educating and having support groups—to talk about the stigmatization—here's always going to be a need for someone to understand the powerful effect of growing up in a culture that's your culture but from which you are banished (Saulnier, 2002, p. 15).

Social workers have written about the effects of racism, classism, sexism, and ageism on our clientele, but this chapter deals with homophobia stemming from our heterosexist society. Herek (1986), looking at the social psychology of homophobia, defined *heterosexism* as a "world-view, a value system that prizes heterosexuality, assumes it is the only appropriate manifestation of love and sexuality, and devalues homosexuality" (p. 924). *Homophobia* is defined as the "prejudice, discrimination, and hostility directed at gay men and lesbian women because of their sexual orientation" (Ellis & Murphy, 1994, p. 50). It should be noted that the experience of homophobia linked with sexism is unique to the lesbian culture and that lesbians of color often experience the triple threat of racism, sexism, and homophobia.

As social group workers, we favor group work as the primary modality offered to the lesbian client, whether or not the leader is a lesbian. Group work (mutual aid) provides a connection with lesbians and other women considering their sexual orientation in a safe, partially controlled environment and places responsibility for the evolution of the content and process on the members, not the leader. Kurland and Salmon (2005) state:

> *The quality of the mutual aid process that occurs in a group is what differentiates group work from casework in a group; Breton (1989) emphasizes the healing and liberating powers of mutual aid and points out that recognition of the process by which members influence and help one another ... leads to strength and actions and change at the social, economic and political levels (p.130).*

Groups allow the diversity needed for individual lesbians, who might be lost in their own identity crises, to appreciate that there are many right choices about how to live one's life as a lesbian. It diffuses the power of the leader and clarifies the need for variety in the role modeling available to women entering the lesbian community. It is an invaluable experience to be in the company of lesbian women talking about their lives because, for all of us, the *invisibility* of the lesbian lifestyle is prominent. Some clients will think that the life of celesbians (celebrity lesbians visible in movies and television) represent the life that all lesbians will have— leading to disappointment, confusion, and, in some, despair. In groups, lesbians can gain perspective on how their choices are similar to or different from those of other lesbians, thereby acquiring more knowledge of the norm of lesbian life in their community. It is important to understand that there is no unified lesbian community, only many distinct lesbian communities. There is no typical lesbian, but rather many unique lesbian women who have developed individually into the type of lesbian that they are today. Good social work practice entails getting the particulars from any woman about her own development as a lesbian without making *any* assumptions. It is empowering to an individual to experience her own journey as being a valid developmental process without trying to impose a societal stereotype, a social work definition, or a lesbian community mandate. Having established that no one person, process, or experience is typical, we can then proceed to look for the commonalities.

There are no universal paths to lesbian identity development, but coming out or disclosure stages have been noted in the literature (Lehman, 1978; Roth, 1985; Roth & Murphy, 1986). Five or six stages are usually noted including disclosure to self/significant family members/intimate others, disclosure at the workplace/ social networks, and identification with the lesbian label and gay community. The Vivienne Cass Identity Model is an example of a nonpathologizing model of homosexual identity formation. Cass proposed a six-stage process: (1) identity awareness, when the individual is conscious of being different; (2) identity comparison, when the individual believes that he or she may be homosexual but tries to act heterosexually; (3) identity tolerance, when the individual realizes that he or she is homosexual; (4) identity acceptance, when the individual begins to explore the gay community; (5) identity pride, when the individual becomes active in the gay community; and (6) synthesis, when the individual fully accepts himself or herself and other (Cass, 1979, 1984, 1990, in Ritter & Terndrup, 2002). It is important to note that not all lesbians go through all stages and not in sequential order.

Social workers referring lesbian clients to groups must be cognizant of the lesbian client's intrapsychic and sociopolitical issues and stage of identity development in order to help her decide whether her presenting problems are primarily:

- Intrapsychic issues, and a therapy group is needed
- Related to her coming-out process, and a group focused on self-acceptance and disclosure strategies is appropriate
- Isolation-based issues so that a support group is needed to connect her to the lesbian subculture
- Issues of oppression and discrimination, so that an action-oriented empowerment group would be helpful
- A combination of these situations requiring more than one type of group intervention

Social workers need to provide opportunities for lesbian women to find their natural processes of self-disclosure and disclosure to others without stigmatization. We need to be able to differentiate the more vulnerable women who could become marginalized during the coming-out process. Even though there is debate about whether lesbianism is caused or created—predetermined genetically or chosen as a preference— everyone does agree that the lesbian woman has to continue to make the choice of self-disclosure or disclosure to others every day. A safe group environment is especially helpful for this process of learning to be vulnerable and expose yourself while setting appropriate boundaries. A group may be composed entirely of lesbian women and formed with this awareness in mind or it may contain lesbians, with or without the knowledge of the non-lesbian members.

The phrase *lesbian women* is used by Murphy (1992) "to affirm the use of the terms gay and lesbian as *adjectives* rather than as *nouns* to highlight that sexual orientation is only one aspect of an individual's life AND to emphasize that lesbian women may have more in common with heterosexual women than with gay men" (p. 242). As noted earlier, only for the lesbian is the experience of homophobia linked with sexism. While this double identity may allow some lesbians to feel comfortable in all women's groups or in all-gay groups, in my experience this does not work for all lesbian women. For example, it is not uncommon for lesbian feminists to feel alienated in a group of heterosexual women even though they identify with the women's movement. Similarly, women who identify strongly with the gay rights movement may resent having to deal with gender differences with their male brothers.

LesBiGay, LGBT, and LBGT are terms used to affirm the gay community, which includes lesbians, gay men, bisexual women and men, and transgendered individuals. LGBTTIQQ is an acronym used to show total inclusion of lesbians, gay males, bisexuals, transgenders, Two Spirits, intersexuals, queers, and questioning. The understanding that "coming out" is a process and is on a spectrum is useful to understanding the various life issues affecting lesbians and their interaction with the gay community. In the past, the mainstream culture's understanding of the lesbian experience (and, therefore, someone trying to learn about lesbianism) had been gained primarily through observation of the gay male lifestyle. Today individuals have the benefit of the Internet, lesbian rock stars, lesbian television talk hosts, and many visible community leaders of gay and lesbian organizations. A difficulty can arise for some that so many possible role models and/or negative stereotypes can be overwhelming and difficult to process easily.

There have always been lesbians who identified with a wide spectrum of the lesbian community and those who identified with only a small part. The paths of many subcommunities may never cross: the sadomasochistic community, the radical lesbian socialists, "dykes on bikes," the bar crowd, the suburban book clubs, the "jocks," the "gay or lesbian" professional network, the feminist woman–identified lesbians (*who may or may not have had sexual relations with a woman*), the college phase choices, etc. Class differences, oppression, and the resultant invisibility have kept these communities separate and isolated; as visibility and numbers increase, work will still need to be done on class and economic differences. Census 2000 revealed that there were 594,391 gay male and lesbian *couples* in the United States, living in 99.3% of all U.S. counties; nearly a quarter of these couples are raising children, and these families live in 96% of U.S. counties (Witeck, 2005). Social group work is the best vehicle to help an individual place herself on this spectrum of possible options and provides support for phases that might occur as the "coming-out" process occurs.

COMMON THEMES

The themes that regularly arise in groups designed for lesbian women will now be considered.

Management of Oppression, Stigma, and Difference

Gay adults often describe themselves as having felt "different" from other children. The factors leading to a sense of difference are diverse.... In boys these tend to be aesthetic and intellectual; in girls, they are athletic. Beginning in children, many gay and lesbian people have feelings of shame at being considered deviant, as well as feelings of self-hatred because they identify with those who devalue them. Such feelings arise from identification with the aggressor, a mental mechanism experienced by many victims of abuse (Friedman & Downey, 1994, p. 926).

The management of shame, self-hatred, and internalized homophobia is required for every lesbian. Internalized homophobia is experienced as internalizing the prejudicial, pejorative views of the homosexual held by the dominant society. Marginalized lesbian women are especially vulnerable if they lack a positive gay identity or do not have access to positive role models in their family or religious or social institutions. Psychologically vulnerable women, teenage girls, and elderly women may resort to alcohol and drug abuse, and there is a higher tendency toward suicide, especially for teenagers (Friedman & Downey, 1994, p. 926). Saulnier (1997) has written of the role of alcohol in the lesbian community and the part that the recovery movement has played in the socialization process for many lesbians. Many of my lesbian couple clients have stressed how significant a source of comfort and support their 12-step programs are for their relationship health. Work performance and career advancement can be seriously impaired by internal and external dilemmas with the development of a lesbian identity. Social group workers must be prepared to deal with despair, alienation, rage, loss, anger, and hostility and to help clients turn these feelings appropriately outward to injustices in the dominant culture.

Invisibility of the Lesbian Woman's Experience

The reality of oppression leads to invisibility of some identified lesbian woman in our society today. In the lesbian community, the formation of an identity is much more difficult when subcommunities are divided, invisible to each other, and stigmatized stereotypes are internalized. In the dominant culture, you may have access to role models for positive gay identity that help build acceptance, or you may be born into the part of the culture that sees only the "evil" and "sinful" aspects of your lifestyle choice. Lesbians themselves tend to underestimate the complexities of the invisibility factor, and the toll it takes on their psychological development. Groups help to normalize the realities and offer pathways to health and empowerment.

Safety and Vigilance Issues

Many lesbians have experienced gay bashing ranging from verbal harassment to physical assault. The threat of physical and emotional harm is a powerful determinant of lesbian women's mental health. The actual experience or the veiled threat can dictate constrictiveness, hiddenness, and paranoia or a reactive, self-conscious, or overexpressive behavior pattern. Sometimes mental health professionals have judged these behaviors to be adolescent and acting out rather than seeing them as coping mechanisms for dealing with harassment, assault, and persecution. Although boys hear "fag" or "queer" more often on the playground than do girls, athletic girls wearing "androgynous" clothes will easily bring out name-calling and harassment.

It should be noted that the humiliation, shame, and lack of empowerment that physical and sexual abuse survivors experience prevents them from easily acknowledging their difficulties with their own safety. The social group worker needs to create a structure that acknowledges the appropriateness of their dilemma and a language for the entire group to use in negotiating trust and emotional closeness.

Lesbian Relationships and Sexual Expression

Lesbian sexuality and sexual behavior in long-term relationships are more frequently written about than perhaps other aspects of lesbian life. Loulan observed that "frequency of sex among lesbian couples drops off dramatically after the first year" and that "it's so much easier to become passionate about the things we don't like about each other. But who would want to have sex with someone who is critical?" (1987, pp. 103, 117). There appears to be a high correlation between a lesbian's satisfaction with her relationship and satisfaction with her sex life. "Even with infrequent sex, it seems that a woman remains satisfied with her sex life because she feels loved" (Loulan, 1987, p. 202). Murphy hypothesized that "although internalized homophobia affects the sexual relationships of both gay and lesbian couples, the differences in amount of sexual activity and sexual exclusivity may be seen as reflections of gender socialization" (1994, p. 21). "Lesbian women report that they are happy with their amount of sexual activity and that they have more affectionate and nongenital sexual contact than heterosexual and gay male couples" (Murphy, 1994, p. 22).

The goal of the social group worker is to reduce the stigma of discussing lesbian sexuality and to increase the ability of the client to develop her own norms. In groups the worker must take an active stance, leading conversation and providing information on sex. Bibliotherapy and structured group exercises can help reduce anxiety for everyone. The value of lesbian couples' groups is immeasurable; because there is little visible role modeling; however, the fear of being seen as "abnormal," "not good enough," or an "immature couple" is high. Good preparation is needed, and a focused educational format with enough time for telling the couple's "story" is optimal.

LIVING WITH DIGNITY AS A DECLARED OUT LESBIAN WOMAN

No one can deny the stress of living as a member of a minority group in an oppressed subculture; physical, psychological, emotional, and spiritual stressors continually occur. Managing conflictual inner and outer messages is the accepted reality for all lesbians over their lifetime. Reaching old age and even the death process do not remove you from the need to make decisions involving "coming out" and/or being visible.

By the time one goes through the coming-out stages, makes peace with one's losses and gains, and accepts a lesbian identity, usually a very strong personal sense of self has developed. The lesbian woman today has gifts to give to the general culture, especially in the area of building self-esteem. Brown, a lesbian ethicist, states:

> *Three intertwined themes I see as defining, cross-situationally, the experience of being lesbian and gay:* biculturalism, *with its requirements of juggling, balance and living in and with ambiguity;* marginality, *with its perspective that is both outside and from within; and normative* creativity, *the ability to create boundaries that will work where none exist or may be only partially suited to the task (1990, p. 2).*

Examples of courage and perseverance are found particularly in multiply oppressed lesbians.

> *A number of clinicians have suggested that the cultural expectations of Asian, African-American, Latino/Latin and Jewish gay men and lesbian women present them (and the couples in which they are members) with unique stress.... Although each community offers some support, each has its own expectations and demands which often conflict with each other. The tension of living in these three communities, in all of which one feels marginalized, adds to identity difficulties (Murphy, 1994, p. 25).*

Although it is not always clear to a lesbian woman whether it is better for her physical health (raises risk to assault and harassment) or her economic health (creates the risk of job discrimination, eviction, and loss of family support) to disclose fully her sexual orientation, living as a declared lesbian has may advantages. One's psychological well-being is greatly enhanced by a reduction of ambivalence and inner anxiety. Removing from one's mind and emotions the constant quandary of when to "come out" frees a significant amount of life energy for other purposes. Comfort with your visibility allows others to interact with you sharing their concerns, fears and worries about your welfare and offering support and acceptance.

PRACTICE PRINCIPLES

Sensitize Your Organization as Well as Yourself

The Council on Social Work Education Curriculum Policy statement states:

> *Special Populations: The social work profession, by virtue of its system of ethics, its traditional value commitments, and its long history of work in the whole range of human services, is committed to preparing students to understand and appreciate cultural and social diversity. The profession has also been concerned about the consequences of oppression.... The curriculum ... should include content on other special population groups ... in particular, groups that have been consistently affected by social, economic and legal bias or oppression. Such groups include those distinguished by age, religions, disablement,* sexual orientation, *and culture (Council on Social Work Education, 1982, cited in Gochros, 1984, p. 154).*

This policy statement means that your social work agency and your social work training/placement should be sensitive to the issues of gay and lesbian populations and that you will not be alone in trying to create opportunities to serve these populations in your agency. Do not be surprised, however, if that is not so. There are many inherent difficulties even in discovering these populations in your caseload. Although it is always supportive to provide opportunities for clients to come out on intake forms or management information systems (MIS) data sheets, do not underestimate the fear of discrimination and homophobia that might prevent a client from choosing to be open early in the intake process. Attention needs to be paid to a range of options guided by the client's needs and preferences. Some clients prefer to include their sexual orientation on the intake sheet, some prefer to speak of it in person, and some are reluctant to bring it up at all. Saulnier (2002) has examined the issue of mental and physical health care providers becoming more *lesbian affirmative*. "Being *lesbian sensitive* meant that providers were able to place a lesbian's concerns or problems in their sociopolitical context ... *lesbian sensitivity* ... is seen "as almost a mirror-opposite of heterosexism. Lesbians are visible; their partners are included in care. Instead of ignorance, practitioners have up-to-date knowledge. Positive images replace negative stereotypes." *Lesbian affirmative* practitioners actively reach out and take special care to make lesbians feel like an important part of their practice (p. 362). Welcoming words included on websites and brochures convey a readiness to create a safe environment for lesbians to come out and fully participate.

Develop Comfort with Learning from Group Members

Do not overstate your knowledge or competencies to your clients or supervisors whether you are heterosexual or homosexual. It is important, when appropriate, to be a beginner about subculture issues, to ask thoughtful questions, and to seek advice about how to prepare for your role as group leader. You may also need to be prepared to clarify to the group your own sexual preferences, or to talk about sexual practices or ask questions that might imply sexual practices. Don't let feelings of shame or embarrassment stop you. Consult with a knowledgeable person and reveal your lack of knowledge of the lesbian woman's experience. Be direct with your supervisor and share concerns that you feel might be limiting your effectiveness with your clients. Do not rely on the clients as your primary source of information; our work is a partnership, and you must supply your own knowledge and experience.

Communicate Your Positions on Issues

For the most part, lesbians appreciate heterosexuals taking the initiative to bring up the subject of gayness, especially in positions that have a possibly negative effect on the status of the lesbian (job or work settings, authority settings like schools, physicians' offices, etc.). A gay-positive atmosphere or environment can be created in which diversity and differences are affirmed. Taking definite stands on antigay jokes and antigay literature is noticed especially in the workplace. Many persons have come to understand gayness through a family member, a close business/work relationship, or a homosexual encounter. While all social workers should be encouraged to work with lesbians in groups, I believe that specialized knowledge, training, and empathetic connection are vital for building trust and being effective.

Lesbians come in every size, shape, and color; variety is the norm. Many women defy the lesbian stereotype. The social group worker's responsibility is to program opportunities to discuss discrimination, stereotypes, and prejudice. Encouraging group interaction and direct feedback to each other is invaluable in helping the individual lesbian understand how she is perceived by others.

Because lesbians are often a hidden minority, it is very important to always assume that someone in your group is a lesbian, has a lesbian mother, sister, aunt, or child, or could be developing any of these options. It is equally important to assume that your boss, your secretary, or your mail carrier is possibly a lesbian or has a lesbian relative. In this way, you will open your eyes to the difficulties of knowing who is actually a lesbian. You will hear antigay jokes and know that someone who is listening is unable to speak out against the ignorance being displayed because of fear of declaring her identity. As you take the subject of lesbianism seriously, you will begin to experience the internal struggles of trying to decide when and where to tackle persons on their homophobia.

You must appreciate the burden of managing the dominant culture's constant and intrusive influence on the lesbian's life. An excerpt from an anxiety reduction group for lesbians follows:

> *Beth:* You don't know what is real or not; are you being paranoid or would my supervisor tell our boss that I'm gay just to further her career? I can't take the chance; I change all of my pronouns, don't let my lover call me at work, and I don't know what I will do when the baby is born. I run out at break and call her because her workplace is much more accepting; they know that she is a lesbian and pregnant. But she doesn't want me to come to her work parties because she thinks that I look too "butch" and that her staff might be uncomfortable with me or with us both present and acting like a couple.
>
> *Yvonne:* Do you think that you look too butch? Could you grow your hair a little longer and that might help? You probably wouldn't be wearing your work boots at the party either, right?

Beth: I don't think that I look 'butch' at work. Most of the workers in my department are men, and we all dress casual; my supervisor is almost the only one in the entire company that wears a dress. I'm afraid that I can't really change how I look that much—sort of androgynous, I hope. To try and change my looks and personality—now that would really make me anxious. Do I really have to 'look different' to feel less anxious?

Group worker: How have others in the group dealt with these issues? Do you sometimes wonder if you are being paranoid? The presence of homophobia in our workplaces is very real, but I would like us to focus here on sharing your tips and strategies for managing this dilemma when it has happened to you.

By acknowledging both the reality of the homophobia/heterosexism and the need for a strategy, the group worker encourages members and emphasizes the need to be proactive. Thus, the group worker is helping members to develop resilient behaviors. Be aware, however, that as some group members share examples of courageous behaviors, some clients are inspired but others may feel depression and more anxiety.

Set Clear Guidelines and Contract for Them

A common experience in lesbian group life is having couples begin to form sexual relationships (subgroups) and create difficulties for those who are being left out, that is, not chosen. Although group workers usually develop "rules" at the beginning of groups against involvement with a member of the group, this continues to occur. The experience of intimacy and closeness in the company of other lesbians in a safe setting is almost overwhelming for some women, and no amount of discussion in advance will deter from them acting on their sexual feelings. The author has found it useful to encourage the group to articulate these issues in the first two sessions, focusing on the experience of being in the group and eliciting feelings about both situations: getting sexually involved and not getting sexually involved. Role playing can be a useful tool, utilizing warm-ups of inclusion/exclusion or "what if" scenarios—What would happen to our group if sexual feelings are acted upon by ____and ____? Encouraging women to get together in small groups only outside the group can also act as a deterrent. Making agreements to share all contacts outside the group immediately, including telephone calls, will make the information available to all members and avoid surprises. Short-term contracts can help manage the push to act out. It is the group's responsibility, along with the worker, to manage the balance of intimacy, intensity, sexuality, and appropriate boundaries.

RECOMMENDED WAYS OF WORKING

Use of Time and the Program

Due to a scarcity of "visibility" and "role modeling" within the dominant culture for lesbians, It is very important to create opportunities within group structures to provide remedial experiences for those women who lack appropriate lesbian role models in the dominant culture. The importance of allowing sufficient time for women to tell their stories cannot be underestimated; to share with other lesbian women and with other lesbian-affirmative women the secret experiences of everyday life is very empowering. Groups often provide a way to have the first contact with a declared lesbian or with the lesbian community; often individuals have been encouraged by their case worker to sign up for a coming-out group or an informational lesbian consciousness group. The worker may have assessed with her client that she is ready to begin contact with other lesbians in the process of clarifying her sexual identity. It is very important for the group leader to screen potential group members to determine what phase of the process they are in; if possible, it is best for the group worker to know the range of experiences that members might have had so that all aspects can be included within the norm. Examples include a 50-year-old woman, married, with three children, who has had a 48-year-old lover, married, with two children, for 12 years; a 27-year-old woman who has never had a sexual relationship with anyone but has had a best friend since college whom she loves and lives with; an 18-year-old woman who has had three short-term relationships with women, but none of whom call themselves lesbian. The program would need to be structured to discuss choice of partners, labels to be considered for oneself, the role of children in the woman's life, and the struggle between the sexual self (perhaps just flowering) and the parental and career roles. Because of the nature of some of the issues involved, I believe that coming-out groups need to be run by lesbian group workers. More needs to be known about the special role of a worker who shares the characteristics of the group being served. Perhaps more could be learned by looking to the substance abuse field, the sexual abuse field, or the disability field. Any group leader, however, might find themselves in a position to help a client engage in these dilemmas; therefore, I consider it important to know how to discuss them. Any worker can support the healthy aspects of the choice and look for any dysfunctional responses (always looking through the lens of oppression and prejudice and listening for a client's actual experience voice).

In the author's experience, short-term groups work best when the purpose is educational or when everyone in the group has one or two pivotal life experiences in common (e.g., being Hispanic, being a mother, being an executive). The formation of a long-term group lends itself to the inclusion of more differences and allows interests to evolve as cohesion is built as part of the group process. The use of program materials can always be used to add variety; for example, an all-white able-bodied mothers' group can learn from a DVD featuring Asian women, disabled women, or gay men in nurturing or mothering roles. Books, videotapes, audiotapes, and websites are wonderful resources for showing healthy role models and helping lesbian women to visualize how their behavior might change. These resources are available from gay and lesbian organizations locally, nationally and on the Internet; catalogs are often available if you live in an inaccessible area.

The use of activities to enhance communication nonverbally and to focus communication verbally has been documented by Middleman (2005) and Lynn and Nisivoccia (1992). Creating a genogram, especially noting to whom one has disclosed one's lesbianism, provides a rapid connection for most people to their problems with the coming-out process and to the issue of shame. By adapting anxiety and depression scales, as well as attitude and fear surveys used to help focus symptoms and to show change, you can help group members focus on how much of their current anxiety and depression appear to be rooted in heterosexism or internalized homophobia. Sometimes it is especially useful to have the group create the instrument together. Collages of society's view of the lesbian lifestyle, created by clients at home and presented to the group, can be very evocative.

Co-leadership is never my first choice of leadership model for women's groups. Although traditionally it has been used in special circumstances where it has served a particular purpose (e.g., to allow a trainee to gain experience with a difficult population, to provide male/female balance), I have not found the usefulness of the method to outweigh the difficulties of trying to coordinate two leadership styles into one leadership role for a group. The primary exception that I have encountered concerns groups where physical safety and controls are needed and where emotional expressions of the group (sexual abuse or domestic violence) are best shared by two leaders.

Ethical Behaviors and Boundaries

Ethical behavior and appropriate boundaries are expected from all social group workers working with groups but are especially important in working with an invisible and marginalized community group.

Relationships that meet the *worker's needs* and are not focused on those of the lesbian client are inappropriate and harmful. More has been written about female sexual abuse perpetrators (Gartrell, 1994) and lesbian domestic violence (Morrow & Hawhurst, 1989). Attention is needed to these issues because of many lesbians' and professionals' denial and avoidance. A sexual relationship and/or sexual behavior is never appropriate between member and group worker; it can be especially destructive in group situations when a secret is being kept by one member of the group and the worker. Sexualizing and flirtatious behavior is destructive in group situations because of the power imbalance between worker and member; it also creates specialness and competition among members. Supervision and consultation should always be sought for help in tricky multiple relationship areas, especially if you have any doubts about whether your behavior is in the best interests of the member and the group.

Initial Screening Session

If possible, an initial individual screening session is always helpful. Gathering data on the following is useful:

- The individual's knowledge of the coming-out process and where she is currently on the continuum. Who are her role models?
- Her current coping skills and social support network
- How shame and internalized homophobia have been addressed. Ask directly: "How have you handled your internalized homophobia and your experiences of shame?"
- Whether alcohol and substance abuse have been part of the client's life and the family history in regard to alcohol, drugs, violence, and neglect
- How the client is managing the balance between privacy, disclosure to self, and disclosure to others. The question to always ask is how will the client "explain" group attendance?

In addition, be conscious of the complexities of multiple oppressions. If you are working with a disabled lesbian woman, you may need to get additional information through self-help groups or disability literature. If you are working with a member of another culture, knowing the customs of dealing with privacy and sexuality will help your communication.

Aligning Yourself with the Member's Perspective

It is crucial to assume that the client is doing the best she can in the coming-out process. It is not wise to push a client to come out, both because the outcome can be so variable and because the choice is better made when the client feels ready and able. With a client who says that she is being persecuted or could be persecuted, always start by believing the statement to be true because so little validation is available for her position within the dominant culture. Even if you know of other lesbians' experiences that seem to conflict with your client's, keep exploring and listening to find out the underlying issues of why this client "believes" her life/livelihood to be threatened. Even liberal colleagues and the social work community can do harm at times by not believing the client's experience and creating hardship for the client and her family

Help with Planning

An important practice principle is to help members realize that they need a *plan* to deal with their families of origin and with their created families. Too often clients sink into despair because they feel they have to take care and be supportive of their families while their families are processing their own losses and expressing dismay about the client's new or continued lesbian identity. The members of the group can give reasons for the correctness of the decision and can also reflect on how difficult it is to hear about anger and emotional turmoil when the woman wants her family of origin to be happy and eager to meet her new lover. Having definite plans for holidays that work for the lesbian woman is crucial. Holidays can be traumatic for lesbians, whether they have declared their status to their families or not. For example:

> *Member:* Even though my mother knows that I am in a relationship now, she still hasn't asked Judy to come to our house for Thanksgiving dinner yet. How long should I wait before I say something? I asked my sister, Kate, and she said that probably since this is the first Thanksgiving since Dad's death, I shouldn't push it. I feel confused because I don't want to upset my mother's holiday, but it is my life, too, and we [she and her lover] have so little time together that I would hate to spend the holiday apart. We have been together for five years, and we have spent the last year coming out in many more places and feeling good about our relationship, and it feels like a step backward.
>
> *Worker:* Could anyone else share how you planned your first few family encounters with a new partner? Did you involve your siblings and friends in the planning or did you do it primarily alone? Did you learn anything in hindsight that you could share with us?

Talking about all of the possibilities in a group of individuals who have experienced many of these options is invaluable to the lesbian woman's learning experience of herself and her motives. Understanding that a range of options is available may be new information for her. It is more effective to have members describe how they have handled or would handle this situation than to have the individual social worker work through this with the lesbian client.

EVALUATION MEASURES

One positive outcome of the managed-care movement in the mental health field has been the emphasis on outcomes and outcome research. At first, it was difficult to change my language and perceptions from intuitions and feelings to numbers and points on a scale. My evaluative expressions of the individual's experience in the group process notes used to be that "she is stuck," "making progress," "having a hard time," and "feeling safe enough to work on her issues." The group evaluative statements used to include "group is stuck," "group is developing leadership," and "group went well tonight." Now I am able to change most of the language on goals, progress, and "stuckness" into scales for the individual in the group and for the group as a whole. More techniques are needed to help us evaluate the group's progress that includes emphasis on group stages.

It is helpful to use specific behavioral terms for goals, group activities, and homework or activities that clients do outside the group. A first attempt to develop statements for how members will know when they have reached their goals begins at intake and at the first or second meeting. Group feedback and anecdotal evidence are still the primary tools used to evaluate effectiveness. I often use the next to the last session to evaluate and encourage members to give each other feedback face to face. We compare the pregroup goals and the postgroup evaluation, and members are often extremely insightful about their own individual changes and changes made by the group as a whole during the life of the group.

RESOURCES

Alternative Family Matters
P.O. Box 390618
Cambridge, MA 02139
(617) 576-6788
www.alternativefamilies.org

(COLAGE) Children of Lesbians and Gays Everywhere
National movement of children and adults with one or more lesbian, gay,
    bisexual, transgender, and/or queer (LGBTQ) parent/s.
1550 Bryant Street, Suite 830
San Francisco, CA 94110
(415) 861-KIDS
www.colage.org

Disabled Womyn's Educational Project
—Dykes, Disability and Stuff
2718 Longview Lane
Madison, WI 53713
(608) 256-8883

Family Equality Council
Formerly Family Pride and Gay and Lesbian Parents
Coalition International (GLPCI), a national advocacy
organization committed to securing family equality for
lesbian, gay, bisexual, transgender, and queer
parents, guardians, and allies

Family Pride Coalition
P.O. Box 50360
Washington, DC 20091
(202) 583-8029
www.glpci.org
www.familypride.org

Lesbian Connection Magazine
Elise Publishing Institute
P.O. Box 811, Dept W.
East Lansing, MI 48826
(517) 371-5257
www.lconline.org

National Center for Lesbian Rights Adoptive and Foster Parent Rights
    http://www.nclrights.org/publications/adoptive-information.htm

National Committee on Lesbian, Gay, Bisexual & Transgender Issues—
National Association of Social Workers (NASW)
750 First Street, NE Suite 700
Washington, DC 20002-4241
www.naswdc.org
www.socialworkers.org
www.helpstartshere.org
(search "lesbian" on sites)

National Gay & Lesbian Task Force
www.thetaskforce.org

Parents and Friends of Lesbians and Gays (P-FLAG)
1726 M Street NW, Suite 400
Washington DC 20036
(202) 467-8180
www.pflag.org

(SAGE) Senior Action in a Gay Environment
305 Seventh Avenue at 28th Street, 16th Floor
New York, NY 10001
(212) 747-2247
www.sageusa.org

The International Foundation for Gender Education
P.O. Box 540229

Waltham, MA 02454
(781) 899-2212
www.ifge.org

http://bentley.umich.edu/research/guides/gaylesbian
(search for "periodicals")
A comprehensive list of periodicals primarily from Michigan

www.GLReview.com
The Gay & Lesbian Review published entirely on the Web

www.biresource.org
(BRC) The BiSexual Resource Center

www.goldenthreads@earthlink.net
Only USA lesbian contact publication

www.gayyellowpages.com
The original lesbian, gay, bisexual & transgender information resource
    since 1973

www.lesbian.org
Meeting places & discussion groups for lesbians

www.welcomingresources.org

www.wowwomen.com
(Lesbians Online) Women Online Worldwide—a place for lesbian women to
    gather and discuss issues significant to the lesbian community

www.mypinkpal.com

www.pinkchoice.com

www.shedate.com

www.ptown.com

REFERENCES

Boenke, M. & Xavier, J. (eds.). (2003). *Transforming families: Real stories about transgen-dered loved ones* (2nd ed.). New Castle, DE: Oak Knoll Press.

Brown, L. S. (1990). Making psychology safe for gays and lesbians. Paper presented at the 98th Annual Convention of the American Psychological Association, Boston.

Cass, V. (1979, 1984, 1990). In K. Ritter & A. Terndrup (eds.), (2002). *Handbook of affirmative psychotherapy with lesbians and gay men.* New York: Guilford Press.

Ellis, P. & Murphy, B. C. (1994). The impact of misogyny and homophobia on therapy with women. In M. Merkin (ed.), *Women in context: Toward a feminist reconstruction of psychology* (pp. 48–73). New York: Guilford Press.

Friedman, R. & Downey, J. (1994). Homosexuality. *New England Journal of Medicine, 331*(14), 923–930.

Gartrell, N. (1994). Boundaries in lesbian therapist-client relationships. In B. Greene & G. Hereck (eds.), *Lesbian and gay psychology*, Vol.1 (pp. 98–117). Thousand Oaks, CA: Sage Publications.

Gochros, H. L. (1984). Teaching social workers to meet the needs of the homosexually oriented. *Journal of Social Work and Human Sexuality, 2*(2/3), 137–156.

Hancock, K. A. (2003). Book review of K. Ritter & A. Tendrup (eds.), *Finally under one roof: Information on the affirmative treatment of lesbian and gay clients: Handbook of affirmative psychotherapy with lesbians and gay men* in *Psychology of Women Quarterly, 27*(2), 189–191.

Herek, G. (1986). The social psychology of homophobia: Toward a practical theory. *Review of Law and Social Change, 14*(4), 923–934.

Kurland, R. & Solomon, R. (2005). Group work vs. casework in a group: Principles and implications for teaching and practice. *Social Work with Groups, 28*(3/4), 121–132.

Lee, J. A. B. (ed.). (1991). *An annotated bibliography of gay and lesbian readings.* New York: Cummings & Hathaway.

Lehman, J. L. (1978). What it means to love another woman. In G. Vida (ed.), *Our right to love* (p. 25). Englewood Cliffs, NJ: Prentice Hall.

Lesbian Review of Books, Jean-Nickolaus Tretter Collection in Gay, Lesbian, Bisexual and Transgender Studies, Special Collections and Rare Books, University of Minnesota Libraries, Minneapolis. *The Lesbian Review of Books* was published from 1994 through 2002 from Hilo, Hawaii, and was edited and published by Dr. Loralee MacPike.

Loulan, J. (1987). *Lesbian passion.* San Francisco: Spinsters, Inc.

Lynn, M. & Nisivoccia, D. (1992). *Activity groups: Integrating the "doing" with special populations.* Paper presented at the 14th Annual Symposium of the Association for the Advancement of Social Work with Groups, Atlanta.

Middleman, R. (2005). The use of program: Review & update. *Social Work with Groups, 28*(3/4), 29–48.

Morrow, S. L. & Hawhurst, D. M. (1989). Lesbian partner abuse—implications for therapists. *Journal of Counseling and Development, 68*(1), 58–62.

Murphy, B. C. (1991). Coming out of the classroom closet. In K. Harbeck (ed.), *Educating mental health professionals about gay and lesbian issues* (pp. 229–246). New York: Haworth Press.

Murphy, B. C. (1994). Difference and diversity: Gay and lesbian couples. *Journal of Gay and Lesbian Social Services, 1*(2), 5–31.

Ritter, K. & Terndrup, A. (2002). *Handbook of affirmative psychotherapy with lesbians and gay men.* New York: Guilford Press.

Roth, S. (1989). Psychotherapy with lesbian couples: Individual issues, female socialization and the social context. In M. McGoldrick, C. M. Anderson, & F. Walsh (eds.), *Women in families: A framework for family therapy.* New York: W. W. Norton.

Roth, S. & Murphy, B. C. (1986). Therapeutic work with lesbian clients: A systemic therapy view. In M. Ault-Riche (ed.), *Women and family therapy* (pp. 78–89). Rockville, MD: Aspen Press.

Ryan, C. & Futterman, D. (1998). *Lesbian & gay youth: care & counseling—The first comprehensive guide to health and mental health care for lesbian and gay youth.* New York: Columbia University Press

Saulnier, C. F. (1997). Alcohol problems and marginalization: Social group work with lesbians. *Social Work with Groups, 20*(3), 37–59.

Saulnier, C. F. (2000). Incorporating feminist theory into social work: Group work examples. *Social Work with Groups, 23*(1), 5–29.

Saulnier, C. F. (2002). Deciding who to see: Lesbians discuss their preferences in health and mental health care providers. *Social Work, 47*(4), 355–365.

Witeck, B. (2005). An encyclopedia of gay, lesbian, bisexual, transgender and queer culture. www.glbtq.com/social-sciences/market_research.html

Part Five

Schools, the Workplace, and the Community

Chapter Nineteen

Group Work With Urban African American Parents in Their Neighborhood Schools

Geoffrey L. Greif and Darnell Morris-Compton

This chapter describes a parenting support group approach used in four different Baltimore city public schools in neighborhoods that have historically been underserved. Dominated by housing projects and young families, the areas are frequently described as some of the worst in Baltimore in terms of crime rate and poverty. Three of the four groups have been held in schools that are composed of a student population that is more than 95% African American. The fourth school has a combination of African American, white, Latino, and Asian students. This chapter will focus primarily on working with African American families, describing the group format and the parenting issues that members have brought to the group over the past 20 years. Discussion of how these issues are handled is included.

The poverty rate for African Americans in 2007 was 24.5%, the highest among all ethnic and racial groups in the United States (DeNavas-Walt, Proctor & Smith, 2008). Poverty, in part, stems from the legacy of racism in the United States, and can be associated with the many problems faced by those African Americans living in the inner-city, including drugs, homelessness, crime, stress, problems with mental and physical well-bring, and being incarcerated (Utsey & Constantine, 2008).

The school systems, often underfunded in major cities due to a shrinking or static tax base, can be ill equipped to meet the educational, much less the emotional, needs of children. Parents and parent figures are also affected by these problems, as well as by the high unemployment rate. Their own resources are sorely depleted. A feeling of powerlessness, a traditional target of social work practice (Cox, 2002), abounds. A cycle is maintained in which parents with diminished resources are raising children in great need. Traditional attempts to assist minority clients often fall short because of a lack of understanding of the culture (Boyd-Franklin, 2006), a lack of resources, and a failure to focus on strengths and a family's resilience (Seccombe, 2002).

In the face of overwhelming problems and needs (Dunlap, Golub & Johnson, 2006), low-income African American families have historically received few or no services (Kalyanpur & Rao, 1991). Group work, based on the concept of mutual aid (Shulman, 2006), provides a forum for parents to join together and help each other. The parenting suggestions emanating from the group will be consistent with the neighborhood's and culture's style of parenting. Group work also has the potential to reduce the isolation so often felt by these parents while providing education and support (Cohen & Graybeal, 2007; Gitterman, 1989). The benefits of groups also include experiences of universality, the instillation of hope, and the feeling of greater strength in numbers. Rehearsal of new parenting behaviors can be attempted, and parents may gain insight into their own approaches to the children they are raising (Cox, 2002; Shulman, 2006). A parenting group can also help parents deal with any personal problems they may be experiencing like depression, which can affect their ability to parent and their child's well being (Sagrestano, Paikoff, Holmbeck, & Fendrich, 2003). In fact, studies have shown parenting groups have been effective at decreasing child conduct problems (Patterson et al., 2002), increasing parental satisfaction and competence (Odom, 1996), and improve interactions between the parent and child (Kaminski et al., 2008).

The social worker as a partner in the school setting is a well-established role, whether functioning as an employee or as a consultant. Leading parent groups to provide both intervention and prevention (see, e.g., O'Donnell, Hawkins, Catalano, Abbott, & Day, 1995) is clearly part of the social work function. Not much has been written, though, about group work specifically with African American parents. Literature on work with the African American family in general has suggested the importance of relationship building, focusing on strengths, keeping interventions concrete, and gathering information about who is considered part of the family (Boyd-Franklin, 2006; Hines, 1989).

The notion of family, particularly for a white worker, often needs to be reconsidered to include more than individuals related by blood (Camille Hall, 2008; Mosley-Howard & Evans, 2000). In addition, race cannot be ignored, whether the worker is of the same race or a different race (Boyd-Franklin, 2006). The worker must show his or her skills, concern, and ability to offer meaningful help during the group meetings.

PRACTICE PRINCIPLES

This group is called "Help! My Kids Are Driving Me Crazy!" The title was selected to convey with humor what parents frequently experience while raising their children. A more straightforward title might have been more threatening. The group is held in several public elementary schools in Baltimore. The attendees are usually mothers and occasionally grandmothers, great-grandmothers, and fathers. It is a 60-minute drop-in group set up to provide mutual aid (see Shulman, 2006), with parents encouraged to help each other. In addition, it functions as a socioeducational group. As Radin (1985) states, such groups can be educative in format, place the worker on a more equal footing with the clients, and are based on non-pathological assumptions. Philosophically, the group is driven by the notion that parenting is a developmental process and that each new stage of a child's growth may pose difficulty for both the child and the parent. The group can help ease that transition by providing support and education about normal stages of development. These parents are also buffeted by the stresses inherent in their environment and by larger social institutions, like Child Protective Services, the Housing Authority, or the Department of Social Services. While these institutions are designed to assist families, they are often perceived as unresponsive and/or intrusive. Thus the group also deals with issues impinging on the family from the outside.

While long-term supportive work is the major purpose of the group, some parents attend only one or two sessions. For this reason, each group should be a learning and supportive experience in itself. Some sessions address a specific topic that is planned in advance, while others have an open format. The members are encouraged to share concerns about their children and are asked to keep confidential all information they hear from other members. Members are informed by the leaders that instances of child maltreatment will be reported to Child Protective Services.

The leader's level of participation is an important component, particularly when working with a client population from a different racial and economic background. Too much input too early in the group process might be construed as controlling. Yet it is also standard practice for a leader to be active at the beginning of a group in order to establish group structure and allay normal anxiety. There was a beginning period at the first school when the members and worker sized each other up. An African American co-leader from the parent body, a key person in the success of that particular group, was more active at the beginning. With the parents (the first author is white, the second author is African American), once the worker was accepted by the group, it was important to be active, as he had been incorporated into the group as a parent and as a person with expertise. The danger of taking a peripheral role during the middle phase of group work, a role often suggested in the literature on group therapy, is that the leader is perceived as withholding or rejecting. The standard approach was modified. Once the leader was accepted, an active role was assumed and parent issues were both discussed by the leader and turned back on the group. At the most recent group, the leader asked for feedback from the group about his level of activity. It became possible to be active during all phases with the group's permission. The leader also met occasionally outside of the group for consultation with parents who did not feel comfortable using the group to discuss their issues. While this approach theoretically might have undermined the work of the group, given the drop-in nature of the group it was seen as accommodating the needs of the parents.

The groups, which have been conducted for different lengths of time since they started in 1990, were set up to meet weekly or monthly (depending on the school). The parents and leader agreed to meet for a certain period of time, and then stop and determine if they wished to continue. This held the parents and worker to a joint commitment and, depending on the culture of the school, proved effective most of the time. The most recent group included MSW students who were completing field education at the elementary school. They were able to follow-up with parents and children when issues were raised in the group in a more thorough way than an outside consultant could.

COMMON THEMES

A number of issues have surfaced at various schools during the years the groups have been in existence. These tend to center on the following themes: disciplining the difficult child; dealing with the noncustodial parent who visits sporadically (usually the father and sometimes the mother if a grandmother was attending the group); parents' feeling undermined by their children's grandparents; being triangulated between a child and Child Protective Services; keeping children safe in the neighborhood; enhancing self-esteem; dealing with stress; and giving a child what he wants when there is little money.

Disciplining the Difficult Child

Perhaps foremost in concern among the parents is unhappiness with the behavior of their children. It is this problem that initially drives parents to attend these groups. Complaints range from the mundane to the extraordinary, from normal developmental concerns to examples of extreme behaviors and exposure to traumatic events that strain the limits of current social work thinking.

Parents raise routine concerns about children who will not sit still during dinner, who do not finish their homework, who balk at doing chores, and who ignore them. They raise more troublesome complaints about teenagers feeling unsafe in schools and getting into fights, dropping out of school, and of running the streets until late at night. Occasionally, striking concerns are brought up. One parent worried about what to tell her 5-year-old daughter who had seen a dead body in a dumpster (see case example later). She also wanted assistance in dealing with the same daughter following sexual abuse by a 7-year-old neighborhood boy. The question of how to handle the parent of the boy after the boy was reported to the police was also raised. One great-grandmother did not know what to do about her great-grandson, who, at the age of 10, often stayed out all night without her knowing his whereabouts.

Underlying these concerns and, in some cases, instigating them is a sense the parents have of feeling totally overwhelmed by their environment. Poverty, unsafe housing, unsafe neighborhoods, inadequate resources, and sometimes their own history of school failure and having been inadequately parented combine to drain the parents of the ability to cope. Their own needs are so great that marshalling strength to cope with the environmental pressures on their children is nearly impossible.

Dealing with the Noncustodial Parent Who Visits Occasionally

Many parents (usually mothers) are raising children alone. As such, their lives often remain entwined with those of the father or fathers of their children, particularly if the father shows an interest in his offspring. Visits pose a problem for two reasons: Some fathers say they will visit and do not. When they do visit, they often have more control over the children than the mother.

As with many separations and divorces, the logistics of contact between the noncustodial parent and the child can be problematic. Even in the best of situations, schedules get lost, communication is confused, and last-minute cancellations wreak havoc on longstanding plans. In these families, where some children have been the product of brief relationships, commitments are kept less often. Thus, promises to visit end up being hollow, leaving the custodial parent to deal with the upset child whose father did not stop by to take the child for the outing he had promised.

Group members also raise the problem of having less control over the child than the father seems to have. Whether married or single, mothers complain that their attempts to discipline fall short, while all the father has to do is "raise his voice," "stamp his foot," or "shout once" and the children fall into line. The seeming power of the father poses a triple threat to the mother: making her feel incompetent, reinforcing the importance of men over women in her community, and angering her, as she is the one who usually spends the most time with the child.

Occasionally it is the grandmother raising her daughter or son's child who discusses this issue. In these situations, the grandmother may complain about her child's lack of concern and sporadic involvement or that when the child does visit, she or he spoils the grandchild.

Parents Feeling Undermined by Their Parents

Many group members live with their parents due to financial constraints and a lack of available child care. These situations lead easily to disagreements over how to parent. Group members sometimes feel undercut by their parents, who invoke certain rules because it is their home. The members, having few options about where else to live, are caught between succumbing to their parents' suggestions about how their grandchildren should be raised and wishing to follow their own rules.

Being Caught Between a Child and Child Protective Services

Parents of older children often feel undermined in their attempts to discipline their child when the child threatens to call 911 or Child Protective Services if the parent is on the verge of physically punishing the child. At times this may be appropriate from the child's perspective. As indicated by the parents, though, it is used even for minor acts of discipline. For the parents, this tips the balance of power in the home and is an example of the state intruding on their family. For some parents, it creates the feeling that life has changed from the time when they were young and parents were in charge of their children.

Keeping Children Safe in the Neighborhood

One of the larger problems in these neighborhoods is the safety of the streets. Members often lament that they were able to play outside until nighttime when they were young, whereas their own children cannot. Yet keeping the children inside in a small apartment or house, especially on a hot evening, poses other problems and adds to the general level of stress in the home. This discussion often results in parents complaining about being unable to control older children who are running the streets. When older children are brought up, and because we are working in an elementary school, we try and reframe the discussion in terms of the family system and how such behavior might affect the elementary school child.

Enhancing Self-Esteem

Some parents have been exposed to other parent education programs in the schools. Chief among these programs' goals is the enhancement of self-esteem. A few group members (who often emerge as internal leaders) are able to use what they have learned in these programs and relate their feelings as parents to their feelings about themselves as people. This can then become a topic of group discussion and lead to a discussion about how making oneself feel better as a person will help them as a parent.

A recent group ended with the leader asking each parent to say something positive about their child or something they took pride in with their child. This ending exercise is meant to have parents leave on a positive note and avoid the sense that sometimes permeates parenting groups that children were out of control and unlovable.

Parents smiled and gave examples ranging from the wonderful art that was hanging outside the child's classroom to the great job a child was doing in keeping his room clean. One father, a recent widower, said his children did not do anything well. A mother in the group who knew the father and his children reminded him that his daughter ran and gave him a big hug the day before when he picked her up after school. The leader helped the father acknowledge this by framing the daughter as someone who showed affection well and gave good hugs. It also meant that the father was a lovable parent, an attempt to get him to view himself differently. This was one example of getting the father to accept a compliment about his child and, indirectly, about himself. The leader must always look for such opportunities to enhance self-esteem.

Dealing with Stress

Parents are constantly bombarded by the chaos in their neighborhoods. They complain that they are stressed out and unable to meet the continuing needs of their children. An ongoing theme is the request for information about how to deal with this stress. In some cases, helping the parent deal with anxiety by helping her understand when she is most anxious will also help reduce anxiety in her interactions with her child (Wood, McLeod, Sigman, Hwang & Chu, 2003).

Giving a Child What He Wants When There Is Little Money

Parents on limited incomes are often scraping the bottom of the barrel by the end of the month to make ends meet. Giving a child even a small bonus for good behavior or a good school performance can be a financial stretch. Finding enjoyable family activities like a visit to a fast food restaurant or a movie is frequently out of a parent's range. As a result, chances to celebrate in a way that is meaningful for a child are few. This makes the parent feel incompetent as a provider and nurturer.

RECOMMENDED WAYS OF WORKING

The approaches used with these group members must be consistent with their culture and cognizant of their inherent strengths. Suggestions for interventions that are outside their resources will not be successful or accepted and may well be experienced as destructive.

Giving instruction about child development is the first stage in helping parents to discipline more effectively. Parents of very young children often interpret rambunctious behavior as disobedience rather than normal exuberance and get into battles with their children. For example, the 18-month-old who looks at the parent and then throws food on the floor is not trying to anger the parent. Messy rooms are not meant to be disrespectful but rather are a reflection of the child's feelings about himself or herself and a lack of interest in cleanliness. In most cases, child development information comes from the group members themselves, and not from the leaders, which helps foster self-esteem in the parents and makes learning feel less like a formal classroom. For some members, depending on their acceptance or rejection of authority, this may make the information more palatable. It also gives a sense of competence and altruism to the provider of the information.

More serious discipline issues are usually handled in two ways. First, the group provides specific suggestions. If these fall short, as sometimes occurs, or if the group is put off by the difficulty of the issue, the leaders step in. If an assessment of the parent has not been made in advance (e.g., this is the parent's first meeting), a few questions about the context of the problem (e.g., who is in the family and who is affected by the problem) sometimes clarify the picture. Family system strengths are often the focus of the conversation. The questions asked include "What has worked for you in the past?" and "When are you most proud of your child?" Ideas from structural family therapy (Nichols, 2009) are often applied. In addition, rituals are prescribed that are intended to enhance enduring family patterns and build closeness (Mackey & Greif, 1994). Encouraging parents to read to their children every night, have a special pizza night once a week, or have a "choose a TV show" night introduces structure to families that often live in chaos. While these rituals do not deal specifically with the discipline problem, they build family strength and set the stage for solving the problem. Concepts underpinning short-term therapy are also applied (Nickerson, 1995), with an eye toward providing a different view of the problem. The role of the leader tends to become more central the more serious the problem. Yet the group, when it is working well, provides support around these intractable problems that can touch a reserve of strength in the parent.

Inadvertently, the timing of some disciplinary interventions may be fortuitous. Something that failed once may work again a year later. The parent who comes occasionally, gets a little information from the group, and does not come back is reminded of that information when he or she sees a sign advertising the group, even if the parent chooses not to return. Over the course of many years of working in the same school, the mere presence of the group, even for one-time attendees, becomes a reminder of suggestions for change.

Dealing with the noncustodial parent, particularly a man, requires an acknowledgment of the differential status men hold in this community, where women so frequently are in the majority. While ventilation is helpful, unless a context and limits for group discussion are set, members tend to spiral off into diatribes about men that are ultimately unproductive. Helping to set the context can include leading discussions about the role of men in the parents' lives when they were younger and focusing on the current precarious position that men occupy in many communities.

Group members often believe that the visiting father should be treated harshly, perhaps reflecting the members' own feelings of anger and helplessness. Ideally, the group can be helped to reach the conclusion that, with most fathers, involvement is a positive experience for the child when it is regulated. If the father visits and undermines the authority of the mother, both parents should be encouraged to work together on setting rules for the child. Often this does not work, though, and the influence of the outside father becomes something that the custodial parent and her children have to learn to live with. In that case, the mother is assisted to view the father's involvement in a way that does not get her so upset. This can include discussing what other behaviors surround the visit that the mother can better understand and change. For example, the mother who finds herself screaming at the father the minute he walks in will be asked to anticipate his visit with a different reaction. The purpose is to handle the visit in a way that makes her feel more in control.

Most recently, talking about how men (and women) are socialized by society has been helpful to group members in understanding the demands on fathers. The impact on sons being raised by single mothers was noted. For example, the members were asked to consider what messages sons receive about how they should behave in the classroom. Care was taken to include the messages that mothers/women/daughters receive from society, too.

In dealing with intrusive grandparents, we return to the ideas of structural family therapy. Boundary issues are emphasized at the same time that group members are asked to explore any unresolved problems they may have with their own parents that affect how they themselves parent. The advantage of the group is that grandmothers caring for grandchildren are also present, giving an intergenerational perspective to the discussion. Sometimes when a mother or grandmother sees the conflict from the another perspective, change can occur.

When group members believe that their attempts to parent are being impeded by a child's threat to call Child Protective Services, we sympathize with them by saying, "It must be hard to be unable to parent the way you want to." The underlying interventions must speak to two themes: helping the members find a way of parenting that will work for them (i.e., increasing their sense of competence) and acknowledging the interference of other institutions in their lives. The first theme is approached by returning the question to the group of what solutions they have found for the particular problem. Then the discussion can turn to other ways in which the members feel that outsiders are interfering, including referring to the group leader as a potential outsider. This sometimes opens up issues about being referred by the school principal to the parenting group and the members' reactions to that suggestion.

When safety concerns keep children cooped up in their homes, suggestions about alternative modes of entertainment in Baltimore are usually given by other group members. The discussion then evolves into how life has changed since the members were young. By broadening the question, members can be asked to discuss how they can recapture part of their past that they enjoyed. These discussions usually occur as parents exchange ideas about how to improve their position on public housing lists so that they can move to a safer neighborhood sooner. For some, a move is the best intervention.

Self-esteem is built within the group process. By supporting the parents' adaptive attempts to parent and by parents finding ways to help other group members, self-esteem does increase. Breaking down parenting into small steps helps the parents gain a sense of control. If the group provides helpful suggestions that are put into action, the members often feel better. Yet some parents are unreachable through the group. They may be what have been called, "help-rejecting complainers." These are people who come to the group and turn back every suggestion, saying "I tried that and it does not work." Others may be in the group because of pressure from a teacher or the principal. The task here is to prevent them from discouraging members working toward change.

Stress is handled the same way. Parents are encouraged to find a small thing they can accomplish that will make their lives more pleasurable. Stress often seems to loom over these parents as a mountain that they can never scale. Suggesting to parents that they have the right to have time for themselves, by asking a trusted neighbor to watch their children one day in exchange for their watching the neighbor's children the next, and stating that they should be allowed to take a shower or go to the bathroom without interruption provides solace to some parents.

Stress is also handled by helping the parent feel more competent, an issue related to self-esteem.

> The parent (referenced earlier) whose young daughter was sexually abused by a neighbor's child had also observed a dead body in a trash dumpster adjacent to their high-rise development. As the child was significantly traumatized and then retraumatized by the second event, the mother wanted assistance in dealing with the child's nightmares and increasingly uncontrollable behavior.
>
> Borrowing from structural family theory, we tried to place the mother in charge of the situation by increasing her feeling of competence. The belief was that if the mother felt more competent, the child would feel less upset. (The child was also in occasional individual treatment related to the sexual trauma.)
>
> We asked the mother to read to her child at bedtime. If she could find books about children successfully coping, so much the better. We also asked her to involve her daughter in other activities where the mother was clearly the expert, like cooking and game playing. The hope was that such activities would enhance the role of the mother and show the child that the mother was competent. The intervention succeeded in reducing the child's nightmares but was less successful with the discipline problem.

Other suggestions for stress-related issues sometimes emerge from the parents' own language rather than our developing an intervention. A parent in a recent group wanted help with her 5-year-old who was acting out. The parent went into a lengthy description of all the child's misdeeds. The mother then talked about her sense of self having a "good mommy" and a "bad mommy" who could respond to her child. We asked her how to bring out the "good mommy" more often. Then we turned to the group and asked the other members to describe their "good" and "bad" sides and when they felt most capable of bringing out their "good" sides. With this approach we were using a common strengths–based, solution-focused approach (see, e.g., Nichols, 2009 & Schwartz, 2007) that asks the group to look for answers. Tuning into what works helps parents to feel more positively about their situation and to see the group as a place to find answers that are transferable to home.

Finally, we try to help parents discuss money management. Groups whose members receive government assistance often have low attendance when checks arrive because parents are making purchases. By the end of the month, little money is left. Parents who can learn to use money more effectively are not bereft the final week of the month when the child wants change for a candy bar. Sound money management by the parent also shows the child that the parent will be consistent in meeting the child's needs, a message that all children need to hear.

EVALUATION AND CONCLUSION

It must be noted that despite the examples given of successful group interventions, some problems presented by the group members are unsolvable in the group context. They push the limits of social work practice because of the extreme nature of the situation and the lack of resources available to families. Some members with intractable problems drop out of the group, perhaps believing that another attempt to help them has failed. Unfortunately, the net result is to reinforce their sense of helplessness.

The success of the drop-in group is judged by the answers to three questions: (1) Do parents return? (2) Do the parents who attend even one session appear to get something out of it? This is often a subjective assessment as paper-and-pencil tests some times scare off potential attendees. At the end of each group, the leaders ask if the group has been helpful. Parents often say they feel better at the end of the group because they have had a chance to vent, have received some ideas about parenting, and have learned that they are not alone in their struggles. The parents' self-report at subsequent sessions is another key gauge. If they are returning with stories of success, even minor success, the group is working for them; and (3) does the principal think it is working?

Many parents return, depending in part on the culture of the school. In three of the four schools, the group has been successful with returning parents; in the fourth school, where attendance is low, the parent-school liaison reports that the parents still request the group, even though they do not always attend. Parents do tend to leave after each session, saying that they enjoyed the meeting. For some principals, the mere presence of the group is greeted warmly because it serves as a statement that the school is trying to meet parents' needs. Some principals may overinflate the impact of the group to maintain its presence in their school. As long as the group is constructive, the principals of all four schools are happy to sponsor it, though the level of support (a quiet room, coffee, signs in the school announcing the group) tends to vary from one school to the next.

Empowering disadvantaged parents through group work can be a key element in any plan to improve the situations of at-risk children. By assisting those who want help and building on their strengths, greater parenting competence may develop throughout the community.

ACKNOWLEDGMENTS

Versions of this chapter appear in G. L. Greif (1993). A school-based support group for urban African American parents. *Social Work in Education, 15*, 133–139; G. L. Greif, (1994). Using family therapy ideas with parenting groups in schools. *Journal of Family Therapy, 16*, 199–207; and J. Mackey & G. L. Greif (1994). Using rituals to help parents in the school setting: Lessons from family therapy. *Social Work in Education, 16*, 171–178.

RESOURCES

Educational Resources Information
Clearinghouse on Disabilities and Gifted Education
1920 Association Drive
Center Reston, VA 20191
http://www.ericec.org

Home and School Institute
1500 Massachusetts Ave., NW
Washington, DC 20002
(202) 466-3633
www.megaskillshsi.org

National Black Child Development Institute
1023 15th Street, NW, Suite 600
Washington, DC 20005
(202) 387-1281
http://www.nbcdi.org

Centers for Disease Control and Prevention
1600 Clifton Road
Atlanta, GA 30333
(800) 232-4636
http://www.cdc.gov/LifeStages/

KidsHealth
The Nemours Foundation
1600 Rockland Road
Wilmington, DE 19803
(302) 651-4046
http://kidshealth.org/

REFERENCES

Boyd-Franklin, N. (2006). *Black families in therapy: Understanding the African American experience* (2nd ed.). New York: Guilford Press.

Camille Hal, J. (2008). The impact of kin and fictive kin relationship on the mental health of black adult children of alcoholics. *Health & Social Work, 33*(4), 259–266.

Cohen, M. B. & Graybeal, C. T. (2007). Using solution-oriented techniques in mutual aid groups. *Social work with groups, 30*(4), 41–58.

Cox, C. B. (2002). Empowering African American custodial grandparents. *Social Work, 47,* 45–54.

DeNavas-Walt, C., Proctor, B. D., & Smith, J. C. (2008). *U.S. Census Bureau current population reports, P60-235, Income, Poverty, and Health Insurance Coverage in the United States: 2007.* Washington, DC: U.S. Government Printing Office.

Dunlap, E., Golub, A., & Johnson, B. D. (2006). The severely-distressed African American family in the crack era: Empowerment is not enough. *Journal of Sociology and Social Welfare, 33*(1), 115–139.

Gitterman, A. (1989). Building mutual support in groups. *Social Work with Groups, 12*(2), 5–21.

Hines, P. M. (1989). The family life cycle of poor black families. In B. Carter & M. McGoldrick (eds.), *The changing family life cycle: A framework for family therapy* (2nd ed., pp. 513–544). Boston: Allyn & Bacon.

Kalyanpur, M. & Rao. S. S. (1991). Empowering low-income black families of handicapped children. *American Journal of Orthopsychiatry, 61,* 523–532.

Kaminski, J. W., Valle, L. A., Filene, J. H., & Boyle, C. L. (2008). A meta-analytic review of components associated with parent training program effectiveness. *Journal of Abnormal Child Psychology, 36,* 567–598.

Mackey, J. & Greif, G. L. (1994). Using rituals to help parents in the school setting: Lessons from family therapy. *Social Work in Education, 16,* 171–178.

Mosley-Howard, G. S. & Evans, C. B. (2000). Relationships and contemporary experiences of the African American family: An ethnographic case study. *Journal of Black Studies, 30,* 428–452.

Nichols, M. P. & Schwartz, R. (2009). *The essentials of family therapy* (4th ed.). Boston: Allyn & Bacon.

Nickerson, P. R. (1995). Solution-focused group therapy. *Social Work, 40,* 132–133.

O'Donnell, J., Hawkins, D., Catalano, R. F., Abbott, R. D., & Day, L. E. (1995). Preventing school failure, drug use, and delinquency among low-income children: Long-term intervention in elementary schools. *American Journal of Orthopsychiatry, 65,* 87–100.

Odom, S. E. (1996). Effects of an educational intervention on mothers of male children with attention deficit hyperactivity disorder. *Journal of Community Health Nursing, 13*(4), 207–220.

Patterson, J., Barlow, J., Mockford, C., Klimes, I., Pyper, C., & Stewart-Brown, S. (2002). Improving mental health through parenting programmes: Block randomized controlled trial. *Archives of Disease in Childhood, 87,* 472–477.

Radin, N. (1985). Socioeducation groups, In M. Sundel, P. Glasser, & R. Vintner (eds.), *Individual change through small groups* (2nd ed., pp. 101–116). New York: Free Press.

Sagrestano, L. M., Paikoff, R. L., Holmbeck, G. N., & Fendrich, M. (2003). A longitudinal examination of familial risk factors for depression among inner-city African American adolescents. *Journal of family Psychology, 17,* 108–120.

Seccombe, K. (2002). "Beating the odds" versus "changing the odds": Poverty, resilience, and family policy. *Journal of Marriage and Family, 64,* 384–394.

Shulman, L. (2006). *The skills of helping individuals, families, and groups and communities* (5th ed.). Belmont, CA, Thomson-Brooks/Cole.

Utsey, S. O. & Constantine, M. G. (2008). Mediating and moderating effects of racism-related stress on the relation between poverty-related risk factors and subjective well-being in a community sample of African Americans. *Journal of Loss and Trauma, 13,* 186–204.

Wood, J. J., McLeod, B. D., Sigman, M., Hwang, W.-C., & Chu, B. C. (2003). Parenting and childhood anxiety: Theory, empirical findings, and future directions. *Journal of Child Psychology and Psychiatry, 44,* 134–151.

Chapter Twenty

Group Work With Victims in Communities Disrupted by Violence and Mass Trauma

John A. Kayser

This chapter examines the benefits and limitations of group work approaches with victims living in communities disrupted by violence and mass trauma. Natural and manmade disasters not only cause death and severe physical injuries and/or psychological damage to individual persons but also can result in severe damage to communities themselves, such as through mass casualties and widespread property loss; disruptions of communication, social networks, routines of daily living, and the functioning of core institutions; and dramatic declines in communities' capacity to provide basic aid (i.e., emergency shelter, food, and water) or assist in reconstruction efforts (Blumenfield & Uransano, 2008; Pfefferbaum et al., 2008; Ritchie, Watson, & Friedman, 2006).

Large-scale natural disasters, while rare, can devastate entire cities (in 2005, Hurricane Katrina killed more than 1800 in New Orleans), large geographic regions (the 2008 earthquake in China killed an estimated 90,000), or even several countries at once (e.g., the 2004 tsunami in the Indian Ocean killed an estimated 230,000 in 11 countries). Preexisting social and structural problems in communities, particularly poverty, significantly exacerbate the impact of natural disasters on communities as well as markedly slow the progress of communities' recovery (Moyo & Moldovan, 2008; Smith, 2008).

According to the *Online Encyclopedia of Mass Violence,* wars and armed conflicts, such as those currently or recently occurring in Iraq, Afghanistan, Pakistan, the Palestinian Territories, Lebanon, and the Darfur region of Sudan, as well as the genocidal conflicts in the 1990s in Rwanda and Bosnia/Herzegovina, result in tremendous loss of life, especially where inflicting massive civilian causalities and death among enemy groups is a specific military/political objective of the combatants (http://www.massviolence.org). In these cases, where existing infrastructures and basic services are destroyed, mass flight of refugees and internally displaced persons often result. While not as destructive to property on the same scale as natural disasters, incidents of mass violence also can have a devastating effect on communities.

According to a 2008 report by the Centers for Disease Control and Prevention (CDC), school shootings remain rare (cdc.gov/injury). They account for less than 1% of violent crimes in American public schools, with an average of 16.5 deaths per year from 2001 to 2008. Nonetheless, 38% of public schools reported at least one violent incident to police during the 2005–2006 school year. In 2005, 628,200 middle school and high school students, between the ages of 12 and 18, were the victims of violent crimes at school, including rape, sexual and aggravated assault, and robbery.

Despite a nationwide overall drop in crime, incidents of mass violence continue to occur in the United States with regularity. In the 5-year period from 2005 through 2009, there have been multiple incidents of mass violence occurring in widely divergent settings, including shootings on college campuses, employment sites, health/recreation centers, and even an army military base. In a number of cases, the perpetrators were individuals with known significant mental health disorders or major adjustment difficulties. In other cases, a mixture of political and criminal motives appears to have been at work. Many perpetrators seek to avoid capture and prosecution through suicide, either through self-inflicted wounds or through "suicide by cop." These disturbing, recurring events of mass violence indicate that there is no place that is safe from unpredictable danger.

Responding to natural and manmade disasters continues to be daunting not only because of the magnitude and severity of events but also because the term *community* refers not only to people in physical proximity to each other but also to those who are connected in other ways, such as through their participation in a common culture (e.g., being members of the same ethnicity, gender, social class, sexual orientation, beliefs, and language) or through having a common interest or activity or even by their regular communication and contact with others in a virtual world, such as online communities and interactive social networks. In these distal communities of interest, it may be a single episode of violence that traumatizes or negatively reverberates throughout members of community of interest.

Bell (2008) notes, for example, that the experience of ethnic and racial groups who live in systems characterized, historically, by oppressed/oppressor relationships have markedly different views of traumatic events compared to whites. Violence directed against individual persons from minority groups can produce traumatic feelings of fear and degradation among other members of the group nationwide. Similarly, attacks on and/or horrific killings of gay men and transgendered persons can be terrorizing to members of the lesbian, gay, bisexual, or transgendered (LGBT) communities. The impacts of these single separate events are cumulative, however, particularly when these communities continue to feel unsafe and vulnerable because of inadequate protection by police and courts.

REVIEW OF PROFESSIONAL LITERATURE

Definitions

The American Medical Association (2005) defines *mass trauma* as multiple injuries, deaths, disability, and emotional stress caused by a catastrophic event, such as a large-scale natural disaster or a terrorist attack. The widespread injuries and deaths result because these events typically are staged in urban settings with dense population, often near large buildings and/or where large groups of people tend to gather (e.g., mass transit centers), which increase the likelihood of a serious disaster involving multiple casualties. In the aftermath of the 2001 terrorist attacks on the United States mainland, the CDC has focused greater attention on "mass casualty events," such as those caused by a bombing, bioterrorist attack, hazardous chemical release, exposure to radiation or radioactive materials, and health pandemics (www.bt.cdc.gov).

The term *community violence* arose in the early 1990s through the efforts of the U.S. surgeon general and the CDC to reframe as a society-wide health concern the violent behaviors of individuals that heretofore had been the primary concern of the criminal justice and mental health systems (CDC, 1993, 2008; Rosenberg & Fenley, 1991). According to Shahinfar, Fox, and Leavitt (2000), *community violence* is defined as "the presence of violence and violence-related events within an individual's proximal development, including home, school, and neighborhood; it may involve direct or threatened harm, be witnessed or experienced, and involve known or unknown perpetrators" (p. 115). These authors suggest that community violence differs from other types of violence in that (a) it is *pervasive*, permeating all micro systems levels, such as home, school, work, and surrounding community; (b) it is *chronic*, characterized by cumulative, repeated exposure to such violent acts as shootings, stabbings, rapes, and beatings. It may also include robbery, kidnapping, school violence, domestic violence, illegal drug activities, child abuse, sexual abuse, hate crimes, homicide, suicide, etc.; (c) it is *random*, presenting a constant threat to community members' safety and security; and (d) it is *alienating*, isolating and fragmenting individuals from their community and sources of social support. Using physical intimidation, threats, or actual harm to take valued possessions increases victims' feelings of vulnerability and fear, and lack of trust in others.

Community violence may result in physical and psychological trauma. *Physical trauma* refers to a serious and critical bodily injury, wound, or shock resulting from an external source such as physical assaults, gun shooting, or stabbings, etc. The effects of physical trauma can be devastating, in that injuries can destroy health, lives, and livelihoods (Bradford, 1999). *Psychological trauma* refers to an experience that is emotionally painful, distressful, or shocking, which often results in lasting mental and physical effects (National Institute of Mental Health, 2001). A traumatic event is any critical incident that causes people to experience unusually strong emotional reactions that have the potential to affect their ability to function at work, at home with family members, or in other areas of their lives (Waldrop, 2001). The event or events may be time-limited, or their impact may be ongoing.

Rates of Exposure

As summarized by Smith (2008), exposure to traumatic events is widespread in the general population. The most common experience is witnessing someone being killed or injured severely, being caught in fire or natural disaster, or being involved in a life-threatening disaster. "Men reported experiencing more of these more commonly than did women, as well as combat, physical attacks, being threatened with a weapon, and being kidnapped. Women were more likely to report rape, sexual molestation, and childhood physical abuse or neglect" (p. 241).

Although an acute stress reaction is extremely common in the aftermath of a traumatic event, only 29% of those who experienced such events had reactions that were deemed serious enough to level requiring clinical intervention (Friedman, Ritchie, & Watson, 2006). Most people exposed to trauma recover spontaneously, "but a sizeable number progress to chronic incapacitating disorders such as PTSD or depression" (p. 10). As summarized by Smith (2008), national co-morbidity studies in 1995 and 2005 place rates for PTSD at between 8% and 9% in the general population. "Hispanics report the lowest rates (5.9%), followed by non-Hispanic Whites (6.8%) and non-Hispanic Blacks (7.1%)" (p. 242). However, the prevalence of psychological distress is considerably higher for acts of terrorism than for natural disasters (Friedman, Ritchie, & Watson, 2006).

Community violence is not confined to poor, urban neighborhoods, however, as can be seen by the number of high profile, multiple-victim school shootings that have occurred in middle class suburban and rural areas since the late 1990s. For example, in the 1999 Columbine High School shooting, in which 13 students and 1 teacher were killed along with two dozen wounded, it was estimated that there were over 10,000 direct and secondary victims of this one single event, just in the Denver metropolitan area alone. (This figure was derived by estimating a minimum of five additional people affected, such as family, relatives, and peers, for each of the approximately1870 students and 95 teachers and staff members at Columbine that day.) Similarly, Paine and Sprauge (2002) reported that the Springfield, Oregon, school shooting in 1998, in which 2 students were killed and 25 others wounded, affected all of the 11,000 students and 1200 employees of the

Eugene-Springfield school district. As these incidents rippled throughout the nation, obviously the number of people affected by community violence occurrences is much, much higher.

PRACTICE PRINCIPLES

Establish Groups as a Major Component in Community Planning Efforts

No single approach to mass trauma and community violence is sufficient, and multiple strategies must be used (Blumenfield & Uranso, 2008; Fraser, 1995; Ritchie, Watson, & Friedman, 2006). Mental health intervention of any kind may be particularly difficult to initiate when there is extensive physical destruction, catastrophic devastation, and collapse of basic services in a large-scale natural disaster.

Broad-based, comprehensive, community-planning efforts, which include emergency preparedness planning for disaster response, can incorporate a variety of group work approaches into the prevention and intervention phases of treatment of mass trauma (Cannon & Gingerich, 2002; Goldstein & Conoley, 1997; Knight, 2006; Layne et al., 2001; Paine & Sprague, 2002; Stewart & Thomson, 2005). In addition, groups can be consciously constructed to work with specific populations who have experienced community violence (i.e., war refugees; victims of juvenile violence; sexual abuse victims, victims of work-place violence, school shootings, rape) (Ceballo, 2000; deYoung & Corbin, 1994; Gabriel, 1996; Hopps & Pinderhughes, 1999; Kinney, 1995; Layne et al., 2001; Murphy, Pynoos, & James, 1997; Ying, 2001). For many group members whose lives contain daily encounters with violence, conflict, and anger, the group experience may be the one consistent place that they experience a sense of safety (Levinsky & McAleer, 1994).

One daunting challenge to community planning efforts is that many people who experience mass trauma and community violence never seek or receive services of any kind. Indeed, the people most likely to benefit from a group experience (i.e., those with no previous exposure to trauma and violence, and who have fewer sources of social support) apparently are those least likely to make use of this experience (Ursano, Fullerton, Vance, & Wang, 2000). Extensive outreach efforts may be required to engage community members following disasters and catastrophes (Naturale, 2008), particularly in communities in which cultural beliefs about mental illness and stigmatization about receiving services make it difficult to engage community members (Fang & Chen, 2004)

Emergency Preparedness, Prevention, and Resilience

Comprehensive community-based planning has increasingly emphasized not only emergency preparedness for disaster relief, but also the fostering of individual and community *resilience* (Pfefferbaum et al., 2008). Seven interrelated factors have been conceptualized as linking the resilience of individuals and communities, and these factors appear highly compatible with the core methods and values of group work approaches. These identified factors are:

- Connectedness, commitment, and shared values
- Participation
- Structure, roles, and responsibilities
- Resources
- Support and nurturance
- Critical reflection and skill building
- Communication

Both large-scale town-hall community meetings and small-scale groups have an important role to play in helping communities clarify and restate their values, achieve greater inclusiveness and participation among all community members, and forge stronger links between individual well-being and the overall health of the community. Prevention groups can decrease school and community violence by strengthening empathy, emotional responsiveness, and affectional bonds among members; promote understanding and tolerance of individual and group differences; teach improved help-seeking behaviors, increased communication and conflict resolution skills; teach about the impact of gangs, guns, and weapons on a community; and reduce members' reactivity to violence, potential for withdrawal and/or reenactment of aggression and violence (Callaway, 2003; Glodich & Allen, 1998; Murphy et al., 1997). Prevention and preparedness groups typically are time-limited, meeting over two or three sessions.

Early Intervention Phase

Early intervention seeks to provide a brief client contact, given as close as possible to the actual site of a disaster (*proximity*), given as soon as possible after the occurrence of the disaster (*immediacy*), which helps victims normalize acute distress reactions as appropriate responses to an overwhelming event (*expectancy*) and which keeps interventions easy to deliver and understand (*simplicity*) (Ruzek, 2006). The overall goal of the early intervention phrase is to promote rapid recovery by establishing safety, reducing the heightened cognitive and affective arousal associated with traumatic distress, and helping clients in the resumption of normal activities (Friedman et al., 2006). Several different methods may be used in this phase:

Peer Support and Defusing

An important distinction has emerged in the trauma literature between *defusing* acute distressful reactions and *debriefing* traumatic experiences.[1] Defusing, which originated in military psychiatry as part of frontline treatment of soldiers experiencing combat (Friedman et al., 2006), is "designed as a brief (10-30 minutes) conversational intervention that can occur informally (e.g., during a meal or while standing in line for services). Defusing is designed to give survivors support, reassurance, and information" (p. 4). It is seen as an effective early intervention during natural and manmade disasters, particularly when survivors become preoccupied with their own internal thoughts about stressful events, and appear open to talking about them.

While defusing appears conceptualized primarily as an individual intervention, its principles are very compatible with spontaneous informal groups (e.g., neighborhood support groups, work peer groups, adolescent "groups on the go") run or co-facilitated by natural helpers or paraprofessionals designed to share stressful experiences; get feedback about their reactions from peers, obtain empathy, support, and validation; problem solve; and regain a sense of safety and control (Jagendorf & Malekoff, 2000; Ursano et al., 2000). Advanced training of and/or consultation to natural helpers by the trained professionals appear crucial for success. These groups typically are of short-term duration.

"Psychological First Aid" Groups

The goals of psychological first aid (PFA) are to (a) to establish contact and engagement with survivors and to provide (b) safety and physical and emotional comfort, (c) stabilization and calming, (d) practical assistance in addressing immediate needs, (e) connections with social supports, (f) information on coping supports, and (g) linkage with collaborative services (Watson, 2008). Group work approaches are a good medium for the application of PFA because the emphasis on groups is developing connections and social supports with others. It is important, however, "to provide opportunities to tailor coping information to specific needs, while not in any way making participants feel that they need to share their experiences" (p. 77). PFA groups can aid members in practical problem-solving, support and understanding for individual members' reactions, normalization of stress reactions, and mutual aid about ways to successfully cope. PFA groups appear to function as a form of very short-term triage screening and immediate responses to mass casualties resulting from community disaster or catastrophe.

Intervention Phase

Psychoeducational Groups

Stewart and Thomson (2005) observe that social disconnection is one of the most prevalent responses to community trauma. Psychoeducational groups, developed as one part of broader efforts in establishing community coalitions and partnerships across agencies and service providers, are often a preferred early intervention method of choice to combat social disconnection, isolation, and withdrawal. According to Knight (2006), "Groups that are more structured, time-limited, and have a clear educational component appear most appropriate to individuals new to treatment.... In this type of psychoeducational groups, feelings are acknowledged and validated, but are deliberately contained" (p. 25). Rather, the emphasis in psychoeducational groups is to assist members in establishing stabilization and safety. Educating group members who have gone through the same type of disaster experience, on the effects of trauma (e.g., acute and/or posttraumatic stress reactions) is helpful. In addition, these short-term psychoeducational groups can be used to assess clients whose pre-trauma histories and/or post-trauma reactions indicate the need for referral for more intensive services. Psychoeducational groups vary in terms of the number of sessions, but typically constitute more than a brief triage contact.

Ongoing Groups for Survivors

Usually begun some weeks or months after a major disaster or violent event, ongoing survivor groups are designed to alleviate suffering and promote a return to healthy functioning by normalizing stress reactions; allow time for mourning and grieving; restore a sense of control over certain aspects of the environment; process anger and rage at the perpetrators; build mutual aid and support to help combat feelings of depression, vulnerability, and helpless; and begin the process of rebuilding one's life (Ceballo, 2000; Dembert & Simmer, 2000; deYoung & Corbin, 1994). Mutual aid groups are useful in helping members process and understand their posttraumatic reactions (Knight, 2006). These ongoing groups provide members a greater opportunity to address bereavement in addition to traumatic stress. The use of cognitive-behavioral techniques in reframing negative cognitions associated with the trauma has good empirical support as an intervention technique (Blumenfield & Urasano, 2008). Typically, these are long-term, closed groups, lasting many months.

Follow-Up Support Groups

Groups designed to deal with the long-term impact of community violence also are essential (Dembert & Simmer, 2000). Group sessions specifically focused on client strengths can be especially helpful. Using solution-focused techniques, such as asking members to share times when they are not experiencing stress- or trauma-related symptoms or reactions, allows the group to focus on the healing and improvement process (Juhnke & Osborne, 1997). Helpful solution-focused therapy techniques include identifying positive changes already occurring; focusing on cognitive decisions regarding improvement (rather than dwelling on external forces or dynamics); identifying common elements in symptom-free times; reminding members of past success in coping with other distressing events; encouraging members to "do something different" when existing coping strategies are not working; and using scaling techniques to help participants identify the degree of improvement since previous sessions.

Forming Groups and Selecting Group Members: Situational, Developmental, and Cultural Considerations

Witnessing, experiencing, or responding to violence and victimization upon one's self, a family member, or a peer typically are deeply distressing events.

A person-environment lens (Fraser, 1995; Wilson & Sigman, 2000) is useful in conceptualizing mass trauma and violence and the complex, interacting situational, developmental, and cultural considerations that must be addressed when practitioners begin to form groups and recruit members.

Situational Factors

When forming groups to respond to acute episodes of, or chronic exposure to, community trauma and violence, it is important to distinguish between *direct victims*, those persons directly injured by disaster and violence, and *secondary victims*, which include witnesses and bystanders, employees at a work site, first responders (i.e., police, fire fighters, paramedics), family members, stakeholders (those that knew victims), and others connected to the event or persons involved (Kinney, 1995). Generally speaking, the more direct the exposure to the traumatic event, the greater is the risk for emotional harm (National Institute of Mental Health, 2001).

Individuals in each category require a different group experience, with their own unique format and structure that best suits their needs for process and recovery. Several authors suggest that iatrogenic effects may occur when individuals with different degrees of exposure are brought together in the same group (Ceballo, 2000; Regher & Hill, 2000). As Raphael and Wilson (2000) observe: "Some [individuals] whose exposure has been minor may be traumatized by vivid accounts of those more intensely involved" (p. 4). Group practitioners, therefore, need to develop a screening process to select individuals most appropriate for the type of group being organized.

Developmental Factors

An individual's cognitive style, pre-event resiliency (i.e., ego strengths and adaptation abilities), available social supports, and the nature of injury or harm will influence his or her subjective reaction to violence (Fraser, 1995). Developmentally, children and adolescents are at particular risks for developing academic difficulties, emotional and behavior problems, and trauma-related symptoms following exposure to violence (Dulmus & Wodarski, 2000; Hopps & Pinderhughes, 1999; Shahinfar, Fox, & Leavitt, 2000). Children witnessing violence are more likely to develop internalizing problems (i.e., depression, anxiety, social withdrawal), whereas children who were attacked or injured by violence are more likely to develop externalizing problems (i.e., aggression, conduct problems, delinquency) (Shahinfar et al., 2000).

Violence not only adversely affects children's sense of safety, it may interfere with development of attachment to adult caretakers and other responsible figures of authority, ability to process painful emotions, and the development of an internalized conscience. Children in the preoperational stage of cognitive development (approximately ages 2 to 7 years), where egocentric thinking is predominant, may believe that they have done something to cause the violence, or that they should have done something to prevent the violence from occurring.

An extensive review of the group therapy literature conducted by Glodich and Allen (1998) stressed the important role groups can have in preventing *reenactment* of violence among children and adolescents exposed to various types of trauma, thus forestalling the movement from "victim" to "perpetrator." Authorities differ, however, in their view regarding whether children should be encouraged to directly speak about trauma-related incidents from their past. Ceballo (2000) cautions against direct exploration with elementary school-aged children, preferring instead that discussions about neighborhood violence occur in *displacement*, that is "one step removed from personal experience" (p. 402). In this approach, group practitioners help normalize and universalize the experience by discussing what "most children or adults would feel" when encountering violence. These techniques help prevent traumatizing some children whose exposure to violence is less severe than other members in the group.

A different view is taken by Murphy, Pynoos, and James (1997), who developed a combined approach of individual treatment, group psychotherapy, and therapeutic mentoring to help children chronically exposed to urban violence. These authors note that children typically respond to invitations to discuss their experiences in one of three ways: (a) sharing minimal details or facts, without processing deeper thoughts and feelings; (b) responding competitively, by sharing "war stories" about their traumatic experiences, without the accompanying appropriate feelings of sadness, anger, or fear; or (c) responding anxiously and avoidently, by seeking to distract themselves and other group members from further discussions of the topic. By drawing attention to when these behaviors occur during group sessions, practitioners help individual members and the group as a whole develop greater ability to tolerate direct discussions of traumatic experiences, eventually leading to the reintegration of painful feelings into their conscious awareness.

Despite their theoretical differences, most group intervention approaches agree that processing underlying feelings and emotional reactions to violence is a crucial component in helping children and adolescents resume the course of their normal development. The advantage of groups is that individual members' emotional needs can be met in a more egalitarian manner through mutual aid and support with peers and caring adults.

Cultural Factors

Group interventions must be adapted to the specific culture and environmental circumstances in which they are to be deployed (Raphael & Wilson, 2000). Several corollaries of this practice principle emerge from this discussion:

First, being a member of a minority cultural group in America may place a person at higher risk for trauma-related symptoms than his/her white counterparts (Abueg, Woods, & Watson, 2000; Naturale, 2008). Acute episodes of violence take place in the context of prior exposure to ongoing chronic forms of social oppression and economic disadvantage for many people of color and other marginalized groups. Group work is the intervention of choice with oppressed populations

(Hopps & Pinderhughes, 1999). "It is critical for the [group] social worker not only to have a general understanding of the history of minority groups and their interactions with each other, but also to have a clear sense of the intergroup factors that exist in the community in which one is working" (Weiss, 1997, p. 126).

Second, perception of events and interpretation of traumatic reactions will vary depending upon the culture of those affected. Similarly, cultural beliefs, traditions, and rituals also will be critical in helping individuals work through and integrate their experiences (Bell, 2008; Perren-Klingler, 2000). Incorporating cultural language and rituals regarding loss, mourning, and death into group interventions may be particularly helpful.

Third, trauma professionals in charge of psychological debriefing or other group crisis intervention approaches typically are outsiders to the indigenous cultural groups and communities in which they work. Further, outside professionals may symbolize to indigenous community members the historic oppression from a dominant culture or country previously involved in colonization or enslavement of the indigenous people (Abueg, Woods, & Watson, 2000). In order to be effective, outside professionals may need to gain credibility by partnering with a cultural expert—a representative of the affected group—who understands the cultural norms (Raphael & Wilson, 2000) or actually training therapists indigenous to the cultural community (Layne et al., 2001). The outside professionals' work in the indigenous community should be time-limited, ending at the point in which the community reestablishes its ongoing functioning.

Fourth, selection of group members should give consideration to matching the cultural diversity of the general school or community populations from which the group is drawn. As Rose (1998) notes, "cultural factors are sometimes a source of homogeneity. As a source of heterogeneity, however, a diversity of cultural factors in composition provides members with an opportunity to relate to peers from dissimilar backgrounds" (p. 37).

Fifth, culture can be a protective factor in mitigating the effects of trauma (Bell, 2008). Culturally specific group intervention can be designed as part of broad coalition or partnerships among multiple agencies and service providers located in the communities themselves (Layne et al., 2001; Stewart & Thomson, 2005). Mutual aid groups may be particularly relevant with some members coming from collectivist cultures, because of the cultural traditions of members helping other members (Bent-Goodley, 2009)

COMMON THEMES

At the risk of blurring the distinctions among the many different types of groups developed to respond to mass trauma and community violence, the following discussion is an amalgamation of themes across group types and populations. Themes are examined within the overlapping theoretical frameworks for the *phases of trauma recovery* (Kinney, 1995) and *stages of group development* (Dembert & Simmer, 2000). While by no means identical, these two have some rough parallels with each other.

"Safety and Control"

The initial phase of trauma recovery is characterized by reactions of shock, horror, and disbelief (Kinney, 1995), as individuals attempt to process extreme events outside of the realm of their previous personal experiences (in the case of acute trauma episodes). For individuals chronically exposed to violence, their first-hand experiences with death and injury may be considerably more extensive, but often, they have had little previous opportunity to process their reactions in an appropriate manner (Ceballo, 2000; Timnick, 1989). Initial themes at the beginning stage of group development typically center on whether the group is a safe place to be together and talk about the things that have happened—both the good and bad. As group members introduce each other and help establish group rules, they begin to create a sense of safety and control (Knight, 2006). The reliability, predictability, and continuity of the group experience are one means by which members begin to reestablish a sense of basic trust in the world around them (Stewart & Thomson, 2005). Group rules may include decisions about who can participate; length of time the group is intended to meet; confidentiality; and how the group will handle individual members who become overwhelmed in talking about their experiences. Ceballo (2000) notes that children exposed to chronic violence may add the rule "no weapons brought to group" to further reinforce the sense of safety and control.

"So Many Thoughts and Feelings"

The second stage of trauma recovery is characterized by individuals experiencing the gamut of emotions and thoughts as they attempt to accommodate their experiences into their existing cognitive schemata or world-view (Kinney, 1995). Emotions may range from numbing to intense anxiety, fear, terror, anger, guilt (at surviving), remorse, and grief. Cognitions may range from confusion, to intrusive thoughts and images, to obsessive ruminations on the same events over and over again. Desire to place blame, seek revenge on perpetrators, or express feelings of betrayal and abandonment at not being protected from harm are common. Feelings of sadness, mourning, and loss over the death of a loved one also predominate (Dembert & Simmer, 2000).

In the middle phase of group development, group facilitators strengthen group cohesion by normalizing common themes and reactions among group members, while also pointing out the uniqueness of each person's individual viewpoints. Themes typically focus on identifying, naming, validating, and expressing these distressing feelings, and on differentiating situations, thoughts, and feelings from each other (Ceballo, 2000; Hopps & Pinderhughes, 1999). In addition, dealing with members' cognitive distortions regarding their personal responsibility for being victimized and/or their potential for becoming violent themselves is critical. For example, some middle school students who knew the Columbine High School shooters worried that because they liked the same kind of music and video games as the two teenage killers, they would become the victims of other students' and parents' wrath, or feared that they would, themselves, subsequently become violent (Kayser, Silver, & Lyon, 2001). Similarly, a persistent theme for many groups is the loss of confidence in one's ability to cope, and feeling inadequate or ineffective in one's role (e.g., spouse, parent, breadwinner, classmate, coworker) (Debert & Simmer, 2000). Feelings of being out of control, or of having no control over one's life may be marked.

"Coping and Reintegration"

The third phase of trauma recovery focuses on developing effective coping strategies to deal with the distressing thoughts and feelings, and restoration of functioning and equilibrium (Kinney, 1995). Themes in this phase typically center on the realization that group members can begin to rebuild their lives, even while recognizing that their lives will never be the same as they were before the violence occurred (Dembert & Simmer, 2000). Highlighting strengths, resilience, and preexisting coping strategies are important (Juhnke & Osborne, 1997; Woodcock, 2001). In the ending phase of group, practitioners need to recognize that, for some members, there is no final closure to the traumatic event, because their lives have been inalterably changed. Providing concrete, tangible reminders of the group experience (e.g., handing out diplomas and bravery awards, developing a group newsletter that summarizes each person's story) are ways of bringing the group experience to an end (Ceballo, 2000).

METHODS

According to Raphael (2008), "the strongest evidence for benefit [to victims exposed to community trauma] is the provision of cognitive behavioral interventions, plus exposure paradigms" (p. 26). These interventions can be incorporated into many group methods and approaches. The keys to successful interventions are respect for the individual members' variation in trauma reactions, and the timing of interventions.

Cognitive Therapy

Cognitive techniques that intervene in and disrupt dysfunctional thoughts (i.e., reframing, evaluating the evidence supporting inaccurate/extreme appraisals of event, challenging distortions, and replacing distortions with accurate information) and which help victims integrate the trauma experience into their existing mental schemas (i.e., redefining experiences, constructing coherent "trauma narratives") have been found to be useful in trauma therapies with children, adolescents, and adults (Nader, 2004; Young, 2006). As Young (2006) notes, however, "care must be given to validating the affective component (the feelings of helplessness, fear, grief, and rage)" (p. 143), in addition to assisting victims in restructuring extreme cognitions and distortions.

Behavioral Therapies

Behavioral techniques include behavior management, stress reduction/relaxation, and teaching safety skills (Nader, 2004; Young 2006). Some survivors may experience guilt when asked to relax, fearing that "relaxing will compromise their coping ... [or will result in] being overwhelmed by intense memories or emotions" (Young, 2006, p. 143). Starting with a brief demonstration of relaxation techniques (e.g., 30 seconds of slow breathing) may be a useful introduction.

Exposure Therapies

Exposure techniques involve "confrontation with the feared stimuli (e.g., traumatic reminders) followed by the introduction of corrective information (e.g., the reminder itself does not represent danger, remembering trauma is not the same as reexperiencing it, anxiety can diminish without avoidance, and experiencing trauma symptoms does not have to lead to loss of control" (Nader, 2004, p. 65).

Other Therapies

Grief and bereavement counseling overlap with but are different from interventions focused on trauma. "Grief counseling requires support for review of the lost relationship, the changes in the bereaved person's life and roles that are a consequence of the loss, and dealings with the yearnings, sadness, anger, and perhaps guilt" (Raphael, 2008, p. 27). Grief, like trauma, can be both intense and prolonged, and clinicians' sensitivity to how these interplay within individual members and in the group as a whole are essential in moving groups forward.

Trauma and grief can also reactivate and intensify pre-trauma existing problems, including drug abuse and antisocial behaviors, and additional therapeutic interventions often are needed to address these problems.

EVALUATION APPROACHES

As Raphael (2008) notes, "testing core elements in real-world post-disaster settings is a research challenge" (p. 27). There is greater evidence for effective interventions with individuals experiencing specific traumas, such as rape, but at present there is "limited scientific basis on which to provide clear guidance for clinical interventions" in instances of mass trauma (p. 27).

Part of the difficulty in measuring the impact of community violence is that, even if people have experienced highly stressful events, they also may have positive, growth-producing experiences as well. Multiple measures, therefore, should be employed in order to understand both the nature and impact of the stressful event and the types of adaptation and growth that may have resulted from the experience. It especially is important to differentially assess the impact of a single traumatic event from multiple traumas and from the accumulated risk of lifetime exposure. The National Center for PTSD's website summarizes a large number of specialized trauma evaluation instruments, including structured clinical interviews, client self-report measures, and clinician-administered scales, for both adult and child-adolescent clients (www.ncptsd.org/treatment/assessment/index.html).

CONCLUSION

This chapter has argued that a *multifaceted group approach at both the macro and micro levels* is needed to prevent and intervene in chronic and acute episodes of community violence and mass trauma. Despite the best efforts of helping professionals, it appears that many people affected by disaster and trauma never seek or receive appropriate help. The ongoing challenge for social workers is to design, coordinate, and implement a flexible array of group approaches that penetrate multiple layers of the community's experience. Formally structured group approaches must also connect more directly to natural, spontaneous groups that develop in response to disasters. Groups are the way communities can provide organized and intense forms of social support to the victims of violence in order to mitigate its impact and to forestall its further spread. Groups are the way communities can begin to heal themselves.

RESOURCES

The following is a list of resources on violence, trauma, and disaster from major national professional or government organizations.

Crisis and Trauma

Baldwin Trauma Pages
David V. Baldwin, PhD
Eugene, OR
(541)-686-2598
www.trauma-pages.com

National Center for PTSD
215 N. Main Street

White River Junction, VT 05009
(802) 296-5132
www.ncptsd.org

Psych Works/Managing Traumatic Stress
1515 University Drive, Suite 115A
Coral Springs, FL 33071-6084
(954) 344-2022
www.psychworks.com

The American Academy of Experts in Traumatic Stress
368 Veterans Memorial Highway
Commack, NY 11724
(631) 543-2217
www.aaets.org

Disaster Mental Health

Center for Mental Health Services
Emergency Services and Disaster Relief Branch
5600 Fishers Lane, Room 17C-20
Rockville, MD 20857
(301) 443-4735
www.mentalhealth.org/cmhs/emergencyservices/index./htm

Federal Emergency Management Agency
500 C. Street. SW
Washington, DC 20472
(202) 566-1600
www.fema.gov

National Institute of Mental Health
Information Resources and Inquiries Branch
6001 Executive Boulevard, Room 8184, MSC 9663
Bethesda, MD 20892-9663
(301) 443-4513
www.nimh.nih.gov

Walter Reed Army Medical Center, Department of Social Work
6900 Georgia Avenue, NW
Washington, DC 20307-5001
(202) 782-6378
www.wramc.amedd.army.mil/departments/socialwork/index.htm

Violence

Centers for Disease Control and Prevention
1600 Clifton Road
Atlanta, GA 30333
(404) 639-3311
www.cdc.gov

Minnesota Center Against Violence and Abuse
School of Social Work
University of Minnesota
105 Peters Hall
1404 Gortner Avenue
St. Paul, MN 55108
(612) 625-1220
www.mincava.umn.edu

National Center for Injury Prevention and Control
Mailstop K60
4770 Buford Highway NE
Atlanta, GA 30341-3724
(770) 488-4362
www.cdc.gov/ncipc

National Center for Victims of Crimes
2111 Wilson Boulevard, Suite 300
Arlington, VA 22201
(703) 276-2880
www.ncvc.org

National Organization for Victims Assistance
1757 Park Road, NW
Washington, DC 20010
(800) 879-6682
(202) 232-6682
www.try-nova.org

UCLA/School Mental Health Project
Center for Mental Health in Schools
Department of Psychology
University of California Los Angeles
P.O. Box 951563
Los Angeles, CA 90095-1563

(310) 825-3634
www.smhp.psych.ucla.edu

REFERENCES

Abueg, F., Woods, G., & Watson, D. (2000). Disaster trauma. In F. Dattilio & A. Freeman (eds.), *Cognitive-behavioral strategies in crisis intervention* (pp. 243–272). New York: Guilford.

American Medical Association. (2005). Mass trauma and explosive events. www.ama-assn.org/ama1/pub/upload/mm/415/05_masstrauma.pdf

Bell, C. (2008). Should culture considerations influence early interventions? In M. Blumenfield & R. Uranano (eds.), *Intervention and resilience after mass trauma* (pp. 127–148). Cambridge, UK: Cambridge University Press.

Bent-Goodley, T. (2009). A black experienced-based approach to gender violence. *Social Work, 54*(3), 262–269.

Blumenfield. M. & Uranao, R. (eds.). (2008). *Intervention and resilience after mass trauma.* Cambridge, UK: Cambridge University Press.

Bradford, A. (1999). REBUILD: An orthopedic trauma support group and community outreach program. *Health and Social Work, 24*(4), 307–311.

Callaway, C. (2003). Peer networking to build resiliency among high school youth: A violence prevention group. In D. Capuzzi (ed.), *Approaches to group work. A handbook for practitioners* (pp. 64–73). Upper Saddle River, NJ: Merrill Prentice Hall.

Cannon, J. & Gingerich, E. (2002). Seeking alternatives to violence: A school-based violence prevention project. In S. Henry, J. East, & C. Schmitz (eds.), *Social work with groups: Mining the gold* (pp. 31–39). New York: Haworth Press.

Ceballo, R. (2000). The neighborhood club: A supportive intervention group for children exposed to urban violence. *American Journal of Orthopsychiatry, 70*(3), 401–407.

Centers for Disease Control and Prevention. (n.d.). *Emergency preparedness and response.* http://www.bt.cdc.gov/

Centers for Disease Control and Prevention. (2008). *Understanding school violence: Fact sheet.* www.cdc.gov/injury

Centers for Disease Control and Prevention. (1993). *The prevention of youth violence: A framework for community action.* Atlanta: Author.

Dembert, M. & Simmer, E. (2000). When trauma affects a community: Group interventions after a disaster. In R. Klein & V. Schermer (eds.), *Group psychotherapy for psychological trauma* (pp. 239–264). New York: Guilford.

deYoung, M. & Corbin, B. (1994). Helping early adolescents tell: A guided exercise for trauma-focused sexual abuse treatment groups. *Child Welfare, 78*(2), 141–154.

Dulmus, C. & Wodarski, J. (2000). Trauma-related symptomatology among children of parents victimized by urban community violence. *American Journal of Orthopsychiatry, 70*(2), 272–277.

Fang, L. & Chen, T. (2004). Community outreach and education to deal with cultural resistance to mental health services. In N. Boyd-Webb (ed.), *Mass trauma and violence: Helping families and children cope* (pp. 234–255). New York: Guilford.

Fraser, M. (1994). Violence overview. In NASW's *Encyclopedia of social work*, Vol. 3 (19th ed., pp. 2453–2460). Washington, DC: NASW Press.

Friedman, M., Ritchie, E., & Watson, P. (2006). Overview. In E. Richie, P. Watson, & M. Friedman (eds.), *Interventions following mass violence and disasters: Strategies for mental health practice* (pp. 3–15). New York: Guilford.

Gabriel, M. (1996). *AIDS trauma and support group therapy*. New York: Free Press.

Glodich, A. & Allen, J. (1998). Adolescents exposed to violence and abuse: A review of the group therapy literature with an emphasis on preventing trauma reenactment. *Journal of Child and Adolescent Group Therapy*, 8(3), 135–154.

Goldstein, A. & Conoley, J. (eds.). (1997). *School violence intervention: A practical handbook*. New York: Guilford.

Hopps, J. & Pinderhughes, E. (1999). *Group work with overwhelmed clients*. New York: Free Press.

Jagendorf, J. & Malekoff, A. (2000). Groups-on-the-go: Spontaneously formed mutual aid groups for adolescents in distress. *Social Work with Groups*, 22(4), 15–32.

Juhnke, G. & Osborne, W. (1997). The solution-focused debriefing group: An integrated postviolence group intervention for adults. *The Journal for Specialists in Group*, 22(1), 66–76.

Kayser, J., Silver, J., & Lyon, M. (2001). From the frying pan into the fire: Three advocacy tales in child and adolescent mental health practice. *Reflections: Narratives of Professional Helping*, 7(1), 48–60.

Kinney, J. (1995). *Violence at work. How to make your company safer for employees and customers*. Englewood Cliffs, NJ: Prentice Hall.

Knight, C. (2006). Groups for individuals with traumatic histories: Practice considerations for social workers. *Social Work*, 51(1), 20–30.

Layne, C., Pynoos, R., Saltzman, W., et al. Trauma/grief-focused group psychotherapy: School-based postwar interventions with traumatized Bosnian adolescents. *Group Dynamics: Theory, Research, and Practice*, 5(4), 227–290.

Levinsky, L. & McAleer, K. (1994). "Listen to us!" Young adolescents in urban schools. In A. Gitterman & L. Shulman (eds.), *Mutual aid groups, vulnerable populations, and the life cycle* (2nd ed., pp. 151–162). New York: Columbia University Press.

Moyo, O. & Modovan, V. (2008). Lessons for social workers: Hurricane Katrina as a social disaster. *Social Development Issues*, 30(17), 1–12.

Murphy, L., Pynoos, R., & James, C. (1997). The trauma/grief-focused group psychotherapy module of an elementary school-based violence prevention/intervention project. In J. Osofsky (ed.), *Children in a violent society* (pp. 223–255). New York: Guildford Press.

Nader, K. (2004). Treating traumatized children and adolescents: Treatment issues, modalities, timing, and methods. In N. Boyd Webb (ed.), *Mass trauma and violence: Helping families and children cope* (pp. 50–73). New York: Guilford.

National Institute of Mental Health. (2001). *Helping children and adolescents cope with violence and disasters: Fact sheet*. Bethesda, MD: Department of Health and Human Services.

Naturale, A. (2006). Outreach strategies: Experiential descriptions of the outreach methodologies used in the September 11, 2001 disaster response in New York. In E. Ritchie, P. Watson, & M. Friedman (eds.), *Interventions following mass violence and disasters: Strategies for mental health practice* (pp. 365–383). New York: Guilford.

Paine, C. & Sprague, J. (2002). Dealing with a school shooting disaster: Lessons learned from Springfield, Oregon. *Emotional and Behavioral Disorders in Youth, 2*(2), 35–40.

Perren-Kilingler, G. (2000). The integration of traumatic experiences: Culture and resources. In J. Violanti, D. Paton, & C. Dunning (eds.), *Posttraumatic stress interventions: Challenges, issues, and perspectives* (pp. 43–64). Springfield, IL: Charles C Thomas Publisher.

Pfefferbaum, R., Reissman, D., Pfefferbaum, B., Wyche, K., Norris, F., & Klomp, R. (2008). Factors in the development of community resilience to disasters. In M. Blumenfield & R. Uranano (eds.), *Intervention and resilience after mass trauma* (pp. 49–68). Cambridge, UK: Cambridge University Press.

Rachael, B. & Wilson, J. (eds.). (2000). *Psychological debriefing: Theory, practice, and evidence.* Cambridge, UK: Cambridge University Press.

Raphael, B. (2008). Systems, science, and populations: Effective early mental health interventions following mass trauma: The roles of government, clinicians, and communities. In M. Blumenfield & R. Uranao (eds.), *Intervention and resilience after mass trauma* (pp. 1–47). Cambridge, UK: Cambridge University Press.

Regehr, C. & Hill, J. (2000). Evaluating the efficacy of crisis debriefing groups. *Social Work with Groups, 23*(3), 69–79.

Ritchie, E., Watson, P., & Friedman, M. (eds.). (2006). *Interventions following mass violence and disasters: Strategies for mental health practice.* New York: Guilford.

Rose, S. (1998). *Group work with children and adolescents: Prevention and intervention in school and community systems.* Thousand Oaks, CA: Sage.

Rosenberg, M. L. & Fenley, M. A. (1991). *Violence in America: A public health approach.* New York: Oxford University Press.

Ruzek, J. (2006). Models of early intervention following mass violence and other trauma. In E. Ritchie, P. Watson, & M. Friedman (eds.), *Interventions following mass violence and disasters: Strategies for mental health practice* (pp. 16–34). New York: Guilford.

Shahinfar, A., Fox, N., & Leavitt, L. (2000). Preschool children's exposure to violence: Relation of behavior problems to parent and child reports. *American Journal of Orthopsychiatry, 70*(1), 115–125.

Smith, N. (2008). Trauma. In T. Mizrahi & L. Davis (eds.), *Encyclopedia of social work,* Vol. 4 (20th ed., pp. 241–245). Washington, DC: NASW Press.

Stewart. D. & Thomson, K. (2005). The FACE YOUR FEAR club: Therapeutic group work with young children as a response to community trauma in Northern Ireland. *British Journal of Social Work, 35*(1), 105–124.

Timnick, L. (1989, September 3). Children of violence. What happens to kids who learn as babies to dodge bullets and step over corpses on the way to school? *Los Angeles Times Magazine,* 6–14.

Ursano, R., Fullerton, C., Vance, K., & Wang, L. (2000). Debriefing: Its role in the spectrum of prevention and acute management of psychological trauma. In B. Raphael and J. Wilson (eds.), *Psychological debriefing: Theory, practice, evidence* (pp. 32–42). Cambridge, UK: Cambridge University Press.

Violanti, J., Paton, D., & Dunning, C. (eds.). *Posttraumatic stress intervention: Challenges, issues, and perspectives.* Springfield, IL: Charles C Thomas Publisher.

Waldrop, D. (2001). *Critical incident stress management.* Washington, DC: Institute for the Advancement of Social Work Research. www.iaswresearch.org

Watson, C. (2008). Psychological first aid. In M. Blumenfield & R. Uranano (eds.), *Intervention and resilience after mass trauma* (pp. 69–84). Cambridge, UK: Cambridge University Press.

Weiss, J. (1997). Working with victims of ethnoviolence. In G. Greif & P. Ephross (eds.), *Group work with populations at risk* (pp. 121–133). New York: Oxford University Press.

Wilson, J. & Sigman, M. (2000). Theoretical perspectives of traumatic stress debriefing. In B. Raphael and J. Wilson (eds.), *Psychological debriefing: Theory, practice, evidence* (pp. 58–68). Cambridge (UK): Cambridge University Press.

Woodcock, J. (2001). Being, noticing, knowing: The emergence of resilience in group work. In T. Kelly, T. Berman-Rossi, & S. Palombo (eds.), *Group work. Strategies for strengthening resiliency* (pp. 5–17). New York: Haworth Press.

Ying, Y. (2001). Psychotherapy with traumatized Southeast Asian refugees. *Clinical Social Work Journal, 29*(1), 65–78.

Young, B. (2006). The immediate response to disaster: Guidelines for adult psychological first aid. In E. Ritchie, P. Watson, & M. Friedman (eds.), *Interventions following mass violence and disasters: Strategies for mental health practice* (pp. 135–154). New York: Guilford.

NOTE

1 Mandatory psychological debriefing groups, which were initially developed in the 1980s for *first responders* (e.g., firefighters, police, rescue workers, emergency medical personnel), and later applied in the 1990s to *victims* of community-wide disasters are no longer recommended as appropriate early intervention approach with survivors (Friedman et al. 2008). "There is little empirical evidence supporting the efficacy of PD [psychological debriefing] or showing that it prevents PTSD. Some research suggests that PD may even exacerbate posttraumatic distress under certain conditions" (Friedman et al., p. 5). Debriefing can exacerbate intrusive recollections or produce secondary traumatization, which may increase the incidence of PTSD. "Group debriefing does help group cohesion, morale, and other important outcomes" (Ruzek, 2006, p. 18), but its efficacy in preventing PTSD has not been demonstrated. Other types of interventions for workers in high-risk occupations, such a police, firefighters, and emergency medical personnel include "thoughtful design of work roles, task rotation, peer support systems, involvement of chaplains and other support personnel, employee assistance services, stress management training, and daily defusing" (pp. 17–18).

Chapter Twenty-One

Group Work in the Workplace Setting

Melissa Back Tamburo

For years, workplaces have noted that "troubled" employees are less productive, consume more management time, and are a greater strain on health insurance costs. Companies recognize that, in order to stay competitive in the fast-paced environment, they need workers who can fully concentrate on their tasks without being distracted by child care, health, financial, or other personal problems (Herlihy & Davidson, 2000). To address these issues, employee assistance programs (EAPs) and/or work/life programs, and more recently workplace wellness programs, have been instituted as resources for both managers and employees to address the personal problems that can impact work performance.

These programs offer a variety of methods, including group work, to address a wide range of employee concerns that can impact work performance. The Employee Assistance Professionals Association defines such an offering as "a work-site-based program designed to assist (1) work organizations in addressing productivity issues and (2) "employee clients" in identifying and resolving personal concerns, including, but not limited to, health, marital, family, financial, alcohol, drug, legal, emotional, stress, or other personal issues that may affect job performance" (http://www.eapassn.org/public/pages/index.cfm?pageid=869).

Work-life programs tend to have more broad organizational impact in that they include both services to assist employees in balancing work and personal life (dependent care resources and referrals as well as legal, financial, and sometimes concierge-like services) and development of workplace policies to recruit and retain employees (flex-time, flex-place, family leave policies). Workplace wellness programs help organizations manage the ever-rising costs of providing healthcare to employees, by providing programming to educate and support employees in improving their health and well-being, thereby reducing the impact on health care (Edington, 2001).

These programs overlap in that they all address issues that impact employee performance, attendance, presenteeism (or measure of productivity while at work), and well-being (Herlihy & Davidson 2000). Common themes among large employee groups are related to developmental stages of families: pregnancy and childbirth, parenting, single-parenting, retirement, eldercare, grief, and loss. Other common themes in large employee groups include addiction recovery support, smoking cessation, and weight loss. The demographics of the organizations' employee population can factor into the trends that affect employees. For example, in an organization with most employees aged 35 or older, issues around eldercare and parenting teens will be more prevalent than in an organization with a younger population. The nature of the work the organization provides may also create specific needs for support groups. For example, in an organization that requires extended lengths of work overseas, deployment away from home can create concerns both prior to and post deployment.

One way in which these issues are addressed is through employee-sponsored support groups. The goal of providing resources for employees with similar concerns is to mitigate any negative impact (or spillover) that these issues might have in the workplace. Negative impacts can include increased absenteeism, distracted employees and loss of productivity time, all leading to decreased overall work performance. These groups are often coordinated by one of the above noted groups (EAP, work/life, wellness), based on a needs assessment or acknowledgment that a trend exists among programs that could be addressed through mutual support.

The current climate of unprecedented economic uncertainty impacts employees in a myriad of ways as they struggle with widespread layoffs, loss of retirement income, and increasing unemployment figures. In such turbulent times, the role of each employee becomes critical to the success of the organization. The American Psychological Association conducted their annual Stress in America survey and reports the following results (2008; http://www.apa.org/releases/women-stress1008.html).

- When asked about the recent financial crisis, almost half of Americans say that they are increasingly stressed about their ability to provide for their families' basic needs.
- Eight of 10 say that the economy is a significant cause of stress, up from 2 of 3 at 6 months earlier.
- Women are most likely to report stress related to the economic climate. Compared with men, more women say they are stressed about money (83% versus 78%), the economy (84% versus 75%), job stability (57% versus 55%), housing costs (66% versus 58%), and health problems affecting their families (70% versus 63%).

This chapter will focus on key elements that comprise effective workplace support groups, and provide specific case examples of two different groups: an eldercare support group and a smoking cessation group. Seasoned professionals that deliver support groups in a variety of different settings were interviewed about their experiences, and themes among their comments will be discussed.

REVIEW OF THE LITERATURE

Irvin Yalom, a leading authority on the dynamics of group practice, identifies several primary factors that make therapy groups effective (Yalom, 1995). Some that are also key elements of support groups include:

- *Installation of hope*—the belief that the group can be effective in helping to resolve their issues
- *Universality*—the understanding that one is not alone in his or her struggles and that others have experienced similar situations and challenges
- *Imparting of information*—educational information regarding group topics, as well as guidance and resources offered by group members
- *Altruism*—group members' participation includes a sense of "receiving through giving" by being a part of helping others through their experience

When seeking current information about the delivery of support groups in the workplace, it is apparent that the traditional social work concept of "group" differs from definitions of many groups found in the workplace. Various disciplines weigh in on the topic, each with its distinct terminology and jargon. Several databases focusing on psychology, business, human resources, organizational development, wellness, as well as social work practice, point to three broad categories of research on groups in the workplace: (1) enhancing and developing effective work groups or teams; (2) employee support groups, including relationship enhancement, parenting, and eldercare groups; and (3) wellness groups, notably around smoking cessation and obesity.

Druskat and Wolff (1999) apply the concepts of emotional intelligence and social capital to team effectiveness and engagement, concluding that a team's ability to develop group emotional intelligence (a shared set of norms that shape interpretation and response to emotions) affects the development of social capital (value added by the quality of social relations among people). This, in turn, impacts the team's effectiveness. Similarly, Chia, Foo, and Fang (2006) discuss the role that membership in a work setting plays in the quality of an individual's life experience. They found that these networks shape information seeking, volunteering, and acceptance among coworkers.

Scamardo and Harnden (2007) focus on developing managerial skills (such as those that deal with interpersonal challenges and communication). They provide a case study of the program developed by the EAP at University of Texas at Austin and apply Yalom's "gold standards" of group practice to examine the outcomes of the managerial support group. From a systems perspective, these studies highlight the importance of membership in work groups as a means of achieving social connections or relationships at work that can lead to improved effectiveness.

Advances in technology have made an impact on accessibility as well as interaction expectations. Kruger and Struzziero (1997) and Tullar, Kaiser, and Balthazard

(1998) discuss the impact of advanced technology on increasing communication of group members, including peer consultations. Better communication allows for a richer experience, shifted from an instructor-centered environment to a student-centered environment where students can more freely interact and provide more peer support than in a traditional classroom setting. Conversely, Masi and Jacobson (2003) report that a study on EAP and work/life program use by 148 managers and human resource (HR) professionals from nine corporations showed a statistically significant difference between HR professionals and managers on use of technology in manager training. Specifically, HR professionals reported preferring classroom training with online training less preferred. It was noted that technology-based programming did not allow for as much group interaction and discussion of specific examples. The role of technology in providing workplace support groups will be discussed further later in this chapter.

The second broad category, employee support groups, addresses issues in employees' personal lives that have the potential to distract them from their work. Peeters, Montgomery, Bakker, and Schaufeli (2005) state that negative experiences in the family might spill over to one's performance at the workplace. Recognizing that there are commonalities among employees' family experiences, many workplaces offer employee support groups to mitigate the potential negative impact. Frase-Blunt (2002) and Shepherd (2007) discuss two common workplace support groups: parenting (of adolescents) and eldercare support groups. Each group focuses on providing information on specific life stage development challenges, allowing resource sharing among group members, and serving as the coordinating facilitator for the group. Schaer, Bodenmann, and Klink (2008) discuss the efficacy of providing a couples' coping training in the workplace, concluding that those that participated scored higher on relationship variables (communication and dyadic coping) and also reduced individual variables including burnout.

Finally, Heinen and Darling (2009) offer a comprehensive review of the employer's perspective on the cost impact of obesity and provide an excellent overview of employer-sponsored wellness and health improvement programs. One of the key aspects to a successful initiative is developing a

> culture of health at work, and activation of social networks to foster positive change using visible leadership participation; strong (usually branded) communications about health and wellness program offerings; site, team and/or individual competition to promote engagement; health champions (peer leaders); affinity groups; and/or other strategies using the social environment at the workplace to promote health (p. 106).

Reilly, Murphy, and Alderton (2006) and Jason, Jayaraj, Blitz, Michaels, and Klett (1990) discuss the delivery of smoking cessation groups in the workplace, both indicating that workplace support (dedication of resources, time, materials) and support groups were found to be significantly associated with positive outcomes.

ESSENTIAL PRACTICE ELEMENTS

Applying a systems perspective to examining group practice in the workplace allows for consideration of the various elements involved in the success of the group. Katz and Kahn (2001) suggest an organization is much like a "live" entity, and consideration should be given to how it uses energy (resources), maintains boundaries, and responds to threats. The environment in which an organization operates is a key concept that will impact decisions. At a time when resources are scarce and many organizations are in "survival mode," workplace support groups can be effective tools in reducing employee stress and distraction.

The presence of organized employee unions adds another dimension when considering the elements of the organization as a system. Labor relations cuts across three domains and, if unions are a part of the workplace, their support of workplace groups is essential to success. By including unions in the planning process and securing their "buy in" to the utility of the group, they can be another "champion" to support the success of the groups. James O'Hair (personal communication, September 1, 2009) notes that his organization (a large employer in Maryland) encourages union members' participation in support groups. The organization recognizes the limitations sometimes inherent in offering workplace groups as they are often given during lunch hour while the union contract stipulates a half-hour lunch break, which precludes them from participation. He underscores the importance of supervisor support to employee involvement in the groups, noting that when supervisors understand the value in the support groups, accommodations will be made.

USING RESOURCES

A fundamental resource to any organization is its employees, and one must consider the cultural and ideological frameworks in which people work. As national demographics shift toward a more diverse and aging workforce (Bond, Thompson, Galinsky & Protos, 2002), organizations face challenges to retain valuable, experienced employees and to attract and recruit the "best of the best" for new hires. Viewing employees as valuable "human capital" assets that keep their organizations on track and producing is an ideology shared by many successful organizations. *Fortune Magazine* publishes a yearly "100 Best Companies" list that is compiled through surveys developed by the Great Place to Work Institute. The surveys include The Trust Index™, which consists of 58 statements that cover credibility, respect, fairness, pride, and camaraderie—the five dimensions that correspond with the Great Place to Work® Model© and the Culture Audit© that collects information about demographics, revenue, benefits, and perks offered to employees (http://www.greatplacetowork.com/best/culture-audit.php). Recognition of the challenges of managing work/life roles of employees is important in an organization receiving a favorable rating.

A second theme for a successful group is organizational support from key stakeholders, including top management. Often, successful workplace groups have a "champion" in the organization's leadership who is a key to accessing decision makers and resources and understands the value of offering support to employees. Applying business models to support the rationale behind a workplace group helps ensure that the group has a distinct purpose and goal and will provide an added value or a return on investment for the organization. It is important to recognize that the purpose of the workplace is to meet the organization's mission and vision, not to provide clinical services for its employees. If the group can successfully demonstrate value by educating and supporting employees, improving essential skills or helping to reduce absenteeism by providing essential resources for employees, its value to the organization will be clearer. Essential resources include a consistent location for the group to be held, investment in a skilled group facilitator that can lead the discussion and provide education and resources as necessary, and time for employees to attend the group.

Next, it is important to examine the support of group programs by managers, who can be resources for "marketing" the groups, and often hold power to dedicate resources (time, scheduling, location) for the groups. A manager's or supervisor's support is a significant factor that impacts job satisfaction (Babbin & Boles, 1996). If managers are supportive of a workplace group, they will be more likely to refer employees and make accommodations if conflicts arise that may prevent an employee's attendance. Again, support from the top is important for group success.

MAINTAINING BOUNDARIES

A fundamental concept for a successful group is the understanding from employer and employees that most workplace based groups are NOT therapy groups. Rather, the purpose is to educate and provide support and resources to employees who have similar needs. This basic tenet is different from the "traditional" social work practice concept of group delivery. Wengener (1992) identifies the purpose of most workplace groups to generally include information exchange, training and consultation, self-help, mutual aid, support, and problem solving. Workers must recognize that there exists an imbalance of power held by the employer, and there is an inherent conflict of interest for the employer to provide clinical services directly to employees. It is imperative for skilled, experienced group leaders to lead the groups, so that in the event that an employee requires services beyond the support group, the leader will have the knowledge base to assess and recommend appropriate resources.

O'Hair (personal communication, September 1, 2009) points out that it is essential for the success of the group that it not become a complaint session about company policies. If group participants express discontent with a situation, the members can use the time to bring forward improvements to existing policies and procedures. Again, a skilled leader can facilitate discussion to help the group develop proactive solutions should the discussion drift toward complaining.

As discussed by Yalom (1995), an expectation of confidentiality is essential in order for participants to speak freely and participate in the group. Workplace support groups differ from therapy groups in that the participants potentially interact with each other as colleagues outside the group. Clarifying expectations for confidentiality at each session is helpful so that all participants understand the framework of the group and make a decision about how much they are willing to share. Most groups hold the expectation that matters discussed within the group remain confidential.

RESPONDING TO THREATS

As noted earlier, changing workforce demographics underscore the utility in an organization working hard to retain valuable employees. Assisting them with support groups based on their specific needs is a step in that direction. The high cost of employee turnover also supports efforts to support them when experiencing common struggles.

Another area that poses a challenge to all organizations is the rising cost of health insurance and the impact on the organization's bottom line. Workplace wellness programs have been created as a means to mitigate health care costs, by working with employees to reduce major health risks, thereby reducing health care claims.

Finally, feedback from the employee level is crucial to determine the utility of offering a group in terms of needs assessment. For a group to be successful, there must be sufficient interest in and need for employees (of all levels) to find it beneficial to attend. Each organization is as different as individual people ... variations on all three systemic levels will create distinct experiences for group facilitators, which should be carefully considered in planning a new program.

Worksite Wellness program

Business Health Services, an EAP, work/life, and wellness vendor based in Baltimore, Maryland, instituted an on-site smoking cessation group at a medium-sized (600 employees) white collar client company that intended to go "smoke free" on their entire corporate campus within 9 months. The initial group consisted of an 8-week classroom style educational program that helps members identify their motivation and readiness for quitting smoking and practical steps to support their success. In addition to the on-site group, members had access to wellness coaches telephonically who could provide another source of support for their goals and wellness kits with concrete tools (books, tip sheets, healthy snacks). All employees were eligible for the program, which was marketed to the workforce through companywide e-mails, posters, and word of mouth. The workplace provided a dedicated room and regular schedule (weekly) for the group to meet. The group was led by a highly skilled trainer, with personal experience in the topic, and a master's level clinician as well. Prior to the completion of the 8-week program, the client company opted to extend the program for another 8 weeks, shifting to more support-based group. The group extension was publicized to the entire employee population again, and two new members joined the group.

Group leaders report great success for group participants; at the present time, two members have quit smoking entirely, and all other members have drastically reduced their daily number of cigarettes, with the goal of quitting completely still ahead (Lindsay Frank, personal communication, August 28, 2009). Leaders attribute the success in group outcomes to participants being highly motivated (for a variety of reasons) to quit, and ready to quit. These two factors (motivation and readiness to quit) are key factors to consider when planning for any kind of group intervention to address behavior change. For in-depth discussion, see Prochaska and DiClemente's (1983) work on change theory.

Eldercare Support Group

This author is the current leader of an eldercare support group that has been provided on site at a quasi-government financial institution for 1 year. The group was initiated by the prior EAP vendor's on-site counselor, upon the request of several employees who were experiencing eldercare issues within the same time frame. The group transitioned seamlessly to the new EAP vendor. The purpose of the group is to provide a regular gathering of employees at the organization who are dealing with eldercare concerns to share their current concerns, learn from others' experiences, get ideas for managing situations, and learn about resources that have been helpful for others. The group meets monthly at a standard time and place, and participation is voluntary and confidential. Attendance varies month to month, mainly around work priorities and the employees' desire to connect with others. The group is held in a common conference room during lunch hour, so employees do not miss work time to attend, and often bring their lunch to eat during the group. "Marketing" for the group has several channels: there is a regular posting on the intranet that all employees have access to; EAP counselors inform clients with eldercare issues about the group, and the Occupation Health Unit refers employees that disclose concerns as well.

At a recent group meeting, a new participant explained that her parents (who lived out of state) had differing levels of care needs. These needs challenged the family with finding appropriate care for both parents that would allow them to remain together as a couple. This led to other participants sharing their experiences about having difficult conversations with their parents, and sometimes equally difficult conversations with hired caregivers. The conversation then moved to how time consuming and exhausted participants felt by their roles as caregivers or coordinators of care, and the impact of their caregiving responsibilities on their leave time and work performance. Group members discussed resources to consider, some of which the new member had not been aware of (including hiring a geriatric care manager, and considering looking into Family Medical Leave Act [FMLA] policies). As noted earlier, Yalom (1995) identifies two of the core functions of group work as normalizing experiences so that group members understand that their struggles are not unique, and learning from others how they've successfully negotiated similar situations. A third core function is to learn from other's experiences, so that the leader's role is essentially more "facilitator" and the group members become the "experts" as they have experienced the situations discussed.

Strong upper management leadership and key department support for the group contribute to its success. Leaders and fellow employees refer colleagues they know are experiencing eldercare concerns to the EAP or the group. Some barriers to employees attending include work requirements taking precedence over group attendance, or employees working in offsite locations that make the commute to the main building longer than a regular lunch hour. Often employees with eldercare concerns have limited leave options, as they have used available leave to attend to their parents' needs. Generally, discussion around consulting with HR and gaining understanding of FMLA policies is part of each meeting.

EVALUATION

When reviewing options to evaluate the effectiveness of a group, stakeholders with differing interests should be considered. Group participant satisfaction survey results are one way to collect information about the utility of the group to meet members' needs, evaluate the effectiveness of the facilitator, and collect feedback on the structure, timing, and other elements that combine to create the group experience. Organization administrators may be more interested in the more quantitative aspects of the groups' impact: the number of employees who attended the group, the average size of each session, and any data indicating improved productivity or reduced employee absenteeism, as well as group member satisfaction data.

Absenteeism data are a key metric used in the workplace; however, being able to access the specific data can be difficult in that it often involves collecting data from various departments. Employee self-report of absenteeism can provide a first glimpse into being able to tie the support group to assisting employees with resources to prevent their missing time from work to attend to family concerns. For example, asking questions on group member surveys such as: "By attending the group, I learned about resources that I would have spent 1–3 hours; 4–6 hours; 7+ hours searching for."

If the support group contained an educational component (such as the smoking cessation group), collecting pre- and post-intervention data on standardized measures helps leaders compare outcome data to other groups, and identify any specific differences between them. Obtaining standardized measures requires group leaders to follow appropriate protocol for their use, including adhering to copyright and licensing requirements. Many measures can be found that are available to the public and do not pose any administrative challenges.

John Reibling, a leader of an internal EAP for a national military organization, notes the importance of collecting data to use to document satisfaction among group members and the challenges associated with such a task in a multisite organization (J. Reibling, personal communication, September 18, 2009). In order for the data to be used in the aggregate, it must be administered and collected in a uniform fashion, which can pose challenges when there are multiple sites and facilitators involved. Group leaders should consider methods to collect outcome and satisfaction data when in the planning stages of the group.

RESOURCES

The Employee Assistance Professionals Association (EAPA) http://www.eapassn. org/i4a/pages/index.cfm?pageid=1
The EEAPA is the world's largest, oldest, and most respected membership organization for employee assistance professionals. With nearly 5000 members in over 30 countries, EAPA is the world's most relied-on source of information and support for and about the employee assistance profession. EAPA publishes the *Journal of Employee Assistance*, hosts professional conferences, and offers training and other resources to fulfill its mission. EAPA's mission is to promote the highest standards of EA practice and the continuing development of employee assistance professionals, programs, and services.

The Alliance for Work-Life Progress (AWLP)
http://www.awlp.org/awlp/home/html/homepage.jsp
The AWLP is dedicated to advancing work-life as a business strategy integrating work, family and community. An entity of World at Work, AWLP defines and

recognizes innovation and best practices, facilitates dialogue among various sectors and promotes work-life thought leadership.

The National Association of Social Workers (NASW)
http://www.socialworkers.org/
The NASW is the largest membership organization of professional social workers in the world, with 150,000 members. NASW works to enhance the professional growth and development of its members, to create and maintain professional standards, and to advance sound social policies.

The Wellness Council of America (WELCOA)
http://www.welcoa.org/
North America's premier resource for worksite wellness, WELCOA is dedicated to helping organizations of all kinds build and sustain results-oriented wellness programs.

REFERENCES

American Psychological Association. (2008, October 7). *Stress in America*. Retrieved August 30, 2009, from http://www.apa.org/releases/women-stress1008.html

Babbin, B. J. & Boles, J. S. (1996). The effects of perceived co-worker involvement and supervisor support on service provider role stress, performance and job satisfaction. *Journal of Retailing, 72*(1), 57–75.

Bond, J. T., Thompson, C., Galinsky, E., & Prottas, D. (2002). *Highlights of the National Study of the Changing Workforce*. New York: Families and Work Institute.

Boston College Center on Work and Family; Chia, H. B., Foo, M. D., & Fang, R. (2006). Workplaces as communities: the role of social networks in who seeks, gives and accepts information on justice issues. *Journal of Community Psychology, 34*(3), 363–377.

Druskat, V. U. & Wolff, S. B. (1999). The link between emotions and team effectiveness: How teams engage members and build effective task processes. *Academy of Management Proceedings*. Briar Cliff Manor, New York: Academy of Management.

Edington, D. W. (2001). Emerging research: A view from one research center. *American Journal of Health Promotion, 15*(5), 341–349.

Employee Assistance Professionals Association. (2003, September 8). EAPA EASNA boards approve consolidation. Retrieved May 12, 2009, from http://www.eapassn.org/public/pages/index.cfm?pageid=1

Frase-Blunt, M. (2002). Workplaces fail to support parents of teens. *HR Magazine*, 102–108.

Herlihy, P. & Davidson, B. D. (2000). Work/life and employee assistance programs: Collaboration or consolidation. In K. Rose (ed.), *Work/life effectiveness: Programs, policies and practices* (pp. 12.3–12.32). Darien, CT: Kubu Communications.

Jason, L. A., Jayaraj, S., Blitz, C. C., Michaels, M. H., & Klett, L. E. (1990). Incentives and competition in a worksite smoking cessation intervention. *American Journal of Publick Health, 80*, 205–206.

Katz, D. & Kahn, R. L. (1966). The social psychology of organizations. In J. M. Shafritz & J. S. Ott (eds.), *Classics of organizational theory* (5th ed., pp. 257–267). Fort Worth: Harcourt College Publishers.

Kruger, L. J. & Struzziero, J. (1997). Computer-mediated peer support of consultation: Case description and evaluation. *Journal of Educational and Psychological Consultation, 8*(1), 75–90.

Masi, D. A. & Jacobson, J. M. (2003). Opinions of managers and human resource professionals of employee assistance and work/life programs. Unpublished Final report for Working Solutions, a division of United Behavioral Health. Baltimore, MD: University of Maryland, Baltimore, School of Social Work.

Peeters, M. C. W., Montgomery, A. J., Baker, A. B., & Schaufeli, W. B. (2005). Balancing work and home: How job and home demands are related to burnout. *International Journal of Stress Management, 12*(1), 43–61.

Prochaska, J. O. & DiClemente, C. C. (1983). Stages and processes of self-change of smoking: Toward an integrative model of changes. *Journal of Consulting and Clinical Psychology, 51*(3), 390–395.

Reilly, P., Murphy, L., & Alderton, D. (2006). Challenging the smoking culture within a mental health service supportively. *International Journal of Mental Health Nursing, 15*, 272–278.

Scamardo, M. & Harnden, S. C. (2007). A manager coaching group model: Applying leadership knowledge. *Journal of Workplace Behavioral Health, 22*(2/3), 127–143.

Schaer, M., Bodenmann, G., & Klink, T. (2008). Balancing work and relationship: Couples coping enhancement training (CCET) in the workplace. *Applied Psychology: An International Review, 57*, 71–89.

Shepherd, L. C. (2007). Helping caregivers help themselves. *Employee Benefit News*, 70–71.

Tullar, W. L., Kaiser, P. R., & Balthazard, P. A. (1998). Group work and electronic meeting systems: From boardroom to classroom. *Business Communication Quarterly, 61*(4), 53–65.

Wengener, N. (1992). Supportive groups services in the workplace: The practice and the potential. In J. Garland (ed.), *Group work reaching out: People, places and power* (pp. 207–221). New York: Haworth Press.

Yalom, I. D. (1985). The theory and practice of group psychotherapy (3rd ed.). New York: Basic Books.

Chapter Twenty-Two

Group Work With Men[1]

Geoffrey L. Greif

Are men an "at-risk" population? Three chapters in this book already focus exclusively or largely on men—Paul Ephross's chapter on sex offenders (Chapter 14), Steve Ball and Ben Lipton's chapter on gay men (Chapter 17), and George S. Getzel and Phillip Osteen's chapter on HIV/AIDS (Chapter 3)—while a few other chapters either include men equally with women or substantially. So why add a separate chapter about men? It is my belief that men, compared with women, are more apt to come to group involuntarily, are more apt to present challenges to the group worker, and are less apt to be understood by group workers, a majority of whom are women. This last point is a reference to the overwhelming number of women who are going into the profession. Finally, from a pure "at-risk" point of view, men are more apt to abuse substances (SAMHSA, 2000), occupy dangerous jobs, work too hard, get killed or injured in Iraq and Afghanistan (Baumeister, 2007), and deny that they need help (e.g., McKelley & Rochlen, 2007).

The socialization of men (as well as women) makes it difficult for them to seek help for a variety of reasons. These include the fear of appearing weak and vulnerable (Addis & Mahalik, 2003) and growing up with the message that men should "go it alone" (Greif, 2009b; Ipsario, 1986). If men talk about feelings, they often believe they are showing weakness. The "go it alone" message prevents them from asking for help (Ipsario, 1986) as they feel they are admitting they cannot take care of themselves. Men do not even like to be interviewed about feelings for research studies (Butera, 2006)—imagine trying to get them to open up given their social conditioning.

It is not only that men are socialized to act like men. They, arguably, are hard-wired differently than women so that processing emotions, a requirement of most group work modalities, is more difficult for them (Brizendine, 2006). Males have higher rates of oppositional defiant disorder and attention-deficit disorder than females (Derks, Dolan, Hudziak, Neale, & Boomsma, 2007). With these characteristics, the treatment process of accepting help, sitting still, listening, and attending in a group context can make treatment a daunting task. (These skills are needed in individual treatment, too, but greater patience is needed in a group where conversation is a shared process.) Until the messages men are given during their upbringing not to seek help are reconciled with them now being in a position where they must seek help, men will have difficulty sorting out their feelings about being in treatment.

Men of color may have traversed a particularly tricky path when they come to treatment due to their experiences growing up in a white dominated society. Specifically, African American boys, recognized as at risk, are more likely to participate in the crime and drug culture as a means for survival (Harvey & Hill, 2004) and are overrepresented in the juvenile justice system (see Chapter 13) (Rozie-Battle, 2002). Homicide is the foremost killer of African American male teenagers (Kunjufu, 2001). African American males are more likely than white males to be removed from their parents, have their parents' rights terminated, exit the child welfare system without being adopted or reunited with their parents, and become homeless as a result (Harvey & Hill, 2004). When they reach adulthood they are likely to bring those histories into a group context. Time in prison and neglect or maltreatment at the hands of the child welfare system may make it especially difficult for them to trust an agency's attempts to help and participate in group therapy.

The context of masculinity also needs to be considered when men meet in groups. Related to socialization, men define themselves and are defined by their behavior and appearance. What are masculine behavior and appearance vary by race and culture. Broadly, the adjectives defining masculinity have not changed *that* much over the past 35 years. According to Bem's (1974) research, masculinity is associated with behaviors that are "assertive," "analytic," "independent," "athletic," "self-reliant," "combative," "tough," "leader-like," "problem-solving," and "emotionally reticent." A subtext is that whites are socialized to be individualistic and African Americans are socialized to be communal (Coleman, Ganong, & Rothrauff, 2006). Race provides a slightly different lens when thinking about the extent to which a black man or a white man should be connected to the community (e.g., a man living alone may be more acceptable in the white community than the African American community) but the above adjectives still largely obtain when thinking about male behavior.

Masculinity plays out in groups in a range of ways. For example, some men will try to gain control over members by putting on a "macho" facade. Uncomfortable with the expectations of group participation, they may present as tough, unapproachable, or overly successful. If they present as tough, they may brag about past sexual or criminal exploits. Involuntary clients may be especially prone to this behavior to gain some control over the situation. Stories about highly successful coping strategies (beating cancer, overcoming unemployment, taking charge of recalcitrant children) may be an attempt to show power and take a leadership position in the group. Showing vulnerability, a prerequisite of some groups, is not an effective survival skill in most families or communities so members overinflate themselves as a defense. Sometimes remarks about moneymaking or derogatory cracks about homosexuals or older people are tossed in to the mix to establish a man's masculinity.

While the definitions of masculinity can vary, variation also exists about the philosophy concerning what men need to develop into men. For example, some argue that young men should be separated from women in order to help them bond with each other. Poet Robert Bly (1992) uses the Brothers Grimm tale of Iron John, in which a young prince lives in the forest with a wild man, to illustrate this point. An opposing view is offered by Australian sociologist Raewyn Connell. Connell (2005) believes that women need to be included in helping men to grow as men. He argues that men help to shape the context in which they live just as they are shaped by the context. Given social work's dedication to nonoppressive practice and the development of frameworks that help social workers and clients reach beyond traditional gender barriers, the worker's understanding of gender expectations will help frame group discussions around how men and women treat each other.

By thinking broadly about the inherent differences and similarities between men and women and the way that culture, race, gender, as well as class, sexual orientation, and age affect how men interact, the context is set for group work with men.

PRINCIPLES OF PRACTICE

What guides practice with men? If we return to the literature review, it is clear that engaging men initially is one of the trickiest parts of treatment. While the notion of therapeutic *resistance* is best viewed as transactional (between the social worker and the client) and not residing solely with the client, an awareness of men's socialization and how that may work against therapeutic engagement needs to drive the initial stages of treatment. Speaking directly to the issue of their socialization is usually the best way to approach men if this is their first time in treatment.

To make such a statement, the social worker has to feel comfortable working with men in groups. The composition of the group—an all-male group, a mixed group, or a primarily female group—will affect the worker's countertransferential feelings as well as the atmosphere of the group. Purely from the point of view of physical safety, a male or female worker may *feel* more at risk with more men in the room. The nature of the group will also affect such feelings. The more that violence is related to the reason for referral, the more anxiety a worker is likely to feel (this would be true of working with women, too).

These beliefs about men and their propensity for violence are part of what makes some social workers reluctant to work with men. Men may control other men and women through their size, physical strength, anger, and threatening demeanor. Depending on the nature of the group, such behaviors (or forms of communication) will have to be addressed as men are given feedback about their presentation. It should be acknowledged that these characteristics are often fed by others. One of the common ways these characteristics are evinced is, for example, by a mother who warns her misbehaving child, "Wait until your father gets home." Asking the group to consider how society constructs roles for men, whether it is a group for men who are violent, abuse substances, have contracted HIV, or are surviving cancer is a core element of practice with men.

Clear ground rules must be established concerning treatment of each other in the group and confidentiality. What type of "posturing" will the leader allow in the group if the leader believes that dysfunctional behaviors that men are socialized to perform are being acted out? For example, will the leader permit talk about sexual exploits? Will the leader allow one-upsmanship? One group of white and African American men that formed to try and break down barriers between men banned jokes that demean others, sports discussions, and hero stories about themselves (Peterson, 2007). It is hard to imagine these particular rules in place in a women's group.

Due to the high level of competition between men (especially younger men), confidentiality, as in all groups, will have to be clearly stated as an expectation. Men have difficulty letting down their guard and until they feel that what they share will be kept within the room, they will not reveal personal material, especially if they live in the same community.

The worker must find a way to connect with his or her own feelings of nurturing as a precursor to connecting therapeutically with men. Exploring past histories with the members (or knowing those past histories but not bringing them up in group if such exploration may be harmful) is one way of building a therapeutic relationship. Was the man abused or neglected as a child? Was he abandoned by one or both of his caregivers or raised in a dangerous neighborhood? Did he always struggle academically? Was he introduced to illegal substances at a young age? Was he born with organic difficulties that made success more challenging? Is there a genetic predisposition to cancer in his family? Knowing the answers to these questions can help the worker who is having a hard time connecting with a man.

COMMON THEMES

The following 11 themes can guide practice with men in groups. They are themes that a worker can anticipate being raised or can look for underneath men's behavior.

1. *Men of color have different life experiences than white men.* Focus groups with youth and staff known to the criminal justice systems (Holley & VanVleet, 2006) as well as focus groups with men who were court-mandated to attend parent education groups (Greif, Finney, Greene-Joyner,

Minor, & Stitt, 2007) reveal that Latino and African American males believe they are treated worse by "the system" because of their race. It is well understood by those reading this chapter that the experiences of people of color in the United States suggest that wariness about services from social work agencies and other societal systems (courts, employers, public housing, etc.) would be appropriate (Schiele, 2005). If men of color are assigned to group treatment involuntarily, they may believe they were treated unfairly because of race. Socioeconomic class, for those of little income, may also be a variable in the way they view their court-mandated treatment—if they had money, they would have hired a better lawyer and avoided mandated treatment.

Parents of color often engage in racial socialization as a way to prepare their children for success in society (Suizzo, Robinson, & Pahlke, 2008). This socialization process can include teaching about the group's history and its religious practices, as well as imparting racial pride. Whatever course the socialization of children specifically takes, the emphasis is often on the differences that exist between people. Such differences may be projected onto workers or agencies that are viewed as aligned with a different race. While the election of an African American president may go a long way toward mitigating some of these feelings, it is too soon to know how the election will impact the way men of color present in treatment in relation to these feelings.

Race is usually raised overtly or covertly by clients. When it is raised overtly, it may come in the form of direct questioning about a worker's experience. When it is raised covertly it may come in the form of statements, such as "all people have this issue" and "you may not understand but...." The social worker must directly address race when it is raised and acknowledge that society treats people differently based on race, as well as neighborhood, gender, religion, sexual orientation, class, (dis)ability, and age. Once addressed, and this may be raised in the beginning stages of the group, the group member can be asked to connect that treatment with the reason for referral. For example, is the man saying that it is harder to deal with prostate cancer, or that noncompliance with medical recommendations is justified, or that medical practitioners are less responsive to the men because of race?

2. *Female social workers and male clients.* Women comprise the vast majority of social work students and beginning workers. A male client is more likely to be treated by a female than a male social worker. Having a female in a nurturing role would be something most males would anticipate as they are apt to have been raised by a mother and taught by female teachers. At the same time, and depending on their experiences with women, men may be accustomed to controlling women. In a group, a range of dynamics may be evident with female social workers.

Some men will take comfort in being nurtured while others will assume a macho posture as a way of maintaining control, particularly if they are involuntary clients.

For men who are comfortable being nurtured, their behavior may manifest itself in seeking advice from the social worker, supporting comments she makes, avoiding conflict with her, and protecting her from other members' attacks. They may look to her for approval instead of assuming responsibility for making their own decisions. The macho posturing may manifest itself in making sexual jokes, harassing the social worker, and attempting to manipulate her in ways they try to control women in their lives. If men are known to influence their female partners in terms of drug abuse and victimization (El-Bassell, Gilbert, Golder, Wu, Fontdevila, & Sanders, 2004), corollaries of these behaviors should be anticipated with other women (leaders and members) in the group. Disclosures about hurting or using women sexually can be upsetting to social workers (female and male) and may raise countertransferential issues that will make helping the men deal with such behavior more vexing. Sweet (2006) believes that women therapists are often unaware of the degree of sadness and frustration that many men experience in their lives and thus misinterpret men's actions. Tuning into this aspect of men's experiences may engender a different response from a female social worker.

One way to address these issues directly is to discuss the social worker's gender in the group and attempt to link it to experiences with women outside of the group. The worker might say, "I see how you are responding to me when I make this comment. When I give you that feedback, does it remind you of other women in your life?" The worker could also say, "I am not sure I understand the range of reactions (note "feelings" are not mentioned here) you are having to this issue. Some men might be frustrated in your shoes." Supervision is often useful in working through countertransferential issues that impede therapy.

3. *Men as financial providers.* Money is a status symbol for men and society socializes them to be the primary breadwinner in the family. Money also provides access to hard core services and benefits to families—clothing, housing, food, educational opportunities, better neighborhoods, travel, entertainment, cars, and home accoutrements like televisions and DVD and CDd players. When men have little money, they are often devalued and feel less masculine.

Helping men get money is beyond the scope of most groups and is the most intractable issue for men, especially in a bad economy. Often undereducated when compared with women and with spotty employment histories, the opportunities for significant change in employment for some men are bleak. Older men have an especially pessimistic outlook for finding work or improving their income. Job training programs have been shown to have some success for the hard to employ (e.g., STRIVE, which is being administered in low-income neighborhoods, like Baltimore).

Even well-educated and financially successful men will bring insecurities around income into a group. In many companies, an employee is only as good as his (or her) last sale, profit period, or cost-cutting suggestion. With companies cutting back or furloughing employees, few men feel as secure financially as they did a few years ago (see Chapter 21).

If employment is an issue that comes up in the group, talking about the difficult job environment is vital as joblessness makes the presenting problems worse. Partializing the process of job skills improvement into interim and achievable small steps should be tried. This is the same philosophy that the man can use to find success with his presenting problem, whether it is parenting skills, substance abuse, or relationship building. Taking things "one step at a time" is a treatment mantra everyone understands.

As mentioned, men sometimes compete with each other in group by discussing money. If they are in legal trouble, they may comment about being able to afford a lawyer as opposed to relying on a public defender. They may talk about the medical care they can afford, the way they take their "lady" out for a celebration, or how they purchase new sneakers for their child. Men may see what cars the other members of the group (or the leaders) are driving and measure their own status in the group hierarchy as a result. A member may reflect his perceived lower status with comments about "rich people" or the "haves and have nots."

Being sensitive to issues that arise around money can help the leader in discussing how men are socialized. The link can then be made between such potential issues as: self-esteem, self-care, social (in)justice, and financial wherewithal.

4. *Men as fathers.* Many men in treatment are also fathers. If parenting is one of the foci of treatment, it is most likely the result of a troubled relationship with their own children (Arenas & Greif, 2000). Men may perceive the "system" to be stacked against them because of their gender and recent research has found, at least in child protective services, a lack of understanding about fathers (Huebner, Werner, Hartwig, White, & Shewa, 2008). Men will complain that women are given preference when it comes to child custody and visitation, in relation to child abuse allegations, and the payment of child support (Greif et al., 2007). They will also complain that they are not taken seriously by the school system as a concerned parent. Lacking affirmation as a parent, they may try and overcontrol their children and end up feeling less competent if that

parenting approach backfires. If they lack developmental knowledge about children, the problems are compounded.

Specific time should be allocated in the group to discuss parenting issues for current as well as future fathers. The emphasis should include the loving and nurturing aspects of parenting, not just the discipline and control issues with which parents often struggle. If the leader has a nurturing style, this will help establish a nurturing tone men can take with their children. Setting a context of love is key. Encouraging fathers to compliment their children for their good behaviors is one way to help them assume a parenting role over which they have control. By emphasizing the nurturing aspects, a metaphor is developed for how the men can interact with others in their lives.

5. *Men and their own fathers.* Whether a father was present or absent in a man's life, the legacy of fatherhood has a profound impact on future generations (Betcher & Pollack, 1993). Usually some of the earliest messages about masculinity, treatment of women, work, and money come from fathers. If a man does not know who is his father or has little contact with him (or receives the message that his father was not responsible in his behavior), the man may have to try especially hard to learn responsible behavior from others.

It is not just physically absent fathers that leave a legacy. Some men have fathers who were physically present but not emotionally available. Those fathers may have been too focused on work, alcohol, or other issues.

Every man has a story to tell about his father, even if it is of being raised in a home where the father was unknown and never discussed. Helping men draw connections between their own behavior and their father's can be facilitated through drawing a family tree (or genogram) and learning that some fathering patterns are intergenerational.

Some of the most powerful discussions can center on what the man would like to tell his father if he were present in the room or what he wished he had received from his father. Such discussions can be highly emotional and are best facilitated when there is group cohesion and a strong connection with the leader.

6. *Men and male friends.* People with friendships live longer, healthier lives (Carstensen, 1991) yet men's lives are shorter than women's. Could stronger social networks help men? Men often talk about hanging out with other guys but are vague about how those relationships operate. Ask men about their friendships with other men, and the response is likely to be that they do not have many friends they can trust (Greif, 2009b). Men's friendships tend to be built on shoulder-to-shoulder interactions—men are raised to do activities with other men (often sports-related) while women are socialized to have face-to-face

interactions, which allow a different level of conversation. When men are raised to compete with men, it is difficult to cooperate with them in a group and achieve insight and behavior change.

Talking to men about their friendships with men can get to the core of the relationships that often lead to peer pressure and drug abuse. Men leaving inpatient facilities are advised to stay away from their old friendships, yet may not be taught about normative friendships between men. Helping men to understand how friendships are started and maintained can lead to new, more adaptive social support systems.

7. *Men and violence.* Most discussions with men in treatment will reveal some history (past or current) with violent behavior where the men were perpetrators, victims, or witnesses. Fights, whether on the playground, within a college or fraternity community, or in a back alley are an unfortunate part of a man's lifespan and can be exacerbated in adulthood when alcohol or drugs are involved. The violence will sometimes also include a history of child abuse (as a perpetrator or a victim). In its simplest form, but one that reinforces aggression, it is admiring a good "hit" in a football game; even this raises the specter of admiring violence.

Interpersonal violence is often a reason for treatment. According to Stosny (2005) who treats domestically violent men in groups, abusive men may view themselves as victims with little choice other than to be violent. They blame others—their partners, society, or the environment in which the violence occurs. In his work with this population, Stosny recommends talking about "personal responsibility, masculinity, intimacy, communication skills, resentment, and forgiveness" (2005, p. 232). In addition, the man must accept the personal power he has in the relationship.

Whether violence is the presenting problem, without understanding the currents of violence inherent in many men's lives and how it appears as a metaphor in group discussions, opportunities to curtail the cycle of violence (both on an individual and a community level) will be missed. Violence can be addressed specifically by asking the men to what extent it has been a part of their life and to what extent they wish to keep it a part of their life as they move forward.

8. *Men don't cry.* For men who have been raised to not show emotions, masking feelings through emotional distancing, drug abuse, or violence may be common. Crying (or appearing vulnerable, fragile, or weak in some other way) would be a sign of weakness. Emotions are not always easy to express for anyone, but men's socialization makes it particularly difficult for them. Ipsario (1986) discusses how men's "restrictive emotionality," as well as their fear of appearing gay, affects their interactions with other men. In some men's views, expressing emotions, and getting

close to other men emotionally and physically, raises their own homophobic reactions.

When new members are first introduced to the group, an early reference to expressing emotions and crying will give men permission to cry in the group. Such behavior will be normalized. Asking men's reactions to someone else crying (it may be a woman or a man in the news or in the group) will further help to pave the way for a range of emotions to be expressed. For example, is it okay for a sports figure to cry when he has been victorious or has been defeated? What about a public figure crying at a funeral? If crying can be normalized and not seen as weakness, the path will be open to the expression of other feelings.

9. *Dealing with loss.* Connected to the expression of feelings, is the way that men mourn losses—they usually don't. Baum (2008) notes that men experience loss from such naturally occurring events as death, divorce, and immigration (see Chapter 7) yet do not know how to express it. Other types of loss men experience include being fired or being underemployed; health-related issues; the normal aging process and its related impact on physical activities and sports; and existential issues (never having achieved their goal of sailing the globe, writing a novel, or starting their own company).

Men may have difficulties even recognizing that they are experiencing loss if they present with symptoms of anxiety or depression. This could be related to the way men are socialized. The social worker needs to be attuned to the themes of denial and lack of insight, how they play out in the group, and look for opportunities to talk about loss as a part of living and loving others.

10. *Sexual issues.* Discussions related to sexual dysfunction may arise either overtly or covertly. Depending on the reason the man is attending group, sexual functioning could be a central theme. Men with chronic disease, substance abuse, or depression frequently experience sexual dysfunction. Substance abuse and violence can be linked to masking sexual dysfunction. Men may hint at dysfunction with comments about an inability to "get it on;" they may talk about fears of dating, being close with women (or men), not wanting to spend the night at women's houses, etc.

Sex is a taboo subject in most groups. Discussions about sexual intimacy can be approached in the same ways as discussions about masculinity and sharing of emotions. The worker can initiate such discussions by talking about the role of men in society and the expectations around performance in *all* arenas—work, the sports arena, and the bedroom. Men can be reassured that it is normal to not always want to go to work, play a sport, or have an interest in sex. The group members may

need to learn how to be close with a significant other without it including sexual intimacy. Information can be given to the group (or the
individual) as a form of education that can help normalize men's (and
women's) experiences in these realms.

11. *Men may clam up when attending a group with their female partner.* In a
recent parenting group I ran (see Chapter 19) which included eight
women and two men, the conversation wound its way around the
group and happened to stop at the female partner in a couple that was
attending. After she spoke about her parenting concerns, her partner
said, "I agree," essentially indicating he had nothing more to offer.
I wonder, because it was a parenting group, if he assumed she was the
expert (see, above, *men as fathers*). I imagine if he had spoken first, that
she would have felt comfortable expanding on his comments or adding
her own. If I could have that moment back again, I would ask him to
speak first. This would have given him the opportunity to be an expert
(or at least offer an opinion) in an area, parenting, in which he might
normally have taken a back seat.

The worker must be aware that if a couple is attending a couples'
therapy group or a parenting group, special efforts must be made to
engage the man who might historically have turned over the emotional
and the parenting work to the female partner. This can be also accomplished by openly commenting on it in the group. A worker might ask,
if there are couples present, "Who takes the lead in dealing with the
feelings (or the nurturing) in each of your homes?" This provides fertile
ground for the group to process roles in couples regardless of the content or the intensity of the group.

CONCLUSIONS

Without a clear understanding of the way that men are socialized and that
socialization varies by culture, opportunities to work with men in groups will be
missed. At the same time, "therapy" in the traditional sense should not be seen as
the only way to help men. Should certain group modalities be adapted to men?
McKelley and Rochlen (2007) suggest coaching as a way to assist men, rather than
"therapy." They see coaching as more collegial and less threatening. For men,
seeing a "coach" has distinctly different connotations than seeing a therapist or a
social worker.

Whatever approach is used should not demean women. By understanding how
men and women influence each other, both in and out of therapy, more and varied
populations of men, presenting with a range of problems, can be helped by this
distinct modality.

RESOURCES

National Center for Fathering
P.O. Box 413888
Kansas City, MO 64141
www.fathers.com

Menstuff—The National Men's Resource
P.O. Box 1080
Brookings, OR 97415
www.menstuff.org

Men's Resources International
1695 Main Street
Springfield, MA 01103
www.mensinternationalresources.org

Local resources are also available for assistance with domestic violence and substance abuse issues. Hospitals often sponsor support groups for men with testicular or prostate cancer. Fathers' rights groups are also available in some areas for men needing assistance with custody.

REFERENCES

Addis, M. E. & Mahalik, J. R. (2003). Men, masculinity, and the contexts of help seeking. *American Psychologist, 58*, 5–14.

Baum, N. (2008). Men's ways of mourning and their implications for psychological counseling. In J. Patterson & I. Lipschitz (eds.), *Psychological counseling research focus* (pp. 95–109). Hauppauge, NY: Nova Science Publishers.

Baumeister, R. F. (2007). Is there anything good about men? Invited address at the American Psychological Association, August 24, San Francisco.

Bem, S. (1974). The measurement of psychological androgyny. *Journal of Consulting and Clinical Psychology, 42*, 155–162.

Betcher, W. & Pollack, W. (1993). *In a time of fallen heroes.* New York: Atheneum.

Bly, R. (1992). *Iron John: A book about men.* New York: Vintage.

Brizendine, L. (2006). *The female brain.* New York: Morgan Road Books.

Butera, K. (2006). Manhunt: The challenge of enticing men to participate in a study of friendship. *Qualitative Inquiry, 12*, 1262–1282.

Carstensen, L. L. (1991). Selectivity theory: Social activity in life-span context. *Annual Review of Gerontology and Geriatrics, 11*, 195–217.

Coleman, M., Ganong, L. H., & Rothrauff, T. C. (2006). Racial and ethnic similarities and differences in beliefs about intergenerational assistance to older adults after divorce and remarriage. *Family Relations, 55*, 576–587.

Connell, R. (2005). *Masculinities* (2nd ed.). Berkeley: University of California Press.

Derks, E. S., Dolan, C. V., Hudziak, J. J., Neale, M. C., & Boomsma, D. I. (2007). Assessment and etiology of attention deficit disorder and oppositional defiant disorder in boys and girls. *Behavior Genetics, 37,* 559–566.

El-Bassell, N., Gilbert, L., Golder, S., Wu, E., Fontdevlia, J., & Sanders, G. 2004. Deconstructing the relationship between intimate partner violence and sexual HIV risk among drug-involved men and their female partners. *AIDS & Behavior, 8,* 429-439.

Greif, G. L. (2009a). One dozen considerations when working with men in substance abuse groups. *Journal of Psychoactive Drugs, 41,* 387-390.

Greif, G. L. (2009b). *Buddy system: Understanding male friendships.* New York: Oxford University Press.

Greif, G. L., Finney, C., Greene-Joyner, R., Minor, S., & Stitt, S. (2007). Fathers who are court-mandated to attend parenting education groups at a child abuse prevention agency: Implications for family therapy. *Family Therapy, 34,* 13–26.

Harvey, A. & Hill, R. (2004). Africentric youth and family rites of passage program: Promoting resilience among at-risk African American youths. *Social Work, 49,* 65–74.

Holley, L. C. & Van Vleet, R. K. (2006). Racism and classism in the youth justice system: Perspectives of youth and staff. *Journal of Poverty, 10,* 45–67.

Hrabowski, F. A., Maton, K. I., & Greif, G. L. (1998). *Beating the odds: Raising academically successful African-American males.* New York: Oxford University Press.

Huebner, R. A., Werner, M., Hartwig, S., White, S., & Shewa, D. (2008). Engaging fathers: Needs and satisfaction in child protective service. *Administration in Social Work, 32,* 87–103.

Ipsaro, A. J. 1986. Male client-male therapist: Issues in a therapeutic alliance. *Psychotherapy, 23,* 257–266.

Kunjufu, J. (2001). *State of emergency: We must save African American males.* Chicago, IL: African American Images.

McKelley, R. A. & Rochlen, A. B. (2007). The practice of coaching: Exploring alternatives to therapy. *Psychology of Men & Masculinity, 8,* 53–65.

Peterson, T. J. (2007). Another level: Friendships transcending geography and race. *The Journal of Men's Studies, 15,* 71–82.

Rozie-Battle, J. (2002). African American teens and the neo-juvenile justice system. *Journal of Health & Social Policy, 15*(2), 69–79.

Stosny, S. (2005). Group treatment of intimate partner abusers. In G. L. Greif & P. H. Ephross (eds.), *Group work with populations at risk* (2nd ed., pp. 226–237). New York: Oxford University Press.

Substance Abuse and Mental Health Services Administration. (2000). *Summary of findings from the 1999 National Household Survey on Drug Abuse* (DHHS Publication No. SMA 00-3466, NHSDA Series H-12). Rockville, MD: Author.

Suisso, M-A., Robinson, C., & Pahlke, E. (2008). African American Mothers' socialization beliefs and goals with young children: Themes of history, education, and collective independence. *Journal of Family Issues, 29,* 287–316.

Sweet, H. (2006). Finding the person behind the persona: Engaging men as a female therapist. In M. Englar-Carlson & M. A. Stevens, (eds.), *In the room with men: A casebook of therapeutic change* (pp. 69–90). Washington, DC: American Psychological Association.

NOTE

1 A version of this article appears as Greif (2009a).

Chapter Twenty-Three

Group Work in Context: Organizational and Community Factors

Elizabeth A. Mulroy

Group work, as seen from an organizational perspective, is a method of practice set in larger systems of organizations and communities. Most groups, such as those for students at risk of dropping out of school, incarcerated mothers, people with mental illness, children of divorce, or people with HIV/AIDS, operate under the auspices of some type of organization or institutional structure. As a method of social work practice, group work is conducted within social programs that operate within, and are supported by, formal and informal organizations. Each program has specific goals, objectives, and outcomes. The success of a specific group depends in part on the viability of the overall social program; that program is itself dependent on the capacity of the sponsoring organization to operate *efficiently, effectively,* and *equitably.* To support its many programs, an organization needs to maintain financial stability, demonstrate program effectiveness through responsiveness to at risk clients, and demonstrate a commitment to social justice.

The dilemma for social work today is that many human service organizations are having trouble meeting these criteria. Whether they are public child welfare agencies, nonprofit settlement houses, YMCAs, or alternative feminist organizations, they operate in a "turbulent institutional environment" (Hasenfeld, 1992, 2010) that also contributes to internal uncertainties and turbulence (Netting & O'Connor, 2003). Social programs and often entire nonprofit organizations have been, or are, at risk of being closed down. Group workers need a working knowledge of their organizations to best understand these external and internal dynamics and their role within the organization.

The purpose of this chapter is to examine some principles of organizations so that the beginning social worker can understand and appreciate the organizational context of group work and social work, and the effects of its community context on program implementation and service delivery.

THE ORGANIZATIONAL CONTEXT

A human service organization has a *transformative* purpose to help clients or consumers fulfill their unmet needs and improve their situations. Hasenfeld (1992) suggests that this transformative quality means human service organizations engage in "moral work" (p. 5), a powerful concept that adds to the complexity of operating human service organizations and measuring their outcomes. A first step in understanding organizations that exist to serve human needs is to know *sector* differences. *Public sector* agencies are governmental agencies that were established and continue to operate through legislative mandate. Some examples include federal, state, and county child welfare departments; family assistance agencies (formerly called public welfare); health; or education. Funding comes from legislative appropriations. *Nonprofit sector* organizations are nongovernmental, tax-exempt, and run by voluntary boards of directors. They are not profit-generating, and they exist to fulfill a particular mission, social purpose, or public benefit. Nonprofit organizations receive funding from a variety of sources, such as charitable contributions, government grants and contracts, fees for service, and fund-raising endeavors.

There is great diversity in types of nonprofit, socially oriented organizations. They may be large or small; highly structured, traditional bureaucracies or informal, nontraditional, alternative organizations; employ professional staffs or use only volunteers; have no geographic affiliation or be closely affiliated with and accountable to one neighborhood or community. Some examples include large, well-established child and family agencies, residential treatment facilities, YMCAs and YWCAs, settlement houses, crisis centers, shelters for the homeless, or relatively new community development organizations.

In contrast, organizations in the *for-profit sector* are commercial and form the backbone of the market economy (Netting & O'Connor, 2003). Their purpose is to make money and they pay taxes. While traditionally not social service providers, large multinational private firms such as Lockheed Martin, Andersen Consulting, and Electronic Data Systems have moved into human services delivery as a result of privatization. Some examples include for-profit residential treatment facilities, hospitals, or employment development agencies with job training programs.

Privatization and Competition

Human service organizations, irrespective of sector, have been affected by privatization—the contracting out of public services to nonprofit and for-profit organizations. Privatization has been operating for years in many public spheres, such as public works in which cities contract with private firms to pick up trash or plow snow; school districts that contract with private bus companies to transport students to and from public schools; transportation, in which counties contract with private construction companies to build or repair roads and highways; or social service departments that contract with private consulting firms to set up management information systems.

The implications of this development for nonprofit organizations and for social work became profound in the 1980s with the convergence of privatization in health and human services *and* deep cuts in federal spending for domestic social programs designed to help the poor. By the end of the 1980s, government contracts had replaced charitable contributions as the major source of funding for many large, established, nonprofit human service organizations such as child and family agencies, as well as for the vast majority of nonprofits that are small, community-based organizations (Perlmutter, 1984; Salamon, 1999; Rathgeb Smith, 2010). By the end of the 1990s, privatization—and the increased competition it generated—had accelerated the commercialization of health and mental health care and shifted social work administrators in public agencies into roles of contract managers (Austin, 2000; Austin, Brody, & Packard, 2009). Increased dependence on these fluctuating public grants and contracts weakened the financial base of small, community-based nonprofit organizations with social justice goals (Fabricant & Fisher, 2002; Gibelman & Demone, 2002). Some large nonprofits maximized opportunities in this environment and managed to grow and thrive. Privatization also enabled the forprofit sector to emerge as a major competitor in the provision of human services (Frumkin & Andre-Clarke, 2000).

With these politically turbulent environmental forces as a backdrop we turn the discussion to the five stages of organizational development.

Organizational Life Stages

Human service organizations adapt in response to the environmental changes just described, and their ability to do this successfully is influenced by their life cycle stage of organizational development. This section will concentrate on the nonprofit sector because of its prominence in human service delivery, and because public agencies and private for-profit firms have different characteristics, roles, and functions. Very large, complex nonprofits, very small, grassroots organizations, and nontraditional organizations with unique circumstances such as non-Western cultures may find the following typology less helpful. It is a model for the majority of nonprofits.

Simon (2001), after conducting a thorough review of the organizational development literature, posits that organizations go through a journey of five life stages:

> *Stage One: Imagine and Inspire.* This is the "I want to do a dream" stage, the inspirational beginning characterized by the enthusiasm and energy of a charismatic, entrepreneurial leader.
> *Stage Two: Found and Frame.* In the start-up phase, the organization gets its official nonprofit tax status and becomes incorporated, formally establishing

the organization. Some staff members may resist moving from an informal, participatory approach to decision making to a more formal arrangement.

Stage Three: Ground and Grow. This stage focuses on establishing procedures, growing the "business," and working through the challenges, opportunities, and choices that present themselves.

Stage Four: Produce and Sustain. Productivity is at its peak as workers are effective and procedures become routine. This has its benefits because systems are needed to keep the organization moving forward. Some employees, however may feel their creativity and opportunities for growth have slowed down.

Stage Five: Review and Renew. In this stage, managers of mature nonprofits engage in continuous surveillance of the organization's external environment (Mulroy, 2004) so that timely reviews and strategic decisions are made for renewal. It is argued that stressful conditions generate possibilities for new patterns of action to form. Thoughtful organizational self-assessment in Stage Five helps revisit the mission, vision, products, services, and structure to make major or minor changes as indicated. It may mean cycling back to earlier stages. For example, if changes to the basic mission and philosophy are needed, then the organization revisits Stage Two. If modifications in services or structure are necessary, then it revisits Stage Four.

Organizations generally move forward in a predictable path, but several factors influence where the organization is in its life cycle: its age, its size, growth rate of its field or domain, social environment, and characteristics of its primary leader (Simon, 2001, p. 9). Younger organizations with few staffers and a small budget, for example, are in the early stages of the life cycle. Those involved in a growth industry such as residential treatment facilities may move through the early life cycle stages quickly. Welfare-to-work programs mandated by the Personal Responsibility and Work Opportunity Reconciliation Act of 1996 created market pressures for both nonprofit and for-profit organizations, and many nonprofits rushed through the life cycle stages to capture these new federal funding streams.

Achieving success in each stage helps the nonprofit grow and thrive. In reality, boundaries between the five stages may blur, so that movement from one stage to another is not obvious. But problems can be expected to emerge in every stage, and a nonprofit organization can *decline and dissolve* in any one of them. The organization can become destabilized through the departure of a charismatic, highly respected founding executive director, loss of program funding, or staff turnover. This model does not predict an end-point for organizational life. "At some point the organization chooses to remain status quo, stagnate, regenerate, or dissolve" (Simon, 2001, p. 10). The extent of environmental turbulence suggests the need for continuous surveillance, review of impacts, and renewal of agency functions to keep the organization responsive and moving forward.

In order to do this well, managers must oversee a number of internal functions that exist in every life cycle stage. These include:

1. *Governance*—legal decision-making structure of a board of directors, agency policies and procedures
2. *Staff leadership*—executive director's role
3. *Financing*—resource development and financial management of multiple grants, contracts, donations, endowments, and fund raising
4. *Administrative systems*—equipment, office space, accounting, support staff, and technology needed to accomplish the mission
5. *Products and services*—design and delivery of services, activities, and products needed to accomplish the mission
6. *Staffing*—size, composition, and pattern of relationships among staff; pay schedules; and use of volunteers
7. *Marketing*—how the organization portrays itself to the public and to consumers.

In sum, we can see the complexity of organizational life and the importance of managing both internal and external factors that affect a nonprofit's well-being so it can be a healthy organization.

Social Programs

Programs are the heart of organizations because it is through programs that social policies passed by federal and state legislative bodies actually get implemented. In effect, social policies are translated into action at the local community level through programs with services that reach intended beneficiaries. Human service programs are concerned with (1) personal development of individuals and families through direct services such as education, training, counseling, therapy, or casework, and (2) social development in communities and with special populations through policy and advocacy, community organizing, planning, interorganizational collaboration, and network formation. The intended outcome of social programs, regardless of the methods used, is to enhance the well-being of clients or consumers, be they individuals, families, organizations, communities, or special populations (Lewis et al., 2001).

The effectiveness of health and human service programs has long been a concern of policy makers and funders. To address this concern, Kettner, Moroney, and Martin (1996; 2008) recommend that, before any new program is developed, social workers systematically take stock of the strengths and weaknesses of their organization's existing programs. Their eight-step effectiveness-based programming guide is outlined next. Primarily designed as a problem assessment tool, it is adapted here to include strengths and assets in the analysis (for further discussion, see Mulroy, 2008).

1. *Define the Organization's Programs*—Learn how the organization defines and organizes its programs. Are they separated by type of client, by geographical region, by type of service provided, or by resources required?

2. *Problem/Issue Analysis*—How well is the issue understood? What is the condition the program seeks to address? Ideally, it should be grounded in a thorough review of research in terms of the type, size, and scope of the issue as it pertains to a target population, as well as historical precedents, community and policy factors, and theories of change on which the intervention is based.

3. *Needs and Assets Assessment*—How well is the need understood—as defined by experts, and as defined by those experiencing the need? What resources (assets) already exist in the community to address the need?

4. *Selecting a Strategy and Selecting Objectives*—Based on data from the foregoing analysis, a program hypothesis is developed. An hypothesis is a statement about what outcomes are expected if a person with the problems or issues outlined above receives the services about to be designed (Kettner et al., 1996, p. 20; 2010). This becomes the framework for the development of precisely stated goals, objectives, and activities. Examine existing programs to see how they accomplished this step.

5. *Program Design*—This important phase allows a social worker or a team of people to creatively assemble services (such as groups) or a combination of services and activities (groups, individual therapy, casework, community activities) that appear to have the best chance of achieving program objectives. This is a critical step in the planning and management of programs because it is based on a carefully thought out assessment of the needs of a particular at-risk population *relative to* the needs and resources of the agency and the community.

6. *Management Information Systems*—To what extent did existing programs use agency resources such as the computer network to design and implement a database for their specific programs? A client data system is essential to produce data and information about the progress of clients throughout each episode of service, which helps determine service effectiveness at termination. When linked to other data sets it facilitates communication and coordinates services among several persons working with a client, while assisting management with its need to measure service effectiveness agency-wide.

7. *Budgeting*—Service delivery costs the agency money, so a social program needs to budget projected costs. An eight-session group could be less expensive to operate than an alternative service, such as one-on-one casework, and therefore more cost-effective. Social workers will want to use available data at an agency to calculate costs for items such as units of service (one group session for 2 hours), achievement of a measurable outcome (for a group), or achievement of a program objective.

8. *Program Evaluation*—In the final analysis, the funders of a social program will want to know how successful the program was in meeting its objectives. Those who render direct services and those who manage the program need to provide evidence of how well the intervention helped achieve program outcomes. Assess the evaluation methods used by existing programs in the agency, and draw lessons learned from their experiences. The point is this: Methods exist to evaluate an individual group; use them, but know that the group is not run in isolation. The group is also evaluated in the context of a social program, and the social program is evaluated in the larger context of the organization's mission and purpose.

Programs usually comprise a number of *services* designed to meet the needs of a population at risk. These services may be concrete, such as emergency financial assistance for rent and utilities for very poor families in public housing, or a transportation system that helps them get food at the food bank, or clothing and furniture at the Salvation Army thrift store. Or they may be less concrete, such as classes in financial literacy, job readiness training, volunteer training, crisis counseling, or leadership development. All of these services work together at various levels of need to keep families at risk of homelessness from being evicted from public housing. We will now turn to community issues because it is from the community that an agency and its social workers draw their clients.

THE COMMUNITY CONTEXT

Since a purpose of group work is to serve clients and the community, knowing the demographics of a community will help guide social workers in deciding who needs to be served by agency programs, what types of services and methods are most appropriate, and whether the agency mission statement is congruent with rapidly changing community conditions and needs. A community analysis can provide social workers with much needed data and should be conducted before a new program or group is created. The following general framework can be used as a beginning point for a community analysis. I call this the *Reconnaissance* phase:

1. Use most recent census data to identify community characteristics of a geographically bounded area.
2. Identify a target at-risk population and its demographic characteristics within this area.
3. Determine resident needs and assets, and existing institutional resources available to meet those needs.
4. Identify leaders within the at-risk population if appropriate.

5. Identify community structure, including presence of potential institutional partners and competitors inside the bounded area and outside of it (adapted from Netting, Kettner, & McMurtry, 2004).

Knowledge of the local scene is important. In very poor communities, residents often have more than one at-risk condition, as discussed in the six parts of this book. In a study of homelessness prevention in public housing, the households in the study sample identified as being at risk of homelessness typically had family members with multiple at-risk conditions at the same time—including health issues, adjusting to change, violence (as victims or perpetrators), substance abuse, or problems with institutions such as schools, the workplace, and the justice system (Mulroy & Lauber, 2002, 2004). One of their most important shared conditions was being very poor and living in unsafe housing and neighborhood environments.

The extent to which the group worker is able to address these multiple layers of at-risk conditions in one group may depend on their organization's community-based orientation, a commitment to serve the very poor as reflected in the organization's mission statement, and their own cultural competence to respond appropriately. For example, the resident population living in the housing project described above was drawn from diverse immigrant groups. At least 19 different languages were spoken. Increased diversity and multiculturalism are central factors in many communities today and are predicted to become more important throughout the next decade.

Keeping close to the pulse of a community—whether defined as the public housing project, a particular neighborhood, or a whole city— opens up opportunities for group workers to serve the public interest.

One example can be found in immigration and refugee movement into cities and towns across America.

Immigrants and Refugees as At-Risk Populations

The international movement of displaced persons who are political refugees or immigrant workers—both legal and illegal—is arguably one of the greatest challenges facing the world, and it will be felt locally because it will alter the realities of diversity in our communities, organizations, and in civic life. Social workers on the front lines, particularly those skilled in group work, case management, community building, program development, and agency management, will be at the center of institutional and community problem-solving and change in the decades to come, as the following examples will illuminate. The presenting problems for a school social worker, for example, may be how to mediate disagreements among students, or between teachers, administrators, parents, and students from many different cultures and religions in a high school beginning to bubble over with tension. Another need will be to work collaboratively and inclusively with all parties, including every immigrant and refugee group represented in the school district, to develop assimilation programs from kindergarten through twelfth grade. A social worker in an Employee Assistance Program of a large nonprofit or for-profit organization or other workplace setting will be asked to help solve misunderstandings and resentments that appear to be getting in the way of productivity and worker retention in its increasingly multicultural and multiethnic work force.

The medical social worker in the hospital emergency department sees an unmet need for trained multilingual staff to improve communication between the rapidly increasing number of immigrant and refugee patients and the medical staff. But the worker must define the problem and create the program with the cooperation and input from the at-risk populations, then appear before several decision-making groups inside the hospital to reframe the issues and offer concrete options that justify the increased costs in cost-cutting times.

City officials in places experiencing "sudden ethnic diversification" (Blais, 2003) are seeking out nonprofit organizations to collaborate in new and different ways. For example, city mayors are looking to nonprofit organizations to help refugees find affordable housing, health care, job training and jobs, help with business startups, and other programs—resources typically located in many different types of organizations, public, nonprofit, and for-profit. From the local government perspective, fresh ways of thinking and acting to resolve civic matters are needed on a *community-wide* basis, and these new approaches are being developed through coalitions and partnerships that must include leaders from the newcomer populations.

Communities with an influx of immigrant and refugee populations seek leadership and guidance in devising programs and services to assimilate newcomer populations. The social work profession's skills, values, and knowledge base prepare practitioners well to respond to these opportunities.

CONCLUSION

Group work with populations at risk requires paying attention to community and organizational factors that will help guide and shape the direction of social work practice. With careful attention to organizational and community contexts, there is no danger of its being marginalized from the profession's social justice core value, an important consideration in the global economy.

RESOURCES

Alliance for Justice
11 Dupont Circle NW, 2nd Floor

Washington, DC 20036
www.afj.org

Association for Community
Organization and Social Administration
www.acosa.org

Center for Community Change
1000 Wisconsin Ave.
Washington, DC 20007
(202) 342-0519
www.communitychange.org

National Community Building Network
8718 Mary Lee Lane
Annandale, VA 22003
(703) 425-6296
www.ncbn.org

REFERENCES

Austin, D. (2000). Social work and social welfare administration: A historical perspective. In R. Patti (ed.), *The handbook of social welfare management* (pp. 27–54). Thousand Oaks, CA: Sage Publications.

Austin, M., Brody, R., & Packard, T. (2009). *Managing the challenges in human service organizations.* Thousand Oaks, CA: Sage Publications.

Blais, P. (2003). The shock of the new: Lewiston, Maine, learns how to treat Somali immigrants like anyone else in town. *Planning, February,* 14–17.

Fabricant, M. & Fisher, R. (2002). *Settlement houses under siege.* New York: Columbia University Press.

Frumkin, P. & Andre-Clarke, A. (2000). When missions, markets, and politics collide: Values and strategy in the nonprofit human services. *Nonprofit and Voluntary Sector Quarterly, 29*(1), 141–163.

Gibelman, M. & Demone, H., Jr. (2002). The commercialization of health and human services: National phenomenon or cause for concern? *Families in Society, 83*(4), 387–397.

Hasenfeld, Y. (1992). *Human services as complex organizations.* Newbury Park, CA: Sage Publications.

Hasenfeld, Y. (2010). *Human services as complex organizations* (2nd ed.). Thousand Oaks: Sage Publications

Kettner, P., Moroney, R., & Martin, L. (1996). *Designing and managing programs.* Thousand Oaks, CA: Sage.

Kettner, P., Moroney, R., & Martin, L. (2008). *Designing and managing programs* (3rd ed.). Thousand Oaks, CA: Sage Publications.

Lewis, J., Lewis, M., Packard, T., & Souflee, F. (2001). *Management of human service programs* (3rd ed.). Belmont, CA: Brooks/Cole.

Mulroy, E. (2004). Theoretical approaches to the social environment for management and community practice: An organization-in-environment approach. *Administration in Social Work—Special Issue: Educating Future Social Work Administrators.*

Mulroy, E. & Lauber, H. (2002). Community building in hard times: A post-welfare view from the streets. *Journal of Community Practice, 10*(1), 1–16.

Mulroy, E. & Lauber, H. (2004). An approach to user-friendly evaluation and community interventions for families at risk of homelessness. *Social Work.*

Netting, E., Kettner, P., & McMurty, S. (1993). *Social work macro practice.* White Plains, NY: Longman.

Netting, E., Kettner, P., & McMurtry, S. (2004). *Social work macro practice* (3rd ed.). Boston: Allyn & Bacon.

Netting, E. & O'Connor, M. K. (2003). *Organization practice: A social worker's guide to understanding human services.* Boston: Allyn & Bacon.

Perlmutter, F. (1984). *Human services at risk.* Lexington, MA: Lexington Books.

Rathgeb Smith, S. (2010). The political economy of contracting and competition. In. Hasenfeld (ed.), *Human services as complex organizations* (2nd ed.) Thousand Oaks, CA: Sage Publications.

Salamon, L. (1999). *America's nonprofit sector: A primer.* New York: The Foundation Center.

Simon, J. S. (2001). *The five life stages of nonprofit organizations.* St. Paul, MN: Amherst Wilder Foundation.

Part Six

Evaluating Practice and Practice Skills

Chapter Twenty-Four

Using Evidence-Based Practice and Intervention Research With Treatment Groups for Populations at Risk

Edna Comer and Andrea Meier

O ver a decade ago, the social work profession joined with other health and human service systems in the call for the incorporation of systematically collected data and research evidence into clinical practice, which is commonly referred to as evidence-based practice (EBP). The National Association of Social Workers (1996) declared that as ethical professionals, social workers are obligated to seek out the most effective interventions for the individuals and groups whom they serve. Achievement of this goal requires the application of conscientious, explicit, and judicious use of the best available evidence in making decisions about the care of the clients so that the treatments offered would have high odds of success (Fraser, 2003; Sackett et al., 1996). Since that time, significant progress has been made toward the adaptation of EBP as part of the standards for social work practice. Numerous publications describe the process and content of EBP (Bretton & Macgowan, 2009; Fraser, 2003; Gambrill, 2006; Macgowan, 2008; Ngo, Langley, Nadeem, Escudero, & Stein, 2008; Pollio; 2006; Rosen & Proctor, 2003). Entire texts are devoted to the conceptualization, development, and implementation of EBP (Fraser, Richman, Galinsky, & Day, 2009; Macgowan, 2008; Rosen & Proctor, 2003). The Council on Social Work Education, the sole accrediting agency for social work education, has specified that knowledge of and practice skills for EBP are competencies that graduating students from MSW programs must have to practice professional social work (Council on Social Work Education, 2006). Current trends in social work education support teaching students the values and skills they need to critically appraise and apply practice-relevant scientific evidence over the course of their professional careers (Howard, McMillen, & Pollio, 2003; Mullen, Bellamy, Bledsoe, & Francois, 2007). Collaborative efforts between social work researchers and educators and human services organizations have been undertaken to implement curriculum changes that reflect the paradigm shift toward evidence-based professional practice. Examples of this include the 2009 Summer Institutes on the Common Elements Approach to Evidence-Based Practice sponsored by the Universities of Maryland and California, Los Angeles. Educators interested in applying the common elements approach to their teaching and research were provided with training on this model. Another example is the *Yale Center for Workforce Development* intended to identify specific strategies to improve the Connecticut workforce. A final example can be found at the Wheeler Clinic, a community agency, which coordinated the project *Current Trends in Family Intervention: Evidence-Based and Promising Practice Models of In-home Treatment in Connecticut*. This state funded project focuses on building a workforce skilled in providing home-based services through coordinated curriculum development, faculty training, university based coursework, experiential learning through internships, and recruitment of graduating students.

In light of the growing interest in research relevant to social work practice and the growing body of knowledge available to guide practice this chapter is intended to help social workers, particularly those who conduct groups, in their efforts toward the use of research evidence in practice situations. General principles of EBP and some strategies for evaluating the quality of research evidence for treatment of individuals and groups are discussed. The authors describe the application of EBP principles in social work with groups and some means for carrying out this process within agency settings. The authors speculate about methodological reasons for the paucity of outcome research in social work with groups. They propose the use of intervention research as an alternative research methodology (Fraser et al., 2009; Rothman & Thomas, 1994) and discuss how social workers can use it to guide them in systematically modifying groups they are currently running or in developing innovative new ones. Information is presented on where social workers can obtain information about EBP principles and procedures and sources of research evidence related to their work with groups.

GENERAL PRINCIPLES OF EVIDENCE-BASED PRACTICE

At the core of the EBP approach is that there is evidence to support the conclusion that an intervention has a reasonable probability of effectiveness (Macgowan, 2008). As purposeful actions toward influencing positive change, interventions may work at the individual, family, group, organizations, or other levels (Fraser et al., 2009). A common goal of social work is to serve populations at risk—peoples with particular physical and psychological conditions, often stigmatized or discriminated against by society or social institutions, or by challenges that arise from their stage of life or personal life situations (Greif & Ephross, 2005). Practice with these populations should include interventions that are unique to their needs and have demonstrated helpfulness in treatment outcomes. An intervention is considered evidence-based when it "has been evaluated using scientific methods, and the cumulative findings from evaluations that demonstrate that the intervention is effective in producing a desired outcome" (Fraser et al., 2009, p. 11).

There are two major components of EBP. First, practitioners make systematic use of clinically relevant research to select accurate and precise diagnostic tests, identify prognostic markers, and assess the potential effectiveness and safety of different kinds of treatments (Sackett et al., 1996). Properly used, this type of information may support or invalidate previously accepted diagnostic tests and treatments, spurring practitioners to modify or replace them with new ones that are more powerful, accurate, and safer. Practitioners can acquire this knowledge by reading professional journals, attending conference presentations about specific populations, and by generating evidence through their own observations and research (Pollio, 2002).

The second component of EBP is that practitioners are expected to draw from multiple sources for information to inform their treatment decisions. That is, they should not use the "cookbook" approach relying on only one source of evidence (e.g., clinical trials). Instead, practitioners are called on to think ecologically, taking into account findings about population characteristics and reports about the social environments in which their clients live (Bilsker & Golsner, 2000). They should try to integrate relevant research evidence, social science theory, and theory-based interventions with "practice wisdom" (Fraser, 2003; Sackett et al., 1996). Their diagnoses and treatment decisions should take into account clients' predicaments, rights, and preferences (Sackett et al., 1996). Practitioners are expected to discuss with their clients the range of treatment options and their associated risks and benefits, to the extent that they are known. Practitioners and clients work together to decide whether and how available evidence applies to their specific circumstances (Fraser, 2003; Sackett et al., 1996).

EVALUATING RESEARCH EVIDENCE

"What is the best evidence available for me to use in making my treatment decisions with the clients? This is the key questions underlying all discussions of EBP. Figure 24.1 lists the three main categories of research evidence: observational, systematic, and preprocessed. Within each category, evidence ranges from weak to strong in the practitioners' confidence in generalizing such findings to a larger population, or to specific clients.

Observational Studies

It should be clear from Figure 24.1 that social workers have a wide variety of sources of evidence. The most common sources are unsystematic clinical observations, in which researchers simply observe the natural course of events and record the results without trying to influence them (Fraser et al., 2009; Guyatt et al., 2000; Macgowan, 2008). For social workers, this type of evidence includes their

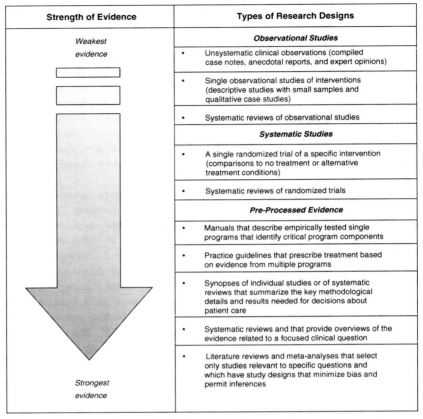

Strength of Evidence	Types of Research Designs
Weakest evidence	**Observational Studies**
	• Unsystematic clinical observations (compiled case notes, anecdotal reports, and expert opinions)
	• Single observational studies of interventions (descriptive studies with small samples and qualitative case studies)
	• Systematic reviews of observational studies
	Systematic Studies
	• A single randomized trial of a specific intervention (comparisons to no treatment or alternative treatment conditions)
	• Systematic reviews of randomized trials
	Pre-Processed Evidence
	• Manuals that describe empirically tested single programs that identify critical program components
	• Practice guidelines that prescribe treatment based on evidence from multiple programs
	• Synopses of individual studies or of systematic reviews that summarize the key methodological details and results needed for decisions about patient care
	• Systematic reviews and that provide overviews of the evidence related to a focused clinical question
Strongest evidence	• Literature reviews and meta-analyses that select only studies relevant to specific questions and which have study designs that minimize bias and permit inferences

Figure 24-1   Types of research designs: strength of evidence for treatment decisions.

compiled case notes, ancillary reports from colleagues and clients, expert opinions, qualitative case studies, and other descriptive studies that have used small samples.

Systematic Studies

In systematic research designs, investigators exert more control over the study variables, using sampling and treatment procedures that enable them to compare samples of participants who had a treatment with participants who did not (Guyatt et al., 2000). Researchers who are able to use these study designs can draw some conclusions about causal relationships between interventions and outcomes. The "gold standard" of systematic intervention research designs is the randomized clinical trial (RCT) that uses experimental designs (Fraser et al., 2009). Here, participants are randomly assigned to a treatment or control group. When it is impossible to use the direct comparisons of an RCT, quasi-experimental research designs can approximate experimental controls by comparing the group that received a particular treatment to a similar sample of participants who were not exposed to the treatment.

Preprocessed Evidence

New resources are being developed to increase the efficiency of the clinical evidence–seeking process. New journals and database services are now made available that include "preprocessed" evidence (Gibbs & Gambrill, 2003; Guyatt et al., 2000). These reports vary in the level of detail they contain to support practitioners' assessments of the strength of the evidence. The particular usefulness to social workers of each type of information source is summarized next:

- Evidence-based treatment manuals, practice guidelines, and textbook summaries of particular practice areas are designed to support systems of care, to help practitioners identify the tradeoff between treatment costs and benefits, and guide them in their decisions through the treatment cycle (Galinsky, Terzian, & Fraser, 2006; Hayward et al., 1995).
- Research synopses of individual studies and summaries provide information on key methodological details and results that practitioners need to apply research evidence to treatment decisions of individual patients (Chorpita, Daleiden, & Weisz, 2005).
- Systematic summaries of research evidence vary in their comprehensiveness and scope, but all include assessments of the methodological rigor of the studies contained in their reviews.
- Compilations of primary studies of specific issues are being compiled that include only those with study designs that minimize bias, enabling readers to have confidence in their clinical inferences.

When they apply research evidence to their treatment decisions, social workers should be mindful of the strengths and limitations of each of these types of evidence (Guyatt et al., 2000). When evidence was not systematically collected, there can be no certainty that it was effective. The apparent benefits of a treatment may be due to other factors: changes in the local environment where the intervention took place, placebo effects, or client and practitioner's expectations. Experts' opinions may be biased if they have not systematically considered the full range of options and possible outcomes. Observational studies may have larger samples and use treatment and nontreatment control groups, but apparent intervention effects may actually be due to differences in the characteristics of participants in each of the groups. Intervention effectiveness from observational studies is stronger when the effect size of a single group is very large, or when a systematic review of similar interventions shows comparable outcomes. Although evidence from clinical trials is considered the strongest evidence of intervention effectiveness, it, too, has its limitations. Recommendations based on those studies reflect the characteristics of the "average client." Social workers who are able to find evidence based on RCTs should keep in mind that those findings are not always applicable to their individual client's particular circumstances.

Most descriptions of EBP principles reflect their historical roots in the medical profession, where EBP has been more fully articulated (Sackett et al., 1996; Sackett, Richardson, Rosenberg, & Haynes, 1997). In the medical context, evidence is used to characterize an individual patient's "clinical status" and guide the selection of treatments and the monitoring of patient progress. In this context, it is possible to use a very high standard of evidence. That is because more laboratories and randomized controlled trials have been done for medical treatments. Research on social interventions rarely achieves this level of rigor, because it is generally impossible to control most of the conditions of the research. This means that social workers must use the best-quality evidence available to them, recognize its limitations, and be conservative in their expectations about its applicability to particular clients or groups.

APPLYING EVIDENCE-BASED PRACTICE PRINCIPLES TO GROUP WORK

Group workers have many opportunities to incorporate research evidence to answer clinical questions that arise as they go through the phases of assessment, treatment planning, and intervention monitoring. Each question requires different kinds of evidence, and, as always, social workers have to adapt their decision-making strategies to the uncertainties inherent in each evidence type (Galinsky, Terzian, & Fraser, 2006; Gambrill, 2000; Macgowan, 2008).

How Are Clients' Needs and Strengths Assessed?

Group workers use assessments for two purposes. They need to identify clients with the characteristics that would make them appropriate for a particular group. They must know how to formulate a client-centered answerable question that is relevant to the health and behavioral status of the individual or target population (Council for Training in Evidence-Based Behavioral Practice, 2008; Gibbs & Gambrill, 2003; Macgowan, 2008). This process is described as being tantamount to a well-defined treatment goal. Having done that, they must determine the stage of development or severity of each individual's problems in order to match them to groups composed of members with similar conditions. They begin to collect data and use that evidence from the moment they meet their clients. They draw on client intake information, biopsychosocial assessments, and, possibly, standardized psychological tests (Gambrill, 2006). The accuracy and soundness of this information depends on the reliability and validity of the instruments used to collect data, the client's willingness to disclose truthful information, and on the social worker's skill in doing assessments and integrating information.

Social workers will not always be familiar with the types of problems their clients present. When social workers are uncertain about aspects of presenting problems, they should consult with more-experienced colleagues and refer to research for studies describing problem etiology (Gambrill, 2006). The worker can seek out reviews and practice guidelines describing alternative treatments for the client's identified problem and the range of probable outcomes for each type of treatment (Macgowan, 2008). Even experienced workers who specialize in a particular kind of clinical problem should check the research literature periodically to see if any progress has been made in their specialty areas.

After reviewing all the evidence, the social worker must decide whether or not any intervention is necessary. If an intervention seems advisable, his or her next question should be "What intervention or interventions can I use to solve it?" The social worker would then review the treatment alternatives. At this stage, the social worker must also take into account what services are available through the agency and within the community. Although a client may have characteristics that make him or her appropriate for group treatment, research evidence may suggest that individual counseling or psychotropic medication may also be effective. Or, a combination of a group and other kinds of individual treatments may be helpful. The information will help the social worker determine the best available treatment (e.g., group, group and some other treatment, or some other treatment rather than a group) for the client.

What evidence could a social worker use to determine whether participation in a treatment group could help remedy the client's problem? Group interventions are most often used to aid clients who are socially isolated, have difficulty with interpersonal relationships, and/or desire to develop their human potential (Nothen & Kurland, 2003;Toseland & Rivas, 2009). Groups are contraindicated when clients are intensely private, have problems that would be difficult for them to disclose to others, or behave in ways that other members might find intolerable.

In some settings, clients are court-mandated into specialized treatment groups, such as addiction treatment or anger management. These clients do not have a choice about being in a group, but they can make choices about whether and how they will take advantage of the group experience. A major goal of the social workers is to help these clients understand how they might be helped through the group process (Chovanec, 2009). They can also help clients understand that by cooperating in the group they may be able to reduce the time they stay under court supervision (Toseland & Rivas, 2009).There is evidence that some types of treatment groups can be effective for some involuntary or mandated populations such as cognitive behavioral groups for multifamily juvenile first offenders (Quinn et al., 2002) and psychotherapy groups for incarcerated offenders (Morgan, 2002). By drawing appropriately on this research, social workers can instill hope in their clients for their ultimate success, while sustaining their own optimism about successful outcomes they can achieve when working with challenging groups.

What Are the Desired Outcomes of Treatment?

After determining that the client is appropriate for group treatment, the social worker and client discuss what the client wants from treatment and how a group treatment could help achieve those goals. In general, the goal of treatment is to reduce the risk of harm or increase the number of protective factors—the resources and strategies the client can draw on to manage her or his problem condition most effectively. The client may have multiple concerns but the social worker needs to clarify which ones can be addressed through group treatment.

Few clinical trials have been conducted to investigate the effectiveness of group treatments. Our knowledge of outcomes is founded primarily on consistent findings of many observational studies (Macgowan, 2008; Pollio et al., 2000). Overall, these findings indicate that treatment groups can alleviate clients' feelings of isolation, restore hope, and, in some cases, empower them (Schopler & Galinsky, 1995). Groups can provide members with accurate information about areas of concern and ways to cope more effectively (Toseland & Rivas, 2009). Members may learn about cognitive self-management and practice new behaviors that improve their communication and social skills. They can develop greater awareness of their psychological processes and insight into their motivations.

What Are the Risks of Each Treatment Alternative?

According to EBP principles, practitioners must help clients understand the possible risks associated with each type of suggested intervention, including costs, the likelihood of no improvement, and possible adverse effects. One reason that treatment groups are such a common type of service is that administrators and program funders view them as economical compared to individual treatments (Crosby & Sabein, 1995), but this advantage must be compared to the relative convenience, effectiveness, and costs of medication or individual therapy.

Systematic studies of group intervention are scarce, making it difficult to judge in advance the likelihood of no improvements or other adverse effects (Macgowan, 2008). Group leaders try to establish guidelines that will assure the safety and well-being of each group member but members are still at risk of experiencing unpleasant situations such as breach of confidentiality, or that other members may not respond to them in constructive ways (Corey & Corey, 2006). For example, a member may be scapegoated or struggle to fit into the group (Konopka, 1983; Nothen & Kurland, 2001; Toseland & Rivas, 2009). Observational studies suggest that some groups do not improve member psychosocial functioning but, instead, promote conformity and dependency. If a group has a few dominant or very talkative members, the group may focus on their needs and neglect those of more passive members (Yalom, & Leszcz, 2005).

Is the Intervention Available to the Client?

Having reached agreement that a group experience is appropriate, the worker and client must then decide which type of group would most likely meet the client's needs and preferences. Their decisions regarding the choice of a group will be based on the client's reasons for joining the group. For example, the client might desire education regarding a particular topic, support in coping with a life situation, to focus on emotional growth or stability, or opportunities for socialization. To make it likelier that the client will receive the full group intervention, the social worker must help the client find a group with the appropriate objectives, and that is held at a convenient location and time. And as much as possible assist the client to deal with challenges (e.g., transportation, child care, etc.) that might prevent him or her from getting to the meetings.

Was the Group Conducted as Planned?

To judge the effectiveness of a group treatment, we must first know whether it was carried off as planned. Researchers refer to this concern as "intervention fidelity." By systematically collecting data from each session (Macgowan, 2008; Meier, 1999; Meier et al., 1995; Toseland & Rivas, 2009), social workers answer a variety of questions about intervention fidelity. What proportion of members attended all the sessions? To what extent and in what ways did members participate in discussions? Were the topics that were supposed to be covered actually discussed? How many members participated in group activities? Group leaders and supervisors, in consultation with group members, can use this information to decide whether and how the group's content or activities should be modified.

In group treatments, the group simultaneously provides the means for providing a service and the setting in which that service takes place (Vinter, 1985). To do this, the group must be viable as a social entity. Groups that function well usually achieve cohesion. Cohesion is not a stage in itself, but the result of all the forces acting on members that motivate them to remain in the group (Toseland & Rivas, 2009). As groups progress toward cohesiveness over time, members shift psychologically from seeing themselves only as individuals to identifying with the group.

Of the group leader's many functions, one of the most important is to help the group achieve cohesion. To do this, the leader must plan and manage the group so that discussions and activities are aligned with the group's developmental processes (Nothen & Kurland, 2002; Toseland & Rivas, 2009). As members get to know and trust one another, they become better able to satisfy their individual needs for affiliation and to help each other in achieving their group's goals. They learn to communicate effectively, interact in constructive ways, and take on roles that are essential to reaching optimum treatment outcomes.

If group cohesion is so important in group treatment, what member behaviors should social workers watch for to determine whether their groups are becoming more cohesive? Group leaders should be familiar with the research describing these behaviors (Berman-Rossi, 1993; Northen & Kurland, 2001). For example, members openly express their satisfaction with the group. They become more willing to invest in and take responsibility for what happens in the group. They take more risks in their self-revelations. Members become more tolerant of individual differences and are better able to resolve conflict using consensus.

Group leaders select activities that they believe will encourage members to engage in these behaviors (Comer & Hirayama, 2008). In keeping with EBP principles, the group leader would also systematically monitor the group's development, documenting his or her observations of each session to determine whether those strategies helped the group to achieve its goals (Toseland & Rivas, 2009). What leaders do in any session of their groups will vary according to the type of the group, its stage of development, and their leadership styles and skill levels (Berman-Rossi, 1993; Toseland & Rivas, 2009). Agencies should collect evidence about their social workers' leadership styles so that leaders will be appropriately matched to the type of group (Toseland & Rivas, 2009).

One variant in group formats calls for two co-leaders. From the EBP perspective, the presence of two leaders means that the group benefits from having a second expert. Co-led groups can offer greater flexibility in meeting members' needs, since leaders can decide whether they would be most effective by sharing the primary leader's role or trading off observer and primary leader roles (Toseland & Rivas, 2009). The co-leader's documented observations could offer additional evidence about intervention fidelity and group functioning.

How Did the Client Respond to the Group?

Treatment groups are opportunities for individual members to learn new information, acquire cognitive self-management and social skills, and receive and give support. Assuming that their assignment to the group was appropriate to begin with, the benefits individual members receive from their groups will be related to how regularly they attend and how actively they participate in discussions and activities. Depending on the context of the service, information about individual members' participation in and reactions to their groups can be compiled from many sources. Group leaders' session report forms are likely to be the most accessible source. Group members' comments about their groups may also be found, however, in case notes of individual counseling sessions, or solicited in group discussions in which members are asked to give each other feedback.

How Will Intervention Outcomes Be Assessed?

In group treatments, social workers should assess process *and* behavioral change outcomes. In process evaluations of groups, we ask "To what extent and in what ways was the group satisfying to group members?" Here, social workers need to distinguish the sources of member satisfaction, (the attractiveness to the group of symptom relief), or some combination of both. In keeping with EBP, group workers may want to collaborate with members to help in developing group self-monitoring procedures, including inventing their own measurement instruments and data collection methods. Or members could be consulted about the best ways to administer standardized measures. Members' reactions to being asked to complete particular instruments may help group workers interpret data collected using them. Group leaders need to document members' comments and incorporate this feedback when planning for future sessions and in assessing the manner in which the group influenced data collecting and analysis.

For a group to be viable, the group leader must be reasonably satisfied with the experience, too. In their session report forms, group leaders should document the challenges they faced as well as successes they achieved (Comer, 1999). After their groups are over, leaders can compare their own perceptions of how well the group worked to members' feedback on evaluation surveys. This evidence can be used as the basis for discussions in supervision sessions or other occasions when leaders need to reflect on their practice.

Individual-Level Behavioral Outcomes

We measure individual outcomes when we want to discover whether an intervention had the desired effect on individual group members. Measures used to assess clients before starting the group (baseline) can be readministered just after the group ends to discover whether there were measurable changes in desired behaviors, and the degree and direction of those changes. If social workers want to know how well changes are sustained over time, they can also administer the measure again at prespecified dates.

Most readers should be familiar with these observational approaches to measuring individual client outcomes. They are variants of the single-subject research design commonly taught in social work programs (Faul et al., 2001; Gambrill, 2006). While very useful for understanding what happened in a specific group, findings based on this kind of evidence would be considered relatively weak. Due to the small sample size, these findings could not be considered representative of the population, and the group would have to have a very large effect in order to be detectable using statistical analyses.

By examining their agency's best practices, social workers can approximate a larger-scale outcome study of their group intervention (Epstein, 2001). This entails reviewing the records of all the clients who participated in past groups and comparing the characteristics and outcomes of the clients who completed a specific kind of group with those who did not receive any group treatment, or with those who did not complete the treatment. Other useful analyses would be to identify the types of clients who have completed their groups and then go on to complete other treatment or service plan goals.

Group-Level Outcomes

When we want to know the overall effectiveness of a group intervention for all members, we can compile and average the differences between pre- and post-group scores of the measures administered to each group member. Here again, however, even if statistically significant changes have occurred, small sample sizes make it unlikely that they would be detected.

Social workers can overcome the problem of small sample size inherent in group treatment outcome studies by using wait-list control designs. This methodology is appropriate when it is impossible to randomly assign members to treatment and nontreatment groups (Rice, 2001). For groups routinely offered in an agency, social workers can take advantage of delays between the time that group members are recruited and when a group starts. In this approach, clients are assessed three times: at intake (Time A), just before the group begins (Time B), and at the end of the group (Time C). The amount and direction of change between Time A and Time B (no-treatment period) is compared to the amount and direction of change between Times B and C. This method enables practitioners to compare individual client outcomes when clients have not received any treatment to the outcomes after they have. Doing wait-list control studies by accumulating data on groups that are routinely offered in an agency results in stronger evidence because findings are based on larger samples.

Thus far, we have devoted the discussion to descriptions of how EBP principles apply to treatment groups. Yet it is important to acknowledge social work with task groups within organizations and social action groups. In these contexts, the desired outcomes of a group could be the team's completion of assigned tasks, or changes in organizations, communities, or policies (Fraser et. al., 2009; Toseland & Rivas, 2009). Although the application of EBP principles to task groups is beyond the scope of this chapter, social workers in macropractice settings should also be alert to the ways they could use evidence systematically. They can apply EBP principles by drawing on administrative data (Meier & Usher, 1998) and research in social psychology on social organizations (Seekins et al., 1984). This evidence can be helpful when deciding how to form teams and committees, facilitate team decisions, monitor team progress toward the achievement of their tasks, or assess the impact of their collective efforts within organizations, and communities, or on policy making.

THE INTERVENTION RESEARCH PARADIGM AND EVIDENCE-BASED PRACTICE

Prevailing trends in social work education are moving toward a paradigm that will help future social workers think critically about the application of practice relevant scientific evidence in practice situations (Howard, McMillen, & Pollio, 2003;

Mullen, Bellamy, Bledsoe, & Francois, 2007). Yet as they begin working toward becoming evidence-based, they may still encounter barriers instead of facilitative conditions and gaps in the available information. In the authors' experiences, MSW students are becoming familiar with the concept of evidence-base practice. However, they have not fully achieved this task and still need help in developing and enhancing skills needed to use evidence competently (Fraser, 1994). Moreover, once on the job, they are unlikely to get experience collecting data systematically or using research evidence.

At present, social workers who are interested in applying EBP principles will find few reports of systematic research or treatment guidelines that apply directly to the kinds of work they do. Group workers, in particular, will have difficulty obtaining systematic evidence on the efficacy of small-group interventions. Most articles in social group work journals are devoted to descriptions of group programming and group dynamics. Outcome studies are relatively rare. Fewer still use experimental or quasi-experimental designs. Experimental research studies need standardized protocols. Because of the nature of the group's developmental processes, it is difficult to maintain such high levels of control. Few studies achieve the statistical power needed to detect treatment effects, in part because researchers have problems obtaining and retaining large enough samples.

Given the scarcity of clinical trials on group interventions and the difficulty in conducting them, what can group workers do to systematically develop evidence to demonstrate the feasibility and value of their groups? One alternative is to employ a research methodology that better accommodates the realities of social work with groups in practice situations. The Intervention Research (IR) Paradigm offers such an alternative. Rothman and Thomas developed the IR Paradigm to provide an integrated perspective for understanding, developing, and examining the feasibility and effectiveness of innovative human service interventions (Bailey-Dempsey & Reid, 1996; Fraser et al., 2009; Rothman & Thomas, 1994). Because IR methodologies take the uncontrollability of practice settings into account, this paradigm is more practical for testing innovative interventions than the social science research paradigm (Rothman & Thomas, 1994). A recent publication, *Intervention Research* by Fraser, Richman, Galinsky, and Day (2009), builds on Rothman and Thomas's work by integrating their own perspective and experiences in developing a school based intervention. It details the *Making Choices* program, an intervention guided by principles of IR and is a specific example of its application in social work.

The conventional social science paradigm ascribes the greatest value to evidence from "black box" experimental studies that allow researchers to say with some confidence that changes in behavior are associated with participation in the intervention and not some other factor. They pay less attention to the intervention's specific mechanisms that may have caused those changes. The IR Paradigm is founded on the principles of industrial research and development. In this context, interventions are seen as "social inventions" that must be systematically pilot-tested and modified until they work as planned under specified conditions. Here, an intervention's reliability and validity are primarily defined in terms of its feasibility under practice conditions (Thomas, 1985). In social work intervention research, social workers systematically test various aspects of their interventions using small-scale studies. Such pilot studies require relatively few resources. Early studies are conducted with abbreviated or simulated versions of the intervention and trial runs of data collection instruments. This design and development process (D&D) allows researcher/practitioners to determine whether their interventions are feasible and promising enough to be worth investing in full-scale field trials (Table 24.1).

In EBP, social workers are not expected to be researchers but rather to draw upon research syntheses in making their treatment decisions (Fraser, 2003). In developmental intervention research, social workers are integral members of research teams. As in EBP, the IR approach embodies a collaborative approach. Practitioners and researchers work as a team, with group members providing vital feedback at many points in the intervention's development. Practitioners may take the lead in identifying problems about their groups that need study. Alternatively, researchers, from within or outside the agency, identify problems through their surveys of the literature and ask practitioners to collaborate in developing new groups. Researchers often (but not necessarily) take the lead in reviewing the research literature and bringing information (or the lack thereof) about population and community characteristics, assessment methods, treatment alternatives, and monitoring strategies back for the team's consideration. People who are members of the intervention's target population may be asked to participate in the focus groups or other simulations to obtain their perspectives about whether and how the group works. Researchers and practitioners collaborate in developing the programming of the group's content, selecting activities, and developing ways to monitor group leader behavior and group development. Once the group is under way, practitioners and group members give feedback periodically on how the intervention design works. If it is not going well, researchers and practitioners work together to modify it to make positive outcomes more likely.

In design and development research on groups, group members are asked frequently for feedback that may, on occasion, prompt the research team to make "midstream" alterations in the group protocol in order to keep the group viable (Comer, 2004; Meier, 1999). Practitioners/researchers are trained to view such modifications not as failures, but as opportunities to extend the understanding about interventions to new populations or conditions (Comer, 2004). At the end of the group, members are assessed to see if their participation in the group helped them achieve their desired outcomes. In addition, members and practitioners are surveyed to find out how satisfied they were with the group experience, and to allow them to offer suggestions about how to improve it. Practitioners and group members' suggestions are incorporated into each successive pilot study, thereby insuring the intervention's acceptability, appropriateness, and validity.

Table.24.1 Intervention Research (IR) Design and Development Activities for Group Interventions

Project Design and Development Stage	Activities	
	Refining an Existing Group	Inventing a New Group
Stage 1: Identify the problem.	Identify the aspects of the current group that are problematic.	Select the problem to remedy. Identify a range of possible strategies for achieving desired outcomes. Is a group a plausible intervention?
Stage 2. Characterize the problem.	Conduct literature reviews and analyze administrative data. • To what extent and in what ways have the characteristics of the client population changed since the group was first offered? Determine whether there has been new research to indicate that: • the content or structure of the group should be modified, or • there are better ways to evaluate the group's effectiveness.	Conduct literature reviews to see what researchers have done to determine the prevalence and severity of the problem, its causes and its etiology. Consult with professional experts, and other people who have lived with the problem to determine whether there are other perspectives not found in the research literature. Identify criteria for an appropriate and effective intervention.

Continued

Table.24.1 Intervention Research (IR) Design and Development Activities for Group Interventions (cont'd)

Project Design and Development Stage	Activities		
	Refining an Existing Group	Inventing a New Group	
	Integrate new information into the intervention design		
Stage 3: Specify the elements of the intervention	Identify the changes to be made in the scope and sequence of the existing group's discussions and activities.	Decide on the scope and sequence of discussion content and the activities of the new group.	
	Modify or design new materials and activity plans.	Design materials and activity plans.	
	Conduct feasibility studies of pilot version of the group.		
Stage 4: Pilot testing	Modify or develop procedures for training and supervising group leaders.		
	Modify or develop procedures for monitoring group processes to insure intervention fidelity.		
	Select or develop evaluation instruments and satisfaction surveys.		
	Analyze pilot-study data to identify the intervention's strengths and flaws.		
	Modify group designs based on these findings to insure that the intervention is as accessible and satisfying as possible for participants.		
	If the pilot study indicates that the intervention is feasible, conduct further small-scale studies to insure that all elements of the intervention can be implemented reliably under real-life conditions.		
Stage 5: Experimental field testing	Conduct full-scale, experimental, or quasi-experimental field tests of the interventions.		
Stage 6: Dissemination of information about the project	Present preliminary findings from early studies at conferences and in publications.		
	Make available manuals and other materials developed along the way to other researchers and practitioners so they can use them to learn how to implement the intervention.		
	Present and publish on findings from the full-scale field tests.		

RESEARCH ON GROUP INTERVENTIONS USING DEVELOPMENTAL INTERVENTION RESEARCH METHODOLOGIES

There have been few published reports of studies that explicitly incorporated D&D strategies to develop innovative group interventions (Comer, 2004). The studies that have been done used D&D procedures to invent groups for varied purposes using face-to-face and technology-mediated communication channels. Face-to-face groups have been developed for people coping with chronic pain and sickle cell disease (Subramanian, 1991) and psychoeducational groups for HIV-affected people (Pomeroy et al., 1995). Telephone support groups have been developed for people with AIDS (Rounds et al., 1995) and family caregivers of people with AIDS (Meier et al., 1995). Meier has developed professionally facili-tated, Internet-mediated support groups for social workers suffering from job stress (Meier, 2000b) and spouses of survivors of colon cancer (Meier, 2003).

In these studies, researchers used the early stages of pilot testing to investigate the appropriateness of specific elements of their research and intervention designs, such as recruitment (Meier, 2000a, 2003); data collection methods (Meier, 1999, 2003; Rounds et al., 1995); participants' comfort levels with the telecommunica-tions technology used to conduct the interventions (Meier, 1999, 2003; Rounds et al., 1995); group discussion formats (Comer, 1999; Meier, 1999, 2003; Pomeroy et al., 1995; Subramanian, 1991; Subramanian et al., 1995); group development issues (Comer, 2004; Comer, Meier, & Galinsky, 1999; Meier, 1999, 2003; Subramanian et al., 1995); and participant satisfaction (Meier, 2003; Meier et al., 1995, 1999; Rounds et al., 1995). All these researchers used findings from their preliminary studies to improve their research designs and data collection tech-niques, and to clarify and extend intervention models.

DESIGNING AND DEVELOPING GROUP INTERVENTION MODELS

Practitioner/researchers can use the D&D procedures prescribed by the IR Paradigm as a map to guide them in refining existing groups or developing new ones. But the map is not the territory. As with any journey, travelers may have to make unexpected detours not shown on the map before they arrive at their desti-nations. The stages shown in Table 24.1 are as if they were discrete and linear, but they are often cyclical and iterative. Practitioner/researchers should expect to make many modifications in their plans for their groups before completing any study. Practitioner/researchers often discover along the way that components in their interventions or their research designs need to be changed. In Meier's early studies of facilitated Internet support groups, for example, she discovered repeatedly that using the Internet as her only communication channel to recruit members was neither effective nor efficient (Meier, 1999, 2003). These findings led her to conclude that, in future studies, she should investigate whether the combination of face-to face and on-line recruitment strategies will work better. In Comer's (1999) study of a face-to-face cognitive-behavioral group intervention for African Americans with sickle cell anemia and depression, she discovered that group members felt the self-management tasks (recording and maintaining journals about their activities) were too burdensome. Because group leader observations and interim measures of members' depression levels showed positive trends, members were allowed to stop doing some of these tasks.

Whether the goal is to improve an existing group or develop a new one, researcher/practitioners who use the IR design and developmental procedures go through similar steps. The greatest difference in procedures for these two types of studies will arise during the early stages of problem identification and definition that precede the actual design or redesign of the intervention model. Table 24.1 summarizes the different starting points of their associated activities and (in stages 4 through 6 at the bottom of the table) shows where the tasks for both types of projects converge.

Modifying an Existing Group

Much of the preliminary work of modifying a group involves field work within the agency. If a group has been offered as a service for a long time, researcher/practitioners should consult coworkers and supervisors and agency records to reconstruct the group's history to answer the following questions: "When was the group first offered?" "Whom was it intended to serve?" "What changes have occurred that prompted the decision to modify the group?" The research team uses the information to clearly define the problem. Has it become more difficulty to recruit and retain participants? If group leaders are reporting problems, what kinds of difficulties are they encountering? Are group members reporting low levels of satisfaction? Are group members not achieving their desired therapeutic outcomes? Answering these questions may illuminate several, interrelated problems that will impel changes in the intervention design.

For example, problems may arise from group composition. A group may stop working well if it was initiated to serve one type of client but was later opened to clients with other needs. In constructing the developmental history of the group, the research team needs to examine client records to see whether recent groups were still composed of members from the original target group. If not, the practitioner/researcher team may suggest reviewing treatment alternatives for the original target population. Alternatively, they may decide that their intervention research studies should focus on developing a group adapted to greater diversity among members.

As group members and group leaders change, so does group structure. Before attempting to modify an existing group, practitioner/researchers must have a clear understanding about how group leaders are running their groups. The research team reviews whatever documentation about the group is available and consults with the leaders. Group leaders are asked to describe the scope and sequence of the discussions and planned activities, their clinical rationales, and how the selection and sequencing of activities are related to group developmental processes. The team also needs to know what group leaders think works well—or badly—and their recommendations for changes. If several group leaders are running the same kind of group, the team may also decide to examine the evidence to see how similar or different the groups are in content and dynamics. Similarly, the team may review whatever data are available about member satisfaction. Afterwards, the team may decide to tap members' reactions to the group by conducting surveys or focus groups.

Practitioner/researchers must also discover what kinds of data have been collected on the group itself, and whether they have been collected systematically. For example, they need to find out whether and how intervention fidelity has been monitored. Are reports on each session required as well as notes in individual client records? If so, what aspects of the session are documented? When and how is this information reviewed? If group leaders or the agency do these kinds of reviews, how are these findings used in ongoing decisions about how the group should be run?

The practitioner/researcher team goes through a similar process to discover whether the client behaviors that the group is supposed to change are systematically assessed. If they have, when and how are these assessments administered? If standardized instruments have been used, are they reliable? Were they normed on the group's target population? Are they valid for use with this particular group, in that items on the instruments tap into the group's content?

Besides learning about the group intervention as it is currently used, the research team gathers the information they will need to help them decide how to modify it. As with EBP, they delve into the current research to update their understanding of the characteristics of the group's target population, the root causes and prevalence of the specific problem, the range of interventions available, and the expected outcomes. To focus this part of the search, practitioner/researchers may also decide to consult with experts in the field.

When they review local census and agency services data, the researcher/practitioner team may find that the community's racial or ethnic composition or its economic health has changed since the group was first offered. Alternatively, recent research on particular health and mental health conditions may suggest new causes of those problems or new opportunities for intervention. Updated information about client and problem characteristics may lead practitioner/researchers to recommend changes in group discussion content or activities. It may turn out that research indicates that a group intervention is no longer considered the most appropriate intervention for a given condition, or that combination therapy regimens, such as groups and antidepressant medications, offer the most benefits. If there are no standardized baseline and outcome measures being used, or the ones that are do not appear to be reliable and valid, the literature review should include a search for better measures.

Developing a New Group

In the previous scenario, the agency had already identified a problem and offered a group intervention to remedy it. Practitioner/researchers were prompted to modify the group because it was not working well in some way. In this second scenario, researcher/practitioners start from scratch, with the realization that there is a problem to be remedied. They must do preliminary investigations to determine its prevalence and severity in the community. Next, they must decide that the problem is significant enough to warrant investing the time and resources needed to develop and implement a new service. Finally, they must decide, based on research into problem prevalence and root causes, agency resources, and client preferences, that a group is the most appropriate intervention.

Designing and Developing the Group Intervention Model

In D&D Stages 1 and 2, practitioner/researchers use EBP strategies to decide on the group format and the information to be conveyed in their groups. In Stage 3, they begin to focus concretely on what group members and group leaders will discuss and do in each session of their groups, coordinating them with the parallel psychosocial group development processes. Group workers will be relying largely on their practice wisdom in this aspect of intervention design. Although experience tells us that the group is the vehicle for individual change through the support and challenge group members give each other, there is very little evidence available to help social workers understand how these processes and dynamics influence the group's outcomes (Macgowan, 2008; Northen & Kurland, 2001; Tolman & Molidor, 1994). Thus, group workers can make important contributions to our understanding of these relationships by systematically collecting evidence and reporting on their experiences with their groups in intervention research studies.

In Stage 3, existing program content is modified or new elements are created. For example, handouts used in sessions may be modified or new ones developed, videos, games or other activities are selected, and group leaders are trained to use them. Once all these elements are in place, the members are recruited for the initial pilot group. Because many aspects of the group are still untested, such pilots are often shortened versions of the full-scale version. These pilots are opportunities to get participant reactions to the discussion content, activities, and written materials, and data collection instruments. At this stage, practitioners and researchers are interested in getting a tentative answer to the feasibility question, "can this group be conducted as planned?"

In Stage 4, practitioners/researchers draw on their experiences implementing the group to identify the group's strength and flaws. If recruiting was not as successful as anticipated, service marketing and recruiting procedures may have to be changed or intensified. Group leaders may discover other things they need to know to be effective facilitators. If they are receiving supervision, they may also learn that a different kind of supervisory support will be needed. Feedback from participants may reveal that they would like a different type, number, or range of activities. Staff and researcher discussions on all these different issues can lead to decisions about what procedures should be modified, with the aim of making the group accessible to participants and the experience as satisfying as possible. If the intervention protocol was changed in response to member feedback, the data collection instruments used to assess outcomes may no longer tap into the group content, and new ones will need to be selected for the next pilot study (Meier, 1999).

Given all the ways that the intervention research plans can go awry, practitioner/researcher teams need to plan for multiple pilot tests of their groups to discover the most workable combination of elements for the research design and the intervention. Practitioner/researchers take advantage of opportunities to pilot different aspects of the group. They can try things out in the groups they run themselves, or collaborate with group workers whom they supervise. Sometimes, they can find small amounts of funding to conduct small studies. With each succeeding pilot, the evidence about what works accumulates.

In Stage 4, practitioner/researchers draw on their experiences implementing the group to identify the group's strengths and flaws. If recruiting was not as successful as anticipated, service marketing and recruiting procedures may have to be changed or intensified. Group leaders may discover other things they need to know to be effective facilitators. If they are receiving supervision, they may also learn that a different kind of supervisory support will be needed. Feedback from participants may reveal that they would like a different type, number, or range of activities. Staff and researcher discussions on all these different issues can lead to decisions about what procedures should be modified, with the aim of making the group accessible to participants and the experience as satisfying as possible. If the intervention protocol was changed in response to member feedback, the data collection instruments used to assess outcomes may no longer tap into the group content, and new ones will need to be selected for the next pilot study (Meier, 1999).

Given all the ways that the intervention research plans can go awry, practitioner/researcher teams need to plan for multiple pilot tests of their groups to discover the most workable combination of elements for the research design and the intervention. Practitioner/researchers take advantage of opportunities to pilot different aspects of the group. They can try things out in the groups they run themselves, or collaborate with group workers whom they supervise. Sometimes, they can find small amounts of funding to conduct small studies. With each succeeding pilot, the evidence about what works accumulates.

Stage 5 calls for practitioner/researchers to conduct full-scale, quasi-experimental evaluations of intervention effectiveness. They only proceed to this stage after multiple pilot studies confirm that the intervention is feasible under practice conditions. Obviously, field testing for IR with groups can only be done if the funding and institutional resources for implementing a larger study are available.

In Stage 6, practitioner/researchers disseminate what they are learning about their interventions. In Table 24.1, dissemination is shown as the last step. Typically, researchers present findings from outcome studies of their projects at conference presentations and scholarly publications when the full-scale field testing has been completed. Researchers following the IR Paradigm will also present and publish articles on preliminary findings from early studies. They also make available manuals and other training materials developed along the way, which other practitioners can use to learn how to implement the intervention.

RESOURCES

EBP and IR both call for social workers to go beyond their daily work routines, to learn more about their clients and interventions and how to improve their practice. Practically speaking, social workers face barriers that may deter them from even beginning. Heavy workloads are common. Many may not have the skills (Fraser, 1994; Fraser et al., 1993; Gambrill, 1999), or the practical experience (Kirk & Penka, 1992; Marino et al., 1998) to do either. Where can social workers acquire the knowledge they need to understand EBP and IR processes? How can they be efficient in their information searches? How can they get help to do IR with their groups? In this final section, we describe how to find help in understanding the principles of EBP, IR design, and development processes as they apply to group work.

Much of the early debate on EBP has taken place within the medical profession. Currently, social work researchers have also begun to express their views on the value and the applicability of EBP principles in social work (Fraser, 2003; Gambrill, 1999; Gibbs & Gambrill, 2002; Pollio, 2002). As with all innovations, the response has been mixed. One of the strongest critiques has been in response to EBP's emphasis on the value of evidence from clinically controlled trials to identify best practices. Social worker critics have argued that this standard of evidence is inappropriate for social work, particularly for group work, where it is rarely available. Moreover, the uncontrollability of practice settings make it difficult to replicate experimentally validated interventions.

In this chapter we have advocated for more realistic ways for social workers to incorporate research evidence in their decisions regarding the use of groups, and for systematically modifying or inventing groups. On-line databases make the search for information about research evidence for social work practice more available through their computers. Social workers who do not have adequate access to the Internet or the skills to use on-line data bases themselves should contact the libraries in their communities to see what resources and help they can offer. The impetus for EBP is leading to investments in the information infrastructure, such as the ongoing professional training and development of knowledge bases needed to support it. All of these developments will make it progressively easier for social workers to know about and take advantage of the evidence that exists when making treatment decisions. It will also support their efforts to conduct research on their groups.

Training to Assess Research Evidence and Use Practice Guidelines

Social workers seeking to learn how to assess research evidence can find lots of help on-line. For example, the Center for Health Evidence (http://www.cche.net/) and the Netting the Evidence (http://www.shef. ac.uk/shar/ir/netting/first.html) websites provide instructions and tools for appraising research evidence. The National Institutes of Health are funding a network of Evidence-Based Practice Centers to review and summarize research for a variety of medical problems, including mental health and substance abuse (http://www.ahcpr.gov/clinic/epcix.htm).

Online Resources for Health and Mental Health Research Evidence

All social workers with Internet access can now delve into numerous health and behavioral sciences research databases. One of the most fully developed is the PubMed website (http://www.ncbi.nlm.nih.gov/ PubMed/), a service of the National Institutes of Health's National Library of Medicine. This database provides access to over 19 million MEDLINE citations dating back to the mid-1960s and additional life science journals, and links to other websites where users can download full text versions of many articles listed in the database (National Library of Medicine, 2003). SCOPUS covers more than 40 million records in life, health, and physical sciences, and over 5000 in social science and humanities (http://info.scopus.com/)

Social workers who have graduated in the past 10 years will also be familiar with other social work–specific computerized or online databases, such as Family and Society Studies Worldwide, PsychInfo, Social Work Abstracts, Social Services Abstracts, and Sociological Abstract. The Cochrane Collaborative offers practitioners free online access to a database (C2SPECTR) of publications containing over 10,000 randomized and possibly randomized trials in education, social work and welfare, and criminal justice. It includes a methodology for conducting systematic reviews of research on psychosocial interventions (Campbell Collaboration, 2003; Howard,

2001). It supports users and reviewers by including useful information about study methods, outcomes, and the rigor of the research designs. These databases are usually not available over the Internet to users who are unaffiliated with a university or college, but they are likely to be available through university libraries. Some of these databases include downloadable full text versions of the publications. By reviewing the abstracts, users can select and receive many of these articles electronically. University libraries may also be able to offer social workers access to the Health and Psychosocial Instruments database, which provides information on measurement instruments, including questionnaires, interview schedules, checklists, index measures, coding schemes/ manuals, rating scales, projective techniques, vignettes/scenarios, and tests, developed for use in the fields of health, psychosocial sciences, and organizational behavior.

Computerized databases make it easy to identify many potentially relevant articles. The challenge is to determine which are the key research studies that address important questions and use the most rigorous research designs. In PubMed and the other databases mentioned above, it is possible to limit the scope of the search results by specifying the topic of interest and "reviews" as the publication type. This search strategy will select only review articles on the specified topic. Systematic reviews of the education. crime and justice, and social welfare research are now in the early development stage. Complete this section by listing some of the sources that are now accessible by Internet. Although these databases are in the early stage of development they do provide beginning knowledge that might be useful to social workers interested in group interventions. Reviewers might not be able to draw conclusions about the efficacy of all group interventions they could find published studies using clinical trials. In most studies, sample sizes were small, or the quality of design and reporting was inadequate. While these conditions are as might not be as helpful for group workers who want to be "EBP-compliant," these sources provide examples of how to conceptualize, develop and implement IR projects and guidelines to so they can create evidence about their interventions.

Collaborative Relationships with Researchers

Collaboration is strongly valued in EBP and the IR Paradigm. Many practitioners know how to design a group intervention, but they may feel less confident about their ability to conduct research on their interventions or analyze data. By developing collaborative relationships with colleges and universities, practitioners can gain access to needed expertise and resources that university faculty and students can provide. Such partnerships between the faculty and practitioners can benefit both groups. The faculty member might wish to collaborate with the practitioner in applying for research grants to develop group interventions or study group outcomes. For social workers, this would also provide opportunities to strengthen their EBP skills. They could get expert advice about what information to look for and how to do efficient literature searches. Social workers would be exposed to role models who could demonstrate and coach them in how to assess research evidence and apply it to the design of future projects and interventions. If these collaborative efforts result in research projects, social workers on research teams could also get experience in selecting appropriate measures and analyzing data.

Collaborative Relationships with Schools of Social Work

In agencies where social work students have field placements, students can be asked to participate in these collaborative research arrangements. Students who chose to join the team would have opportunities to learn about intervention design and development in the context of group work. For example, if the agency decides to modify a group, students could be asked to compile the information about the group's developmental history within the agency, or data on changes in community, population, and client characteristics. Students could help practitioners update their knowledge by identifying alternative interventions and new assessment tools. In the process, students would get to practice their skills with online research data bases. Since design and development work with group interventions usually extends over several years, these projects could provide an opportunity for a number of students to gain knowledge and training in IR research methodologies on a single project. Meanwhile, the agency would also benefit from the accumulation of data from a larger sample that would enable them to conduct rigorous analyses of their group's outcomes.

CONCLUSION

All scientific work is incomplete—whether it be observational or experimental. All scientific work is liable to be upset or modified by advancing knowledge. This does not confer upon us the freedom to ignore the knowledge we already have, or to postpone the action that it appears to demand at a given time (Hill, 1965, p. 300).

This chapter discusses the importance of EBP in social work practice and some of the advances made toward its adaptation to the social work practice standards. It provides basic elements of EBP and ways of discerning the quality of research evidence. Guidelines are suggested for the application of EBP in practice situations. Evidence-based social work with groups is seem as being most helpful to people in group treatment. Emphasis is placed on Intervention Research as an alternate research methodology that is uniquely suited to the development or modification of treatment strategies in practice situations. Gaps in our knowledge about what makes social work group interventions work makes using EBP and IR with groups challenging. We have much to learn about who benefits the most from what groups, and under what conditions. Clearly, filling those gaps using intervention research methodologies will be time-consuming and energy-intensive. Yet social workers' efforts to incorporate evidence in their treatment decisions and in conducting developmental research on groups are also intrinsically valuable. When they seek out the best available evidence to back their clinical judgments, or develop pilot studies on their groups, they are mining the knowledge bases that can help them better understand the people and communities they serve and the range of possible treatments they can offer. Moreover, it is judicious to use our best practice techniques to make a difference in the lives of the peoples we serve.

REFERENCES

Bailey-Dempsey, C. & Reid, W. J. (1996). Intervention design and development: A case study. *Research on Social Work Practice, 6*(2), 208–228.

Berman-Rossi, T. (1993). The tasks and skills of the social worker across stages of group development. *Social Work with Groups, 16*(1–2), 69–81.

Bretton, E. & Macgowan (2009). A critical review of adolescent substance abuse group treatments. *Journal of Evidence-based Social Work, 6*(3), 217–243.

Chorpita, B., Daleiden, E. & Weiscz, J. (2005). Identifying and selecting the common elements of evidence-based interventions: A distillation and matching model. *Mental Health Services Research, 7*(1), 5–20.

Chovanec, M. (2009). Involuntary clients. In A. Gitterman & R. Salmon (eds.), *Encyclopedia of social work with groups.* New York: Routledge.

Comer, E. (2004). Integrating the health and mental health needs of the chronically ill: A group for individuals with depression and sickle cell disease. *Social Work and Health Care, 38*(4), 57–76.

Comer, E. & Hirayama, K. (2008). Activity use and selection. In A. Gitterman & R. Salmon (eds.), *Encyclopedia of social work with groups* (pp. 62–64). New York: Routledge.

Comer, E., Meier, A. & Galinsky, M. J. (1999). Studying innovations in group work practice: Applications of the intervention research paradigm. Paper presented at the American Association for the Advancement of Social Work with Groups, 21st Annual Symposium, Denver, CO.

Comer, E., Meier, A. & Galinsky, M. J. (2004). Development of innovative group work practice using the Intervention Research Paradigm: Two cases. *Social Work, 49*(2), 250–260.

Comer, E. E. (1999). Effects of a cognitive behavioral group intervention on the reduction of depressive symptoms in individuals with sickle cell disease. Unpublished dissertation, University of North Carolina, Chapel Hill, NC.

Corey, M. & Corey, G. (2006). *Groups: Process and practice* (7th ed.). Belmont, CA: Thomson Higher Education.

Crosby, G. & Sabein, J. E. (1995). Developing and marketing time-limited groups. *Psychiatric Services, 47*(1), 7–8.

Council for Training in Evidence-Based Behavioral Practice. (2008). Definition and competencies for evidence-based behavioral practice (EBBP). Retrieved April 13, 2010, from http://www.ebbp.org/documents/EBBP_competencies.pdf.

Epstein, I. (2001). Using available clinical information in practice-based research: Mining for silver while dreaming for gold. *Social Work in Health Care, 33*(3/4), 15–32.

Faul, A. C., McMurtry, S. L., & Hudson, W. W. (2001). Can empirical clinical practice techniques improve social work outcomes? *Research on Social Work Practice, 11*(3), 277–299.

Fraser, M. (2003). Intervention research in social work: A basis for evidence-based practice and practice guidelines. In A. Rosen & E. K. Proctor (eds.), *Developing practice guidelines of social work interventions: Issues, methods and research agenda* (pp. 17–36). New York: Columbia University Press.

Fraser, M. W. (1994). Scholarship and research in social work: Emerging challenges. *Journal of Social Work Education, 30*, 252–266.

Fraser, M. W., Jenson, J. M., & Lewis, R. E. (1993). Research training in social work: The continuum is not a continuum. *Journal of Social Work Education, 29*(1), 46–62.

Fraser, M., Richman, J., Galinsky, M., & Day, S. (2009). *Intervention research.* New York: Oxford University Press.

Galinsky, M., Terizan, M., & Fraser, M. (2006). The art of group work practice using manualized curricula. *Social Work Practice with Groups, 29*(1), 11–26.

Gambrill, E. (1999). Evidence-based practice: An alternative to authority-based practice. *Families in Society, 89*(4), 341–350.

Gambrill, E. (2000). The role of critical thinking in evidence-based social work. In P. Allen-Meares & C. Garvin (eds.), *The handbook of social work direct practice* (pp. 43–63). Thousand Oaks, CA: Sage.

Gambrill, E. (2006). *Social work practice: A critical thinker's guide* (2nd ed.). New York: Oxford University Press.

Gibbs, L. & Gambrill, E. (2002). Evidence-based practice: Counterarguments to objections. *Research on Social Work Practice, 12*(3), 452–476.

Gibbs, L. & Gambrill, E. (2003). *Evidence-based practice for the helping professions.* Pacific Grove, CA: Thompson Learning.

Greif, G. & Ephross, P. (2005). *Group work with populations at risk* (2nd ed.). New York: Oxford University Press.

Guyatt, G. H., Haynes, B., Jaescheke, R. Z., Cook, D. J., Green, L., Nayolor, C. D., Wilson, M. C., & Richardson, W. S. (2000). *EBM: Principles of applying users' guides to patient care.* Centre for Health Evidence. Retrieved March 14, 2003, from http://www.cche.net/userguide/applying.asp

Hayward, R. S. A., Wilson, M. C., Tunis, S. R., Bass, E. G., & Guayatt, G. (1995). *How to use a clinical practice guideline.* Centre for Health Evidence. Retrieved March 3, 2003, from http://www.cche.net/userguides/guideline.asp

Hill, A. B. (1965). The environment and disease: Association or causation? *Proceedings of the Royal Society of Medicine, 58*, 295–300.

Howard, M. O. (2001). First Annual Campbell Collaboration Colloquium, Philadelphia, PA. *SSWR News, 8*, 12.

Howard, M., McMillian, C., & Pollio, E. E. (2003). Teaching evidence-based practice: Toward a new paradigm for social work education. *Research in Social Work Practice, 13*(2), 234–259.

Kirk, S. & Penka, C. E. (1992). Research utilization and MSW education: A decade of progress? In A. J. Grasso & I. Epstein (eds.), *Research utilization in the social services* (pp. 497–421). New York: Haworth Press.

Konopka, G. (1983). *Social group work: A helping process* (3rd ed.). Englewood Cliffs, NJ: Prentice Hall.

Macgowan, M. (2008). *A guide to evidence-based group work*. New York: Oxford University Press.

Marino, R., Green, R. G., & Young, E. (1998). Beyond the scientist-practitioner model's failure to thrive: Social workers' participation in agency-based research activities. *Social Work Research, 22*(3), 188–192.

Meier, A. (1999). A multi-method evaluation of a computer-mediated, stress management support group for social workers: Feasibility, process, and effectiveness. Unpublished dissertation, University of North Carolina, Chapel Hill.

Meier, A. (2000a). Offering social support via the Internet: A case study of an online support group for social workers. *Journal of Technology in Human Services, 17*(2/3), 237–266.

Meier, A. (2000b). Offering social support via the Internet: A case study of an online support group for social workers. In J. Finn & G. Holden (eds.), *Human services online: A new arena for service delivery* (pp. 237–266). New York: Haworth Press.

Meier, A. (2003). *Colon cancer caregivers' online support group project: Research feasibility, and intervention feasibility and outcomes* (final report). Chapel Hill: University of North Carolina, Lineberger Comprehensive Cancer Center.

Meier, A., Galinsky, M. J., & Rounds, K. (1995). Telephone support groups for caregivers of persons with AIDS. In M. J. Galinsky & J. H. Schopler (eds.), *Support groups: Current perspectives on theory and practice* (pp. 99–108). Binghamton, NY: Haworth Press.

Meier, A. & Usher, C. L. (1998). New approaches to program evaluation. In R. L. Edwards & J. A. Yankey (eds.), *Skills for effective nonprofit organizations* (pp. 371–405). Washington, DC: NASW Press.

Morgan, R. D. (2002). Group psychotherapy with incarcerated offenders: A research synthesis. *Group Dynamics, 6*(3), 203–218.

Mullen, E. J., Bellamy, S. E., & Francois, J. J. (2007). Teaching evidence-based practice. *Research on Social Work Practice, 17*, 574–582.

National Association of Social Workers. (1996). *Code of ethics*. Washington, DC: National Association of Social Workers.

National Library of Medicine. (2003). *Entrez PubMed*. Retrieved March 3, 2003, from www.ncbi.nlm.nih.gov/PubMed/

Northen, H., & Kurland, R. (2001). *Social work with groups* (3rd ed.). New York: Columbia University Press.

Ngo, V., Langley, A., Nadeem, E., Escudero, P., & Stein, B. (2008. Providing evidence-based practice to ethnically youths: Examples fro the cognitive behavioral intervention for trauma in school programs. *Journal of the American Academy of Child and Adolescent Psychiatry, 47*(8), 858–862.

Pollio, D. E. (2002). The evidence-based social worker. *Social Work with Groups, 25*(4), 57–70.

Pollio, D. E. (2006). The art of evidence-based practice. *Research on social work, 16*(2), 224–232.

Pollio, D. E., Brower, A. M., & Galinsky, M. J. (2000). Change in groups. In P. Allen Meares & C. Garvin (eds.), *The handbook of social work direct practice* (pp. 281–300). Thousand Oaks, CA: Sage Publications.

Pomeroy, E. C., Rubin, A., & Walker, R. J. (1995). Effectiveness of a psychoeducational and task-centered group intervention for family members of people with AIDS. *Social Work Research, 19*(3), 142–151.

Quinn, W. H., Van Dyke, D. J., & Kurth, S. T. (2002). A brief multiple family group model for juvenile first offenders. In C. R. Figley (ed.), *Brief treatments for the traumatized: A project of the Green Cross Foundation* (pp. 226–251). Westport, CT: Greenwood Press.

Rice, A. H. (2001). Evaluating brief structured group treatment of depression. *Research on Social Work Practice, 11*(1), 53–78.

Rosen, A. & Proctor, E. (2003). *Developing practice guidelines for social work intervention.* New York: Columbia Press.

Rothman, J. & Thomas, E. J. (1994). *Intervention research: Design and development for human service.* New York: Haworth Press.

Rounds, K., Galinsky, M. J., & Despard, J. R. (1995). Evaluation of telephone support groups for persons with HIV disease. *Research on Social Work Practice, 5*(4), 442–459.

Sackett, D. L., Ricardson, W. S., Rosenberg, W., & Haynes, R. B. (1997). *Evidence-based medicine: How to practice and teach evidence-based medicine.* New York: Churchill Livingstone.

Sackett, D. L., Richardson, W. M. C., Gray, J. A. M., Haynes, R. B., & Richardson, W. S. (1996). Evidence-based medicine: What it is and what it isn't. *British Medical Journal, 312,* 71–72.

Schopler, J. H. & Galinsky, M. J. (1995). Group practice overview. In R. L. Edward & J. G. Hopps, et al. (eds.), *Encyclopedia of social work*, Vol. 1 (pp. 1129–1143). Washington, DC: NASW Press.

Seekins, T., Mathews, R. M., & Fawcett, S. B. (1984). Enhancing leadership skills for community self-help organizations through behavioral instruction. *Journal of Community Psychology, 12,* 155–163.

Subramanian, K. (1991). Structured group work for the management of chronic pain: An experimental investigation. *Research on Social Work Practice, 1*(1), 32–45.

Subramanian, K., Hernandez, S., & Martinez, A. (1995). Psychoeducational group work for low-income Latina mothers with HIV infection. *Social Work with Groups, 18*(2/3), 53–64.

The Campbell Collaboration. (2003). *The Campbell Collaboration Homepage.* Retrieved March 2, 2003, from http://www.campbellcollaboration.org/

Thomas, E. J. (1985). The validity of design and development and related concepts in developmental research. *Social Work Research and Abstracts, 21*(2), 50–55.

Tolman, R. & Molidor, C. (1994). A decade of social group work research: Trends in methodology, theory, and program development. *Research on Social Work Practice, 4*(2), 142–159.

Toseland, R. W. & Rivas, R. F. (2009). *An introduction to group work practice* (6th ed.). Boston: Allyn and Bacon.

Vinter, R. (1985). Essential components of social group work practice. In M. Sundel, P. Glasser, R. Sarri, & R. Vinter (eds.), *Individual change through small groups* (2nd ed., pp. 11–34). New York: The Free Press.

Yalom, I. D. & Leszcz, M. (2005). *The theory and practice of group psychotherapy* (5th ed.). New York: Basic Books.

Chapter Twenty-Five

Skills for Working across Populations at Risk

Geoffrey L. Greif and Paul H. Ephross

This is a skills book intended to assist practitioners in working with a wide range of populations. Each chapter includes specific recommendations for how to help people in pain or who share a common condition of need. Just as there are recurring themes that emerge when working with each of these populations, we believe that common skills are needed for working *across* populations. In essence, each chapter is a look at the trees in the forest. The chapters, taken together, become the forest. In reading across the chapters, skills emerge from the whole forest that can serve practitioners well, both when intervening in the group and on behalf of the group. While no particular skill is guaranteed to work with all populations all the time, these skills are sufficiently generic to apply to most situations. We have collected these skills, borrowed in part from the chapter authors, and present them as guideposts for practice.[1]

The list of skills that follows is not ranked in order of importance. They do go from the general to the specific. Some need no explanation.

1. *Understanding the relationship of the worker to the agency (or practice setting) and understanding where both worker and agency fit into the overall service component of the community.* Such an understanding sets the context for social work practice that never occurs in a vacuum devoid of awareness of corollary services.
2. *Understanding how groups flow from beginning to end.* Workers should be familiar with how members begin with a group, continue with a group (the middle stage), and terminate with a group, including where the member goes next if service is still needed. Social work service takes place in the context of phases of group development and these phases, when the member is made aware of them, can optimize growth in the member. These phases also guide the worker in using herself or himself in relation to the group member. In turn, the group as an entity goes through phases in relation to the agency context. For example, some agencies have long-standing groups and others are starting groups de novo. The agency's

knowledge about these groups will affect, for example, whether other agency workers refer clients to the group and what they tell the clients about how the group operates.

3. *Operating with cultural awareness and sensitivity.* The ability to appreciate and convey respect for clients' differences, whether they be in the areas of race, class, ethnicity, sexual orientation, age, and/or (dis)ability is a central skill that, hopefully, has been reenforced by the chapter authors' insights.

4. *Advocating for and on behalf of the client, the group, and the agency.* Workers should represent client and group interests to the agency, as well as agency interests in the larger social service context. When a social worker is employed by the agency, an obligation exists to work on behalf of those served by the agency and to know agency policies in relation to those served (e.g., Brown, 1991). An obligation also exists to further the cause of the agency in the community in a manner that is consistent with the profession's commitment to social justice.

5. *Practicing in an ethical manner.* Workers should abide by standards that are consistent not only with the NASW Code of Ethics but also with ethical practices mandated by the licensing statutes of the state within which he or she is practicing and with the broad ethical goals of the agency.

6. *Helping the group establish adaptive norms.* Clients should be able to modify norms for use in achieving their individual goals, as well as group goals.

7. *Self-disclosing in an appropriate manner.* Workers should always be aware of the stage of the group and the purpose of the group when they and/or members are self-disclosing. The worker self-discloses all the time, including by how she dresses and describes her role within the agency. In the simplest form, telling the group that one is a student or just finished one's master's degree, conveys a value on education. Self-disclosure must be consistent with agency procedures and policies and should be used judiciously to advance the group, not only to meet the needs of the worker.

8. *Using self to reflect back to the group and to role model for the group.* Use of self requires insight into the worker's own feelings and history and how that background affects *every* action the worker takes with the group.

9. *Engaging group members in setting goals for the group and for themselves that are consistent with the purpose of the group.*

10. *Seeking feedback from the group.* Workers should inquire about how well members feel the group is working and what else they would like to have occur in the group; While accepting a leadership role, workers should also help group members accept and actualize their own responsibilities for what the group does and how it does it.

11. *Assisting clients in setting goals.* Workers should help with long and short-term objectives both in and out of the group.

12. *Being aware of the temporal issue and using it to the advantage of the group.* The meaning of time varies from one culture to the next. "Soon" to one person may mean 30 minutes and to another person a few weeks in the future. Change, then, may be expected more quickly by some than others. Members' conception of time frames (e.g., how long before I start to feel better?) should be addressed.

13. *Educating group members in relation to issues relevant to the group.* For example, teaching parents about normal developmental stages in young children, informing cancer patients about depression that may be common following surgery (without the leader practicing medicine), and helping young women understand societal pressures in relation to body image are all appropriate ways to educate.

14. *Admitting a lack of knowledge or confusion about an issue.* Workers who pretend to be "all knowing" may take away the group members' ability to admit that they do not know something and may set unrealistically high expectations about what any one group member should know. When the worker does not have an answer to a question, has to do some research on something, or must think about it for some period of time, she models for group members that they do not need to have an immediate answer to every issue that arises. In addition, when the worker points out he is confused by something, it allows other members to be confused—a normal state for many members who are dealing with complex situations with often conflicting information and conflicting motivations.

15. *Helping members gain insight through a variety of interventions.* Techniques include art projects, music (especially useful with youth), role-playing, providing direct feedback to the member and the group, and, most significantly, connecting current behaviors and feelings to past behaviors and feelings.

16. *Encouraging relevant expression.* Group members should share feelings and thoughts that reflect the group purpose. Workers should redirect members when it is clear those expressions are not within the purview of the group.

17. *Showing positive regard for the expression of feelings and thoughts.* Such regard is best shown through active listening, reflecting back to the client, and tracking. Tracking refers to making specific references to what the client has said earlier in the meeting or at previous meetings.

18. *Normalizing feelings for members.* For example, by conveying to the returning Afghan conflict veteran that what she is feeling is typical given her combat experiences, the worker reassures the veteran. Such reassurance helps the veteran feel more connected to and less isolated

from others. Normalizing feelings permits the group member to look more cognitively at what is being experienced by pulling the feeling away from the member and spreading it around.

19. *Engaging members cognitively.* Asking a group member what he is thinking, and not what he is feeling, engages a different part of a group member's experience and opens up other ways of approaching the presenting problem. (When intellectualization is used consistently as a defense, asking about feelings may be more appropriate.) Asking other group members what they think about one member's presenting problem will also push the group in a different direction than asking them what they *feel* about what a member is experiencing. Here members will generate ideas for solutions. This skill is also related to reframing where the leader provides a different view of a problem presented by a member.

20. *Reaching for feelings by drawing on past experiences and family history.* When members are asked to talk, for example, about past traumatic experiences related to abuse (see Chapter 10), feelings are intentionally being tapped. Recounting family history can also bring out strong emotional reactions. The sharing of feelings can lead to catharsis and an opening up of previously taboo subjects. When it is known that the sharing of feelings will result in painful expressions, topics should be approached sensitively and with the permission of the members. Starting off the discussion by saying, "I know this may be painful today but I was wondering if anyone wanted to talk about their experience or their feelings when they were first diagnosed with HIV." This acknowledges at the beginning that the discussion to follow may be difficult.

21. *Partializing the presenting problems.* A common skill in working with others is asking members, when they bring in a host of problems, to take them one at a time and to prioritize which one they would like to talk about first. Partializing helps group members who feel overwhelmed to gain some small control and a sense of competence over at least one of the issues they are facing.

22. *Confronting the group members and the group as a whole.* Much has been written about this key skill and how the leader might confront individuals about their behavior (nonconformity to group norms, absenteeism, lack of engagement, etc.) and the group about its own processes (avoiding work, staying superficial, scapegoating, etc.). While an in-depth discussion is beyond the purpose of this list of skills, the leader must be clear about the reasons for confrontation and do it in a manner that is growth promoting and not attacking. The leader who actively avoids confrontation may send the group a message that they do not need to work on their issues. Supervision will be useful to the leader who is struggling with how to confront.

23. *Using programming effectively.* Programming (such as videos, speakers, role plays, or ice-breaking exercises) must be timed to fit with the group's developmental stage. Using an exercise that is too revealing too early in the group would be inappropriate just as ending a group with an initial ice-breaking exercise would be ill timed.

24. *Focusing on the here and now.* Sometimes group members wander back in time and recycle their stories to no purpose when they are better aided if they are kept in the present.

25. *Teaching relaxation techniques.* Techniques can range from those to be used across situations—deep breathing and visualization techniques, for example—to those to be used in specific situations—"Take a walk around the block one time before you go into your home so you are ready for your children."

26. *Suggesting ways to resolve interpersonal conflict.* Workers can assist with conflicts among group members during a meeting and between group members and their significant others outside of the group;

27. *Teaching the importance of "I" messages.*

28. *Modeling empathetic responses when painful issues are raised.*

29. *Using national events to teach about human nature and social justice.* The shootings at Virginia Tech, the aftermath of Hurricane Katrina, the BP Gulf of Mexico oil spill, and the death of Michael Jackson are all events that may be grist for the group's mill when linked to the purpose of the group. For example, following Michael Jackson's death, a group could be asked how they wish to be remembered after they die.

30. *Teaching about contracting.* As the leader sets limits, constructs boundaries, and forms contracts with the group around the maintenance of the group, the leader is role modeling for members how to do the same in their own lives.

31. *Using videotaping to advance the group.* Some groups, particularly those with younger members, enjoy being taped. When used appropriately, videotaping can provide a powerful feedback loop to members about their in-group behavior.

32. *Tracking changes in members through research instruments.* Brief questionnaires can be effective in getting members to consider their own progress and the group's progress as a whole. An awareness of evidence-based practices in approaching the group's presenting problems can guide the worker in deciding which research instruments to use and how to apply them.

33. *Building and reenforcing self-esteem and competence in individual group members and the group as a whole.* Creating an atmosphere of positive regard for members in a supportive context is vitally important to the effectiveness of the group.

We believe that these skills can be applied across populations and across group purposes. While the emphasis may appear to be on the use of these skills in clinical groups, many of them are appropriate in community organizing and task-oriented groups. Ethical leadership is not confined to any one setting or approach. Positive regard for others is the sine qua non of social work. As new populations arise with new challenges, we hope the skills learned in this volume can be adapted to meet the needs of tomorrow's underserved.

REFERENCES

Brown, L. N. (1991). *Groups for growth and change*. New York: Longman.

Ephross, P. H. & Greif, G. L. (2009). Group process and group work techniques. In A. R. Roberts (ed.), *Social workers' desk reference* (pp. 679–685). New York: Oxford University Press.

NOTE

1 Some of the information in this chapter appears in Ephross and Greif (2009). We thank Dr. Al Roberts, who died in 2008, for his significant contributions to the group work method and the profession of social work.

Index

CPSIA information can be obtained at www.ICGtesting.com
Printed in the USA
BVOW021637200613

323841BV00003B/4/P

9 780195 398564